The New York Public Library Book of

HOW AND WHERE TO LOOK IT UP

The New York Public Library Book of

HOW AND WHERE TO LOOK IT UP

Sherwood Harris
Editor-in-Chief

A STONESONG PRESS BOOK

Prentice Hall
New York   London   Toronto   Sydney   Tokyo   Singapore

Publisher Nina Hoffman
Managing Editor William Hamill
Associate Managing Editor Jill Schoenhaut

Senior Production Manager Robin B. Besofsky
Production Editor Lisa Wolff
Designer Levavi & Levavi, Inc.

First Edition

Copyright © 1991 by The Stonesong Press, Inc., Sherwood Harris, and The New York Public Library

The name "The New York Public Library" and the representation of the lion appearing in this work are trademarks and the property of The New York Public Library, Astor, Lenox and Tilden Foundations.

Prentice Hall General Reference
15 Columbus Circle
New York, NY 10023

A Prentice Hall Reference Book

Prentice Hall and colophons are registered trademarks
of Simon & Schuster, Inc.

1 2 3 4 5 6 7 8 9 10

Library of Congress Cataloging-in-Publication Data

The New York Public Library book of how and where to look it up /
    Sherwood Harris, editor.—1st ed.
        p.   cm.
    Includes index.
    ISBN 0-13-614728-3
    1. Libraries—Handbooks, manuals, etc. 2. Research—Methodology—Handbooks, manuals, etc. 3. Bibliography—Methodology—Handbooks, manuals, etc. I. Harris, Sherwood. II. New York Public Library.
    Z710.N48   1991
    025.5'24'072—dc20
                                                            91-25660
                                                                CIP

Editor-in-Chief: Sherwood Harris

Editors

Reference Books: Michael Zwiebach
Telephone Sources: Elizabeth A. Caldwell
Government Sources: Beatrice Rieser
Picture Sources: Judith A. Posner
Special Collections: Sherwood Harris
Electronic Databases: Sally Bell, John Fink

Associate Editors:

Lorna B. Harris   Jon-Holcomb Noble
Marianne Losch   Lisa Wolf

Word Processing

Carol Hudson   Arline Llewellyn
A Word Away: Teresa Mamone Colavito

Contents

Foreword

In today's data-minded world, there is so much material now available—not just in public libraries but also in electronic sources, in specialized libraries, by telephone, and through museums, organizations, and government agencies—that there is a great need for a comprehensive book to explain, detail, and simplify the task of research. That is the basic intent and scope of *The New York Public Library Book of How and Where to Look It Up*. Further, we hope our work can help a researcher at any level of skill quickly find the right source.

Standing behind every listing in this book is a dedicated person, or, more often, a dedicated group of people, whose high standards provide information resources of incalculable value for us all. To those of you whom we contacted during the preparation of *How and Where to Look It Up*, my personal thanks for your interest in the project and your generous assistance. To those whom we did not personally contact, my thanks also. Without you all, a book like this simply would not have been possible.

The concept for *How and Where to Look It Up* originated with Paul Fargis of The Stonesong Press in consultation with the staff of the New York Public Library. It is the third title in a new series of general reference books

published under the aegis of the New York Public Library; the two preceding books were *The New York Public Library Desk Reference* and *The New York Public Library Book of Chronologies*. I am indebted to Richard Newman, director of the Publications Department of the New York Public Library, for his support and help in making the resources of the Library available, and to Library staff members Barbara Berliner, John Hawker, Andrew H. Lee, Rodney Phillips, and Julia van Haaften, for their comments and assistance. Thanks also to Ron Schick for help on "Picture Sources."

Your attention is directed to the masthead on the copyright page. This is one of the most capable groups of editors I have had the pleasure of working with, and I thank them again for their long hours and their dedication to an extremely demanding project. I would like to add a note of personal thanks to Lee Ash, editor of *Subject Collections* since its inception, for his help and encouragement with my own work on the "Special Collections" chapter of this book.

Every attempt was made to ensure that this publication is as accurate as possible. Making it complete as well as accurate was a difficult task. We had to be highly selective to create a useful one-volume work; reference books and special collections alone could have filled several volumes. We made our final choices as objectively as we could, guided always by our goal of providing users with help in their search for information that would be easy to find, authoritative, and not overly redundant. If errors or omissions are discovered, please let us know so that future editions can be amended. Address any such information to The Stonesong Press, Inc., in care of Prentice Hall, 16th floor, 15 Columbus Circle, New York, NY 10023.

Sherwood Harris
Editor-in-Chief

Part 1

How to Look It Up

THERE IS AN ALMOST OVERWHELMING AMOUNT of information available now, more than at any time in the history of civilization. It is preserved and made accessible in many ways: through public libraries, electronic databases, photographic archives, associations, museums, special collections, and bookstores, and, more and more frequently these days, over the telephone.

But the vastness of this body of information creates problems. How can someone readily look up the information he or she needs without spending an inordinate amount of time and still be sure of finding the best, most accurate source?

Finding the right resources is not just a problem for the layperson who occasionally needs a piece of information, such as where to write for a college admissions application or where to find facts for a special company presentation or report. It is a problem as well for journalists, librarians, public relations people, lawyers, and professional researchers. Information professionals, perhaps more than anyone else, frequently find themselves overwhelmed by the sheer quantity of information—and often underwhelmed by the inappropriateness of what they find.

How and Where to Look It Up provides a solution to these problems for laypersons and professionals at any level. Presented herein is a careful selection of information sources in six major categories: (1) Reference Books, (2) Telephone Sources, (3) Government Sources, (4) Picture Sources, (5) Special Collections, and (6) Electronic Databases. The information is not meant to be exhaustive or all-inclusive. Instead, sources in the six categories were winnowed from the hundreds of thousands available to give you, the user, a concise, easy-to-look-up set of authoritative references that will provide information on just about any subject under the sun.

Special Features

The most important feature of *How and Where to Look It Up* is its subject-by-subject organization. Each section is like a mini-encyclopedia, with A-to-Z listings for that type of source.

To make the search for information easier and faster, each of the six "Where to Look It Up" sections has its own index at the beginning of the listings. All you have to do is decide what type of source is the most appropriate for your inquiry, then turn to the index for that type of source, and it will lead you directly to your subject. Page numbers of subject indexes are given on the contents page.

For further ease of use, the subjects covered in each subject category are arranged alphabetically, with many cross-references. The listings under each subject are also alphabetical. In addition, there is an alphabetical index of all the individual listings at the end of the book. If you need to find the telephone number of a source you have used before, for example, all you have to do is look up the name of the source in the alphabetical index of listings, then turn to the specific page where the information is located.

For those who wish to delve deeper into the material covered in the six listings sections, the names of authoritative, well-established source books and directories are given in the introductory sections of each of the six listings sections. For example, *Guide to Reference Books* by Eugene P. Sheehy is given as the source of additional information for the first listings section, "Reference Books."

There is an exception. No guides or directories were available for "Telephone Sources." Although you will find information in the introduction to that section on the *AT&T Toll Free 800 Directory*, an excellent telephone directory, most of the 800 numbers are for business purposes, not reference. The "Telephone Sources" section in *How and Where to Look It Up* is, at the time of this writing, the *only* up-to-date guide to telephone information sources. This unique section is a very important special feature in *How and Where to Look It Up*.

Another important special feature, developed especially for *How and Where to Look It Up*, is the group of listings in the "States and Territories" category in the "Government Sources" section. For the first time, central telephone numbers are given that can refer you directly to the appropriate state agency. The introduction to "Government Sources" also provides up-to-date information on the federal government's new centralized Federal Information Center, whose computers and information specialists can answer a wide variety of questions using government sources.

Finding What You Want

Information professionals have learned, over the years, how to cope with the overwhelming amount of information and reference material now available. And they have learned how to do this without squandering that most precious quantity, time.

This knowledge has been graciously shared and passed along to the editors of *How and Where to Look It Up* by the staff of the New York Public Library and many, many others. In one sense, *How and Where to Look It Up* is like a master Rolodex® compiled by the best researchers in the country. But also contained herein are the strategies, techniques, and tips these professionals make use of every day. These are discussed broadly in "Part One: How to Look Things Up." The discussion continues in the introductions to each of the six "Where to Look It Up" sections. These introductions provide detailed "how to" tips and information, tailored specifically to the type of source. Locating and obtaining photographs, for example, requires a substantially different approach than, say, obtaining information from an electronic database. You will find the details you need to work with these two types of sources—as well as the other four—in the introductions that precede the alphabetical listings.

The Time Factor

From the experiences of professional researchers emerges a broad underlying principle that is almost instinctive and taken for granted but that deserves examination and better understanding. And that is: Every search for information is limited by time.

At one end of the scale, researchers are often expected to come up with facts immediately. When people call the Telephone Reference Service of the New York Public Library, for example, they expect—and get—answers to their questions while still on the line. Reporters and editors for daily newspapers must track down facts in a matter of hours, or even minutes, as press time approaches. For weekly and monthly magazine writers and editors, the time available to check out a story may be days or even weeks. But it is amazing how often even they face last-minute scrambles to look something up just before press time. Book authors and editors have more time to checks things out, but for them, too, there is always a deadline, a due date. Even for scholarly projects that may involve years of work, there inevitably comes the time when the work must be completed and shipped off for review or publication.

So the first step in looking up information is to decide how much time is available. Time available determines the type of source to be consulted. On a general scale of fastest to slowest:

1. A small desktop library. With a dictionary, a good, small general reference such as the *World Almanac* or the *The New York Public Library Desk Reference,* and an atlas—even an inexpensive paperback edition such as the Rand McNally *Road Atlas*—a large number of questions can be answered very quickly. Add a book or two on the subject that concerns you most, such as a style manual for someone who does a lot of writing and editing or a medical guide for someone in the health field, and most of your routine information needs are at your fingertips.

The desktop library can be expanded easily into a small office library that can efficiently serve the information needs of a wider group of people. See section 1, "Reference Books," for publications that can form the core of an office library specializing in the subjects you deal with most frequently.

2. Telephone sources. A call to your local library or to one of the many listings in the "Telephone Sources" section may produce a quick, authoritative answer to your question.

The public information numbers in the "Government Sources" section can also provide information quickly.

If you have not worked with a telephone source, however, give yourself as much lead time as possible. Sometimes it takes several calls to locate the person who has the information you want. Once you have located that helpful person, be sure to write down his or her number for future reference. A card file—such as the ubiquitous Rolodex®—is excellent for this purpose.

Another important reason for giving yourself sufficient lead time is that it may not be possible to answer your query quickly or at the length you desire by telephone. Sometimes the telephone or government source can send you a publication containing the information you want or direct you to a reference book. This takes more time, of course, so plan for it.

It is also a good idea to query a picture source first by telephone to find out how to acquire the picture you want and approximately how long it will take to receive it. Many picture sources will expedite your request for an additional fee.

3. Electronic databases. These are ranked midway on our scale of fastest to slowest. On the one hand, they can provide voluminous information very quickly if you or your office has a subscription to an online service or you have your own CD-ROM equipment. But if you must route your request through a library or professional database search company, it will take more time. When considering this alternative, always ask the library or search firm how long it will take to process your query—and how much it will cost. In no other area of information gathering is the phrase "time equals money" more to the point.

4. Personal visits. Going to libraries, government agencies, and special collections takes more time, but it is frequently the most productive method of looking things up, especially if you are researching a subject in some depth. A personal visit to an information center not only provides access to many more publications, but it also gives you the opportunity to talk over your needs with the best people to help, the reference librarians and specialists that staff the center.

Special collections—especially private ones—may be open to the public only on a limited basis, so call ahead and find out what the limitations are. In some cases, you may have to write a letter describing your project in order to obtain permission to use the special collection.

We begin a search for information with a subject in mind for which we wish to find specific facts. *How and Where to Look It Up* enables you to go directly to the medium that will produce the best results for you in the time available. Be sure to read the introductions to each of the six listings sections. They are rich in ideas and tips provided by some of the best professionals in the country. Be sure to allow yourself enough time to browse through the listings themselves. This representative collection of America's vast information resources is full of fascinating and surprising things, and you may well come across something unexpected that will make your search for information even more rewarding.

Part 2

Where to Look It Up

1.

Reference Books

The new york public library operates one of the largest open-access reference collections in the United States, if not the world. Located across Fifth Avenue and a few doors down from the main building, the General Reference Service at the Mid-Manhattan Library has a collection of about 56,000 books and periodicals. It maintains subscriptions to about 40 newspapers.

The main reading room on the second floor of the Mid-Manhattan Branch is one of the New York Public Library's busiest information centers. Hundreds of visitors are drawn daily to its open stacks and extensive collection. Some drop in briefly for a quick fact check in a familiar reference book; others browse for hours and return frequently for deeper and more detailed research. Many are young people searching for information on education and job opportunities, for the General Reference Service also provides specialized services in these fields.

The NYPL Public Library Basic Reference List

The General Reference Service does much more than provide easy access to reference books and periodicals. It operates a busy Telephone Reference Service that answers thousands of inquiries every year. The General Reference Service staff also reviews and evaluates major new references as well as significant new editions of older books. Publications that meet the Library's high standards are listed in a "Basic Reference List of Reference Books for Branch Libraries." This compilation is circulated to the many branches of the Library to provide them with guidance in building and maintaining a strong core of reference books.

The Library's unique "Basic Reference List of Reference Books for Branch Libraries" is a concise, informative, and carefully designed guide to the most useful of the thousands of books in print in the reference category. For these reasons, it was chosen as the basis for the A-to-Z list of reference books in this section. Additional titles that experienced librarians and professional researchers have found to be useful have been added, while some titles of purely local interest have been dropped.

Included in the "Reference Books" listings that follow are almanacs, atlases, bibliographies, dictionaries, encyclopedias, and periodicals (weekly, monthly, or quarterly), as well as subject-specific references, such as the *Norton/Grove Concise Encyclopedia of Music*. For ease of use, references are arranged alphabetically by subject, then alphabetically by title within each subject. The "General Reference Books" category lists references that cover many subjects, such as *The World Almanac*. Books in the "General References" category are especially good sources for quick fact checking.

Users of this section should keep in mind that it is not intended to be a record of all reference works in print on any particular subject. Instead, it represents a careful selection of books that will be of greatest help in a search for information.

Finding the Information You Want

Use the following A-to-Z list of reference books to select the titles that cover your subject. Write down the information on these titles and take your notes to the nearest library—or easier still, flag the books you are interested in with slips of paper and take *How and Where to Look It Up* with you when you go to the library. In addition to public libraries, many business, corporate, college, and government libraries also have very useful general reference collections.

To locate the books you want, consult the library's catalog. The old, familiar card catalog, like the buggy whip, has become almost obsolete in the onrush of new information technology. Many mourn the passing of the card catalog. It was comfortable to work with, easy to use, and full of fascinating information. But card catalogs were almost impossible to keep up to date, and the cataloging of new acquisitions required a substantial amount of time and attention from librarians who often felt their skills could be put to better use. Even more frustrating, when you needed a

specific card, its drawer was often being used by someone else!

Microfiche and Computer Catalogs

You can still find card catalogs in local libraries. But more and more, the card catalog is being replaced by computer-based catalogs or by microfiche systems, in which small sheets of film containing microimages are enlarged by special optical readers.

Some of the new electronic library catalogs contain millions of entries that are better organized, more up-to-date, and accessed far more easily than any card catalog could ever hope to be. One popular system, the OCLC (Online Computer Library Center) Union Catalog, contains 18,000,000 records. It is updated weekly and is available on a membership basis.

The Library of Congress's REMARC (Retrospective Machine Readable Cataloging) system contains 4,280,000 Library of Congress records from 1897 to 1980; its basic MARC system contains more recent entries as well as records from various specialized collections. These Library of Congress catalogs are available through commercial online services.

Regardless of the cataloging system in use, the basic elements remain the same. Books are cataloged three ways: by author (last name first), by title, and by subject. A "call number," or locator code, is always given. This code will tell you where to find what you want if the library has open stacks, or where a librarian will find it for you if the stacks are not open.

Here is the information on a typical author card in the computerized catalog available to the public in the General Research Division in Room 315 of the main building:

FA   Eugene Sheehy
                      Items found: 334   Item 1.

TITLE   Guide to reference books/ edited by Eugene P. Sheehy; with the assistance of Rita G. Keckeissen . . . [and others]; science, technology, and medicine compiled by Richard J. Dionne . . .

PUBLICATION   10th ed. Chicago: American Library Association, 1986.

CALL NUMBER   Pub. Cat.87-855 . . . [and 13 more]

This record indicates that there are a total of 334 items in the library by author Eugene P. Sheehy. This card, "Item 1.," concerns his well-known reference book *Guide to Reference Books*, 10th edition. To have a look at it, you would fill out a call slip and present it to one of the librarians at the call desk.

Identical information appears on the title and subject cards, except that the first line is different. The first line of the title card is:

FT   Guide to Reference Books
           Items found: 334

And the first line of the subject card is:

FS   Reference Books
           Items found: 334

Along with the basic catalog information, some of the newer microfiche and computer cataloging systems often list other libraries in the area that have the book. This is a major benefit of the new technology. If the book you want is not available at your local library, you can see, in the same block of information on the screen, a list of other libraries where it can be found. You can then ask your library to order the book for you through its interlibrary loan program.

It should be noted, however, that most reference books are not available through interlibrary loan. They cannot be taken out of the library that owns them; they must be used at that branch. The newer cataloging systems at least tell you the nearest available library where you can go to work with the book you want.

CD-ROM

One of the most exciting new developments in information technology is the CD-ROM— the Compact Disk-Read Only Memory. CD-ROMs are laser-readable compact disks that look very much like those disks used for music recordings. CD-ROMs are formatted so that they can store millions of computer-generated words. The 13 volumes of the 1933 edition of the *Oxford English Dictionary*, for example, are stored on just one CD-ROM disk. The ROM feature—Read Only Memory—means just that: the disk can only be read. The information on it cannot be edited, corrected, or changed in any way.

CD-ROMs are ideal media for storing large amounts of information in compact, easily accessible form. The information for a publication such as the *Oxford English Dictionary* is first stored in a computer database, where it can be updated systematically. When the time comes to issue a new edition, it is faster, simpler, and cheaper to transfer the electronic data from the computer database to disks than to print and bind conventional books. The ease with which the central database can be updated also means that references such as the *Physicians' Desk Reference* can be kept current much more easily. *PDR* subscribers receive quarterly updates on new medicines and drugs.

While the number of reference books available on CD-ROM is still small, this medium is so useful that many libraries have begun subscribing to services that provide CD-ROMs and regular updates or are making plans to do so.

The Reference Librarian

If you are unsure about how to use call numbers or how to operate computer, microfiche, microfilm, or CD-ROM equipment—or are working in an unfamiliar library with a system you have not seen before—ask one of the librarians to show you how to get what you want. You can save a lot of time by simply asking for help.

All libraries, large or small, have reference sections and reference librarians or others on staff who are familiar with reference books. Find out who they are and ask them to help you locate the book you want. A personal visit to the library is best, but most libraries welcome telephone requests for information if they are not too complicated or time-consuming.

Tips on Using Reference Books

---

1. If the library does not have the exact book you are looking for, check the catalog subject heading for other possibilities or ask the reference librarian for advice.

Even if the library has exactly what you want, browse the subject headings anyway. They are an excellent source of ideas. You may find books that are even better suited to your needs than the one you were looking for.

2. Edition dates given are for the most recent edition available at the time **How and Where to Look It Up** *was prepared.* These dates are included as a guide to the currency of the information in the editions actually available in your library. Not all information is "perishable," but if the editions you locate in your library are older, you should con-

sider whether the information you seek will remain the same or change over time and conduct additional research as needed.

3. For additional information on reference books, consult **Guide to Reference Books** *by* **Eugene P. Sheehy,** as referred to in our example of catalog information above. Published by the American Library Association, "Sheehy" has come to be known by generations of library science students as the bible of reference books. The *Guide to Reference Books* is organized by subject and gives details and brief descriptions of more than 16,000 reference books.

4. Experienced researchers know that one good source frequently leads to another. Most of the books listed in *How and Where to Look It Up* have bibliographies. When you look up something in a reference book, make it a point to check the bibliography to see what other sources might be useful. This is particularly important when conducting in-depth research.

5. Major newspapers are usually available on microfilm and/or microfiche in the communities they serve, but not all are fully indexed. The most widely available newspaper is the *New York Times*, which has an index that is so detailed and comprehensive that researching it frequently eliminates the need to call up the individual articles on microfilm. The *Times's* coverage of national and international news is so extensive that it can often be used as a guide to when events are covered in other newspapers that do not have extensive indexes.

6. Most libraries have photocopying facilities, so there is no longer the need to hand-copy quotes and bibliographic information onto file cards. Simply photocopy the pages that contain the information you want and take them home or to your office to work with at your own pace. The copies can be placed in manila folders by subject or chapter or any other convenient arrangement. Experienced researchers *always copy the title page and copyright page* of the reference books they use and attach them to the other copied pages. This eliminates any confusion later about the source of the material. The copyright information remains with the material in case permissions must later be obtained for quoting or reprinting.

At one time photocopying of copyrighted material was prohibited under U.S. copyright laws. This is no longer the case. Extensive revisions were made to the copyright law in 1976; among them were modifications of the "fair use" doctrine to permit photocopying for research puposes.

Bring plenty of change when you go to the library to copy something. This will avoid delays when the "exact change" indicator comes on.

7. For in-depth research in a large group of reference books and periodicals, consider using an online service, such as DIALOG, to conduct a database search. Online services can tailor a search to your needs precisely and can print out bibliographies of sources, abstracts, and, in many cases, the full text of the source you want. See Section 6, "Electronic Databases," for information on how to conduct a search and what is available through several online services.

8. If your project requires use of the traditional file-card approach for citations and bibliographic material, consult one of the many guides to writing a research paper. Two good ones are:

MLA Handbook for Writers of Research Papers, Theses, and Dissertations. Modern Language Association, 1988.

A Manual for Writers of Term Papers, Theses, and Dissertations, by Kate Turabian. University of Chicago Press, 5th edition, 1987. Available in paperback, this book complements the venerable *Chicago Manual of Style,* 13th edition, also published by the University of Chicago.

9. Create your own mini reference library. If you find yourself going to the library to look up the same reference book again and again, consider purchasing that book for your personal or office library. Most information professionals have a small desktop library of their own for quick research of the information they most frequently need. These desktop libraries commonly include a dictionary, a style guide, a small atlas, the *World Almanac,* and, more and more these days, a computer manual or two.

Reference Books
Subject Index

A

ABBREVIATIONS

Abbreviations Dictionary, edited by Ralph De Sola. Elsevier, 7th edition, 1985. Covers most standard abbreviations, including euphemisms, slang, some technical and professional shorthand, historical/mythological references, geographical data, eponyms, airlines/airports of the world—in short, 1,200 pages of miscellaneous information of all kinds.

Acronyms, Initialisms and Abbreviations Dictionary, edited by Jennifer Mossman, four volumes and supplement. Gale, biennial. Gives meaning of abbreviations and acronyms with English translations, when necessary, and location or country of origin. Includes symbols such as chemical elements, but not local institutions or associations.

ACRONYMS. *See* ABBREVIATIONS.

AFRICAN AMERICANS. *See also* ETHNIC GROUPS.

Blacks in American Films and Television: An Encyclopedia, by Donald Bogle. New York: Garland, 1988. An introduction to the history of Blacks in the media and the evolution of their role in films, television, and radio. Includes listings of radio shows, films, and television shows with critical analyses of Black actors and directors.

Black Writers of America: A Comprehensive Anthology, edited by Richard Barksdale and Keneth Kinnamon. Macmillan, 1972. Collection of Afro-American literature from the eighteenth century to the last half of our own. Most works are given complete. Introductions to chronological periods provide overviews of the literature of the time and its sociohistorical context. Biographical facts and critical assessments are given for each writer. Diversity of selections include folk tales and oratory. Includes bibliography and index.

Ebony Pictorial History of Black America, three volumes plus 1973 yearbook. Johnson, 1971–73. An "extended essay" with extraordinarily vivid illustrations.

From Slavery to Freedom: A History of Negro Americans, by John Hope Franklin. Knopf, 4th edition, 1974. A history of African-Americans from Africa to the present. It also explores the history of Blacks in Canada, Latin America, and the Caribbean. Covers the African homelands and their sociology, the slave trade, the Caribbean, and slavery as an American institution. In the 20th century, the author documents the Harlem Renaissance, the New Deal, and developments up to the death of Martin Luther King, Jr.

Negro Almanac, edited by Harry A. Ploski and James Williams. Bellweather, 5th edition, 1989. Reference covering the cultural and political history of Black Americans. Includes generous amount of statistical information and biographies of Black Americans, both historical and comtemporary. Indexed.

Reconstruction: America's Unfinished Revolution, by Eric Foner. Harper, 1988. Incorporating much eyewitness material, this book emphasizes the centrality of the Black experience. The book also examines the themes of race and class, the remodeling of Southern society, and the national context. A complete, modern, scholarly text. Includes bibliography and index.

AIDS

AIDS: A Self-Care Manual, edited by BettyClare Moffat et al. AIDS Project, Los Angeles, 1987. A practical and medically authoritative book on AIDS. Discusses epidemiological questions, AIDS myths, caring for people with AIDS, and current medical treatments. Contains glossary of AIDS-related terms, appendices, and index.

The AIDS Information Sourcebook, edited by H. Robert Malinowsky and Gerald J. Perry. Oryx, 3rd edition, 1991. Provides general information about AIDS, including a historical overview

of key events and research. Includes bibliography and subject index.

ALCOHOLISM

Drugfree: A Unique Positive Approach to Staying off Alcohol and Drugs, by Richard B. Seymour and David E. Smith. Facts on File, 1987. Geared to the recovering abuser, the heart of the book deals with how to stay off alcohol and drugs and conquer "white knuckle sobriety." Also deals with physical and psychological effects of alcohol and drug use and addiction and ways of getting help. Includes bibliography and index.

The Encyclopedia of Alcoholism, by Morris Chafitz, M.D., Robert O'Brien, and Glen Evans. Facts on File, 2nd edition, 1991. Updated edition of the standard reference on alcoholism, with alphabetically arranged essays and definitions. Has appendices and index.

ALMANACS. *See* GENERAL REFERENCE BOOKS.

ANATOMY

ABC's of the Human Body, Reader's Digest, 1987. Includes interesting facts, quick reference, basic medical and biological information, and practical advice about the human body. Written for a general audience. Illustrated and indexed.

Gray's Anatomy of the Human Body, edited by Carmine D. Clemente. Febiger, 30th edition, 1984. Comprehensive, standard title with illustrations, definitions, and descriptions. Considered a classic.

Kimber-Gray-Stackpole's Anatomy and Physiology, by Marjorie A. Miller, Anna B. Drakontides, and Lutie C. Lowell. Macmillan, 17th edition, 1977. Textbook designed for nursing students. Attempts to integrate micro- and macroscopic views of anatomy. Illustrated and indexed.

ANIMALS. *See also* ZOOLOGY.

Audubon Society Field Guide to North American Fishes, Whales, and Dolphins, by the Audubon Society Staff and others. Knopf, 1983.

Audubon Society Field Guide to North American Mammals, by the Audubon Society Staff and John O. Whitaker. Knopf, 1980.

Dictionary of Animals, edited by Michael Chinery. Arco, 1984. Alphabetical descriptions and classifications of animals written for young people. Illustrated and indexed.

The Encyclopedia of Mammals, edited by Dr. David Macdonald. Facts on File, 1984. Written for a general audience, this comprehensive sourcebook has signed articles on all known species of mammals, from mice to elephants, from whales to bats, with pertinent facts given in tables at the beginning of each article. Has more than 1,000 color illustrations and appendices, glossary, bibliography, and index.

A Field Guide to the Mammals, by William H. Burt. Houghton Mifflin, 1980. Houghton Mifflin, 3rd edition, 1976.

A Field Guide to Animal Tracks, by Murie J. Olaus. Houghton Mifflin, 2nd edition, 1975.

Grzimek's Animal Life Encyclopedia, edited by Bernhard Grzimek, 13 volumes. Van Nostrand Reinhold, 1972–75. Each volume deals with a group classification (e.g., "Lower Animals," "Insects"). Using minimal connective text to explain zoological concepts, encyclopedia presents detailed information on known animals. Contains accompanying illustration of each animal discussed. Includes appendices and index.

Grzimek's Encyclopedia of Mammals, edited by Bernard Grzimek, five volumes. McGraw Hill, 2nd edition, 1989. Updated from the 1964 version, this work benefits from and incorporates 25 years of recent zoological study. More than two hundred of the world's leading biologists, zoologists, ecologists, and photographers contribute.

Larousse Encyclopedia of the Animal World, Larousse, 1975. Older but useful reference that describes animal species in layperson's terms. Illustrated. Organized taxonomically.

The Life of Vertebrates, by John Z. Young. Oxford University Press, 3rd edition, 1981. Synoptic natural history of the evolution of vertebrates. Treats the increasing complexity and adaptability of vertebrates. College-level text. Indexed.

Macmillan Illustrated Animal Encyclopedia, edited by Dr. Philip Whitfield. Macmillan, 1984. Catalog of vertebrate animals selected to represent the diversity of the group. Organized by taxonomic family. Includes short descriptions with accompanying illustrations. Indexed.

Walker's Mammals of the World, by Ronald M. Nowak and John L. Paradiso, two volumes. Johns Hopkins University Press, 4th edition, 1983. Includes concise descriptions and accompanying photographs. Organized by taxonomic family. Indexed.

ANIMALS—PREHISTORIC

Dinosaur!, by David Norman, Ph.D. Prentice Hall, 1991. Conveys the geological time scale, evolution, and natural history of dinosaurs, as well as the paleontological discoveries that have enabled their story to be reconstructed. Extensively illustrated; indexed.

Dinosaurs, An Illustrated History, by Edwin H. Colbert. Hammond, 1983. A short illustrated outline of the natural history of the dinosaurs—beginnings, evolutionary development, their world, and their extinction. Written for the layperson. Also contains additional background information on the Mesozoic era and its other nonlizard inhabitants. Includes glossary and index.

The Dinosaur Heresies: New Theories Unlocking the Mystery of the Dinosaurs and Their Extinction, by Robert T. Bakker, Ph.D. Morrow, 1986. One of the most-discussed books on popular science in recent years. Bakker analyzes the controversies surrounding dinosaur extinction and advances original theories of his own, while painting a picture of very active, adaptable animals. Easily understandable, well illustrated, and without scientific jargon.

Field Guide to Dinosaurs: The First Complete Guide to Every Dinosaur Now Known, by The Diagram Group. Avon, 1983.

ANTHROPOLOGY. *See also* SOCIAL SCIENCES.

Encyclopedia of Anthropology, Harper & Row, 1976. Unique, one-volume treatment of anthropology and related areas, with clear, unbiased information. Entries cover terms, concepts, theories, and biographies. For high school students and undergraduates.

ANTIQUES AND COLLECTIBLES

The Dictionary of Antiques and the Decorative Arts, by Louise A. Boger. Scribner, revised edition, 1979. Short articles and illustrations covering furniture, glass, ceramics, styles, terms, and biographies; international in scope.

Kovel's Antiques and Collectibles Price List, by Ralph Kovel and Terry Kovel. Crown, annual.

Recent appraiser-approved prices for over 50,000 antiques and collectible items.

Kovel's Know Your Antiques, by Ralph Kovel and Terry Kovel. Crown, updated edition, 1990. How to recognize and evaluate any antique, large or small, like an expert. Covers pottery, porcelain, silver, pewter, country and formal furniture, pressed and cut glass, prints, bottles, ironware, tinware, letters, sheet music, autographs, books, magazines, and more. Provides advice about caring for antiques and recognizing frauds. Has bibliographies for each specialty.

Kovel's Know Your Collectibles, by Ralph Kovel and Terry Kovel. Advises on what collectible objects are likely to increase in value and how to preserve, protect, and sell them. Covers ceramics, pottery, furniture, glass, toys, print advertisements, and many other items. Has bibliographies for each major specialty.

ARCHAEOLOGY

Cambridge Encyclopedia of Archeology, edited by Andrew Sherratt. Crown, 1980. Entries cover the major themes raised by archaeological research and the development of the discipline; the terminology, methods, and history of archaeology, and the process of analysis; and the details of major archaeological discoveries in India, Western Europe, the Mediterranean, Asia, the Arctic, and Australia. Explains dating methods and chronological atlases.

Facts on File Dictionary of Archaeology, edited by Ruth D. Whitehouse. Facts on File, 1983. Over 3,500 entries covering themes, concepts, and discoveries. Illustrated; useful to both students and professionals. Covers prehistory to the colonization of the Americas.

ARCHITECTURE

Architecture Through the Ages, by Talbot Hamlin. Putnam, 1953. College text; a survey history from the social point of view. Indexed and illustrated.

Encyclopedia of Architecture: Design, Engineering and Construction, edited by Joseph A. Wilkes and Robert T. Packard, five volumes. New York: Wiley, 1988. This work not only addresses the history of Western architecture over the last 200 years, but it also explores modern concerns such as day-care centers and handicapped-access build-

ing codes. The work covers 500 different topics, and each article was written and edited by experts in the field. Accessible to both the art historian and the weekend do-it-yourselfer. Contains 3,000 photographs. Sponsored by American Institute of Architects.

Macmillan Encyclopedia of Architects, edited by Adolf K. Placzek, four volumes. Free Press, New York/Collier Macmillan, London, 1982. A social and historical view of ancient, medieval, Renaissance, and modern architecture of Europe, the Middle East, and North America. Includes biographical entries.

Old House Dictionary: An Illustrated Guide to American Domestic Architecture (1600–1940), by Steven J. Phillips. American Source Books, 1989. Definitions of more than 1,500 terms relating to American architecture. Cross-referenced and topically arranged.

Sir Bannister Fletcher's A History of Architecture, edited by John Musgrove. Butterworth's, 19th edition, 1987. Title refers to the famous creator of this reference. Overarching view of architectural history, newly rewritten and expanded to include worldwide coverage. Extensively illustrated, with glossary, index, and bibliographies appended to each chapter. Includes general introductions and background for each chapter.

ART. *See* FINE ARTS; GRAPHIC ARTS.

ASSOCIATIONS. *See* ORGANIZATIONS.

ASTROLOGY. *See* OCCULT.

ASTRONOMY

The Amateur Astronomer's Handbook, by James Muirden. Harper, 3rd edition, 1982. For beginners who want to select equipment and set up their own observatories. Includes celestial chart tables of eclipses and planetary positions.

Contemporary Astronomy, by Jay M. Pasachoff. CBS College Publishing, 3rd edition, 1985. Textbook for beginners who have no background in mathematics or physics. Plunges right into astronomy, in clear, colloquial English. Well illustrated. Includes appendices, glossary, index, and bibliography.

A Field Guide to the Stars and Planets, by Jay M. Pasachoff and Donald M. Menzel. Houghton Mifflin, 1980. Houghton Mifflin, 1983.

The International Encyclopedia of Astronomy, edited by Patrick Moore. Orion, 1987. Popular reference work that condenses difficult concepts into readable prose. No prior knowledge of astronomy is assumed. Several major essays are included as well as shorter entries. Illustrated in full color.

The Universe From Your Backyard: A Guide to Deep-Sky Objects from *Astronomy* **Magazine,** by David J. Eicher. Cambridge University Press, 1988. A useful guide for all amateur astronomers.

ATLASES

Commercial Atlas and Marketing Guide. Rand McNally, annual. Maps of U.S. states and metropolitan areas showing transportation patterns, population, and other useful demographic data. Substantial tables give other commercial and marketing information such as per capita income. Includes extensive, keyed index.

Goode's World Atlas, edited by Edward B. Espenshade, Jr. and Joel L. Morrison. Rand McNally, 18th edition, 1989. Contains thematic maps and tables showing distribution of population, minerals, manufacturing, and other subjects. Also included are metropolitan-area maps, physical-political maps of regions, geographic tables, and ocean-floor maps showing earth movement. Pronouncing index included.

Hammond Ambassador World Atlas, Hammond, 1987. Political, physical, and thematic maps. Has both alphabetical index and individual indexes for each map giving some gazetteer information.

National Geographic Atlas of the World. National Geographic Society, 6th edition, 1990. Thoroughly revised and modernized since the 5th edition, the new *National Geographic Atlas of the World* reflects a growing interest in and concern with global ecology. Unique state-of-the-art satellite images provide spectacular views of the earth's major regions as seen from space. The physical and cultural maps are related to these satellite images. Has extensive supporting text, including factual articles on all the countries. Gazetteer locates some 150,000 places.

Rand McNally New International Atlas, edited by John Leverenz. Rand McNally, anniversary edition, 1990. Up-to-date physical, political, and thematic maps. Also contains tables with population

and other demographic information. Gives local forms of names with conventional English derivations for major places. Includes full index.

Rand McNally Road Atlas: United States, Canada, Mexico. Rand McNally, annual. Maps of states, provinces, national parks, and city and metropolitan areas. Includes tourist information with keys to points of interest and complete index.

The Times Atlas of the World. Times Books, 7th edition, 1985. Large-scale maps are presented in a large format from John Bartholomew & Son of Edinburgh, United Kingdom, one of the world's oldest and most respected cartographers. The scale permits more detail; there are more than 200,000 locations clearly labeled on the maps and listed in the Index-Gazetteer with latitude and longitude coordinates for locating them precisely.

ATLASES—HISTORICAL

Atlas of American History, edited by James Truslow Adams. Scribner, 2nd edition, 1985. Development of the United States illustrated by maps. Provides coverage through the Vietnam War. Includes some demographic maps. Indexed.

Historical Atlas of the United States, National Geographic Society, 1988. Maps, photographs, charts, and text on the history, boundaries, land, people, economics, and communities of the United States.

Shepherd's Historical Atlas, by William R. Shepherd. Harper, 9th edition, 1980. Maps illustrating Western political history from Mycenaen Greece to the mid-20th century. Indexed.

Times Atlas of World History, edited by Geoffrey Barraclough. Hammond, 3rd edition, 1989. Maps showing movements in world history. Emphasis is on Europe and America. Maps are accompanied by explanatory essays. Includes glossary and index.

ATMOSPHERE

A Field Guide to the Atmosphere, by Vincent J. Schaefer and John A. Day. Houghton Mifflin, 1983.

AUTHORS. *See also* LITERATURE.

American Authors 1600–1900, edited by Stanley J. Kunitz and Howard Haycraft. H.W. Wilson, 8th edition, 1977. Biographical dictionary of American literature from the Jamestown settlement to the close of the 19th century. Length of essays varies according to the importance of the writer. Short, critical appraisals are sometimes given. Bibliographies appended to essays.

Contemporary Authors, Gale, annual. A biographical dictionary series, begun in 1960, which presents writers living or deceased since then. Entries are short and factual, unless the author's importance warrants an extended critical commentary.

    Autobiography Series (1st volume, 1984) collects 10,000-to-15,000-word autobiographical essays from important contemporary writers. Each volume is fully indexed and functions as a companion volume to the main series.
    Bibliographical Series (1st volume, 1986) is another companion series that surveys the writings by and about important contemporary authors. Each bibliography is accompanied by an essay, giving other sources of information. Indexed.

Cyclopedia of World Authors, edited by Frank N. Magill, three volumes. Salem, 1974. Compilation of biographical sketches of 1,000 major world authors, with lists of their works.

European Authors, 1000–1900, edited by Stanley J. Kunitz and Vineta Colby. H.W. Wilson, 1967. Biographical dictionary of European literature. Bibliographies appended to each article. Treats minor and major figures.

Twentieth Century Authors, by Stanley Kunitz and Howard Haycraft. H.W. Wilson, 1942, 1st supplement, 1955. Popularly written sketches of authors of all nations whose books are familiar to readers of English; includes bibliographies of major books by and about each author.

World Authors, 1950–1970, H.W. Wilson, 1975; 1970–1975, H.W. Wilson, 1980; 1975-1980, H.W. Wilson, 1985. These three volumes are updatings of the original, *Twentieth Century Authors,* by Stanley Kunitz. Entries are comprehensive and often include comments by the author.

    Index to the Wilson Authors Series, H.W. Wilson, revised edition, 1986. Name index to the 10-volume Wilson authors series of American, British, European, Greek, Latin, and world authors.

AUTOMOBILES

Automotive Encyclopedia, edited by William K. Toboldt and others. Goodheart, 1989. Textbook on basic principles of automotive design, construction, operation, maintenance, and repair; covers American models and some foreign cars.

Chilton's Auto Repair Manual. Chilton, annual. Covers all mass-produced American cars of the past six or seven years plus the current year. Illustrated; includes charts to help diagnose problems. Useful for both novices and experts.

Chilton's Import Car Repair Manual. Chilton, annual. Covers imported cars.

The Complete Car Cost Guide, compiled by IntelliChoice, annual. Presents model-by-model charts of purchase costs and dealer costs, plus projected expenditures and devaluations. Good to have when negotiating with car dealers.

B

BALLET

Balanchine's Complete Stories of the Great Ballets, by George Balanchine and Francis Mason. Doubleday, revised edition, 1977. Stories and some notes and comments on well-known ballets by the most influential choreographer of the twentieth century. Included are essays on such subjects as "How to Enjoy Ballet" and "How I Became a Dancer and Choreographer." Some of Balanchine's comments shed light on the author as well as the ballet in question. Illustrated; includes index and glossary of ballet terms.

The Concise Oxford Dictionary of Ballet, by Horst Koegler. Oxford University Press, 2nd edition, 1982. Entries on a variety of ballet-related topics. Originally a translation of a German work, this edition adds information to make it pertinent to English-speaking readers.

BANKING. *See* FINANCE.

BASEBALL

The Baseball Encyclopedia: The Complete and Official Record of Major League Baseball, edited by Joseph Reichler. Macmillan, 7th edition, 1988. A big book—2,875 pages. Covers everything about

Major League baseball, including awards and special achievements, all-time leaders, teams, players, home/road performance, championships, and major changes in playing and scoring rules, back to 1876.

The Sports Encyclopedia: Baseball, by David S. Neft and Richard M. Cohen. St. Martin's, 10th edition, 1990. Contains team statistics for each season, with alphabetical registers for batters and pitchers in each era and short summation of each season.

Total Baseball, by John Thjorn and Pete Palmer. Warner, 1989. Another big book—2,294 pages. First part has features such as "Scandals and Controversies" and "Tragedies and Shortened Careers"; second part has statistics, including many developed especially for this book, such as "Clutch Hitting Index" and "Relief Rankings," plus more conventional statistics on teams, players, and awards.

BASKETBALL

The Official NBA Basketball Encyclopedia, edited by Zander Hollander and Alex Sachare. Villard, 1989. "The most complete historical work ever created about professional basketball." Covers history, Hall of Fame, all-time records, all-star games, and official NBA rules. Includes complete statistical profile of every player who has ever appeared in the NBA. Illustrated with photographs; indexed.

BENEFITS. *See also* MEDICARE.

Catalog of Federal Domestic Assistance, Office of Management and Budget. U.S. Government Printing Office. Looseleaf with updating pages. Comprehensive description of federal programs and activities that provide assistance or benefits to Americans.

What Every Veteran Should Know, annual with monthly supplements, Veterans' Information Service. Provides general information on laws and programs relating to veterans.

BIBLE REFERENCES. *See also* BIBLES; CHRISTIANITY.

Almanac of the Bible, edited by Geoffrey Wigoder. Prentice Hall, 1991. Ecumenical scholarship in a thorough study of the Bible that covers the books of the Bible, biography, natural history, quotations, archaeology, and many other aspects.

Dictionary of the Bible, by James Hastings. Macmillan, revised edition, 1963. Based on the Revised Standard Version; Protestant scholarship for the general reader.

Dictionary of the Bible, by John L. MacKenzie. Macmillan, 1965. Catholic scholarship for the general reader. Complements James Hastings's *Dictionary of the Bible,* above.

Harper's Bible Dictionary, edited by Paul J. Achtemeier. Harper, 1985. Explains terms of current biblical scholarship. Extended entries define terms in relation to their biblical usage, then explain where problems, if any, arise from that usage. Entries also give the general or specific background of names and places, as well as their location in the Bible. The books of both Old and New Testaments are outlined and key texts given. Designed to be compatible with any translation; entries written by Protestant, Catholic, and Jewish authorities.

The Interpreter's Dictionary of the Bible, four volumes plus supplement. Abingdon, 1962. Scholarly and encyclopedic; refers to the King James version and the Revised Standard Version, with Apocrypha. For the general reader.

The Interpreter's One Volume Commentary on the Bible, Abingdon, 1971. Ecumenical scholarship for the layperson; specific as well as general topics are covered.

The Jerome Biblical Commentary, by Raymond Edward Brown. Prentice-Hall, 1968. Roman Catholic scholarship. Book-by-book commentary for the scholar and the general reader.

Strong's Exhaustive Concordance, by James Strong. Broadman, 1979. Most complete concordance of the King James version along with key word comparisons of selected words and phrases in the Revised Standard Version, the New English Bible, the Jerusalem Bible, and the New American Standard Bible.

BIBLES. *See also* BIBLE REFERENCES; CHRISTIANITY.

The Holy Bible, King James version. Oxford University Press, 1965. Authorized texts of Old and New Testaments and Apocrypha.

The Holy Scriptures According to the Masoretic Text, two volumes. Jewish Publication Society of America, 1955. Hebrew-English Bible (Old Testament). Completely modern translation with the Hebrew in parallel columns.

The New American Bible, edited by the Catholic Biblical Association of America. Kenedy, 1970. Roman Catholic version based on modern English translations; replaces the Douay edition.

The New Oxford Annotated Bible with the Apocrypha, Oxford University Press, 1973. Ecumenical study edition of Revised Standard Version. Modern translation with scholarly notes for all faiths.

Tanakh. Jewish Publication Society of America, 1985. A recent translation of the Old Testament according to traditional Hebrew text. This edition is in contemporary English.

BIBLIOGRAPHIES—GENERAL. *See also* BIBLIOGRAPHIES—PERIODICALS; LITERATURE.

Books in Print, Bowker, annual. Comprehensive author-and-title index to all U.S. books in print during the year covered by the edition. Lists both hardcover and paperback editions. (*See also* SUBJECT GUIDE TO BOOKS IN PRINT, below.)

Subject Guide to Books in Print, Bowker, annual. Companion to *Books in Print* (above). Indexes by subject all U.S. books in print during the year covered by the edition. Lists both hardcover and softcover editions.

Subject Guide to Major U.S. Government Publications, American Library Association, 2nd edition, 1987. Emphasis is on period since 1968; items were chosen "with an eye toward enduring significance."

BIBLIOGRAPHIES—PERIODICALS

Gale Directory of Publications, Gale, annual. Comprehensive geographical list of major print media in United States and Canada; supersedes the *Ayer Directory of Publications* and *The IMS . . . Ayer Directory of Publications.*

Magazines for Libraries, edited by William A. Katz and Linda S. Katz. Bowker, 6th edition, 1989. Annotated classified guide to recommended periodicals for the general reader and school, college, and public libraries. Provides comparative evaluations and grade- and age-level recommendations for all periodicals included.

Reader's Guide to Periodical Literature, H.W. Wilson, annual. Complete indexing of articles, book reviews, essays, poems, and short stories published in 191 leading U.S. magazines. Indexed by author and subject.

Ulrich's International Periodicals Directory, Bowker. Kept up to date by *Ulrich's Quarterly.* A classified guide to more than 60,000 current periodicals, foreign and domestic.

BICYCLES

The Complete Book of Bicycling, by Eugene A. Sloane. Simon & Schuster, 4th edition, 1988. How-to book covering all subjects, including maintenance, new technology, and sports-medicine aspects. Includes appendix, bibliography, and index.

BIOGRAPHY. *See also* GENEALOGY *and specific subjects, such as* SCIENCE.

Biography and Genealogy Master Index, edited by Miranda C. Herbert and Barbara McNeil. Gale, 1980. The purpose of this book is to indicate where to find biographical material about a given person. Individuals are arranged alphabetically. Many different sources are indexed. Has annual supplements.

Biography Index, H.W. Wilson. Cumulative index to biographical material in books and magazines from January 1946 to present. Includes index by profession. Updated with interim issues.

Current Biography, H.W. Wilson, annual. Biographies of prominent people written in lively, popular prose. Emphasis is on entertainers, star athletes, politicians, and other celebrities. Series is cumulative, with biographies revised and updated occasionally. Each volume has seven-year index.

Dictionary of American Biography, Scribner, 17 volumes, 1964–81. Long articles, with appended bibliographies, on noted individuals who died prior to 1965. A complete index lists all entries in the series in one alphabet.

> **Concise Dictionary of American Biography,** Scribner, 3rd edition, complete to 1960. Entries range from the minimal, giving only the basic factual information, to extended commentaries that preserve the style and context of the original 17-volume *Dictionary of American Biography.*

Dictionary of American Negro Biography, edited by Rayford W. Logan and Michael R. Winston. Norton, 1983. Biographies of black Americans who have had an impact on history, excluding those still living. Bibliographies follow entries. Includes index of entries by profession or field of endeavor.

Dictionary of National Biography: The Concise Dictionary. Vol. I (to 1900), Oxford University Press, 1953; Vol. II (1901–70), Oxford University Press, 1982; supplement, 1971–80, Oxford University Press, 1986 (includes cumulative index 1901–80). Volumes I and II are extremely condensed outlines (taken from the parent work) of the lives of famous Britons who died during the given period. The volume 1971–80 is representative of the whole set of dictionaries but covers the latest period. In addition to basic biographical facts, the entries give critical appreciations of the subject's career and life work. This volume has an index that covers the 20th century to 1980.

The International Who's Who, Europa, annual. Dictionary of biography of famous and influential contemporaries. Information mainly on individual's career.

Notable American Women, 1607–1950, edited by Edward T. James, three volumes. Harvard University Press, 1971. Long scholarly articles on women "whose work in some way took them before the public." Includes notorious underworld and demimonde personages and adventurers as well. Bibliographies appended to each entry.

> **Notable American Women, The Modern Period,** edited by Barbara Sicherman and Carol Hurd Green. Harvard University Press, 1980. This volume makes a special effort to include minority women.

Our Foreign-Born Citizens, by Annie S. Beard. Crowell, 6th edition, 1968. Short celebratory biographies of a handful of famous and influential Americans of foreign birth. For high school students.

Webster's American Biographies, edited by Charles Van Doren. Merriam-Webster, 1975. Full-scale critical biographies of notable Americans, including contemporaries. Indexes list entries by place of birth and profession.

Webster's New Biographical Dictionary, Merriam-Webster, 1983. Dictionary of famous and influential individuals excluding living persons. Emphasis is on historical importance. Pronouncing index included.

Who Was Who in America, 1897–1985, eight volumes. Marquis, 1943–85. **Historical Volume,** *1607–1896,* Marquis, 1963. **Index,** *1607–1985,* Marquis, 1985. These volumes contain all the biographies that were removed from *Who's Who* because of death of the individual. The *Historical Volume* also includes tables, time lines, maps, and other references useful to the study of American biographical history. The series provides entries on Americans from the founding of the Jamestown settlement in 1607. The *Index* lists the entries of all the volumes in one alphabetized list.

Who's Who, St. Martin's, annual. Dictionary of biography that recognizes Britons whose careers "affect the political, economic, scientific, and artistic life of the country."

Who's Who Among Black Americans, by Iris Lloyd. Gale, annual. Short entries focusing on career achievements and positions. Indexes list entries by place of birth and profession.

Who's Who in America, Marquis, two volumes. Biennial. Entries on contemporaries who hold important positions or whose achievements are considered significant. Indexes break down entries by category and list retirees and the recently deceased. *See also* WHO'S WHO IN THE WORLD and WHO'S WHO IN AMERICAN WOMEN, Marquis.

BIOLOGY

Biology, by Helena Curtis and Sue N. Barnes. Worth, 5th edition, 1989. Introductory biology textbook for college students. Begins with cell biology and evolutionary theory and moves on to substantial discussions of genetics, taxonomy, plant and animal biology, population genetics and dynamics, and finally, ecology.

Exploring Biology, by Pamela S. Camp and Karen Arms. CBS College Publishing, 1984. Introductory text for nonmajors that begins with familiar topics before heading into unfamiliar waters.

BIRDS

Audubon Society Encyclopedia of North American Birds, by John K. Terres. Knopf, 1980.

Audubon Society Field Guide to North American Birds, two volumes. Knopf, 1977.

Volume 1: Eastern Region, by the Audubon Society Staff and John Bull.
Volume 2: Western Region, by the Audubon Society Staff and M.D. Udvardy.

Audubon Society Master Guide to Birding, edited by John Farrand, Jr., three volumes. Knopf, 1983.
Volume 1: Loons to Sandpipers.
Volume 2: Gulls to Dippers.
Volume 3: Old World Warblers to Sparrows.

The Birder's Handbook: Field Guide to the Natural History of North American Birds, by Paul R. Ehrlich, David S. Dobkin, and Darryl Wheye. Simon & Schuster, 1988. Details all bird species known to nest regularly on the North American continent north of the Mexican border, as well as all the extinct birds that had nested there since the Europeans arrived. Includes 60-page bibliography plus Index to North American Birds.

The Encyclopedia of Birds, edited by Christopher M. Perrins and Dr. Alex L.A. Middleton. Facts on File, 1985. A total of 180 bird families worldwide are catalogued, with details about their distribution, physical characteristics, feeding habits, social organization, and reproductive behavior. Illustrated with 335 color photographs. Has glossary and index.

A Field Guide to Advanced Birding, by Kenn Kaufman. Houghton Mifflin, 1980.

A Field Guide to Birds of Britain and Europe, by Roger Tory Peterson. Houghton Mifflin, 4th edition, 1988.

A Field Guide to the Birds: A Completely New Guide to All the Birds of Eastern and Central North America, by Roger Tory Peterson. Houghton Mifflin, 1980.

A Field Guide to Birds' Nests, by Hal H. Harrison. Houghton Mifflin, 1988.

Field Guide to the Birds of North America, edited by Shorley Scott. National Geographic, 1983.

A Field Guide to Eastern Birds, by Roger Tory Peterson. Houghton Mifflin, 1984.

A Field Guide to Hawks, by William S. Clark. Houghton Mifflin, 1987.

A Field Guide to Mexican Birds, by Roger Tory Peterson and Edward A Chalif. Houghton Mifflin, 1973.

A Field Guide to Western Birds, by Roger Tory Peterson. Houghton Mifflin, 1990.

BLACKS. *See* AFRICAN AMERICANS.

BONDS. *See* INVESTMENTS.

BOOKS. *See* BIBLIOGRAPHIES—GENERAL; PUBLISHING.

BOTANY. *See also* HORTICULTURE.

A Dictionary of Botany, by R. John Little and C. Eugene Jones. Van Nostrand Reinhold, 1980. Definitions of terms for general use.

BUSINESS. *See also* EMPLOYMENT; FINANCE; FRANCHISING; INVESTMENTS; LABOR; MANAGEMENT; PERSONAL FINANCE.

The Business One Irwin Business and Investment Almanac, edited by Sumner N. Levine. Business One Irwin, annual. Formerly entitled *Dow Jones-Irwin Business and Investment Almanac.* Covers stock-market averages, price/earnings ratios, futures markets, mutual fund performance, foreign stock markets, and many other topics relating to investments.

Business Rankings and Salary Index, Business Library Compilation. Gale, 1988. Ranks corporations, products, and people. Includes descriptions of ranking criteria and salaries for 150 occupations.

Dun's Directory of Service Companies, Dun's Marketing Services, 1989. Provides information on approximately 50,000 businesses in service industries that employ over 50 people. Listed alphabetically, by geography, and by industry.

How to Run a Small Business, J.K. Lasser Tax Institute, McGraw-Hill, 6th edition, 1989. Practical advice for small businesses and for people considering opening them. Details everything from choosing a location to financing to tax management, bookkeeping, accounting, personnel management, and computer technology. Concisely written and well-organized. Indexed.

Louis Rukeyser's Business Almanac, edited by Louis Rukeyser and Joan Cooney. Simon & Schuster, annual. Compilation of facts and figures of the business world, covering who owns what and controls what, where and how the investment money is moving, and many other related topics.

Moody's Industrial Manual. Moody's Investors Service, twice a week, annual bound volume. Covers

U.S., Canadian, and foreign companies listed on U.S. exchanges; includes corporate history, subsidiaries, principal plants, business and products, and financial data.

The Practical Guide to Joint Ventures and Corporate Alliances, by Robert Porter Lynch. Wiley, 1989. This is a handbook to guide the businessperson through the creation and operation of a joint venture. Covers strategy, legal structure, and corporate restructuring.

Roberts' Dictionary of Industrial Relations, by Harold S. Roberts. BNA, 3rd edition, 1986. Provides terms and other information in the labor–management field; includes summaries of important cases.

Small Business Sourcebook, edited by Charity Anne Dorgan, two volumes. Gale, 3rd edition, 1989. Lists of trade associations, periodicals, seminars, and trade shows for small businesses.

Standard and Poor's Register of Corporations, Directors and Executives. Standard and Poor's, annual. Published continuously since 1928, this three-volume reference provides essential information on virtually all of the nation's corporations and their key people. Updated with supplements in April, July, and October.
   Volume 1: Profiles of more than 55,000 corporations in alphabetical order.
   Volume 2: Brief biographies of directors and executives.
   Volume 3: Indexes according to geography, industry, and other parameters.

Thomas' Register of American Manufacturers, Thomas, annual. Classified section, brand-names index, and catalogs of companies appearing in the alphabetical section.

C

CAREERS. *See* EMPLOYMENT.

CARS. *See* AUTOMOBILES.

CATS. *See* PETS.

CHEMISTRY

General Chemistry, by James Brady. Wiley, 1986. Nontechnical treatment for senior high school and college students; includes history.

C.R.C. Handbook of Chemistry and Physics: A Ready Reference Book of Chemical and Physical Data, CRC Press, annual. Compilation of essential tables and chemical and physical properties of elements and compounds.

General Chemistry: Principles and Structure, by James E. Brady and Gerard E. Humiston. Wiley, 5th edition, 1990. General chemistry textbook with built-in teaching aids. Study guides are printed in margins and review problems are given at the end of each topic. Complete package of teaching supplements is available. Covers both inorganic and organic chemistry. Thoroughly illustrated. Includes appendices, glossary, and index.

Hawley's Condensed Chemical Dictionary, Van Nostrand Reinhold, 11th edition, 1987. Revised by N. Irving Sax and Richard J. Lewis. Describes industrial and scientific chemicals, terms, processes, reactions, and related terminology and phenomena. Charts chemical structures; gives uses and trademarked products that employ these chemicals. Some emphasis is on environment and energy sources. Includes appendices.

Van Nostrand Reinhold Encyclopedia of Chemistry, edited by Douglas M. Considine. Van Nostrand Reinhold, 4th edition, 1984. Illustrated articles define and explain major topics in chemistry. Entries indexed.

CHILD CARE

Baby and Child Care, by Dr. Benjamin Spock and Dr. Michael B. Rothenberg. Dutton, 40th anniversary edition, 1985. The classic guide now deals with divorce, single and step-parents, and the role of fathers in childbirth. New sections cover child abuse and neglect, and there is a chapter on the importance of the mother–father relationship.

Childhood Symptoms: Every Parent's Guide to Childhood Illnesses, by Edward R. Brace and John P. Pacanowski, M.D., F.A.A.P. Harper, 1985. Easy-to-follow references guide the parent or caregiver through an analysis of the potential problem and alert the reader as to when medical help is needed. Specific symptoms are cross-referenced to conditions in which the symptom plays a part.

New Child Health Encyclopedia: the Complete Guide for Parents/Boston Children's Hospital, by the Boston Children's Hospital Medical Center staff. Delacorte, 1987. Specialized, practical advice book for parents. Divided into four sections: "Keeping Children Healthy," "Finding Health Care for Children," "Emergencies," and "Diseases and Symptoms." Provides reliable, up-to-date information on every subject by experts associated with one of the nation's leading child-care facilities. Indexed.

The New York Times Parent's Guide to the Best Books for Children, by Eden Ross Lipson. Random House, 1988. A guide for book-loving parents, this work has a specialized set of indexes that direct you to the right book for the child you have in mind. Covers picture books, wordless books, storybooks, and books for beginning to expert readers.

The Parent's Desk Reference, by Irene Franck and David Brownstone. Prentice Hall, 1991. An encyclopedic guide covering the rearing of children from prenatal to college age. Covers such major topics as health, psychology, education, and law. Has resource sections on emergency procedures, reading lists, curriculum samples, hotline numbers, and other vital information.

Your Baby and Child: From Birth to Age Five, by Penelope Leach. Knopf, revised edition, 1989. Described in a *New York Times* article as offering "a Britannica of information combined with motherly reassurance," *Your Baby and Child* tells you not only what to do, but why you should do it. Traditional advice is backed up or refuted by a compilation of clearly explained research studies.

CHRISTIANITY. *See also* BIBLE REFERENCES; BIBLES; RELIGION.

Catholic Almanac, Doubleday, annual. Provides information on news events of the year; current information on the activities of the Catholic Church, its members and its clergy; and statistics, documents, Catholic communications information, and church views on world issues.

Dictionary of Saints, by John J. Delaney. Doubleday, 1980. Short biographies of Roman Catholic saints. Indexes.

Handbook of Denominations in the United States, edited by Frank S. Mead and Samuel S. Hill. Abingdon, 8th edition, 1988. History and present structure of Christian religious bodies in the United States. Reports on doctrines of different churches. Provides bibliography and index.

The New Catholic Encyclopedia, 17 volumes, two supplements. McGraw-Hill, 1967. Completely new encyclopedia featuring articles on scripture, theology, liturgy, church history, canon, and civil law. Also contains entries on literature, science, art, and music, as they pertain to Catholicism. Includes biographies, excluding living persons, of significant figures in Church history. Cross-referenced, with illustration and maps. Bibliographies appended to each article.

Oxford Dictionary of the Christian Church, by Frank Leslie Cross. Oxford University Press, 2nd edition, 1974. Provides broad coverage of history, doctrines, biographies, terms, and other topics.

CHRONOLOGIES

The New York Public Library Book of Chronologies, edited by Bruce Wetterau. Prentice Hall, New York, 1990. The history of the world—from the Big Bang to the present—is presented in 14 groups of related historical topics that cover subjects as diverse as literature, Antarctic exploration, the development of airplanes, football, and the motion pictures industry. An extensive index locates subjects in all chronologies in which they appear.

Timetables of History, by Bernard Grun. Simon & Schuster, revised edition, 1987. Series of chronological tables showing historical events in history and politics, literature, religion and philosophy, and science and technology. Coverage is from the beginning of time to the present in 50- to 500-year jumps. Beginning 501 A.D., the table becomes yearly. Emphasis is on Western history and culture. Indexed.

The Time Tables of Science: A Chronology of the Most Important People and Events in the History of Science, by Alexander Hellemans and Bryan Bunch. Simon & Schuster, 1988. Contains over 10,000 entries organized chronologically and by discipline, interspersed with more than 100 short essays on science and technology and nine overviews of the main periods of scientific history. Indexed by subject and name.

CIVIL RIGHTS. *See also* LAW: CONSTITUTIONAL.

State by State Guide to Women's Legal Rights, McGraw-Hill, 1987. Covers four main areas: home and family, education, employment, and women in the community.

CLEANING

How to Clean Everything, by Alma Moore. Simon & Schuster, 3rd edition, 1977. Includes detailed descriptions of how to clean everything in the home and the materials needed. A second section deals with removing stains from textiles.

CLOTHING AND TEXTILES

The Encyclopedia of Textiles, by Judith Jerde. Facts on File, 1991. Reference source for all varieties of textiles, their manufacture, and their value both historically and in modern use. Written by a former curator of costume for New York City's Metropolitan Museum of Art.

Fairchild's Dictionary of Textiles, by Dr. Isabel B. Wingate. Fairchild Publications, 6th edition, 1979. Reference source for all branches of the industry. Includes entries on fibers, yarns, fabric construction, finishing and sale, inventors and developers, and government standards and regulations. Includes appendix of organizations involved with the textile industry.

Folk and Festival Costume of the World, by R. Turner Wilcox. Scribner, 1977. Covers ethnic costumes from 150 countries and groups.

Historical Encyclopedia of Costumes, by Auguste Racinet. Facts on File, 1988. Details not only the history, but the geography of costume throughout the world from ancient times to the late 19th century.

History of Costume: From the Ancient Egyptians to the Twentieth Century, Harper, 1965. Fully illustrated with photos and paintings; covers accessories; has 50 pages of draft patterns.

The Mode in Costume, by R. Turner Wilcox, Scribner, 1974. A history of European fashion from 3000 B.C. A basic, factual text with drawings of representative costumes. Useful for costume designers looking for period authenticity.

20,000 Years of Fashion, by Francis Boucher. Harry N. Abrams, expanded edition, 1983. Begins divided into historical-regional sections but quickly moves to the history of European costume. Discusses materials, ornaments, accessories, and functions. Illustrated. Includes glossary and index.

COINS. *See* MONEY.

COLLEGES AND UNIVERSITIES. *See also* EDUCATION: FINANCIAL AID.

Barron's Guide to Colleges, compiled by Barron's Educational Services, annual. Gives sample SAT questions, colleges-at-a-glance, and more detailed descriptions of each college, including tuition costs, admission requirements, and rankings of competitiveness relative to other colleges.

The College Cost Book, compiled by The College Board, annual. Covers 3,000 colleges and universities. Provides information on what each college really costs, including personal expenses, travel, and books; how to get financial aid; and how to interpret financial aid packages. Includes tables in the back to help you work out applications for financial aid.

The College Handbook, compiled by The College Board. College Entrance Examination Board, annual. Since 1963, *The College Handbook* has offered detailed information for college-bound students on such subjects as freshman admissions requirements and procedures, enrollment, majors, expenses, financial aid, and many other areas of interest.

Comparative Guide to American Colleges, by James Cass. Harper, 13th edition, 1987. Descriptions of four-year college programs. Ranks institutions by admissions selectivity and lists those granting largest numbers of baccalaureate degrees in selected fields.

Guide to American Graduate Schools, by Harold R. Doughty. Penguin, 6th edition, 1990. Describes over 600 institutions with graduate and professional programs.

Higher Education Directory, annual, Higher Education Publications. "Contains listings of accredited institutions of post-secondary education in the United States and its outlying areas which meet the U.S. Dept. of Education eligibility requirements." Gives general information about the schools, such as addresses, names of administrators, type of program and degrees available, and tuition fees.

Index of Majors, compiled by The College Board, annual. Lists nearly 600 undergraduate and graduate majors and the colleges, state by state, that currently offer them.

Lovejoy's College Guide, by Charles T. Straughn II and Barbarasue Lovejoy Straughn. Monarch, 20th edition, 1991. Celebrating its 50th anniversary with this edition, Lovejoy's provides profiles of more than 2,500 four-year and two-year colleges and universities, along with admissions requirements, application procedures, tuition figures, selectivity rankings, and information on many other topics.

Peterson's Guide to Colleges, edited by Theresa C. Moore. Peterson's Guides, annual. Alphabetized by state, gives information on entrance requirements, tuition, and financial aid.

The Right College, by the College Research Group. Arco, annual. Lists more than 2,500 colleges and universities, with information on applications and admissions.

COMMODITIES. *See* INVESTMENTS.

COMMUNICATIONS. *See also* JOURNALISM.

International Encyclopedia of Communications, edited by Erik Barnouw, Oxford University Press, 1989. A collaborative effort by contributors from 29 countries, this work gives information on topics as diverse as pre-Columbian Indian writing and modern animation. Includes biographical sketches of important contributors to the field. Cross-referenced material; topical guide.

Webster's New World Dictionary of Media and Communications, by Richard Weiner. Simon & Schuster, 1990. A comprehensive work that lists and explains trade slang, organizations, trademarked services and products, parent companies, and acronyms. Cross-referenced.

COMPUTER DATABASES. *See also* COMPUTERS.

Computer-Readable Databases, edited by Kathleen Young Marcaccio. Gale, annual. A directory and data sourcebook covering more than 5,000 electronic databases. Gives names, addresses, and telephone numbers for database producers and services, with description of the material provided, how to access or obtain the database, and other pertinent information. Has information on CD-ROMs.

COMPUTERS. *See also* COMPUTER DATABASES.

The Complete Handbook of Personal Computer Communications, by Alfred Glossbrenner. St. Martin's, 1985. Covers equipment, such as modems and software, needed to communicate over telephone lines with personal computers. Has chapters devoted to online utilities; business, financial, and investment services; electronic mail; and related subjects.

Computer Dictionary, by Charles J. Sippl. Sams, 4th edition, 1985. Provides brief definitions in lay language.

Encyclopedia of Computer Science and Engineering, Van Nostrand Reinhold, 2nd edition, 1982. A reference work for the nonspecialist, consisting of 500 signed survey articles.

CONSTITUTION. *See* LAW: CONSTITUTIONAL.

COOKBOOKS. *See also* FOOD AND NUTRITION.

Better Homes and Gardens New Cookbook, by the editor of *Better Homes and Gardens*. Meredith, 10th edition, 1990. A standard cookbook in its latest editon, with staple recipes and types of cooking.

Betty Crocker's Cookbook, Prentice Hall, 40th Anniversary edition, 1991. The best-selling cookbook in its latest form, this book gives easily readable and understandable recipes. Also has a glossary of cooking terms in back, as well as nutritional guidelines and "special helps."

The Fanny Farmer Cookbook, revised by Marion Cunningham with Jeri Laber. Knopf, 12th edition, 1989. In more than 1,800 recipes for American dishes, this book pays attention to healthful eating, emphasizing cereals and grains, and has an expanded fish section. Has helpful hints throughout, along with guides to what to look for in ingredients.

Joy of Cooking, by Irma S. Rombauer and Marion Rombauer Becker. Macmillan, revised edition, 1986. All-purpose cookbook for informal and formal use with American and foreign recipes. Includes menu planning suggestions, nutrition, basic information on foods, basic cooking terminology, and methods of preparation.

Larousse Gastronomique, edited by Jennifer Harvey Lang. Crown, 1988. Complete culinary encyclopedia, including histories of foods and preparation techniques, definitions, recipes (294 ways to prepare eggs), and articles on international cuisines. The emphasis remains French, but information and recipes are adapted for American kitchens.

The New Basics Cookbook, by Julee Rosso and Sheila Lukins. Workman, 1989. The authors of *The Silver Palate Cookbook* have compiled the recipes that made them famous, along with updates, additions, shopping tips, and suggestions for entertaining. A collection of tried and true recipes covering soup to nuts. Easy and interesting to read, as well as being a helpful source of information.

COPYRIGHT

Copyright Handbook, by Donald F. Johnston. Bowker, 2nd edition, 1982. Copyright law explained simply. Treated along with other topics are remedies for infringement, how to register, restrictions, and duration. Includes lengthy appendices and index.

COSTUME. *See* CLOTHING AND TEXTILES.

CURRENT EVENTS. *See* NEWS AND CURRENT EVENTS.

D

DEMOGRAPHICS. *See also* ATLASES.

County and City Data Book, U.S. Government Printing Office, revised irregularly. Statistics on population, housing, trade, finance, climate, etc. of U.S. counties and cities with populations of more than 25,000.

Historical Statistics of the United States: Colonial Times to 1970, U.S. Government Printing Office, 1975. Comprehensive compilation of social and economic statistics. Historical complement to *Statistical Abstract.*

Lifetrends, by Jerry Gerber, Janet Wolff, Walter Klores, and Gene Brown. Macmillan, 1990. Describes the phenomenon of the baby boomers and the impact of this pivotal generation on social planning, business, medicine, advertising, and related concerns on into the 21st century.

Market Guide, Editor & Publisher, annual. Market surveys of 1,500 largest cities in the United States and Canada; provides demographic and economic information.

State and Metropolitan Area Data Book 1986, U.S. Government Printing Office, 1986. A presentation of statistics from almost 50 government and private agencies on a multiplicity of political, economic, and social topics. Published as a supplement to the *Statistical Abstract of the United States;* released annually.

Statistical Abstract of the United States, U.S. Government Printing Office, annual. More than 1,500 tables summarizing U.S. social, political, and economic statistics from governmental and nongovernmental sources.

United Nations Statistical Yearbook. Unipub, annual. Master digest of statistics for over 200 countries on a variety of subjects such as population, manpower, education, and prices.

DENTISTS

American Dental Directory, American Dental Association, annual. Lists American dentists by state and city and gives dental specialization and schools.

DICTIONARIES—BIOGRAPHICAL. *See* BIOGRAPHY.

DICTIONARIES—ENGLISH LANGUAGE. *See also* RHYME; SLANG; STYLE AND USAGE; SYNONYMS; *and specialized subjects, such as* MEDICINE AND HEALTH; SCIENCE.

The American Heritage Dictionary of the English Language, edited by William Morris. Houghton Mifflin, 10th revision, 1981. Includes articles on the English language and usage, dialects, and history. Etymologies follow word definitions. Pronunciation key appears at the bottom of every page. Sometimes synonyms are included after the definition of a word. Illustrated. Includes appendices.

The Barnhart Dictionary of Etymology, edited by Robert K. Barnhart. H.W. Wilson, 1987. Traces the origins of over 30,000 words.

The Concise Oxford Dictionary of English Etymology, edited by T.F. Hoad. Oxford University Press, 1986. Based on *The Oxford Dictionary of English Etymology,* edited by C.T. Onions. Oxford University Press, 1966. Provides concise statements on the origins of words and their development once they became part of the English language.

Dictionary Buying Guide, by Kenneth F. Kister. Bowker, 3rd edition, 1977. Consumer guide to general English-language word books in print.

Includes critical reviews and comparisons of dictionaries, usage handbooks, style manuals, and secretary's handbooks.

Dictionary of Foreign Phrases and Abbreviations, by Kevin Guinagh. H.W. Wilson, 3rd edition, 1982. Contains 45,000 entries covering foreign phrases and abbreviations occurring in English.

Foreignisms, by Tad Tuleja. Macmillan, 1988. A guide to the foreign expressions in our speech, not only in everyday conversation but in law, business, politics, theater, dance, and music. Lists over 1,000 words and phrases from twenty different languages, along with word origins and pronunciation.

Morris Dictionary of Word and Phrase Origins, by William Morris and Mary Morris. Harper, 2nd edition, 1988. Provides connotations, definitions, and roots of English words and phrases. A popular presentation that also covers foods, foreign terms, sports, and given names.

Oxford American Dictionary, compiled by Eugene Ehrlich et al. Oxford University Press, 1980. Emphasis is on everyday use. Spellings and pronunciations are mainly American.

The Oxford Dictionary of English Etymology, edited by C.T. Onions. Oxford University Press, 1966. A one-volume etymological dictionary by one of the original lexicographers of the first edition of the 20-volume *Oxford English Dictionary*.

The Oxford English Dictionary, prepared by J.A. Simpson and Edmund S. Weiner, 20 volumes. Oxford University Press, 2nd edition, 1989. The publication of this reference is an event in the English-speaking literary world. Briefly, this is an etymological or word-source dictionary. In addition to definitions, this work gives the history of 290,500 words, both current and archaic, in the English language. Slang entries are very limited. Word histories include early forms, variant forms and roots, and first or exemplary usages in English from ancient to modern times. Short explanatory notes are provided for more common words.

The Shorter Oxford English Dictionary of Historical Principles, by Sir James Augustus Henry Murray. Oxford University Press, 3rd edition, 1973. This is a two-volume abridgment of the 1st edition of the *Oxford English Dictionary;*

includes revised etymologies and extensive additions of new words.

The Random House Dictionary of the English Language (unabridged), edited by Stuart Berg Flexner. Random House, 2nd edition, 1987. A wide-ranging, up-to-date unabridged dictionary. In addition to the standard features of any standard dictionary, it incorporates concise dictionaries of French, Spanish, Italian, and German, an atlas, and basic information on the natural sciences, American and world geography, and American government.

Third Barnhart Dictionary of New English, edited by Robert K. Barnhart et al. Has thousands of entries covering words not included, or inadequately explained, in standard dictionaries, such as *groupie, nerd,* and *yuppie.* Gives etymologies.

Webster's New World Dictionary of American English, edited by Victoria Neufeldt. Simon & Schuster, 3rd college edition, 1988. In addition to definitions, the dictionary gives roots, synonyms, context sentences, some simple illustrations, and some acronyms and abbreviations, as well as parts of speech, plurals, and syllabification.

Webster's Ninth New Collegiate Dictionary, Merriam-Webster, 9th edition, 1983. Most recent, best-selling edition in the collegiate series of Merriam-Webster dictionaries dating back to 1898. Contains 45,000 entries based on 13,000,000 citations. Definitions conform to a classic Webster principle: the sense known to have been first used in English is given first.

Webster's Third New International Dictionary, Unabridged, Merriam-Webster, 1976. Approximately 450,00 entries.

12,000 Words: A Supplement to Webster's Third New International Dictionary, New American Library, 1986. Includes new words and meanings, as well as older words omitted from main volume.

DICTIONARIES—FOREIGN LANGUAGE

Arabic:

English-Arabic and Arabic-English Dictionary, by John Wortabet. Ungar, 1954.

Chinese:

Pinyin Chinese-English Dictionary, Wiley, 1979. Extensive coverage of present-day Chinese. The pinyin system for romanizing Chinese ideograms was introduced in the 1960s.

Dutch:

Cassell's New Dutch Dictionary: English-Dutch, Dutch-English, by the Cassell's editors, Macmillan, 1982.

French:

Cassell's French Dictionary, edited by Dennis Girard et al. Macmillan, 1972. French-English and English-French.

The Concise Oxford French-English Dictionary, edited by Henry Ferrar. Oxford University Press, 2nd edition, 1980. Concise, usable, and current. Etymology reduced in the interests of space. Updated from the 1st edition (1934) to reflect recent changes in the French language, modern French usage, and new technical vocabularies.

Harper Collins French Dictionary, HarperCollins, 1990. French-English, English-French.

Harrap's Concise French Dictionary, Prentice-Hall, 1990. French-English, English-French.

German:

Cassell's German Dictionary: German-English, English-German, by Harold T. Betteridge. Macmillan, 1978.

Harper Collins German Dictionary, HarperCollins, 1990. German-English, English-German.

Harrap's Concise German Dictionary, Prentice-Hall, 1990. German-English, English-German.

Greek—Classical:

Greek-English Lexicon, by Henry George Liddell. Oxford University Press, 1940. A standard work for classical Greek. A supplement edited by E.A. Barber, published in 1968, updates the original.

Greek—Modern:

Divry's Modern English-Greek, Greek-English Desk Dictionary, by George Divry. Divry, 1976.

Hebrew:

Complete English-Hebrew Dictionary: Complete Hebrew-English Dictionary, by Reuben Alcalay, three volumes. Prayer Book, 1968.

Italian:

Cassell's Italian Dictionary: Italian-English, English-Italian, compiled by Piero Rebora. Macmillan, 1977.

Harper Collins Italian Dictionary. HarperCollins, 1990. Italian-English, English-Italian.

Harrap's Concise Italian Dictionary, Prentice-Hall, 1990.

Japanese:

Modern Reader's Japanese-English Character Dictionary, by Andrew N. Nelson. Tuttle, 2nd revised edition, 1966.

Latin:

Cassell's Latin Dictionary: Latin-English, English-Latin, edited by D.P. Simpson. Macmillan, 1977.

A Latin Dictionary, by Charlton Thomas Lewis and Charles Short. Oxford University Press, 1879. Founded on Andrews edition of Freund's Latin dictionary.

A Latin Dictionary, revised by Charlton T. Lewis and Charles Short. Oxford University Press, 1980. Includes definitions of mythological characters, places, and names, as well as words. Word definitions also give use in sentences and places in Latin literature to find the word in context.

Russian:

English-Russian, Russian-English Dictionary, by Kenneth Katzner. Wiley, 1984. First full-sized, one-volume Russian-English, English-Russian dictionary published in the United States and based on American English.

Spanish:

American Heritage Larousse Spanish Dictionary, Houghton Mifflin, 1986. A bilingual dictionary based on the *American Heritage Dictionary* and *Pequeño Larousse Ilustrado.*

Cassell's Spanish Dictionary: Spanish-English, English-Spanish, revised by Anthony Gooch and Angel Carcía de Paredes. Macmillan, 1978.

Harper Collins Spanish Dictionary, HarperCollins, 1990. Spanish-English, English-Spanish.

Simon & Schuster's International Dictionary, Simon & Schuster, 1973. English-Spanish, Spanish-

English desk dictionary with more that 200,000 entries. Distinction is made between American and British usage and pronunciation.

The Spanish and English, English and Spanish Dictionary—Self Pronouncing, by Mariano Velasquez de la Cadena et al. Prentice-Hall, revised edition, 1973. For advanced language students.

   Vietnamese:

Essential Vietnamese-English Dictionary, by Dinh Hoa Nguyen. Tuttle, 1983.

   Yiddish:

Modern English-Yiddish, Yiddish-English Dictionary, by Uriel Weinrich. McGraw-Hill, 1968. Scholarly.

DICTIONARIES—GEOGRAPHICAL

The United States Dictionary of Places, Somerset Publishers, 1988. "A national place name directory." Gives location, population, zip code, and available information on origin of the names of incorporated towns and cities.

Webster's New Geographical Dictionary, Merriam-Webster, revised edition, 1984. Basic geographic, demographic, economic, and (in some of the entries) historical notes on world countries, regions, cities, and natural features. Includes maps. Cross-referenced.

DINOSAURS. *See* ANIMALS—PREHISTORIC.

DISABILITIES

Access America: An Atlas and Guide to the National Parks for Visitors with Disabilities, by Peter Shea et al. Northern Cartographic, 1988. Guide evaluates the accessibility of National Parks. Includes charts and maps, comments on medical services, transportation, and climate.

Directory of National Information Services on Handicapping Conditions and Related Services, U.S. Government Printing Office, 1986. Descriptive directory of national organizations concerned with the physically handicapped, mentally retarded, or learning disabled.

Directory for Exceptional Children, Porter Sargent, 12th edition, 1990. Guide to educational and training facilities for the emotionally disturbed, mentally retarded, and physically handicapped.

Financial Aid for the Disabled and Their Families, by Gail Ann Schlacter and David Weber. Reference Service, 1988. Provides information on a wide range of funding needs in such areas as education, career development, research, and travel. Includes multiple indexes; cross-referenced.

DOCTORS. *See* MEDICINE AND HEALTH.

DOGS. *See* PETS.

DO-IT-YOURSELF GUIDES. *See* HOME BUILDING, MAINTENANCE, AND REPAIR.

DRAMA. *See* LITERATURE—SPECIFIC CATEGORIES: DRAMA; THEATER.

DRUG ABUSE

Cocaine, by Roger D. Weiss and Steven M. Mirin. American Psychiatric Press, 1987. Covers cocaine processing and use, its medical effects on mind and body, and dependence and treatment. Appendices list U.S. drug-treatment centers and give a self-test for cocaine dependence. Includes index and bibliography.

Drugfree: A Unique Positive Approach to Staying off Alcohol and Drugs, by Richard B. Seymour and David E. Smith. Facts on File, 1987. Geared to the recovering abuser, the heart of the book deals with how to stay off alcohol and drugs and conquer "white knuckle sobriety." Also deals with physical and psychological effects of alcohol and drug use and addiction and ways of getting help. Includes bibliography and index.

Encyclopedia of Drug Abuse, by Glen Evens et al. Facts on File, 2nd revised edition, 1990. Comprehensive work that provides facts about the medical, legal, social, and biological aspects of drug abuse.

DRUGS AND MEDICINES

The Essential Guide to Generic Drugs, by M. Laurence Lieberman, R.Ph. Harper, 1986. Layperson's guide to generic equivalents of major prescription drugs, with information on cost savings, if any.

The Essential Guide to Nonprescription Drugs, by David R. Zimmerman. Harper, 1983. Consumer directory to over-the-counter drugs, describing uses, relative effectiveness (as compared to manufacturers' claims), recommended dosages, and safety evaluations of products. Indexed.

The Essential Guide to Prescription Drugs, by James W. Long. Harper, updated annually. Layperson's guide to prescription drugs, product types, their use, and the conditions they treat.

Handbook of Nonprescription Drugs, compiled by the American Pharmaceutical Association. 8th edition, 1986. Chapters are organized by the type of preparation (cold and allergy, contact lens) and describe the conditions they are designed to treat, relevant symptoms, physiology, treatments, ingredients, effectiveness, and safety guidelines. Addressed to the pharmacist, but very useful to the layperson.

The Merck Index: An Encyclopedia of Chemicals, Drugs, and Biologicals, edited by Martha Windholz. Merck & Co., 10th edition, 1983. Technical descriptions of the preparation, properties, uses, commercial names, and toxicity of drugs and medicines. Published continuously since 1889; updated every seven to eight years.

Orphan Drugs, by Kenneth Anderson and Lois Anderson. Body Press, 1991. Describes over 1,500 drugs, both generic and brand-name, that have been tested and approved by countries outside the United States. These drugs are used to treat over 800 different conditions and diseases. Listings include names of companies licensed to produce the drugs and their availibility.

Physician's Desk Reference, Edward R. Barnhart, publisher. Medical Economics, annual. Latest available information intended for physicians on over 2,000 products. Covers dosage, contraindications, precautions, side effects, and undesirable interactions. The information is furnished by the manufacturers of the various products. Product identification in color.

Physician's Desk Reference for Nonprescription Drugs, Van Nostrand Reinhold, annual. A companion to the *Physician's Desk Reference.* Provides essential information on nonprescription drugs. Indexed by manufacturer, product name, product category, and active ingredients.

E

EARLY MAN. *See also* ANTHROPOLOGY; ARCHAEOLOGY.

Encyclopedia of Human Evolution and Prehistory, edited by Ian Tattersall, Eric Dilson, and John Van Convering. Garland, 1988. Provides comprehensive coverage of all aspects of human evolution and prehistory. Appendices, index.

The Field Guide to Early Man, by David Lambert and the Diagram Group. Facts on File, 1988. Covers the development of the human species for the general reader, with 500 illustrations, maps, charts, diagrams, and photographs.

EARTH SCIENCES. *See also* METEOROLOGY; MINERALOGY; OCEANOGRAPHY.

The Cambridge Encyclopedia of Earth Sciences, edited by David G. Smith. Cambridge University Press, 1982. Designed as an introduction to earth sciences. Emphasizes the theory of plate tectonics and its current theoretical ramifications. Illustrated, with glossary, index, and bibliography.

ECOLOGY

Environmental Hazards: Air Pollution, by Willard E. Miller and Ruby M. Miller. ABC-Clio, 1989. An encyclopedic reference source, with a general review introduction and chronology of the ecology movement. Includes biographies of key figures and annotated bibliography. Excellent for students.

Natural Resource Conservation, by Oliver S. Owen and Daniel D. Chiras. Macmillan, 5th edition, 1990. College textbook on environmentalism and resource conservation. Emphasizes biological approach. Covers pollution, waste disposal, the energy crisis, and nuclear energy. Also has a chapter on environmental crises and economic growth. Illustrated; includes glossary and index.

ECONOMICS. *See also* SOCIAL SCIENCES.

American Economic History, by Harold V. Faulkner. Quest Editions, 9th edition, 1976. College text covering the subject from colonial times to the present with numerous graphs, maps, and tables. Includes full coverage of post-World War II economic changes.

Comparative Economic Systems, by William N. Loucks. Harper, 9th edition, 1973. College textbook; includes succinct coverage of major economic systems.

Economics, by Paul A. Samuelson and William D. Nordhaus. McGraw-Hill, 13th edition, 1989. An introduction to capital economics. Integrates macro- and micro-economic theory and history with a chapter on Marxism and the Soviet economy. Summary and questions for discussion at the end of each chapter. Illustrated; includes glossary and index.

History of Economic Theory and Method, by Robert Ekelund. McGraw-Hill, 2nd edition, 1983. History of economic thought from ancient times to the present; for college and graduate students.

A History of Economic Thought, by John Fred Bell. Ronald Press Co., 2nd edition, 1967. After a short survey of its beginnings, Bell begins his narrative with the beginnings of mercantilism. A critical history with a strong ideological identification with modern capitalism. Includes bibliography and indexes.

McGraw-Hill Dictionary of Modern Economics: A Handbook of Terms and Organizations, McGraw-Hill, 3rd edition, 1983. Over 1,400 terms and organizations clearly explained for the non-specialist.

What's Ahead for the Economy?, by Louis Rukeyser. Simon & Schuster, 1983. The host of "Wall Street Week" explains major economic trends in taxes, spending, banking and credit, labor law, and business regulations and restrictions and how they affect all of us.

EDUCATION

Dictionary of Education, by Carter V. Good. McGraw-Hill, 3rd edition, 1973. Definitions of technical and professional terms and concepts in all areas of education.

Digest of Education Statistics, Thomas D. Snyder, project director. U.S. Department of Education, National Center for Education Statistics, annual. A wealth of educational information, some of going back as far as 1869, is offered every year in this government publication. More than 350 tables, with supporting text, cover all aspects and levels of public and private education: enrollment, revenues, expenditures, teachers' salaries, and many other topics.

The Educator's Desk Reference: A Sourcebook of Educational Information and Research, by Melvyn N. Freed et al. Macmillan, 1989. A reference source for over 100 educational journals, this book is also a one-stop reference with information on computer software, intelligence and standardized tests, and educational organizations.

Patterson's American Education, annual, Educational Directories. Comprehensive list of schools at all levels, private and public; educational associations; and school systems.

Financial Aid:

Directory of Financial Aids for Minorities, by Gail A. Schlachter and Sandra E. Goldstein. Reference Service Press, 1989. Minorities included are Asians, Blacks, Hispanics, and Native Americans.

Directory of Financial Aids for Women 1989–1990, by Gail Ann Schlachter. Reference Service Press, 1989. Profiles of grant-giving institutions, foundations, and internships designed primarily or exclusively for women. Cross-referencing and indexing allows specific grant information (such as programs designed for women of a particular nationality) to be researched. Includes bibliography of general financial aids.

Private Schools:

The Handbook of Private Schools, Porter Sargent, annual. Describes more than 2,000 private elementary and secondary school in the United States; includes directory of summer programs and camps.

ELDERLY. *See* OLD AGE.

ELECTRONICS

Modern Dictionary of Electronics, by Rudolf F. Graf. Howard W. Sams and Co., 6th edition, 1984. Definitions and explanations of technical terminology used by engineers and electricians, students and hobbyists.

EMPLOYMENT

The American Almanac of Jobs and Salaries, by John Wright and Edward J. Dwyer. Avon, 1990. Gives valuable information on the present status, salaries, and outlook for a wide variety of career opportunities, including federal employment.

Career Information Center, 13 volumes. Glencoe, 3rd edition, 1987. A handy and quick reference tool with many occupations not listed in *Occupational Outlook Handbook* (below).

Dictionary of Occupational Titles, U.S. Government Printing Office, 4th edition, 1983; supplement; 1986. The four volumes contain standardized descriptions of job duties and related information for 20,000 occupations, plus data on training time, physical demands, and environmental conditions for occupations.

Directory of Special Programs for Minority Group Members, Garrett Park, annual. Includes information on general employment and educational assistance programs, federal aid programs, etc.; covers Asians, Blacks, Hispanics, Native Americans, and other groups.

Home Study Course for Civil Service Jobs, by Hy Hammer. Arco, 6th edition, 1984. Provides general information on federal, state, and local government jobs with sections on tests of vocabulary, mathematics, clerical skills, reasoning, and leadership.

The Jobs Rated Almanac, edited by Les Krantz. World Almanac, 1988. Rankings of 250 jobs, from actuaries to zoologists, on the basis or workplace stress, salary, outlook, perks, and physical demands.

A Manager's Guide to Employee Privacy: Laws, Policies, and Procedures, by Kurt H. Decker. Wiley, 1989. Covers various situations (immigration, AIDS, skill testing, medical records policies, for example) and the laws that apply, as well as policies that should be implememted. Especially useful for small businesses.

Occupational Outlook Handbook, biennial, U.S. Government Printing Office. Descriptions of job duties, education requirements, employment outlook and earnings.

ENCYCLOPEDIAS

Best Encyclopedias: A Guide to General and Specialized Encyclopedias, by Kenneth F. Kister. Oryx, 1986, updated every three or four years. Encyclopedia comparison chart provides differences in price, number of volumes, and other criteria.

The Encyclopedia Americana, edited by David Holland, 30 volumes. Grolier, 1989. First published in 1829, *Americana's* 30 volumes contain nontechnical articles on tens of thousands of subjects, arranged alphabetically and backed by the input of hundreds of expert advisory editors and contributors. There is an extensive and thorough index in the last volume. Updated each year by the *Americana Annual.*

Encyclopaedia Britannica, 32 volumes. Encyclopaedia Britannica, Inc., 15th edition, 1987. In three sections: Propaedia, or outline of knowledge; Macropaedia, with longer in-depth articles covering major topics; and Micropaedia, with shorter A-to-Z ready reference entries. *Britannica's* reputation as the basic encyclopedia for all libraries and reference collections is based on the writing and knowledge of thousands of expert contributors and consultants. Updated between major editions by the Britannica *Book of the Year.*

The New Columbia Encyclopedia, edited by William H. Harris and Judith S. Levey. Columbia University Press, 4th edition, 1975. This work set the standard for one-volume quick-reference encyclopedias. In more than 3,000 illustrated pages, it contains some 50,000 A-to-Z short articles covering a wide range of topics.

ENVIRONMENT. *See* ECOLOGY.

ETHICS

Encyclopedia of Bioethics, edited by Warren T. Reich, two volumes. Macmillan, 1982. Presents major conflicts between basic human values and technology. A four-volume version was published by Free Press in 1978.

ETHNIC GROUPS. *See also* AFRICAN AMERICANS; JEWS; NATIVE AMERICANS.

Harvard Encyclopedia of American Ethnic Groups, edited by Stephan Thernstrom and others. Harvard University Press, 1980. Defining *ethnic* in the widest possible way, this book contains substantial articles on American ethnic groups. Origins, migration and settlement, history in America, socioeconomic structure, religion and politics, and many other topics are addressed. Includes demographic information, individual bibliographies, and appendices.

We the People: An Atlas of America's Ethnic Diversity, by James Paul Allen and Eugene James Turner. Macmillan, 1988. An atlas devoted to ethnic settlement in the United States. Maps show the distribution of ethnic groups in America, while the text discusses the immigration, history in the United States, and migrations of the ethnic populations. Includes references, appendices, and indexes.

ETIQUETTE

The Amy Vanderbilt Complete Book of Etiquette, revised by Letitia Baldridge. Doubleday, 1978. Contains rules, guidelines, and suggestions on every-thing from wedding etiquette to entertaining to table manners. The book even tells you how to conduct yourself in an audience with the Pope. Indexed.

Emily Post's Complete Book of Wedding Etiquette, by Elizabeth L. Post. Harper, 1982. A guide that takes you from the proposal to the honeymoon, including pre-wedding parties, wedding attendants, ceremonies and receptions, and many other topics.

Emily Post's Etiquette, by Elizabeth L. Post. Harper, 14th edition, 1984. The classic reference for which fork to use has been expanded to in-clude such modern situations as dating, living together, second marriages, and co-ed business traveling. Has a unique chapter on how to figure out who is your second cousin once removed.

ETYMOLOGY. *See* DICTIONARIES—ENGLISH LAN-GUAGE. *See also* LANGUAGE.

F

FAMILY PLANNING

The New Birth-Control Book: A Complete Guide for Men and Women, by Howard Shapiro. Pren-tice Hall, 1988. An update of the 1978 edition, detailing the recent advances made in birth-control methods. Includes chapters on reproduction in general, birth-control pills, IUDs, rhythm method, sterilization, and abortion.

FASHION. *See* CLOTHING AND TEXTILES.

FEDERAL GOVERNMENT. *See also* POLITICS.

Black Elected Officials, Unipub, annual. Blacks in elected office as of June 30 of the edition year.

Congress and the Nation, six volumes. Congres-sional Quarterly, 1965-. Overview and detailed cov-erage of presidential, legislative, and political events in every major subject area. Based on *Con-gressional Quarterly Weekly Report* and the *Congres-sional Quarterly Almanac.*
    Volume 1: 1945–1964
    Volume 2: 1965–1968
    Volume 3: 1969–1972
    Volume 4: 1972–1976
    Volume 5: 1977–1980
    Volume 6: 1981–1984

Congressional Directory, U.S. Government Print-ing Office, biennial with supplement. Covers biographical information, committee assignments of members of Congress, and officers of Con-gress.

The Dorsey Dictionary of American Government and Politics, by Jay M. Shafritz. Irwin, 1987. 4,000 entries on current terms and issues in American politics. Appendixes refer the reader to statistical information guides, online databases, and key con-cepts by subject.

Guide to Congress, Congressional Quarterly, 3rd edition, 1982. Covers history and workings of Con-gress, with biographical data on all members of Congress.

United States Government Manual, U.S. Govern-ment Printing Office, annual. Lists departments, agencies, commissions, etc. of the federal govern-ment and provides the names of senior officials. Describes origins and functions of these govern-mental bodies.

Washington Information Directory, Congressional Quarterly, annual. Lists names, telephone num-bers, addresses, and responsibilities of 5,000 key personnel and agencies, both private and govern-mental, in the Washington, DC area; includes detailed indexes.

FICTION. *See* LITERATURE: FICTION.

FIELD GUIDES

Animals:

Audubon Society Field Guide to North American Fishes, Whales, and Dolphins, by the Audubon Society Staff and others. Knopf, 1983.

Audubon Society Field Guide to North American Mammals, by the Audubon Society Staff and John O. Whitaker. Knopf, 1980.

A Field Guide to the Mammals, by William H. Burt. Houghton Mifflin, 3rd edition, 1976.

A Field Guide to Animal Tracks, by Murie J. Olaus. Houghton Mifflin, 2nd edition, 1975.

Astronomy:

A Field Guide to the Stars and Planets, by Jay M. Pasachoff and Donald M. Menzel. Houghton Miff-lin, 1980. Houghton Mifflin, 1983.

Atmosphere:

A Field Guide to the Atmosphere, by Vincent J. Schaeffer and John A. Day. Houghton Mifflin, 1983.

Birds:

Audubon Society Encyclopedia of North American Birds, by John K. Terres. Knopf, 1980.

Audubon Society Field Guide to North American Birds, two volumes. Knopf, 1977.

> Volume 1: Eastern Region, by the Audubon Society Staff and John Bull.
> Volume 2: Western Region, by the Audubon Society Staff and M.D. Udvardy.

Audubon Society Master Guide to Birding, edited by John Farrand, Jr., three volumes. Knopf, 1983.

> Volume 1: Loons to Sandpipers.
> Volume 2: Gulls to Dippers.
> Volume 3: Old World Warblers to Sparrows.

A Field Guide to Advanced Birding, by Kenn Kaufman. Houghton Mifflin, 1980.

A Field Guide to Birds of Britain and Europe, by Roger Tory Peterson. Houghton Mifflin, 4th edition, 1988.

A Field Guide to the Birds: A Completely New Guide to All the Birds of Eastern and Central North America, by Roger Tory Peterson. Houghton Mifflin, 1980.

A Field Guide to Birds' Nests, by Hal H. Harrison. Houghton Mifflin, 1988.

Field Guide to the Birds of North America, edited by Shorley Scott. National Geographic, 1983.

A Field Guide to Eastern Birds, by Roger Tory Peterson. Houghton Mifflin, 1984.

A Field Guide to Hawks, by William S. Clark. Houghton Mifflin, 1987.

A Field Guide to Mexican Birds, by Roger Tory Peterson and Edward A. Chalif. Houghton Mifflin, 1973.

A Field Guide to Western Birds, by Roger Tory Peterson. Houghton Mifflin, 1990.

Ferns. *See* PLANTS AND FLOWERS *(below).*

Fish:

Audubon Society Field Guide to North American Fishes, Whales, and Dolphins, by the Audubon Society Staff and others. Knopf, 1983.

A Field Guide to Atlantic Coast Fishes, by G. Carleton Ray and C. Richard Robbins. Houghton Mifflin, 1986.

A Field Guide to Coral Reefs of the Caribbean and Florida, by Eugene H. Kaplan. Houghton Mifflin, 1988.

Field Guide to Freshwater Fishes of North America, by A.J. McClane. Holt, 1978.

A Field Guide to Pacific Coast Fishes of North America, by William N. Eschmeyer and Earl S. Herald. Houghton Mifflin, 1983.

Field Guide to Saltwater Fishes of North America, by A.J. McClane. Holt, 1978.

Fossils:

Audubon Society Field Guide to North American Fossils, by the Audubon Society Staff and Ida Thompson. Knopf, 1982.

A Field Guide to Prehistoric Life, by David Lambert and The Diagram Group. Presents to the amateur fossil hunter a complete, systematic means of identifying and understanding fossil life. More than 500 illustrations, maps, and charts.

The Illustrated Encyclopedia of Fossils, by Giovanni Pinna. Facts on File, 1990. Covers every aspect of the field, including the formation of fossils, their significance in the paleologic record, their excavation, and their classification. Over 1,300 color illustrations. Has glossary, bibliography, and index.

Insects and Spiders:

Audubon Society Field Guide to North American Butterflies, by the Audubon Society Staff and Robert M. Pyle. Knopf, 1981.

Audubon Society Field Guide to North American Insects and Spiders, by the Audubon Society Staff and Lorus Milne. Knopf, 1980.

A Field Guide to Beetles, by Richard E. White. Houghton Mifflin, 1983.

A Field Guide to the Butterflies, by Roger Tory Peterson. Houghton Mifflin, 1983.

A Field Guide to the Insects of America North of Mexico, by Donald J. Borror and Richard E. White. Houghton Mifflin, 1974.

A Field Guide to Moths of Eastern North America, by Charles V. Covell, Jr. Houghton Mifflin, 1984.

A Field Guide to Western Butterflies, by J.W. Tilden and Arthur C. Smith. Houghton Mifflin, 1986.

Mushrooms:

Audubon Society Field Guide to North American Mushrooms, by the Audubon Society Staff and Gary H. Lincoff. Knopf, 1981.

A Field Guide to Mushrooms: North America, by Kent H. McKnight and Vera B. McKnight. Houghton Mifflin, 1987.

Plants and Flowers:

Audubon Society Field Guide to North American Wildflowers, by the Audubon Society Staff, two volumes. Knopf, 1979.

Volume 1: Eastern Region.
Volume 2: Western Region.

A Field Guide to Eastern Edible Wild Plants, by Lee A. Peterson. Houghton Mifflin, 1982.

A Field Guide to Ferns and Their Related Families: Northeastern and Central North America, by Boughton Cobb. Houghton Mifflin, 1975.

A Field Guide to Edible Plants, by Steven Foster. Houghton Mifflin, 1990.

A Field Guide to Medicinal Plants: Eastern and Central North America, by Steven Foster and James A. Duke. Houghton Mifflin, 1990.

A Field Guide to Pacific States Wildflowers, by Theodore F. Niehaus. Houghton Mifflin, 1976.

A Field Guide to Rocky Mountain Wildflowers, by John A. Craighead et al. Houghton Mifflin, 1974.

A Field Guide to Southwestern and Texas Wildflowers, by Theodore F. Niehaus et al. Houghton Mifflin, 1984.

A Field Guide to Wildflowers of Northeastern and North Central North America, by Roger Tory Peterson and Margaret McKenny. Houghton Mifflin, 1975.

Reptiles and Amphibians:

Audubon Society Field Guide to North American Reptiles and Amphibians, by the Audubon Society Staff and F. Wayne King. Knopf, 1979.

A Field Guide to Reptiles and Amphibians, by Robert B. Stebbins. Houghton Mifflin, 2nd edition, 1985.

A Field Guide to Reptiles and Amphibians of Eastern and Central North America, by Roger Conant. Houghton Mifflin, 2nd edition, 1975.

Rocks and Minerals:

Audubon Society Field Guide to North American Rocks amd Minerals, by the Audubon Society Staff and Charles W. Chesterman. Knopf, 1979.

A Field Guide to Rocks and Minerals, by Frederick H. Pough. Houghton Mifflin, 4th edition, 1976.

Shellfish:

Audubon Society Field Guide to North American Seashells, by the Audubon Society Staff and Harold A. Rehder. Knopf, 1981.

A Field Guide to Atlantic Coast Shells, by Percy A. Morris. Houghton Mifflin, 3rd edition, 1973.

A Field Guide to Coral Reefs of the Caribbean and Florida, by Eugene H. Kaplan. Houghton Mifflin, 1988.

A Field Guide to Pacific Coast Shells, by Percy A. Morris. Houghton Mifflin, 1974.

Trees:

Audubon Society Field Guide to North American Trees, by the Audubon Society Staff and Elbert A. Little, Jr., two volumes. Knopf, 1980.

Volume 1: Eastern Region.
Volume 2: Western Region.

A Field Guide to Eastern Forests, by John C. Kricher. Houghton Mifflin, 1988.

A Field Guide to Eastern Trees, by George A. Petrides. Houghton Mifflin, 1988.

A Field Guide to Trees and Shrubs, by George A. Petrides. Houghton Mifflin, 1973.

FILM. *See* MOVIES.

FINANCE. *See also* BUSINESS; PERSONAL FINANCE.

Encyclopedia of Banking and Finance, by Glenn G. Munn. Bankers Publishing, 8th edition, 1983. Definition of terms and articles on money, credit, banking, investments, insurance, and other financial matters.

FINE ARTS

Britannica Encyclopaedia of American Art. Encyclopaedia Britannica, 1973. Articles on all aspects of American fine and applied arts. Cross-referenced and illustrated, with glossary, bibliography, and guide to museums and public collections.

A Dictionary of Art Terms and Techniques, by Ralph Mayer. Crowell, 1969. Presents short definitions of terms from the fine arts and allied fields. Information given covers materials, methods, history, and technology. Geared to art students and artists.

Dictionary of Subjects and Symbols in Art, by James Hall. Harper, revised edition, 1979. Entries concern basic themes (mainly Classical and Christian) in Western art. Cross-referenced.

Encyclopedia of Painting, edited by Bernard S. Myers. Crown, 4th revised edition, 1979. Provides general information on movements, styles, techniques, and important painters, from prehistoric times to the present. This edition includes more contemporary and women artists. Copiously illustrated.

Everyman's Dictionary of Pictorial Art, edited by William Gaunt, two volumes. Dutton, 1962. Quick reference to painters, periods, forms, and techniques from all over the world. Illustrated. Articles are concise, with some critical commentary.

Gardner's Art Through the Ages, two volumes, by Horst De la Croix and Richard Tansey. Harcourt Brace Jovanovich, 8th edition, 1986. Generously illustrated beginner's history of art. With glossary, index, and bibliography.

History of Art, by Horst W. Janson. Harry N. Abrams, 3rd edition, 1986. Extensively illustrated work that emphasizes the scholarly discipline of art history as well as the history itself. Covers mainly Western art.

> **History of Art for Young People,** by Horst W. Janson. Harry N. Abrams, 3rd edition, 1987. Abridgment of book above for young people.

History of Modern Art, by H. Horvard Arnason and Daniel Wheeler. Prentice Hall, 3rd edition, 1986. Comprehensive history of art and architecture in Europe and America from the Impressionists to date. For laypersons and college students.

McGraw-Hill Dictionary of Art, edited by Bernard S. Myers, five volumes. McGraw-Hill, 1969. Illustrated encyclopedic entries on all aspects of art. Includes extensive treatment of Far Eastern, Middle Eastern, and African art. Also has entries on museums, archaeology, decorative arts, and many other related fields. Illustrated and cross-referenced.

The Oxford Companion to Art, edited by Harold Osborne. Oxford University Press, 1970. Nonspecialist's introduction to fine arts. Includes entries on all of the world of art from prehistory to present. Illustrated, with bibliography.

Oxford Dictionary of Art, edited by by Ian Chilvers and Harold Osborne; consulting editor, Dennis Farr. Oxford University Press, 1988. Compiled from three Oxford Guides—Art, 20th Century Art, and Decorative Art. Offers 3,000 entries on nearly every aspect of Western art and the essentials of Asian art. Provides information on artists, schools, techniques, periods, major museums, and philosophers. Includes extensive cross-references.

FINE ARTS—AMERICAN

Who's Who in American Art, Bowker, annual. Profiles representatives of all segments of the art world including artists, administrators, and librarians. Entries give vital statistics, professional education and training, commissions and exhibitions, and membership in art societies. Includes geographic and professional classification indexes and cumulative necrology.

FIRST AID

First Aid Book, Alton Thygerson. Prentice Hall, 2nd edition, 1986. Treats all types of injury-related and emotional or trauma health emergencies. For advanced students or beginners.

FISH

Audubon Society Field Guide to North American Fishes, Whales, and Dolphins, by the Audubon Society Staff and others. Knopf, 1983.

Dr. Axelrod's Mini-Atlas of Freshwater Aquarium Fishes, by Dr. Herbert R. Axelrod et al. T.F.H.

Publications, 3rd edition, 1989. Has photographs of all kinds of freshwater fishes, grouped by characteristics. Information, in symbols, is given on the conditions necessary for maintaining and caring for each fish. A second section is devoted to aquarium maintenance and fish breeding. Includes special section on photography for aquarists, plus indexes.

Encyclopedia of Tropical Fishes, by Dr. Herbert R. Axelrod and William Vorderwinkler. T.F.H. Publications, 27th edition, 1983. How to breed and care for tropical fishes. Fishes classified by breeding procedures. Includes several chapters on how to set up and maintain an aquarium. Illustrated.

A Field Guide to Atlantic Coast Fishes, by G. Carleton Ray and C. Richard Robbins. Houghton Mifflin, 1986.

A Field Guide to Coral Reefs of the Caribbean and Florida, by Eugene H. Kaplan. Houghton Mifflin, 1988.

Field Guide to Freshwater Fishes of North America, by A.J. McClane. Holt, 1978.

A Field Guide to Pacific Coast Fishes of North America, by William N. Eschmeyer and Earl S. Herald. Houghton Mifflin, 1983.

Field Guide to Saltwater Fishes of North America, by A.J. McClane. Holt, 1978.

The Simon & Schuster Pocket Guide to Aquarium Fishes, by Gwyne Vevers. Simon & Schuster, 1984. Description of various aquarium fishes with recommendations for care and feeding. Includes an essay on how to equip and maintain an aquarium. Illustrated.

FLAGS

Guide to Flags of the World, by Mauro Talocci; translated by Robert Strom. Morrow, revised edition, 1982. Descriptions and histories of national, state, and provincial flags, coats of arms, and international flags. Arranged by continent, then by country.

So Proudly We Hail, by Rear Admiral William Rea Furlong and Commodore Byron McCandless. Smithsonian Institution Press, 1981. A history of the U.S. flag and its predecessors, going back to the first explorations of the New World. Richly illustrated, with index of protocols and

laws concerning the flag. Includes bibliography and index.

FLOWERS. *See* GARDENING; HORTICULTURE; PLANTS AND FLOWERS.

FOLKLORE. *See also* MYTHOLOGY.

A Guide to Folktales in the English Language: Based on the Aarne-Thompson Classification System, by D.L. Ashliman. Greenwood, 1987. A numerical system used to cross-reference folk and fairy tales by basic plot. "Sleeping Beauty," for example, cross-references to 22 other tales with the same basic plot. Includes lists of secondary sources, collections of tales in print, and all 210 Grimm tales with classification numbers in the back.

FOOD AND NUTRITION. *See also* COOKBOOKS.

The Calorie Factor: A Dieter's Companion, by Margo Felder. Simon & Schuster, 1989. The ultimate calorie counter—details the calories found in everything, even army food.

The Columbia Encyclopedia of Nutrition, by the Institute of Human Nutrition, Columbia University, College of Physicians and Surgeons. Edited by Myron Winick and others. Putnam, 1989. Clear, readable prose gives an accessible guide to vitamins, additives, dieting, hypertension, and other nutrtionally related disorders. Includes section on nutrition for nursing and pregnant women.

Complete Book of Food, by Carol Ann Ringler. World Almanac, 1987. Dictionary of foods that "gives the reader the ability to evaluate each food as an individual health product." Provides nutritional, medical, and consumer information.

Foods and Nutrition Encyclopedia, by Audrey Ensminger and M.E. Ensminger, two volumes. Pegus Press, 1983. In-depth source of information on diet, nutrition, and health. Discusses the relationship of athletics and exercise to nutrition; gives a history of nutrition; and discusses nutrition-related diseases, important minerals and vitamins, and other related topics. Directed at consumer laypersons, but would be useful to medical and other health professionals. Illustrated.

Food Values of Portions Commonly Used, by Jean A.T. Pennington and Helen Nichols Church. Harper, 15th edition, 1989. Tables of nutritive values of foods and their mineral and vitamin contents.

FOOTBALL

The Encyclopedia of Football, by Roger Treat. A.S. Barnes, 14th edition, 1976. Gives a comprehensive year-by-year history, including players, coaches, records, teams, and other leagues.

The Sports Encyclopedia: Pro Football, by David S. Neft and Richard M. Cohen. St. Martin's, 6th edition, 1988. Follows same format as *Baseball* (above). Includes team and individual statistics, Hall-of-Famers, and Super Bowls.

FOREIGN POLICY. *See* INTERNATIONAL RELATIONS.

FOSSILS

Audubon Society Field Guide to North American Fossils, by the Audubon Society Staff and Ida Thompson. Knopf, 1982.

A Field Guide to Prehistoric Life, by David Lambert and The Diagram Group. Presents to the amateur fossil hunter a complete, systematic means of identifying and understanding fossil life. More than 500 illustrations, maps, and charts.

The Illustrated Encyclopedia of Fossils, by Giovanni Pinna. Facts on File, 1990. Covers every aspect of the field, including the formation of fossils, their significance in the paleologic record, their excavation, and their classification. Over 1,300 color illustrations. Has glossary, bibliography, and index.

FOUNDATIONS. *See* ORGANIZATIONS.

FRANCHISING

Franchise Annual, edited by Edward L. Dixon. Info Press. Lists franchises by popular name for Canada, the United States, and overseas. Gives start-up costs.

The Rating Guide to Franchises, by Dennis L. Foster. Facts on File, revised edition, 1991. Updated version of standard directory of American and Canadian franchises and franchise opportunities, from AAMCO to Wendy's fast food.

Source Book of Franchise Opportunities 1990–1991, by Robert S. Bond and Christopher E. Bond. Dow Jones-Irwin, 1990. Covers the history, financial start-up, and training for some 400 American and Canadian businesses offering franchises.

FURNITURE. *See also* ANTIQUES AND COLLECTIBLES.

Encyclopedia of Furniture, by Joseph Aronson. Crown, 3rd edition, 1965. Has short descriptive entries on furniture styles, development, and designers. Liberally illustrated in black and white. Includes bibliography and glossary.

Sotheby's Concise Encyclopedia of Furniture, edited by Christopher Payne. Harper, 1989. An illustrated history of furniture from the Renaissance to the present, written by international experts. Details major styles, trends, and innovations. Illustrated dictionary explains furniture styles and construction.

G

GAMES. *See also* SPORTS.

Hoyle's Rules of Games, edited by Albert H. Morehead and Geoffrey Mott-Smith. New American Library, 2nd revised edition, 1983. Latest guide to card and parlor (board) games, with rules and information on how to score. Includes the official new contract bridge rules and glossary.

GARDENING. *See* HORTICULTURE; PLANTS AND FLOWERS.

GEMOLOGY

Color Encyclopedia of Gemstones, by Joel E. Arem. Van Nostrand Reinhold, 1987. The standard reference source on gemstones, now updated to include such subjects as synthetic gems, scientific color grading and testing, and thermal properties of gems as "diagnostic tools." Has listings of 250 gem species with 300 full-color photographs.

GENEALOGY

How to Find Your Family Roots, by Timothy Field Beard. McGraw-Hill, 1977. Guide to specific genealogical research. Gives resources, research techniques, and hints on how to ferret out information and deal with foreign governments.

The Library: A Guide to the LDS Family History Library, edited by Johni Cerny and Wendy Elliott. Ancestry Publishing, 1988. An explanatory guide to the largest single collection of genealogical works, detailing the services offered by this organization, how its information is gathered and classified, and what records are available in its local, state, and foreign branches. The Family History Library, run by the Church of Jesus Christ of

Latter Day Saints, is accessible to both amateur and professional researchers.

The Source: A Guidebook of American Genealogy, by Arlene Eakle and Johni Cerny. Ancestry, 1984. A compilation of resources, research techniques, and record sources for American genealogical study. Useful for beginners and professionals. Includes extensive appendices, glossary, and bibliography. Most complete work in the field.

GENERAL REFERENCE BOOKS. *See also* ENCYCLOPEDIAS.

Famous First Facts, by Joseph Nathan Kane. H.W. Wilson, 4th edition, 1981. Helpful for locating the unusual.

Guinness Book of World Records, Sterling, annual. Has information on numerous biggests, smallest, longests, shortests, etc.

Information Please Almanac, edited by Otto Johnson. Houghton Mifflin, annual. Statistical and factual material organized by subject area; contains special articles by experts. Illustrated, with a color map section and detailed index.

The New York Public Library Desk Reference, Simon & Schuster, 1989. Each of the 26 sections is a mini-encyclopedia covering, in tables, illustrations, and text, such subjects as the animal world, math and science, the arts, religion, sports, health, the United States, and the world. Each section ends with a list of "Additional Sources of Information" for those who wish to pursue a subject in greater detail. Has a map section in color. Indexed.

The World Almanac and Book of Facts, edited by Mark S. Hoffman. Pharos, annual. First published in 1868, this is the most comprehensive and well-known of almanacs. A book of general statistics and information, it contains "more than 1 million up-to-date facts." Contains a chronology of the year's events, consumer information, historical anniversaries, annual climatological data, and forecasts. Color section has flags and maps. Includes detailed index.

GEOGRAPHY. *See* ATLASES; DICTIONARIES—GEOGRAPHICAL.

GOVERNMENT—FEDERAL. *See* FEDERAL GOVERNMENT.

GOVERNMENT—STATE. *See* STATE GOVERNMENTS.

GRAMMAR. *See also* STYLE AND USAGE.

Harper's English Grammar, by John B. Opdycke. Warner, revised by Stewart H. Benedict, 1965. Follows the conventional classification of the parts of speech and treats each one individually. The second part of the book explains sentences, syntax, phrases, and similar matters. Indexed.

GRANTS. *See* PHILANTHROPY.

GRAPHIC ARTS

Britannica Encyclopaedia of American Art. Encyclopaedia Britannica, 1973. Articles on all aspects of American fine and applied arts. Cross-referenced and illustrated, with glossary, bibliography, and guide to museums and public collections.

Illustration Index, by Marsha C. Appel. Scarecrow, 5th edition, 1984. Lists illustrations that have appeared in publications. Arranged by subject. Publications selected for "richness of illustration and for the availability of back issues in libraries."

Index to Illustrations of Living Things Outside North America: Where to Find Pictures of Flora and Fauna, by Lucile Thompson Munz and Nedra G. Slauson. Archon, 1981. An index of pictures of animals and plants in over 200 books, categorized by common usage, scientific name, and genus. As implied by the title, extinct species and those found in North America only are not included. Complements *Index to Illustrations of the Natural World,* listed below.

Index to Illustrations of the Natural World, by John W. Thompson; edited by Nedra Slauson. Gaylord Professional Publications, 1977. An index to still-surviving North American species of flora and fauna, both native and introduced.

The Oxford Companion to the Decorative Arts, edited by Harold Osborne. Oxford University Press, 1975. Handbook giving introductory survey of craftsmanship. Entries concentrate on cultures, history, techniques, and materials. Excludes mass-produced items.

Symbol Sourcebook, by Henry Dreyfuss. McGraw/Van Nostrand Reinhold, 1972. An extensive guide to international graphic symbols.

H

HANDICAPPED SERVICES. *See* DISABILITIES.

HEALTH. *See* MEDICINE AND HEALTH.

HEALTH CARE

Guide to the Health Care Field, annual, American Hospital Association. National directory of hospitals, health organizations, and agencies.

HEALTH EDUCATION

Allied Health Education Directory, AMA, annual. Contains information on educational programs in allied health occupations and on the accreditation process used to certify schools. Includes glossary and appendices.

HERALDRY

A Dictionary of Heraldry, edited by Stephen Friar, illustrated by John Ferguson, Andrew Jamieson, and Anthony Wood. Harmony/Crown, 1987. Provides explanations of both the traditional and current terms of heraldry, from classic coats-of-arms to airline trademarks.

HISTORY. *See also* ATLASES—HISTORICAL.

An Encyclopedia of World History, Ancient, Medieval and Modern, edited by William L. Langer. Houghton Mifflin, 5th edition, 1972. Divides history into eight periods and treats each period chronologically, with encyclopedic entries on important events and personages. Includes appendices and index.

World Civilizations: Their History and Their Culture, by Edward Burns et al, three volumes. Norton, 7th edition, 1986. Broad survey of history. High school-level text. Illustrated. Includes appendices and index.

African:

Africa in History, By Basil Davidson. Macmillan, 1974. General narrative history going back to earliest times and the dawn of man. Concentrates on debunking a lot of myths about African civilization. Includes index and bibliography.

A History of the African People, by Robert W. July. Scribner, 2nd edition, 1974. Although it begins with ancient Africa, this history concentrates mainly on the social and political movements of modern Africa from about 1800. A very general, basic history, useful as a textbook. Illustrated. Includes bibliography and index.

American. *See also* ATLASES—HISTORICAL.

Dictionary of American History, eight volumes. Scribner, revised edition, 1976. Entries provide quick identification of a subject and related information. Many entries, however, go into more detail. Cross-referenced; includes index volume. *See also* its abridgment, THE CONCISE DICTIONARY OF AMERICAN HISTORY (Scribner, 1983).

Documents of American History, edited by Henry Steele Commager. Prentice-Hall, 1973. Compilation of official and archival documents that illustrate American history. All constitutional amendments, important Supreme Court decisions, and many presidential addresses are included. Useful for beginning documentary research.

The Encyclopedia of American Facts & Dates, by Gorton Carruth. Harper, 8th edition, 1987. 1,006 pages, with extensive index. Organized chronologically and concurrently from 986 A.D. to the present, according to four major fields of interest:

    I: Exploration and Settlement, Government, Civil Rights, Statistics.

    II: Publishing, Arts and Music, Popular Entertainment, Architecture, Theater.

    III: Business and Industry, Science, Education, Philosophy and Religion.

    IV: Sports, Social Issues and Crime, Folkways, Fashion, Holidays.

Encyclopedia of American History, edited by Richard B. Morris. Harper, 6th edition, 1982. The first part contains a basic chronology from the first explorations and settlements. Part II presents the nonpolitical history of American life including intellectual, cultural, economic, and scientific development. Part III is a biographical dictionary of important Americans. Part IV analyzes the structure of American government and reprints the Constitution and the Declaration of Independence. Enlarged edition includes more information on minorities and women.

Facts About the Presidents, by Joseph Nathan Kane. H.W. Wilson, 5th edition, 1989. Part I contains data on birth, education, private life, elections, and public administration for each President. Part II presents collected facts in comparative tables. Also contains information on the presidency, such as salaries, cabinet officers, power of veto, and electoral and popular votes for every election.

The Growth of the American Republic, by Samuel Eliot Morison, Henry Steele Commager, and William E. Leuchtenberg, two volumes. Oxford University Press, 7th edition, 1980. Written by three of the most respected scholars of American history, this work has been updated through the Carter presidency. Very scholarly, with appendices, bibliography, and index for each volume.

Harvard Guide to American History, edited by Frank Freidel. Harvard University Press, revised edition, 1974. Directory of historical publications, primary sources, and archives. Has extensive bibliographies for biographies and other critical writings on a variety of research topics.

A History of the American People, by Norman A. Graebner, Gilbert C. Fite, and Philip L. White, two volumes. McGraw-Hill, 1975. General history conceived as a basic textbook for high schools (a teacher's manual is available). Well illustrated and concise. Includes appendices and index.

The Oxford Companion to American History, by Thomas H. Johnson. Oxford University Press, 1966. Concise introductory articles on a variety of topics and historical personages.

The Oxford History of the United States, edited by C. Vann Woodward. Oxford University Press, 1982—. Incomplete as yet, the first volumes are *Battle Cry of Freedom: The Civil War Era,* by James McPherson, and *The Glorious Cause: The American Revolution, 1763–1789,* by Robert Middlekauf. For readers more interested in a particular period rather than a general overview of American history.

Reconstruction: America's Unfinished Revolution, by Eric Foner. Harper, 1988. Incorporating much eyewitness material, this book emphasizes the centrality of the Black experience. The book also examines the themes of race and class, the remodeling of Southern society, and the national context. A complete, modern, scholarly text. Includes bibliography and index.

Ancient:

Civilization of the Ancient Mediterranean: Greece and Rome, three volumes, edited by Michael Grant and Rachel Kitzinger. Scribner, 1988. Series of essays on various historical and cultural topics. Volume I features a chronology and Volume III has an index. Illustrated.

A History of the Ancient World, by Chester G. Starr. Oxford University Press, 1965. Comprehensive survey of the history of Western civilization from its beginnings to 400 A.D. Illustrated. Includes bibliography and index.

The Oxford Classical Dictionary, edited by N.G.L. Hammond and H.H. Scullard. Oxford University Press, 2nd edition, 1970. This work contains articles on Greek and Latin literature, history, religion, art, and sciences up to the death of Constantine (337 A.D.). Also includes places and biographies of major people. Bibliographies appended to articles; includes index of place names.

Asian:

Encyclopedia of Asian History, edited by Ainslee T. Embree (under the auspices of the Asia Society), four volumes. Scribner, 1988. This reference undertakes to "make available the highest level of contemporary scholarship on Asia to a nonspecialist audience." Political, socioeconomic, and intellectual movements are treated equally, but with an emphasis on historical significance. Includes illustrations, appendices, and index.

British:

The Cambridge Historical Encyclopedia of Great Britain and Ireland, edited by Christopher Haigh. Cambridge University Press, 1985. From the earliest Britons to 1975, this liberally illustrated work is aimed at high school students. Includes Who's Who of important people, bibliography, and index.

English Social History, by G.M. Trevelyan. Longman Group Ltd., 1978. This groundbreaking work has been reset with copious illustrations. It portrays the social life of the English from the time of Chaucer through the death of Queen Victoria. Indexed.

A History of England, by David Harris Willson and Stuart E. Prall. Holt, 3rd edition, 1984. Single-volume history that tries to balance political narrative and economic and social history. Includes appendices, genealogical tables, maps, bibliography, and index.

Oxford Illustrated History of Britain, edited by Kenneth O. Morgan. Oxford University Press,

1984. 2,000 years of British history as told by ten leading historians. Details how the past has shaped British character, patriotism, and ethnocentrism. Includes over 250 illustrations, chronologies, genealogies of monarchs, and a table of Prime Ministers.

The Oxford Illustrated History of the British Monarchy, by John Cannon and Ralph Griffiths. Oxford University Press, 1988. A dynastic account of the history, public and private, of the British monarchy. Augmented by many illustrations that show the visual magnificence that is a part of the monarchy. Includes appendices, bibliography, and index.

Chinese:

The Cambridge History of China, 15 volumes. Cambridge University Press, 1976. The newest and most comprehensive history of China. Each volume has a glossary-index, maps and tables, a bibliography, and bibliographical essays. As always with Cambridge, the approach is impeccably scholarly.

Encyclopedia of China Today, by Fredric M. Kaplan and Julian M. Sobin. Harper, 3rd edition, 1980. Handy, quick, factual introduction to history, politics, culture, and economic system, with section on "Doing Business with the PRC." Includes maps, illustrations, appendices, and index.

Cuban:

Cuba, Between Revolution and Reform, by Louis A. Perez, Jr. Oxford University Press, 1988. A narrative history that emphasizes the antecedents of the Cuban revolution and concludes with an analysis of Fidel Castro's successes and failures. Includes bibliographical essay and index.

Cuba: From Columbus to Castro, by Jaime Suchlicki. Pergamon, 2nd revised edition, 1985. Summary of Cuba's development, with special attention to the 20th century and the Cuban revolution.

European:

Europe From the Renaissance to Waterloo, Europe Since Waterloo, by Robert Ergang and Donald G. Rohr. D.C. Heath, 3rd edition, 1967. Taking the rise of nation states as its starting-off point, this history is a general overview of European history, ending with a chapter on "New Directions in Europe, 1960–66." Includes bibliographies and indexes. Illustrated.

French:

France: A Modern History, by Albert Guerard, revised by Paul A. Gagnon. University of Michigan Press, 1969. A general history with an emphasis on the 1789 Revolution. Includes bibliography and index.

German:

Germany: A Modern History, by Marshall Dill, Jr. University of Michigan Press, revised edition, 1970. Disposing quickly of pre-nineteenth-century history, this work concentrates its attention on the formation of the German state (under Bismarck) to the end of World War II. (Roughly 280 of its 450 pages are spent on this era.) A good overview for the general reader, with a bibliography of works in English and an index.

A History of Modern Germany, by Hajo Holbern, three volumes. Princeton University Press, 1982. Volume 1 covers the Reformation, volume 2 covers the period 1648–1840, and volume 3 covers the years 1840–1945. Each volume includes coverage of the socioeconomic and political changes that led to the rise and fall of the era.

Italian:

Italy: A Modern History, by Denis Mack Smith. University of Michigan Press, revised edition, 1969. This history concentrates on Italy after unification, from 1861 through the fall of the Fascists, with a short overview of the nation since World War II. General, popular history. Includes bibliography and index.

Latin American:

The Cambridge Encyclopedia of Latin America and the Caribbean, edited by Simon Collier, Harold Blakemore, and Thomas E. Skidmore. Cambridge University Press, 1985. Broad coverage for the general reader of history and economic development, culture and society, and flora and fauna. Includes illustrations, glossary, and index.

The Cambridge History of Latin America, edited by Leslie Bethell, seven volumes. Cambridge University Press, 1985–90. History of the areas south of the United States from just prior to the European invasions to the present. The last three volumes are not yet published. Covers general themes in Latin American history with chronological accounts of the individual countries. Bibliographical essays are appended to each chapter.

Mexican:

The Course of Mexican History, by Michael C. Meyer and William L. Sherman. Oxford University Press, 3rd edition, 1987. General overview of Mexican history from pre-Columbian times through the 1985 earthquake and the fall of oil prices. Incorporates sociocultural as well as political history. Well illustrated; intended for college students as an introduction. Includes index and bibliography in Spanish. An English bibliography is appended to each chapter.

Middle Eastern:

The Middle East: A History, by Sydney Nettleton Fisher and William L. Ochsenwald. McGraw-Hill, 4th editon, 1989. Beginning with the rise of Islam, this history covers the Middle Eastern Crescent and adjoining Arab lands to the present time. Emphasizes the role of history in the current debates and conflicts. Indexed.

Puerto Rican:

Historical Dictionary of Puerto Rico and the U.S. Virgin Islands, by Kenneth Farr. Scarecrow, 1973. A dictionary of political and cultural terms. Includes data on persons, events, places, and geographical and political subdivisions of both Puerto Rico and, to a lesser extent, the U.S. Virgin Islands.

Puerto Rico: A Political and Cultural History, by Arturo Morales Carrion et al. Norton, 1983. Narrative history that begins at the beginning (not the cession of the island to the United States in 1898). Explores "problems related to the Puerto Rican search for identity." Discusses sociocultural and political factors that give Puerto Rico its character. Includes bibliography and index.

Russian:

A History of Russia, by Nicholas V. Riasanovsky. Oxford University Press, 1977. A strong narrative history that blends discussions of economics, social organization, religion, and culture into the story. Modern and satisfactorily impartial. Includes illustrations, bibliography, and index.

South Asian:

Cambridge Encyclopedia of India, Pakistan, Bangladesh, Sri Lanka, Nepal, Bhutan, and the Maldives, edited by Francis Robinson. Cambridge University Press, 1989. A regional encyclopedia focusing on the history and sociology of the area. Seventy contributors provide an in-depth and comprehensive picture of South Asia and the Indian subcontinent. Includes 75 maps, 69 tables, and dynastic charts from 500 B.C. to the present.

United States. *See* AMERICAN (ABOVE).

HOCKEY

The Hockey Encyclopedia, by Stan Fischler and Shirley Walton Fischler. Macmillan, 1983. Opens with a brief history of the game, then gives lists of players, coaches, records, achievements, Stanley Cup playoffs, and statistics.

The National Hockey League Official Guide and Record Book, Running Press, annual. Provides complete statistics, plus features on NHL history and rule changes. Covers back to the 1917–28 season.

HOLIDAYS

The American Book of Days, edited by Jane M. Hatch. H.W. Wilson, 3rd edition, 1978. Chronological arrangement of descriptive articles on holidays and other special observances.

Anniversaries and Holidays, by Ruth W. Gregory. American Library Association, 4th edition, 1983. International in scope; describes more than 2,500 historical and contemporary holidays and religious festivals.

Celebrations: the Complete Book of American Holidays, by Robert J. Myers. Doubleday, 1972. Origins and descriptions of all major American holidays.

Chases's Annual Events, Contemporary Books, annual. Day-by-day listing of national and state holidays, religious observances, special events, festivals and fairs, and historical anniversaries and birthdays. Covers U.S. events primarily, but some international occasions and anniversaries are included.

HOME BUILDING, MAINTENANCE, AND REPAIR

The Complete Illustrated Guide to Everything Sold in Hardware Stores, by Tom Philbin and Steve Ettlinger. Macmillan, 1988. Provides complete details on all tools, fasteners, materials, and other home-repair items on the market today, including those for specialized work, where the correct specific tools or materials can make the difference between a successful job and a failure.

Formulas, Methods, Tips and Data for Home and Workshop, by Kenneth Swezey. Harper, revised edition, 1979. Practical information for do-it-yourself enthusiasts.

McGraw-Hill's National Electrical Code Handbook, by Joseph F. McPartland et al. McGraw-Hill, 1984. Explains and clarifies National Electrical Code regulations. Designed for professionals, this handbook is also accessible for do-it-yourselfers contemplating electrical changes and improvements.

Reader's Digest New Complete Do-It-Yourself Manual, Reader's Digest, 1991. First published 1973, this best-selling single-volume guide to home maintenance and repair has been completely revised and updated for the 1990s. For homeowner and apartment dweller alike, it provides details, photographs, and diagrams for projects within the capability of the do-it-yourselfer. It also offers guidance as to when a contractor or specialist is needed.

Reader's Digest Fix-It-Yourself Manual. Reader's Digest, 1981. Information how to repair, clean, and maintain anything in and around your home. Has major sections on furniture repair and upholstering; covers small and large appliances. Illustrated with clear, step-by-step diagrams and photographs. Indexed.

The Simon and Schuster Complete Guide to Home Repair and Maintenance, by Bernard Gladstone. Simon & Schuster, 1984. New text and illustrations, not to be confused with Gladstone's earlier work, published by the *New York Times* (for whom he is an editor). Begins with a chapter on tools and techniques and works through basic repair operations to more complex renovations. Includes appendix on furniture refinishing. Indexed and illustrated.

Time-Life Books Complete Home Improvement and Renovation Manual. Time-Life Books, 1991. A compilation of the most useful material in Time-Life's best-selling earlier 36-volume series. Major sections cover interior improvements; kitchens and bathrooms; doors and windows; heating, cooling, and electrical systems; exterior improvements; and major additions. Extensively illustrated with clear how-to illustrations and diagrams; indexed.

HOMOSEXUALITY

Gay American History, by Jonathan Katz. Harper, 1976. Extensive collection of documents with commentary covering the past 350 years.

HORTICULTURE. *See also* BOTANY; PLANTS AND FLOWERS.

Hortus Third: A Concise Dictionary of Plants Cultivated in the United States and Canada, by the staff of the L.H. Bailey Hortorium, Cornell University. Macmillan, 1976. More than 34,000 A-to-Z listings cover all plants cultivated in North America, from a botanical point of view. Almost 200 general entries treat such subjects as bulbs, evergreens, and propagation. Illustrated, and has glossary of terms.

Manual of Cultivated Plants, by L.H. Bailey. Macmillan, revised edition, 1949. Handbook for identification of plants commonly grown in the United States and Canada. Includes taxonomic information and detailed description of each plant. Organized by taxonomic classification. With glossary and index.

Wildflowers Across America, by Lady Bird Johnson and Carlton B. Lees. Abbeville, 1988. A guide to using wildflowers and plants in private and public gardens. Color photographs compiled by Johnson, active in the National Wildflower Research Center, and Lees, a horticulturalist.

The Wise Garden Encyclopedia. Harper, revised edition, 1991. An A-to-Z reference for specialists and backyard gardeners alike. The new edition has 600 new line drawings and 64 pages of new color photographs. Covers flowers, trees, shrubs, lawns, herbs, soil, fertilizers, pesticides, garden design, and many other topics.

Wyman's Gardening Encyclopedia, by Donald Wyman. Macmillan, 1977. Horticultural manual for everybody. Contains articles on individual plants, gardening practices, and garden chemicals and their ecological consequences.

HOSPITALS. *See* HEALTH CARE.

HOTELS AND MOTELS

Hotel and Motel Red Book, American Hotel Association, annual. The main section is a "destination index" for the United States, Canada, Mexico, and the Caribbean: an alphabetical listing of travel destinations giving basic travel information. Hotels/motels are rated for quality and information such as rates, services, and facilities for handicapped travelers. The Red Book contains airport and major city maps, rail and airline information, and other travel information.

I

ILLUSTRATION. *See* GRAPHIC ARTS.

INDIANS. *See* NATIVE AMERICANS.

INSECTS AND SPIDERS

Audubon Society Field Guide to North American Butterflies, by the Audubon Society Staff and Robert M. Pyle. Knopf, 1981.

Audubon Society Field Guide to North American Insects and Spiders, by the Audubon Society Staff and Lorus Milne. Knopf, 1980.

The Encyclopedia of Insects, edited by Christopher O'Toole. Twenty expert contributors cover the awesome variety of insects, which have evolved into more than 750,000 species. Topics include the evolution and classification of arthropods, their common physical features, their reproductive cycles, and many other subjects. Illustrated with color photographs and specially commissioned illustrations.

A Field Guide to Beetles, by Richard E. White. Houghton Mifflin, 1983.

A Field Guide to the Butterflies, by Roger Tory Peterson. Houghton Mifflin, 1983.

A Field Guide to the Insects of America North of Mexico, by Donald J. Borror and Richard E. White. Houghton Mifflin, 1974.

A Field Guide to Moths of Eastern North America, by Charles V. Covell, Jr. Houghton Mifflin, 1980. Houghton Mifflin, 1984.

A Field Guide to Western Butterflies, by J.W. Tilden and Arthur C. Smith. Houghton Mifflin, 1986.

INTERNATIONAL RELATIONS. *See also* UNITED NATIONS.

A Diplomatic History of the American People, by Thomas Andrew Bailey. Prentice-Hall, 10th edition, 1980. College text; narrative history of American foreign relations.

The Statesman's Yearbook, St. Martin's, annual. Concise compendium of descriptive and statistical information about countries of the world.

Treaties and Alliances of the World: An International Survey Covering Treaties in Force and Communities of States, Gale, 4th edition, 1986. Concise summaries of international treaties and agreements, with discussion of history and later development of the agreements.

INVENTIONS. *See also* PATENTS.

The History of Invention: From Stone Axes to Silicon Chips, by Trevor I. Williams. Facts on File, 1987. Broad survey covering all areas of the globe, relating inventions to the (mythical) progress of civilization. Well-illustrated. Contains biographical dictionary in appendix. Indexed.

The Second World Almanac of Inventions, by Valerie-Anne Giscard d'Estaing. World Almanac, 1986. Inventions grouped by purpose. Entries describe how and when inventions were imagined and constructed. Illustrated and indexed.

INVESTMENTS. *See also* BUSINESS; PERSONAL FINANCE.

The Business One Irwin Business and Investment Almanac, edited by Sumner N. Levine. Business One Irwin, annual. Formerly entitled *Dow Jones-Irwin Business and Investment Almanac.* Covers stock market averages, price/earnings ratios, futures markets, mutual fund performance, foreign stock markets, and many other topics relating to investments.

Investor's Guide to Stock Quotations, by Gerald Warfield. Harper, 3rd edition, 1990. Provides explanation and interpretation of newspaper financial sections.

Moody's Handbook of Common Stocks. Moody's Investors Service, quarterly. Each issue has price charts and concise financial statistics for over 1,000 common stocks, with data covering a 10-year period.

ISLAM. *See also* RELIGION.

The Concise Encyclopedia of Islam, by Cyril Glasse. Harper, 1989. A standard reference work with short dictionary-style entries on various topics. Includes a series of maps, extensive charts, genealogical tables, a bibliography, and a chronology.

Islam, edited by John Alden Williams. Washington Square, 1963. A selection of texts with brief introductions and explanations by a well-known scholar of Islamic history and art. Included are short passages from the *Qur'an* (the Arberry translation, see below); the sayings and actions of the Prophet Muhammad, known as *hadith;* interpretations of Islamic law, *fiqh;* some material on mysticism in Islam, popularly known as Sufism; and text from what Williams calls the "dissidents" of Islam, the sects.

Islam and the Arab World: Faith, People, Culture, edited by Bernard Lewis. Knopf, 1976. A collection by thirteen respected academics on various aspects of Islamic civilization and culture, including major treatments of art, urban development, the sciences, music, literature, and the three great later empires of Islamic civilization: Turkey, India, and Iran. Illustrated, with many pictures in color. Includes a chronology, several maps, and a select bibliography.

Islam: the Straight Path; by John Esposito. Oxford University Press, 1988. Written by a college instructor to fill the gap in materials in English, this work is an explanation of Islam for the general reader. It provides a balanced picture of Islamic history and society from the beginnings to the present. Includes an introductory bibliography and maps.

The Koran Interpreted, translated by A.J. Arberry. Collier, 1986. Retains the poetic style of the Qu'ran, but without any commentary.

The Qur'an: the First American Version, translation and commentary by T.B. Irving. Amana, 1985. This is a modern translation intended for English-speaking Americans. It was developed by Irving, a Muslim, to convey the meaning and spirit of the original for a contemporary audience.

The Holy Scriptures According to the Masoretic Text, two volumes. Jewish Publication Society of America, 1955. Hebrew-English Bible (Old Testament). Completely modern translation with the Hebrew in parallel columns.

J

JEWS. *See also* ETHNIC GROUPS; JUDAISM.

American Jewish Yearbook, Jewish Publications Society, annual. Has directory information, statistics, and the year's events with biographies and special articles. Worldwide coverage with emphasis on American Jewish communities.

Encyclopedia of Judaism, edited by Geoffrey Wigoder. Macmillan, 1989. A large, comprehensive work that covers, in clear and concise entries, Jewish culture, Judaism as a religion, and the history of the Jewish people. Illustrated, with a glossary.

A History of the Jews, by Abram Leon Sachar. Knopf, 5th edition, 1964. Complete history from earliest times. Interweaves religious heritage with sociopolitical background. Includes bibliography and index.

JOBS. *See* EMPLOYMENT.

JOURNALISM

Encyclopedia of American Journalism, by Donald Paneth. Facts on File, 1983. An in-depth view of the Fourth Estate, from Ben Franklin to Walter Cronkite. Includes more than 1,000 entries on newspapers, magazines, radio, TV, and documentaries and newsreels. Also has articles on trends, concepts, and jargon.

World Press Encyclopedia, edited by George Thomas Kurian, two volumes. Facts on File, 1982. Contributions from 2,000 sources analyze the press in different nations, under different regimes, and in all cultural contexts.

JUDAISM. *See also* JEWS; RELIGION.

Encyclopedia Judaica, 16 volumes plus yearbooks and Decennial Book. Macmillan, 1971–72. Provides comprehensive, up-to-date coverage of all areas related to Jewish culture and religion. Decennial Book updates the set to 1982 but does not repeat the articles that are in the yearbooks; only the calendars of events are incorporated.

Encyclopedia of Judaism, edited by Geoffrey Wigoder. Macmillan, 1989. A large, comprehensive work that covers, in clear and concise entries, Jewish culture, Judaism as a religion, and the history of the Jewish people. Illustrated; includes a glossary.

New Standard Jewish Encyclopedia, Doubleday, 5th edition, 1977. Short articles on all aspects of Jewish history, religion, and life.

L

LABOR. *See also* EMPLOYMENT.

Labor in America: A History, by Foster R. Dulles. Harlan Davidson, 4th revised edition, 1984. Concise account from colonial times to the present, with emphasis on national level; college text.

LANGUAGE. *See also* DICTIONARIES.

The American Language, by H.L. Mencken. Knopf, 4th edition, 1936; two supplements published in 1945–48. When it was written, even the phrase "the *American* language" was a major critical departure. This is a seminal work in the study of etymological and linguistic differences between American and British English. Although many of Mencken's ideas were modified or disproved by later research, the work remains influential. Mencken was a great stylist himself, so the book's value lies as much in its brilliant prose as in its usefulness as a reference.

> The American Language, by Henry L. Mencken, abridged edition. Knopf, 4th edition, 1963. Some updating of the parent set.

American Sign Language: A Comprehensive Dictionary, by Martin Sternberg. Harper, 1981. Five thousand entries containing a pronunciation guide, an explanation of the meaning of the sign, and several other features, including illustrations and an appendix of words in seven foreign languages.

The Cambridge Encyclopedia of Language, by David Crystal. Cambridge University Press, 1987. An introduction to linguistic studies organized into parts such as "The Structure of Language," "The Language of the World," and "Language, Brain and Handicap." Illustrated. Includes short bibliography, glossary, and indexes.

LAW. *See also* CIVIL RIGHTS.

Black's Law Dictionary, by Henry Campbell Black et al. West, 6th edition, 1990. Clear definitions of legal terminology from all fields of law. Also includes some historical words and phrases from British and American jurisprudence. Includes appendices.

Encyclopedia of Legal Information Sources, edited by Paul Wasserman et al. Gale, 1988. A large, annotated bibliography of over 19,000 books, articles, films, research centers, online databases, and professional societies and associations. Emphasis is on federal law, but legal sources are also listed by state.

Reader's Digest Family Legal Guide: A Complete Guide for the Layman, edited by Inge N. Dobelis. Reader's Digest, 1981. Practical guidance for the average person. Includes contracts, wills, bankruptcy, arrests, and many other areas of interest to the layperson.

United States Code Congressional and Administrative News. West Publishing, monthly issues, annual bound volumes. Includes texts of laws and legislative history, presidential proclamations, and administrative regulations.

United States Code 1982, with annual supplements. U.S. Government Printing Office, new edition every six years. Official compilation of U.S. law in effect under 50 titles, or subjects.

You and the Law, Reader's Digest, 3rd edition 1984. A practical guide to everyday law and how it affects you and your family. Has 651 sections that cover, in clear, understandable terms, all the legal problems that confront the average person. Includes charts and tables that show differences from state to state. Has a glossary of more than 1,000 legal terms and an index.

Constitutional:

American Constitutional Law, by Martin Shapiro. Macmillan, 6th edition, 1983. Covers constitutional law and its evolution; has excerpts of cases, with extensive analysis.

Civil Liberties Under the Constitution, by Mabra G. Abernathy. University of South Carolina Press, 4th edition, 1985. Excerpts with commentary on important court decisions and relevant congressional actions on all aspects of civil liberty.

Encyclopedia of the American Constitution, edited by Leonard W. Levy, four volumes. Macmillan, 1986. A collection of essays by historians, lawyers, and political scientists on doctrinal concepts, legislation, people, historical periods, and decisions of the Supreme Court involving the American Constitution. Most essays should be accessible to the general reader.

Leading Constitutional Decisions, by Robert F. Cushman. Prentice Hall, 17th edition, 1987. Abridged texts of Supreme Court decisions, with notes.

Family:

The Complete Legal Guide to Marriage, Divorce, Custody and Living Together, by Steven Mitchell Sack. McGraw-Hill, 1987. Comprehensive guide to family law. Contains everything from legal rights of cohabitation to protecting children from domestic violence. Written by a lawyer, it nevertheless concentrates on remedial and precautionary measures that can be taken without the aid of a lawyer. Written in simple English, it explains the law by relating it to actual problems.

LIQUORS. *See* WINES AND SPIRITS.

LITERATURE. *See also* AUTHORS.

Benet's Reader's Encyclopedia, by William R. Benet. Harper, 3rd edition, 1987. Handbook of terms, writers, schools, movements, plots, fictional characters, allusions, and other subjects. International in scope.

Cassell's Encyclopedia of World Literature, Beekman, 1973. Histories of national literatures, literary genres, and literary movements, plus brief biographical sketches of literary figures.

Columbia Dictionary of Modern European Literature. Columbia University Press, 2nd edition, 1980. Has signed articles on 1,800 authors who write or wrote in European languages other than English from the late 19th century to the present, as well as general articles on literature.

A Handbook to Literature, by C. Hugh Holman and William Harmon. Macmillan, 1986. Alphabetical listing of words and phrases pertaining to English and American literature. Gives definitions and examples. Cross-referenced; includes index of proper names and other appendices.

Reader's Adviser, Bowker, 13th edition, 1988. A layperson's guide to literature.
Volume 1: The best in American and British fiction, poetry, essays, literary biography, bibliography, and reference.
Volume 2: The best in American and British drama and world literature in translation.
Volume 3: The best in general reference literature, the social sciences, history, and the arts.
Volume 4: The best in the literature of philosophy and world religion.
Volume 5: The best in the literature of science, technology, and medicine.
Volume 6: Indexes to volumes 1–5.

African:

African Authors: A Companion to Black African Writing, by Donald E. Herdeck, two volumes. Black Orpheus, 1973. Comprehensively indexed reference book surveying all of African literature including popular and folk genres. Contains biographies and discussions of authors and their bibliographies.

American:

American Authors and Books, 1640 to the Present Day, by William Jeremiah Burke. Crown, 3rd revised edition, 1972. Provides very brief information on authors, illustrators, editors, periodicals, and other literary and book-related topics.

Black Women Writers (1950–1980): A Critical Evaluation, edited by Mari Evans. Anchor, 1984. Fifteen women authors speak of their writings and ideas.

Columbia Literary History of the U.S., edited by Emory Elliot. Columbia University Press, 1988. Replaces *Literary History of the United States*, by Robert Spiller, a longtime standard reference. Expands the traditional subjects of literary history by incorporating current theoretical ideas and newly discovered writers. Includes treatment of recently explored subjects, such as the role of women and minorities in U.S. literature. No separate bibliography other than what is found in the text. Indexed.

Modern American Literature, by Dorothy N. Curley, three volumes plus Supplement. Frederick Ungar, 4th edition, 1969–76. Critical reviews on 20th-century authors.

Norton Anthology of American Literature, edited by Nina Baym et al., two volumes. Norton, 2nd edition, 1985. Selected works of American literature, edited to "make them readily accessible to students." Includes essays and introductions to the authors and works, a bibliography, indexes, and a variety of appendices.

Oxford Companion to American Literature, by James D. Hart. Oxford University Press, 5th edition, 1983. Entries on American fiction, authors, and literary schools and movements. Emphasizes sociocultural context.

> **Concise Oxford Companion to American Literature,** by James D. Hart. Oxford University Press, 1986. Abridgment of parent work.

Reader's Encyclopedia of American Literature, by Max J. Herzberg et al. Crowell, 1962. Surveys American and Canadian literature with entries on authors, works, fictional characters, literary magazines, schools and movements, and more general topics. Cross-referenced.

Children's:

The New York Times Parent's Guide to the Best Books for Children, by Eden Ross Lipson. Random House, 1988. A guide for book-loving parents, this work has a specialized set of indexes that direct you to the right book for the child you have in mind. Covers picture books, wordless books, storybooks, and books for beginning to expert readers.

Writers for Children: Critical Studies of Major Authors Since the Seventeenth Century, edited by Jane M. Bingham. Scribner, 1988. Critical and biographical essays on 84 writers of children's books. The work addresses mainly American and British authors, but Europeans are also covered. The essays delve into relevant social, political, aesthetic, and moral issues. Includes complete index in the back.

Classical:

Crowell's Handbook of Classical Literature, by Lillian Feder. Crowell, 1964. Encyclopedic entries that fill in historical background of authors and works and give critical analyses of a few works. Major works are given synopses. Related subjects are also treated.

A History of Greek Literature, by Albin Lesky, translated by James Willis and Cornelis de Heer. Crowell, 2nd edition, 1966. Covers the Greeks from the Homeric epic onwards. Emphasizes impact of Greeks on Western writing in general.

A History of Latin Literature, by Moses Hadas. Columbia University Press, 1952. Surveys all of Latin literature from classic times through the early Christian period.

The Oxford Classical Dictionary, edited by N.G.L. Hammond and H.H. Scullard. Oxford University Press, 2nd edition, 1970. This work contains articles on Greek and Latin literature, history, religion, art, and sciences up to the death of Constantine (337 a.d.). Also includes places and biographies of major people. Bibliographies appended to articles; includes index of place names.

The Oxford Companion to Classical Literature, edited by M.C. Howatson. Oxford University Press, 2nd edition, 1989. Entries on authors, characters, plots, literary forms, and cultural and historical background. Also contains a chronological table and maps, plus translations of Latin and Greek words.

Criticism:

Book Review Digest, 1905–present, H.W. Wilson, annual. Digests of major book reviews, with an index to reviews in about 75 English and American periodicals.

Contemporary Literary Criticism. Gale, new volumes added annually. Reprints passages of published criticism by living writers or writers who have died since 1960.

Library of Literary Criticism of English and American Authors, edited by Martin Tucker, four volumes. Frederick Ungar, 1966. Excerpts of critical writings on major literary figures. This is an abridgment and updating of the original work by Charles W. Moulton.

The Critical Temper: A Survey of Modern Criticism on English and American Literature from the Beginning to the Twentieth Century, three volumes plus supplement. Frederick Ungar, 1969–79. Supplements Moulton's *Library of Literary Criticism of English and American Authors*; emphasizes 20th-century criticism.

Modern Black Writers, Frederick Ungar, 1978. Excerpts from critical writings about Black writers; provides international coverage.

Modern Romance Literatures, by Dorothy N. Curley. Frederick Ungar, 1967. Excerpts from reviews and criticism of 20th-century French, Italian, and Spanish (Spain) writers.

Drama. *See also* SHAKESPEARE *(below).*

Crowell's Handbook of Classical Drama, by Richmond Y. Hathorn. Crowell, 1967. Has brief entries on dramatists, terms, plays, and characters. Emphasizes Greek classical drama.

Contemporary Dramatists, edited by James Vinson and D.L. Kirkpatrick. St. James, 4th edition, 1988. Biographies, published work, and critical essays on living dramatists, with supplements for screen, radio, and television writers, musical librettists, and theater groups.

Guide to Great Plays, by Joseph T. Shipley. Public Affairs Press, 1956. Gives information on authors, plot synopses, analysis, and critical opinion, and notes on production history. Alphabetical by author.

Masters of the Drama, by John Gassner. Dover, 3rd edition, 1954. Comprehensive critical study of drama from beginnings to modern times. Emphasis is on analysis and evaluation. Relates theater and dramatists to their social and cultural milieux.

Modern World Drama: An Encyclopedia, by Myron Matlaw. Dutton, 1972. Articles on plays, playwrights, national dramatic literature, and technical terms from the late 19th century to the present. Includes synopses of plays.

Ottemiller's Index to Plays in Collections, by John H. Ottemiller. Scarecrow, 7th revision, 1988. Standard index to plays in collections; no subject index.

Play Index, H.W. Wilson, new volume every four years. Lists plays for children and adults; includes single collected plays and one-act plays. Indexed by subject.

The Reader's Encyclopedia of World Drama, edited by John Gassner and Edward Quinn. Crowell, 1969. Has entries on playwrights, critics, national dramatic literatures, and histories. Emphasis is on drama as literature.

World Drama From Aeschylus to Anouilh, by Allardyce Nicoll. Harcourt, Brace, 1949. Provides a general historical account of theater from its beginnings to modern times. Emphasis is on historical significance of particular plays and writers.

English:

British Authors Before 1800, edited by Stanley J. Kunitz and Howard Haycraft. H.W. Wilson, 1952. Short biographical essays on principal and marginal figures in British literature. Bibliographies appended to essays.

The Cambridge Guide to Literature in English, edited by Ian Ousby. Cambridge University Press, 1988. A concise encyclopedia, this book provides biographical information on authors, brief plot descriptions, and criticism of individual works. Other entries cover genres, movements, literary schools, and critical concepts. Covers the great works and female and minority authors from all English-speaking cultures.

The Concise Cambridge History of English Literature, by George Sampson. Cambridge University Press, 2nd edition, 1965. Based on the 14-volume *Cambridge History of English Literature*, this one-volume reference provides background and history of authors and important works, but without the extensive criticism and commentary of the source work. It is divided into topics and eras, and then by author, up to the time of T.S. Eliot. Indexed.

The English Novel, by Walter Allen. Dutton, 1954. Literary history of novel form in England from John Bunyan through James Joyce.

A Literary History of England, edited by Albert C. Baugh. Prentice-Hall, 2nd edition, 1967. One-volume survey with bibliography and index.

Modern British Literature, by Ruth Z. Temple, three volumes. Frederick Ungar, 1966–75. Excerpts from critical writings on 20th-century British authors; volume four includes more recent criticism and more recent authors.

Norton Anthology of English Literature, edited by M.H. Abrams et al., three volumes. Norton, 5th edition, 1987. Selected works of English literature, edited to "make them readily accessible to students." Includes essays and introductions to the authors and works, bibliography, indexes, and a variety of appendices.

Norton Anthology of Literature by Women: The Tradition in English, edited by Sandra M. Gilbert and Susan Gubar. Norton, 1985. Heavily annotated selections of women's writing in English from the Middle Ages to the present. Follows the Norton format, with introductions for every writer and period and selected bibliographies and indexes.

The Oxford Companion to English Literature, edited by Margaret Drabble. Oxford University Press, 5th edition, 1985. Has entries on English fiction, authors, and literary schools and movements. Emphasizes cultural-historical background.

The Stanford Companion to Victorian Fiction, by John Sutherland. Stanford University Press, 1989. Alphabetical guide to authors, novels, magazines and periodicals, publishers, illustrators, and miscellaneous information of the period. Includes much new and previously undiscussed material on this most complex literary era. Indexed.

Fiction:

Contemporary Novelists, edited by D.L. Kirkpatrick and James Vinson. St. Martin's, 4th edition, 1986. Provides brief biographical and bibliographical information on novelists writing in English.

Cyclopedia of Literary Characters, edited by Frank N. Magill, two volumes. Salem, 1963. Has over 16,000 entries for characters from major Western works of fiction. Complements *Masterpieces of World Literature in Digest Form,* below.

Dickinson's American Historical Fiction, by A.T. Dickinson. Scarecrow, 5th edition, 1986. Historical novels and other fiction are classified by chronological periods from the Colonial period to the 1980s.

Fiction Catalog, H.W. Wilson, 11th edition, 1986. Annotated list of titles recommended for library use, with subject index. Updated by annual paperbound supplements.

Masterpieces of World Literature in Digest Form, by Frank N. Magill, four volumes. Harper, 1952–69. The 500 synopses in each volume cover a wide range of fiction in English. Complemented by *Cyclopedia of Literary Characters* (above) and *Cyclopedia of World Authors* (see AUTHORS).

French:

The Concise Oxford Dictionary of French Literature, edited by Joyce M. Reid. Oxford University Press, 1985. Condensed, updated version of *The Oxford Companion to French Literature,* below, with 200 new articles.

The Oxford Companion to French Literature, edited by Paul Harvey and J.E. Heseltine. Oxford University Press, 1969. Comprehensive scholarly coverage from medieval times to 1939; includes authors and their works; survey articles, terms, and movements.

German:

A History of German Literature, by Ernst Rose. New York University Press, 1960. History of German literature with bibliography and index.

The Oxford Companion to German Literature, by Henry Garland and Mary Garland. Oxford University Press, 2nd edition, 1986. German writers and their works, with cultural and historical background.

Italian:

Dictionary of Italian Literature, edited by Peter and Julia Bondanella. Greenwood, 1979. Short reference guide to Italian writers, fiction, critical schools, and genres. Includes appendices and index.

A History of Italian Literature, by Ernest H. Wilkins. Harvard University Press, revised 1974. This history includes folk literature and minstrelsy along with discussions of recognized authors and general topics. Includes appendices and index.

Nonfiction:

Essay and General Literature Index, 1900–1989, H.W. Wilson, new volume every five years. Detailed index by author, subject, and some titles to essays and selected articles published in books.

Poetry. *See also* RHYME.

Contemporary Poets, edited by James Vinson and D.L. Kirkpatrick. St. Martin's, 4th edition, 1985. Biographies, published work, and critical essays on living poets. A separate appendix lists several poets who have died since 1960. Indexed.

Granger's Index to Poetry, by Edith Granger. Columbia University Press, 8th edition, 1986. Poems are indexed by title, first line, author, and subject. More than 400 anthologies are reviewed.

The Home Book of Modern Verse, edited by Burton Egbert Stevenson. Holt, 2nd edition, 1953. 1,000-page companion to *The Home Book of Verse,* organized by subject categories in a similar fashion. Covers American and English poetry of the 20th century. Has indexes of first lines, titles, and authors.

The Home Book of Verse, edited by Burton Egbert Stevenson, two volumes. Holt, 9th edition, 1953. A combination of the best and the most popular English-language poetry, from Spenser to the present, excepting those "too free for modern taste." Poems are grouped by subject categories, such as babyhood, satire, love of various kinds, reflection, and legend. Indexes of first lines, authors, and titles are provided.

Norton Anthology of Modern Poetry, edited by Richard Ellman and Robert O'Clair. Norton, 2nd edition, 1973. Provides many works by major English-speaking poets and a wide selection of lesser ones. Includes representative Native American, Chicano, and Harlem Renaissance poets. Book is arranged by poet, chronologically from the poet's birthdate; a brief paragraph of biographical information is given for each poet.

Norton Anthology of Poetry, edited by Alexander W. Allison et al. Norton, 3rd edition, 1983. Chronologically arranged collection of British and American poetry, from pre-Chaucer to the present. Annotated and indexed.

Princeton Encyclopedia of Poetry and Poetics, edited by Alex Preminger et al. Princeton University Press, 1974. Contains entries on history, theory, technique, and criticism of poetry. Omits articles on individual authors and poems.

Princeton Handbook of Poetic Terms, edited by Alex Preminger et al. Princeton University Press, 1986. Concise guide to rhyme, meter, form, and other essentials of poetic composition.

A Treasury of Great Poems, edited by Louis Untermeyer, two volumes. Simon & Schuster, 1955. English and American poetry from Chaucer to Dylan Thomas. Organized by poet, and prefaced by brief critical and biographical essays.

Reviews. *See* CRITICISM (*above*).

Russian:

The Epic of Russian Literature, by Marc L'vovich Slonim. Oxford University Press, 1950. Volume 1 of a literary history of Russia, relating past to present.

Volume 2: From Chekhov to the Revolution, by Marc L'vovich Slonim. Oxford University Press, 1962. Covers 1900–17.

Volume 3: Soviet Russian Literature, by Marc L'vovich Slonim. Oxford University Press, 1977. Covers 1917–77.

A History of Soviet Literature, by Vera Alexandrova, translated by Mira Ginsburg. Greenwood, 1963. Study of the development of Russian literature from the revolution to 1964. Divided into two periods: pre- and post-World War II.

Shakespeare:

The Arden Shakespeare, edited by Harold F. Brooks and Harold Jenkins. Routledge. The revised and reedited texts of this edition are copiously annotated. Each play is published separately (with an additional volume for the sonnets and narrative poems). Introductions, in-depth consideration of historical questions surrounding the plays, critical essays, and appendices are always provided. Shows differences between textual sources.

The Cambridge Companion to Shakespeare Studies, edited by Stanley Wells. Cambridge University Press, 1986. The revision of the *New Companion to Shakespeare Studies*. Includes new articles and revisions of the older essays. Some topics from the older work have been omitted.

Complete Works of Shakespeare, edited by David M. Bevington. Scott, Foresman, 3rd edition, 1980. Includes interpretive essays that highlight the critical issues of each play.

The Harvard Concordance to Shakespeare, edited by Marvin Spevack. Belknap, 1974. This reference lists all the words in the plays and poems and all the individual lines. Useful for researching such things as rhyme or puns and wordplay. Gives words' frequency of appearance in the works. Includes appendices.

A New Companion to Shakespeare Studies, edited by Kenneth Muir and S. Schoenbaum. Cambridge University Press, 1971. Series of essays covering everything from the playwright's life to criticism of the plays. Clearly written and informative. Includes bibliography, chronology, and index.

Reader's Encyclopedia of Shakespeare, edited by Oscar J. Campbell. Crowell, 1966. Compilation of period documents, essays, chronology of historical events, bibliography, and other information related to the life and works of Shakespeare.

The Riverside Shakespeare, edited by G. Blakemore Evans. Houghton Mifflin, 1974. The standard one-volume modern edition to which most contemporary scholarship refers. In addition to meticulously edited and annotated texts, *Riverside* contains introductory essays on and plot synopses of each play, several general introductory essays on essential topics, period illustrations, a glossary, a bibliography, and substantial indexes. Required for many college courses in Shakespeare.

Shakespeare: An Illustrated Dictionary, by Stanley Wells. Oxford University Press, 1978. Short entries on a variety of Shakespeare-related subjects. Quick reference material. Illustrated. Includes selected character index for the plays.

A Shakespeare Commentary, by Arthur E. Baker, two volumes. Frederick Ungar, 1957. Scholarly notes on 13 better-known plays, including excerpts of plot sources.

Short Stories:

Short Story Index, H.W. Wilson, new volume every five years. Indexes collections of short stories and individual stories by title and author. Also available are interim annual updates.

Short Story Index, cumulative, 1900–78, H.W. Wilson, 1979. Alphabetical author, editor, and title index to the 8,400 collections listed over the years in *Short Story Index.*

Spanish:

Modern Latin American Literature, two volumes, edited by David W. Foster and Virginia R. Foster. Frederick Ungar, 1975. Excerpts from reviews of 137 20th-century Latin American authors.

A New History of Spanish Literature, by Richard E. Chandler and Kessel Schwartz, Louisiana State University Press, 1961. Treats each literary genre separately. Written with college students in mind. Includes discussion of culture and history, with appendices and index.

Oxford Companion to Spanish Literature, edited by Philip Ward. Oxford University Press, 1978.

Covers literature written in the languages of Spain, from Roman times to the present, including that of Central and South America. Articles are on authors, specific works, movements, styles, and terms.

Spanish-American Literature, by Enrique Anderson-Imbert, translated by John V. Falconien, two volumes. Wayne State University Press, 1969. Survey of the literature of Hispanic America from the time of the Conquistadores to the present. Indexed.

M

MAGAZINES. *See* BIBLIOGRAPHIES—PERIODICALS.

MANAGEMENT. *See also* BUSINESS.

Encyclopedia of Management, edited by Carl Heyel. Van Nostrand Reinhold, 1982. Entries range from short essays on such topics as alcohol and drug abuse in the workplace and collective bargaining, to biographical information on famous industrialists and business people, to short entries on terms and jobs. Includes appendices and index.

Management Handbook, edited by Paul Mali. Wiley, 1981. Collection of essays on all aspects of business management. Emphasis is on analysis of problems and techniques of solving them. Contains "problem-solving index."

MATERIALS

Materials Handbook, by George S. Brady and Henry R. Claus. McGraw-Hill, 12th edition, 1985. Has capsule descriptions of commercially available substances. This includes almost anything, even short entry headed "foodstuffs." Directed at purchasing agents, foremen, production managers, and others. Indexed.

MATHEMATICS

The VNR Encyclopedia of Mathematics, edited by W. Gellert et al. Van Nostrand Reinhold, 1977. Not exactly a textbook, but useful to students. Text is extensively color-coded to make reading easier. Clearly written. Considers topics in elementary and higher mathematics and continues with reports on other topics such as number theory and algebraic geometry.

Essentials of Mathematics, by Russell Person. Wiley, 5th edition, 1989. Basic elementary mathematics, clearly explained.

Mathematics Dictionary, by Glenn James and Robert C. James, Van Nostrand Reinhold, 4th edition, 1976. Standard work for students and professionals; includes biographies and English equivalents for foreign terms.

Practical Mathematics, by Claude I. Palmer. McGraw-Hill, 7th edition, 1986. Textbook for technical schools and community colleges covering arithmetic, algebra, geometry, and trigonometry.

Prentice-Hall Encyclopedia of Mathematics, Prentice-Hall, 1982. Clearly written coverage of subject from arithmetic to calculus.

MEDICARE

Medicare Explained, Commerce Clearing House, annual. Concise, thorough explanation for the average reader of all aspects of federal health insurance for the aged and disabled. Includes recent legal changes. Also includes inpatient/outpatient benefits, nursing home services, services excluded from coverage, and miscellaneous provisions. Information is presented with examples. Indexed.

Medicare Made Easy, by Charles B. Inlander and Charles K. McKay. Addison Wesley, 1989. Guide for Medicare recipients and advocates. A tour through the system strips away the confusion and helps recipients get the benefits to which they are entitled.

MEDICINE AND HEALTH. *See also related subjects, such as* AIDS, ANATOMY, FIRST AID, *and* DRUGS AND MEDICINES.

American Medical Association Encyclopedia of Medicine, edited by Charles B. Clayman, M.D. Random House, 1989. A clear, systematic account of current medical knowledge and terminology. Gives descriptions of common and not-so-common diseases, their causes, and their symptoms. Also includes biological and anatomical descriptions, uses of drugs, chemical interactions, and other information.

American Medical Association Family Medical Guide, edited by Jeffrey R.M. Kung and Asher J. Finkel. Random House, revised and updated, 1987. Layperson's text featuring articles on diseases and disorders, diagnostic charts, and an index of drugs and medications. Extensively illustrated; uses charts when possible. Emphasizes prevention.

American Medical Association Home Medical Advisor, edited by Charles B. Clayman, Jeffrey R.M. Kinz, and Harriet S. Meyer. Random House, 1988. Self-help guide to symptoms, disorders, diseases, and medical emergencies. The main sections of the book are presented as charts.

Columbia University College of Physicians and Surgeons Complete Home Medical Guide, by Donald F. Tapley et al. Crown, 1985. Deals with the nature of health and the health system, what to do until the doctor comes, general physiology, maintaining health, disease, treatment and health, drugs, and resources. Includes glossary of medical terms, an atlas of organ systems, appendices, and index.

Dorland's Illustrated Medical Dictionary. W.B. Saunders, 27th edition, 1988. One of the oldest of the medical dictionaries, the latest edition has been updated to include terms such as AZT and HIV. This is considered one of the most comprehensive medical dictionaries in print. Includes 53 plates, tables, and illustrations throughout. Contains indexes and tables. For specialists; entries tend to be technical. Also includes pronunciation and etymology guide.

Health Care U.S.A., by Jean Carper. Prentice Hall, 1987. Information on 480 health-related conditions or disorders. Each entry gives information on causes, symptoms, and treatments, as well as information on clinics, relevant organizations, research centers, and names and numbers of specialists.

Melloni's Illustrated Medical Dictionary, by Biagio John Melloni, Ida Dox, and Gilbert M. Eisner. Williams and Wilkins, 2nd edition, 1985. Includes phonetic pronunciation table; table of prefixes, suffixes, and combining forms; and table of abbreviations. Has accessible entries on medical topics and terms.

The Merck Manual of Diagnosis and Therapy, edited by Robert Berkow. Merck and Co., 15th edition, 1987. A one-volume reference that attempts to cover all but the most obscure diseases. Sections are organized by type of disease or medical specialty.

Mosby's Medical and Nursing Dictionary, by Walter D. Glanze. C.V. Mosby, 3rd edition, 1990. Complete and geared towards nurses and other health professionals. Has exhaustive appendices, including a 44-page color atlas of human anatomy.

The Patients' Guide to Medical Tests, by Cathy Pinckney and Edward R. Pinckney. Facts on File, 3rd edition, 1986. Alphabetical index to and dictionary of 700 tests most commonly used in medical diagnosis. Intended primarily for patients, this reference gives risks, costs, accuracy, and the symptoms and conditions for which a test may be prescribed.

Stedman's Medical Dictionary, by Thomas L. Stedman et al. Williams and Wilkins, 25th edition, 1990. A standard medical dictionary; indexed, with a (now classic) section on the etymology of medical terms.

The Wellness Encyclopedia, edited by the staff of the University of California, Berkeley, Wellness Letter. Houghton Mifflin, 1991. Comprehensive resource that focuses on preventive health, not illness. Has chapters on healthy eating, reducing risk for certain diseases, designing an exercise program, and prevention and treatment of minor illnesses.

Diagnosis and Treatment:

Current Medical Diagnosis and Treatment, edited by Steven A. Schroeder et al. Appleton and Lange, annual. Provides concise information on the diagnosis and treatment of diseases and disorders for medical practitioners. Uses common medical terminology, but is generally understandable to the layperson. Indexed.

The Merck Manual, edited by Robert Berkow. Merck, Sharp and Dohme Research Laboratories, 15th edition, 1987. Covers diagnosis and treatment of diseases and disorders for medical practititioners. Used worldwide, it covers conditions not commonly found in the United States. Portable size for hospital staff use. Indexed.

Volume 1: General Medicine.
Volume 2: Obstetrics, Gynecology, Pediatrics, Genetics.

Doctors:

Directory of Medical Specialists, three volumes. Marquis Who's Who, biennial. Comprehensive listing of physicians certified by the individual boards of the American Board of Medical Specialties. Pro-

vides current professional and biographical information.

History:

Encyclopedia of Medical History, by Roderick McGrew. McGraw-Hill, 1985. Historical treatment of selected medical topics in essay form. Combines history with modern scientific knowledge related to topic. Bibliography appended to each essay. Indexed.

MEDICINES. *See* DRUGS AND MEDICINES.

METEOROLOGY. *See also* EARTH SCIENCES.

The Weather Almanac, edited by James A. Ruffner and Frank E. Blair. Gale, 6th edition, 1990. Definitions and articles on major weather events and meteorological issues. Includes layperson's guide to "weather fundamentals" and a glossary. Provides meteorological and climatological information and statistics for major U.S. and world cities. Indexed.

MILITARY. *See* WAR.

MINERALOGY. *See also* EARTH SCIENCES.

Simon & Schuster's Guide to Rocks and Minerals, edited by Martin Prinz et al. Simon & Schuster, 1978. Basic mineralogical information very succinctly presented. Text is always opposite full-color picture of rock or mineral in question. Includes glossary and index.

MONEY

The Comprehensive Catalog of U.S. Paper Money, by Gene Hessler. BNR Press, 4th revision, 1983. Includes illustrations and histories of all paper bills issued (or planned) since 1861, when paper money was introduced. Includes information on modern notes, how they're printed, and types. With appendices and bibliography.

Standard Catalog of World Coins, Krause Publications, annual. Comprehensive country-by-country listing from 1800 to the present; includes values. Covers U.S. coins from 1793 to date.

Walter Breen's Complete Encyclopedia of U.S. and Colonial Coins, by Walter Breen. Doubleday, 1988. Covers 8,000 coins arranged chronologically, with technical and historical information. Includes 4,000 photographs.

MOVIES

The American Film Institute Catalogue of Motion Pictures Produced in the United States: Fea-

ture Films, 1911–1920, two volumes, edited by Patricia K. Hanson. University of California Press, 1988. A continuation of the American Film Institute Catalogue, documenting 1911–20, for which information is scarce. Contains an alphabetical index with detailed information. Volume 2 is a series of indexes on both general topics and personalities.

The Film Encyclopedia, by Ephraim Katz. Harper, 1979. Covers directors, producers, actors, composers, and screenwriters, as well as major studios and film centers. There are also entries on technical topics such as Cinemascope. Does not list individual movies.

Halliwell's Film and Video Guide, by Leslie Halliwell. Scribner, 6th edition, 1988. Lists English-language feature-length films, giving credits, casts, synopses, and country of origin. Complements *Halliwell's Filmgoer's Companion,* below.

Halliwell's Filmgoer's Companion, by Leslie Halliwell. Scribner, 9th edition, 1989. Mainly gives concise information on actors—supporting as well as stars. Also has entries on individual movies, directors, and photographers. Concerned entirely with Hollywood and Britain and the popular film industry. Illustrated.

MUSEUMS. *See also* SPECIAL COLLECTIONS.

Official Museum Directory, American Association of Museums, annual. Lists over 6,000 museums of art, history, and science.

MUSHROOMS

Audubon Society Field Guide to North American Mushrooms, by the Audubon Society Staff and Gary H. Lincoff. Knopf, 1981.

A Field Guide to Mushrooms: North America, by Kent H. McKnight and Vera B. McKnight. Houghton Mifflin, 1987.

MUSIC. *See also* OPERA.

Dictionary of Music, edited by Alan Isaacs and Elizabeth Martin. Facts on File, 1983. A layperson's or beginning student's guide to all of music. Concise, clear entries cover composers, descriptions of genres, and definitions of terminology. Some popular and jazz figures are also covered.

A History of Western Music, by Donald J. Grout and Claude V. Paliska. Norton, 4th edition, 1988.

A standard college text on music history, featuring short introductions to each historical period.

The International Cyclopedia of Music and Musicians, edited by Oscar Thompson. Dodd, Mead, 11th edition, 1985. For general reading as well as reference. Has summaries of periods, composers, and compositions; bibliographies appended to articles. Many entries are devoted to contemporary developments. Section for addenda in the back of the volume.

Musical Instruments, by Sibyl Marcuse. Doubleday, 1964. Selected instruments of the world, briefly described. Also includes historical instruments no longer in use. See also *A Survey of Musical Instruments,* by Sibyl Marcuse (Doubleday, 1975).

The New Grove Dictionary of Musical Instruments, edited by Stanley Sadie, three volumes. Macmillan, 1984. More complete and recent than Marcuse (see above). Scholarly, like the other series. Illustrated. Also contains instruments of historical interest. Articles are more extensive than in Marcuse.

The New Grove Dictionary of Music and Musicians, edited by Stanley Sadie, 20 volumes. Macmillan, 6th edition, 1980. Traditionally the standard multivolume music reference in English. Compared to "Old Grove," *New Grove* has twice the amount of information, reflecting the tremendous growth in the field of musicology. Expanded sections include ethnomusicology, popular music, biographies, early music, and bibliographies. The final volume contains multiple appendices and indexes. Very scholarly but accessible to the general reader.

The Norton/Grove Concise Encyclopedia of Music, edited by Stanley Sadie and Alison Latham. Norton, 1988. A quick reference book for music lovers and students. Includes music terminology, musicians, composers and musicologists, and specific pieces of music. Originally published in Britain, so favors British terminology over American (e.g., *crochet* and *quaver* for *quarter note* and *eighth note*). Consult the 20-volume *New Grove Dictionary of Music and Musicians* (1980) for in-depth, serious academic work.

The New Harvard Dictionary of Music, edited by Don Randel. Harvard University Press, 1988. Quick reference entries contrast with longer encyclopedia-length articles on all topics of music including history, popular music, mixed media, and instruments. Also covers non-Western music. Bibliographies appended to many articles.

The New Oxford Companion to Music, edited by Denis Arnold, two volumes. Oxford University Press, 1983. Includes biographies of composers, opera synopses, analyses of compositions, historical articles, and essays on popular music, jazz, and ethnomusicology. Also has definitions of musical terms, illustrations, and musical examples. Bibliographies appended to major articles.

American:

American Music: A Panorama, by Daniel Kingman. Schirmer Books, 1979. "Panoramic survey" of the "parallel streams of American music, folk, classical and popular." A textbook for high school students, it emphasizes the interconnectedness of American music. At the end of each chapter is a bibliography and a suggested list of projects.

The New Grove Dictionary of American Music, edited by H. Wiley Hitchcock and Stanley Sadie, four volumes. Macmillan, 1986. In an effort to catch the essence of American music and its more pluralistic base, the New Grove published this dictionary, which consists of some expanded material from the 20-volume *The New Grove Dictionary of Music and Musicians*, above, and some altogether new material. Covers American folk music, patriotic and political music, rock, the American music industry, and musical institutions. Scholarly and complete.

Jazz:

Encyclopedia of Jazz, by Leonard Feather. Horizon, revised edition, 1960. The insider guide to jazz with complete discographies of major artists, articles on jazz history, and more. Now has two follow-up editions, *The Encyclopedia of Jazz in the Sixties* (Horizon, 1966) and *The Encyclopedia of Jazz in the Seventies* (Horizon, 1976). Includes appendices, illustrations, and bibliographies.

The New Grove Dictionary of Jazz, two volumes, edited by Barry Kernfeld. Macmillan, 1988. The largest dictionary of jazz ever published. Has extensive bibliographies; discographically accurate (although not complete). Musical terms, procedures, and structures are precisely defined, using musical examples, but without overly technical language.

Some artists, such as George Gershwin, Scott Joplin, and Aretha Franklin, are not included because they are beyond the scope of jazz as defined here. Instruments, record companies and labels, and styles are included. Includes bibliographies and indexes.

Musicians:

Baker's Biographical Dictionary of Musicians, edited by Nicholas Slonimsky. Schirmer Books, 7th edition, 1984. Classic reference, full of facts and critical insights. Includes scholars, critics, and teachers and extends recognition to famous jazz, rock, folk, and other popular performers and composers —"everyone with an operative larynx short of singing whales."

Biographical Dictionary of Afro-American and African Musicians, by Eileen Southern. Greenwood, 1982. Reference that collects much disparate information and presents it together. For example, one can find entries not only on Duke Ellington, but also on his sidemen. Black musicians have had such a profound effect on American music that this reference, the only one of its kind that I know of, is invaluable.

Popular:

American Popular Songs from the Revolutionary War to the Present, edited by David Ewen. Random House, 1966. Listing by title of 3,600, including composer, date, and source.

Encyclopedia of Pop, Rock, and Soul, by Irwin Stambler. St. Martin's, 1989. Up-to-date, wide-ranging coverage of every star of modern pop from Paul Anka to ZZ Top. Entries concentrate on a performer's more recent activities. Includes appendices.

Encyclopedia of the Musical Theater, by Stanley Green. DaCapo, 1976. Quick reference guide to Broadway musicals and their stars, writers, producers, and songs. Includes appendices and addenda.

The Harmony Illustrated Encyclopedia of Country Music, by Fred Deller, Alan Cackett, and Roy Thompson. Harmony, revised edition, 1986. Completely revised, this book includes some of the latest bands and singers in country-and-western music. Illustrated and indexed.

The Harmony Illustrated Encyclopedia of Rock. Harmony, 3rd edition, 1983. Includes artists and bands that "best represent the rock movement of the day." Illustrated and indexed.

The Rolling Stone Illustrated History of Rock and Roll, edited by Jon Pareles and Patricia Romanowski. Rolling Stone Press, 1983. Devoted mainly to musicians and pop group biographies. Also has entries on other aspects of rock.

MYTHOLOGY

Brewer's Dictionary of Phrase and Fable, edited by Igor Evans. Harper, 14th edition, 1989. Gives origins and meanings for 20,000 common phrases, allusions, and mythical and fictitious characters.

Bulfinch's Mythology, by Thomas Bulfinch. Crowell, 1955. The classic work on mythology, Bulfinch's gives brief summations of Greek, Roman, Norse, Arthurian, and other miscellaneous myths and includes notes on the *Iliad*, the *Odyssey*, and the *Aeneid*.

Crowell's Handbook of Classical Mythology, by Edward Tripp. Crowell, 1970. Alphabetical guide to brief information on Greek and Roman classical myths, including characters, events, places, and retelling of stories.

The Facts on File Encyclopedia of World Mythology and Legend, by Anthony Mercatante. Facts on File, 1988. A comprehensive reference on world mythologies covered in thematic, biographical, and narrative essays. Illustrated.

Funk & Wagnalls Standard Dictionary of Folklore, Mythology and Legend. Funk & Wagnalls, 1972. Originally in two volumes; provides comprehensive coverage of plots, characters, and folklore of many countries.

Larousse World Mythology, by Pierre Grimal. Bookthrift, 1965. Essays on mythologies of the countries of the world.

N

NAMES

A Dictionary of Surnames, by Patrick Hanks and Flavia Hodges. Oxford University Press, 1988. Has 100,000 entries on names from Europe, Australia, North America, and the British Isles. Lists alternate spellings as well.

The Facts on File Dictionary of First Names, by Leslie Dunkling and William Gosling. Facts on File, 1983. Entries on English first names give gender, linguistic origin, variations, and history of each name. Includes bibliography and appendices.

The New Century Cyclopedia of Names, edited by Clarence L. Barnhart, three volumes. Prentice-Hall, 1954. "Provides information about proper names having importance in the English-speaking world." This includes names of persons, places, and historical events.

New Dictionary of American Family Names, by Elsdon C. Smith. Crown, 1988. Derivations of common American names. Gives nation of origin and original language meaning.

NATIONAL PARKS

Access America: An Atlas and Guide to the National Parks for Visitors with Disabilities, by Peter Shea et al. Northern Cartographic, 1988. Guide evaluates the accessibility of National Parks. Includes charts and maps, with comments on medical services, transportation, and climate.

National Geographic Guide to the National Parks of the United States. National Geographic Society, 1989. Provides practical information on America's 50 national parks: how to get there, when to go, how to visit, and "Time-tailored Tours"—tours to fit the time you have to spend. The guide includes details on weather and road information, facilities for the disabled, things to do, and campgrounds and accommodations. Contains 429 color photographs and 72 maps, and is indexed. Initial purchase includes videocassette "Our National Parks: A Seasonal Tour."

NATIONS OF THE WORLD. *See also* HISTORY; TRAVEL. *See also coverage of specific countries in* ATLASES; GENERAL REFERENCE BOOKS; *and* ENCYCLOPEDIAS.

Encyclopedia of Latin America, edited by Helen Delpar. McGraw-Hill, 1974. Concise entries on a variety of subjects relating to Latin America. Intended as an overview of Latin American civilization. Emphasis is on national period of Latin American history. Brief bibliographies appended to some entries.

Encyclopedia of the Third World, by George Thomas Kurian, three volumes. Facts on File, 3rd edition, 1987. Each Third World country (that is, economically developing, less industrialized nation) is given a detailed entry. Articles include basic census and political, economic, and historical information and descriptions of principal languages and religions. Includes glossary and bibliography for each country. Articles have subheads for easy reference.

NATIVE AMERICANS. *See also* ETHNIC GROUPS.

The American Indian Index, by Gregory N. Frazier. Arrowstar, 1985. Directory of federally recognized tribes, Indian commissions and agencies, Indian publications, museums, reservation services, and other subjects.

Atlas of the North American Indian, by Carl Waldman. Facts on File, 1985. Details the migration of prehistoric tribes to North America from Asia. A unique section on "Lifeways" provides information on all socioeconomic and religious aspects of Native American cultures, both pre- and post-contact with European Americans. Covers the Indian Wars, the Land Cessions, and contemporary Native American conditions.

A Concise Dictionary of Indian Tribes of North America, by Barbara Leitch. Reference Publications, 1979. Complete guide to North American Indians. Entries on every known tribe give brief history and information on culture, religion, and economy. Also includes census information on modern descendants. Illustrated and indexed.

Encyclopedia of Native American Tribes, by Carl Waldman. Facts on File, 1988. Discusses more than 150 tribes of North America and gives summaries of the historic record including locations, migrations, languages, war, culture, contact with Europeans, and present conditions.

NATURAL RESOURCES. *See* ECOLOGY.

NEWS AND CURRENT EVENTS

Facts on File, Facts on File, biweekly. Digest of news events compiled from various newspapers and sources. Broadly descriptive and brief. Useful as a supplement and index to the *New York Times.* A bound volume of the same material appears annually.

NEWSPAPERS. *See* BIBLIOGRAPHIES—PERIODICALS.

NUMISMATICS. *See* MONEY.

NUTRITION. *See* FOOD AND NUTRITION.

O

OCCULT

Encyclopedia of the Unexplained: Magic, Occultism, and Parapsychology, edited by Richard Cavendish. McGraw-Hill, 1974. Covers developments over the past 200 years in parapsychology and psychical research; spiritualism, magic, and the occult; and divination-astrology, the Tarot, and other subjects. The author applies a scientific method to his inquiries. Includes bibliography and index. Illustrated.

The Encyclopedia of Witches and Witchcraft, by Rosemary Ellen Guiley. Facts on File, 1989. A comprehensive and objective coverage of the long and varied history of witchcraft in 500 illustrated historical articles and biographies.

Larousse Encyclopedia of Astrology, by Jean-Louis Brau, Helen Weaver, and Allan Edmonds. McGraw-Hill, 1980 (English translation). A dictionary accessible to the novice and helpful to students and devotees. Includes instructions for calculating a horoscope, definitions and technical terms, explanations of various systems, and cultural and historical information.

OCEANOGRAPHY. *See also* EARTH SCIENCES.

Ocean World Encyclopedia, by Donald G. Groves and Lee M. Hunt. McGraw-Hill, 1980. Nonspecialist's illustrated reference to major subjects in oceanography. Indexed.

OLD AGE

Aging Well: A Guide for Successful Seniors, by James F. Fries. Addison-Wesley, 1989. Provides answers to the most commonly asked questions about the risks and challenges of growing older. Legal forms are included, along with statistics on life expectancy and recommendations for staying healthy.

The Retirement Sourcebook: Your Complete Guide to Health, Leisure, and Consumer Information, by Edward Palder. Woodbine House, 1989.

A sourcebook covering the main concerns of senior citizens. Information is organized under five main headings, providing information on everything from con artists to free services at public libraries. Lists addresses, phone numbers, and hotlines for agencies serving retirees.

OPERA. *See also* MUSIC.

The Definitive Kobbe's Opera Book, edited by The Earl of Harewood. Putnam, revised edition, 1987. Reference guide to the world's great operas with plot synopses, performance data, some critical commentary on each opera, and some biographical details about the composers. Indexed.

ORGANIZATIONS. *See also* FEDERAL GOVERNMENT.

Encyclopedia of Associations, Gale, 25th edition, 1991. Volume 1: *National Organizations of the U.S.* Comprehensive source of detailed information on nonprofit national membership organizations.

P

PARLIAMENTARY PROCEDURES

Robert's Rules of Order Newly Revised, by Henry M. Robert. Scott, Foresman, 1985. Standard handbook of parliamentary procedures.

PATENTS. *See also* INVENTIONS.

Patent It Yourself, by David Pressman. Nolo, 1985. Legal guide for inventors. Provides information on how to patent, protect, and market an invention in the United States. Systematically laid out for easy reference. Indexed.

PERSONAL FINANCE. *See also* FINANCE; TAXES.

Marshall Loeb's Money Guide, by Marshall Loeb. Little, Brown, annual. The managing editor of *Fortune* and former managing editor of *Money* magazine writes clearly and lucidly about such complex subjects as investments, financing a home, taxes, retirement, estates, and many other subjects relating to personal and family finances. Organized by topic, with an index.

Sylvia Porter's Your Finances for the 90s, by Sylvia Porter. Prentice Hall, 1990. Comprehensive guide to all aspects of personal money management for the layperson.

What's Ahead for the Economy?, by Louis Rukeyser. Simon & Schuster, 1983. The host of "Wall Street Week" explains major economic trends in taxes, spending, banking and credit, labor law, and business regulations and restrictions and how they affect all of us.

PETS

The Complete Book of Cat Health, by the Animal Medical Center. Macmillan, 1985. Veterinary specialists address basic concerns of cat care. Includes encyclopedia of symptoms and diseases and information on caring for newborn or older cats; has a section on "people–pet relationships." Indexed.

The Complete Cat Book, by Richard H. Gebhardt. Howell House, 1991. Official standards for every breed, from an internationally recognized cat show judge. Also covers health and maintenance, as well as other related topics. Illustrated with photographs; has an appendix, glossary, and index.

The Complete Dog Book, by the American Kennel Club. Howell House, 17th edition, 1985. Official publication of the American Kennel Club, frequently revised. Lists recognized breeds with standards and a short history. Includes limited information on care and feeding.

Pets: Every Owner's Encyclopedia, by The Diagram Group. Paddington Press, 1978. Describes and illustrates more than 500 species and varieties, from familiar household pets to exotic animals of every kind. Has bibliographies and an index.

The Ultimate Cat Book, by David Taylor with Daphne Negus. Simon & Schuster, 1989. Guide to the origins and specifics of each breed of domestic cat, as well as technical information on health, behavior, reproduction, and showing and traveling. Includes 750 color photographs.

PHARMACOLOGY. *See* DRUGS AND MEDICINES.

PHILANTHROPY. *See also* ORGANIZATIONS.

Foundation Directory, edited by Stan Olson. Foundation Center, biennial. Compilation of detailed information on foundations or organizations making grants; includes indexes by subject and name.

PHILATELY. *See* STAMPS AND STAMP COLLECTING.

PHILOSOPHY

Encyclopedia of Philosophy, four volumes, edited by Paul Edwards. Free Press, 1973. Clear, readable compendium of articles by authorities in many areas; includes Eastern and Western thought.

Masterpieces of World Philosophy in Summary Form, by Frank N. Magill. Harper, 1961. Over 200 synopses and commentaries on basic Western philosophy arranged chronologically.

Thales to Dewey, by Gordon H. Clark. Baker, 1957. A history of philosophy.

PHOTOGRAPHY

History of Photography, by Beaumont Newhall. New York Graphic Society, 1982. Compact history from beginnings in 1830 to present day. Indexed, with bibliography.

Photography: A Handbook of History, Materials and Processes, by Charles Swedlund. Holt, 2nd edition, 1981. A condensed history is included, but book concentrates on introducing students to photography basics. Includes glossary, index, and bibliography.

A World History of Photography, by Naomi Rosenblum. Abbeville, 1989. Complete history covering the entire world. Extensively illustrated; includes technical history. With glossary, bibliography, index, and charts identifying photographic processes.

PHYSICS

C.R.C. Handbook of Chemistry and Physics: A Ready Reference Book of Chemical and Physical Data, CRC Press, annual. Compilation of essential tables and chemical and physical properties of elements and compounds.

Encyclopedia of Physics, edited by Rita G. Lerner and George L. Trigg. Addison-Wesley, 2nd revised edition, 1986. Extended, scholarly articles on a variety of subjects. Although all the articles begin with basic definitions, most assume a general grounding in physics. Indexed.

Fundamentals of Physics, by David Halliday and Robert Resnick. Wiley, 3rd edition, 1988. Beginning textbook. Has study notes in the margins, accessible text, and problem sets. Separate study guide and supplements available. Includes appendices and index.

Physics: Its Methods and Meanings, by Alexander Taffel. Allyn & Bacon, 5th edition, 1986. Textbook for the beginning student. Covers everything from measuring mass to quantum theory and nuclear physics. Includes appendices, glossary, and index. Illustrated.

PLACES. *See* ATLASES.

PLANTS AND FLOWERS. *See also* BOTANY; HORTICULTURE; TREES.

Audubon Society Field Guide to North American Wildflowers, by the Audubon Society Staff, two volumes. Knopf, 1979.
   Volume 1: Eastern Region.
   Volume 2: Western Region.

A Field Guide to Eastern Edible Wild Plants, by Lee A. Peterson. Houghton Mifflin, 1982.

A Field Guide to Ferns and Their Related Families: Northeastern and Central North America, by Boughton Cobb. Houghton Mifflin, 1975.

A Field Guide to Edible Plants, by Steven Foster. Houghton Mifflin, 1990.

A Field Guide to Medicinal Plants: Eastern and Central North America, by Steven Foster and James A. Duke. Houghton Mifflin, 1990.

A Field Guide to Pacific States Wildflowers, by Theodore F. Niehaus. Houghton Mifflin, 1976.

A Field Guide to Rocky Mountain Wildflowers, by John A Craighead et al. Houghton Mifflin, 1974.

A Field Guide to Southwestern and Texas Wildflowers, by Theodore F. Niehaus et al. Houghton Mifflin, 1984.

A Field Guide to Wildflowers of Northeastern and North Central North America, by Roger Tory Peterson and Margaret McKenny. Houghton Mifflin, 1975.

Manual of Cultivated Plants, by L.H. Bailey. Macmillan, revised edition, 1949. Handbook for identification of plants commonly grown in the United States and Canada. Includes taxonomic information and detailed description of each plant. Organized by taxonomic classification. With glossary and index.

Wildflowers Across America, by Lady Bird Johnson and Carlton B. Lees. Abbeville, 1988. A guide to using wildflowers and plants in private and public gardens. Color photographs compiled by Johnson, active in the National Wildflower Research Center, and Lees, a horticulturalist.

Wyman's Gardening Encyclopedia, by Donald Wyman. Macmillan, 1977. Horticultural manual for everybody. Contains articles on individual plants, gardening practices, and garden chemicals and their ecological consequences.

PLAYS. *See* LITERATURE: DRAMA.

POETRY. *See* LITERATURE: POETRY.

POLITICS. *See also* FEDERAL GOVERNMENT; INTERNATIONAL RELATIONS.

Almanac of American Politics, Dutton, biennial. Has political profile of every state and every congressional district and biography, key votes, and ratings by large special-interest groups for each senator and representative.

The American Political Dictionary, by Jack Plano. Holt, 7th edition, 1985. Combination dictionary and subject-arranged overview of important terms, concepts, and court cases.

Colonial America: Essays in Politics and Social Development, edited by Stanley N. Katz. Little, Brown, 1971. A series of essays focused on the sociopolitical development of the American colonies in the 17th and 18th centuries. The book covers the origins of colonial society (17th century), politics and the imperial relationship, and politics and sociology of the 18th century. Other subjects include family structure in the different colonies, witchcraft, slavery, legal transformation, and economic development; in short, covers major sociopolitical developments in colonial society.

Political Handbook of the World, McGraw-Hill, annual. Includes coverage of national political parties and current political issues of the independent nations; also social and economic facts and statistics.

Safire's Political Dictionary, by William Safire. Random House, 1978. The language of politics according to *New York Times* columnist William Safire. Covers some historical terms and much Washington jargon; includes terms coined by Presidents and other political figures.

POPULATION AND VITAL STATISTICS. *See* DEMOGRAPHICS.

POST OFFICES. *See* ZIP CODES.

PREHISTORY. *See* ANIMALS—PREHISTORIC; EARLY MAN; FOSSILS.

Audubon Society Field Guide to North American Fossils, by the Audubon Society Staff and Ida Thompson. Knopf, 1982.

PRONUNCIATION

NBC Handbook of Pronunciation, by Eugene Ehrlich and Raymond Hand, Jr. Harper, 4th edition, 1991. Developed more than forty years ago by radio broadcasters facing the challenge of pronouncing difficult words over the air, the *Handbook* has since become the standard reference on American pronunciation. The latest edition contains 21,000 words and proper names, including such pronunciation demons as Lech Walesa.

PROVERBS

Early American Proverbs and Proverbial Phrases, by Bartlett Jere Whiting. Harvard University Press, 1977. Covers pre-1820 American proverbs.

Macmillan Book of Proverbs, Maxims, and Famous Phrases, edited by Burton Stevenson. Macmillan, 1987. Provides sources for more than 73,000 English proverbs and traces their development and variations. Arranged by subject or key word. Indexed.

Oxford Dictionary of English Proverbs, by Frank P. Wilson. Oxford University Press, 3rd edition, 1970. Arranged alphabetically by first word, including "a," "an," and "the."

PSYCHIATRY

Longman Dictionary of Psychology and Psychiatry, edited by Robert M. Goldenson. Longman, 1984. Has almost 16,000 entries covering terms, phrases, drugs, tests, therapies, and other related subjects. Has biographies of major figures in the psychosciences.

Psychiatric Dictionary, edited by Robert J. Campbell. Oxford University Press, 6th edition, 1989. Encyclopedic entries on all aspects of mental health.

Written for professionals. Uses the new official nomenclature of disorders.

PSYCHOLOGY. *See also* SOCIAL SCIENCES.

Encyclopedia of Human Behavior, by Robert H. Goldenson, two volumes. Doubleday, 1970. 1,000 terms clearly defined for the nonspecialist and student.

Encyclopedia of Psychology, four volumes. Wiley, 1984. 2,100 signed articles by authorities in many areas; for professionals and laypersons.

Introduction to Psychology, by Clifford T. Morgan et al. McGraw-Hill, 7th edition, 1986. General textbook dealing with the basics of psychology. Opening chapter addresses the subject as a whole and explores such questions as what psychology is and what psychologists do. From there, the text explores such basic topics in psychology as behavioral science, sensory processes, memory, and socialization. Each chapter begins with an outline and concludes with a summary, a glossary of terms, and a selected bibliography. Illustrated. Includes appendices, glossary, and indexes.

Longman Dictionary of Psychology and Psychiatry, edited by Robert M. Goldenson, Longman, 1984. Has almost 16,000 entries covering terms, phrases, drugs, tests, therapies, and other related subjects. Has biographies of major figures in the psychosciences.

The New Harvard Guide to Modern Psychology. Belknap, 1988. Scientific discussion of mental disorders from biological, sociological, and psychological perspectives. Includes extended articles on behavior, principles of treatment, and management. Indexed.

Penguin Dictionary of Psychology, by Arthur S. Reber. Viking/Penguin, 1985. Written for both the layperson and the expert reading outside his/her field, this book defines words and concepts used in psychology and psychiatry, as well as relevant terms from other disciplines. Items are listed alphabetically by key terms. Includes names of people only when used as adjectives (such as Freudian or Jungian) or as relating to laws, principles, or syndromes. Full explanations are provided for controversial usages and terms used differently by various schools.

PUBLISHING

Literary Market Place, Bowker, annual. Directory of U.S. and Canadian book publishers and related businesses such as book clubs, literary agents, translators, and manufacturers. Gives names of executives and addresses, telephone numbers, and fields of specialization for each publishing company.

Q

QUOTATIONS. *See also* PROVERBS.

Bartlett's Familiar Quotations, by John Bartlett. Little, Brown, 15th edition, 1980. Chronological arrangement of passages, phrases, and proverbs traced to their sources in ancient and modern literature. Includes over 20,000 quotations up through the present, with author and keyword indexes.

The Home Book of Quotations, by Burton E. Stevenson. Dodd, Mead, 1967. Arranged by subject. Includes over 50,000 quotations, with a keyword index.

The Oxford Dictionary of Quotations, Oxford University Press, 3rd edition, 1979. Alphabetical sequence includes authors writing in English and foreign authors. Omits proverbs and phrases. Fully indexed.

Respectfully Quoted: A Dictionary of Quotations Requested by the Congressional Research Service. Library of Congress, 1989. Compiled by librarians. Includes 2,100 quotations arranged by subject, keyword, and author.

Simpson's Contemporary Quotations, compiled by James B. Simpson. Houghton Mifflin, 1988. 10,000 entries alphabetically arranged by both author and subject. Concentrates on memorable quotes from 1964 to the present.

They Never Said It, by Paul F. Boller, Jr. and John George. Oxford University Press, 1989. A book of fake quotes, misquotes, and misleading attributions. Thomas Jefferson never said, "That government is best which governs least," and Horace Greeley never said, "Go west young man." Sets the record straight on these and similar examples of misquotes that have come to be accepted as the truth.

R

REFERENCE BOOKS

Guide to Reference Books, edited by Eugene P. Sheehy. American Library Association, 10th edition, 1986. The most complete compilation of reference books currently available. More than 16,000 entries provide details on general reference works and on reference books on specialized subjects in the humanities, social and behavorial sciences, history and area studies, and science, technology, and medicine.

Guide to Reference Books for School Media Centers, by Christine G. Wynar. Libraries Unlimited, 3rd edition, 1986. Evaluative annotations of reference titles suitable for high school students.

RELIGION. *See also* CHRISTIANITY; ISLAM; JUDAISM.

Dictionary of Comparative Religion, edited by S.G.F. Brandon. Scribner, 1978. Descriptions of the history and current practices of world religions and denominations, together with related subjects. Provides detailed coverage of eastern and ancient religions. Many terms are defined under one heading and these are cross-referenced and indexed (alphabetically and synoptically). Bibliographies are appended to entries.

Dictionary of Non-Christian Religions, by Geoffrey Parrinder. Westminster, 1973. Concise discussions of terms, gods, and concepts of contemporary and historical religions.

Encyclopedia of Religion, 16 volumes. Macmillan, 1987. The most current of the standard encyclopedias of religion.

Encyclopedia of Religion and Ethics, 13 volumes. Scribner, 1961. Comprehensive discussions of religions and ethical systems, including folklore.

Encyclopedia of the American Religious Experience: Studies of Traditions and Movements, edited by Charles H. Lippy and Peter W. Williams. Scribner, 1988. 105 commissioned essays by 100 authors represent the best of current scholarship. Excellent for students and the general reader. Extensive bibliographies, cross-references, and cross-disciplinary analyses.

Facts on File Dictionary of Religions, edited by John Hinnells. Facts on File, 1984. Definitions of terms used in various world religions. Entries run from several descriptive sentences to many paragraphs. Terms are defined within one heading, and these are cross-referenced and indexed (alphabetically and synoptically). Includes extensive bibliography.

Handbook of Denominations in the United States, edited by Frank S. Mead and Samuel S. Hill. Abingdon, 8th edition, 1985. History and present structure of Christian religious bodies in the United States. Reports on doctrines of different churches. Includes bibliography and index.

Man's Religion, by Davis S. Noss and the late John B. Noss. Macmillan, 7th edition, 1984. Introductory text describing world religions. Organized by area of origin. Ecumenical and unbiased, with coverage of Asiatic religions. Bibliography at the end of each chapter. Includes index. Illustrated.

What the Great Religions Believe, by Joseph Gaer. New American Library, 1963. Explanations, brief biographies of founders of 11 religions, and selections from sacred literature. For students and general readers.

Yearbook of American and Canadian Churches, Abingdon, annual. Statistical and historical data and directories to all religious bodies in the United States and Canada. Lists religious periodicals, accredited seminaries and religious schools, and activities of various churches.

REPORT WRITING. *See* WRITING.

REPTILES AND AMPHIBIANS

Audubon Society Field Guide to North American Reptiles and Amphibians, by the Audubon Society Staff and F. Wayne King. Knopf, 1979.

The Encyclopedia of Reptiles and Amphibians, edited by Dr. Tim Halliday and Dr. Kraig Adler. Facts on File, 1986. Expert contributors provide a survey of these two classes of animals, once the dominant life forms on Earth. The entries cover their incredible diversity of form and behavior; their evolution, feeding, and predatory habits; their reproduction and life cycles; and their distribution and survival status. Includes more than 150 color photographs and specially commissioned illustrations.

A Field Guide to Reptiles and Amphibians, by Robert B. Stebbins. Houghton Mifflin, 2nd edition, 1985.

A Field Guide to Reptiles and Amphibians of Eastern and Central North America, by Roger Conant. Houghton Mifflin, 2nd edition, 1975.

RÉSUMÉS

The Perfect Résumé, by Tom Jackson. Doubleday, 1980. Goes beyond the rules of résumé-writing and helps the reader discover potential career objectives, understand the theory and process behind résumé-writing, and target specific employers. The book is not designed simply to be read—the reader is constantly involved through questionnaires and exercises. Sample résumés included.

Your Resume: Key to a Better Job, by Leonard Corwen. Arco, 4th edition, 1991. Designed mainly for higher-level executives and professionals, this bestselling guide has been updated for the 1990s. It features more than 35 sample résumés and 20 model cover letters, worksheets for assessing personal strengths, a resource list for tapping the hidden job market, and a directory of information sources by occupation.

RHYME

Clement Wood's Unabridged Rhyming Dictionary, by Clement Wood. Simon & Schuster, 1943. Accompanying this dictionary are an analysis of various poetic forms, a chapter on the vocabulary of poetry, and a concluding section on versification. The rhyming dictionary differentiates words by vowel sounds and subsequent sounds, and then for the preceding consonant sounds. The dictionary thus allows one to choose a rhyme-word that is also metrically right.

ROCK AND ROLL. *See* MUSIC: POPULAR.

ROCKS AND MINERALS

Audubon Society Field Guide to North American Rocks and Minerals, by the Audubon Society Staff and Charles W. Chesterman. Knopf, 1979.

A Field Guide to Rocks and Minerals, by Frederick H. Pough. Houghton Mifflin, 4th edition, 1976.

RULES OF ORDER. *See* PARLIAMENTARY PROCEDURES.

S

SCHOOL PAPERS. *See* WRITING.

SCIENCE. *See also* EARTH SCIENCES; *and specific subjects, such as* BIOLOGY; CHEMISTRY; *and* PHYSICS.

American Men and Women of Science, seven volumes. Bowker, 16th edition, 1986. Standard biographical source on living scientists from the fields of biological and physical sciences, as well as medicine and the health sciences.

Asimov's Biographical Encyclopedia of Science and Technology, by Isaac Asimov. Doubleday, 2nd revised edition, 1982. Covers lives and achievements of 1,195 scientists and technologists from ancient times to the present.

Asimov's Chronology of Science and Discovery, by Isaac Asimov. Harper, 1989. A chronology of scientific discoveries that places each discovery in a sociopolitical context, detailing not only the positive effects, but the negative as well.

Chamber's Science and Technology Dictionary, edited by Peter M.B. Walker. Cambridge University Press, 4th edition, 1988. One-volume dictionary devoted to science and technology, with 45,000 entries in over 100 fields. Includes trade names.

Concise Dictionary of Scientific Biography, Scribner, 1981. An alphabetical list of 5,000 scientists with short biographical information.

A History of Science, and Its Relation to Philosophy and Religion, by Sir William Cecil Dampier. Cambridge University Press, 4th edition, 1968. Covers history of scientific thought, concentrating on theories and ideas. Includes bibliography and index.

McGraw-Hill Dictionary of Scientific and Technical Terms, edited by Sybil P. Parker. McGraw-Hill, 4th edition, 1988. Standard general science dictionary; emphasizes computer science, technology, and modern electronics. A new feature in this edition is the pronunciation guide for all defined terms. Includes 100,000 entries, 7,500 of which are new.

McGraw-Hill Encyclopedia of Science and Technology, 20 volumes. McGraw-Hill, 6th edition, 1987. Comprehensive treatment of science topics except for medicine and behavorial science.

McGraw-Hill Yearbook of Science and Technology, McGraw-Hill, annual. Updates the *McGraw-Hill Encyclopedia of Science and Technology.*

Science Year, The World Book Annual Science Supplement, World Book. Articles on the year's developments and projects in science. Illustrated and indexed.

The Time Tables of Science: A Chronology of the Most Important People and Events in the History of Science, by Alexander Hellemans and Bryan Bunch. Simon & Schuster, 1988. Contains over 10,000 entries organized chronologically and by discipline, interspersed with more than 100 short essays on science and technology and nine overviews of the main periods of scientific history. Indexed by subject and name.

Van Nostrand's Scientific Encyclopedia, two volumes. Van Nostrand Reinhold, 7th edition, 1988. Short, informative articles on more than 16,000 science and technology topics.

SEAMANSHIP

The Norton Encyclopedic Dictionary of Navigation, by David F. Tver, edited by Hewitt Schlereth. W.W. Norton, 1987. The book is divided into four sections: Navigation Terms, Weather Terms, Navigation Astronomy, and Navigation Alphabet. All sections are completely cross-referenced and alphabetized.

SECRETARIAL SKILLS. *See also* STYLE AND USAGE.

Complete Secretary's Handbook, by Lillian Doris and Besse May Miller, revised by Mary A. DeVries. Prentice Hall, 6th edition, 1988. Contains chapters on filing and follow-up techniques, typing skills, using computers and other automated equipment, and other general secretarial duties. Two sections deal with writing skills and another provides quick reference to information needed on a daily basis. Includes glossary of business terms and index.

Webster's New World Secretarial Handbook, Simon & Schuster, 4th edition, 1989. Guide to many diverse aspects of the profession. Includes information on several professional fields for specialized secretaries, easy-to-understand essay on general legal principles, travel information, and a strong chapter on English usage, including a spelling and syllabification list of 33,000 words. Includes handy general reference section. Indexed.

SEX

Masters and Johnson on Sex and Human Loving, by William H. Masters, Virginia E. Johnson, and Robert C. Kolodny. Little Brown, 2nd edition, 1985. Provides complete coverage of the biologi-cal, psychological, and social aspects of human sexuality. Examines both cultural and historical trends and practices. Has a selected bibliography and an index.

SHAKESPEARE. *See* LITERATURE: SHAKESPEARE.

SHELLFISH

Audubon Society Field Guide to North American Seashells, by the Audubon Society Staff and Harold A. Rehder. Knopf, 1981.

A Field Guide to Atlantic Coast Shells, by Percy A. Morris. Houghton Mifflin, 3rd edition, 1973.

A Field Guide to Coral Reefs of the Caribbean and Florida, by Eugene H. Kaplan. Houghton Mifflin, 1988.

A Field Guide to Pacific Coast Shells, by Percy A. Morris. Houghton Mifflin, 1974.

SHORT STORIES. *See* LITERATURE: SHORT STORIES.

SIGN LANGUAGE. *See* LANGUAGE.

SLANG

Dictionary of Slang and Unconventional English, by Eric Honeywood Partridge. Macmillan, 8th edition, 1985. Includes more than 72,000 terms of British origin. Scholarly.

New Dictionary of American Slang, edited by Robert L. Chapman. Harper, 1986. A well-known lexicographer's attempt to keep up with the ever-changing spoken nonstandard English. Scholarly, but basic and accessible. Introduction deals with the problem of defining the type of language usage indicated by "slang." Includes some etymological explanations.

SNAKES. *See* REPTILES AND AMPHIBIANS.

SOCIAL SCIENCES. *See also* ANTHROPOLOGY; ECONOMICS; PSYCHOLOGY; SOCIOLOGY.

International Encyclopedia of the Social Sciences, eight volumes (originally issued in 17 volumes), plus Biographical Supplement and Supplemental Volumes, Macmillan, 1968–79. Comprehensive, scholarly coverage of all aspects of the social sciences, including demography, international relations, and law.

A New Dictionary of the Social Sciences, by Geoffrey Mitchell. Aldine, 2nd edition, 1979. Has long entries discussing philosophical and historical aspects of major concepts and theories with emphasis on sociology and anthropology. Includes some biographies.

SOCIAL SECURITY. *See* BENEFITS.

SOCIAL WORK

Encyclopedia of Social Work, three volumes. National Association of Social Workers, 18th edition, 1987. Theoretical and practical approach to societal problems, including family and housing, for social workers and social-science students and practitioners.

SOCIOLOGY. *See also* SOCIAL SCIENCES.

Encyclopedia of Sociology, Dushkin, 1981. For the nonscholar; 1,300 entries on sociological terms, theories, institutions, and biographies. Provides comprehensive coverage with simplified explanations.

Sociology, by Donald Light, Jr. and Suzanne Keller. Knopf, 4th edition, 1985. An introductory college text. From a close examination of the sociological perspective and discussions of fundamental methods and techniques, the book moves into the major sociological topics: culture, socialization, social institutions, and change. Illustrated. Includes summary and glossary at the end of each chapter, references, and index.

SOUTH AMERICA. *See also* HISTORY: LATIN AMERICAN.

South American Handbook. Trade and Travel Publications, annual. Complete information for travelers on what to see, how to get there, and where to eat and stay. Also includes a variety of other information a visitor might need to know and a general introduction with hints about safety, health risks, money, language, and law enforcement. Includes maps, appendices, and index.

SPACE TECHNOLOGY

The Illustrated Encyclopedia of Space Technology, by Kenneth Gatland. Orion, 1989. History of space exploration and a discussion and explanation of the technology involved. Amply illustrated; includes glossary and index.

SPECIAL COLLECTIONS. *See also* MUSEUMS.

Directory of Special Libraries and Information Centers, edited by Brigitte T. Darnay and Janet A.

DeMaggio. Gale, annual. Two-volume directory of more than 19,000 special libraries and research centers, archives, information centers, computer-based retrieval systems, and many specialized collections of films, artifacts, computer tapes, and special objects. Covers collections maintained by business firms, nonprofit organizations, educational institutions, government agencies, and many other types of organizations.

Subject Collections, edited by Lee Ash and William G. Miller. Bowker, 6th edition, 1985. A guide to special book collections and subject emphases as reported by university, college, public, and special libraries and museums in the United States and Canada. Valuable for locating the papers of individuals and organizations within larger collections and libraries.

SPEECHES

A Treasury of the World's Great Speeches, edited by Houston Peterson. Simon & Schuster, revised edition, 1965. Anthology of speeches from history, each with a preface placing it in historical perspective and relating the dramatic setting. Indexed.

SPORTS. *See also specific sports, such as* BASEBALL; BASKETBALL; *and* FOOTBALL.

The Complete Book of the Olympics, by David Wallechinsky. Penguin, 1984; revised edition, 1988. Complete records of summer and winter Olympics, back to the first games in Athens in 1896. Gives statistics and brief write-ups of each event and each winning performance. Includes essays on history and issues.

The Encyclopedia of Sports, A.S. Barnes, 3rd revised edition, 1963. A complete history of nearly 80 sports, the basic rules and equipment used, and lists of champions and championship teams.

Sports Lingo, by Harvey Frommer. Atheneum, 1979. Comprehensive dictionary of technical and cultural sports terms from archery through wrestling, noting how they vary in usage from sport to sport.

Webster's Sports Dictionary, Merriam-Webster, 1976. Limits itself to strict definitions of terms; does not provide historical background or statistics. Includes terms used in sports played in English-speaking countries. (*Sport* is defined as anything reasonably expected to be found in the sports section of a newspaper.) Cross-referenced; has lists of sportswriting abbreviations and referee signals.

STAMPS AND STAMP COLLECTING

Scott Standard Postage Stamp Catalogue, four volumes. Scott Publishing, annual. Provides descriptions, photographs (where possible), and monetary values for all known world stamps, past and present.

The Stamp Atlas, by W. Raife Wellsted and Stuart Rossiter. Facts on File, 1986. Written by postal historians, this comprehensive work details (globally) when and where stamps were issued, the operations of postal systems, and changing political boundaries from earliest times.

STATE GOVERNMENTS

Book of the States, The Council of State Governments, biennial. Source of information about the governments and constitutions of the state governments. Information is presented in tabular form or in articles. State finances, judiciary, and legislatures are all covered. Includes statistics on population and land area and historical data. Indexed.

STOCKS. *See* INVESTMENTS.

STYLE AND USAGE. *See also* DICTIONARIES—ENGLISH LANGUAGE; GRAMMAR; PRONUNCIATION; SECRETARIAL SKILLS; WRITING.

The Chicago Manual of Style, University of Chicago Press, 13th edition, 1982. First published in 1906, this style manual has become recognized as a reliable standard for writers and editors preparing manuscripts for publication. Major sections cover bookmaking, style, and production and printing. Includes extensive index.

A Dictionary of Modern English Usage, by Henry Watson Fowler, revised by Ernest Gowers. Oxford University Press, 2nd edition, 1965. Respected A-to-Z guide to English usage, with a British slant, first published in 1926.

The Harper Dictionary of Contemporary Usage, by William Morris and Mary Morris. Harper, 2nd edition, 1985. Provides comments by famous writers and experts on the state of English today and preferred forms of usage. Includes answers to questions raised by the Morrisses' syndicated newspaper column. Includes bibliography.

A Manual for Writers of Term Papers, Theses, and Dissertations, by Kate Turabian. University of Chicago Press, 5th edition, 1987. Available in paperback, this book complements the venerable *Chicago Manual of Style*, 13th edition, also published by the University of Chicago. The emphasis of the Turabian book is on the correct forms and techniques for the preparation of scholarly and technical work. The 5th edition devotes substantial attention to computerized word processing.

Modern American Usage: A Guide, by Wilson Follett, completed by Jacques Barzun. Hill and Wang, 1966. Many famous English critics worked on this book. Encyclopedic entries cover many aspects of formal composition.

The MLA Style Manual, by Walter S. Achtert and Joseph Gibaldi. Modern Language Association of America, 1985. Comprehensive guide to style, mechanics, manuscript preparation, and documentation. Intended for humanities scholars.

SYNONYMS

Roget's International Thesaurus, Crowell/Harper, 4th edition, 1977. First published by Dr. Peter Mark Roget in 1852, and revised and updated numerous times over the years. The first reference book to group words according to ideas rather than alphabetically.

Webster's Collegiate Thesaurus, Merriam-Webster, 1976. Has alphabetical arrangement; gives antonyms as well as synonyms; provides illustrative sentences.

Webster's New Dictionary of Synonyms, Merriam-Webster, 1984. Lists synonyms with notes on connotational distinctions; some antonyms also given. Includes context sentences, as well as contrasted and analogous words. Features long introductory article on distinctions. Cross-referenced. This is not just a basic word list, but more a reference concerning distinctions between related words and word groups.

Webster's New World Dictionary of Synonyms, edited by David B. Guralnick. Simon & Schuster, 1984. Defines *synonym* as "words that mean *almost* the same thing." The more than 4,000 entries include the subtle nuances that make proper word choice easier.

T

TAXES

H & R Block Income Tax Guide, Collier, annual. Takes you line by line through the most frequently used personal income tax forms, includes a special-interest chapter covering specific situations, and has an A-to-Z glossary of tax terms.

J.K. Lasser's Your Income Tax, Simon & Schuster, annual. Clarifies federal income-tax law for the layperson.

U.S. Master Tax Guide, Commerce Clearing House, annual. Detailed reference for personal and business taxes.

TECHNOLOGY

Chamber's Dictionary of Science and Technology, Cambridge University Press, 1988. Covers terms from acoustics to zoology; includes trade names.

Encyclopedia of Modern Technology, edited by Dr. David Blackburn and Prof. Geoffrey Holister. G.K. Hall, 1987. Nontechnical articles on the practical uses to which science has been put—and is being put. Divided by fields of endeavor. The authors survey technological problems and the development of key ideas. Includes short glossary and index; illustrated.

Henley's Twentieth Century Book of Ten Thousand Formulas, Processes and Trade Secrets, by A. Henley. Gordon Press, 1986. Publisher's Agency (revised and enlarged), 1981. Amateur's guide to technology. Tables, appendices, and index included. Buying guide for useful chemicals and supplies also included.

McGraw-Hill Dictionary of Scientific and Technical Terms, edited by Sybil P. Parker. McGraw-Hill, 4th edition, 1988. Standard general science dictionary; emphasizes computer science, technology, and modern electronics.

McGraw-Hill Encyclopedia of Science and Technology, 20 volumes. McGraw-Hill, 6th edition, 1987. Comprehensive treatment of science topics except for medicine and behavioral science.

McGraw-Hill Yearbook of Science and Technology, McGraw-Hill, annual. Updates the *McGraw-Hill Encyclopedia of Science and Technology.*

The Way Things Work, two volumes, Simon & Schuster, 1967. Descriptions and diagrams explain more than 1,000 mechanical, electrical, and electronic devices clearly and simply. Related machines and principles are grouped together.

TELECOMMUNICATIONS

ARRL Handbook for the Radio Amateur, American Relay Radio League, annual. Comprehensive reference beginning with radio principles and continuing through construction and maintenance of radios and assembling and operating a radio station. Indexed.

TELEVISION

Les Brown's Encyclopedia of Television, by Les Brown. Zoetrope, 1982. Complete guide to the history, technology, and programming of television and the personalities behind it. Illustrated. Includes short bibliography and appendices.

TENNIS

Bud Collins' Modern Encyclopedia of Tennis, by Bud Collins. Doubleday, 1988. Gives an excellent brief history of the game, detailing its origins, development, and evolution to its current professional level. Includes separate chapters on roots, players, records, officials, statistics, and rules.

TERRORISM

Directory of International Terrorism, by George Rosie. Paragon House, 1986. Emphasis is on post-World War II terrorist activities.

TEXTILES. *See* CLOTHING AND TEXTILES.

THEATER. *See also* LITERATURE: DRAMA.

Cambridge Guide to World Theatre, edited by Martin Banham. Cambridge University Press, 1989. Useful for both scholars and general readers, this dictionary emphasizes performance, detailing both individual and company efforts. Contains biographical sketches of actors, directors, and playwrights. Notes entire countries with strong theater traditions.

The Oxford Companion to Theatre, edited by Phyllis Hatnoll. Oxford University Press, 4th edition, 1983. Articles on all aspects of the theater, including theater architecture, technical theater, terminology, individual theaters, and experimental theater. Also includes articles on history, national dramatic literature, plays, actors, playwrights, and teachers. Illustrated.

Theatre World. Crown, annual. A theater yearbook that gives a complete pictorial and statistical record of each Broadway season from 1944–45 through the present.

THESAURUSES. *See* SYNONYMS.

TRAVEL

Birnbaum guides, by Stephen Birnbaum and Alexandra Mayes Birnbaum. Houghton Mifflin. Expanding series of guides provides detailed travel and sightseeing information and extensive listings of accommodations, restaurants, museums, and other tourist attractions. Updated annually. The Birnbaum titles currently are: *Canada; Caribbean, Bermuda, and the Bahamas; Disneyland; Europe; Europe for Business Travelers; Florida for Free; France; Great Britain; Hawaii; Ireland; Italy; Mexico; South America; Spain and Portugal; United States; USA for Business Travelers;* and *Walt Disney World*.

Fodor's guides. Fodor Travel Publications. Fodor's offers more than 300 guides to the world's nations, regions, and cities—from Acapulco to Williamsburg. The books give details on how to get to all these places and where to stay, where to eat, and what to see once you get there. The line also includes a series of *Budget Guides*.

TREATIES. *See* INTERNATIONAL RELATIONS.

TREES

Audubon Society Field Guide to North American Trees, by the Audubon Society Staff and Elbert A. Little, Jr., two volumes. Knopf, 1980.
  Volume 1: Eastern Region.
  Volume 2: Western Region.

A Field Guide to Eastern Forests, by John C. Kricher. Houghton Mifflin, 1988.

A Field Guide to Eastern Trees, by George A. Petrides. Houghton Mifflin, 1988.

A Field Guide to Trees and Shrubs, by George A. Petrides. Houghton Mifflin, 1973.

TROPICAL FISH. *See* FISH.

TV. *See* TELEVISION.

U

UNITED NATIONS

Everyone's United Nations, United Nations, 1986. Covers structure, functions, and activities of the organization and its related agencies from 1945, with special emphasis on the 1965–78 period.

V

VETERANS. *See* BENEFITS.

VITAL STATISTICS. *See* DEMOGRAPHICS.

W

WAR

Dictionary of Wars, by George C. Kohn. Facts on File, 1986. Who fought whom, when, where, and why, from 2000 B.C. to the present. An authoritative and concise source of information on the major wars, rebellions, and revolutions down through history.

The Encyclopedia of Military History, by R. Ernest Dupuy and Trevor N. Dupuy. HarperCollins, 2nd edition, 1986. Covers warfare and military affairs from 3500 B.C. to the present in chronologically and geographically arranged chapters. Illustrated, and has a general index plus an index of battles and sieges.

The Encyclopedia of Modern War, by Roger Parkinson. Stein and Day, 1977. This reprint of a classic A-to-Z reference covers battles, weapons, and personalities from 1793 to the mid-1970s, as well as stategy and tactics.

Historical Encyclopedia of WWII, edited by Hendrik Brugmans et al. Facts on File, 1980. Begins with an essay on the origins of the war, then goes into alphabetical listings with brief informational entries and longer articles. A concluding essay on the immediate and long-range consequences of the war appears at the end of the alphabetical listings. Chronology and bibliography included.

Korean War Almanac, by Harry G. Summers, Jr. Facts on File, 1990. This reference book on the war contains an overview of the entire conflict, a chronology of events, and 375 articles on the people, battles, weapons, military units, and key concepts of the war. Includes maps and photos.

The Times Atlas of the Second World War, edited by John Keegan. Harper, 1989. Uses new computer mapping techniques for clear, more comprehensive treatment of nearly every conflict. Eastern Front coverage is more complete due to Soviet cooperation. Provides extensive treatment of socioeconomic issues and detailed treatment of the Holocaust and the various underground and resistance movements.

Vietnam War Almanac, by Harry G. Summers, Jr. Facts on File, 1985. Provides a clear, accessible, and objective look at the conflict that shaped a generation. Includes an introductory history of the country and a description of the physical and historical conditions that shaped American policy there; a chronology of events, both in Vietnam and in the United States; and 500 articles.

Warfare in the Ancient World, edited by General Sir John Hackett. Facts on File, 1990. This comprehensive survey spans nearly eighteen centuries, covering all regions of the ancient world, from the armies of the Egyptian pharaohs to the defenders of the crumbling Roman empire in the fifth century A.D. Each chapter is written by an authority in the field. Illustrated; has maps, bibliography, and index.

Webster's American Military Biographies, edited by Robert McHenry. Merriam, 1978. Has more than 1,000 biographies of persons important to the military history of the nation. Addenda give chief service officers, list of wars, battles, and expeditions.

World Almanac of World War II, edited by Brigadier Peter Young. World Almanac, 1986. Gives chronology, information on weapons and equipment, biographies, and a summation. Has full-color photographs, maps, and clear analysis.

World War I, by S.L.A. Marshall. Houghton Mifflin, 1985. A step-by-step documentation of the events leading up to the war itself and the Treaty of Versailles. A thorough, fairly personal account of the war, it delves into the personalities and possible motivations of the war's leading characters.

WEATHER. *See* METEOROLOGY.

WELFARE. *See* BENEFITS.

WINES AND SPIRITS

Alexis Lichine's New Encyclopedia of Wines and Spirits, by Alexis Lichine. Knopf, 5th edition, 1987. Has entries on all major wines and spirits, thoroughly described. Includes essay chapters on related subjects such as the history of wine; appendices including a chart of French wine vintages; and a conversion table of measures. Also has selected bibliography and index.

Hugh Johnson's Modern Encyclopedia of Wine, by Hugh Johnson. Simon & Schuster, 2nd edition, 1987. Accepted as the most comprehensive, usable, and well-written book on wine, this version is revised and updated to take into account the changes in the wine world. A companion to the *World Atlas of Wine* (below), this work tells you who makes it, where, how good it is, how much it costs, and whether it's worth the price.

The World Atlas of Wine, by Hugh Johnson. Simon & Schuster, 1978. Locates wine regions on country maps, then shows districts within regions and locations of vineyards within districts on small-scale maps. Covers the major wine-producing nations of the world. Supporting text gives the specific characteristics of wines grown in each region, district, and vineyard. Indexed.

WITCHCRAFT. *See* OCCULT.

WOMEN. *See also* BIOGRAPHY.

American Woman: Her Changing Social, Economic, and Political Roles, 1920–70, by William H. Chafe. Oxford University Press, 1974. Narrative history of the period with good documentation; of interest to the historian, general reader, and student from high school up.

State-by-State Guide to Women's Legal Rights, by the NOW Legal Defense and Education Fund and Renee Cherow-O'Leary. McGraw-Hill, 1987. A historic overview of women's changing legal status and a state-by-state guide to women's rights in education, family, employment, and the community. Appendices list factors considered by the courts in divorce and custody, and list civil rights offices around the country.

We, the American Women, Science Research, 1983. Brief narrative history in simple style followed by documents edited to be read easily. Includes all aspects of women's life and contributions. Especially useful for high school.

WRITING. *See also* STYLE AND USAGE.

A Manual for Writers of Term Papers, Theses, and Dissertations, by Kate L. Turabian. University of Chicago Press, 5th edition, 1987. Guide to the preparation and presentation of scholarly research papers.

Simon & Schuster Handbook for Writers, by Lynn Quitman Troyka. Prentice Hall, 1987. Concentrates on mechanics, grammar, and style. Intended for classroom and student use.

Student's Guide for Writing College Papers, by Kate L. Turabian. University of Chicago Press, 3rd edition, 1977. Simplified manual for younger students.

The Term Paper, Step by Step, by Donald J. Mulkerne. Anchor, 3rd edition, 1983. Guide to writing research papers. Geared to high school students and first- and second-year college students.

Writer's Market. Writer's Digest Books, annual. On how to sell what you write. Contains pub-

lisher listings and much practical advice and information on how to get published.

X, Y, Z

ZIP CODES

National Zip-Code and Post Office Directory, annual, U.S. Postal Service. Lists post offices with street listings and zip codes. Also gives other information about postal services such as charges, abbreviations, and how to address mail.

ZOOLOGY. *See also* ANIMALS.

General Zoology, by Claude A. Villiee, Warren F. Walker, and Robert D. Barnes. CBS College Publishing, 1984. Textbook of animal function and behavior. Begins with principles of cell biology; continues through organ systems. The third part discusses genetics and population genetics and the theory of evolution. Finally, the book samples the diversity of animal forms from protozoa to human beings and examines the relation of animals to their environment. Illustrated, with index/glossary.

2.

Telephone Sources

THIS SECTION LISTS TELEPHONE NUMBERS THAT have been set up specifically to respond to queries from the general public. A call to one of these numbers will be answered by a trained operator whose job it is to answer questions and, in some cases, to make referrals if professional help is needed. More and more frequently these days, the operator at the other end of the line is sitting in front of a computer terminal that can display a wide range of information while you talk.

One of the best ways to start a telephone search for information is with a call to a library. The information experts at the Telephone Reference Service of the New York Public Library handle an average of 800 questions a day, from local as well as long-distance callers—some from as far away as Australia. With a core library of about 1,500 reference books at their fingertips, the Library's Telephone Reference Service operators are prepared to provide information quickly on all but the most esoteric subjects.

Large libraries without specific telephone reference departments will direct incoming calls for information to the appropriate division. (See the "General Telephone Sources" listing below.) Most smaller libraries also welcome queries, as long as they are not too complex or too time-consuming. Simply ask for the reference department and your call will be routed to a reference librarian. If a small library does not have a formal reference department, there will almost always be someone familiar with reference books who can help you. Make a personal visit to your local library and get to know the people you will be talking to by telephone. You may be surprised at the extent of the information available through a local telephone call.

Conducting Telephone Research

Telephone research is the fastest and simplest way to obtain information, but it can also be extremely frustrating and time-consuming if done in a haphazard way. Think about it: Which of these two questions is more likely to produce a useful answer?

How much do teachers get paid?
or

Which states pay the highest and lowest average teacher salaries?

The second question is obviously much more to the point. So as you set out to obtain information by telephone, work out specific, rather than general, questions. The more specific the question, the easier it is for the researcher at the other end of the line to provide exactly what you want.

Keep a Log of Your Calls

Experienced researchers *always* keep a log of their telephone calls. It sometimes takes calls to several numbers to reach the most helpful person. With a record of these calls, you may be able to skip most of the numbers if you have to call back for further information or assistance. One thing is certain: the one time you neglect to write down the number of someone helpful will be the very time you will need to get in touch with that person again.

The telephone log need not be formal or complicated; many researchers simply use a blank pad of paper to jot down dates, numbers called, names of people who responded, and the information provided. Especially useful numbers can be transferred from the log to a Rolodex® or other telephone file system if you expect to use them frequently.

Tips on Telephone Research

1. Telephone numbers change more rapidly than any other information resource. If a number has changed or been discontinued, note this in the margin alongside the entry in this book. Write it right in the book! This is a lot simpler than keeping a separate card file and noting the change on a card.

2. After your questions have been answered, ask whether the source has anything it can send you on the subject. Many telephone sources have useful brochures and pamphlets that they will send free of charge, or at minimal cost. Ask the telephone source for information on reference books and articles that might provide more information if you need to pursue a subject more thoroughly than is possible by telephone. Libraries are especially helpful in this respect.

3. Addresses of telephone sources are provided so that telephone queries can by followed up by mail if necessary.

4. Government agencies can be very helpful. Specific government hotlines and telephone reference services are included in this chapter along with other telephone sources. For broader inquiries, consult the "Government Sources" section, which lists main numbers and public information numbers of federal, state, and foreign governmental offices.

5. The federal government operates a toll-free Federal Information Center: 800/347-1997. This number welcomes queries on all aspects of the federal government. The hours are 9 A.M. to 10:30 P.M. Monday through Friday. See the "Federal Government" listing below for additional details.

6. If a source is not listed here and you believe it exists, call the nationwide information number for 800 toll-free listings: 800/555-1212. You can also purchase your own copy of the *AT&T Toll-Free 800 Directory*, which comes in two editions: Business and Consumer. For prices and ordering instructions, call 800/426-8686.

Note on 800 numbers: Some exchanges require that you dial 1 before long-distance and 800 numbers (1-800/XXX-XXXX), and some do not. To simplify matters the numeral 1 is not included with the numbers in this section. If you need to use 1 with your calls, simply add it mentally when you make the call.

7. If you need to talk to a manufacturer about how to assemble, use, maintain, or repair a product, get the company's 800 num-

ber and call it. More and more companies are now offering this service.

   8. Cooperative Extension Services have become a powerful and easy-to-reach source of information on an unusually broad spectrum of subjects, including appliances, cleaning, do-it-yourself projects, fabric handling and care, family life development, gardening and horticulture, and nutrition. Cooperative Extension Services tend to specialize in information of greatest usefulness to the counties they serve, so not all offices can answer questions in all areas.

   Every county throughout the United States has a Cooperative Extension Services number that can be reached through a local call; simply look up "Cooperative Extension" in your local telephone directory (sometimes the number will be in the "Government Listings" section). If you need assistance obtaining the number for the nearest Cooperative Extension, call 212/340-2900, 9 A.M. to 5 P.M. EST, Monday through Friday. This branch, operated by Cornell University, maintains a national directory of Cooperative Extension numbers and addresses.

   9. Hearing- and speech-impaired persons who use a telecommunications device for the deaf (known as TTD or TTY) can get help with calls made from one TDD to another by calling the following service:
TDD/TTY Operator Services
800/855-1155

   The TDD operator can help place calls, assist if there is a problem with a number, obtain TDD numbers not listed in the telephone book, and report problems with your telephone.

   TDD numbers are given in the listings below whenever available.

Telephone Sources
Subject Index

A

ABORTION. *See* FAMILY PLANNING.

ABUSE. *See* CHILDREN—ABUSE; DOMESTIC VIOLENCE.

ACOUSTICS

Acoustical Society of America
500 Sunnyside Boulevard
Woodbury, NY 11797
516/349-7800
    weekdays: 9 A.M.–4 P.M. EST
The society seeks to increase and diffuse the knowledge of acoustics. In so doing they will answer inquiries and make referrals.

ADOPTION

Adoption Crossroad
401 East Seventy-fourth Street, Suite 17D
New York, NY 10021
212/988-0110
    weekdays: 9 A.M.–9 P.M. EST
Provides psychological support and worldwide search services to aid for families separated by adoption.

ALMA Society
Adoptees' Liberty Movement Association
P.O. Box 154
Washington Bridge Station
New York, NY 10033
212/581-1568
    24 hours a day
Supports the position that the adult adoptee has an inalienable right to knowledge about his or her origins. Provides information on how to search for biological parents; maintains the ALMA International Reunion Registry Databank.

Orphan Voyage
2141 Road 2300
Cedaredge, CO 81413
    weekdays: 9 A.M.–5:30 P.M. MST
303/856-3937
Provides information on searches for relatives and adoption issues; in business for 38 years.

AERONAUTICS

American Institute of Aeronautics and Astronautics Technical
Information Service/Library
555 West Fifty-seventh Street
New York, NY 10019
212/247-6500
    weekdays: 9 A.M.–5 P.M. EST
Answers inquiries on all aspects of aeronautics and astronautics.

Smithsonian Institution
National Air and Space Museum Library
Seventh Street and Independence Avenue SW, Room 3100
Washington, DC 20560
202/357-3133
    weekdays: 10 A.M.–4 P.M. EST
Reference services will answer questions on aviation, astronautics, early pioneers of flight and early aircraft, astronomy, the earth, and planetary sciences. A division of the Smithsonian Institution.

AFRICA

African-American Institute
833 United Nations Plaza
New York, NY 10017
212/949-5666
    weekdays: 9 A.M.–5 P.M. EST
Answers inquiries about Africa, including its development, and offers referrals.

AGRICULTURE

Department of Agriculture
National Agricultural Library
Reference and User Services, Room 1200
10301 Baltimore Boulevard
Beltsville, MD 20705-2351
301/344-3755
    weekdays: 8 A.M.–4:30 P.M. EST
    D.C. Reference Center:
    Department of Agriculture
    Fourteenth Street and Independence Avenue SW
    South Building, Room 1052
    Washington, DC 202250
    202/447-3434
    weekdays: 8 A.M.–4:30 P.M. EST
Answers over 25,000 questions each year. Library has 2 million books on agriculture and related subjects, making it the largest such collection in the United States. The library also has the original

works of Linnaeus. Agricola database provides information services.

AIDS

Gay Men's Health Crisis Hotline
129 West Twentieth Street
New York, NY 10011
212/807-6655
TDD: 212/645-7470
    Monday–Friday: 10 A.M.–9 P.M. EST
    Saturday: 12 P.M.–3 P.M. EST
Provides basic information about acquired immune deficiency symptoms, possible causes, and preventive measures.

Women in Crisis
133 West Twenty-first Street, Suite 11
New York, NY 10011
212/242-4880
    Weekdays: 9 A.M.–5 P.M.
Provides information to community agencies and the public on AIDS transmission and prevention as it affects women and their families. Provides counseling for women with AIDS and their care givers.

ALCOHOLISM

Alcohol and Drug Problems Association of North America
1400 I Street NW
Washington, DC 20005
202/289-6755
    weekdays: 9 A.M.–5 P.M. EST
Answers questions on legislation, public policy, and issues in the field of drugs and alcohol.

Association of Halfway House Alcoholism Programs of North America, Inc.
786 East Seventh Street
St. Paul, MN 55106
612/771-0933
    weekdays: 10 A.M.–4 P.M. CST
Provides referrals to halfway houses throughout the country for recovery from alcoholism and other drug abuse. Publishes a newsletter.

Boost Alcohol Consciousness Concerning the Health of University Students
P.O. Box 100430
Denver, CO 80250-0430
303/871-3068
    weekdays: 8 A.M.–4:30 P.M. MST
Will answer general questions on alcohol educa-

tion and on drinking tendencies of 18- to 25-year-olds. Provides newsletter.

Employee Assistance Professionals Association, Inc.
4601 North Fairfax Drive, Suite 1001
Arlington, VA 22203
703/522-6272
    weekdays: 9 A.M.–5 P.M. EST
Employee Assistance Programs (EAPS) are designed to help all employees and their families who are alcohol or drug abusers or affected by substance abuse. Will provide referrals for members to chapters throughout the country.

Families Anonymous
P.O. Box 528
Van Nuys, CA 91408
818/989-7841
    weekdays: 9 A.M.–4 P.M. PST; answering service after office hours
Will refer friends and families of people with drug, alcohol, or behavioral problems to local support groups around the country.

National Association for Children of Alcoholics
31582 Coast Highway, Suite B
South Laguna, CA 92677
714/499-3889
    weekdays: 9 A.M.–5 P.M. PST; answering service after office hours
Provides general information for children of alcoholics. Referrals to therapists, programs, treatment centers, and local chapters.

National Clearinghouse for Alcohol and Drug Information
P.O. Box 2345
Rockville, MD 20852
301/468-2600
    weekdays: 9 A.M.–5 P.M. EST
Does database searches for specific topics as well as general information and statistics on alcohol and other drug-related problems. Will send literature in English or Spanish.

ALLERGIES AND RESPIRATORY DISEASES

The American Academy of Allergy and Immunology
611 East Wells Street
Milwaukee, WI 53202
800/822-ASMA (822-2762)—24-hour answering service for general information

414/272-6071—weekdays: 8 A.M.–5 P.M. EST for specific inquiries
Offers information for allergy suffers and the general public through pamphlets and telephone services.

Emphysema Anonymous, Inc.
P.O. Box 3224
Seminole, FL 34642
813/391-9977
    weekdays: 8 A.M.–5 P.M. EST
Answers questions regarding emphysema and related respiratory problems. Will recommend doctors and places to live in the United States where climate is compatible. Also publishes newsletter.

Lung Line
National Jewish Center For Immunology and Respiratory Medicine
1400 Jackson Street
Denver, CO 80206
800/222-LUNG (222-5864) (including Colorado, except Denver)
In Denver only: 303/355-LUNG (355-5864)
    weekdays: 8 A.M.–5 P.M. MST
Answers questions regarding asthma, emphysema, chronic bronchitis, juvenile rheumatoid arthritis, and other respiratory and immune-system disorders.

The National Heart, Lung and Blood Institute Education Programs Information Center
4733 Bethesda Avenue, Suite 530
Bethesda, MD 20814-4820
301/496-4236
    weekdays: 8:30 A.M.–5 P.M. EST
Answers calls regarding high blood pressure, high cholesterol, smoking, asthma, and blood resources. Will provide pamphlet by mail.

APPLIANCES. *See also* HOME BUILDING, MAINTENANCE, AND REPAIR.

Whirlpool Corporation
Consumer Assurance Assistance Line
2303 Pipestone Road
Benton Harbor, MI 49022
800/253-1301
In Alaska and Hawaii: 800/253-1121
In Michigan: 800/632-2243
    24 hours a day
One of the first companies to set up a national toll-free number for queries on everything relating to their products.

GE Answer Center
9500 Williamsburg Plaza
Louisville, KY 40222
800/626-2000
   24 hours a day
Provides advice and tips on GE, RCA, and Hotpoint products—buying, maintenance, and do-it-yourself repairs.

ARTHRITIS

Arthritis Consulting Service
4620 North State Road 7, Suite 206
Fort Lauderdale, FL 33319
800/327-3027
   weekdays: 8:30 A.M.–4 P.M. EST
Provides information on latest research and on how to cope.

ARTS—GENERAL

National Endowment For the Arts
Research Division
1100 Pennsylvania Avenue NW
Washington, DC 20506
202/682-5400
   weekdays: 9 A.M.–5:30 P.M. EST
Program specialists can help with questions on dance, design arts, expansion arts, folk arts, interarts, literature, media arts, museums, and visual arts. They can also provide information about grants. Division does research on artists, art organizations, and audiences.

AUTOMOBILES—MAINTENANCE AND REPAIR

Center for Auto Safety
2001 S Street NW, Suite 410
Washington, DC 20009
202/328-7700
   weekdays: 9 A.M.–5:30 P.M. EST
Answers inquiries on design and defects of new cars and legal rights of owners of defective cars.

Insurance Institute for Highway Safety
Communications Department
1005 North Glebe Road, Suite 800
Arlington, VA 22201
703/247-1500
   weekdays: 9 A.M.–4:45 P.M. EST
Answers questions about the crashworthiness of almost any model car, theft histories, and performance statistics.

National Safety Council
444 North Michigan Avenue
Chicago, IL 60611
312/527-4800, ext. 8706
   weekdays: 8:30 A.M.–4:45 P.M. CST
Provides information on seat-belt use for children, state laws affecting drivers and children, and current research.

AUTOMOBILES—TIRES

Tire Industry Safety Council
529 Fourteenth Street NW, Suite 844
Washington, DC 20045
202/783-1022
   weekdays: 8:30 A.M.–5 P.M. EST
Will answer questions about any aspect of tires and tire safety, such as tire rotation, how to buy tires, sizes, side-walls, and proper inflation pressure. Has instructions on how to diagnose tire problems and information on tire history.

AVIATION. *See* AERONAUTICS.

B

BANKING. *See* FINANCE.

BASEBALL

National Baseball Hall of Fame
P.O. Box 590
Cooperstown, NY 13326
607/547-9988
   weekdays: 9 A.M.–5 P.M. EST November–April;
   9 A.M.–9 P.M. EST May–October
Answers general questions about the history, the players, or the game of baseball.

BASKETBALL

Hickox Library
1150 West Columbus Avenue
P.O. Box 179
Springfield, MA 01101-0179
413/781-6500
   weekdays: 9 A.M.–5 P.M. EST
Questions about basketball can be answered over the phone. Visits to the collection are by appointment only.

National Basketball Associations
645 Fifth Avenue
New York, NY 10022
212/826-7000

weekdays: 9 A.M.–5 P.M. EST
Answers questions on NBA players, schedules, games, and rules and regulations.

BEVERAGES—ALCOHOLIC. *See* WINES AND SPIRITS.

BIRDS

National Audubon Society
Information Services Department
950 Third Avenue
New York, NY 10022
212/832-3200
weekdays: 10 A.M.–4 P.M. EST
Answers general questions about birds and bird clubs, conservation of natural resources, and natural history.

BIRTH DEFECTS

National Network to Prevent Birth Defects
National Coalition Against the Misuse of
Pesticides
701 E Street SE, Suite 200
Washington, DC 20003
202/543-5450
weekdays: 9 A.M.–5 P.M. EST
These two nonprofit organizations share the same office and share information. They can answer many questions about toxic chemicals, birth defects, and pesticides.

Spina Bifida Information and Referral
1700 Rockville Pike, Suite 250
Rockville, MD 20852
800/621-3141
weekdays: 9 A.M.–5 P.M. EST
Provides general information to consumers and parents on this birth defect of the spine.

BLINDNESS

RP Foundation Fighting Blindness
1401 Mt. Royal Avenue, Fourth Floor
Baltimore, MD 21217
800/638-2300
TDD: 301/225-9409
weekdays: 8:30 A.M.–5 P.M. EST
Part of National Retinitis Pigmentosa Foundation. Answers questions about genetics of eye diseases, current research, and retina-donor programs.

BLOOD. *See also* HEMOPHILIA.

The National Heart, Lung and Blood Institute
Education Programs Information Center

4733 Bethesda Avenue, Suite 530
Bethesda, MD 20814-4820
301/496-4236
weekdays: 8:30 A.M.–5 P.M. EST
Answers calls regarding high blood pressure, high cholesterol, smoking, asthma, and blood resources. Will provide pamphlet by mail.

BOATING

Boating Safety Hotline
Office of Boating, Public, and Consumer Affairs
U.S. Coast Guard Office, G-NAB-5
2100 2nd Street SW
Washington, DC 20593-0001
800/368-5647
In Washington, DC: 202/267-0780
weekdays: 8 A.M.–4 P.M. EST
Provides safety information on any recreational craft regulated as a boat. Staff also takes complaints and reports on possible safety defects, assists consumers who are having difficulty getting action or recalls, and provides literature.

BONDS. *See* INVESTMENTS.

BOWLING

Professional Bowlers Association of America
1720 Merriman Road, P.O. Box 5118
Akron, OH 44334-0118
216/836-5568
weekdays: 8:30 A.M.–5:30 P.M. EST
Answers questions on how to become a PBA member, PBA tours, scores of professional tournaments, and general questions on bowling.

BOXING

International Boxing Hall of Fame
1 Hall of Fame Drive
Canastota, NY 13032
315/697-7095
7 days a week: 10 A.M.–5 P.M. EST, answering machine
Answers questions on fighters, records, and dates of fights; provides statistical information on major boxing matches and boxers.

BUSINESS. *See also* EMPLOYEE ASSISTANCE; FINANCE; FRANCHISING.

U.S. Department of Commerce
Office of Business Liaison
Fourteenth Street and Constitution Avenue NW,
Room 5898C

Washington, DC 20230
202/377-3176
  weekdays: 8:00 A.M.–5 P.M. EST
Offers information on various federal policies and
programs of interest to business people.

U.S. International Trade Commission (ITC)
500 E Street SW
Washington, DC 20436
800/343-9822
In Washington, DC: 202/252-2200
  weekdays: 8:45 A.M.–5:15 P.M. EST
The ITC has volumes of information on domestic
production and consumption and has publications
on various commodities. They can also provide
information to business people who are having
problems.

C

CANCER

AMC Cancer Research Center
1600 Pierce Street
Denver, CO 80214
800/525-3777
303/233-6501
  weekdays: 8:00 A.M.–5 P.M. MST
Provides latest information on cancer causes, prevention, and methods of detection and diagnosis,
as well as counseling.

National Cancer Institute
Cancer Information Service
Bethesda, MD 20892
800/4-CANCER (422-6237)
  Monday–Friday: 9 A.M.–10 P.M. (all time zones)
  Saturday: 10 A.M.–6 P.M. (all time zones)
Staff will provide you with information about treat-
ment options, prevention, and coping strategies.
Publications are available (free), as are referrals to
counseling centers.

CARS. *See* AUTOMOBILES.

CEMETERIES. *See* FUNERALS.

CEREBRAL PALSY

United Cerebral Palsy Association, Inc.
7 Penn Plaza
Suite 804
New York, NY 10001

800/872-5827
In New York City: 212/268-6655
  weekdays: 9 A.M.–5 P.M. EST
Provides information about cerebral palsy and guidance programs for cerebral palsy sufferers.

CHILD ABUSE. *See also* DOMESTIC VIOLENCE.

American Bar Association
National Resource Center for Children and the Law
1800 M Street NW, Suite S-300
Washington, DC 20036
202/331-2250
  weekdays: 8 A.M.–5 P.M. EST
Provides legal advice about child abuse.

Childhelp USA IOF Hotline
P.O. Box 630
Hollywood, CA 90028
800/4 A CHILD (422-4453)
  24 hours a day
Because responsibility for investigating reports of
suspected child abuse and neglect rests at the
state level, each state has established a child-
protective-services reporting system. Call the national number above for the telephone number in
your state. Hotline is also a resource for literature
and crisis counseling.

Illusion Theater
528 Hennepin Avenue, Suite 704
Minneapolis, MN 55403
612/339-4944
  weekdays: 8:30 A.M.–5 P.M. CST
A preventive organization that educates and refers, but does not counsel. National touring theater company promotes healthy sexuality through
prevention of sexual abuse, interpersonal violence,
and AIDS. Provides publications.

National Center for Missing and Exploited
Children
2101 Wilson Boulevard
Suite 550
Arlington, VA 22201
800/843-5678
In Virginia: 703/235-3900
  24 hours a day
National clearing center for information on and
reporting of child abuse and missing children.
Also has information on exploitation of minors.

National Child Abuse Hotline
Child-Help, USA

64-63 Independence Avenue
Woodland Hills, CA 91367
800/422-4453
    24 hours a day
Provides adults and children with information and counseling on physical, sexual, or emotional abuse.

National Committee for the Prevention of Child Abuse
332 South Michigan Avenue, Suite 1600
Chicago IL 60604
312/663-3520
    weekdays: 9 A.M.–5 P.M. CST
Publishes some 60 pamphlets for parents and professionals. Maintains a national chapter network dedicated to the prevention of child abuse.

CHILDBIRTH. *See also* BIRTH DEFECTS; FAMILY PLANNING.

American Society for Psychoprophylaxis in Obstetrics, Inc.
(ASPO/LAMAZE)
1101 Connecticut Avenue NW, Suite 700
Washington, DC 20036
800/368-4404
In Washington, DC: 202/857-1128
    weekdays: 9 A.M.–5 P.M. EST
Call the above toll-free number for the phone number of the nearest Lamaze instructor. He or she will be able to answer your questions concerning the method.

Cesareans/Support, Education and Concern (C/SEC)
22 Forest Road
Framingham, MA 01701
508/877-8266
    weekdays: 9 A.M.–5 P.M. EST, answering machine
Informs people about cesareans and their prevention.

CHILD CARE

La Leche League International
9616 Minneapolis Avenue
Franklin Park, IL 60131
708/455-7730
    24 hours a day
Provides information about breastfeeding.

Totline
Raritan Bay Mental Health Center
570 Lee Street
Perth Amboy, NJ 08861

201/442-1666, ask for Children's Unit
    Monday–Thursday: 8:30 A.M.–8:30 P.M. EST
    Friday–8:30 A.M.–4:15 P.M. EST
Therapists answer questions about children 18 years or younger.

CHILDREN—FOSTER CARE

Child Welfare Institute
1365 Peachtree Street, Suite 700
Atlanta, GA 30309
404/876-1934
    8:30 A.M.–5 P.M. EST
Provides information and advice about foster care, adoption, and child abuse.

CIVIL RIGHTS. *See* DISCRIMINATION.

CLOTHING AND TEXTILES.

American Apparel Manufacturers Association
2500 Wilson Boulevard, Suite 301
Arlington, VA 22201
703/524-1864
    weekdays: 9 A.M.–5 P.M. EST
Answers questions about the care, handling, fit, sizing, content, country of origin, and performance record of various kinds of apparel. Also has economic and technical information.

COMPUTERS

3M Data Storage Products Hotline
P.O. Box 709
Weatherford, OK 73096
800/328-9438
    weekdays: 7 A.M.–7 P.M. CST
Answers questions about proper use of diskettes—not just 3M products.

CONSUMER PROTECTION

Federal Trade Commission
Public Reference Section
Pennsylvania Avenue at Sixth Street NW
Washington, DC 20580
202/326-2222
    weekdays: 9 A.M.–5 P.M. EST
Provides information and advice regarding consumer problems and complaints, especially in areas such as deceptive advertising, unordered merchandise, and franchise and credit problems.

COOKING. *See* FOOD AND NUTRITION.

COPYRIGHT

Library of Congress
Copyright Public Information Office
101 Independence Avenue SE
Washington, DC 20559
202/479-0700
    weekdays: 8:30 A.M.–5 P.M.EST
Will provide information about copyright law and about the procedures for registering and securing copyrights. If you need to order forms and know their numbers, dial the copyright forms hotline ordering number (202/707-9100) and follow the instructions for placing your order. Forms hotline operates 24 hours a day.

COSMETICS

Food and Drug Administration
Office of Consumer Affairs, HFE-88
5600 Fishers Lane
Rockville, MD 20857
301/443-3170
    weekdays: 8 A.M.–4:30 P.M. EST
Provides information on those cosmetics regulated by the FDA.

CRAFTS

American Craft Council
72 Spring Street
New York, NY 10012
212/274-0630
    Tuesday–Friday: 1 P.M.–5 P.M. EST
Answers inquiries on all aspects of contemporary (post-World War II) American crafts.

CREDIT UNIONS

National Credit Union Administration
1776 G Street NW
Washington, DC 20456
202/682-9600
    weekdays: 9 A.M.–5 P.M. EST
Provides information on what credit unions are, how to find one, and how to organize one.

CULTS

Cult Awareness Network
2421 West Pratt Boulevard, Suite 1173
Chicago, IL 60645
312/267-7777
    weekdays: 9 A.M.–5 P.M. CST
Offers information, counsel, and a national refer-

ral network for concerned families of those in destructive cults.

Fundamentalists Anonymous
P.O. Box 20324
Greeley Square Station
New York, NY 10001
212/696-0420
    weekdays: 10 A.M.–6 P.M. EST, answering machine
Operating from a belief that fundamentalism can pose a mental health hazard due to strict regimentation of members' lives and extreme authoritarian leadership, this group offers support to those injured by the fundamentalist experience. The organization also has information about nearby support groups.

D

DEAFNESS. *See* HEARING AND SPEECH IMPAIRMENT.

DEATH. *See also* FUNERALS.

National Hospice Organization Hotline
1901 North Moore Street, Suite 901
Arlington, VA 22209
800/658-8898
    weekdays: 9 A.M.–5:30 P.M. EST
Provides information on hospices and hospice programs around the country.

Parents of Murdered Children
100 East Eighth Street, Suite B41
Cincinnati, OH 45202
513/721-5683
    24 hours a day
Self-help organization that provides support for families and others cruelly bereaved. Staff will work with professionals in law, mental health, social work, medicine, education, religion, and mortuary service.

DEMOGRAPHICS

Population Institute
110 Maryland Avenue NE, Suite 207
Washington, DC 20002
202/544-3300
    weekdays: 9:30 A.M.–5:30 P.M. EST
Answers questions dealing with international overpopulation and the balance between population growth, environment, and resources. Can

also answer questions regarding education on population.

DENTISTRY

National Institute of Dental Research
Building 31, Room 2C-35
9000 Rockville Pike
Bethesda, MD 20892
301/496-4261
   weekdays: 8:30 A.M.–5 P.M. EST
As a research organization, provides information about the latest dental problems and research.

DIABETES

American Diabetes Association
National Service Center
1660 Duke Street
Alexandria, VA 22314
800/232-3472
In Virginia: 703/549-1500
   weekdays: 8:30 A.M.–5 P.M. EST
Provides information on diabetes, its symptoms, and possible treatment. Can direct callers to state affiliates.

**Juvenile Diabetes Foundation
International Hotline**
432 Park Avenue South
New York, NY 10016
800/223-1138
In New York City: 212/889-7575
   weekdays: 8:30 A.M.–5:30 P.M. EST
Answers questions on juvenile diabetes; provides referrals to physicians and clinics.

DIETHYLSTILBESTROL (DES) EXPOSURE

DES Action USA (East Coast)
Long Island Jewish Medical Center
New Hyde Park, NY 11040
516/775-3450
   Tuesdays and Thursdays: 9 A.M.–2 P.M. EST

DES Action USA (West Coast)
1615 Broadway, Suite 510
Oakland, CA 94612
415/465-4011
   Wednesdays: 10 A.M.–4 P.M. PST
Nonprofit consumer group dedicated to informing the public and health officials about the effects of DES exposure. Recommends physicians, support groups, and screening centers, in addition to providing information about the known

effects of DES in children and grandchildren of mothers who have taken the drug during pregnancy.

DIETS. *See* FOOD AND FOOD PREPARATION; NUTRITION.

DISABILITIES

The Orton Dyslexia Society
724 York Road
Baltimore, MD 21204
800/ABCD123 (222-3123)
In Maryland: 301/296-0232
   9 A.M.–5 P.M. EST
Answers questions about dyslexia and provides referrals.

**Educational Testing Service
A.T.P. Services for Handicapped Students**
P.O. Box 6226
Princeton, NJ 08541-6226
609/771-7137
TDD: 609/771-7150
   weekdays: 8 A.M.–4 P.M. EST; after 4 P.M. calls
   are transferred to California for assistance.
Provides information for handicapped high school students about preparing for SAT and achievement tests.

Job Accommodation Network
West Virginia University
809 Allen Hall
P.O. Box 6123
Morgantown, WV 26506-6123
800/526-7234
In West Virginia: 800/526-4698
In Canada: 800/526-2262
   Monday–Thursday: 8 A.M.–8 P.M. EST
   Friday: 8 A.M.–5 P.M.
Not an employment agency. Network provides employers, schools, and governments with ideas for accommodating handicapped people.

Mainstream, Inc.
1030 Fifteenth Street NW, Suite 1010
Washington, DC 20005
202/898-0202
   weekdays: 9 A.M.–5 P.M. EST
For disabled consumers who would like tips on resume writing, the job search, and legal services.

National Center for Learning Disabilities
99 Park Avenue, Sixth Floor
New York, NY 10016
212/687-7211

weekdays: 9 A.M.–5 P.M. EST
Answers questions on learning disabilities and where to get diagnostic testing done. Provides referrals to support groups and specialized organizations and information on higher education or high school equivalency. Pamphlets available and can send information on children's rights.

National Information Center for Children and Youth with Disabilities
P.O. Box 1492
Washington, DC 20013
800/999-5599
   weekdays: 9 A.M.–5:30 P.M. EST
Answers questions on all issues regarding children and young people with disabilities.

TASH Inc.
70 Gibson Drive
Unit 12
Markham, Ontario
Canada
416/475-2212
   weekdays: 8:30 A.M.–4:30 P.M. EST
A nonprofit corporation owned by voluntary organizations that manufacture and market electronic equipment for severely handicapped individuals; provides information about this equipment.

DISCRIMINATION

Department of Education
Office of Civil Rights
330 C Street SW, Suite 5000
Washington, DC 20202
202/732-1213
   weekdays: 8:30 A.M.–5 P.M. EST
Answers questions regarding discrimination against women in schools or educational programs. Also provides referrals to regional offices around the country.

NAACP Legal Defense and Educational Fund, Inc.
99 Hudson Street, Sixteenth Floor
New York, NY 10013
212/219-1900
   weekdays: 9 A.M.–5 P.M. EST
If you feel you have been discriminated against due to your race or nationality, the NAACP Legal Defense and Educational Fund can give you information and refer you to a lawyer.

Special Counsel for Immigration-Related Unfair Employment Practices
P.O. Box 65490
Washington, DC 20035-5490
800/255-7688
   weekdays: 9 A.M.–5:30 P.M. EST
Provides information about employment discrimination against immigrants.

DOGS. *See* PETS.

DOMESTIC VIOLENCE. *See also* CHILD ABUSE.

Domestic Violence Hotline
P.O. Box 463100
Mt. Clemens, MI 48046
800/333-SAFE (333-7233)
   24 hours a day
Each state, Puerto Rico, and the Virgin Islands has a local crisis center. Call above number to obtain the location of the nearest crisis center.

National Child Abuse Hotline
Child-Help, USA
64-63 Independence Avenue

Woodland Hills, CA 91367
800/422-4453
   24 hours a day
Provides adults and children with information and counseling on physical, sexual, or emotional abuse.

Parents Anonymous Hotline
6733 South Sepulveda Boulevard, Suite 270
Los Angeles, CA 90045
800/421-0353
In California: 800/352-0386
   weekdays: 8:30 A.M.–5 P.M. PST, answering machine after hours
Provides information on self-help groups for parents involved in child abuse or general frustrations with the job of parenting.

DOWN SYNDROME

National Down Syndrome Hotline
National Down Syndrome Society
666 Broadway, Suite 810
New York, NY 10012
800/221-4602
In New York City: 212/460-9330
   weekdays: 9 A.M.–5 P.M. EST
Provides general information on Down syndrome and referrals.

DRUG ABUSE. *See also* ALCOHOLISM.

Alcohol and Drug Problems Association of North America
1400 I Street NW, Suite 1275
Washington, DC 20005
202/289-6755
  weekdays: 8 A.M.–4 P.M. EST
Answers questions on legislation, public policy, and issues in the field of drug and alcohol abuse.

American Council for Drug Education
204 Monroe Street, Suite 110
Rockville, MD 20850
800/488-DRUG (488-3784)
In Maryland: 301/294-0600
  weekdays: 9 A.M.–5 P.M. EST
Answers general questions on drug education and prevention services. Also provides pamphlets.

Association of Halfway House Alcoholism Programs of North America, Inc.
786 East Seventh Street
St. Paul, MN 55106
612/771-0933
  weekdays: 10 A.M.–4 P.M. CST
Provides referrals to halfway houses throughout the country for recovery from alcoholism and other drug abuse. Publishes a newsletter.

Families Anonymous
P.O. Box 528
Van Nuys, CA 91408
818/989-7841
  weekdays: 9 A.M.–4 P.M. PST; answering service after office hours
Will refer friends and families of people with drug, alcohol, or behavioral problems to local support groups around the country.

Narcotics Anonymous
World Service Office
P.O. Box 9999
Van Nuys, CA 91409
818/780-3951
  weekdays: 8 A.M.–5 P.M. PST
Provides information on Narcotics Anonymous and on where to find local chapters throughout the country. Pamphlets also available.

National Association on Drug Abuse Problems, Inc.
355 Lexington Avenue
New York, NY 10017
212/986-1170
  weekdays: 9 A.M.–5 P.M. EST
Answers drug-, alcohol-, and AIDS-related questions and performs research. Conducts and provides referrals to vocational rehabilitation programs following treatment. Provides referrals to programs and treatment centers. Also answers questions on AIDS that are drug-related. Pamphlets are available.

National Clearinghouse for Alcohol and Drug Information
P.O. Box 2345
Rockville, MD 20852
800/729-6686
In Maryland: 301/468-2600
  weekdays: 9 A.M.–7 P.M. EST
Provides general information on alcohol and other drug-related problems. Will send literature and search for and provide publications on alcohol and drug topics.

National Cocaine Hotline
National Drug Abuse Treatment Referral and Information Service
P.O. Box 100
Springfield Avenue
Summit, NJ 07902-0100
800/COCAINE (262-2463)
  24 hours a day
Provides information on cocaine abuse and its symptoms and is a source of referral information for counselors and treatment centers.

National Institute on Drug Abuse
5600 Fishers Lane, Room 10A-54
Rockville, MD 20857
301/443-6245
Workplace hotline: 800/843-4971—answers calls for employers who are implementing drug-free workplace programs
  weekdays: 9 A.M.–8 P.M. EST
National Hotline for Drug Users: 800/662-HELP (662-4357) — answers calls for information on drug abuse
  weekdays: 9 A.M.–3 P.M. EST
  Saturday and Sunday: 12 P.M.–3 P.M. EST

National Parents' Resources Institute for Drug Education (PRIDE)
50 Hurt Plaza, Suite 210
Atlanta, GA 30303
900/988-7743
In Atlanta: 404/577-4500
  weekdays: 9 A.M.–5 P.M. EST

Provides information on prevention through education of all age groups.

DRUGS AND MEDICINE

Food and Drug Administration
(CDER Executive Secretariat)
HFD 8
5600 Fishers Lane
Rockville, MD 20857
301/295-8012
> weekdays: 8 A.M.–4:30 P.M. EST

Provides information on prescription and over-the-counter drugs, side effects, labeling requirements, and drug problems.

Johnson & Johnson Information Center
199 Grandview Road
Skillman, NJ 08558
800/526-3967
> weekdays: 8 A.M.–6 P.M. EST

Information center answers questions regarding Johnson & Johnson products and such subjects as skin and sun care, child care, wound management/first aid, consumer dental care, and feminine hygiene/menstruation.

National Association of Retail Druggists
205 Daingerfield Road
Alexandria, VA 22314
703/683-8200
> weekdays: 9 A.M.–5 P.M. EST

Provides information on prescription drugs, drug labels, package inserts, and effective storage measures.

DYSLEXIA. *See* DISABILITIES.

E

ECOLOGY

Center for Environmental Information
46 Prince Street
Rochester, NY 14607
716/271-3550
> weekdays: 9 A.M.–4:30 P.M. EST

Clearinghouse with specialists versed in all aspects of acid rain, including atmospheric sciences, environmental aspects, social aspects, and engineering.

Citizens' Clearinghouse for Hazardous Wastes, Inc.
P.O. Box 6806
Falls Church, VA 22040

703/237-2249
> weekdays: 9 A.M.–5 P.M. EST

Answers questions about hazardous waste, polluters, solid waste, recycling, water testing, medical waste, landfills, and organization information.

Environmental Protection Agency
Public Information Center
401 M Street SW
Washington, DC 20460
202/382-2080
> weekdays: 8 A.M.–5:30 P.M. EST

If the information center cannot answer your question, your call will be transferred to the appropriate desk. Subjects: air and radiation, pesticides, toxic substances, acid deposits, environmental monitoring and quality assurance, solid waste and emergency response, water, and noise control.

TSCA Hotline
Office of Toxic Substances, TS-799
U.S. Environmental Protection Agency
401 M Street SW
Washington, DC 20460
202/554-1404
> weekdays: 8:30 A.M.–5 P.M. EST

Provides general and technical information on the Toxic Substances Control Act to the chemical industry, labor and trade organizations, schools, and general public. Answers questions about asbestos and toxic substances. Call the number above to obtain the number for the regional office of the U.S. Environmental Protection Agency, which may be in a better position to answer your questions.

EDUCATIONAL FILMS

American Film and Video Association
920 Barnsdale Road, Suite 152
La Grange Park, IL 60525
708/482-4000
> weekdays: 8 A.M.–5 P.M. CST

Answers questions from the general public on a one-time basis about educational films and documentaries and how to obtain them.

ELECTIONS

Federal Election Commission
999 E Street NW
Washington, DC 20463
800/424-9530
> weekdays: 8:30 A.M.–5 P.M. EST

Provides information on election laws and campaign financing.

EMPLOYEE ASSISTANCE

Employee Assistance Professionals Association (EAPA)
4601 North Fairfax Drive
Suite 1001
Arlington, VA 22203
703/522-6272
  weekdays: 9 A.M.–5 P.M. EST
Assists employers and employees with programs that will help employees with drug, mental, or health problems with the goal of assisting employers to increase productivity. EAPA can provide medical and treatment referrals and establish programs to smooth out problems in the workplace. Information available to the general public.

ENERGY AND POWER GENERATION

Department of Energy
NATAS (National Appropriate Technology Assistance Service)
P.O. Box 2525
Butte, MT 59702-2525
800/428-2525
In Montana: 800/428-1718
  weekdays: 8 A.M.–5 P.M. MST
Answers specific questions about implementing energy conservation and renewable energy projects.

ENTOMOLOGY

American Museum of Natural History
Department of Entomology
Central Park West and Seventy-ninth Street
New York, NY 10024
212/769-5613
  weekdays: 9 A.M.–5 P.M. EST
Experts in entomology will answer questions about ants, flies, spiders, and other insects.

ENVIRONMENT. *See* ECOLOGY.

EPILEPSY

Epilepsy Foundation of America
4351 Garden City Drive
Landover, MD 20785
800/EFA-1000 (332-1000)
  weekdays: 9 A.M.–5 P.M. EST
Provides information, referrals, and counseling on epilepsy.

F

FAMILY PLANNING

National Abortion Federation
NAF Consumer Hotline
1436 U Street NW, Suite 103
Washington, DC 20009
800/772-9100
  weekdays: 9:30 A.M.–5:30 P.M. EST
Answers questions on pregnancy, abortion, clinics, costs, Medicaid coverage, and parental and spousal consent. Booklets are also available.

Planned Parenthood Federation of America, Inc.
810 Seventh Avenue
New York, NY 10019
800/829-PPFA (829-7732)
In New York City: 212/541-7800
  weekdays: 9 A.M.–5 P.M. EST
No advice. Provides information only on family planning, sexuality, and contraception.

FEDERAL GOVERNMENT

Federal Information Center
P.O. Box 600
Cumberland, MD 21501-0600
800/347-1997
TDD:800/326-2996
  weekdays 9 A.M.–4 P.M. EST; also available until 10:30 P.M. for calls from West Coast, Alaska, and Hawaii
Provides information on all activities and agencies of the federal government. If the query cannot be answered immediately by operators accessing the databases at the Center, they will call you back. The 800 toll-free operation is new in 1990; it replaces a network of regional centers located throughout the country. The new system handles about 10,000 calls per day.

FINANCE. *See also* PERSONAL FINANCE.

Federal Deposit Insurance Corporation Hotline
550 Seventeenth Street NW
Washington, DC 20429
800/424-5488
202/898-3536
weekdays: 9 A.M.–4 P.M. EST
Provides general banking information on consumer banking laws.

Financial Women International
500 N. Michigan Avenue
Suite 1400
Chicago, IL 60611
312/661-1700, ext. 738
    Monday–Thursday: 8:30 A.M.–5:30 P.M. CST
    Friday: 8:30 A.M.–5 P.M. CST
Devoted to the professional interests and advancement of women in the financial services industry. FWI welcomes calls from anyone interested in banking or in need of information on educational programs, career development, management skills, or statistics.

U.S. Securities and Exchange Commission
Public Reference Branch
450 Fifth Street NW, Room 1024
Washington, DC 20549
202/272-7450
    weekdays: 9 A.M.–5 P.M. EST
Provides information on filing by publicly traded companies, information on registration statements, and registering as investment advisors or broker/dealers.

FISHING

The American Museum of Fly Fishing Library
P.O. Box 42
Manchester, VT 05254
802/362-3300
    weekdays: 9 A.M.–5 P.M. EST
Provides answers to questions about fly fishing and its history, as well as fish lore and angling in general.

FOOD AND NUTRITION

The Butterball Turkey Talk-line
Swift-Eckrich, Inc.
1919 Swift Drive
Oak Brook, IL 60522
800/323-4848
    October 29–December 31 only
Will advise on buying, basting, stuffing, carving, and storing any kind of turkey, goose, chicken, or Cornish hen.

Cookware Manufacturers Association
P.O. Box 1177
Lake Geneva, WI 53147
414/248-9208
    weekdays: 8 A.M.–4:30 P.M. CST
Answers general questions about qualities, prop-

erties, and uses of both metal and nonmetal cooking utensils. Also advises on care of such utensils.

Food and Drug Administration
Office of Consumer Inquiries, HFE-88
5600 Fishers Lane, Room 1663
Rockville, MD 20857
301/443-3170
    weekdays: 8 A.M.–4:30 P.M. EST
Provides information on foods.

National Peanut Council
1500 King Street, Suite 301
Alexandria, VA 22314
703/838-9500
    weekdays: 9 A.M.–5 P.M. EST
Provides information on consumption, nutritional value, and economic value of peanuts.

North American Vegetarian Society
P.O. Box 72
Dolgeville, NY 13329
518/568-7970
    weekdays: 9 A.M.–5 P.M. EST
Provides information on vegetarianism and healthy diets.

Nutrition Information Center
New York Hospital—Cornell Medical Center
Memorial Sloan-Kettering Cancer Center
515 East Seventy-first Street
Room S-904
New York, NY 10021
212/746-1617
    weekdays: 9 A.M.–5 P.M. EST
Designed to serve as a resource in clinical nutrition, nutrition research, and general nutrition. Can provide referrals.

Sugar Association
1101 Fifteenth Street NW, Suite 600
Washington, DC 20005
202/785-1122
    weekdays: 9 A.M.–5 P.M. EST
Provides information on sugar and cooking.

United Fresh Fruit and Vegetable Association
727 North Washington Street
Alexandria, VA 22314
800/336-3065
703/836-3410
    weekdays: 8:30 A.M.–5:30 P.M. EST
Provides information on the nutritional value and seasonal buying of fruits and vegetables.

U.S. Department of Agriculture
Meat and Poultry Hotline
South Building, Room 1165
Washington, DC 20250
800/535-4555
In Washington, DC: 202/447-3333
    weekdays: 10 A.M.–4 P.M. EST, except week-
    days in November: 9 A.M.–5 P.M. EST
Answers questions about safe handling of meat,
poultry, and eggs, their wholesomeness and stor-
age, and labeling.

FOOTBALL

National Football Foundation and College Hall
of Fame
Bell Tower Building
1865 Palmer Avenue
Larchmont, NY 10538
914/834-0474
    weekdays: 8 A.M.–5 P.M. EST
Answers historical questions on college football
Hall of Fame inductees and provides information
on memberships and nominations of players and
coaches to the Hall of Fame.

National Football League
410 Park Avenue
New York, NY 10022
212/758-1500
    weekdays: 8:30 A.M.–7 P.M. EST
Public relations office will answer general questions on football and provide football rules. Provides team phone numbers and addresses, history
of current or former players, and information on
Super Bowls and Pro Bowls.

Pro Football Hall of Fame Library and Research
Center
2121 George Halas Drive NW
Canton, OH 44708
216/456-8207
    7 days a week: 9 A.M.–5 P.M. EST, except Me-
    morial Day through Labor Day: 9 A.M.–8 P.M.
Research center provides information on professional football.

FOSTER CARE. *See* CHILDREN—FOSTER CARE.

FRANCHISING

International Franchise Association
1350 New York Avenue NW, Suite 900
Washington, DC 20005
202/628-8000

weekdays: 8:30 A.M.–5:30 P.M. EST
Supplies information on how to evaluate a franchise opportunity.

FUNERALS

Cemetery Consumer Service Council (CCSC)
P.O. Box 3574
Washington, DC 20007
703/379-6426
    Weekdays: 9 A.M.–5:30 P.M. EST
Provides information and can assist in disputes
between consumers and cemeteries.

Funeral Service Consumer Assistance Program
(FSCAP)
2250 East Devon Avenue, Suite 250
Des Plaines, IL 60018
800/662-7666
    Weekdays: 9 A.M.–4:30 P.M. CST
Provides facts and figures, and will also mediate
if disputes develop and provide binding arbitration if necessary. Also provides statistics.

G

GAMBLING

Gamblers Anonymous International Service Office
P.O. Box 17173
Los Angeles, CA 90017
213/386-8789
    weekdays: 7 A.M.–4 P.M. PST
Provides literature on how to recover from gam-
bling compulsion.

National Council on Problem Gambling
445 West Fifty-ninth Street, Room 1521
New York, NY 10019
800/522-4700
In New York City: 212/765-3833
    weekdays: 9 A.M.–5 P.M. EST
Provides general information about compulsive
gambling and bibliography of most recent studies
on gambling and its effects. Also provides referrals.

GARDENING. *See* HORTICULTURE.

GENERAL TELEPHONE SOURCES

Boston Public Library
666 Boylston Street
Boston, MA 02117
617/536-5400

Monday–Thursday: 9 A.M.–9 P.M. EST
Friday–Saturday: 9 A.M.–5 P.M. EST

An operator will direct you to the desk that answers questions about the subject of your inquiry.

Brooklyn Public Library
Central Library, Telephone Reference
Grand Army Plaza
Brooklyn, NY 11238
718/780-7700
Tuesday–Thursday: 9 A.M.–8 P.M. EST
Friday–Saturday: 10 A.M.–6 P.M. EST
Sunday: 1 P.M.–5 P.M. EST (closed June 9 to September)

Provides telephone information on a variety of subjects. Particular strengths includes their archival and nonarchival collection of information on Brooklyn.

Chicago Public Library
400 North Franklin
Chicago, IL 60610
312/269-2800
Monday–Thursday: 9 A.M.–7 P.M. CST
Friday: 9A.M.–6 P.M. CST
Saturday: 9 A.M.–5 P.M. CST

The operator will direct you to the desk that answers questions about the subject of your inquiry.

Detroit Public Library
5201 Woodward Avenue
Detroit, MI 48202
313/833-1010 and 313-833-4000
Tuesday and Saturday: 9:30 A.M.–5:30 P.M. CST
Wednesday: 1 A.M.–9 P.M. CST

The operator will direct you to the desk that answers questions about the subject of your inquiry.

Library of Congress
General Reference
10 First Street SE, Room LJ 122
Washington, DC 20540
202/707-5522
weekdays: 8:30 A.M.–5 P.M. EST

The Library of Congress is primarily devoted to answering the reference questions of Congress, foreign embassies, and the press. The General Reference number provides the general public with information on the collection and services of the Library of Congress only.

Los Angeles Public Library
Central Library
433 South Spring Street

Los Angeles, CA 90013
213/612-3200
Monday–Thursday: 10 A.M.–8 P.M. PST
Friday–Saturday: 10 A.M.–5:30 P.M. PST

The operator will direct you to the desk that answers questions about the subject of your inquiry.

The New York Public Library
Telephone Reference Service
Mid-Manhattan Library
455 Fifth Avenue
New York, NY 10016
212/340-0849
Monday–Friday: 9 A.M.–6 P.M. EST
Saturday:9:30 A.M.–5:30 P.M. EST

Answers questions on all but the most esoteric subjects quickly and authoritatively. If these telephone reference experts cannot answer your question right away, they will direct you to the appropriate divisions of the New York Public Library.

Queens Public Library
89-11 Merrick Boulevard
Jamaica, NY 11432
718/990-0714
Monday–Friday: 10 A.M.–9 P.M. EST
Saturday: 10 A.M.–5:30 P.M. EST
Sunday: 12 P.M.–5 P.M. EST (closed mid-May to September)

Provides telephone information service on many topics. Particular strengths include black culture and history (the Carter-Woodson Collection) and information about Long Island.

GEOGRAPHY

National Geographic Society Library
Seventeenth and M Streets NW
Washington, DC 20036
202/857-7783 for general information
202/857-7059 for maps
202/775-6175 for magazine index
weekdays: 8:30 A.M.–5 P.M. EST

Large library on geography, natural sciences, travel, exploration, and polar material.

GLAUCOMA

Foundation for Glaucoma Research
490 Post Street, Suite 830
San Francisco, CA 94102
415/986-3162
weekdays: 9 A.M.–5 P.M. PST

The executive director, educational director, or research director can answer questions about glaucoma.

GOLF

U.S. Golf Association
Liberty Corner Road
Far Hills, NJ 07931
908/234-2300
   weekdays: 8:30 A.M.–5 P.M. EST
The operator will transfer you to the appropriate desk to answer questions on such subjects as the history of golf, its rules, or the state of the art.

GOVERNMENT—FEDERAL. *See* FEDERAL GOVERNMENT.

GOVERNMENT—LOCAL. *See* LOCAL GOVERNMENT.

GRAMMAR AND SPELLING

Grammar Hotline
Tidewater Community College
1700 College Crescent
Virginia Beach, VA 23456
804/427-7170
   weekdays: 10 A.M.–12 P.M. EST; summer hours Monday, Wednesday, and Friday: 8:30 A.M.–10:30 A.M. EST
Sponsored by colleges and universities around the nation, grammar hotlines provide answers to questions about punctuation, spelling, capitalization, grammar, and usage. Office hours vary due to college schedules. There are approximately 30 such hotlines. Call the number above, the headquarters, for the hotline number nearest you.

GROWTH—HUMAN

Human Growth Foundation
7777 Leesburg Pike, Suite 202 South
Falls Church, VA 22043
800/451-6434
In Virginia: 703/883-1773
   weekdays: 8:30 A.M.–5 P.M. EST
Provides information about growth problems.

H

HAIR

Clairol Hotline
Clairol, Inc.

345 Park Avenue
New York, NY 10154
800/223-5800 and 800/252-4765
   weekdays: 8:30 A.M.–8 P.M. EST
Answers hair-care product questions and gives advice on hair care, hair coloring, and remedial measures.

HANDICAPS. *See* DISABILITIES.

HAZARDS. *See also* ECOLOGY.

National Network to Prevent Birth Defects
National Coalition Against the Misuse of Pesticides
701 E Street SE, Suite 200
Washington, DC 20003
202/543-5450
   weekdays: 9 A.M.–5 P.M. EST
These two nonprofit organizations share the same office and share information. They can answer many questions about toxic chemicals, birth defects, and pesticides.

HEARING AND SPEECH IMPAIRMENT. *See also* STUTTERING.

American Speech-Language-Hearing Association
10801 Rockville Pike
Rockville, MD 20852
800/638-8255
In Maryland, Hawaii, and Alaska, and for TDD: 301/897-5700
   weekdays: 8:30 A.M.–4:30 P.M. EST
Provides information on hearing, language, and speech problems.

National Association of the Deaf
814 Thayer Avenue
Silver Spring, MD 20910
301/587-1788
   8:45 A.M.–5 P.M. EST
Provides information on rehabilitation programs, counseling, education, employment, discrimination, and the law. Will also answer questions.

National Hearing Aid Society
Hearing Aid Helpline
20361 Middlebelt Road
Livonia, MI 48152
800/521-5247
In Michigan: 313/478-2610
   weekdays: 9 A.M.–4:30 P.M. EST
Provides information on hearing aids and referrals to hearing specialists, sources of financial assistance, and support groups.

HEMOPHILIA

National Hemophilia Foundation
110 Greene Street, Room 303
New York, NY 10012
212/219-8180
   weekdays: 9 A.M.–5 P.M. EST
Answers calls regarding hemophilia, its diagnosis, and its treatment. Will also provide information on AIDS and hemophilia. Referrals to treatment centers and information on summer camps for kids available.

HERPES

National Herpes Hotline
American Social Health Association
P.O. Box 13827
Research Triangle Park, NC 27709
919/361-8488
   weekdays: 9 A.M.–7 P.M. EST
Provides information on herpes to those infected in childhood and those to whom the disease was transmitted sexually. Makes referrals to support groups.

HIGH BLOOD PRESSURE. *See* HYPERTENSION.

HOCKEY

American Hockey League
425 Union Street
West Springfield, MA 01089
413/781-2030
   weekdays: 9 A.M.–5 P.M. EST
Answers questions about schedules, rules and regulations, and the status of current or former players.

National Hockey League
960 SunLife Building
1155 Metcalfe Street
Montreal, PQ, Canada H3B2W2
514/871-9220
   weekdays: 9 A.M.–5 P.M. EST
Answers general questions about the NHL and its statistics.

U.S. Hockey Hall of Fame
P.O. Box 657
801 Hat Trick Avenue
Eveleth, MN 55734
218/744-5167
   Monday–Saturday: 9 A.M.–5 P.M. CST
   Sunday: 11 A.M.–5 P.M.

Although the Hockey Hall of Fame Library does not have an index system, it does have hundreds of periodicals, programs, press guides, and books. The librarian will be happy to try to answer any question.

HOME BUILDING, MAINTENANCE, AND REPAIR. *See also* APPLIANCES; MOBILE HOMES; WOODWORKING.

Conservation and Renewable Energy Inquiry and Referral Service (CAREIRS)
P.O. Box 8900
Silver Spring, MD 20907
800/523-2929
   weekdays: 9 A.M.–5 P.M. EST
Funded by the U.S. Department of Energy, CAREIRS provides general information on how to make the home more energy efficient. Booklets are available on home heating and lighting, alternate energy sources, insulation, energy-efficient landscaping, and other topics.

Loctite Hotline
Automotive and Consumer Group
4450 Cranwood Court
Cleveland, OH 44128
800/321-9188
In Ohio: 216/475-3600
   weekdays: 8 A.M.–5 P.M. EST
Offers information on products such as chemicals, superglue, epoxies, acrylics, polyesters, and other home-repair products.

Public Service Electric and Gas Company
Energy Conservation Center
80 Park Plaza
Newark, NJ 07101
800/854-4444
   weekdays: 9 A.M.–5 P.M. EST
Provides information on conserving energy, including weatherization services, air-conditioner and furnace efficiency, and rebates. Also upon request will send publications on air-conditioner and heat-pump rebates, loans, and home energy audits.

Shelter Institute
38 Center Street
Bath, ME 04530
207/442-7938
   Monday–Friday: 8 A.M.–4:30 P.M. EST
   Saturday: 9 A.M.–3 P.M. EST

Resource and education center for consumer-built housing engineered for efficiency. The goals of the Institute are to demystify house building and teach everything one needs to know to build a house for one-fourth to one-half the national average cost.

HOMEOPATHY

National Center for Homeopathy
801 North Fairfax Street, Suite 306
Alexandria, VA 22314
703/548-7790
   weekdays: 9 A.M.–5 P.M. EST
Provides information on the medical specialty that treats persons through the use of natural medicines that stimulate one's own healing process.

HORTICULTURE

American Rose Society Library
P.O. Box 30,000
Shreveport, LA 71130-0030
318/938-5402
   weekdays: 8 A.M.–5 P.M. CST, except April–October, 7 days a week: 9 A.M.–6 P.M.
Answers questions relating to roses, rose diseases, and coping strategies (or will provide number of local rosarian who can provide better counsel due to shared climatic problems, at no charge).

New York Botanical Garden
Plant Information Service
Bronx, NY 10458
212/220-8681
   weekdays: 11 A.M.–4 P.M. EST
Horticulturists are on hand to answer questions about indoor and outdoor plants.

Scott Lawn Hotline
Scotts Companies
Marysville, OH 43041
800/543-TURF (543-8873)
   weekdays: 8 A.M.–5 P.M. EST
Answers questions about grass seed, fertilizer, and insect and weed controls. Not limited to Scott lawn products.

HOSPICES. *See* DEATH.

HUMANITIES

National Endowment for the Humanities
Public Affairs Office
1100 Pennsylvania Avenue NW
Washington, DC 20506
202/786-0438
   weekdays: 8:30 A.M.–5 P.M. EST
Provides information on grants for the study of the humanities.

HYPERTENSION

The National Heart, Lung and Blood Institute
Education Programs Information Center
4733 Bethesda Avenue, Suite 530
Bethesda, MD 20814-4820
301/951-3260
   weekdays: 8:30 A.M.–5 P.M. EST
Answers calls regarding high blood pressure, high cholesterol, smoking, asthma, and blood resources. Will provide pamphlet by mail.

I

IMMIGRATION

Contact Center
P.O. Box 81826
Superior Industrial Park
Lincoln, NE 68501
402/464-0602
TDD: 800/552-9097
   weekdays: 6 A.M.–midnight CST
Amnesty Hotline—800/842-2924 links immigrants to certified educational services in communities.
Literacy Hotline—800/228-8813 provides help on reading.

INCONTINENCE

Continence Restored
Dr. E. Douglas Whitehead
785 Park Avenue
New York, NY 10021
212/879-3131
   Monday: 9 A.M.–11 A.M. EST
   Wednesday: 2:30 P.M.–5 P.M.
Private urologist's office that helps men and women with incontinence and/or sexual dysfunction. Has established several groups with professionals and doctors to assist with various problems beyond telephone information.

The Geriatric Division
Department of Medicine of Brigham and Women's Hospital
75 Francis Street

Boston, MA 02115
617/732-6844
 weekdays: 9 A.M.–5 P.M. EST
University-based research center that provides information about incontinence, bladder control, and a wide variety of other medical problems affecting the elderly. Gvies consultations and some referrals.

INSURANCE

Federal Crime Insurance Program
P.O. Box 6301
Rockville, MD 28050
800/638-8780
 weekdays: 8:30 A.M.–5:30 P.M. EST
Will quote cost of crime insurance and areas of the country in which it is available.

National Flood Insurance Program
10101 Senate Drive
Lanham, MD 20706
800/638-6620
 weekdays: 8 A.M.–8 P.M. EST
Provides general information, premium quotations, and directions for finding individual flood zones.

National Insurance Consumer Helpline
American Council of Life Insurance
1001 Pennsylvania Avenue NW
Washington, DC 20004
800/942-4242
In Washington, DC: 202/624-2004
 weekdays: 9 A.M.–5 P.M. EST
Answers questions about life insurance; does not act on complaints. If you have a complaint, contact the insurance department of the state in which the policy was bought.

National Insurance Consumer Helpline
Insurance Information Institute
110 William Street
New York, NY 10038
800/942-4242
In New York City: 212/669-9200
 weekdays: 8 A.M.–8 P.M. EST
Provides information about assessing various types of property and casualty insurance policies and more detailed information about individual policies.

INTERSTITIAL CYSTITIS. *See* URINARY TRACT INFECTIONS.

INVESTMENTS

American Stock Exchange
Rulings Department

86 Trinity Place
New York, NY 10006
212/306-1450
 weekdays: 9 A.M.–5 P.M. EST
Provides general information about the rules, regulations, and interpretation of stock trading at this exchange. For complaints that will be acted upon, contact the Investor Inquiries Office at the address above, telephone 212-306-1452.

Commodity Exchange, Inc. (Comex)
4 World Trade Center, Eighth Floor
New York, NY 10048
212/938-2935
 weekdays: 9 A.M.–5 P.M. EST
Offers current prices on gold, silver, copper, and aluminum as well as futures and options on gold, silver, and copper.

Commodity Futures Trading Commission
Office of Proceedings
2033 K Street NW
Washington, DC 20581
202/254-3067
 weekdays: 8 A.M.–4:45 P.M. EST
Provides histories and background checks of commodities brokerage houses and brokers. Will also accept complaints about brokers.

National Association of Securities Dealers (NASD)
1735 K Street NW
Washington, DC 20006
301/590-6500
 weekdays: 9 A.M.–5 P.M. EST
Call this number to find the proper procedure for filing a complaint about a stockbroker through the NASD.

U.S. Department of the Treasury
Bureau of the Public Debt
P.O. Box 1328
Parkersburg, WV 26106-1328
304/420-6112
 weekdays: 8 A.M.–4 P.M. EST
Provides general information about U.S. savings bonds, their loss, theft, or mutilation, reissuing, redemption, and the going rates.

U.S. Securities and Exchange Commission
Public Reference Branch
450 Fifth Street NW, Room 1024
Washington, DC 20549
202/272-7450

weekdays: 9 A.M.–5 P.M. EST

Provides information on filing by publicly traded companies, on registration statements, and on registering as investment advisors or broker/dealers.

J

JEWELRY

American Gem Society
5901 West Third Street
Los Angeles, CA 90036-2898
213/936-4367
  weekdays: 8:30 A.M.–5 P.M. PST
Advances the jewelry industry and protects the consumer. Will provide local addresses and numbers of qualified gemologists and appraisers.

L

LACTOSE INTOLERANCE

Lactaid Inc.
P.O. Box 111
Pleasantville, NJ 08232
800/LACTAID (522-8243)
  weekdays: 9 A.M.–5 P.M. EST
Gives advice and information about lactose intolerance and the Lactaid product made by this company.

LAW

Gay and Lesbian Advocates and Defenders (GLAD)
P.O. Box 218
Boston, MA 02112
617/426-1350
  weekdays: 9 A.M.–5 P.M. EST
Provides free legal advice to gay men and lesbians. Also makes referrals. The AIDS law project gives legal help to people experiencing discrimination because they are, or are perceived to be, HIV positive.

Legal Services Corporation
400 Virginia Avenue SW
Washington, DC 20024-2751
202/863-1820
  weekdays: 9 A.M.–5:30 P.M. EST

Created by Congress, the Legal Services Corporation helps provide equal access to America's judicial system by furnishing "high-quality legal services to those who would be otherwise unable to afford adequate legal counsel in civil cases." The headquarters in Washington maintains a network of offices around the country and can direct requests for assistance to the nearest local office.

National Center for Youth Law
114 Samson Street, Suite 900
San Francisco, CA 94104
415/543-3307
  weekdays: 9 A.M.–5 P.M. PST
Attorneys can answer questions, including those from other attorneys, on laws about children.

Women's Legal Defense Fund
1875 Connecticut Avenue NW, Suite 710
Washington, DC 20009
202/986-2600
  Weekdays: 9 A.M.–5 P.M. EST
Counselors will provide free legal advice on women's issues such as domestic violence and employment discrimination.

Family Law:

Children's Defense Fund
122 C Street NW, Suite 400
Washington, DC 20001
202/628-8787
  weekdays: 9 A.M.–5 P.M. EST
Strictly a public policy organization that can answer questions concerning such subjects as current legislation and programs.

Concern for Dying
250 West Fifty-seventh Street, Room 831
New York, NY 10107
212/246-6962
  weekdays: 9 A.M.–5 P.M. EST
An educational council that provides information and will answer questions about living wills.

LAWYERS

National Resource Center for Consumers of Legal Services
1444 I Street NW

Washington, DC 20005
202/842-3503 and 804/693-9330
   weekdays: 9 A.M.–5 P.M. EST
Provides help choosing a lawyer, counseling on how to complain about an incompetent lawyer, and information on group legal insurance. Makes referrals amd can send literature.

LEARNING DISABILITIES. *See* DISABILITIES.

LEPROSY

American Leprosy Mission
1 ALM Way
Greenville, SC 29601
800/543-3131
In South Carolina: 803/271-7040
   weekdays: 8 A.M.–5 P.M. EST
Provides information on Hansen's disease (leprosy).

LIBRARIES. *See* GENERAL TELEPHONE SOURCES; SPECIAL COLLECTIONS.

LITERACY

Contact Center
P.O. Box 81826
Superior Industrial Park
Lincoln, NE 68501
402/464-0602
TDD: 800/552-9097
   weekdays: 6 A.M.–midnight CST
Literacy hotline—800/228-8813; provides help on reading.
Amnesty hotline—800/842-2924; links immigrants to certified educational services in communities.
National GED Hotline—800/626-9433; gives information on high school equivalency process.

LOCAL GOVERNMENT

National Civic League
1445 Market Street, Suite 300
Denver, CO 80202-1728
303/571-4343
   weekdays: 8 A.M.–5 P.M. MST
Provides information on innovations and techniques to address local problems.

M

MEDICAL CARE

Corporate Angel Network, Inc.
Building One

Westchester County Airport
White Plains, NY 10604
914/328-1313
   weekdays: 8:30 A.M.–4:30 P.M. EST
Provides free airplane transportation to and from recognized cancer treatment facilities, using empty seats on corporate flights. Questions answered about services.

Shriners Hospital for Crippled Children
Referral Line
P.O. Box 31356
Tampa, FL 33631-3356
800/237-5055
In Florida: 800/282-9161
   weekdays: 8 A.M.–5 P.M. EST
Provides information on free hospital care available to children under 18 who need orthopedic care or burn treatment.

MEDICAL COSTS

Department of Health and Human Services
Hill Burton Hospital Care Hotline
Public Health Service
Health Resources and Services Administration
Rockville, MD 20857
800/638-0742
   weekdays: 9:30 A.M.–5:30 P.M. EST
Answers questions on the Hill Burton Hospital care program. This program assists low-income people with medical bills.

MEDICARE AND MEDICAID. *See also* OLD AGE—ASSISTANCE.

Health and Human Services Department
Health Care Financing Administration
200 Independence Avenue SW
Washington, DC 20201
202/245-6161
   weekdays: 9 A.M.–5:30 P.M. EST
Provides information on Medicare and Medicaid.
Non-Emergency Surgery hotline: 800/638-6833—provides information on second opinions.
   weekdays 9 A.M. –5:30 P.M. EST.

MEDICINE AND HEALTH. *See also related subjects; such as* AIDS, ALCOHOLISM, *and* DRUGS AND MEDICINE.

American Medical Association
515 North State Street

Chicago, IL 60610
312/464-5000
   weekdays: 8:30 A.M.–4:30 P.M.CST
Answers questions about doctors and the practice of medicine. Directs complaints about physicians to state branches.

MISSING PERSONS

Child Find of America, Inc.
P.O. Box 277
New Paltz, NY 12561
800/426-5678
In New York: 914/255-1848
   24 hours a day
An international locator service for missing children.

Missing Children Help Center
410 Ware Boulevard, Suite 400
Tampa, FL 33619
813/623-KIDS (623-5437)
   weekdays: 9 A.M.–5 P.M. EST
Answers questions on parental abductions, criminal or stranger abductions, and runaways; provides general information on child safety. Pamphlets available.

National Runaway Switchboard
3080 North Lincoln Avenue
Chicago, IL 60657
800/621-4000
800/621-3230
   24 hours a day
Counsels and assists runaways.

Runaway Hotline
Box 12428
Austin, TX 78711
800/231-6946
In Texas: 800/392-3352
   24 hours a day
Volunteers serve as a life-line to distressed children and teenagers, providing services for food, shelter, and health care and acting as go-betweens with parents.

MOBILE HOMES

Manufactured Housing Institute
1745 Jefferson Davis Highway
Suite 511
Arlington, VA 22202
703/979-6620

   weekdays: 8:30 A.M.–5:30 P.M. EST
An organization of manufacturers and suppliers of factory-built homes. Supplies information about mobile-home safety and construction standards, zoning, and land development.

MONEY

Department of the Treasury
Bureau of Engraving and Printing
Fourteenth and C Streets SW
Washington, DC 20228
202/447-0193
   weekdays: 9 A.M.–2 P.M. EST
Government agency that answers questions about history, design, engraving, and printing of paper money.

Department of the Treasury
U.S. Mint
633 Third Street NW
Washington, DC 20220
202/874-6450 for general information
202/874-6210 for historical data
   weekdays: 9 A.M.–5:30 P.M. EST
Answers inquiries on mint functions, including manufacture and distribution of coins and medals; provides historical information.

MOUNTAINEERING

Appalachian Mountain Club Library
5 Joy Street
Boston, MA 02108
617/523-0636
   weekdays: 8:30 A.M.–5:30 P.M. EST
Provies information on mountaineering, mountains, and the history and exploration of mountain areas.

MULTIPLE SCLEROSIS

National Multiple Sclerosis Society
Information Resource Center
205 East Forty-second Street, Third Floor
New York, NY 10017
800/227-3166
In New York: 212/986-3240
   weekdays: 10 A.M.–5 P.M. EST
Provides information about MS's causes and prevention.

MUSCULAR DYSTROPHY

Muscular Dystrophy Association
3561 East Sunrise Drive

Tucson, AZ 85718
602/529-2000
   weekdays: 7:30 A.M.–5:30 P.M. MST
Provides information about muscular dystrophy
and professional and public education programs.

N

NUCLEAR ENERGY

Nuclear Information and Resource Service (NIRS)
1424 Sixteenth Street NW, Suite 601
Washington, DC 20036
202/328-0002
   weekdays: 9 A.M.–5:30 P.M. EST
Provides information on commercial nuclear power
plants and some information on military power
plants. Has information on radioactivity at all plants
and on general nuclear issues.

NUTRITION. *See* FOOD AND NUTRITION.

O

OCCUPATIONAL SAFETY

Department of Labor
Occupational Safety and Health Administration
Information Office
2000 Constitution Avenue NW
Washington, DC 20210
202/523-8151
   weekdays 8:30 A.M.–5:30 P.M. EST
Answers general questions on occupational safety
and current cases of violations of regulations. Also
provides information on general filing of complaints.

OLD AGE—ASSISTANCE. *See also* MEDICARE AND
MEDICAID.

American Association of Retired Persons (AARP)
601 E. Street NW
Washington, DC 20049
202/434-2277
   weekdays: 9 A.M.–5 P.M. EST
Provides information on a variety of nationwide
services and resources available to retired people
over 50.

University of Southern California
Andrus Gerontology Center
University Park
Los Angeles, CA 90089-0191
213/740-6060
   weekdays: 8:30 A.M.–5 P.M. PST
Will refer calls on questions regarding services,
such as in-home health care, meals-on-wheels,
doctors, lawyers, insurance, or day-care centers
to another department at the center. Also provides counseling and will answer questions for
people having problems with their parents.

Elderhostel, Inc.
75 Federal Street
Boston, MA 02110
617/426-7788
   weekdays: 9 A.M.–4 P.M. EST
An education program that offers noncredit courses
on a variety of liberal arts and sciences subjects at
1,600 colleges and universities. Call to book at a
catalogue—free for one year—and to find out more
information.

National Council of Senior Citizens
1331 F Street NW
Washington, DC 20004-1171
202/347-8800
   weekdays: 8:30 A.M.–6 P.M. EST
Information about such subjects as nursing-home
standards and regulations, patients' rights, legislation, and social security.

National Council on the Aging
Senior Community Service Program
409 Third Street SW
Washington, DC 20024
202/479-1200
   weekdays: 9 A.M.–5 P.M. EST
Agency helping older people secure employment and
income. Provides information on training programs
and advice on where to find out about community-
service employment programs in local areas. They
will also provide information on programs specifically designed to help the elderly with legal assistance. (Most phone books have listings of local
chapters of the National Council on the Aging.)

Social Security Administration
Office of Public Inquiries
6401 Security Boulevard
Baltimore, MD 21235
800/234-5772

weekdays: 7 A.M.–7 P.M. EST
The 800 number can answer questions about social security or Medicare, be it personal or generic. Also try calling your local Social Security office or consult your post office for the schedule of visits of Social Security representatives.

P

PARKINSON'S DISEASE

National Parkinson Foundation
1501 Northwest Ninth Avenue
Miami, FL 33136
800/327-4545
In Florida, except Miami: 800/433-7022
In Miami: 305/547-6666
    weekdays: 9 A.M.–5 P.M. EST
Answers questions about Parkinson's disease, distributes pamphlets, and provides referrals.

PATENTS AND TRADEMARKS

Department of Commerce
Patent and Trademark Office
Crystal Plaza Building 2
2021 Jefferson Davis Highway
Arlington, VA 20231
703/557-3158
    weekdays: 8:30 A.M.–5 P.M. EST
Provides information on filing for patents or trademarks.

PEACE CORPS

Peace Corps Library
1990 K Street NW
Washington, DC 20526
202/606-3307
    weekdays: 9 A.M.–5 P.M. EST
Provides information about the Peace Corps and its programs.

PERFORMING ARTS

Performing Arts Library
Roof Terrace Level
John F. Kennedy Center for the Performing Arts
Washington, DC 20566
202/416-8780
    Tuesday–Friday: 11 A.M.–8:30 P.M. EST
    Saturday: 10 A.M.–6 P.M. EST
A joint project of the Library of Congress and the

Kennedy Center, the library provides information and reference assistance for queries about dance, theater, music, film, broadcasting, and related areas. No nonperforming arts subjects.

PERSONAL FINANCE. *See also* FINANCE; INSURANCE; TAXES.

Family Economics Research Group (FERG)
439A Federal Building
6505 Belcrest Road
Hyattsville, MD 20782
301/436-8461
    weekdays: 8 A.M.–4:30 P.M. EST
Part of the U.S. Department of Agriculture, FERG provides research information about the economic aspects of family living, family resources, budgets, insurance, and child-care costs.

International Association for Financial Planning (IAFP)
2 Concourse Parkway, Suite 800
Atlanta, GA 30328
404/395-1605
    weekdays: 9 A.M.–5 P.M. EST
Industry and professional organization devoted to educating people about the profession of financial planning. It can put you in touch with financial planners who have good records and can mail you information about financial planning.

PESTICIDES

National Coalition Against the Misuse of Pesticides
701 E Street SE, Suite 200
Washington, DC 20003
202/543-5450
    weekdays: 9 A.M.–5 P.M. EST
Clearinghouse for pesticide information. Shares office with National Network to Prevent Birth Defects.

National Pesticide Telecommunications Network (NPTN)
3601 Fourth Street
Lubbock, TX 79430
800/858-7378
    24 hours a day
Operates "Verbal Library" on specific pesticides and their toxicity; has information on the recognition and management of pesticide poisonings and other safety information.

PETS

American Dog Owners Association
1654 Columbia Turnpike
Castleton, NY 12033
518/477-8469
   Monday–Thursday: 9 A.M.–2:30 P.M. EST
   Friday: 9:15 A.M.–1:45 P.M. EST
An educational and legislative association prepared
to answer questions about dogs.

PHILANTHROPY

Philanthropic Advisory Service
Council of Better Business Bureaus, Inc.
4200 Wilson Boulevard, Suite 800
Arlington, VA 22203
703/276-0100
   weekdays: 9 A.M.–5 P.M. EST
Provides people interested in giving with data on
more than 200 national, nonprofit organizations
and how they spend their money. For a $2 fee
will send publication, a bimonthly list of organizations about which the most inquiries have been
received from the public, media, government, and
other better business bureaus.

PLASTIC SURGERY

**American Academy of Facial Plastic and
Reconstructive Surgery**
1110 Vermont Avenue NW, Suite 220
Washington, DC 20005
202/842-4500
   weekdays: 8:30 A.M.–5 P.M. EST
Answers inquiries on plastic surgery (as on costs
and risks), with focus on the face and neck.

POETRY

Academy of American Poets
177 East Eighty-seventh Street
New York, NY 10128
212/427-5665
   weekdays: 9:30 A.M.–5:30 P.M. EST
If they cannot answer a question about poetry or
a poet, they can refer you to a resource.

POISON CONTROL CENTERS

Dial "0" for operator who will connect you immediately to the nearest Poison Control Center. In
some areas, 911 may also provide this service.
Trained Poison Control Center staff members will
provide you with instant information about anti-
dotes and treatment if someone you know has
ingested a poison. Consult your telephone directory or contact your local information operator
(555-1212) for the full telephone number of the
Poison Control Center nearest you.

POPULATION. *See* DEMOGRAPHICS.

PREGNANCY

Nutrition Action Group (NAG)
66 High Street
Exeter, NH 03833
603/778-1476
   weekdays: 9 A.M.–5 P.M. EST
Dr. Tom Brewer and other volunteers operate a
24-hour hotline for women, families, educators,
midwives, and doctors on everything concerning
pregnancies.

R

RADIO. *See* TELECOMMUNICATIONS.

S

SCANDINAVIA

American-Scandinavian Foundation
725 Park Avenue
New York, NY 10021
212/879-9779
   weekdays: 9 A.M.–5:30 P.M. EST
Provides cultural and educational information about
Denmark, Finland, Iceland, Norway, and Sweden.

SECURITIES. *See* INVESTMENTS.

SEXUALLY TRANSMITTED DISEASES. *See also*
AIDS.

National STD Hotline
American Social Health Association
P.O. Box 13827
Research Triangle Park, NC 27709
800/227-8922
   weekdays: 8 A.M.–11 P.M. EST
Provides free and confidential information on sexually transmitted diseases, with referrals. Also
available are pamphlets on prevention.

SIDS. *See* SUDDEN INFANT DEATH SYNDROME.

SKIING

The U.S. Ski Hall of Fame and Museum
P.O. Box 191
Ishpeming, MI 49849-0190
906/486-9281
    weekdays: 9 A.M.–4 P.M. EST
Provides information on many aspects of skiing, including its history and protocol.

SMOKING

Action on Smoking and Health (ASH)
2013 H Street NW
Washington, DC 20006
202/659-4310
    weekdays: 9 A.M.–5 P.M. EST
Provides information about antismoking campaigns, smoking hazards, and nonsmokers' rights.

SOCIAL SECURITY. *See* OLD AGE—ASSISTANCE.

SOUND. *See* ACOUSTICS.

SPACE TECHNOLOGY

American Institute of Aeronautics and Astronautics Technical Information Service Library
555 West Fifty-seventh Street
New York, NY 10019
212/247-6500
    weekdays: 9 A.M.–5 P.M. EST
Answers inquiries on all aspects of aeronautics and astronautics.

Smithsonian Institution
National Air and Space Museum Library
Seventh Street and Independence Avenue SW
Room 3100
Washington, DC 20560
202/357-3133
    weekdays: 10 A.M.–4 P.M. EST
Reference services will answer questions on aviation, astronautics, early pioneers of flight and early aircraft, astronomy, the earth, and planetary sciences.

SPECIAL COLLECTIONS

Association of College and Research Libraries (ACRL)
50 East Huron Street
Chicago, IL 60611
800/545-2433, ext. 2521
In Chicago: 312/280-2521
    weekdays: 8:30 A.M.–4:30 P.M. CST

The Association research library will help you find college and research libraries with special collections in your subject of interest.

SPELLING. *See* GRAMMAR AND SPELLING.

SPINA BIFIDA. *See* BIRTH DEFECTS.

SPORTS. *See also specific sports such as* BASEBALL, FISHING, *or* FOOTBALL.

Amateur Athletic Foundation Library
2141 West Adams Boulevard
Los Angeles, CA 90018
213/730-9696
    weekdays: 10 A.M.–5 P.M. PST, except Wednesday: 10 A.M.–8:30 P.M. PST
Provides general information, including trivia, on sports, athletics, and Olympic Games.

The President's Council on Physical Fitness and Sports
450 Fifth Street NW
Suite 7103
Washington, DC 20001
202/272-3430
    8 A.M.–5:30 P.M. EST
Although the Council cannot provide you with personal advice, it can give you general information about exercise, physical education programs, and physical fitness regimens for youth and older people.

Women's Sports Foundation
342 Madison Avenue
Suite 728
New York, NY 10173
800/227-3988
In New York: 212-972-9170
    weekdays: 9 A.M.–5 P.M. EST
Founded by Billie Jean King and other female athletes, the foundation can provide information and referrals on issues concerning women and sports, such as pregnancy, careers, and athletic scholarships.

STOCKS. *See* INVESTMENTS.

STUTTERING

National Center For Stuttering
200 East Thirty-third Street
New York, NY 10016
800/221-2483
In New York City: 212/532-1460

weekdays: 9:30 A.M.–5 P.M. EST
Provides information to parents of young children who stutter and referral service to treatment centers for older children and adults.

SUDDEN INFANT DEATH SYNDROME (SIDS)

The SIDS Alliance
10500 Little Patuxent Parkway, Suite 420
Columbia, MD 21044
800/221-SIDS (800/221-7437)
In Maryland: 301/964-8000
    weekdays: 9 A.M.–5 P.M. EST, answering service after hours
Provides general and medical information about sudden infant death syndrome counseling, support groups, and research. Makes referrals.

SWIMMING

International Swimming Hall of Fame
1 Hall of Fame Drive
Fort Lauderdale, FL 33316
305/462-6536
    weekdays: 9 A.M.–5 P.M. EST
Answers questions about swimming, its history, pool care and management, diving, water polo, swimmers' biographies, and swim-meet officiating.

T

TAXES. *See also* PERSONAL FINANCE.

Internal Revenue Service (IRS)
Taxpayer Service Division
1111 Constitution Avenue NW
Washington, DC 20224
800/829-1040
    weekdays: 8 A.M.–4:30 P.M.
Answers general questions on taxes. The number above will automatically switch you to the tax region in which you live.

TELECOMMUNICATIONS

Federal Communications Commission (FCC)
Library
1919 M Street NW, Room 639
Washington, DC 20554
202/632-7100
    weekdays: 1 P.M.–4 P.M. EST
The FCC Library provides information on various telecommunications issues, but it can answer only *short* reference questions.

Federal Communications Commission
Consumer Assistance and Small Business Division
1919 M Street NW
Washington, DC 20554
202/632-6999
    weekdays: 9 A.M.–5:30 P.M. EST
Answers questions concerning all aspects of communications regulations. Can also advise on how to start your own broadcast station.

TELEPHONES. *See also* TELECOMMUNICATIONS.

Tele-Consumer Hotline
1910 K Street NW
Suite 610
Washington, DC 20006
800/332-1124
TDD, Spanish, and Italian assistance: 800/332-1124
In Washington, DC: 202/223-4371
    weekdays: 9 A.M.–8 P.M. EST
Provides information about long-distance options and service, telephone equipment and repairs, ways to cut costs, and billing problems. Much of their information revolves around "special needs," helping people who have handicaps get equipment and discounts. This organization was formed as a result of the breakup and divestiture of ATT, which left many holes in telephone services. Only the following states are covered by this service: Arkansas, Alabama, California, Delaware, District of Columbia, Kansas, Kentucky, Louisiana, Maryland, Mississippi, Missouri, Oklahoma, New Jersey, New York, Pennsylvania, Tennessee, Texas, Virginia, and West Virginia.

TELEVISION. *See also* TELECOMMUNICATIONS.

Museum of Television and Radio
1 East Fifty-third Street
New York, NY 10022
212/752-4690
    weekdays: 4 P.M.–5 P.M. EST
Answers questions about the media.

TENNIS

International Tennis Hall of Fame and Tennis Museum Library
194 Bellevue Avenue
Newport, RI 02840
401/846-4567
    weekdays: 9 A.M.–5 P.M. EST
Will answer questions about the history, etiquette, and rules of tennis.

TEXTILES. *See* CLOTHING AND TEXTILES.

TIRES. *See* AUTOMOBILES—TIRES.

TOXIC WASTE. *See* ECOLOGY.

TRAVEL

American Society of Travel Agents (ASTA)
Consumer Affairs Department
1101 King Street
Alexandria, VA 22314
703/739-2782
    weekdays: 9 A.M.–5 P.M. EST
ASTA will mediate between travel suppliers and consumers if the problem is at least six months old and the travel supplier has not resolved it. Their specialty is problems with travel agents, tour operators, cruises, and airlines.

U.S. Department of Transportation
Consumer Affairs Division
400 Seventh Street SW, Room 10405
Washington, DC 20590
202/366-2220
    weekdays: 8 A.M.–4:30 P.M. EST
Handles complaints about all aspects of airplane travel, including bumping, lost luggage, on-time performance, and smoking. Department will investigate your problem and take action.

Interstate Commerce Commission
Office of Compliance and Consumer Assistance
Twelfth Street and Constitution Avenue NW
Washington, DC 20423
202/275-7844
    weekdays: 9 A.M.–5 P.M. EST
Complaints about bus or train transportation and interstate movers are filed and investigated. This office will also offer advice as to how to avoid problems.

Department of State
Citizens Emergency Center
Main State Building, Room 4800
2201 C Street NW
Washington, DC 20520
202/647-5225
    weekdays: 8:15 A.M.–10 P.M. EST
    Saturday: 9 A.M.–3 P.M.
    after hours, call main State Department number:
    202/647-4000
Assists Americans who are in distress abroad. This includes arrests, deaths, and whereabouts of U.S. citizens abroad. Also issues travel advisories for specific countries and visa requirements to all countries.

U

URINARY TRACT INFECTIONS

Dr. Larrian Gillespie, M.D.
The Interstitial Cystitis Foundation
120 South Spalding Drive
Suite 210
Beverly Hills, CA 90212
213/274-6294
    weekdays: 9 A.M.–5 P.M. PST
Nonprofit foundation founded by a urologist, Dr. L. Gillespie, that assists with information and support in the treatment of interstitial cystitis, the inflammation of the bladder surface caused by the use of antibiotics in the absence of infection.

V

VETERANS

Vietnam Veterans of America
1224 M Street NW
Washington, DC 20005
800/424-7275
In Washington, DC: 202/628-2700
    weekdays: 9 A.M.–5:30 P.M. EST
Answers to questions about Agent Orange, post-traumatic stress disorder, and legal and other related matters. Provides information about filing claims and referrals to local chapters where counseling is available.

VOLUNTEERING. *See also* PEACE CORPS.

ACTION
1100 Vermont Avenue NW
Washington, DC 20525
202/634-9380
    weekdays: 8:30 A.M.–5 P.M. EST
Call above number for nearest regional office to you. ACTION provides Americans with information on programs that accept volunteers.

W

WILLS. *See* LAW: FAMILY LAW.

WINES AND SPIRITS

Distilled Spirits Council of the United States
1250 I Street NW, Suite 900
Washington, DC 20005
202/628-3544
  weekdays: 9 A.M.–5 P.M. EST
A trade council that provides information on safe and moderate consumption of alcohol, cooking with alcohol, and alcohol-related issues.

WOMEN. *See also* LAW; SPORTS; WOMEN'S HEALTH.

American Women's Economic Development Corp. (AWED)
641 Lexington Avenue, Ninth Floor
New York, NY 10022
800/222-AWED (222-2933)
In New York City: 212/692-9100
  weekdays: 9 A.M.–6 P.M. EST
Nationwide nonprofit organization that counsels women over the telephone or in person, for a fee: $10 for 15 minutes, $35 for one half-hour of individual counseling on business growth, development, and management.

WOMEN'S HEALTH

National Women's Health Network (NWHN)
1325 G Street NW, Lower Level
Washington, DC 20005
202/347-1140
  weekdays: 8 A.M.–5 P.M. EST
Staffed by laypersons, the NWHN is a clearinghouse that provides factual information pertaining to women's health. Referrals and literature also available.

PMS ACCESS
P.O. Box 9326
Madison, WI 53715
800/222-4PMS (222-4767)
  weekdays: 9 A.M.–5 P.M. CST
Provides information on premenstrual syndrome, support, and referrals.

WOODWORKING. *See also* HOME BUILDING, MAINTENANCE, AND REPAIR.

Shopsmith, Inc.
3931 Image Drive

Dayton, OH 45414
800/543-7586
  Monday–Friday: 9 A.M.–12 midnight EST
  Saturday: 9 A.M.–6 P.M. EST
Helps with questions about woodworking. A maker of bandsaws, jigsaws, joiners, and other woodworking tools, Shopsmith has technicians who will research your problem (even if unrelated to their tools) and call you back.

YOUTH. *See also* CHILDREN—ABUSE; DRUG ABUSE.

Contact Center
P.O. Box 81826
Superior Industrial Park
Lincoln, NE 68501
402/464-0602
TDD: 800/552-9097
Youth Hotline: 800/235-0795
  weekdays: 6 A.M.–midnight CST
Provides information on problems of youth, including teenage pregnancy, drug abuse, and normal growing challenges.

ZIP CODES

U.S. Postal Service
900 Brentwood Road NE
Washington, DC 20066
202/682-9595
  weekdays: 8 A.M.–8 P.M. EST
  Saturday: 8 A.M.–5 P.M. EST
Call your local post office for rates and ZIP codes for anywhere. If no one can help you, call the above number.

U.S. Postal Service
Consumer Advocate
Consumer Affairs Department
475 L'Enfant Plaza, Room 5821
Washington, DC 20260-2200
202/268-2284
  weekdays: 8 A.M.–5 P.M. EST
Complaints about any aspect of the postal service should be registered with your local postal service. If the response is not satisfactory, call the number above. This office will investigate and help seek a solution. It also provides information on specific products and services.

3.

Government Sources

WHILE NOT EXPLICITLY STATED IN THE CONSTI-
tution or the Bill of Rights, Americans have a
fundamental right to know about the activities of government and to obtain information
from government sources. We pay the taxes
that generate information used by government at all levels in carrying out its many
functions; we must have access to this information in order to vote intelligently. As President James Madison once wrote:

> "A popular government without popular
> information or the means of acquiring it, is
> but a Prologue to a Farce or a Tragedy or
> perhaps both. Knowledge will forever gov-
> ern ignorance, and a people who mean to
> be their own Governors, must arm them-
> selves with the power knowledge brings."

Information about some subjects, of course,
cannot be made available. These include national security matters, trade secrets, ongoing criminal investigations, and, in time of
war, military plans. In World War II, the
security surrounding invasion preparations
and top-secret agencies such as the Manhattan Project, which developed the atomic

bomb, was extremely tight and highly effective in preventing leaks that might have been
disastrous.

Unfortunately, the security habit was hard
to break. Long after World War II, much
more information in government files re-
mained classified than was really necessary.
Even in unclassified areas, the dissemination
of information to the public was not always
given a very high priority.

The Freedom of Information Act

The first major effort to improve the public's
access to government information was the
Freedom of Information Act (FOIA) of 1966,
which set standards for determining which
records must be made available for public
inspection and which could be withheld from
disclosure. The FOIA required federal agencies to provide the fullest possible disclosure
of information to the public, and it provided

administrative and judicial remedies for those denied access to records. (See tip 8, below, for further details on the FOIA.)

Many states and local governments followed with their own "sunshine laws." Finally, one important consequence of the Watergate scandal of 1972–74 was to make government officials *want* to operate more openly, with the public more aware and better informed about what officials were doing. Lapses in this trend, such as the secret sale of arms to Iran and the illegal diversion of funds to the Nicaraguan Contras in 1986–87, have underscored the importance of keeping the public informed in areas in which it has legitimate concerns.

Nowadays it is rare when a government agency does not have an officially designated public affairs or public information official. More importantly, there has been a change in attitude throughout all levels of government. Where formerly one might have encountered reluctance, even resistance, to answering queries from the public, now there is a much greater willingness to help.

Government Sources

The first section of "Government Sources" covers the U.S. federal goverment. The main branches of the federal government are organized alphabetically: executive branch; independent agencies, commissions, and governmental corporations; judicial branch; and legislative branch. Entries within each of these major divisions are alphabetical.

Following the main section on the federal government is the section on foreign governments. This section gives the addresses and telephone numbers of foreign embassies and legations. If you call the embassy and ask to speak to the public affairs or public information office, your call will be routed to the appropriate desk for handling requests for information.

The final major section in this chapter covers state governments. The telephone numbers given are usually main numbers of the Governor's office, whose operators can direct your request for information to the appropriate state agency.

When no public information number is given for a government agency, direct your queries to the main number to be referred to the appropriate office. Addresses of government sources are provided so that telephone queries can by followed up by mail or personal visit if necessary.

Tips on Government Research

1. The telephone numbers for government offices change frequently, especially when a new administration comes in. If a number has changed or been discontinued, note this in the margin alongside the listing in this book so that the change can be spotted easily next time you look up the listing. This is a lot simpler than keeping a separate card file and noting the change on a card.

2. Always get the names and direct telephone numbers or extensions of the government people you deal with. It is much easier to follow up a request, or obtain additional information later on, if you can get back in touch with a specific person.

3. Government personnel change frequently. Professional researchers will tell you that all too often a good source will move on to another job or retire just when he or she becomes most useful. There is nothing you can do about this, of course, but keeping a log of the calls you make will help you track down someone else when your good source disappears.

The log of calls need not be formal or complicated. Many researchers simply use a blank pad of paper to jot down dates, numbers called, names of people who responded, and the information provided. The sheets can then be filed away against that inevitable day when your source has moved on and you have to track down a new one. Especially useful numbers can be transferred from the log to a Rolodex® or other telephone file system if you expect to use them frequently.

4. Always ask whether a government source can send you a publication dealing with your subject. Many government offices that handle large numbers of queries from the public have brochures or reports that they can mail to you free of charge, or at nominal cost. Also ask the source for additional information on major references that might be available through the Government Printing Office.

5. Ask also whether another government office might have information on the subject you are checking out. The first source you contact may not always be the best.

6. The federal government operates a central toll-free Federal Information Center, 800/347-1997. This number welcomes queries on all aspects of the federal government. The hours are 9 A.M. to 10:30 P.M., Monday through Friday, all time zones. If the query cannot be answered immediately by operators accessing the databases at the Center, they will call you back. The 800 toll-free operation became operational in 1990; it replaced a former network of regional centers located throughout the country. The new system handles about 10,000 calls per day. Mailing address:

Federal Information Center
P.O. Box 600
Cumberland, MD 21502-0600

7. For more detailed information on federal government agencies, consult the current edition of **The United States Government Manual,** available through the U.S. Government Printing Office (GPO). Telephone directories for the Senate and the House of Representatives are also published by the Government Printing Office. Order them through:

Superintendent of Documents
Government Printing Office
Washington, DC 20402

Or contact your nearest GPO bookstore. For addresses and telephone numbers of regional GPOs, see the listings of Government Printing Offices under the "Federal Government—Legislative Branch" section.

8. For details on obtaining material under the Freedom of Information Act and its companion legislation, the Privacy Act, obtain a copy of the booklet "A Citizen's Guide on Using the Freedom of Information Act and the Privacy Act of 1974 to Request Government Records." Prepared by the House of Representatives Committee of Government Operations and printed by the Government Printing Office, this booklet is "one of the most widely read congressional committee reports in history," according to its authors—striking evidence of the public's thirst for government information. Ask for House Report 101-193.

9. Many government agencies, such as the Library of Congress, have special collections and reading rooms. See section 5 in this book on "Special Collections."

Government Sources
Subject Index

FEDERAL GOVERNMENT— EXECUTIVE BRANCH

AGRICULTURE

Department of Agriculture
Fourteenth Street and Independence Avenue SW
Washington, DC 20250
Main number: 202/447-2791
Public Affairs: 202/447-4026

Agriculture agencies:

Agricultural Cooperative Service
P.O. Box 96576
Washington, DC 20090-6576
Information Services: 202/653-6973; 202/653-6976

Agricultural Marketing Service
P.O. Box 96456
Washington, DC 20250
Information: 202/447-8999

Agricultural Research Service
B-005, BARC
Beltsville, MD 20705
Information Office: 301/344-2264

Agricultural Stabilization and Conservation Service
P.O. Box 2415
Washington, DC 20013
Information Division: 202/447-5237

Animal and Plant Health Inspection Service
Department of Agriculture
South Building, Room 1147
Fourteenth Street and Independence Avenue SW
Washington, DC 20250
Legislative and Public Affairs: 202/447-2511

Commodity Credit Corporation
P.O. Box 2415
Washington, DC 20013
Information Division: 202/447-5237

Cooperative State Research Service
Aerospace Building

901 D Street SW
Washington, DC 20250-2200
Information: 202/447-4587; 202/447-4423

Economics Management Staff
Department of Agriculture
South Building
Fourteenth Street and Independence Avenue SW
Washington, DC 20005-4789
Public Affairs: 202/786-1504

Extension Service
Director, Communication, Information and Technology
Department of Agriculture
Fourteenth Street and Independence Avenue SW
Room 3328
Washington, DC 20250
Communications: 202/447-3029

Farmers Home Administration (FmHA)
Department of Agriculture
South Building, Room 5037
Fourteenth Street and Independence Avenue SW
Washington, DC 20250
Legislative Affairs and Public Information:
202/447-4323

Federal Crop Insurance Corporation
Department of Agriculture
South Building, Room 4416
Fourteenth Street and Independence Avenue SW
Washington, DC 20250
Information and Governmental Affairs:
202/447-3287

Food and Nutrition Service
3101 Park Center Drive
Alexandria, VA 22302
Consumer Advisor: 202/382-9681
Public Information: 703/756-3276

Food Safety and Inspection Service
Department of Agriculture

Fourteenth Street and Independence Avenue SW
Room 327E
Washington, DC 20250
Information and Legislative Affairs: 202/447-7943

Foreign Agricultural Service
Department of Agriculture
Fourteenth Street and Independence Avenue SW
Room 5074
Washington, DC 20250
Information Division: 202/447-3448

Forest Service
P.O. Box 96090
Washington, DC 20090-6090
Public Affairs: 202/447-3760

Human Nutrition Information Service
6505 Belcrest Road
Hyattsville, MD 20782
Public Affairs: 301/436-8617

International Cooperation and Development, Office of
Department of Agriculture
Fourteenth Street and Independence Avenue SW
Washington, DC 20250-3800
Information: 202/653-7589; 202/653-9312

National Agricultural Library
Reference and User Services, Room 1200
10301 Baltimore Boulevard
Beltsville, MD 20705
Information: 301/344-3755
   D.C. Reference Center:
   Department of Agriculture
   Fourteenth Street and Independence Avenue SW
   South Building, Room 1052
   Washington, DC 202250
   202/447-3434

Rural Electrification Administration
Department of Agriculture
Fourteenth Street and Independence Avenue SW
Room 4042
Washington, DC 20250
Public Information: 202/382-1255

Soil Conservation Service
P.O. Box 2890
Washington, DC 20013
Public Information: 202/447-4543

World Agricultural Outlook Board
Department of Agriculture

South Building, Room 5143
Fourteenth Street and Independence Avenue SW
Washington, DC 20250-3800
Information Office: 202/447-5447

COMMERCE

Department of Commerce
Fourteenth Street and Constitution Avenue NW
Washington, DC 20230
Main number: 202/377-2000
Director of Public Affairs: 202/377-3263
Public Information: 202/377-4901

   Commerce agencies:

Bureau of the Census
Federal Office Building #3D
Suitland, MD 20233
Public Information: 301/763-4040; 301/763-4051

Bureau of Economic Analysis
Fourteenth Street and Constitution Avenue NW
Washington, DC 20230
Public Information: 202/523-0777; 202/523-0539

Bureau of Export Administration
Fourteenth Street and Constitution Avenue NW
Room 3893
Washington, DC 20230
Public Affairs: 202/377-2721

Economic Development Administration
Fourteenth Street and Constitution Avenue NW
Washington, DC 20230
Public Affairs: 202/377-5113

International Trade Administration (ITA)
Fourteenth Street and Constitution Avenue NW
Washington, DC 20230
Public Affairs: 202/377-3808

Minority Business Development Agency
Fourteenth Street and Constitution Avenue NW
Washington, DC 20230
Information Clearing House: 202/377-2414
Public Affairs: 202/377-1936
Office of Program Support: 202/377-5122

National Institute of Standards and Technology
Route I-270 and Quince Orchard Road
Gaithersburg, MD 20899
Main number: 301/975-2000
Information Resources: 301/975-3058

**National Oceanic and Atmospheric
Administration** (NOAA)
Fourteenth Street and Constitution Avenue NW
Washington, DC 20230
202/377-2985
Public Affairs: 202/377-4190

National Weather Service
8060 Thirteenth Street
Silver Spring, MD 20910
202/377-8090
Public Affairs: 301/427-7622

National Technical Information Service
5285 Port Royal Road
Springfield, VA 22161
Public Affairs: 703/487-4650

**National Telecommunications and Information
Administration**
Fourteenth Street and Constitution Avenue NW
Washington, DC 20230
Public Affairs: 202/377-1832; 202/377-1551

Patent and Trademark Office
Crystal Plaza Building 2
2021 Jefferson Davis Highway
Arlington, VA 20231
Public Affairs: 703/557-3341

U.S. Travel and Tourism Administration
Fourteenth Street and Constitution Avenue NW
Washington, DC 20230
Public Affairs: 202/377-3811

DEFENSE

Department of Defense
The Pentagon
Washington, DC 20301-1155
Main number: 202/545-6700
   Directorate for Public Communications:
   202/697-5737; 202/697-6462
   Directorate for Community Relations:
   202/695-2113
   Directorate for Defense Information:
   202/697-2902; 202/697-2528
   Armed Forces News Division: 202/697-5131
   Directorate for Editorial Services, Speechwriters:
   202/697-9105

Defense agencies:

Armed Services Board of Contract Appeals
5109 Leesburg Pike

Skyline Six
Falls Church, VA 22041-3208
Chairman: 202/756-8501

Defense Advanced Research Projects Agency
1400 Wilson Boulevard
Arlington, VA 22209-2308
Information: 202/694-5469

Defense Communications Agency
Eighth Street and South Courthouse Road
Arlington, VA 22204
Main number: 202/692-9012
Information: 202/692-0018

Defense Contract Audit Agency
Building 4
Cameron Station
Alexandria, VA 22304-6178
Director: 202/274-6785
Public Affairs: 202/274-7319

Defense Intelligence Agency
The Pentagon
Washington, DC 20340-0001
Main number: 202/697-8844
Secretariat: 202/697-9348

Defense Investigative Service
Buzzard's Point
1900 Hall Street SW
Washington, DC 20324-1700
Main number: 202/475-0966
Public Affairs: 202/475-1062

Defense Logistics Agency
Cameron Station, Room 3A150
Alexandria, VA 22304-6100
Main number: 202/274-6000
Executive Office: 202/274-6115

Defense Mapping Agency
8613 Lee Highway
Fairfax, VA 22031-2137
Main number: 703/756-9368
Public Affairs: 202/653-1131; 202/653-1132
For purchase of maps and charts: 1/800/826-0342
   *Maps also available through the Interior
   Department:*
   U.S. Geological Survey
   Federal Center
   P.O. Box 25286
   Denver, CO 80255
   303/236-7477

Defense Nuclear Agency
6801 Telegraph Road
Alexandria, VA 22310
Washington number: 202/325-7095
Public Affairs: 703/325-7095

National Security Agency
9800 Savage Road
Fort Meade, MD 20755-6000
Information: 301/688-6311

Strategic Air Command (SAC)
Offutt Air Force Base, NE 68113
Public Affairs: 402/294-4130

Strategic Defense Initiative Organization (SDI)
The Pentagon
Washington, DC 20301-7100
Main number: 202/697-4040
External Affairs: 202/695-8737

U.S. Space Command
Peterson Air Force Base, CO 80914-5001
Public Affairs: 303/554-3022

Department of the Air Force
The Pentagon
Washington, DC 20330-1000
Main number: 202/545-6700
Public Affairs: 202/697-6061
Public Communications: 202/697-2769

   Air Force Service Information and News Center
   Building 1500
   Kelly Air Force Base, TX 78241-5000
   512/925-6161

Department of the Army
The Pentagon
Washington, DC 20310-1500
Main number: 202/545-6700
Information during non-office hours: 202/695-0441
Public Affairs: 202/694-0741
   Command Information Division: 202/695-3952
   Community Relations Division: 202/697-5716

Department of the Navy
The Pentagon
Washington, DC 20350-1200
Main number: 202/545-6700
Office of Information: 202/697-7391
Public Liaison: 202/695-0965

U.S. Marine Corps
Department of the Navy

Headquarters, Code AR
Washington, DC 20380-0001
Main number: 202/694-2500
Public Affairs: 202/694-1492

EDUCATION

Department of Education
400 Maryland Avenue SW
Washington, DC 20202
Main number: 202/708-5366
Public Affairs: 202/401-1576

ENERGY

Department of Energy
The Forrestal Building
1000 Independence Avenue SW
Washington, DC 20585
Main number: 202/586-5000
Energy Information Center: 202/586-8800
Program Public Affairs:
   Defense: 202/586-2295
   Energy Research: 301/353-4944
   Fossil Energy: 301/353-2617
   International Affairs and Emergencies:
   202/586-5924
   Nuclear Energy: 202/586-9720
   Radioactive Waste Management: 202/586-9116

   Energy agencies:

Federal Energy Regulatory Commission
825 North Capitol Street NE
Washington, DC 20426
Public Affairs: 202/357-8088; 202/357-8055
Public Records: 202/357-8118

HEALTH AND HUMAN SERVICES

Department of Health and Human Services
Hubert H. Humphrey Building
200 Independence Avenue SW
Washington, DC 20201
Main number: 202/245-6296
General Information: 202/475-0257
Public Affairs: 202/245-1850; 202/245-1853
News Office: 202/245-6343
Community Services: 202/252-5238
Health and Human Services offices and administrations: 202/474-0257

Family Support Administration
370 L'Enfant Promenade SW
Washington, DC 20447

Main number: 202/252-4500
Communications Office: 202/252-4518

Office of Refugee Resettlement
Family Support Administration
370 L'Enfant Promenade SW
Washington, DC 20447
Main Information number: 202/252-4545
Public Affairs: 202/426-6510

Health Care Financing Administration
(Medicare and Medicaid)
200 Independence Avenue SW
Washington, DC 20201
Main number: 202/245-6113
Information: 301/966-3000

Office of Human Development Services
200 Independence Avenue SW
Washington, DC 20201
Main number: 202/245-7246
Public Information: 202/472-7257
Mental Retardation Programs: 202/245-7634

Public Health Service (PHS)
200 Independence Avenue SW
Washington, DC 20201
Main number: 202/245-6296
Public Affairs: 202/245-6867

Alcohol, Drug Abuse & Mental Health Administration
5600 Fishers Lane, Parklawn Building
Rockville, MD 20857
Main number: 301/443-4797; 301/443-3875
Public Information at National Institutes of:
Alcohol Abuse: 301/443-4373
Drug Abuse: 301/443-6487
Mental Health: 301/443-3877

Centers for Disease Control
Office of Assistant Secretary for Health
1600 Clifton Road NE
Atlanta, GA 30333
Main number: 404/639-3311
Press and Public Relations: 404/639-3286

Food and Drug Administration (FDA)
5600 Fishers Lane, Parklawn Building
Rockville, MD 20857
Main number: 301/443-1544
Consumer Information: 301/443-3170
Associate Commissioner for Public Relations:
301/443-4177
Consumer Affairs: 301/443-3170

National Institutes of Health (NIH)
9000 Rockville Pike
Bethesda, MD 20892
Main number: 301/496-4000
Director, Division of Public Information:
301/496-5787

Social Security Administration
6401 Security Boulevard
Baltimore, MD 21235
Main number: 301/965-1234
Information, Personal Accounts (phone only):
800/234-5772
Office of Public Inquiries: 301/965-7700
Office of Research and Statistics:301/965-0179

HOUSING AND URBAN DEVELOPMENT (HUD)

Department of Housing and Urban Development
451 Seventh Street SW
Washington, DC 20410
Main number: 202/755-5111
Program and Information Center: 202/755-6420
Public Affairs: 202/755-6980; 202/755-5713
Press Office: 202/755-6685

INTERIOR

Department of the Interior
1800 C Street NW
Washington, DC 20240
Main number: 202/343-3171

Bureau of Indian Affairs
1800 C Street NW
Washington, DC 20240
General Information: 202/343-4576

Bureau of Land Management
1800 C Street NW
Washington, DC 20240
General Information: 202/343-5717
Public Affairs: 202/343-9435

Bureau of Mines
2401 E Street NW
Washington, DC 20241
General Information: 202/634-1004
Public Affairs: 202/634-1001

Bureau of Reclamation
1800 C Street NW
Washington, DC 20240
Public Affairs: 202/343-4662

also:

Engineering and Research Center
Building 67
Denver Federal Center
Denver, CO 80225
Public Affairs: 303/236-6741

Minerals Management Service
Room 4443, MS 612
Fourteenth and C Streets NW
Washington, DC 20240
Public Affairs: 202/343-3983

National Park Service
P.O. Box 37127
Washington, DC 20013-7127
Park Publication Information: 202/343-4747
Public Affairs: 202/343-7394

Surface Mining, Office of
1951 Constitution Avenue NW
Washington, DC 20240
Public Affairs: 202/343-4953

Territorial and International Affairs
1800 C Street NW
Washington, DC 20240
Office of Legislative and Public Affairs:
202/343-3003
Public Information: 202/343-4822

U.S. Fish and Wildlife Service
1800 C Street NW
Washington, DC 20240
Public Affairs: 202/343-5634
Publications: 703/358-1711

U.S. Geological Survey
119 National Center
12201 Sunrise Valley Drive
Reston, VA 22092
Main number: 703/648-4000
Public Affairs: 703/648-4460
For maps:
U.S. Geological Survey
Federal Center
P.O. Box 25286
Denver, CO 80255
303/236-7477
(*See also:* DEPARTMENT OF DEFENSE, DEFENSE
MAPPING AGENCY.)

JUSTICE

Department of Justice
Constitution Avenue and Tenth Street NW

Washington, DC 20530
Main number: 202/633-2000
General Information: 202/633-2007
Public Affairs: 202/633-2015; 202/633-2018;
202/633-4389

National Criminal Justice Reference Service
National Institute of Justice
Box 6000
Rockville, MD 20850
301/251-5500
800/851-3420

Justice Statistics Clearinghouse
800/732-3277

Juvenile Justice Clearinghouse
800/638-8736

Justice agencies and divisions:

Antitrust Division
FOIA Unit
Tenth Street and Pennsylvania Avenue NW
Washington, DC 20530
Information: 202/633-2692

Civil Rights Division
Tenth Street and Pennsylvania Avenue NW
Washington, DC 20530
Executive Office: 202/633-4224

Drug Enforcement Administration
1600-700 Army Navy Drive
Arlington, VA 22202
Main number: 202/307-1000
Public Affairs: 202/307-7977

Federal Bureau of Investigation (FBI)
J. Edgar Hoover Building
Ninth Street and Pennsylvania Avenue NW
Washington, DC 20535
Main number: 202/324-3000
Public Affairs: 202/324-3691
Research Unit: 202/324-5611

Immigration and Naturalization Service
425 I Street NW
Washington, DC 20536
Main number: 202/633-2000
Public Affairs: 202/633-4316
Alien Information Office: 202/633-4330;
202/633-4316

Office of Justice Programs
633 Indiana Avenue NW

Washington, DC 20531
Main number: 202/633-2000
Public Affairs: 202/724-7782

Bureau of Prisons
320 First Street NW
Washington, DC 20534
Public Affairs: 202/724-3198

U.S. Marshals Service
600 Army Navy Drive, Suite 1260
Arlington, VA 22202-4210
Main number: 202/307-9000
Congressional and Public Affairs Office:
202/307-9065

Tax Division
Tenth Street and Pennsylvania Avenue NW
Washington, DC 20530
Office of the Assistant Attorney General:
202/633-2901

LABOR

Department of Labor
200 Constitution Avenue NW, Room S-1032
Washington, DC 20210
Main number: 202/523-8165
Information and Public Affairs: 202/523-7316
Publication Information: 202/523-6871

Labor Department agencies:

Bureau of Labor-Management Relations
200 Constitution Avenue NW
Washington, DC 20210
Main number: 202/523-8165
Public Affairs: 202/523-6045

Bureau of Labor Statistics
Accounting Office Building
441 G Street NW
Washington, DC 20212
Main number: 202/523-1327
Public Affairs: 202/523-1221
Public Information: 202/523-1221

Employment Standards Administration
200 Constitution Avenue NW
Washington, DC 20210
Main number: 202/523-8165
Public Affairs: 202/523-8743

Employment and Training Administration
200 Constitution Avenue NW
Washington, DC 20210

Main number: 202/523-8165
Public Affairs: 202/523-6871

Mine Safety and Health Administration
4015 Wilson Boulevard, Room 601
Arlington, VA 22203
Public Affairs: 703/235-1452

Occupational Safety and Health Administration
(OSHA)
200 Constitution Avenue NW
Washington, DC 20210
Main number: 202/523-8017
Public Affairs: 202/523-8151; 202/523-6027

Pension and Welfare Benefits Administration
200 Constitution Avenue NW
Washington, DC 20210
Main number: 202/523-8165
Public Affairs: 202/523-8921

Veterans' Employment and Training Service
200 Constitution Avenue NW
Washington, DC 20210
Assistant Secretary: 202/523-9116

THE PRESIDENT

The President
The White House
1600 Pennsylvania Avenue NW
Washington, DC 20500
202/456-1414
Photo Office: 202/456-2594
Office of Public Affairs and Media Relations:
202/456-7150
Office of Research: 202/456-7750
    Library: 202/456-7000
White House Press Office: 202/456-2100

Executive offices:

Council of Economic Advisers
Old Executive Office Building
Washington, DC 20500
Main number: 202/395-5804
Special Asst. to Chairman: 202/395-5084

Council on Environmental Quality
722 Jackson Place NW
Washington, DC 20503
Main number: 202/395-5750
General Counsel: 202/395-5754

Office of Management and Budget (OMB)
Executive Office Building

Washington, DC 20503
Main number: 202/395-3000
Director of External Affairs: 202/395-3080

National Critical Materials Council
Fourteenth and C Streets NW
Washington, DC 20240
Main number and Information: 202/347-1847

National Drug Control Policy, Office of
Executive Office of the President
Washington, DC 20500
Main number: 202/673-2520
Director of Public Affairs: 202/673-2823

National Security Council (NSC)
Old Executive Office Building
Washington, DC 20506
Main number and Information: 202/395-4974

Office of Science and Technology Policy
New Executive Office Building
Washington, DC 20506
Main number and Information: 202/395-7347

Office of the U.S. Trade Representative (USTR)
600 Fourteenth Street NW
Washington, DC 20506
Main number: 202/395-3000
Public Affairs: 202/395-3230

STATE

Department of State
2201 C Street NW
Washington, DC 20520
Main number: 202/647-4000
Overseas Citizens Service: 202/647-5225 (24 hours)
Assistant Secretary, Public Affairs: 202/647-9606

Main information address:
Public Information Division
Department of State
Room 5819
2201 C Street NW
Washington, DC 20520-1853
202/647-6575; 202/647-6576

State Department bureaus and offices:

Bureau of Consular Affairs

Visa Services
Public Inquiries
2401 E Street NW

Washington, DC 20520-0113
Main number: 202/647-0510
Information: 202/326-6060; 202/326-1488

Passport Services
1425 K Street NW
Room G-62
Washington, DC 20524
Main information number: 202/647-0518

Passport Services Field Offices: (listed alphabetically by city)

Boston, MA:
Passport Office
Thomas P. O'Neill Federal Building
Boston, MA 02222
617/565-6990

Chicago, IL:
Passport Office
Federal Building
Chicago, IL 60604
312/353-7155

Honolulu, HI:
Passport Office
Federal Building
Honolulu, HI 96850
808/541-1918

Houston, TX:
Passport Office
1919 Smith Street
Houston, TX 77002
713/653-3153

Los Angeles, CA:
Passport Office
11000 Wilshire Boulevard
Los Angeles, CA 90024-3615
213/209-7075

Miami, FL:
Passport Office
Federal Office Building
Miami, FL 33130
305/536-4681

New Orleans, LA:
Passport Office
701 Loyola Avenue
New Orleans, LA 70130
504/589-6161

New York, NY:
Passport Office
Rockefeller Center
New York, NY 10111-0031
212/541-7710

Philadelphia, PA:
Passport Office
Federal Building
Philadelphia, PA 19106
215/597-7482

San Francisco, CA:
Passport Office
525 Market Street
San Francisco, CA 94105-2773
415/974-9941

Seattle, WA:
Passport Office
Federal Building
Seattle, WA 98174
206/442-7945

Stamford, CT:
Passport Office
1 Landmark Square
Stamford, CT 06901
203/325-3530

Washington, DC:
Passport Office
1425 K Street NW
Washington, DC 20524-0002
202/647-0518

For the following State Department offices, requests for information should be routed through the main information office:

Public Information Division
Department of State
Room 5819
2201 C Street NW
Washington, DC 20520-1853

For mail inquiries, use the main address above, but give the individual ZIP codes below:

Economic and Business Affairs
202/647-2720
ZIP code: 20520-4216

Human Rights and Humanitarian Affairs
202/647-2126
ZIP code: 20520-7812

International Communications and Information Policy
202/647-5832
ZIP code: 20520

International Organization Affairs
202/647-6400; 202/647-6394

Oceans and International Environmental and Scientific Affairs
202/647-3529

Passport Services. *See* Bureau of Consular Affairs.

Protocol, Office of the Chief of
202/647-2663

Refugee Programs
202/633-1520

Regional Bureaus:

African Affairs
202/647-7371
ZIP code: 20520-3430

East Asian and Pacific Affairs
202/647-2538
ZIP code: 20520-6310

European and Canadian Affairs
202/647-6925
ZIP code: 20520-6511

Inter-American Affairs
202/647-4726
ZIP code: 20520-6258

Near Eastern and South Asian Affairs
202/647-5150
ZIP code: 20520-6243

TRANSPORTATION

Department of Transportation
400 Seventh Street SW
Washington, DC 20590
Main number: 202/366-4000
Public Affairs: 202/366-5580

Consumer Information:

Airplane Safety: 202/267-3489
Airplane Complaints: 202/366-2220
Automobile Defects: 1/800/424-9393
Boat Safety: 1/800/368-5647
Environmental Programs: 202/366-4366
Fraud, Waste and Abuse: 1/800/424-9071

Transportation Agencies:
(Addresses and main telephone numbers are the same as listed above for the Department of Transportation, unless otherwise noted.)

Federal Aviation Administration (FAA)
800 Independence Avenue SW
Washington, DC 20591
Public Affairs: 202/267-3883
Public Information Center: 202/267-3484

Federal Highway Administration
Main number: 202/366-0660
Public Information: 202/366-0630

Federal Railroad Administration
Public Affairs: 202/366-0881

Maritime Administration
Public Information: 202/366-5807

National Highway Traffic Safety Administration
Main number: 202/366-9550
Technical Reference: 202/366-2768

Saint Lawrence Seaway Development Corporation
Main number: 202/366-0091
Communications: 202/366-0110

U.S. Coast Guard
2100 Second Street SW
Washington, DC 20593
Main number: 202/267-1587
Public Affairs: 202/267-2229

Urban Mass Transportation Administration
Public Information: 202/366-4043
Transit Research Information: 202/366-9157

TREASURY

Department of the Treasury
1500 Pennsylvania Avenue NW
Washington, DC 20220
Main number: 202/566-2000
Public Affairs Office: 202/566-2041; 202/566-5252

Treasury agencies:

Bureau of Alcohol, Tobacco and Firearms
1200 Pennsylvania Avenue NW
Washington, DC 20226
Main number: 202/566-2000
Public Affairs: 202/566-7135
Public Information: 202/566-7777

Office of the Comptroller of the Currency
490 L'Enfant Plaza East SW

Washington, DC 20219
Communications: 202/447-1800
Information: 202/447-1810

Bureau of Engraving and Printing
Fourteenth and C Streets SW
Washington, DC 20228
Program Analysis and External Affairs:
202/447-1093

Federal Law Enforcement Training Center
Glynco, GA 31524
Main number: 912/267-2100
Public Affairs: 912/267-2447
Washington, DC Public Affairs: 202/566-2951

Financial Management Service
401 Fourteenth Street SW
Washington, DC 20227
Main number and Public Affairs: 202/287-0669

Internal Revenue Service
Headquarters
1111 Constitution Avenue NW
Washington, DC 20224
Information: 202/566-5000

Bureau of Public Debt
999 E Street NW
Washington, DC 20239-0001
Main number: 202/376-4300
Public Affairs: 202/376-4302

U.S. Customs Service
1301 Constitution Avenue NW
Washington, DC 20229
Public Affairs: 202/566-8195

U.S. Mint
Judiciary Square Building
633 Third Street NW
Washington, DC 20220
Main number: 202/376-0560
Public Affairs: 202/376-0837

U.S. Savings Bonds Division
1111 Twentieth Street NW
Washington, DC 20226
Main number: 202/634-5350
Public Affairs: 202/634-5377; 202/634-5389
Current Rate Information: 1/800/US-BONDS
(1/800/872-6637)

U.S. Secret Service
1800 G Street NW

Washington, DC 20223
Main number and Public Affairs: 202/535-5708

VETERANS AFFAIRS

Department of Veterans Affairs
810 Vermont Avenue NW
Washington, DC 20420
Main number: 202/233-2300
Public Affairs:
    Atlanta, GA: 404/374-3236
    Chicago, IL: 312/353-4076
    Dallas, TX: 214/372-7084
    Denver, CO: 303/980-2995
    Los Angeles, CA: 213/824-4497
    New York, NY: 212/620-6525
    Washington, DC: 202/233-2741

FEDERAL GOVERNMENT—INDEPENDENT AGENCIES, COMMISSIONS, AND GOVERNMENTAL CORPORATIONS

ACTION
1100 Vermont Avenue NW
Washington, DC 20525
Main number: 202/634-9380
Public Affairs: 202/634-9108

AMTRAK, National Railroad Passenger Corporation
60 Massachusetts Avenue NE
Washington, DC 20002
Main number: 202/906-3000
Public Affairs: 202/906-3860

Appalachian Regional Commission
1666 Connecticut Avenue NW
Washington, DC 20235
Main number: 202/673-7893
Public Affairs: 202/673-7968

Central Intelligence Agency
Washington, DC 20505
Main number: 703/482-1100
Public Affairs: 703/482-7676

Civil Rights, Commission on
1121 Vermont Avenue NW
Washington, DC 20425
Main number: 202/376-8177
Public Affairs: 202/376-8312

Consumer Product Safety Commission
5401 Westbard Avenue
Bethesda, MD 20207
Main number and Public Affairs: 202/492-6580

Environmental Protection Agency
401 M Street SW
Washington, DC 20460
Main number: 202/382-2090
Public Affairs: 202/382-4361

Equal Employment Opportunity Commission
1801 L Street NW
Washington, DC 20507
Main number: 202/634-6036; 1/800/USA-EEOC
Public Affairs: 202/634-6922

Export-Import Bank
811 Vermont Avenue NW
Washington, DC 20571
Main number: 202/566-8990
Public Affairs: 202/566-8990

Farm Credit Administration
1501 Farm Credit Drive
McLean, VA 22102-5090
Main number: 703/883-4000
Public Affairs: 703/883-4056

Federal Communications Commission
1919 M Street NW
Washington, DC 20554
Main number: 202/632-7000
Public Affairs: 202/632-5050

Federal Deposit Insurance Corporation
550 Seventeenth Street NW
Washington, DC 20429
Main number: 202/393-8400
Office of Corporate Communications: 202/898-6995

Federal Emergency Management Agency
500 C Street SW
Washington, DC 20472
Main number and Public Affairs: 202/646-4600

Federal Labor Relations Authority
500 C Street SW
Washington, DC 20424
Main number: 202/382-0711
Information Resources: 202/382-0715
(*See also* NATIONAL LABOR RELATIONS BOARD.)

Federal Maritime Commission
1100 L Street NW
Washington, DC 20573
Main number: 202/523-5773
Office of the Chairman: 202/523-5911

Federal Mediation and Conciliation Service
2100 K Street NW

Washington, DC 20427
Main number and Public Affairs: 202/653-5290
(*See also* NATIONAL MEDIATION BOARD.)

Federal Reserve System
Twentieth Street and Constitution Avenue NW
Washington, DC 20551
Main number: 202/452-3000
Public Affairs: 202/452-3204; 202/452-3215

Federal Trade Commission
Pennsylvania Avenue at Sixth Street NW
Washington, DC 20580
Public Reference Branch: 202/326-2222
Public Affairs: 202/326-2180; 202/326-2181

General Services Administration (GSA)
General Services Building
Eighteenth and F Streets NW
Washington, DC 20405
Main number: 202/472-1082
Public Affairs: 202/566-0705

Interstate Commerce Commission (ICC)
Twelfth Street and Constitution Avenue NW
Washington, DC 20423
Main number and Public Affairs: 202/275-7119
Consumer Assistance: 202/275-7849

Legal Services Corporation
400 Virginia Avenue SW
Washington, DC 20024-2751
Information: 202/863-1820

National Aeronautics and Space Administration (NASA)
600 Independence Avenue SW
Washington, DC 20546
Main number: 202/453-1000
Associate Administrator for Communications:
202/453-1898
Public Affairs: 202/453-8536

National Archives and Records Administration
Seventh Street and Pennsylvania Avenue NW
Washington, DC 20408
Main number: 202/501-5400
Office of Presidential Libraries: 202/501-5700
Publication and Sales: 202/501-5240

National Credit Union Administration
1776 G Street NW
Washington, DC 20456
Main number: 202/682-9600
Public Affairs: 202/682-9650

National Endowment for the Arts
Nancy Hanks Center
1100 Pennsylvania Avenue NW
Washington, DC 20506
Public Information Office: 202/682-5400

National Endowment for the Humanities
Nancy Hanks Center
1100 Pennsylvania Avenue NW
Washington, DC 20506
Public Information Office: 202/786-0438

National Labor Relations Board
1717 Pennsylvania Avenue NW
Washington, DC 20570
Main number: 202/655-4000
Information Division: 202/632-4950
(*See also* FEDERAL LABOR RELATIONS AUTHORITY.)

National Mediation Board
1425 K Street NW
Washington, DC 20572
Main number: 202/523-5920
Public Affairs: 202/523-5335
(*See also* FEDERAL MEDIATION AND CONCILIATION
Service.)

National Science Foundation
1800 G Street NW
Washington, DC 20550
Main number: 202/357-5000
Public Information: 202/357-9498

National Transporation Safety Board
800 Independence Avenue SW
Washington, DC 20594
Main number and Public Affairs: 202/382-6600

Nuclear Regulatory Commission
Office of Governmental and Public Affairs
Washington, DC 20555
Main number: 301/492-7000
Public Affairs: 301/492-0240
Information on Pending Regulations:
1/800/368-5642

**Occupational Safety and Health Review
Commission**
1825 K Street NW
Washington, DC 20006
Main number and Information: 202/634-7943
(*See also* DEPARTMENT OF LABOR, OCCUPATIONAL
SAFETY AND HEALTH ADMINISTRATION [OSHA].)

Peace Corps
1990 K Street NW

Washington, DC 20526
Main number: 202/254-6886
Public Information: 202/254-5010

Personnel Management, Office of
1900 E Street NW, Room 5F12
Washington, DC 20415
Main number: 202/632-1212
Public Affairs: 202/632-7433; 202/632-1214

Postal Rate Commission
1333 H Street NW
Washington, DC 20268-0001
Main number: 202/789-6800
Information: 202/789-6840

Postal Service, U.S.
475 L'Enfant Plaza SW
Washington, DC 20260-3121
Main number: 202/268-2000
Communications Dept.: 202/268-2143
Library: 202/268-2900

President's Committee on Employment of People With Disabilities
1111 Twentieth Street NW, Suite 636
Washington, DC 20036
Public Affairs: 202/653-5044

President's Council on Physical Fitness and Sports
450 Fifth Street NW, Suite 7103
Washington, DC 20001
Information Office: 202/272-3430: 202/272-3421

Securities and Exchange Commission (SEC)
450 Fifth Street NW
Washington, DC 20549
Main number: 202/272-3100
Public Affairs: 202/272-2650

Selective Service System
1023 Thirty-first Street NW
Washington, DC 20435
Main number: 202/724-0820
Public Information: 202/724-0419

Small Business Administration (SBA)
Imperial Building
1441 L Street NW, Rm 926
Washington, DC 20416
Main number: 202/653-7561; 800/368-5855
Public Communications: 202/653-6832

Smithsonian Institution
1000 Jefferson Dr. SW, Room 2410

Washington, DC 20560
Main number: 202/357-1300
Libraries: 202/357-2139
Public Affairs: 202/357-2627
Visitor Information: 202/357-2000

Thrift Supervision, Office of
(formerly Federal Home Loan Bank Board)
1700 G Street NW
Washington, DC 20552
202/906-6000
Public Affairs: 202/906-6677; 202/906-6678

U.S. Information Agency
301 Fourth Street SW
Washington, DC 20547
Main number: 202/485-7700
Public Liaison Office: 202/485-2355
   Voice of America
   Public Affairs: 202/485-8238; 202/485-6231

U.S. International Development Cooperation Agency

   Agency for International Development (AID)
   320 Twenty-first Street NW
   Washington, DC 20523-0001
   Main number and External Affairs: 202/647-1850
   Overseas Private Investment Corporation
   1615 M Street NW
   Washington, DC 20527
   202/457-7200
   Information Office: 202/457-7010

U.S. International Trade Commission
500 E Street SW
Washington, DC 20436
Main number: 202/252-1000
Public Affairs: 202/252-1820

FEDERAL GOVERNMENT—JUDICIAL BRANCH

Supreme Court of the United States
U.S. Supreme Court Building
1 First Street NE
Washington, DC 20543
Main number: 202/479-3000
Clerk: 202/479-3011
Public Information: 202/479-3211

   Administrative Office of the United States Courts
   811 Vermont Avenue NW
   Washington, DC 20544

Public Information: 202/633-6040

Federal Judicial Center
1520 H Street NW
Washington, DC 20005
Main number: 202/633-6011
Information Specialist: use main number, ask
for Information Specialist

Temporary Emergency Court of Appeals
Clerk
U.S. Courthouse
Washington, DC 20001
202/535-3390

U.S. Claims Court
Clerk
717 Madison Place NW
Washington, DC 20005
202/633-7257

U.S. Court of International Trade
Clerk
1 Federal Plaza
New York, NY 10007
212/264-2814

U.S. Court of Military Appeals
Clerk
450 E Street NW
Washington, DC 20442-0001
202/272-1448

U.S. Tax Court
Administrative Office
400 Second Street NW
Washington, DC 20217
202/376-2751

FEDERAL GOVERNMENT—LEGISLATIVE BRANCH

CONGRESSIONAL AGENCIES

Architect of the Capitol
U.S. Capitol Building
Washington, DC 20515
Main number and Information: 202/225-1200

Botanic Garden. *See* UNITED STATES BOTANIC
GARDEN.

Congressional Budget Office
Second and D Streets SW
Washington, DC 20515

Main number: 202/226-2621
Office of Intergovernmental Relations: 202/226-2600

Copyright Royalty Tribunal
1111 Twentieth Street NW, Suite 450
Washington, DC 20036
Main number and Information: 202/653-5175

District of Columbia
District Building
1350 Pennsylvania Avenue NW
Washington, DC 20004
Main number and Information: 202/727-6224
Mayor's office: 202/727-6424

General Accounting Office
441 G Street NW
Washington, DC 20548
Main number: 202/275-5067
Public Information: 202/275-2812

Government Printing Office (GPO)
North Capitol and H Streets NW
Washington, DC 20401
Main number: 202/275-2051
Public Affairs: 202/275-3204

Regional Bookstores: (listed by city)

Government Printing Office Bookstore
Room 100
275 Peachtree Street NE
Atlanta, GA 30343
404/331-6947

Government Printing Office Bookstore
2021 Third Avenue North
Birmingham, AL 35203
205/731-1056

Government Printing Office Bookstore
10 Causeway Street, Room 179
Boston, MA 02222
617/565-6680

Government Printing Office Bookstore
Room 1365, Federal Building
219 South Dearborn Street
Chicago, IL 60604
312/353-5133

Government Printing Office Bookstore
Room 1653, Federal Building
1240 East Ninth Street
Cleveland, OH 44199
216/522-4922

Government Printing Office Bookstore
Room 207, Federal Building
200 North High Street
Columbus, OH 43215
412/469-6956

Government Printing Office Bookstore
Room 1C46, Federal Building
1100 Commerce Street
Dallas, TX 75242
214/767-0076

Government Printing Office Bookstore
Room 117, Federal Building
1961 Stout Street
Denver, CO 80294
303/844-3964

Government Printing Office Bookstore
Suite 160, Federal Building
477 Michigan Avenue
Detroit, MI 48226
313/226-7816

Government Printing Office Bookstore
Texas Crude Building
801 Travis Street
Houston, TX 77002
713/653-3100

Government Printing Office Bookstore
Room 158, Federal Building
400 West Bay Street
Jacksonville, FL 32202
904/791-3801

Government Printing Office Bookstore
120 Bannister Mall
5600 East Bannister Road
Kansas City, MO 64137
816/765-2256

Government Printing Office Bookstore
Retail Sales Outlet
8660 Cherry Lane
Laurel, MD 20707
301/953-7974

Government Printing Office Bookstore
ARCO Plaza, C-Level
505 South Flower Street
Los Angeles, CA 90071
213/894-5841

Government Printing Office Bookstore
Room 190, Federal Building

517 East Wisconsin Avenue
Milwaukee, WI 53202
414/291-1304

Government Printing Office Bookstore
Room 110, Federal Plaza
New York, NY 10278
212/264-3825

Government Printing Office Bookstore
Robert Morris Building
100 North Fourteenth Street
Philadelphia, PA 19103
215/597-0677

Government Printing Office Bookstore
Room 118, Federal Building
1000 Liberty Avenue
Pittsburgh, PA 15222
412/644-2721

Government Printing Office Bookstore
1305 Southwest First Avenue
Portland, OR 97201
503/221-6217

Government Printing Office Bookstore
World Savings Building
720 North Main Street
Pueblo, CO 81003
719/544-3142

Government Printing Office Bookstore
Room 1023
450 Golden Gate Avenue
San Francisco, CA 94102
415/556-0643

Government Printing Office Bookstore
Room 194
915 Second Avenue
Seattle, WA 98174
206/442-4270

Government Printing Office Bookstore
710 North Capitol Street
Washington, DC 20401
202/275-2091

Government Printing Office Bookstore
1717 H Street NW
Washington, DC 20005
202/653-5075

Library of Congress
101 Independence Avenue SE

Washington, DC 20540
Main number: 202/707-5000
Information Office: 202/707-2905

Office of Technology Assessment
600 Pennsylvania Avenue SE
Washington, DC 20510-8025
Main number: 202/224-8713
Public Affairs: 202/224-9241
Publications: 202/224-8996

United States Botanic Garden
Office of the Director
245 First Street SW
Washington, DC 20024
Main number: 202/225-8333
Information: 202/225-1200

THE U.S. HOUSE OF REPRESENTATIVES
The Capitol
Washington, DC 20515
Main number: 202/224-3121
Clerk: 202/225-7000 (for information about the House)

Standing Committees of the House:
(Address individual committee by title and use the main U.S. House address above.)

Agriculture: 202/225-2171
Appropriations: 202/225-2771
Armed Services: 202/225-4151
Banking, Finance and Urban Affairs: 202/225-4247
Budget: 202/225-7200
District of Columbia: 202/225-4457
Education and Labor: 202/225-4527
Energy and Commerce: 202/225-2927
Foreign Affairs: 202/225-5021
Government Operations: 202/225-5051
House Administration: 202/225-2061
Interior and Insular Affairs: 202/225-2761
Judiciary: 202/225-3951
Merchant Marine and Fisheries: 202/225-4047
Post Office and Civil Service: 202/225-4054
Public Works and Transportation: 202/225-4472
Rules: 202/225-9486
Science, Space, and Technology: 202/225-6371
Small Business: 202/225-5821
Standards of Official Conduct: 202/225-7103
Veterans' Affairs: 202/225-3527
Ways and Means: 202/225-3625

THE U.S. SENATE
The Capitol

Washington, DC 20510
Main number: 202/224-3121
Secretary of the Senate: 202/224-2115 (for information about the Senate)

Standing Committees of the Senate:
(Address individual committee by title and use the main U.S. Senate address above.)

Agriculture, Nutrition, and Forestry: 202/224-2035
Appropriations: 202/224-3471
Armed Services: 202/224-3871
Banking, Housing, and Urban Affairs: 202/224-7391
Budget: 202/224-0642
Commerce, Science, and Transportation: 202/224-5115
Energy and Natural Resources: 202/224-4971
Environment and Public Works: 202/224-6176
Finance: 202/224-4515
Foreign Relations: 202/224-4651
Governmental Affairs: 202/224-4751
Judiciary: 202/224-5225
Labor and Human Resources: 202/224-5375
Rules and Administration: 202/224-6352
Small Business: 202/224-5175
Veterans' Affairs: 202/224-9126

FOREIGN GOVERNMENTS

Afghanistan:
Embassy of the Republic of Afghanistan
2341 Wyoming Avenue NW
Washington, DC 20008
202/234-3770
FAX: 202/328-3516

Algeria:
Embassy of the Democratic and Popular Republic of Algeria
2118 Kalorama Road NW
Washington, DC 20008
202/328-5300
   Iranian Interests Section:
   2209 Wisconsin Avenue NW
   Washington, DC 20007
   202/965-4990

Antigua and Barbuda:
Embassy of Antigua and Barbuda
3400 International Drive NW, Suite 4M
Washington, DC 20008

202/362-5211
FAX: 202/362-5225

Argentina:
Embassy of the Argentine Republic
1600 New Hampshire Avenue NW
Washington, DC 20009
202/939-6400

Australia:
Embassy of Australia
1601 Massachusetts Avenue NW
Washington, DC 20036
202/797-3000
FAX: 202/797-3168

Austria:
Embassy of Austria
2343 Massachusetts Avenue NW
Washington, DC 20008
202/483-4474
FAX: 202/483-2743

Bahamas:
Embassy of The Commonwealth of The Bahamas
600 New Hampshire Avenue NW, Suite 865
Washington, DC 20037
202/944-3390
FAX: 202/333-7487

Bahrain:
Embassy of the State of Bahrain
3502 International Drive NW
Washington, DC 20008
202/342-0741

Bangladesh:
Embassy of the People's Republic of Bangladesh
2201 Wisconsin Avenue NW
Washington, DC 20007
202/342-8372

Barbados:
Embassy of Barbados
2144 Wyoming Avenue NW
Washington, DC 20008
202/939-9200

Belgium:
Embassy of Belgium
3330 Garfield Street NW
Washington, DC 20008
202/333-6900

Belize:
Embassy of Belize

3400 International Drive NW, Suite 2J
Washington, DC 20008
202/363-4505
FAX: 202/362-7468

Benin:
Embassy of the People's Republic of Benin
2737 Cathedral Avenue NW
Washington, DC 20008
202/232-6656

Bolivia:
Embassy of Bolivia
3014 Massachusetts Avenue NW
Washington, DC 20008
202/483-4410
FAX: 202/328-3712

Botswana:
Embassy of the Republic of Botswana
4301 Connecticut Avenue NW, Suite 404
Washington, DC 20008
202/244-4990
FAX: 202/244-4164

Brazil:
Brazilian Embassy
3006 Massachusetts Avenue NW
Washington, DC 20008
202/745-2700
FAX: 202/745-2827

Brunei:
Embassy of the State of Brunei Darussalam
2600 Virginia Avenue NW, Suite 300
Washington, DC 20037
202/342-0159

Bulgaria:
Embassy of the People's Republic of Bulgaria
1621 Twenty-second Street NW
Washington, DC 20008
202/387-7969
FAX: 202/234-7973

Burkina Faso:
Embassy of Burkina Faso
2340 Massachusetts Avenue NW
Washington, DC 20008
202/332-5577

Burundi:
Embassy of the Republic of Burundi
2233 Wisconsin Avenue NW, Suite 212

Washington, DC 20007
202/342-2574

Cameroon:
Embassy of the Republic of Cameroon
2349 Massachusetts Avenue NW
Washington, DC 20008
202/265-8790

Canada:
Embassy of Canada
501 Pennsylvania Avenue NW
Washington, DC 20001
202/682-1740
FAX: 202/682-7726

Cape Verde:
Embassy of the Republic of Cape Verde
3415 Massachusetts Avenue NW
Washington, DC 20007
202/965-6820
FAX: 202/965-1207

Central African Republic:
Embassy of Central African Republic
1618 Twenty-second Street NW
Washington, DC 20008
202/483-7800

Chad:
Embassy of the Republic of Chad
2002 R Street NW
Washington, DC 20009
202/462-4009
FAX: 462-4009

Chile:
Embassy of Chile
1732 Massachusetts Avenue NW
Washington, DC 20036
202/785-1746

China: *See also* TAIWAN.
Embassy of the People's Republic of China
2300 Connecticut Avenue NW
Washington, DC 20008
202/328-2500

Colombia:
Embassy of Colombia
2118 Leroy Place NW
Washington, DC 20008
202/387-8338
FAX: 202/232-8643

Comoros:
Embassy of the Federal and Islamic Republic of the Comoros
c/o Permanent Mission of the Federal and Islamic Republic of the Comoros to the United Nations
336 East Forty-fifth Street, Second Floor
New York, NY 10017
212/972-8010

Congo, People's Republic of:
Embassy of the People's Republic of Congo
4891 Colorado Avenue NW
Washington, DC 20011
202/726-5500

Costa Rica:
Embassy of Costa Rica
1825 Connecticut Avenue NW
Washington, DC 20009
202/234-2945
FAX: 202/234-8653

Côte d'Ivoire:
Embassy of the Republic of Côte d'Ivoire
2424 Massachusetts Avenue NW
Washington, DC 20008
202/797-0300

Cuba:
No diplomatic relations; affairs are handled by Switzerland.

Cyprus:
Embassy of the Republic of Cyprus
2211 R Street NW
Washington, DC 20008
202/462-5772

Czechoslovakia:
Embassy of Czechoslovak Socialist Republic
3900 Linnean Avenue NW
Washington, DC 20008
202/363-6315
FAX: 202/966-8540

Dahomey: *See* BENIN.

Denmark:
Royal Danish Embassy
3200 Whitehaven Street NW
Washington, DC 20008
202/234-4300
FAX: 202/328-1470

Djibouti:
Embassy of the Republic of Djibouti
1430 K Street NW, Suite 600

Washington, DC 20005
202/347-0254

Dominica:
Permanent Mission to the United Nations of the Commonwealth of Dominica
820 Second Avenue, Suite 900b
New York, NY 10017
212/949-0853

Dominican Republic:
Embassy of Dominican Republic
1715 Twenty-second Street NW
Washington, DC 20008
202/332-6280

Ecuador:
Embassy of Ecuador
2535 Fifteenth Street NW
Washington, DC 20009
202/234-7200

Egypt:
Embassy of the Arab Republic of Egypt
2310 Decatur Place NW
Washington, DC 20008
202/232-5400

El Salvador:
Embassy of El Salvador
2308 California Street NW
Washington, DC 20008
202/265-3480

Equatorial Guinea:
Embassy of Equatorial Guinea
801 Second Avenue, Suite 1403
New York, NY 10017
212/599-1523

Estonia:
Legation of Estonia
9 Rockefeller Plaza
New York, NY 10020
212/247-1450

Ethiopia:
Embassy of Ethiopia
2134 Kalorama Road NW
Washington, DC 20008
202/234-2281

European Communities, Delegation of the Commission of the
2100 M Street NW, Seventh Floor

Washington, DC 20037
202/862-9500
FAX: 202/429-1766

Fiji:
Embassy of Fiji
2233 Wisconsin Avenue NW, Suite 240
Washington, DC 20007
202/337-8320

Finland:
Embassy of Finland
3216 New Mexico Avenue NW
Washington, DC 20016
202/363-2430

France:
Embassy of France
4101 Reservoir Road NW
Washington, DC 20007
202/944-6000

Gabon:
Embassy of the Gabonese Republic
2034 Twentieth Street NW
Washington, DC 20009
202/797-1000

Gambia, The:
Embassy of The Gambia
1030 Fifteenth Street NW, Suite 720
Washington, DC 20005
202/842-1356
FAX: 202/842-2073

Germany:
Embassy of the Federal Republic of Germany
4645 Reservoir Road NW
Washington, DC 20007
202/298-4000

Ghana:
Embassy of Ghana
3512 International Drive NW
Washington, DC 20008
202/686-4520
FAX: 202/939-5824

Great Britain: *See* **United Kingdom of Great Britain and Northern Ireland**.

Greece:
Embassy of Greece
2221 Massachusetts Avenue NW

Washington, DC 20008
202/667-3168
FAX: 202/939-5824

Grenada:
Embassy of Grenada
1701 New Hampshire Avenue NW
Washington, DC 20009
202/265-2561

Guatemala:
Embassy of Guatemala
2220 R Street NW
Washington, DC 20008
202/745-4952
FAX: 202/745-1908

Guinea:
Embassy of the Republic of Guinea
2112 Leroy Place NW
Washington, DC 20008
202/483-9420

Guinea-Bissau:
Embassy of the Republic of Guinea-Bissau
c/o Permanent Mission of Guinea-Bissau
211 East Forty-third Street, Suite 604
New York, NY 10017
212/661-3977

Guyana:
Embassy of Guyana
2490 Tracy Place NW
Washington, DC 20008
202/265-6900

Haiti:
Embassy of Haiti
2311 Massachusetts Avenue NW
Washington, DC 20008
202/332-4090
FAX: 202/745-7215

Honduras:
Embassy of Honduras
3007 Tilden Street NW
Washington, DC 20008
202/966-7702
FAX: 202/966-9751

Hungary:
Embassy of the Republic of Hungary
3910 Shoemaker Street NW
Washington, DC 20008
202/362-6730

Iceland:
Embassy of Iceland
2022 Connecticut Avenue NW
Washington, DC 20008
202/265-6653
FAX: 202/265-6656

India:
Embassy of India
2107 Massachusetts Avenue NW
Washington, DC 20008
202/939-7000

Indonesia:
Embassy of the Republic of Indonesia
2020 Massachusetts Avenue NW
Washington, DC 20036
202/775-5200

Iran:
No diplomatic relations; affairs are handled by
Algeria.

Iraq:
Embassy of the Republic of Iraq
1801 P Street NW
Washington, DC 20036
202/483-7500
FAX: 202/462-5066

Ireland:
Embassy of Ireland
2234 Massachusetts Avenue NW
Washington, DC 20008
202/462-3939

Israel:
Embassy of Israel
3514 International Drive NW
Washington, DC 20008
202/364-5500
FAX: 202/364-5610

Italy:
Embassy of Italy
1601 Fuller Street NW
Washington, DC 20009
202/328-5500

Ivory Coast: *See* CÔTE D'IVOIRE.

Jamaica:
Embassy of Jamaica
1850 K Street NW, Suite 355
Washington, DC 20006

202/452-0660
FAX: 202/452-0081

Japan:
Embassy of Japan
2520 Massachusetts Avenue NW
Washington, DC 20008
202/939-6700
FAX: 202/939-6788
Information Center:
Lafayette Center
1155 Twenty-first Street NW
Washington, DC 20036
202/939-6904

Jordan:
Embassy of the Hashemite Kingdom of Jordan
3504 International Drive NW
Washington, DC 20008
202/966-2664
FAX: 202/966-3110

Kenya:
Embassy of Kenya
2249 R Street NW
Washington, DC 20008
202/387-6101

Korea:
Embassy of Korea
2370 Massachusetts Avenue NW
Washington, DC 20008
202/939-5600

Kuwait:
Embassy of the State of Kuwait
2940 Tilden Street NW
Washington, DC 20008
202/966-0702
FAX: 202/966-0517

Laos:
Embassy of the Lao People's Democratic Republic
2222 S Street NW
Washington, DC 20008
202/332-6416

Latvia:
Legation of Latvia
4325 Seventeenth Street NW
Washington, DC 20011
202/726-8213

Lebanon:
Embassy of Lebanon

2560 Twenty-eighth Street NW
Washington, DC 20008
202/939-6300
FAX: 202/939-6324

Lesotho:
Embassy of the Kingdom of Lesotho
2511 Massachusetts Avenue NW
Washington, DC 20008
202/797-5533
FAX: 202/234-6815

Liberia:
Embassy of the Republic of Liberia
5201 Sixteenth Street NW
Washington, DC 20011
202/723-0437

Lithuania:
Legation of Lithuania
2622 Sixteenth Street NW
Washington, DC 20009
202/234-5860
FAX: 202/328-0466

Luxembourg:
Embassy of Luxembourg
2200 Massachusetts Avenue NW
Washington, DC 20008
202/265-4171
FAX: 202/328-8270

Madagascar:
Embassy of the Democratic Republic of Madagascar
2374 Massachusetts Avenue NW
Washington, DC 20008
202/265-5525

Malawi:
Malawi Embassy
2408 Massachusetts Avenue NW
Washington, DC 20008
202/797-1007

Malaysia:
Embassy of Malaysia
2401 Massachusetts Avenue NW
Washington, DC 20008
202/328-2700
FAX: 202/483-7661

Mali:
Embassy of the Republic of Mali
2130 R Street NW

Washington, DC 20008
202/332-2249

Malta:
Embassy of Malta
2017 Connecticut Avenue NW
Washington, DC 20008
202/462-3611
FAX: 202/387-5470

Marshall Islands:
Embassy of the Republic of the Marshall Islands
1901 Pennsylvania Avenue NW, Suite 1004
Washington, DC 20006
202/223-4952
FAX: 202/785-5083

Mauritania:
Embassy of the Islamic Republic of Mauritania
2339 S Street NW
Washington, DC 20008
202/387-1220

Mauritius:
Embassy of Mauritius
4301 Connecticut Avenue NW, Suite 134
Washington, DC 20008
202/244-1419
FAX: 202/966-0983

Mexico:
Embassy of Mexico
2829 Sixteenth Street NW
Washington, DC 20009
202/234-6000

Micronesia:
Embassy of the Federated States of Micronesia
706 G Street SE
Washington, DC 20003
202/544-2640

Morocco:
Embassy of Morocco
1601 Twenty-first Street NW
Washington, DC 20009
202/462-7979
FAX: 202/265-0161

Mozambique:
Embassy of the People's Republic of Mozambique
1990 M Street NW, Suite 570
Washington, DC 20036
202/293-7146
FAX: 202/235-0245

Myanmar:
Embassy of the Union of Myanmar
2300 S Street NW
Washington, DC 20008
202/332-9044

Nepal:
Royal Nepalese Embassy
2131 Leroy Place NW
Washington, DC 20008
202/667-4550

Netherlands:
Embassy of the Netherlands
4200 Linnean Avenue NW
Washington, DC 20008
202/244-5300
FAX: 202/362-3430

New Zealand:
Embassy of New Zealand
37 Observatory Circle NW
Washington, DC 20008
202/328-4800

Nicaragua:
Embassy of Nicaragua
1627 New Hampshire Avenue NW
Washington, DC 20009
202/387-4371

Niger:
Embassy of the Republic of Niger
2204 R Street NW
Washington, DC 20008
202/483-4224

Nigeria:
Embassy of the Federal Republic of Nigeria
2201 M Street NW
Washington, DC 20037
202/822-1500

Norway:
Royal Norwegian Embassy
2720 Thirty-fourth Street NW
Washington, DC 20008
202/333-6000
FAX: 202/337-0870

Oman:
Embassy of the Sultanate of Oman
2342 Massachusetts Avenue NW
Washington, DC 20008
202/387-1980

Pakistan:
Embassy of Pakistan
2315 Massachusetts Avenue NW
Washington, DC 20008
202/939-6200
FAX: 202/387-0484

Panama:
Embassy of Panama
2862 McGill Terrace NW
Washington, DC 20008
202/483-1407
FAX: 202/483-8413

Papua New Guinea:
Embassy of Papua New Guinea
1330 Connecticut Avenue NW, Suite 350
Washington, DC 20036
202/659-0856
FAX: 202/466-2412

Paraguay:
Embassy of Paraguay
2400 Massachusetts Avenue NW
Washington, DC 20008
202/483-6962

Peru:
Embassy of Peru
1700 Massachusetts Avenue NW
Washington, DC 20036
202/833-9860

Philippines:
Embassy of the Philippines
1617 Massachusetts Avenue NW
Washington, DC 20036
202/483-1414
FAX: 202/328-7614

Poland:
Embassy of the Polish People's Republic
2640 Sixteenth Street NW
Washington, DC 20009
202/234-3800

Portugal:
Embassy of Portugal
2125 Kalorama Road NW
Washington, DC 20008
202/328-8610

Qatar:
Embassy of the State of Qatar
600 New Hampshire Avenue NW, Suite 1180

Washington, DC 20037
202/338-0111

Romania:
Embassy of the Socialist Republic of Romania
1607 Twenty-third Street NW
Washington, DC 20008
202/232-4747

Russia: *See* UNION OF SOVIET SOCIALIST REPUBLICS.

Rwanda:
Embassy of the Republic of Rwanda
1714 New Hampshire Avenue NW
Washington, DC 20009
202/232-2882

Saint Kitts and Nevis:
Embassy of St. Kitts and Nevis
2501 M Street NW, Suite 540
Washington, DC 20037
202/833-3550

Saint Lucia:
Embassy of St. Lucia
2100 M Street NW, Suite 309
Washington, DC 20037
202/463-7378
FAX: 202/887-5746

São Tomé and Principe:
Embassy of Sao Tome and Principe
801 Second Avenue, Suite 1504
New York, NY 10017
212/697-4211
FAX: 212/687-8389

Saudi Arabia:
Embassy of Saudi Arabia
601 New Hampshire Avenue NW
Washington, DC 20037
202/342-3800

Senegal:
Embassy of the Republic of Senegal
2112 Wyoming Avenue NW
Washington, DC 20008
202/234-0540

Seychelles:
Embassy of the Republic of Seychelles
c/o Permanent Mission of Seychelles to the United
Nations
820 Second Avenue, Suite 900F
New York, NY 10017

212/687-9766
FAX: 212/808-4975

Sierra Leone:
Embassy of Sierra Leone
1701 Nineteenth Street NW
Washington, DC 20009
202/939-9261

Singapore:
Embassy of Singapore
1824 R Street NW
Washington, DC 20009
202/667-7555
FAX: 202/265-7915

Somalia:
Embassy of the Somali Democratic Republic
600 New Hampshire Avenue NW, Suite 710
Washington, DC 20037
202/342-1575

South Africa:
Embassy of South Africa
3051 Massachusetts Avenue NW
Washington, DC 20008
202/232-4400

Spain:
Embassy of Spain
2700 Fifteenth Street NW
Washington, DC 20009
202/265-0190

Sri Lanka:
Embassy of the Democratic Socialist Republic of Sri Lanka
2148 Wyoming Avenue NW
Washington, DC 20008
202/483-4025
FAX: 202/232-7181

Sudan:
Embassy of the Republic of Sudan
2210 Massachusetts Avenue NW
Washington, DC 20008
202/338-8565

Suriname:
Embassy of the Republic of Suriname
4301 Connecticut Avenue NW, Suite 108
Washington, DC 20008
202/244-7488
FAX: 202/244-5878

Swaziland:
Embassy of the Kingdom of Swaziland
3400 International Drive NW
Washington, DC 20008
202/362-6683
FAX: 202/244-8059

Sweden:
Embassy of Sweden
600 New Hampshire Avenue NW, Suite 1200
Washington, DC 20037
202/944-5600
FAX: 202/342-1319

Switzerland:
Embassy of Switzerland
2900 Cathedral Avenue NW
Washington, DC 20008
202/745-7900
FAX: 202/387-2564
Cuban Interests Section
2630 and 2639 Sixteenth Street NW
Washington DC 20009
202/797-8518

Syria:
Embassy of the Syrian Arab Republic
2215 Wyoming Avenue NW
Washington, DC 20008
202/232-6313
FAX: 234-9548

Taiwan (Republic of China):
Coordination Council for North American Affairs
4201 Wisconsin Avenue NW
Washington, DC 20016
202/895-1800

Tanzania:
Embassy of the United Republic of Tanzania
2139 R Street NW
Washington, DC 20008
202/939-6125

Thailand:
Embassy of Thailand
2300 Kalorama Road NW
Washington, DC 20008
202/483-7200

Togo:
Embassy of the Republic of Togo
2208 Massachusetts Avenue NW
Washington, DC 20008
202/234-4212

Trinidad and Tobago:
Embassy of Trinidad and Tobago
1708 Massachusetts Avenue NW
Washington, DC 20036
202/467-6490
FAX: 202/785-3130

Tunisia:
Embassy of Tunisia
1515 Massachusetts Avenue NW
Washington, DC 20005
202/862-1850

Turkey:
Embassy of The Republic of Turkey
1606 Twenty-third Street NW
Washington, DC 20008
202/387-3200

Uganda:
Embassy of the Republic of Uganda
5909 Sixteenth Street NW
Washington, DC 20011
202/726-7100
FAX: 202/726-1727

Union of Soviet Socialist Republics (USSR):
Embassy of the Union of Soviet Socialist
Republics
1125 Sixteenth Street NW
Washington, DC 20036
202/628-7551

United Arab Emirates:
Embassy of the United Arab Emirates
600 New Hampshire Avenue NW, Suite 740
Washington, DC 20037
202/338-6500

United Kingdom of Great Britain and Northern Ireland:
British Embassy
3100 Massachusetts Avenue NW
Washington, DC 20008
202/462-1340
FAX: 202/898-4255

Upper Volta: *See* BURKINA FASO.

Uruguay:
Embassy of Uruguay
1918 F Street NW
Washington, DC 20006
202/331-1313

Venezuela:
Embassy of Venezuela
2445 Massachusetts Avenue NW
Washington, DC 20008
202/797-3800

Western Samoa:
Embassy of Western Samoa
c/o Permanent Mission of Samoa to the United
Nations
820 Second Avenue
New York, NY 10017
212/599-6196

Yemen:
Embassy of the Yemen Arab Republic
600 New Hampshire Avenue NW, Suite 840
Washington, DC 20037
202/965-4760
FAX: 202/337-2017

Yugoslavia:
Embassy of the Socialist Federal Republic of
Yugoslavia
2410 California Street NW
Washington, DC 20008
202/462-6566

Zaire:
Embassy of the Republic of Zaire
1800 New Hampshire Avenue NW
Washington, DC 20009
202/234-7690

Zambia:
Embassy of the Republic of Zambia
2419 Massachusetts Avenue NW
Washington, DC 20008
202/265-9717

Zimbabwe:
Embassy of Zimbabwe
2852 McGill Terrace NW
Washington, DC 20008
202/332-7100

STATE GOVERNMENTS

Alabama:
Office of the Governor
11 South Union Street, Room 219
Montgomery, AL 36130
205/242-7139; 8 A.M.–5 P.M. CST
Operator directs calls to appropriate offices.

Alaska:
Office of the Governor
P.O. Box A
Juneau, AK 99811-0101
907/465-3500; 8 A.M.–5 P.M. Alaska Standard Time
Operator refers calls to Office of Ombudsman.
   Office of Ombudsman
   P.O. Box WO
   Juneau, AK 99811-3000
   907/465-4970; 8 A.M.–5 P.M.
   Alaska Standard Time
Answers all constituency calls.

Arizona:
Office of the Governor
1700 West Washington Avenue
Phoenix, AZ 85007
602/542-4331; 8 A.M.–5 P.M.
Operator directs calls to appropriate offices.

Arkansas:
Office of the Governor
State Capitol, Room 250
Little Rock, AR 72201
501/682-2345; 8 A.M.–5 P.M. CST
Operator directs calls to appropriate offices.

California:
Office of the Governor
State Capitol
Sacramento, CA 95814
916/445-2841; 8 A.M.–5 P.M. PST
Operator directs calls to appropriate offices.

Colorado:
Office of the Governor
State Capitol Building, Room 136
Denver, CO 80203
303/866-2471; 8 A.M.–5 P.M. MST
Citizen's Advocate Office: 303/866-2885

Connecticut:
Office of the Governor
210 Capitol Avenue
Hartford, CT 06106
203/566-4840; 8:30 AM–5:30 P.M. EST
Operator directs calls to appropriate offices.

Delaware:
Office of the Governor
820 North French Street
Wilmington, DE 19801
302/736-4101; 8 A.M.–5 P.M. EST
Constituent services: 800/292-9510

Florida:
Office of the Governor
Capitol Building
Tallahassee, FL 32399-0001
904/488-4441; 8 A.M.–5 P.M. EST
Citizen's assistance: 904/488-7146

Georgia:
Office of the Governor
203 State Capitol
Atlanta, GA 30334
404/656-1776; 8 A.M.–5 P.M. EST
Operator directs calls to appropriate offices.

Hawaii:
Office of the Governor
Executive Chambers
State Capitol
Honolulu, HI 96813
808/548-3170; 7:45 A.M.–4:30 P.M. Hawaii Standard Time
Citizen's assistance: 808/548-6222

Idaho:
Office of the Governor
State House
Boise, ID 83720
208/334-2100; 8 A.M.–5 P.M. MST
Operator directs calls to appropriate offices.

Illinois:
Office of the Governor
207 State House
Springfield, IL 62706
217/728-6830; 8:30 A.M.–5 P.M. CST
Citizen's assistance: 217/782-0244

Chicago Citizen's Assistance
Office of the Governor
100 West Randolph Street
Chicago, IL 60601
312/814-2121; 8:30 A.M.–5 P.M. CST

Indiana:
Office of the Governor
State House, Room 206
Indianapolis, IN 46204
317/232-4567
Citizen's assistance: 800/333-8357 (records message 24 hours per day)

Iowa:
Office of the Governor
State Capitol

Des Moines, IA 50319
515/281-5211; 8:30 A.M.–4 P.M. CST
Operator directs calls to appropriate offices.

Kansas:
Office of the Governor
State House
Topeka, KS 66612
913/296-3232; 8 A.M.–5 P.M. CST
Constituent assistance: 913/296-4030

Kentucky:
Office of the Governor
Capitol Building, Room 100
Frankfort, KY 40601
502/564-2611; 8 A.M.–5:30 P.M. CST
Ask for constituent services.

Louisiana:
Office of the Governor
P.O. Box 94004
Baton Rouge, LA 70804
504/342-7015; 8 A.M.–5:30 P.M. CST
Constituent services: 800/LA-CARES

Maine:
Office of the Governor
State House Station #1
Augusta, ME 04333
207/289-3531; 8 A.M.–5 P.M. EST
Constituent services: 800/452-4617

Maryland:
Office of the Governor
State House
Annapolis, MD 21401
301/974-3431; 8:30 A.M.–5 P.M. EST
Operator directs calls to appropriate offices.

Massachusetts:
Office of the Governor
State House, Room 360
Boston, MA 02133
617/727-3600; 9 A.M.–5 P.M. EST
Constituent services: 617/727-2776

Michigan:
Office of the Governor
P.O. Box 30013
Lansing, MI 48904
517/373-3400; 8 A.M.–6 P.M. EST
Operator directs calls to appropriate offices.

Minnesota:
Office of the Governor

State Capitol, Room 130
St. Paul, MN 55155
612/296-3391; 8 A.M.–5 P.M.

Mississippi:
Office of the Governor
P.O. Box 139
Jackson, MS 39205
601/359-3100
Citizen's assistance: 601/354-4540 (records messages
24 hours per day, 7 days per week)

Missouri:
Office of the Governor
Constituency Service Section
P.O. Box 720
Jefferson City, MO 65102
314/751-3222; 8 A.M.–5 P.M. CST

Montana:
Office of the Governor
State Capitol
Helena, MT 59620
406/444-3111; 8 A.M.–5 P.M. MST
  Dept. of Commerce
  Consumer Affairs Unit
  1424 North Avenue
  Helena, MT 59620
  406/444-4312; 8 A.M.–5 P.M. MST

Nebraska:
Office of the Governor
State Capitol
Division of Policy Research
Lincoln, NE 68509
402/471-2414; 8 A.M.–5 P.M. CST

Nevada:
Office of the Governor
State Capitol Complex
Carson City, NE 89710
702/687-5670; 8 A.M.–5 P.M. PST
Operator directs calls to appropriate offices.

New Hampshire:
Office of the Governor
State House, Room 208
Concord, NH 03301
603/271-2121; 8 A.M.–5 P.M. EST
Citizen's Services: in NH, 800/852-3456
out of NH, 603/271-3130

New Jersey:
Office of the Governor

Constituency Relations
State House
125 West State Street
Trenton, NJ 08625
609/292-6000; 9 A.M.–5 P.M. EST

New Mexico:
Office of the Governor
Constituency Services
State Capitol
Santa Fe, NM 87503
505/827-3000; 8 A.M.–5 P.M. MST
Office of the Lieutenant Governor
State Ombudsman
State Capitol
Sante Fe, NM 87503
505/827-3000; 8 A.M.–5 P.M. MST

New York:
Executive Chamber
State Capitol
Albany, NY 12224
518/474-8390; 8:30 A.M.–5 P.M. EST
Consumer Problems:
State Consumer Protection Board
Consumer Problems
250 Broadway
New York, NY 10013
212/587-4908; 9 A.M.–5 P.M. EST

North Carolina:
Office of the Governor
Executive Chamber
State Capitol
Raleigh, NC 27603-8001
919/733-4240; 8 A.M. 5 P.M. EST

North Dakota:
Office of the Governor
600 East Boulevard
Bismarck, ND 58505
701/224-2200; 8 A.M.–5 P.M. CST

Ohio:
Office of the Governor
77 South High Street, 30th Floor
Columbus, OH 43266-0601
614/466-3555; 8 A.M.–5 P.M. EST
Operator directs calls to appropriate offices.

Oklahoma:
Office of the Governor
Room 212

Oklahoma City, OK 73105
405/521-2342; 8 A.M.–5 P.M. CST

Oregon:
Office of the Governor
State Capitol Building
Salem, OR 97310
503/378-3111; 8 A.M.–5 P.M. PST

Pennsylvania:
Office of the Governor
The Capitol, Room 225
Harrisburg, PA 17120
Governor's Action Line: 800/932-0784 (PA residents
only); 8 A.M.–5 P.M. EST
Commonwealth Information Center: 717/787-2121;
8 A.M.–5 P.M. EST
Operator directs calls to appropriate offices.

Rhode Island:
Office of the Governor
State House
Providence, RI 02903
401/277-2080; 9 A.M.–5 P.M. EST

South Carolina:
Office of the Governor
P.O. Box 11369
Columbia, SC 29211
803/734-9818; 8 A.M.–6:30 P.M. EST

South Dakota:
Office of the Governor
500 East Capitol
Pierre, SD 57501
605/773-3212; 8 A.M.–5 P.M. CST

Tennessee:
Office of the Governor
State Capitol
Nashville, TN 37219
615/741-2001; 8:00 A.M.–4:30 P.M. CST

Texas:
Office of the Governor
P.O. Box 124-28
State Capitol
Austin, TX 78711
512/463-2000; 8 A.M.–5 P.M. CST
Citizen's assistance: 512/463-2000

Utah:
Office of the Governor
210 State Capitol

Salt Lake City, UT 84114
801/538-1000; 7:30 A.M.–6 P.M. MST

Vermont:
Office of the Governor
109 State Street
Montpelier, VT 05602
802/828-3333; 8 A.M.–4:30 P.M. EST

Virginia:
Office of the Governor
State Capitol, Third floor
Richmond, VA 23219
804/786-2211; 8 A.M.–5:30 P.M. EST

Washington:
Office of the Governor
Legislative Building
Olympia, WA 98504
206/753-6780; 7:30 A.M.–5:30 P.M. PST

West Virginia:
Office of the Governor
State Capitol Building
Charleston, WV 25305
304/340-1600; 8 A.M.–6 P.M. EST

Wisconsin:
Office of the Governor
State Capitol
P.O. Box 7863
Madison, WI 53707
608/266-1212; 8 A.M.–5 P.M. CST
Constituency Relations: 608/266-1212

Wyoming:
Office of the Governor
State Capitol Building
Cheyenne, WY 82002
307/777-7434; 8 A.M.–5 P.M. MST

4.

Picture Sources

THE PIONEERING PHOTOJOURNALISM OF *LIFE* magazine in the late 1930s and its coverage of World War II demonstrated, once and for all, the effectiveness of pictures as an important and meaningful source of information. And then came television! Now, we rely on graphic images as a primary source of information about the world we live in. And so the process of looking up information these days frequently requires finding pictures to make a point, to document a story, to lend visual content to a presentation, and to enhance the written word in countless other ways.

There are more than 1,000 sources of pictures throughout the United States—and many, many more if you add libraries, museums, and historical societies with collections of regional and local interest. As with other chapters in this book, "Picture Sources" presents a selection of sources—both commercial and non-commercial—that information professionals have found to be especially useful. There are literally millions of images available through the sources listed below.

Sources that have particularly strong collections in one area or another are listed alphabetically by subject, then alphabetically by organization within each subject. Large, nonspecialized, multisubject collections are grouped in the "General Picture Sources" category, with information about the major subjects to be found in each general collection.

Some sources are listed under two or more subjects when they have more than one strong specialty.

Additional Sources

Additional picture sources may be found in the following places:

1. The "Special Collections" section in this book. For example, at the New York Public Library, the Schomburg Center for Research in Black Culture and the Billy Rose Theatre collections have extensive picture archives in black history and performing arts, respectively. Many other libraries and museums throughout the country also offer pictures as adjuncts to their main collections.

2. The "Government Sources" section. Contact the public affairs or public information number listed to find out about the availability of pictures.

3. Local libraries, museums, and historical societies. Many of these institutions have picture archives. Call the main number listed in the telephone directory and ask for the person who can tell you what pictures are available. If that source doesn't have what you want, ask whether there are other sources that might be helpful.

4. College and university libraries. Call the main college or university library number and ask for the person or department in charge of the picture collection.

5. State and regional tourist bureaus. These are good sources of regional pictures. Call the number listed in your telephone directory. If you can't find a number, call the main information number listed for the state under "State Governments" in the "Government Sources" section of this book.

6. Presidential libraries. These are not only good sources for the life and political career of each President for which there is a library, but also for historical and social events that occurred during his lifetime. For a complete listing of these, see "Presidential Libraries" in the "Special Collections" section of this book.

7. Major corporations. Many have excellent collections of photographs and art, and most of the time their pictures will be furnished free of charge. Check with the public relations departments or archivists of major companies in an industry for which you need images. Call the toll-free information number, 800/555-1212, to obtain the corporation headquarters' number. Explain what you want and your request will be routed to the appropriate office. Not all corporate collections are open to the public, however, so you may have to call several companies to locate the most helpful source.

8. Airlines. These are often a good, free source of images of foreign countries. Call the U.S. headquarters of the airlines operating in the countries in which you are interested and ask for public relations.

9. Public relations departments—or photographic archives—of television networks and movie studios. These are good sources for pictures of movie and TV personalities and scenes from movie and TV productions.

Some commercial agencies have catalogs and will be happy to send them to you free of charge. This is a good way to get an overview of an agency's collection. Many agencies now number each photograph reproduced in a catalog so that you can order an image directly or tell an agency that you would like to see a selection of pictures similar to a number displayed in the catalog.

Museums also have catalogs of their collections or exhibits. Some museums charge for these catalogs, but the charge is usually minimal. Reproductions can be ordered directly from the catalog.

Conducting Picture Research

1. If the picture you want to use has been published, photocopy it from the publication in which it appeared and send the copy to the source credited. This will speed things up considerably and increase your chances of getting exactly what you want. Write on the photocopy (1) the title and date of the publication in which the picture appeared, (2) the page number, and (3) the source of the picture as credited in the publication. You will find the source on the same page as the picture or in the section of the publication that lists illustration credits.

2. Jot down the names and telephone numbers of all the people contacted while working on a specific assignment. You may have to get back to them to ask for further information or to follow up on a request. Write the names and numbers in this book alongside the appropriate listing. It is also a good idea to jot down the date and project name every time you call a contact.

No people's names are provided for the

listings in this book because they change so frequently.

3. Be sure to find out how long it will take to receive your order. Try to give your sources as much lead time as possible—they may not be able to fill your order adequately if you call at the very last minute with a request. Some sources will expedite an order for an extra charge.

4. Count the number of photographs received in each shipment, making sure that the count matches up with the number on the consignment memo. Call the agency immediately if it does not—otherwise you may find yourself being charged for "missing" pictures when you return them. Some agencies have a form to fill out to confirm the number of pictures received; be sure to complete and return this form as soon as you receive a package.

5. Make certain that your production department understands that images must never be cut, marked, or permanently altered in any way; otherwise you may have to pay a stiff penalty for damages when you return such pictures. Be sure you have permission to remove slides or transparencies from their mounts; most agencies will not allow this. If transparencies must be removed from their mounts, insist that your printer put each transparency back in its proper mount and tape it up. If he or she returns a batch of unmounted slides and a pile of empty mounts, it will be extremely difficult to match them up, and they cannot be returned to the source in this manner. Also, as long as slides and transparencies are unmounted, they are much more likely to be scratched or damaged.

6. When you return photographs, the number you return and the number you are holding should always add up to the total sent to you. Original photographs should be returned via certified mail, return receipt requested, unless the agency specifies otherwise.

7. It is considerate to return immediately all images that you initially reject so that the source can send them to someone else for consideration. You should then make a second return as soon as the final selection of pictures has been made so that you do not needlessly hold onto images you are not going to use while waiting to return those you do. Make a third and final return when the pictures used have come back from the printer.

With each return, include a copy of the original consignment memo (showing any corrections necessary in the total count of pictures sent to you). On each copy accompanying each return, indicate the date you are making the return, the number of pictures being returned, and the the number you are still holding. On the final return, indicate that you are holding none, and specify exactly how each image was used.

8. All sources from which you obtain photographs will want you to give them a credit in the publication—either alongside the reproduction itself or in a special illustration credit section. Museums may request a longer credit than others, because they may require a specific collection to be credited as well as the museum itself. When you credit an agency, you will usually have to credit the photographer as well. Assigning credit is an important part of the permission process; should you fail to give credit, you may find yourself fined an additional fee for the oversight—sometimes double the original cost!

9. When you reproduce a painting or other work of art, most museums will not permit you to crop the work or to superimpose anything over it. Generally, museums will permit the reproduction of a *detail* of a work, provided it is so labeled. You will need to specify that you are reproducing a detail when you contact the museum for permission to reproduce. Similarly, if you wish to use a work of art on the cover of a publication, you must get special permission to set the title or other print matter over the image.

10. Museums may require approval of proofs

of a piece of art reproduced from a color transparency. Your production schedule should allow enough time to send proofs to the museum and to make any changes required, and still meet your deadlines.

Many picture sources ask for one or two copies of the publication in which their pictures appear as part of their conditions of use. If that is not feasible, send tear sheets instead.

11. Be sure to ask for fees and other charges **before** *ordering pictures,* or you may be in for a surprise when the bill arrives. There are almost *always* charges for providing pictures for reproduction. This is true of nonprofit organizations as well as commercial agencies.

Checklist of picture fees and charges

1. Reproduction fees. Fees to reproduce an image vary tremendously—from less than one hundred dollars to thousands of dollars, depending upon a number of factors, such as:

• Type of use: editorial, advertising, promotional, or house organ.

• Type of medium: book (trade or textbook), magazine, newspaper, television, film, video, brochure, or annual report.

• Circulation: print run, magazine circulation, or number of weeks the image will be aired in an ad on TV.

• Number of languages in which the publication will appear.

• The geographical area of distribution of the publication in which the picture will appear: United States, North America, or the world, for example.

• Specific special uses: magazine cover or interior, book cover or interior, chapter opener, opening or end paper, or dust jacket.

• Size of reproduction: one-quarter, one-half, three-quarter, full, or double-page.

• If you pay a reproduction fee for use of an image on the cover of a publication, you *may* have to pay an additional fee for the second use (full or detail) of that same image inside the same publication or if you use a detail from the work.

• If an image is being used in a second edition of a book, you may have to pay for reproduction rights again, even if for the same picture in the same context. The fee for reuse may be negotiated at a lower rate than for the original use.

2. Holding fees. If you hold onto pictures sent to you beyond the date you are expected to return them, you may have to pay a daily or weekly charge per image or consignment until the return is made. If you realize you may need to hold pictures beyond the return, call the source and ask for an extension.

3. Lost, damaged, or stolen pictures. These may cost up to $1,500 per image for an original, $150 for a duplicate.

4. Comp fees. Agencies expect to be paid for the use of their images in comprehensive layouts that are prepared and presented for decision but turned down prior to reproduction. A typical comp fee is $75.

5. No-credit fees. If you fail to give a source proper credit, you may be charged up to double the reproduction fee.

6. Service or research fees. These can range from $50 to $75 per consignment or order, even if more than one order is placed over a period of time for a single project. A service/research fee is *always* charged if *no* pictures are used. It may or may not be charged if images are reproduced, in addition to the reproduction fee itself.

7. Print fees. Noncommercial agencies, such as the U.S. government and many museums and libraries, may charge fees for processing your request and making the prints. News services (for example, Wide World, part of the Associated Press) may charge print fees, apart from reproduction fees, even if the prints made for you from their negatives are to be returned after consideration or use.

For more detailed information on fees and

charges, consult the latest edition of the *ASMP Stock Photography Handbook*. To obtain a copy, contact:

American Society of Magazine Photographers (ASMP)
419 Park Avenue South, Suite 1407
New York, NY 10016
212/889-9144

Picture Sources
Subject Index

A

AERONAUTICS. *See also* SPACE TECHNOLOGY.

National Air and Space Museum Library
Seventh Street and Independence Avenue SW
Washington, DC 20560
202/357-3133
FAX: 202/786-2835
Collection of more than 600,000 items includes black-and-white photographs, color prints, transparencies, and other media, covering aviation and space exploration from 1800 to the present. A division of the Smithsonian Institution.

AFRICAN AMERICANS

Moorland-Spingarn Research Center
Prints and Photographs Department
Howard University
500 Howard Place NW

Washington, DC 20059
202/806-7480
Collection covers international black history and experience from 1800 to the present.

New York Public Library
Schomburg Center for Research in Black Culture
515 Lenox Avenue
New York, NY 10037
212/491-2200
FAX: 212/491-6760
Collection covers black history and culture in Africa and the United States from the 17th century to the present.

AGRICULTURE. *See also* GENERAL PICTURE SOURCES.

Grant Heilman Photography
Box 317
Lititz, PA 17543
717/626-0296
FAX: 717/626-0971
Covers all aspects of American agriculture from 1959 to the present, including related topics such as botany and zoology. General file and landscapes also available.

U.S. Department of Agriculture
Office of Communications, Photography Division
Fourteenth Street and Independence Avenue SW
Washington, DC 20250-1300
202/447-6633
FAX: 202/382-8902
Covers all aspects of agriculture and conservation.

AMERICAN HISTORY. *See* HISTORY.

AMERICAN INDIANS. *See* NATIVE AMERICANS.

AMERICAN WEST

Arizona Photographic Associates
2344 West Holly Avenue
Phoenix, AZ 85009
602/258-6551
Covers American West plus Alaska, Hawaii, and Mexico, 1860s to present. Collection includes natural, animal, and human scenes; some coverage of Africa, Antarctica, Asia, England, and Italy.

National Archives and Records Service
Still Picture Branch
Seventh Street and Pennsylvania Avenue NW, Room 18-N
Washington, DC 20408
201/501-5455

The Archives is the depository of the permanent records of the federal government. Included are photographs and other materials relating to the American West from government agencies through 1912.

Stock Imagery
711 Kalamath
Denver, CO 80204
303/592-1091
FAX: 303/592-1278
Has large general stock of scenics, recreation, American West, and many other categories in modern times.

ANIMALS. *See also* BIRDS; GENERAL PICTURE SOURCES; NATURAL HISTORY.

All Stock
1530 Westlake Avenue North
Seattle, WA 98109
800/248-8116
In Washington: 206/282-8116
FAX: 206/286-8502
Has three main files: animals for use in advertising, Alaska, and general coverage. All three categories include historical and modern photos.

Animals, Animals/Earth Scenes
17 Railroad Avenue
Chatham, NY 12037
518/392-5500
FAX: 518/392-5550
Covers all kinds of animals and other natural history subjects with modern photographs in color and black-and-white.
Also:
Animals, Animals/Earth Scenes
580 Broadway, Suite 1111
New York, NY 10012
212/925-2110
FAX: 212/925-2796

Animals Unlimited
11 West Nineteenth Street
New York, NY 10011
800/828-4545
In New York: 212/633-0300
FAX: 212/633-0408
Specialty is animal photographs of all kinds. A division of SuperStock, Inc.

Anthro-Photo File
33 Hurlbut Street

Cambridge, MA 02138
617/868-4784, 617/495-5243
Extensive collection of primates, plus archaeology, anthropology, and field biology.

Bruce Coleman
117 East Twenty-fourth Street, 5th Floor
New York, NY 10010
212/969-6252
FAX: 212/979-5468
Extensive collection includes animals, travel, science, and nature. Contemporary photographs; color only.

E.R. Degginger
40 Laura Lane
P.O. Box 186
Convent Station, NJ 07961
Morristown, NJ 07960
201/267-4165
Has broad general stock, especially in natural sciences, including wildlife. No current events or politics.

Leonard Rue Enterprises
138 Millbrook Road
Blairstown, NJ 07825
201/362-6616
FAX: 201/362-5808
Stock of color and black-and-white nature and wildlife photographs available.

Photo Researchers
60 East Fifty-sixth Street
New York, NY 10022
800/833-9033
In New York: 212/758-3420
FAX 212/355-0731
Collection of 60,000 science and more than 500,000 nature photographs; repository for the National Audubon Society collection. General collection includes travel and contemporary people and subjects; color and black-and-white.

ANTHROPOLOGY

Anthro-Photo File
33 Hurlbut Street
Cambridge, MA 02138
617/868-4784, 617/495-5243
Specialties are archaeology, anthropology, primate behavior, and field biology.

National Museum of Natural History
National Anthropological Archives

Tenth Street and Constitution
Avenue NW (MRC 152)
Washington, DC 20560
202/357-1976
A division of the Smithsonian Institution. Contains over 400,000 images, including photographs, drawings, and other media relating to anthropology and the history of anthropology, including a large percentage relating to American Indians.

ART. *See* FINE ARTS.

AUTOMOBILES

Detroit Public Library
National Automotive History Collection
5201 Woodward Avenue
Detoit, MI 48202
313/833-1456
Has more than 130,000 photographs relating to automotive history, technology, and related subjects.

Henry Ford Museum and Greenfield Village
The Edison Institute Archives
P.O. Box 1970
Dearborn, MI 48121
313/271-1620
FAX: 313/271-8013
Large museum collection covers transportation, agriculture, and general history, plus photographs and literature about the Ford family, automobiles, and Edison memorabilia.

Motor Vehicles Manufacturers Association
7430 Second Avenue, Suite 300
Detroit, MI 48202
313/872-4311
FAX: 313/872-5400.
Accepts inquiries from member companies, museums and other associations, and media only. Collection of 25,000 black-and-white photographs, prints, and clippings covers all aspects of motor vehicles from 1890 to the present.

AVIATION. *See* AERONAUTICS.

B

BIRDS

National Audubon Society Collection
Photo Researchers
60 East Fifty-sixth Street

New York, NY 10022
800/833-9033
In New York: 212/758-3420
FAX: 212/355-0731
Has more than 500,000 color and black-and-white photographs. Collection handled by Photo Researchers.

BLACKS. *See* AFRICAN AMERICANS.

C

CELEBRITIES. *See also* PERFORMING ARTS.

Camera 5
6 West Twentieth Street
New York, NY 10011
212/989-2004
FAX: 212/727-1858
Extensive collection includes current photographs of people in all walks of life and other general subjects. Will work on assignment.

Magnum Photographs Inc.
72 Spring Street
New York, NY 10012
212/966-9200
FAX: 212/941-9325
Archive of more than 6,000,000 color transparencies and black-and-white photographs on all subjects, historical and modern, both editorial and commercial. Will work on assignments.

Outline Press Syndicate
596 Broadway, 11th Floor
New York, NY 10022
212/226-8790
FAX: 212/226-8944
Stock agency specializing in personality portraiture; photographs include celebrities back to 1980.

People Weekly Syndication
Time and Life Building
1271 Avenue of the Americas
New York, NY 10020
212/522-2453, 212/522-2569
FAX: 212/522-0884
Collection covers celebrities and ordinary people, with some location shots for specific events. Mostly black-and-white, but some color available. Research assistance can be obtained for a fee. Normal service is 24 hours, but same-day service is available for extra fee.

Photofest
47 West Thirteenth Street, 2nd Floor
New York, NY 10011
212/633-6330
FAX: 212/366-9062
Collection includes mostly performing-arts personalities in all fields. Black-and-white and color coverage is from early 1900s through current times.

Photoreporters
875 Avenue of the Americas
New York, NY 10001
212/736-7602
Collection is 90 percent color, and for commercial use only. Covers celebrities, politicians, and current events worldwide.

Retna Ltd.
36 West Fifty-sixth Street, Suite 3A
New York, NY 10019
212/489-1234
FAX: 212/974-8437
Specializes in musical performers back to the 1940s and celebrities back to the 1960s, including some movie stills. Some other media figures are also covered.

Shooting Star International
P.O. Box 93368
Hollywood, CA 90093
213/876-2000
FAX:213/874-7366
Collection concentrates on entertainment personalities and location coverage, mostly in color. Historical archives date back to 1960s with some earlier movie stills. Will work on assignment.

Star File
1501 Broadway, Suite 1405
New York, NY 10036
212/869-4901
FAX: 212/354-8376
Has stock and current images of celebrities, performers, pop music stars, and politicians worldwide; '40s and '50s movie stars; and major celebrity events.

Life Picture Sales
Time and Life Building
1271 Avenue of the Americas, Room 2858
New York, NY 10020
212/522-4800
FAX: 212/522-0328
Has all photographs appearing in *Life* magazine,

1936–72, plus some that appeared in *Life* from 1978 to the present. Coverage is in the millions, mostly black-and-white. Outtakes available of staff photographers' work.

Visages
560 Broadway, #407
New York, NY 10012
212/941-7550
FAX: 212/941-7568
Large current and archival collection of celebrity photographs from many fields, with an emphasis on performing arts; full service agency, will work on assignments.

COMPUTER-GENERATED IMAGES. *See* SPECIAL EFFECTS.

CURRENT EVENTS. *See* NEWS AND CURRENT EVENTS.

D

DANCE. *See* PERFORMING ARTS.

E

ELECTRON MICROGRAPHY. *See* PHOTOMICROGRAPHY.

EUROPE

The Photo Source
11 West Nineteenth Street
New York, NY 10011
800/828-4545
In New York: 212/633-0300
FAX: 212/633-0408
Specialty is photographs of European travel, business, industry, lifestyles, and more. A division of SuperStock, Inc.

F

FINE ARTS

Art Resource
65 Bleecker Street, 9th Floor
New York, NY 10012
212/505-8700
FAX: 212/420-9286

Collection of stock fine-arts photographs, historical and modern, covering the United States, England, and Europe. Will help with research. Represents some museums in the United States and abroad.

Boston Museum of Fine Arts
Department of Photographic Services
Slide and Photograph Collection
465 Huntington Avenue
Boston, MA 02115
617/267-9300, ext. 317
FAX (for Museum): 617/267-0280
Extensive slide collection covers much of Museum collection.

The Bridgeman Art Library
11 West Nineteenth Street
New York, NY 10011
800/828-4545
In New York: 212/633-0300
FAX: 212/633-0408
Specialty is fine art and artifacts from galleries and museums worldwide. A division of Super-Stock, Inc.

Museum of Modern Art
Photographic Archive
11 West Fifty-third Street
New York, NY 10019
212/708-9458
Includes majority of Museum of Modern Art collection; however, architecture/design, film stills, and photography are housed in their respective departments. No photographs available for promotional purposes.

National Gallery of Art
Office of Photographic Services
Sixth Street and Constitution Avenue NW
Washington, DC 20565
202/842-6231
FAX: 202/842-2356
Holds slides and photographs of the permanent collection; a division of the Smithsonian Institution.

National Museum of American Art
Eighth and G Streets NW
Washington, DC 20560
202/357-1626
FAX: 202/786-2607
Collection includes American art only, historical to modern. Slides and prints available. A division of the Smithsonian Institution.

National Portrait Gallery
Prints and Photographs Collection
Eighth and F Streets NW
Washington, DC 20560
202/357-2791
Collection includes only prints of items owned by the National Portrait Gallery. A division of the Smithsonian Institution.

Philadelphia Museum of Art
Rights and Reproductions Department
Twenty-sixth and Franklin Parkway
Box 7646
Philadelphia, PA 19101-7646
215/787-5428
FAX: 215/236-4465
Photographs available of museum collection; major part of collection is on slides.

Yale University
Photographs/Rights and Reproductions Department
1111 Chapel Street
Box 2006 Yale Station
New Haven, CT 06520
203/432-0630
Transparencies and black-and-white photographs available of wide-ranging collection. Callers should have specific requests for items in collection only.

FISH. *See* UNDERWATER PHOTOGRAPHY.

FLAGS

The Flag Research Center
3 Edgehill Road
Winchester, MA 01890
617/729-9410
FAX: 617/721-4817
Collection covers U.S. and foreign flags, contemporary as well as historical.

FORESTRY AND FOREST PRODUCTS

U.S. Department of Agriculture
Forest Service
Audio Visual Services
P.O. Box 96090
Washington, DC 20090-6090
202/447-3959
FAX: 202/497-3610
Photographs are in two files: (1) current activities in forestry and related environmental issues, and (2) historical file, which includes many related photographs in other fields.

G

GENERAL PICTURE SOURCES

Actuality
1 Fifth Avenue
New York, NY 10003
212/979-9102
General international file with emphasis on contemporary issues and human development. Color plus black-and-white.

All Stock
1530 Westlake Avenue North
Seattle, WA 98109
800/248-8116
In Washington: 206/282-8116
FAX: 206/286-8502
Has three main files: general coverage, Alaska, and animals for use in advertising. All three files include historical and modern subjects.

The Bettmann Archive
902 Broadway
New York, NY 10010
212/777-6200
FAX: 212/533-4034
Stock house with archive and current news divisions covering all subjects. Historical images cover American and world history. Repository for the photographs of United Press International (1907–present) and Reuters (1985–present), as well as International News Photos (1912–1958), Underwood and Underwood (1880–1955), and others.

Black Star
116 East Twenty-seventh Street
New York, NY 10016
212/679-3288
FAX: 212/889-2052
Has more than 4,000,000 contemporary and historical photographs in all subjects, including politics and current events; worldwide coverage.

Bruce Coleman
117 East Twenty-fourth Street, 5th Floor
New York, NY 10010
212/969-6252
FAX: 212/979-5468
Extensive collection includes animals, travel, science, and nature. Contemporary photographs; color only.

Camerique
1701 Skippack Pike
P.O. Box 175
Blue Bell, PA 19422
215/272-7649
FAX: 215/272-7651
General file includes contemporary and historical subjects in color and black-and-white.

Comstock, Inc.
The Comstock Building
30 Irving Place
New York, NY 10003
800/225-2727
In New York: 212/353-8600
FAX: 212/353-3383
Has stock of both editorial and commercial photographs. More than 3,000,000 photographs, including animals, business and industry, lifestyles, natural history, science, medicine, sports, travel, and more. Free catalog.

Design Photographers International
19 West Twenty-first Street, Suite 901
New York, NY 10010
212/627-4060
FAX: 212/645-9619
Has wide selection of high-tech and travel photographs; large general file. No personalities, news, or fashion.

E.R. Degginger
40 Laura Lane
P.O. Box 186
Convent Station, NJ 07961
Morristown, NJ 07960
201/267-4165
Has broad general stock, especially in natural sciences, including wildlife. No current events or politics.

FPG International
251 Park Avenue South
New York, NY 10010
212/777-4210
FAX: 212/995-9652
Large general file of more than 4,000,000 photographs includes history, human interest, world travel, business and industry, and more. Color and black-and-white available.

Four by Five
11 West Nineteenth Street

New York, NY 10011
800/828-4545
In New York: 212/633-0300
Fax: 212/633-0408
Large stock file specializes in advertising, corporate, and publishing needs. A division of SuperStock, Inc.

Gamma-Liaison
11 East Twenty-sixth Street
New York, NY 10010
212/447-2500
FAX: 212/447-2534
Collection covers foreign and domestic travel, news, and personalities; advertising and corporate stock photographs available. Will do work on assignment.

H. Armstrong Roberts Stock Photographs
4203 Locust Street
Philadelphia, PA 19104
215/386-6300
FAX: 215/386-3521
Main office. Large general collection includes contemporary people, travel, and vintage lifestyles; color and black-and-white.
Also:
H. Armstrong Roberts Stock Photographs
233 East Wacker Drive, Room 4305
Chicago, IL 60601
312/938-4466
FAX: 312/938-1903
Serves Illinois, Iowa, Michigan, Minnesota, and Wisconsin.

H. Armstrong Roberts Stock Photographs
1181 Broadway
New York, NY 10001
212/685-3870
FAX: 212/779-7056
Serves New York, New Jersey, and New England.

The Image Bank
111 Fifth Avenue
New York, NY 10003
212/529-6700
FAX: 212/529-8886
Large collection includes industry, scenics, people, sports, travel, futuristic backgrounds, food, still lifes. Slides and transparencies only. Over 50 offices worldwide, including 12 in United States. Services also include stock illustrations, film footage, and book packaging.

Library of Congress
Prints and Photographs Division
First and Independence Avenue SE
Washington, DC 20540
202/707-6394
Photoduplication service: 202/707-5640
One of the largest collections in the world, basically historical, with worldwide coverage. Most material can be reproduced, and much of it is in the public domain. Limited reference service by mail; a personal visit is suggested if at all possible.

Magnum Photographs Inc.
72 Spring Street
New York, NY 10012
212/966-9200
FAX: 212/941-9325
Archive of more than 6,000,000 color transparencies and black-and-white photographs in all subjects, historical and modern, both editorial and commercial. Will work on assignments.

Monkmeyer Press Photo Service
118 East Twenty-eighth Street
New York, NY 10016
212/689-2242
FAX: 212/779-2549
Collection includes human-interest occupations and subjects such as education, family life, foreign countries, and psychology.

New York Public Library
Mid-Manhattan Library
Literature and Language Department
Picture Collection
455 Fifth Avenue
New York, NY 10016
212/340-0877
Circulating collection of 2,500,000 items covers all topics; strong on costume and design. Note: this is a tearsheet collection only. All material is sourced.

Peter Arnold
1181 Broadway, 4th Floor
New York, NY 10001
212/481-1190
FAX: 212/481-3409
General file, with strong emphasis on science, medicine, and the environment; photomicrography available.

Photo Researchers
60 East Fifty-sixth Street

New York, NY 10022
800/833-9033
In New York: 212/758-3420
FAX 212/355-0731
Collection of 60,000 science and more than 500,000 nature photographs; repository for the National Audubon Society collection. General collection includes travel and contemporary people and subjects; color and black-and-white.

PhotoSource International
Pine Lake Farm
Osceola, WI 54020
715/248-3800
FAX: 715/248-7394
Information service for people who need photographs and people who sell photographs. Four newsletters available based on budget for picture purchases. Photo databank available for wide variety of subjects. Clients will deal directly with referred sources. Listing is free for buyers of photographs.

PhotoTake
4523 Broadway
New York, NY 10040
212/942-8185
FAX: 212/942-8186
Collection covers natural history, biology, medicine, technology, industry, and special effects.

Photri, Inc.
3701 South George Mason Drive, Suite C2 North
Falls Church, VA 22041
703/931-8600
FAX: 703/998-8407
Covers all subjects, especially space, aerospace, military, and Washington, DC. Locations worldwide.

The Picture Cube
89 Broad Street, Suite 1131
Boston, MA 02110
617/367-1532
FAX: 617/482-9266
General collection includes worldwide travel, education, occupations, Boston, family life, lifestyles, New England, and more.

The Picture Group
830 Eddy Street
Providence, RI 02905
401/461-9333

401/461-8848 (corporate division)
FAX: 401/461-9060
Stock file covers business, current issues, national and international events, and politics. Will take assignments. Corporate division provides assignment photography for annual reports and corporate publications.

Rainbow
1079 Main Street
P.O. Box 573
Housatonic, MA 01236
413/274-6211
FAX: 413/274-6689
General file includes computers and high-tech subjects, medicine, robotics, youth, and locations.

Shostal Associates
11 West Nineteenth Street
New York, NY 10011
800/828-4545
In New York: 212/633-0300
FAX: 212/633-0408
Large stock of photographs includes scenics, people, lifestyles, and industry worldwide. A division of SuperStock, Inc.

Stock, Boston
36 Gloucester Street
Boston, MA 02115
617/266-2300
FAX: 617/353-1262
Large general file of contemporary photographs in all area, including international subjects.

The Stock Broker
450 Lincoln Street, Suite 110
Denver, CO 80203
303/698-1734
FAX: 303/733-6748
Has more than 250,000 general photographs on recreation, adventure, sports, nature, worldwide travel, business and industry, and the American West. Covers mostly modern times; color and black-and-white.

Stock Imagery
711 Kalamath
Denver, CO 80204
303/592-1091
FAX: 303/592-1278
Has large general stock of scenics, recreation, American West, and many other categories in modern times.

The Stock Market
360 Park Avenue South
New York, NY 10010
800/999-0800
In New York: 212/684-7878
FAX:800/283-0808
FAX in New York: 212/532-6750
Large collection includes business, industry, travel, people, lifestyles, and nature.

Stock Stock
7041 East Hornblossom Lane
Scottsdale, AZ 85253
602/941-2903
FAX: same
Broad general file of stock photographs, illustrations, and videos; specializes in the Southwest. Computer capability.

Stockphotographs
111 Fifth Avenue
New York, NY 10003
212/477-7901
FAX: 212/477-7908
An Image Bank company. Large collection includes industry, scenics, people, sports, travel, futuristic backgrounds, food, still lifes. Slides and transparencies only. Over fifty offices worldwide, including twelve in the United States. Services also include stock illustrations, film footage, and book packaging.

The Stock Shop/Medichrome
232 Madison Avenue
New York, NY 10016
212/679-8480
FAX: 212/532-1934
Collection includes medicine, industry, lifestyles, travel, scenics, and sports.

SuperStock, Inc.
11 West Nineteenth Street
New York, NY 10011
800/828-4545
In New York: 212/633-0300
FAX: 212/633-0408
Millions of photographs cover all subjects, historical and contemporary, worldwide. For specialties of SuperStock divisions, see separate listings for Animals Unlimited, the Bridgeman Art Library, Four by Five, the Kobal Collection, the Photo Source, Shostal Associates, and Three Lions.

Sygma Photo News
225 West Fifty-seventh Street
New York, NY 10019
212/765-1820
FAX: 212/459-9362
Collection covers celebrities and current world events.

Tony Stone Worldwide
233 East Ontario Street
Chicago, IL 60611
312/787-7880
FAX: 312/787-8798
Has general international contemporary photographs.

Tony Stone Worldwide/After Image
6100 Wilshire Boulevard, Suite 240
Los Angeles, CA 90048
213/938-1700
FAX: 213/938-0731
Collection covers general international contemporary subjects.

Uniphoto Picture Agency
3205 Grace Street NW
Washington, DC 20007
202/333-0500
FAX: 202/338-5578
Large stock covers all subjects; can provide contacts with assignment photographers worldwide. Owned by Pictor International, London.

Westlight
2223 South Carmelina Avenue
Los Angeles, CA 90064
213/477-0421
FAX: 213/820-2687
Collection includes advertising backgrounds, computer graphics, high tech, industry, people, scenic backgrounds, and more.

GEOGRAPHY. *See also* GENERAL PICTURE SOURCES; NATURAL HISTORY.

University of Wisconsin, Milwaukee
American Geographical Society Collection
Golda Meir Library
Box 399
Milwaukee, WI 53201
800/558-8993
In Wisconsin: 414/229-6282, or 414/229-3984
Subjects include nature, people, and more, all related to geography worldwide. 150,000 photographs, slides, LANDSAT images, and other media.

Mark MacLaren
430 East Twentieth Street
New York, NY 10009
212/674-8615; 212/674-0155
Has more than 100,000 slides, with emphasis on travel, cities, and people worldwide. Covered areas include Eastern Europe, South America, Scandinavia, South Pacific, and more.

H

HISTORY. *See also* AMERICAN WEST; MILITARY; WOMEN.

The Bettmann Archive
902 Broadway
New York, NY 10010
212/777-6200
FAX: 212/533-4034
Stock house with archive and current news divisions covering all subjects. Historical images cover American and world history. Repository for the photographs of United Press International (1907–present) and Reuters (1985–present), as well as International News Photos (1912–1958), Underwood and Underwood (1880–1955), and others.

Brown Brothers
100 Bortree Road
P.O. Box 50
Sterling, PA 18463
717/689-9688
FAX: 717/689-7873
Collection of more than 12,000,000 images in black-and-white and color covering past and present. Covers early New York political movements and politicians, rural and urban life, early technology, inventors, science, American fads, celebrities, and movie stills.

Culver Pictures
150 West Twenty-second Street, Suite 300
New York, NY 10011
212/645-1672
FAX: 212/627-9112
Historical archive of 7,000,000 images in many media, many subjects through World War II; includes movie stills.

Drake Well Museum
RD #3
Titusville, PA 16354
814/827-2797

Collection covers oil industry, historical and current.

Granger Collection
1841 Broadway
New York, NY 10023
212/586-0971
FAX: 2212/262-8103
Historical picture library for commercial and professional users only. Collection of 6,000,000 illustrations covers world history in many media.

Hagley Museum and Library
Pictorial Collections
P.O. Box 3630
Wilmington, DE 19807
302/658-2401
FAX: 302/658-0568
Collection of more than 500,000 black-and-white photographs emphasizing business and industry.

Henry Ford Museum and Greenfield Village
The Edison Institute
Archives
P.O. Box 1970
Dearborn, MI 48121
313/271-1620
FAX: 313/271-8013
Large museum collection covers transportation, agriculture, and general history, plus photographs and literature about the Ford family, automobiles, and Edison memorabilia.

Historical Pictures Service
921 West Van Buren Street, Room 201
Chicago, IL 60607
312/346-0599
FAX: 312/733-2844
Has images from prehistory to early 1900s. Collection is worldwide with emphasis on American history and portraits of historical figures. Limited number of current images.

Library of Congress
Prints and Photographs Division
First and Independence Avenue SE
Washington, DC 20540
202/707-6394
Photoduplication service: 202/707-5640
One of the largest collections in the world, basically historical, with worldwide coverage. Most material can be reproduced, and much of it is in the public domain. Limited reference service by mail.

Mariners Museum
The Library
100 Museum Drive
Newport News, VA 23606
804/595-0368
FAX:804/591-8212
Collection covers maritime history.

National Archives and Records Service
Still Picture Branch
Seventh Street and Pennsylvania Avenue NW, Room 18-N
Washington, DC 20408
202/501-5455
The Archives is the depository of the permanent records of the federal government. The Still Picture Branch has several million photographs and other pictorial materials relating to the social, cultural, economic, environmental, technological, and political history of the United States.

New-York Historical Society
Department of Prints, Photographs, and Architectural Collections
170 Central Park West
New York, NY 10024
212/873-3400
FAX: 212/874-8706
More than 250,000 prints from the 1700s to the early 1900s; photographs cover the 1840s through the early 1900s. Collection covers New York City mainly, but includes some general U.S. subjects. By appointment only.

Peabody Museum
East India Square
Salem, MA 01970
508/745-1876
FAX: 508/744-6776
Collection covers American maritime history, ethnology of South and Central Pacific peoples, Asian export art, and the natural history of New England.

Three Lions
11 West Nineteenth Street
New York, NY 10011
800/828-4545
In New York: 212/633-0300
FAX: 2212/633-0408
Specialties are nostalgia, history, Americana, and religious and inspirational subjects. A division of SuperStock, Inc.

I

INDIANS. *See* NATIVE AMERICANS.

J

JEWS

The Jewish Museum
c/o Art Resource
65 Bleecker Street, 9th Floor
New York, NY 10012
212/505-8700
FAX: 212/420-9286
Collection includes Judaica, ceremonial objects, and paintings of Jewish subjects.

M

MAPS

Library of Congress
Geography and Map Division
First and Independence Avenue SE
Washington, DC 20540
202/707-6277
Largest collection of maps in the world, many of which can be reproduced.

MEDICINE AND HEALTH

Camera M.D. Studios
Library Division
8290 Northwest Twenty-sixth Place
Fort Lauderdale, FL 33322
305/741-5560
Collection includes more than 250,000 images, mostly color with some black-and-white, in medical sciences only. Covers all major medical specialties, including modern imaging techniques. Personnel are trained in medicine as well as writing.

National Library of Medicine
Prints and Photographs Collection
8600 Rockville Pike
Bethesda, MD 20894
301/496-5961
FAX: 301/402-0872
Comprehensive collection of 57,000 images of people and events relating to the history of medicine and medical developments; some modern images are included.

Peter Arnold
1181 Broadway, 4th Floor
New York, NY 10001
212/481-1190
FAX: 212/481-3409
General file, with strong emphasis on science, medicine, and the environment; includes photomicrography.

Rainbow
1079 Main Street
P.O. Box 573
Housatonic, MA 01236
413/274-6211
FAX: 413/274-6689
General file includes computers and high-tech subjects, medicine, robotics, youth, and locations.

Stock Shop/Medichrome
232 Madison Avenue
New York, NY 10016
212/679-8480
FAX: 212/532-1934
Collection includes medicine, industry, lifestyles, travel, scenics, and sports.

MILITARY

Anne S.K. Brown Military Collection
Brown University Library
Box A
Brown University
Providence, RI 02912
401/863-2414
FAX: 401/863-1272
More than 60,000 images cover all aspects of world military history, including uniforms and naval history, plus coverage of royalty. Library also has an extensive collection of reference books.

Department of Defense
Still Media Records Center
Building 168, Room 116
Anacostia Naval Station
Code SSRC
Washington, DC 20374-1681
202/433-2166
Central Department of Defense repository for photographs and other still media of the U.S. military services from 1982 to the present. (National Archives, below, covers the years prior to 1982.)

National Archives and Records Service
Still Picture Branch
Seventh Street and Pennsylvania Avenue NW,
Room 18-N
Washington, DC 20408
201/501-5455
The Archives is the depository of the permanent records of the federal government and is the repository for photographs, paintings, and illustrations for the U.S. military services from the American Revolution through 1981.

Naval History Center
Washington Navy Yard
Washington, DC 20374-0571
202/433-2765
Collection of 250,000 photographs covering all aspects of naval history. Can usually help with research. Copies of photographs are available, but not quickly.

U.S. Army Center of Military History
Attn: DAMH-HSA
Building 159
SEFC/Washington Navy Yard
Washington, DC 20374-5088
703/274-8290; 703/274-8291
Combat art collection covers World War II to present, paintings only. Photographs available of some paintings.

U.S. Army Military History Institute
Carlisle Barracks, PA 17013
717/245-3434
Collection includes 730,000 photographs plus posters and other media covering the history of the U.S. Army from the Mexican War to the present.

MONEY

American Numismatic Society
One Hundred Fifty-fifth Street and Broadway
New York, NY 10032
212/234-3130
FAX: 212/234-3381
The Society's museum collection covers past and present; photographs are available of the museum collection. The museum library is one of the largest in the world in this field.

National Museum of American History
Numismatic Division, Room 4000
Twelfth Street and Constitution Avenue NW

Washington, DC 20506
202/357-1798
A division of the Smithsonian Institution. Collection of about 1,000,000 items includes coinage and monetary and medallic art from worldwide sources beginning in ancient Greece; photographs may be ordered.

Bureau of Engraving and Printing
Fourteenth and C Streets SW, Room 533-M
Washington, DC 20228
202/447-0193
FAX: 202/287-0131
Collection covers government securities, U.S. currency, and postage stamps; historical file from the late 1800s. Photographs and reproductions restricted; call or write for further information.

MOVIES. *See* PERFORMING ARTS.

N

NATIONAL PARKS

National Park Service
History Collection (Graphics)
Office of Library, Archives, and Graphics Research
Harpers Ferry Center
Harpers Ferry, WV 25425
304/535-6491, 304/535-6494
FAX: 304/535-6492
Collection of 1,500,000 items covers National Parks and related areas throughout the United States in color and black-and-white. Photographs document National Parks locations and history from 1929 with a few earlier photographs.

NATIVE AMERICANS

Museum of the American Indian, Heye Foundation
Broadway at One Hundred Fifty-fifth Street
New York, NY 10032
212/283-2420
FAX: 212/491-9302
Collection covers the culture, life, and art of the Native Americans of North, Central, and South America. Includes black-and-white photographs of live subjects and color transparencies of artifacts.

National Archives and Records Service
Still Picture Branch
Seventh Street and Pennsylvania Avenue NW,
Room 18-N

Washington, DC 20408
201/501-5455
The Archives is the depository of the permanent records of the federal government and include pictorial records from fifteen government agencies, including the Bureau of Indian Affairs, the Bureau of American Ethnology, and the U.S. Army.

National Museum of Natural History
National Anthropological Archives
Tenth Street and Constitution Avenue NW
(MRC 152)
Washington, DC 20560
202/357-1976
A division of the Smithsonian Institution. Contains over 400,000 images, including photographs, drawings, and works in other media relating to anthropology and its history, including a large percentage relating to Native Americans.

NATURAL HISTORY

All Stock
1530 Westlake Avenue North
Seattle, WA 98109
800/248-8116
In Washington: 206/282-8116
FAX: 206/286-8502
Has three main files: animals for use in advertising, Alaska, and general coverage. All three categories include historical and modern photographs.

American Museum of Natural History
Photographic Collection
Library Services Department
Central Park West at Seventy-ninth Street
New York, NY 10024
212/769-5419
Large collection of black-and-white and color prints available for purchase or rental covering all areas of natural history except botany. Personal visit or letter preferred.

Animals, Animals/Earth Scenes
17 Railroad Avenue
Chatham, NY 12037
518/392-5500
FAX: 518/392-5550
Covers all kinds of animals and other natural history subjects with modern photographs in color and black-and-white.

Also:
Animals, Animals/Earth Scenes
580 Broadway, Suite 111
New York, NY 10012
212/925-2110
FAX: 212/925-2796

Bruce Coleman
117 East Twenty-fourth Street, 5th Floor
New York, NY 10010
212/969-6252
FAX: 212/979-5468
Extensive collection includes animals, travel, science, and nature. Contemporary photographs, color only.

Comstock, Inc.
The Comstock Building
30 Irving Place
New York, NY 10003
800/225-2727
In New York: 212/353-8600
FAX: 212/353-3383
Has stock of both editorial and commercial photographs. More than 3,000,000 photographs include animals, business and industry, lifestyles, natural history, science, medicine, sports, travel, and more. Free catalog.

E.R. Degginger
P.O. Box 186
Convent Station, NJ 07961
201/267-4165
Has broad general stock, with a specialty in natural and physical sciences, including wildlife. No current events or politics.

Field Museum of Natural History
Photography Department
Roosevelt Road at Lake Shore Drive
Chicago, IL 60605-2496
312/922-9410, ext. 248
Collection of 500,000 photographs covers anthropology, botany, and geology; includes photographs of artifacts, early expedition photographs (back to 1871), and current subjects.

Leonard Rue Enterprises
138 Millbrook Road
Blairstown, NJ 07825
201/362-6616
FAX: 201/362-5808
Stock of color and black-and-white nature and wildlife photographs.

Photo Researchers
60 East Fifty-sixth Street
New York, NY 10022
800/833-9033
In New York: 212/758-3420
FAX 212/355-0731
Collection of 60,000 science and more than 500,000 nature photographs; repository for the National Audubon Society collection. General collection includes travel and contemporary people and subjects in color and black-and-white.

PhotoTake
4523 Broadway
New York, NY 10040
212/942-8185
FAX: 212/942-8186
Collection covers natural history, biology, medicine, technology, industry, and special effects.

NAVY. *See* MILITARY.

NEWS AND CURRENT EVENTS

Associated Press: *See* WIDE WORLD PHOTOGRAPHS, below.

Gamma-Liaison
11 East Twenty-sixth Street
New York, NY 10010
212/447-2500
FAX: 212/447-2534
Collection covers foreign and domestic travel, news, and personalities; advertising and corporate stock photographs available. Will do work on assignment.

Magnum Photographs Inc.
72 Spring Street
New York, NY 10012
212/966-9200
FAX: 212/941-9325
Archive of more than 6,000,000 color transparencies and black-and-white photographs on all subjects, historical and modern, both editorial and commercial. Will work on assignments.

Reuters. *See* GENERAL: THE BETTMANN ARCHIVE.

SIPA Press
30 West Twenty-first Street
New York, NY 10010
212/463-0150
FAX: 212/463-0160
Collection of photographers' work in many fields; worldwide coverage. Photographs are available for rental by publications; they are available to commercial sources only with research help from SIPA staff. Collection covers events throughout the world from mid-1900s to current files.

Sygma Photo News
225 West Fifty-seventh Street
New York, NY 10019
212/765-1820
FAX: 212/459-9362
Collection covers celebrities and current world events.

Time Picture Syndication
Time and Life Building
1271 Avenue of the Americas, Room 2311
New York, NY 10020
212/522-3593
FAX: 212/522-0150
Collection based on photographs that have appeared in *Time* magazine throughout its history plus materials that are not from the magazine. All subjects covered.

Also:
Life Picture Sales
Time and Life Building
1271 Avenue of the Americas, Room 2858
New York, NY 10020
212/522-4800
FAX: 212/522-0328
Has all photographs appearing in *Life* magazine, 1936–72, plus some that appeared in *Life* from 1978 to the present. Coverage is in the millions, mostly black-and-white. Outtakes available of staff photographers' work.

United Press International (UPI). *See* GENERAL PICTURE SOURCES: THE BETTMANN ARCHIVE.

Wide World Photographs
50 Rockefeller Plaza
New York, NY 10020
212/621-1930
FAX: 212/621-1955
Wide World is the commercial photographic branch of The Associated Press. The collection of 60,000,000 images covers news events from the early 1900s to the present, concerning sports, film stars, entertainment, political figures, and many other subjects.

P

PEOPLE. *See* CELEBRITIES; PERFORMING ARTS.

PERFORMING ARTS

Academy of Motion Picture Arts and Sciences
Margaret Herrick Library
333 South La Cienaga Boulevard
Beverly Hills, CA 90211
213/247-3020
FAX: 213/657-5193
A source of motion-picture history, biography, and production since 1927. Collection contains 5,000,000 photographs.

Hoblitzelle Theater Arts Library
Harry Ransom Humanities Research Center
University of Texas at Austin
P.O. Box 7219
Austin, TX 78713-7219
512/471-9124
FAX: 512/471-9646
Three collections include (1) photography—more than 5,000,000 photographs, plus an extensive literature and equipment collection, covering the entire history of photography; (2) theater—photographs, printed items, original designs, and literature dating back to the 17th century; (3) film—photographs, film stills, and footage, both archival and current.

The Kobal Collection
11 West Nineteenth Street
New York, NY 10011
800/828-4545
In New York: 212/633-0300
FAX: 212/633-0408
Specialty is movie stars and scenes, historical and current, worldwide. A division of SuperStock, Inc.

Memory Shop
109 East Twelfth Street
Box 365, Cooper Station
New York, NY 10003
212/473-2404
Movie, theater, TV, and rock star photographs from 1920s to present.

New York Public Library for the Performing Arts
Billy Rose Theatre Collection
111 Amsterdam Avenue
New York, NY 10023
212/870-1639
Has photographs and other images of personalities connected with performing arts, exclusive of music, dance, and sound recordings. Write for more detailed information.

New York Public Library for the Performing Arts
Dance Collection
111 Amsterdam Avenue
New York, NY 10023
212/870-1657
FAX: 212/799-7975
Collection of 260,000 photographs and negatives covers wide range of subjects relating to dance—persons, companies, musical productions, and folk dances.

Photofest
47 West Thirteenth Street, 2nd Floor
New York, NY 10011
212/633-6330
FAX: 212/366-9062
Collection includes mostly performing arts personalities in all fields. Black-and-white and color coverage is from early 1900s through current times.

PHOTOGRAPHY

Hoblitzelle Theater Arts Library
Harry Ransom Humanities Research Center
University of Texas at Austin
P.O. Box 7219
Austin, TX 78713-7219
512/471-9124
FAX: 512/471-9646
A major part of this large performing-arts collection is devoted to photography. More than 5,000,000 photographs and an extensive literature and equipment collection cover the history of photography.

International Museum of Photography at George Eastman House
900 East Avenue
Rochester, NY 14607
716/271-3361
FAX: 716/271-3970
Historic home of George Eastman plus the International Museum. Extensive collection covers 150 years of photography, including equipment, photographs, film stills and footage, and literature.

Museum of Modern Art
Department of Photography
11 West Fifty-third Street
New York, NY 10019
212/708-9626
More than 20,000 photographs cover the history of photography from the earliest years to the present.

National Museum of American History
Division of Photographic History
Twelfth Street and Constitution Avenue NW
Washington, DC 20560
202/357-2059
Collection of approximately 100,000 images focuses on the history of photography, with 12,000 pieces of equipment. The collection dates from 1839 to the present, with an emphasis on the the 1800s. A division of the Smithsonian Institution.

PHOTOMICROGRAPHY

Camera M.D. Studios
Library Division
8290 Northwest Twenty-sixth Place
Fort Lauderdale, FL 33322
305/741-5560
Collection includes more than 250,000 images, mostly color with some black-and-white, in medical sciences only. Covers all major medical specialties including modern imaging techniques. Personnel are trained in medicine as well as writing.

Peter Arnold
1181 Broadway, 4th Floor
New York, NY 10001
212/481-1190
FAX: 212/481-3409
General file has photomicrography on scientific and medical subjects.

R

RAILROADS

Association of American Railroads Library
50 F Street NW
Washington, DC 20001
202/639-2334
FAX: 202/639-2312
Extensive files of photographs and slides of historic and current railroad equipment.

S

SPACE TECHNOLOGY

National Aeronautics and Space Administration (NASA)
Broadcast and Audio-Visual Branch

400 Maryland Avenue SW
Washington, DC 20546
202/453-8375
Collection covers NASA from its beginning to the present; very large collection of still photographs from all areas of space technology.

Also:
National Aeronautics and Space Administration
Lyndon B. Johnson Space Center
AP3/Building 2, Room 187
P.O. Box 58425
Houston, TX 77258
713/483-4876
FAX: 483-4876
Coverage emphasizes manned space flight.

SPECIAL EFFECTS

Comstock, Inc.
The Comstock Building
30 Irving Place
New York, NY 10003
800/225-2727
In New York: 212/353-8600
FAX: 212/353-3383
Has stock of both editorial and commercial photographs. Special effects are included in large stock of more than 3,000,000 photographs covering animals, business and industry, lifestyles, natural history, science, medicine, sports, and travel. Free catalog.

FPG International
251 Park Avenue South
New York, NY 10010
212/777-4210
FAX: 212/995-9652
Special effects are included in large general file of more than 4,000,000 photographs covering history, human interest, world travel, business and industry, and more. Color and black-and-white available.

The Image Bank
111 Fifth Avenue
New York, NY 10003
212/529-6700
FAX: 212/529-8886
Special effects are included in large collection of industry, scenics, people, sports, travel, futuristic backgrounds, food, and still lifes. Slides and transparencies only. Over 50 offices worldwide, in-

cluding 12 in the United States. Services also include stock illustrations, film footage, and book packaging.

PhotoTake
4523 Broadway
New York, NY 10040
212/942-8185
FAX: 212/942-8186
Collection covers natural history, biology, medicine, technology, industry, and special effects.

The Stock Market
360 Park Avenue South
New York, NY 10010
800/999-0800
In New York: 212/684-7878
FAX: 800/283-0808
FAX in New York: 212/532-6750
Large collection of business, industry, travel, people, lifestyles, and nature includes special effects.

SuperStock, Inc.
11 West Nineteenth Street
New York, NY 10011
800/828-4545
In New York: 212/633-0300
FAX: 212/633-0408
Millions of photographs cover all subjects, including special effects. For specialties of SuperStock divisions, see separate listings for Animals Unlimited, the Bridgeman Art Library, Four by Five, the Kobal Collection, the Photo Source, Shostal Associates, and Three Lions.

SPORTS

Baseball Hall of Fame
National Baseball Library
Cooperstown, NY 13326
607/547-9988
FAX: 607/547-5980
Collection of 200,000 black-and-white photographs and 5,000 slides covers baseball from mid-1800s to present with emphasis on 1900–60.

Focus on Sports
222 East Forty-sixth Street, Room 401
New York, NY 10017
212/661-6860
FAX: 212/983-3031
Large collection covers athletes, locations, and other related topics in all sports.

Sports Illustrated Picture Sales
Time & Life Building, Room 2059
1271 Avenue of the Americas
New York, NY 10020
212/522-4781, 212/522-2803
FAX: 212/522-0102
Makes available photographs published in *Sports Illustrated* since its inception in 1954; represents photographers whose work appears in this magazine. Outtakes available.

Wide World Photographs
50 Rockefeller Plaza
New York, NY 10020
212/621-1930
FAX: 212/621-1955
Wide World is the commercial photographic branch of the Associated Press. The collection of 60,000,000 images covers news events from the early 1900s to the present concerning sports, film stars, entertainment, political figures, and many other subjects.

T

TELEVISION. *See* PERFORMING ARTS.

U

UNDERWATER PHOTOGRAPHY

Al Grotell Underwater Photography
170 Park Row, #15D
New York, NY 10038
212/349-3165
Underwater photographs of natural and manufactured objects. Worldwide coverage includes approximately 10,000 prints. Will work on assignment.

Jeffrey L. Rotman, Underwater Photographer
14 Cottage Avenue
Somerville, MA 02144
617/666-0874
FAX: 617/666-4811
Collection of 150,000 slides emphasizes underwater photography, but also includes nature, history, scenics, and sociological photojournalism. Coverage is worldwide.

W

WEST. *See* AMERICAN WEST.

WOMEN

Arthur and Elizabeth Schlesinger Library on the History of Women in America
Radcliffe College
10 Garden Street
Cambridge, MA 02138
617/495-8647
With more than 45,000 photographs from the 1840s to the present, the collection covers women's movements, women in all career areas, and families.

WORLD HISTORY. *See* HISTORY.

5.

Special Collections

THE SPECIAL COLLECTIONS RESIDING IN MORE than 16,000 libraries across the land comprise a competitive resource that no other country can equal. No other nation has special collections with the depth, variety, and excellence of those in the United States. The range is almost unbelievable. You can browse through the newspapers of George Washington's day, catch up on the latest developments in thermonuclear energy, leaf through the original manuscripts of Emily Dickinson's poetry, read Chinese history in the original Chinese version, and experience much, much more in the reading rooms of America's special collections. These collections may range from less than 1,000 items to the millions of items in the Library of Congress, a special collection so large that it is, in turn, subdivided into many separate specialized divisions.

With an information resource as vast and as varied as this—and one that is scattered across the land—it can be a problem to locate exactly what you need without spending a lot of time. The "Special Collections" section of *How and Where to Look It Up* is designed to solve this problem. The collec-

tions listed here have been carefully selected from the thousands open to the public throughout the United States. Organized by subject, they are outstanding resources for that subject. Whenever possible, collections have been added from all parts of the country for greater convenience. For this reason, "Special Collections" contains many more listings than the other sections in *How and Where to Look It Up*.

A distinction should be made between private collections and those maintained by public libraries. Public libraries are open to the public and staffed accordingly to handle large numbers of people and their needs. On the other hand, private collections are not always equipped to do this and may place many more limitations on their accessibility. Always call ahead to see what, if any, limitations are in effect at the special collection you want to use.

For those who wish to review the full range of special collections in the United States, two books are recommended:

Directory of Special Libraries, two volumes. Gale, annual. An alphabetical listing of more than 18,500 special libraries, research libraries, information centers, archives, and data centers. Includes a subject index.

Subject Collections, compiled and edited by Lee Ash and William G. Miller. Bowker, 6th edition, 1985. Two volumes containing 2,196 pages of collections in academic, public, and special libraries and museums, listed alphabetically according to subjects. A greatly enlarged 7th edition is in preparation.

Tips on Working with Special Collections

1. Always call ahead before you visit a special collection. Most such collections—especially private ones—are not staffed to handle large numbers of unscheduled visitors, so you may have to make an appointment to come in and discuss your needs at a time convenient for the librarian. And you may have to request an appointment in writing, with a full description of your project and your qualifications. This is especially true of collections with rare books or classified government material.

2. When you call, ask for hours of operation and other limitations. Smaller collections, particularly, may not be open full time.

3. Don't expect to borrow books as you would at a public library. Most special collections make their material available for reference use only on the premises. Inquire about photocopying facilities—most special collections have a copier—and any other services you may need. Then bring enough change to operate the copier; the library is probably not equipped to make change.

4. Community hospitals frequently have excellent small medical and health libraries that are open to the public on a limited basis. If the special collections listed below in the "Medicine and Health" category are not con-

venient, call your local hospital; it may have just what you need.

5. Nearby colleges and universities may also have special collections that are more convenient than those listed below. This is especially true of institutions that have large departments or graduate schools devoted to a specific subject, such as art, business, engineering, law, medicine, and so forth. Again, call ahead of time to see whether the college or university has what you want and whether or not the collection is open to the public.

6. Local public libraries, state libraries, and historical societies are often excellent sources of local and regional information. Call your local public library. The librarians can tell you what they have and what they know of the material available through other local sources.

Special Collections Subject Index

A

ACCOUNTING

**American Institute of Certified Public Accountants
Library Services Division**
1211 Avenue of the Americas
New York, NY 10036-8775
800/223-4155
Collection covers accounting, auditing, taxation, finance, and management; it includes 23,000 books, 3,600 bound periodical volumes, 95,000 pamphlets, 130 tax and business looseleaf services, and all New York Stock Exchange, American Stock Exchange, and Over-The-Counter annual reports since 1977 on microfiche. There is also a special collection of old accounting texts.

National Association of Accountants Library
10 Paragon Drive
Montvale, NJ 07645-1760
201/573-6235
FAX: 201/573-8185
Collection includes works on accounting and financial management and a special collection of trade manuals.

**University of Chicago
Business and Economics Collection**
Joseph Regenstein Library

1100 East Fifty-seventh Street
Chicago, IL 60637
312/702-8716
Covers economics, management, finance, and accounting. Holds 375,000 books.

**University of Southern California
Crocker Business and Accounting Libraries**
University Park
Los Angeles, CA 90089-1421
213/743-6792
Covers accounting, taxation, finance, marketing, and organizational behavior. Library holds 71,000 books, in addition to other research materials.

ADOLESCENCE

**University of North Carolina, Chapel Hill
Center for Early Adolescence—Information
Services Division**
Carr Mill Mall, Suite 223
Carrboro, NC 27510
919/966-5678
Holds 7,000 books and clippings on the physical and social development of young adolescents.

ADVERTISING. *See also* COMMUNICATIONS.

American Association of Advertising Agencies
Member Information Service
666 Third Avenue
New York, NY 10017
212/682-2500
Covers advertising and marketing. Holds 2,000 books and 400 vertical file drawers of clippings, reports, and pamphlets.

University of Illinois
Communications Library
122 Gregory Hall
Urbana, IL 61801
217/333-2216
Holds 16,000-volume library on communications—advertising, broadcasting, publishing, public relations, and film. Special collections include the D'Arcy Collection of advertising clippings 1890–1970.

AERONAUTICS. *See also* AVIATION MEDICINE; SPACE TECHNOLOGY.

American Institute of Aeronautics and
Astronautics Technical Information Service
AIAA Library
555 West Fifty-seventh Street
New York, NY 10019
212/247-6500
FAX: 212/582-4861
Covers aeronautics, aerospace, space sciences, physics, chemistry, earth sciences, and engineering. Includes 35,000 books, 1,000 bound periodical volumes, 50,000 conference papers, and 750,000 microfiche.

California Institute of Technology
Aeronautics Library
1201 East California Boulevard
Pasadena, CA 91125
818/356-4521
Contains technical works on aeronautics and related subjects. Special collections hold reports by NASA and other national research institutions.

International Civil Aviation Organization Library
1000 Sherbrooke Street, West, Suite 400
Montreal, Quebec, Canada H3A 2R2
514/286-6231
Holds 16,500 books relating to aeronautics, aviation, air law, and international law and organizations. Special collections include holdings of transport, aeronautical, and international societies.

Massachusetts Institute of Technology
Aeronautics and Astronautics Library
Room 33-316
Cambridge, MA 02139
617/253-5666
Covers practical and theoretical aspects of aeronautical engineering. Special collections include publications of the National Advisory Committee for Aeronautics and NASA since 1915 and complete sets of technical papers from the Institute of the Aeronautical/Aerospace Sciences, the American Rocket Society, and the American Institute of Aeronautics and Astronautics.

Museum of Flight Research Facility
9404 East Marginal Way, South
Seattle, WA 98108
206/764-5705
Holds 6,000 books, 500 bound periodical volumes, and 10,000 photographs about aviation and aerospace, plus plane and plane manufacturing company data, history and specifications, and historical aviation materials. Includes special collection of juvenile aviation books, 1920-30.

Smithsonian Institution
National Air and Space Museum Library
National Air and Space Museum, Room 3100
Seventh Street and Independence Avenue SW
Washington, DC 20560
202/357-3133
In addition to its superb display of authentic, historic aircraft, the library holds 40,000 books, 7,000 bound periodical volumes, and a large collection of photographs covering all aspects of aeronautics and astronautics, with special emphasis on early aviation history.

U.S. Air Force
Air Force Systems Command
Air Force Geophysics Laboratory
Research Library
GL/SULL
FL 2807
Hanscom Air Force Base, MA 01731
617/377-4895
Holds over 250,000 volumes, 100,000 technical reports, and supporting materials on physics and geophysics, astronomy, electrical engineering, meteorology, computer science, and materials science. Includes special collections on early ballooning and aeronautics.

U.S. Space Education Association Media Center
746 Turnpike Road
Elizabethtown, PA 17022-1161
717/367-3265
Houses research materials on NASA space program, space sciences, solar power, and even science fiction. Includes technical abstracts and NASA reports, photographs, brochures, and other materials. Publishes a bimonthly periodical.

AFRICA. *See also* AFRICAN ART.

Library of Congress
African and Middle Eastern Division
John Adams Building, Room 1015
101 Independence Avenue SE
Washington, DC 20540
202/707-7937
Holds 600,000 volumes in general collections supplemented by area newspapers, manuscripts, and related material. Divided into African, Hebraic, and Near East sections, each of which has materials in the corresponding area languages as well as Western languages.

Northwestern University
Melville J. Herskovits Library of African Studies
University Library
Evanston, IL 60208
312/491-7684
All aspects of Africa—anthropology, history, linguistics, geography, sociology, economics, and other subjects—are covered in the collection's 182,000 volumes and thousands of other holdings.

Smithsonian Institution
National Museum of African Art
950 Independence Avenue SW
Washington, DC 20560
202/357-4654
This is the only museum in the United States devoted exclusively to portraying the cultural heritage of Africa. In addition to its large collection of sub-Saharan art, there is a specialized library of 18,000 volumes and periodicals. The museum also is the repository for the Eliot Elisofon Photographic Archives, which include some 100,000 slides, photographs, and film segments on Africa.

Yale University
African Collection
Sterling Memorial Library, Room 317
New Haven, CT 06520

203/432-1883
FAX: 203/432-9652
Covers all aspects of Africa, including its history and culture. Holds 90,000 books, 85,000 bound periodical volumes, 150 manuscript collections, plus microfilm of newspapers, pamphlets, and government documents, photographs, posters, postcards, broadsides, and maps. Includes special collections on Rhodesia and South Africa.

AFRICAN AMERICANS

Amistad Research Center Library/Archives
Tulane University
6823 St. Charles Avenue
New Orleans, LA 70118
504/865-5535
Covers ethnic minorities of America, with emphasis on African Americans. Has more than 17,000 volumes and other materials, including 500,000 clippings.

Chicago Public Library
Carter G. Woodson Regional Library
Vivian G. Harsh Research Collection of Afro-American History and Literature
9525 South Halsted Street
Chicago, IL 60628
312/881-6910
Covers history, literature, religion, sociology, art, and music of Afro-Americans. Holds 32,000 books, more than 500 bound periodical volumes, and 2,500 pamphlets, plus 2,600 records and tapes. Includes special collections on history 1684 to present, children's literature, and international black affairs.

Fisk University
Special Collections Department
Seventeenth Street at Jackson Street
Nashville, TN 37203
615/329-8646
Special collections include the Black Oral History Collection and many other materials on the African American experience.

Howard University
Moorland-Springarn Research Center
Library Division
500 Howard Place NW
Washington, DC 20059
202/636-7260
Founded in 1916, this collection covers all aspects of the African American experience. The library

has 150,000 volumes, plus periodicals, microforms, and theses.

New York Public Library
Schomburg Center for Research in Black Culture
515 Lenox Avenue
New York, NY 10037
212/491-2200
FAX: 212/491-6760
Holdings include 87,000 volumes on social sciences, the humanities, and the black experience around the world. Special collections: the Haitian Collection, African and Caribbean music, and authors and artists of the Harlem Renaissance. Also has large holdings of recordings, photographs, oral history tapes, and other media.

AFRICAN ART

Smithsonian Institution
National Museum of African Art
950 Independence Avenue SW
Washington, DC 20560
202/357-4654
This is the only museum in the United States devoted exclusively to portraying the cultural heritage of Africa. In addition to its large collection of sub-Saharan art, there is a specialized library of 18,000 volumes and periodicals. The museum also is the repository for the Eliot Elisofon Photographic Archives, which include some 100,000 slides, photographs, and film segments on Africa.

AGING. *See* OLD AGE.

AGRICULTURE. *See also* LAND TENURE.

Cornell University
New York State Agricultural Experiment Station Library
Geneva, NY 14456
315/787-2214
Holds over 50,000 volumes, journals, and other materials relating to agriculture. Has a large collection on grapes and wine.

Stanford University
Food Research Institute Library
Stanford, CA 94305
415/723-3943
Devoted to the economic aspects of agriculture, food supply, population, and underdeveloped areas. Holds documents of foreign governments and international organizations.

U.S. Department of Agriculture
National Agriculture Library
10301 Baltimore Boulevard
Beltsville, MD 20705
301/344-3755
Holds 2 million volumes and 27,000 journal volumes, all devoted to agriculture, food and nutrition, horticulture, animal husbandry, veterinary medicine, alternative farming, engineering and rural development, and agricultural trade and marketing. Special collections cover foreign and domestic nursery and seed trade catalogs and flock, herd, and stud books.

University of Alaska, Fairbanks
Agricultural and Forestry Experiment Station
Palmer Reseach Center
533 East Fireweed
Palmer, AK 99645
907/745-3257
Contains books, periodicals, and abstracts on agriculture, including crop and soil science, and animal husbandry, among other topics.

University of Arizona
Arid Lands Information Center
845 North Park Avenue
Tucson, AZ 85719
602/621-1955
Library specializes in deserts of the world. Covers agriculture, including special collections items on summer rainfall agriculture; international research, including the West Africa Collection; and forestry, mainly the Dryland Forestry Collection. Houses environmental reports as well.

University of California, Berkeley
Giannini Foundation of Agricultural Economics
Research Library
248 Giannini Hall
Berkeley, CA 94720
415/642-7121
FAX: 415/643-8911
Specializes in economic studies in agriculture—land use and valuation, labor, marketing and production, resources conservation, and other allied subjects.

University of California, Riverside
Bio-Agricultural Library
Riverside, CA 92521
714/787-3238
Covers biochemistry and biomedical sciences as

they relate to agriculture. Horticulture collection relates particularly to citrus and desert plants, environmental sciences, and agricultural engineering. Includes special collection on arid land research.

University of Georgia
Science Library
Athens, GA 30602
404/542-4535
Holds 700,000 volumes on science and technology, agriculture, medicine, veterinary medicine, and economics.

University of Illinois
Agriculture Library
226 Mumford Hall
1301 West Gregory
Urbana, IL 61801
217/333-2416
Covers agriculture, economics, animal husbandry, engineering, horticulture, food science, forestry, and agricultural history. Holds 70,000 volumes.

ALCOHOLISM. *See* SUBSTANCE ABUSE.

AMERICAN HISTORY. *See* HISTORY—AMERICAN.

AMERICAN SOUTH

University of Southern Mississippi
McCain Library and Archives
Southern Station, Box 5148
Hattiesburg, MS 39406-5148
601/266-4345
Covers Mississippiana, Civil War, and Confederate history. Special collections cover Confederate literature, railroads, children's literature, rare books, and genealogy. Holds 65,000 volumes, plus archival materials.

University of Mississippi
Archives and Special Collections/Mississippiana
University, MS 38677
601/232-7408
Houses 32,000 volumes, 3,000 bound periodical volumes, and many special collections devoted to Mississippi and Southern subjects and authors, including African American fiction.

University of Virginia
Special Collections Department
University of Virginia Library
Charlottesville, VA 22903-2498
804/924-3025
Houses the Tracy W. McGregor Library devoted to the history of the Southeastern United States

from 1607 to the 20th century. This collection holds 21,000 books and manuscripts.

AMERICAN WEST

Denver Public Library
Western History Department
1357 Broadway
Denver, CO 80203-2165
303/571-2009
Collection of 65,000 books and pamphlets, 300,000 prints and photographs, and other material covers U.S. history west of the Mississippi River, with emphasis on Rocky Mountain region.

National Cowboy Hall of Fame and Western Heritage Center
Research Library of Western Americana
1700 North East Sixty-third Street
Oklahoma City, OK 73111
405/478-2250
Houses materials on cowboys, gauchos, and Western history. Includes special collection of American Western art.

University of California, Berkeley
Bancroft Library
Berkeley, CA 94720
415/642-3781
Houses the Bancroft Collection, covering the history of Western North America with an emphasis on California and Mexico; also has Regional Oral History Office records and covers history of science and technology related to California. Special collections include the Mark Twain Papers.

University of California, Davis
Michael and Margaret B. Harrison Western Research Center
Department of Special Collections
Shields Library
Davis, CA 95616
916/752-1621
Includes material on history and development of the American West from 19th century to present, Native Americans, ethnic studies, folklore, literature, art and architecture, and history of printing.

University of Oklahoma
Western History Collections
630 Parrington Oval, Room 452
405/325-3641
Covers Native American, Oklahoma, American Southwest, and recent U.S. history. Includes spe-

cial collections of Cherokee nation papers. Holds 50,000 books, 250,000 photographs in archives, and other historical documents.

University of New Mexico
Special Collections Department
General Library
Albuquerque, NM 87131
505/277-6451
Covers history of the American Southwest, Mexico, and Latin America. Holds 36,700 books and 1,000 oral histories.

University of Southern California
Department of Special Collections
University Park
Los Angeles, CA 90089-0182
213/743-0966
Covers general, western, and aeronautical history. 120 special collections include oral histories and the Darwin collection. Holds 51,000 volumes, 50,000 manuscripts, and other materials.

University of Texas, Austin
Barker Texas History Center
General Libraries, SRH 2.109
Austin, TX 78713-7330
512/471-5961
FAX: 512/471-9241
Covers Texas history, literature, and folklore and Southern and Western history. Holds 142,000 books, sound archives, Texas documents, historic newspapers, and photographs.

ANESTHESIOLOGY

American Society of Anesthesiologists
Wood Library
Museum of Anesthesiology
515 Busse Highway
Park Ridge, IL 60068
312/825-5586
Covers anesthesiology, resuscitation, shock, medical applications of hypnotism, inhalation therapy, and history of anesthesiology. Includes special collections of anesthesiological equipment and apparatus and the Living History of Anesthesiology on videocassette.

ANIMAL RIGHTS

National Anti-Vivisection Society Library
53 West Jackson Boulevard, Suite 1550
Chicago, IL 60604-3703
312/427-6065

Library contains educational materials on "the evils of vivisection of animals."

ANTHROPOLOGY. *See also* SOCIAL SCIENCES.

Harvard University
Tozzer Library
21 Divinity Avenue
Cambridge, MA 02138
617/495-2253
Formerly the Library of the Peabody Museum of Archaeology and Ethnology. Covers materials on anthropology, ethnology, and prehistoric archaeology. Holds 171,000 volumes.

Smithsonian Institution
National Museum of Natural History
Anthropology Division Library
Natural History Building, Rooms 330/331
Tenth Street and Constitution Avenue NW
Washington, DC 20560
202/357-1819
Covers physical anthropology, ethnology, and archaeology. Holdings of 68,000 volumes and other materials include the Bureau of American Ethnology Library Collection.

University of California
Anthropology Library
230 Kroeber Hall
Berkeley, CA 94720
415/642-2400
Library specializing in anthropology.

Yale University
Anthropology Library
Kline Science Library
Box 6666
New Haven, CT 06511
203/432-3439
Holds 19,000 volumes on anthropology.

APPLIED SCIENCE. *See* TECHNOLOGY.

AQUACULTURE. *See also* FISH AND FISHERIES; MARINE BIOLOGY; OCEANOGRAPHY.

University of Rhode Island
International Center for Marine Resource Development Library
Main Library
Kingston, RI 02881
401/792-2938
Covers aquaculture, fisheries, and coastal zone

management in developing countries. Holds 13,000 books and documents.

ARBITRATION

American Arbitration Association
Eastman Arbitration Library
140 West Fifty-first Street
New York, NY 10020
212/484-4127
Covers arbitration, mediation, and other forms of alternative dispute resolution. Includes special collections on early history and development in the United States, arbitration rules of trade associations, and arbitration institutions throughout the world. Holds 16,000 volumes and 19,500 microfiche.

ARCHITECTURE. *See also* FINE ARTS; LANDSCAPE ARCHITECTURE.

American Institute of Architects Information Center
1735 New York Avenue NW
Washington, DC 20006
202/626-7493
FAX: 202/783-8247
Covers American architecture and architectural practice, building technology, and urban planning. Holds 26,000 volumes, 20 vertical file drawers of pamphlets and clippings, and 17,000 slides, films, and videotapes. Special collections include AIA archives and the Richard Morris Hunt Collection.

Clemson University
Emery A. Gunnin Architectural Library
College of Architecture
Lee Hall
Clemson, SC 29634-0501
803/656-3933
Subjects include building science and city and regional planning. Holds 29,000 books, a large slide collection, and other research materials.

Columbia University
Avery Architectural and Fine Arts Library
Broadway and 116th Street
New York, NY 10027
212/854-3501
Houses 235,000 volumes plus 100,000 manuscripts and papers on architecture, planning, fine arts, and archaeology. Special collections holdings include 130,000 original architectural drawings of major firms.

Harvard University
Graduate School of Design
Frances Loeb Library
Gund Hall
Cambridge, MA 02138
617/495-2574
Subjects include architecture and landscape architecture and city and regional planning. Holds 244,000 volumes, 20,000 maps, 5,000 architectural drawings, and supporting materials.

Massachusetts Institute of Technology
Rotch Library of Architecture and Planning
Room 7-238
Cambridge, MA 02139
617/258-5599
Covers architectural history and design, urban and environmental studies, and regional planning. Holds more than 100,000 books, bound periodical volumes, technical reports, pamphlets, maps and plans, and M.I.T. theses.

Stanford University
Art and Architecture Library
Nathan Cummings Art Building
Stanford, CA 94305-2018
415/723-3408
Covers architectural history and art. Holds 125,000 volumes.

University of Arizona
College of Architecture Library
Tucson, AZ 85721
602/621-2498
Holds works on design, particularly desert architecture, urban planning, and historic preservation. Includes 24,500 slides as well as books and other materials.

University of California, Los Angeles
Architecture and Urban Planning Library
1302 Perloff Hall
Los Angeles, CA 90024-1467
213/825-2747
Holds 25,000 volumes on architecture and urban planning.

University of Houston
Architecture and Art Library
Houston, TX 77204-4431
713/749-7551
FAX: 713/749-3867
Has 45,000 works on architecture and urban design, art, and photography.

University of Kansas
Murphy Library of Art and Architecture
Helen Foresman Spencer Museum of Art
Lawrence, KS 66045-2800
913/864-3020
Covers architecture, design, photography, art, and art history. Holds 84,000 volumes.

University of Michigan
Art and Architecture Library
2106 Art and Architecture Building
Ann Arbor, MI 48109
313/764-1303
Covers architecture, urban planning, design, landscape architecture, art, photography, and graphic design. Special collection owns Jens Jenson landscape drawings. Holds 55,000 volumes, software programs, maps, and other supporting materials.

University of Southern California
Helen Topping Architecture and Fine Arts Library
University Park
Los Angeles, CA 90089-0292
213/743-2798
Holds 60,000 books and 200,000 slides on history of art and architecture in Southern California.

University of Virginia
Fiske Kimball Fine Arts Library
Bayly Drive
Charlottesville, VA 22903
804/924-7024
Holds 108,000 volumes and 140,000 architecture slides on art, architecture, theater, and allied arts.

University of Wisconsin, Madison
Kohler Art Library
General Library System
800 University Avenue
Madison, WI 53706
608/263-2256
Holds 103,000 volumes and 16,000 microforms on art, architecture, dance, and photography.

ART. *See* AFRICAN ART; FINE ARTS; GRAPHIC ARTS. *See also* ARCHITECTURE.

ASIA. *See* FAR EAST; MIDDLE EAST.

ASTRONOMY. *See also* SCIENCE.

Harvard University
Observatory Library
60 Garden Street
Cambridge, MA 02138

617/495-5488
FAX: 617/495-7199
Covers astronomy, astrophysics, and related sciences such as physics, mathematics, and optics. Holds 70,000 volumes and 500,000 telescope photographs.

Princeton University
Astronomy Library
Peyton Hall
Princeton, NJ 08544
609/452-3820
FAX: 609/243-7333
Holds more than 17,000 books on astronomy and astrophysics. Includes special collections on the European Southern Observatory, Atlas of the Southern Sky, and Mount Palomar Sky Atlas.

Smithsonian Astrophysical Observatory Library
60 Garden Street
Cambridge, MA 02138
617/495-7264
Covers astonomy, astrophysics, and related subjects. Holds 30,000 books, 10,000 bound periodical volumes, and a large microfiche collection.

University of Arizona
Space Imagery Center
Lunar and Planetary Laboratory
Tucson, AZ 85721
602/621-4861
Specializes in space photography and planetary science. Holds over 750,000 photographs, 1,000 maps, 23 atlases, and 3,000 slides.

University of Chicago
Yerkes Observatory Library
Williams Bay, WI 53191
414/245-5555
Covers astronomy and astrophysics. Holdings include 15,000 books.

University of North Carolina, Chapel Hill
Alfred T. Brauer Library
CB 3250 Phillips Hall
Chapel Hill, NC 27599
919/966-2323
Covers mathematics, statistics, computer science, operations research, and astronomy. Holds more than 78,000 volumes, reports, microfiche, and audiotapes.

University of Rochester
Physics-Optics-Astronomy Library
374 Bausch and Lomb Building

Rochester, NY 14627
716/275-4469
Covers astronomy and astrophysics and optics, with special collection of preprints in high-energy physics. Holds more than 12,000 books, 11,000 bound periodical volumes, plus patents, theses, and reports. Also has quarterly list of new publications.

Yale University
Astronomy Library
J.W. Gibbs Laboratory
260 Whitney Avenue
Box 6666
New Haven, CT 06511
203/432-3000
Covers astronomy, astrophysics, celestial mechanics, physics, and mathematics. Holds more than 16,000 books, 6,000 bound periodical volumes, and 800 shelf feet of observatory reprints. Includes extensive collection of domestic and foreign observatory publications.

AUTOMOBILES

Detroit Public Library
National Automotive History Collection
5201 Woodward Avenue
Detroit, MI 48202
313/833-1456
All aspects of automobiles—their history, technology, and the people and companies that pioneered them. Holds 213,500 books and other materials, including 80,000 advertising catalogs for cars and accessories.

AVIATION. *See* AERONAUTICS.

AVIATION MEDICINE

U.S. Air Force
Air Force Systems Command
Human Systems Division
School of Aerospace Medicine
Strughold Aeromedical Library
Brooks Air Force Base, TX 78235-5301
516/536-3725
Holds books and technical reports on aerospace medicine, clinical medicine, the life sciences, and related subjects such as bioastronautics.

U.S. Army Medical Research and Development Command
Aeromedical Research Laboratory Scientific Information Center

Box 577
Ft. Rucker, AL 36362
205/255-6907
Dedicated to the study of aerospace medicine and related subjects such as optics, audiology, aviation psychology, and the like. Contains all the Laboratory's reports.

B

BANKING. *See* FINANCE.

BASEBALL. *See also* SPORTS.

National Baseball Hall of Fame and Museum, Inc.
National Baseball Library
Box 590
Cooperstown, NY 13326
607/547-9988
In addition to comprehensive collection of biographies, histories, and reference books, library has complete runs of baseball and sports magazines, issues of 19th- and early 20th-century sports magazines, biographical data on minor-league players, umpires, executives, and films. Special collections include history and documents from the Negro Leagues and the official records of Major League Baseball.

BIOLOGY. *See also* LIFE SCIENCES; NATURAL HISTORY; SCIENCE.

Princeton University
Biology Library
Guyot Hall
Princeton, NJ 08544
609/452-3235
Covers biology—micro, molecular, plant, and population; biochemistry; zoology; genetics; and ecology. Holds more than 18,000 books and 21,000 bound periodical volumes.

Stanford University
Falconer Biology Library
Stanford, CA 94305
415/723-1528
Holds more than 85,000 volumes relating to biology, biochemistry, population genetics, and ecology.

University of Nebraska, Lincoln
Biological Sciences Library
Manter Hall 402

Lincoln, NE 68588-0118
402/472-2756
Covers biology, botany, and zoology and related subjects. Holds 30,000 volumes.

BIRDS

National Audubon Society Library
950 Third Avenue
New York, NY 10022
212/546-9108
Holds references on ornithology and natural history, including the Society's archives and Audubon manuscripts.

BLACKS. *See* AFRICAN AMERICANS.

BLINDNESS. *See* DISABILITIES.

BOTANY. *See also* HORTICULTURE.

Harvard University
Arnold Arboretum and Gray Herbarium Library
22 Divinity Avenue
Cambridge, MA 02138
617/495-2366
Holds 152,500 volumes on botany and horticulture.

New York Botanical Garden Library
Bronx, NY 10458
212/220-8751
In addition to its magnificent gardens, this institution has a library of half a million books, periodicals, nursery catalogs and seed lists, microforms, photographs, and other materials relating to botany, horticulture, environmental sciences, and other subjects.

Smithsonian Institution
National Museum of Natural History
Botany Library
Natural History Building
Tenth Street and Constitution Avenue NW
Washington, DC 20560
202/357-2715
Holds 35,000 volumes on taxonomic botany and the history of botany plus 14 shelves of collectors' field notebooks.

University of Wisconsin, Madison
Botany Department
Herbarium Library
158 Birge Hall
430 Lincoln Drive
Madison, WI 53706
608/262-2792

Covers taxonomy of flowering plants, gymnosperms, and ferns, including local and world flora. Holds 2,000 volumes, bound periodical volumes, and 938,000 dried specimens.

BROADCASTING. *See also* PERFORMING ARTS; TELECOMMUNICATIONS.

National Association of Broadcasters Library and Information Center
1771 N Street NW
Washington, DC 20036
202/429-5490
Holds books and periodicals concerning radio and television broadcasting and related subjects.

National Public Radio
Broadcast Library
2025 M Street NW
Washington, DC 20036
202/822-2064
FAX: 202/822-2064
Holds 80,000 audiotapes and 7,000 phonograph records on current events, drama, and music.

BUDDHISM

American Buddhist Movement Archives
301 West 45th Street
New York, NY 10036
212/489-1075
Covers Buddhism, Buddhist art and culture, Tibetan Buddhism, Asian meditation, and Zen. Holds 8,000 volumes plus dissertations and Buddhist lectures on cassette tape.

BUSINESS. *See also* FINANCE; LABOR; MANAGEMENT.

Boston Public Library
Kirsten Business Branch
20 City Hall Avenue
Boston, MA 02108
617/523-0860
Covers all aspects of business, business administration, banking, finance, business law, investments, accounting, and taxation. Has the last 60 years of *Moody's Manuals*; the last 30 years of *Commercial and Financial Chronicle*; the *Bank and Quotation Record* since 1928; *Standard and Poor's New York Stock Exchange and American Stock Exchange Daily Stock Price Record* since 1962; over-the-counter stocks since 1968; New York Stock Exchange and American Stock Exchange companies' annual and 10K reports; the last 10 years of the *Wall*

Street Journal; and the last five years of the Wall Street Transcript.

Brooklyn Public Library
Business Library
280 Cadman Plaza West
Brooklyn, NY 11201
718/780-7800
Library covers all business-related subjects including accounting, management, and finance. Special collection has annual reports of foreign companies and many foreign telephone directories. The Business Library is also a U.S. Government Documents depository. Publishes a monthly newsletter.

Chicago Public Library Central Library
Business/Science/Technology Division
400 North Franklin Street
Chicago, IL 60611
312/269-2814
312/269-2865
Library covers all business topics, including marketing, small business, investments, and personnel, as well as related scientific topics: technology, patents, medicine, physics and biology, and computer science. Has more than 60,000 volumes and SEC reports and 50 drawers of corporate annual reports. Includes special collections of complete U.S. and British patents, gazettes, domestic and foreign auto manuals, career information, electrical and computer schematics, and industrial, corporate and product directories.

Columbia University
Thomas J. Watson Library of Business and Economics
130 Uris Hall
New York, NY 10027
212/280-4000
Library covers all business-related subjects including finance and management, marketing, labor relations, agriculture, banking, and transportation. Holds nearly 360,000 volumes and 566,000 microforms.

Harvard University
Harvard Business School
Baker Library
Soldiers Field Road
Boston, MA 02163
617/495-6044
Holds 540,000 volumes on all aspects of business

management and economics. Special collections include corporate reports, manuscripts, and archives.

New York Public Library
Economic and Public Affairs Division
Fifth Avenue and Forty-second Street, Room 228
New York, NY 10018
212/930-0750
Covers business-related subjects such as marketing, labor, banking, and insurance; also covers government publications and demography, and has census and other statistical information. Holds 1.5 million books and 1 million microforms.

Seattle Public Library
Business and Science Department
1000 Fourth Avenue
Seattle, WA 98104
206/386-4655
Covers regional business and economics, skilled trades, and investments. Holds 250,000 books, as well as other research materials.

Stanford University
J. Hugh Jackson Library
Graduate School of Business
Stanford, CA 94305-5016
415/723-2161
Special collections emphasize Pacific Northwestern economics and business. More than 364,000 volumes.

University of Alabama
Business Library
Box 870266
Tuscaloosa, AL 35487-0266
205/348-6096
Covers all aspects of business including accounting, banking, economics, marketing, real estate, insurance, business law, and statistics. Owns collection of corporate reports.

University of California, Los Angeles
John E. Anderson Graduate School of Management Library
Los Angeles, CA 90024-1460
213/825-3138
Holds material on all fields of business and management, including accounting, finance and investments, labor relations, marketing, arts management, and urban land economics. Houses Robert E. Gross Collection of Rare Books in Business

and Economics and Kress Collection of Rare Books in Business and Economics, among others.

University of Chicago
Business and Economics Collection
Joseph Regenstein Library
1100 East Fifty-seventh Street
Chicago, IL 60637
312/702-8716
Covers economics, management, finance, and accounting. Holds 375,000 books.

University of Michigan
Kresge Business Administration Library
School of Business Administration
Tappan and Monroe Streets
Ann Arbor, MI 48109-1234
313/764-7356
Covers accounting, finance, marketing, management, banking, and related subjects. Holds 208,000 volumes, government documents, corporate financial reports, other reports, and supporting materials.

University of Pennsylvania
Lippincott Library of the Wharton School
3420 Walnut Street
Philadelphia, PA 19104-6207
215/898-5924
Founded in 1927, the Wharton School's Lippincott Library covers business, management, finance, economics, multinational enterprises, and many other related subjects. The Library holds more than 202,000 volumes and 215,000 microform records.

University of Virginia
Colgate Darden Graduate School of Business Administration Library
Box 6550
Charlottesville, VA 22906
804/924-7321
Covers business finance, accounting, management, marketing, and organization behavior. Holds 65,000 books, bound periodical volumes, corporate annuals, and 10K reports.

University of Washington
Business Administration Library
100 Balmer Hall DJ-10
Seattle, WA 98195
206/543-4630
Library holds 48,000 volumes, including U.S. corporate records relating to management, marketing, personnel and labor, international business, and labor law.

C

CANCER

American Cancer Society
Medical Library
261 Madison Avenue
New York, NY 10016
212/599-3600
Covers oncology, biochemistry, cytology, public health, rehabilitation of the cancer patient, smoking, radiobiology, and general medicine. Holds 18,000 books, 7,000 bound periodical volumes, plus reports from foundations, institutes, and laboratories.

University of Texas
M.D. Anderson Hospital and Tumor Institute
Research Medical Library
Texas Medical Center
Houston, TX 77030
713/792-2282
FAX: 713/797-6513
Covers cancer, radiological physics, and cell biology. Library holds 45,000 books, special collection of rare books, and early treatises on cancer.

CAREERS. *See* EMPLOYMENT.

CARTER, JIMMY. *See* PRESIDENTIAL LIBRARIES.

CARTOONS

Museum of Cartoon Art Research Library
Comly Avenue
Rye Brook, NY 10573
914/939-0234
Covers comic-strip and comic-book art, political/editorial cartooning, caricature, magazine cartoons, illustration, and animation. Holds 500 books, 300 bound periodical volumes, 800 animated cartoons, three vertical file drawers of clippings and articles, and over 50,000 pieces of original artwork. *Note:* Relocating to Boca Raton, FL in late 1991.

CENSUS STATISTICS. *See* DEMOGRAPHICS.

CHEMICAL ENGINEERING. *See also* CHEMISTRY; ENGINEERING.

Stanford University
Swain Library of Chemistry and Chemical Engineering
Stanford, CA 94305
415/723-9237
Holds 42,500 volumes relating to chemistry and chemical engineering.

University of Illinois
Chemistry Library
257 Noyes Laboratory
305 South Matthews
Urbana, IL 61801
217/333-3737
Covers general chemistry and chemical engineering. Holdings include 70,000 volumes, over 900 films, and other materials.

University of Washington
Chemistry Library and Information Services
60 Chemistry Building BG-10
Seattle, WA 98195
206/543-1603
Holds 49,000 volumes and microfiche covering chemistry and chemical engineering.

CHEMISTRY. *See also* CHEMICAL ENGINEERING; SCIENCE.

American Chemical Society Library
1155 Sixteenth Street NW
Washington, DC 20036
202/872-4509
Holds 10,000 books, 7,300 bound periodical volumes, and 350,000 photographs concerning chemistry, chemical engineering, and related subjects.

University of California, Berkeley
Chemistry Library
100 Hildebrand Hall
Berkeley, CA 94720
415/642-3753
Covers chemistry, thermodynamics, chemical engineering, electrochemistry, and more specialized subjects. Special collections have Russian monographs as part of exchange program; also U.S. chemical patents.

University of California, Los Angeles
Chemistry Library
4238 Young Hall
Los Angeles, CA 90024-1569
213/825-3342
All fields in chemistry represented—organic, inorganic, and biochemistry, among others. Special collections house the Morgan Memorial Collection on history of chemistry. Also owns copies of U.S. chemical patents, 1952 to present.

University of Illinois
Chemistry Library
257 Noyes Laboratory

305 South Matthews
Urbana, IL 61801
217/333-3737
Covers general chemistry and chemical engineering. Holdings include 70,000 volumes, over 900 films, and other materials.

University of Michigan
Chemistry Library
2000 Chemistry Building
Ann Arbor, MI 48109-1055
313/764-7337
Holds 53,000 volumes, technical reports, and periodicals on chemistry. Special collections include Sadtler Proton NMR Spectra.

University of Texas, Austin
Chemistry Library
General Libraries, WEL 2.132
Austin, TX 78713-7330
512/471-1303
FAX: 512/471-9241
Holds more than 25,000 books, bound periodical volumes, and other research materials.

University of Washington
Chemistry Library and Information Services
60 Chemistry Building BG-10
Seattle, WA 98195
206/543-1603
Holds 49,000 volumes and microfiche covering chemistry and chemical engineering.

CHILDREN. *See also* LITERATURE: CHILDREN'S.

New York Public Library
Early Childhood Resource and Information Center
66 Leroy Street, 2nd Floor
New York, NY 10014
212/929-0815
Has more than 13,000 books and other materials on all aspects of the care, development, and education of children, including parent–child activities.

CHILDREN'S LITERATURE. *See* LITERATURE: CHILDREN'S.

CHIROPRACTIC

Cleveland Chiropractic College
Ruth R. Cleveland Memorial Library
6401 Rockhill Road
Kansas City, MO 64131
816/333-8230
Covers chiropractic, orthopedics, and allied sci-

ences. Holds 8,600 books, bound periodical volumes, and radiographic films.

National College of Chiropractic
Learning Resource Center
200 East Roosevelt Road
Lombard, IL 60148
312/629-2000
Specializes in chiropractic medicine and related fields such as orthopedics and radiology. Also contains general medical volumes.

CHRISTIANITY

American Baptist Historical Society
American Baptist–Samuel Colgate Historical Library
1106 South Goodman Street
Rochester, NY 14620
716/473-1740
Covers Baptist history, theology, and authors. Holds 30,000 books, 15,000 bound periodical volumes, 200,000 annual reports and pamphlets, and 6,000 manuscripts, plus clippings, photographs, and oral history cassette tapes. Includes special collections of 17th- and 18th-century English Baptist materials.

American Congregational Association
Congregational Library
14 Beacon Street
Boston, MA 02108
617/523-0470
Holds 200,000 books, pamphlets, and periodicals about Congregationalism, 16th- to 18th-century religion and theology, plus modern writings on religion and theology. Includes special collections of church records, hymnals, town and local church histories, and works of Richard, Increase, and Cotton Mather, plus the minor Mathers.

Assemblies of God Theological Seminary
Cordas C. Burnett Library
1445 Boonville Avenue
Springfield, MO 65802
417/862-3344
Covers Bible, theology, Holy Spirit, missions, and the Assemblies of God. Holds more than 58,000 volumes, 2,000 reels of microfilm, 46,000 microfiche, and 2,000 cassette tapes.

Associated Mennonite Biblical Seminaries Library
3003 Benham Avenue
Elkhart, IN 46514

219/295-3726
Subjects include biblical studies, theology, church history, ethics, Christian education, and mission work, with special collections devoted to Mennonites and the Studer Bible Collection. Holds 100,000 books.

California Lutheran University
Pearson Library Special Collections
60 Olsen Road
Thousand Oaks, CA 91360-2787
805/493-1595
Holds 92,000 government documents. Library also owns materials on history of Scandinavian Lutheranism.

California Province of the Society of Jesus
Jesuit Center Library
300 College Avenue
Box 128
Los Gatos, CA 95031
408/354-9240
Library holdings of Catholic theology and ecclesiastical history. Includes special collection of Jesuitica.

Chicago Theological Seminary
Hammond Library
5757 South University Avenue
Chicago, IL 60637
312/752-5757
Covers theology, social ethics, personality and religion, Congregational Church history, and sociology and religion. Holds more than 104,000 volumes, plus church records from Midwest congregations and audiovisual programs. Includes special collections on Puritan and Congregational history and psychiatry, psychology, and religion.

Christian Theological Seminary Library
1000 West Forty-second Street
Box 88267
Indianapolis, IN 46208-0267
317/924-1331
Covers religion, theology, and Disciples of Christ historical materials. Holds 115,000 books and other research materials.

Church of Jesus Christ of Latter-Day Saints
Historical Department
Church Library/Archives
50 East North Temple Street
Salt Lake City, UT 84150
801/531-2745

Holds 170,000 books, pamphlets, 290,000 minute books, and other handwritten documents, including manuscripts and records of Mormonism.

General Theological Seminary
St. Mark's Library
175 Ninth Avenue
New York, NY 10011
212/243-5150
Holds 215,000 books relating to biblical studies, theology, and church history. Special collections include 800 editions of the Latin Bible, the Early English Theology Collection, and materials from the Protestant Episcopal Church in the United States.

Harvard University
Divinity School
Andover-Harvard Theological Library
45 Francis Avenue
Cambridge, MA 02138
617/495-5788
Contains studies in theology, the Bible, Protestantism, and allied subjects. Special collections hold materials from American Congregational, Unitarian, and Universalist ministries. Holds 388,000 volumes.

Princeton Theological Seminary
Speer Library
Mercer Street and Library Place
Box 111
Princeton, NJ 08542
609/497-7940
Covers theology, Presbyterianism, Semitic philology, biblical studies, and church history. Holds more than 335,000 volumes, 59,000 bound pamphlets, 100,000 manuscripts, and 3,000 cuneiform tablets. Includes special collections of Puritan and English theological literature, early American pamphlets, hymnology, and the Baptism Controversy.

Union Theological Seminary
Burke Library
3041 Broadway at Reinhold Niebuhr Place
New York, NY 10027
212/662-7100
Founded in 1838, the Burke Library's 570,000 volumes and other materials cover the Bible, theology, sacred music, church history, ecumenics, and related subjects.

University of the South
School of Theology Library
Sewanee, TN 37375-4006
615/598-5931
Holds 102,000 books relating to theology and church history, liturgy, ritual, art, and music. Includes journals and archives of the Episcopalian Church.

Yale University
Divinity School Library
409 Prospect Street
New Haven, CT 06520
203/432-5290
Holds 351,000 volumes and 300 linear feet of personal papers and archives about theology, history of doctrine, biblical studies, and missions. Includes extensive collections of archives of various world missions and missions to Asia, plus historical sermons.

CIVIL ENGINEERING. *See also* ENGINEERING.

U.S. Army Corps of Engineers
Cold Regions and Engineering Laboratory Library
72 Lyme Road
Hanover, NH 03755-1290
603/646-4221
FAX: 603/646-4278
Covers civil engineering emphasizing cold-weather construction problems. Holdings include topics in geology, hydrology, meteorology, mathematics, and other related sciences.

U.S. Bureau of Reclamation
Denver Office Library
Denver Federal Center
Denver, CO 80225
303/236-6963
In addition to books, this collection holds the Bureau's technical reports and has government publications, technical specifications, and other materials basically on development of water resources—dams, power plants, canals, and the like.

CIVIL RIGHTS

American Civil Liberties Union Library/Archives
132 West Forty-third Street
New York, NY 10036
212/354-5290
Holds 5,000 books, plus ACLU board and committee minutes and reports, press releases, an-

nual reports, and pamphlets and newsletters from 1920 to the present.

Commission on Civil Rights
National Clearinghouse Library
1121 Vermont Avenue NW
Washington, DC 20425
202/376-8110
Holdings pertain to civil rights and related problems, such as economics and education. Special collections contain all Commission publications from 1957 to present. Pertinent legal references also available.

Equal Employment Opportunity Commission Library
2401 East Street NW
Washington, DC 20507
202/634-6990
FAX: 202/634-4259
Covers employment discrimination and labor law. Holds Equal Employment Opportunity Commission reports.

CLASSICAL LITERATURE. *See* LITERATURE: CLASSICAL.

CLOCKS AND WATCHES

National Association of Watch and Clock Collectors, Inc.
Watch and Clock Museum of the NAWCC Library
514 Poplar Street
Box 33
Columbia, PA 17512
717/684-8261
Holds books on horology, business records of the Hamilton Watch Company, documents, periodicals, and ephemera.

CLOTHING AND TEXTILES

American Textile Manufacturers Institute
1801 K Street NW, Suite 900
Washington, DC 20006
202/862-0500
FAX: 202/862-0570
Holds 1,200 books; also historical records relating to the textile industry, its history, and safety.

Fashion Institute of Technology Library
Seventh Avenue at Twenty-seventh Street
New York, NY 10001-5992
212/760-7884
Covers costume, fashion, interior design, man-

agement, engineering, and technology. Includes special collections of photographs, drawings, and sketches. Holds more than 103,000 books and other support materials.

M. Lowenstein Corporation
Design Research Library
1430 Broadway
New York, NY 10018
212/930-5610
Holds 2,500 books and 1 million swatches of material from 1800 to 1983. Subjects include design and decorative arts.

Museum of American Textile History
800 Massachusetts Avenue
North Andover, MA 01845
508/686-0191
Houses special collection of trade catalogs, maps, prints, and photos. Holds 35,500 volumes, as well as other supporting materials.

Philadelphia College of Textiles and Science
Pastore Library
School House Lane and Henry Avenue
Philadelphia, PA 19144
215/951-2840
FAX: 215/848-1144
Holds 75,000 books, 12,000 bound periodical volumes, and 6,000 reels of microfilm, about textiles and the textile business. Includes special collection on textile history.

University of Texas, Austin
Natural Fibers Information Center
University Station, Box 7459
Austin, TX 78713
512/471-1616
FAX: 512/471-3034
Covers agricultural and economic statistics and production data on cotton, wool, mohair, and oilseeds.

COLLEGES AND UNIVERSITIES. *See also* EDUCATION.

American Council on Education
Library and Information Services
One Dupont Circle, Suite 640
Washington, DC 20036
202/939-9405
FAX: 202/833-4760
Holds more than 7,000 books on higher education policy and administration, plus college catalogs

on microfilm. Includes special collections of reports from educational foundations, the archives from 1918 to 1977, and complete publications of the American Council on Education.

COMMUNICABLE DISEASES

U.S. Army Medical Research and Development Command
Walter Reed Army Institute and Research Library
Walter Reed Army Medical Center
Washington, DC 20307-5100
202/576-3314
Concentration is in communicable diseases and immunology; also has works in general and clinical medicine, biochemistry, psychology, and the veterinary sciences.

U.S. Centers for Disease Control
CDC Information Center
1600 Clifton Road NE
Atlanta, GA 30333
404/639-3534
Concentration is in communicable diseases and epidemiology. Also has holdings on microbiology, virology, veterinary sciences, and biochemistry. Has collection of U.S. Department of Health and Human Services publications.

COMMUNICATIONS. *See also* TELCOMMUNICATIONS.

University of Illinois
Communications Library
122 Gregory Hall
Urbana, IL 61801
217/333-2216
16,000-volume library on communications—advertising, broadcasting, publishing, public relations, and film. Special collections include the D'Arcy Collection of advertising clippings 1890–1970.

University of Pennsylvania
Annenberg School of Communications Library
3620 Walnut Street
Philadelphia, PA 19104-6220
215/898-7027
Holds more than 23,000 volumes, pamphlets, clippings, dissertations, tapes, and disks relating to communications theory and history.

COMPUTERS. *See also* TECHNOLOGY.

Massachusetts Institute of Technology
Lincoln Laboratory Library

244 Wood Street
Box 73
Lexington, MA 02173-0073
617/981-7171 or 617/981-2300
FAX: 617/981-0427
Covers electronics, electrical engineering, computer science, physics, mathematics, and space science. Holds 108,000 volumes, 400,000 technical reports, 3,000 maps, plus 1 million other cataloged items.

Stanford University
Mathematical and Computer Sciences Library
Building 380, Sloan Mathematics Center
Stanford, CA 94305
415/723-4672
Holds more than 56,000 volumes and 60,000 reports on computer science and related subjects such as mathematics, statistics, and operations research.

University of California, Los Angeles
Computer Science Department Archives
3440 Boelter Hall
Los Angeles, CA 90024-1596
213/825-4317
Contains books and periodicals, 10,000 technical reports, dissertations, and theses. Holds Institute of Electrical and Electronics Engineers Repository Collection.

University of Illinois
Mathematics Library
216 Altgeld Hall
1409 West Green Street
Urbana, IL 61801
217/333-0258
Covers pure and appled mathematics, statistics, and computer sciences. Has 69,000 volumes.

University of Maryland, College Park
Computer Science Center
Program Library
College Park, MD 20742
301/454-4261
Covers computer science and mathematics and statistics. Special collections include System Reference Library for UNIVAC 1100 series, reference manuals for the IBM 4300, and Maryland State Data Center for U.S. Census Bureau publications and tapes of census statistics. Holdings include 3,500 books, 5,000 technical reports, programs, and assorted materials.

University of Washington
Computing Information Center
Academic Computing Services, HG-45
Seattle, WA 98195
206/543-5818
FAX: 206/545-8049
Covers computing, programming languages, hardware, software, artificial intelligence, and electronic music. Holds 8,700 books, 1,700 bound periodical volumes, and 8,600 technical reports.

CONSUMER PRODUCTS INFORMATION

Consumer Product Safety Commission Library
5401 Westbard Avenue, 4th Floor
Washington, DC 20207
301/492-6544
Library concerned with product safety standards and law, product testing, and related business and technology subjects. Holds the Commission's Archives. Publishes monthly newsletter.

Consumers Union of United States, Inc. Library
256 Washington Street
Mount Vernon, NY 10553
914/667-9400
FAX: 914/667-2701
Holdings mainly on consumer economics, history of consumer movement, and related areas such as public health. Retains laboratory test data, documents, and archives of the Center for the Study of the Consumer Movement. Publishes monthly magazine *Consumer Reports*.

COTTON. *See* CLOTHING AND TEXTILES.

CRAFTS

American Craft Council Library
45 West 45th Street, Room 201
New York, NY 10036
212/869-9422
FAX: 212/956-3699
Covers contemporary crafts, all media: fiber, clay, metal, wood, glass, enamel, and plastic. Holds 4,000 books, 300 bound periodical volumes, 5,000 exhibition catalogs, 67 vertical file drawers of clippings and archives, and 300 slide study sets. Includes special collections of biographical and visual data on contemporary American craftspeople and archives of the American Craft Museum and the American Crafts Council.

CRIME. *See* LAW ENFORCEMENT.

D

DANCE

New York Public Library for the Performing Arts
Dance Collection
111 Amsterdam Avenue
New York, NY 10023
212/870-1657
Dozens of special collections cover all forms of dance and most major individuals, groups, and movements, among them American Ballet Theater, Ballet Russe de Monte Carlo, Agnes De Mille, and Isadora Duncan. Holdings include 40,000 books plus films and videotapes, photographs, manuscripts, programs, scrapbooks, and oral history tapes.

DEFENSE. *See* MILITARY.

DEMOGRAPHICS

Brown University
Population Studies and Training Center—
Demography Library
Box 1916
Providence, RI 02912
401/863-2668
FAX: 401/863-3700
Holds 9,200 books, reports, and 450 foreign census reports. Subjects include population, human ecology, and urbanization.

Johns Hopkins University
Population Information Program
527 St. Paul Place
Baltimore, MD 21202
301/659-6300
FAX: 301/338-7570
Holds books and periodicals on family planning, world population, and related law and policy issues. Publishes *Population Reports*, bimonthly.

Princeton University
Office of Population Research Library
21 Prospect Avenue
Princeton, NJ 08544
609/452-4874
Holds 26,000 volumes, 5,500 reprints, 10,000 manuscripts and pamphlets, and 1,100 reels of microfilm, about population studies, demography, fertility, mortality, census, and vital statistics.

University of Texas, Austin
Population Research Center Library
1800 Main Building
Austin, TX 78712
512/471-5514
Subjects include census data, human fertility, and ecology. Special collections include international census publications. Holds 7,000 books, plus supporting materials.

U.S. Bureau of the Census
Library and Information Services Branch
Federal Building No. 3, Room 2455
Washington, DC 20233
301/763-5042
Holds publications of the U.S. Census, 1790 to the present, plus references on population, economics, statistics, and urban studies. Includes some foreign statistical data, all complete censuses, Congressional materials, and statistical yearbooks.

DENTISTRY

American Dental Association
Bureau of Library Services
211 East Chicago Avenue
Chicago, IL 60611
312/440-2642
Holds 20,000 books and 35,000 bound periodical volumes on dentistry. Includes special collection of ADA archives and portraits.

National Institute of Dental Research
Research Data and Management Information
Bethesda, MD 20892
301/496-7220
FAX: 301/496-9241
Holdings on dental research are project summaries and technical reports only.

Northwestern University
Dental School Library
311 East Chicago Avenue
Chicago, IL 60611
312/649-6896
Houses special collection of rare books on dentistry; major holdings of 69,000 volumes and other materials cover oral hygiene, oral surgery, prosthetics, orthodontics, forensic dentistry, and other related subjects.

University of Connecticut
Health Center
Lyman Maynard Stowe Library

Farmington, CT 06032-9984
203/679-2547
FAX: 203/679-4046
Holds 52,000 volumes on medicine, nursing, dentistry, and allied health sciences. Includes special audiovisual collection.

University of Florida
Health Science Library
Box J-206
Gainesville, FL 32611
904/392-4016
Covers medicine, nursing, dentistry, pharmacy, veterinary medicine, and allied health sciences; holds 222,000 volumes and other materials.

University of Illinois at Chicago
Health Sciences Center
Library of the Health Sciences
1750 West Polk Street
Chicago, IL 60612
312/996-8974
FAX: 312/733-6440
Covers medicine, dentistry, nursing, pharmacy, and allied health sciences. Special collections includes 500 volumes of herbals and pharmacopeias, Bailey Collection in neurology and psychiatry, and Kiefer Collection in urology. Library holds 563,000 volumes, 35,000 documents, the medical center archives, and other materials.

University of Minnesota
Biomedical Library
Diehl Hall
505 Essex Street, SE
Minneapolis, MN 55455
612/626-3260
Covers medicine, nursing, dentistry, and allied health sciences; also biology. Holds 354,000 volumes and other materials.

University of Oklahoma
Health Sciences Center Library
1000 Stanton L. Young Boulevard
Box 26901
Oklahoma City, OK 73190
405/271-2285
FAX: 405/271-3297
Covers medicine, dentistry, nursing, public health, pharmacy, and allied health subjects. Holds 63,886 books and 124,541 bound periodical volumes.

University of Pennsylvania
School of Dental Medicine

Leon Levy Library
4001 Spruce Street
Philadelphia, PA 19104-6041
215/898-8969
Library devoted to dental practice and history. Holds more than 50,000 volumes, including 1,400 rare books.

University of Rochester
School of Medicine and Dentistry
Edward G. Miner Library
601 Elmwood Avenue
Rochester, NY 14642
716/275-3364
FAX: 716/275-4799
Holds 200,000 volumes on a variety of medical disciplines: medicine, dentistry, nursing, psychiatry, and dental research. Includes special collection on history of medicine, journals, and bound periodical volumes.

University of Tennessee, Memphis
Health Sciences Library
877 Madison Avenue
Memphis, TN 38136
901/528-5638
Holds over 40,000 volumes, bound periodical volumes, and other research materials on medicine, dentistry, nursing, pharmacy, allied health subjects and disciplines, and social work.

University of Texas
Health Science Center, Houston
Dental Branch Library
6516 John Freeman Avenue
Houston, TX 77225
713/792-4094
Holds more than 13,000 books and 12,000 bound periodical volumes on dentistry. Includes special collection on history of dentistry.

University of Washington
Health Sciences Library and Information Center
T-227 Health Sciences, SB-55
Seattle, WA 98195
206/543-5530
FAX: 206/543-8066
Covers medicine, nursing, dentistry, and allied health subjects. Holds 84,000 books, 186,000 bound periodic volumes, and other research materials.

DISABILITIES

American Foundation for the Blind
M.C. Migel Memorial Library

15 West Sixteenth Street
New York, NY 10011
212/620-2162
Holds 40,000 volumes on the education, psychology, and rehabilitation of the blind. Includes special collection of American Foundation for the Blind photographs.

International Center for the Disabled
Bruce Barton Memorial Library
340 East Twenty-fourth Street
New York, NY 10010
212/679-0100
Holds 6,000 books and other supporting materials relating to physical therapy, psychology, psychiatry, chemical dependency, job placement, and other allied subjects.

National Information Center for Children and Youth with Handicaps
Box 1492
Washington, DC 20013
703/893-6061
Provides information and referral services and educational materials on disabilities and special education. Publishes two digests, semiannually and quarterly.

National Institute on Disability and Rehabilitation Resources
National Rehabilitation Information Center
8455 Colesville Road, Suite 935
Silver Spring, MD 20910
800/346-2742
In Maryland: 301/588-9284
Holds special materials, prepared especially for the National Institute on Disability and Rehabilitation, on rehabilitation of handicapped individuals. Also contains 350 journals and serials.

National Society to Prevent Blindness
Conrad Berens Library
500 East Remington Road
Schaumburg, IL 60173
312/843-2020
Ophthalmological library emphasizing eye safety and health. Holds the National Society to Prevent Blindness archives.

New York Public Library
Mid-Manhattan Library
Project Access
455 Fifth Avenue

New York, NY 10016
212/340-0843
Has collection of directories of organizations, services, equipment, and information sources for the blind, deaf, and mobility-impaired.

New York Public Library
Regional Library for the Blind and Physically Handicapped
166 Avenue of the Americas
New York, NY 10013
212/925-1014
A major regional library in the Library of Congress's National Library Service for the Blind and Physically Handicapped. Offers many special services.

University Affiliated Cincinnati Center for Developmental Disorders
Research Library
Pavilion Building
3300 Elland Avenue
Cincinnati, OH 45229
513/559-4626
Covers mental retardation, learning disabilities, and other developmental disabilities. Related subjects include special-education pediatrics, neurology, nutrition, psychology, and other sciences. Has special library of material about gifted children and bibliotherapy. Includes audiovisual material as well as printed works.

DOGS. *See* PETS.

DRAMA. *See* PERFORMING ARTS; THEATER.

DRUG ABUSE. *See* SUBSTANCE ABUSE.

DRUGS AND MEDICINES. *See also* SUBSTANCE ABUSE.

Philadelphia College of Pharmacy and Science
Joseph W. England Library
42nd Street and Woodland Avenue
Philadelphia, PA 19104
215/596-8960
FAX: 215/222-5060
Holds 56,000 volumes, 35,000 microforms, 24 vertical file drawers, and audiovisual programs on pharmacology, chemistry, and toxicology. Includes special collection on the history of pharmacy.

U.S. Food and Drug Administration
Center for Drugs and Biologics
Medical Library/HFN-98

5600 Fishers Lane, Room 11B-07
Rockville, MD 20857
301/443-3180
Pharmacology, pharmacy, and pharmaceutical technology are main subjects, supported by toxicology, carcinogeneity, food and drug law, veterinary medicine, epidemiology and related sciences, biochemistry, and microbiology. Repository for FDA archives and U.S.–foreign drug compilations.

University of Houston
College of Pharmacy Library
Houston, TX 77204-5511
713/749-1566
FAX: 713/749-3867
Holds references on pharmacy and pharmacology, toxicology, and general chemistry, with special history of pharmacy collection. Owns 14,000 volumes.

University of Iowa
College of Pharmacy
Iowa Drug Information Service
Westlawn, Box 330
Iowa City, IA 52242
319/335-8913
Holds 240,000 articles on microfilm on drugs and drug therapy.

University of Mississippi
John Davis Williams Library
Austin A. Dodge Pharmacy Library
215A Faser Hall
University, MS 38677
601/232-7381
Subjects include pharmacy, organic chemistry, botany, pharmacognosy, and related subjects. Holds 28,000 volumes.

University of Wisconsin, Madison
F.B. Power Pharmaceutical Library
School of Pharmacy
425 North Charter Street
Madison, WI 53706
608/262-2894
Covers pharmacy and related subjects. Special collections include catalogs of drugs and pharmaceutical equipment, 1860 to present, and Kremers reference files, 1870 to present. Holds more than 12,000 books plus other research materials.

E

EARTH SCIENCES. *See also* GEOLOGY; ECOLOGY; METEOROLOGY; OCEANOGRAPHY; SCIENCE; SEISMOLOGY.

American Geological Institute
GeoRef Information System
4220 King Street
Alexandria, VA 22302
703/379-2480
FAX: 703/379-7563
Covers earth sciences, geophysics, hydrology, paleontology, and environmental geology. GeoRef is a worldwide bibliographic database of 1.4 million citations in earth science, from 1785 to the present.

Library of Congress
Science and Technology Division
John Adams Building, Room 5104
101 Independence Avenue SE
Washington, DC 20540
202/707-5639
Oversees all science and technology collections, which total 3.5 million volumes and 3.7 million technical reports, including those of NASA, the Department of Defense and its contractors, the International Science Organization, and others.

Massachusetts Institute of Technology
Dynamics of Atmospheres and Oceans Library
Room 54-1427
Cambridge, MA 02139
617/253-2450
Subjects include meteorology, oceanography, geophysics, and allied sciences.

Stanford University
Branner Earth Sciences Library
School of Earth Sciences
Stanford, CA 94305
415/723-2746
Covers geology, geophysics, and allied sciences, theoretical and applied. Holds Hayden, King, and Wheeler surveys, state geological open-file reports, and geothermal technical reports.

University of California, Berkeley
Earth Sciences Library
230 Earth Sciences Building
Berkeley, CA 94720
415/642-2997
Covers all earth sciences, including geology, geophysics, seismology, climatology, and paleontology. Holds 51,000 maps, pamphlets, and other supporting materials.

University of Massachusetts, Amherst
Morrill Biological and Geological Sciences Library
214 Morrill Science Center
Amherst, MA 01003
413/545-2674
Covers biology and biochemistry, botany, entomology, environmental sciences, forestry, geography and geology, earth sciences, public health, veterinary sciences, and zoology. Holds 100,000 volumes and 125,000 maps and other materials. Includes special collection on ornithology.

University of Missouri, Rolla
Curtis Laws Wilson Library
Rolla, MO 65401
314/341-4227
FAX: 314/341-4233
Subjects include mining and metallurgy, engineering, geology, and the earth sciences. Special collections include U.S. Geological Survey and U.S. Bureau of Mines publications. Holdings include 411,000 volumes.

U.S. National Oceanic and Atmospheric Administration
Library and Information Services Division
Main Library
6009 Executive Boulevard
Rockville, MD 20852
301/443-8288
FAX: 301/443-0237
Covers oceanography, meteorology, and related subjects, such as surveying, hydrographic surveying, geodesy, nautical and aeronautical cartography, geodetic astronomy, hydrology, and mathematics. Includes special rare book collection of scientific treatises from the 16th and 17th centuries. Holds nearly 654,000 books, as well as reports, maps, charts, and documents.

ECOLOGY

California Air Resources Board Library
Box 2815
Sacramento, CA 95812
916/323-8377
Devoted exclusively to problems of air pollution and the environment.

Conservation Districts Foundation
Davis Conservation Library
408 East Main Street
Box 776
League City, TX 77573
409/332-3402
FAX: 713/332-5259
Holdings on conservation and ecology, resources development, and related studies, as well as history of water conservation in America.

Environmental Protection Agency
Andrew W. Breidenbach Environmental Research Library
26 West Martin Luther King Drive
Cincinnati, OH 45268
513/569-7707
Holds more than 17,000 books and other materials relating to various hazards to the environment.

National Institute for Urban Wildlife Library
10921 Trotting Ridge Way
Columbia, MD 21044
301/596-3311
Has works on ecology, wildlife management, and land use in urban environments. Holdings include slides, pamphlets, catalogs, and newspaper clippings in addition to books and periodicals. Publishes several newsletters and the proceedings of a 1986 symposium.

National Institute of Environmental Health Sciences Library
Box 12233
Research Triangle Park, NC 27709
919/541-3426
FAX: 919/541-0669
Holds reference works on environment and pollution-related sciences such as pharmacology, toxicology, cell biology, and carcinogenesis. A branch of the U.S. Public Health Service.

National Wildlife Federation Library
8925 Leesburg Pike
Vienna, VA 22180
703/790-4446
Holds books and theses on wildlife management, conservation of natural resources, ecology, and related environmental sciences.

Stanford University
Hopkins Marine Station Library
Cabrillo Point

Pacific Grove, CA 93950
408/373-0460
Holds 25,000 books, maps, reports, and other supporting materials relating to marine biology, neurobiology, ecology and population biology, and allied subjects.

University of Alaska, Anchorage
Arctic Environmental Information and Data Center
707 A Street
Anchorage, AK 99501
907/257-2733
FAX: 907/276-6847
Has works on Alaska's environment—geology, glaciology, land use, pollution, Arctic research, climate records, and energy resources. Depository for Arctic Petroleum Operators Association and Alaska Oil and Gas Association reports.

University of California, Los Angeles
Laboratory of Biomedical and Environmental Sciences Library
900 Veteran Avenue
Los Angeles, CA 90024-1786
213/825-8741
Holdings on environmental science and energy science, nuclear medicine, and biochemistry. Repository for U.S. Atomic Energy Commission reports. Operates with cooperation of U.S. Department of Energy.

U.S. Department of Agriculture Animal and Plant Inspection Service
Animal Damage Control Program
Denver Wildlife Research Center Library
Federal Center, Building 16
Box 25266
Denver, CO 80225-0266
303/236-7873
Works on the animal sciences—zoology, ornithology, mammalogy, and environmental issues such as ecology and animal damage control (e.g., use of pesticides and land use). Owns technical reports and Fish and Wildlife Services publications.

U.S. Department of the Interior
Natural Resources Library
Eighteenth and C Streets NW
Washington, DC 20240
202/343-5815
Holds 600,000 books and other material on national parks, conservation and ecology, energy, land use, Native Americans, wildlife management,

and law. Includes Department of the Interior published archives.

ECONOMICS. *See also* SOCIAL SCIENCES.

Massachusetts Institute of Technology
Dewey Library
Hermann Building, E53-100
Cambridge, MA 02139
617/253-5677
Covers economics, management and finance, sociology, psychology, law, and political science. Holds more than 375,000 volumes, 123,000 pamphlets, 26,000 technical reports, and 6,000 M.I.T. theses, plus more material on microfilm and microfiche. Includes special collections on industrial relations, United Nations documents, and corporate financial reports.

University of Chicago
Business and Economics Collection
Joseph Regenstein Library
1100 East Fifty-seventh Street
Chicago, IL 60637
312/702-8716
Covers economics, management, finance, and accounting. Holds 375,000 books.

EDUCATION. *See also* COLLEGES AND UNIVERSITIES.

Harvard University
Graduate School of Education
Monroe C. Gutman Library
6 Appian Way
Cambridge, MA 02138
617/495-4225
Broad coverage of all aspects of education, including tests and urban and minority education, in a collection of 150,000 books and 300,000 microforms. Has a special collection of 18th- and 19th-century textbooks.

New York Public Library
Mid-Manhattan Library
Learner's Advisory Service and Job Information Center
455 Fifth Avenue
New York, NY 10016
212/340-0836
Has special collections of college and university directories, continuing education information, and a wide range of job- and career-related guides, national clipping files of job ads, and business directories.

Stanford University
Cubberly Education Library
Stanford, CA 94305
415/723-2121
Devoted to education and allied social sciences and has a collection of 19th-century textbooks. Holds more than 137,000 volumes, historical documents, and curriculum materials.

Teachers College
Milbank Memorial Library
Columbia University
New York, NY 10027
212/678-3494
Established in 1897. The holdings of 424,000 volumes and many other materials cover all aspects of education and include many special collections.

ELDERLY. *See* OLD AGE.

ELECTRICAL ENGINEERING. *See also* ENGINEERING.

Massachusetts Institute of Technology
Lincoln Laboratory Library
244 Wood Street
Box 73
Lexington, MA 02173-0073
617/981-7171 or 617/981-2300
FAX: 617/981-0427
Covers electronics, electrical engineering, computer science, physics, mathematics, and space science. Holds 108,000 volumes, 400,000 technical reports, 3,000 maps, plus 1 million other cataloged items.

ELECTRONICS. *See also* TECHOLOGY.

General Electric Company
Information Resources Center
Electronics Park, Building 3, Room 154
Syracuse, NY 13221
315/456-2023
Holds 13,000 books and other materials devoted to electronics and related subjects, such as microwave engineering, physics, mathematics, and business.

Massachusetts Institute of Technology
Research Laboratory of Electronics
Document Room
Room 36-412
Cambridge, MA 02139
617/253-2566
FAX: 617/258-7864

Covers electronics and allied fields: acoustics, optics and quantum electronics, neurophysiology, cognitive information processing, plasma dynamics, radio astronomy, lasers, molecular beams, microwave electronics, and computers. Holds 4,000 volumes, 1,700 technical reports, and 2,600 dissertations. Includes special collections of Radiation Laboratory reports and RLE reprints.

EMPLOYMENT

New York Public Library
Mid-Manhattan Library
Learner's Advisory Service and Job Information Center
455 Fifth Avenue
New York, NY 10016
212/340-0836
Has special collections covering career planning, job searches, vocational test guides, national clipping files of job ads, business directories, and career-oriented periodicals. Also has an educational section with college and university directories and continuing education information.

ENERGY AND POWER GENERATION. *See also* NUCLEAR ENERGY.

Conservation and Renewable Energy Inquiry and Referral Service Library
Advanced Sciences, Inc.
2000 North Fifteenth Street, Suite 407
Arlington, VA 22201
703/243-4900
FAX: 703/998-7674
Contains references on energy conservation with emphasis on solar energy. Contractually attached to the Department of Energy.

Consolidated Edison Company of New York, Inc.
Library
4 Irving Place, Room 1650-S
New York, NY 10003
212/460-4228
Has more than 35,000 books, periodicals, and pamphlets relating to public utilities and power generation and use.

Solar Energy Research Institute Technical Library
1617 Cole Boulevard
Golden, CO 80401
303/231-1415
FAX: 303/231-1199

Concentration on renewable energy sources. Holds 15,000 books and 400,000 reports.

ENGINEERING. *See also* CHEMICAL ENGINEERING; CIVIL ENGINEERING; ELECTRICAL ENGINEERING.

Massachusetts Institute of Technology
Barker Engineering Library
Room 10-500
Cambridge, MA 02139
617/253-5663
Covers all aspects of engineering, plus transportation, energy, computer science, and applied mathematics. Holds 162,000 volumes, 19,000 M.I.T. theses, 59,000 technical reports, and more material on microfilm and microfiche.

United Engineering Trustees, Inc.
Engineering Societies Library
345 East Forty-seventh Street
New York, NY 10017
212/705-7611
Collection of 300,000 volumes covers all branches of engineering. The Library is the depository for the following engineering societies: American Society of Civil Engineers; American Society of Mechanical Engineers; Institute of Electrical and Electronics Engineers; American Institute of Mining, Metallurgical, and Petroleum Engineers; American Institute of Chemical Engineers; Illuminating Engineering Society; and Society of Women Engineers.

University of Minnesota
Science and Engineering Library
206 Walter Library
117 Pleasant Street, Southeast
Minneapolis, MN 55455
612/624-0224
Covers engineering, general sciences, and history of science. Special collections includes the Archive for the History of Quantum Physics. Holds 331,000 volumes, 91,500 maps, 200,000 government documents, and other materials.

ENTOMOLOGY. *See also* LIFE SCIENCES.

Smithsonian Institution
National Museum of Natural History
Entomology Library
Natural History Building, Room W629C
Tenth Street and Constitution Avenue NW
Washington, DC 20560
202/357-4696

Has 23,000 volumes on the taxonomy and medical aspects of insects.

University of California, Berkeley
Entomology Library
Wellman Hall, Room 210
Berkeley, CA 94720
415/642-2030
Covers entomology and allied subjects, including parasitology and insect pathology.

ENVIRONMENT. *See* ECOLOGY.

EPILEPSY

National Epilepsy Library
4351 Garden City Drive, Suite 406
Landover, MD 20785
800/332-4050
In Maryland: 301/459-3700
Covers all aspects of epilepsy and works on neurology. Holds the Archives of the Epilepsy Movement.

F

FAMILY PLANNING

Columbia University
Center for Population and Family Health
Library/Information Program
60 Haven Avenue
New York, NY 10032
212/305-6960
FAX: 212/305-7024
Specializes in family planning; also demography and related studies. Holds 5,000 books, 27,000 reports, and other supporting materials.

Margaret Sanger Center
Planned Parenthood, New York City

Abraham Stone Library
380 Second Avenue
New York, NY 10010
212/677-6474
Library owns materials on abortion and family planning, demography, sexuality and infertility, handicapped sexuality, and related subjects.

FAR EAST. *See also* MIDDLE EAST.

Columbia University
C.V. Starr East Asian Library
300 Kent Hall

116th Street and Amsterdam Avenue
New York, NY 10027
212/854-4318
Covers humanities, social sciences, and history of China, Japan, and Korea. Special collections include Chinese local histories and genealogies and Korean collection of Yi Song-ui. Holds 248,000 volumes in Chinese, 187,000 volumes in Japanese, 29,000 volumes in Korean, and 33,000 volumes in Western languages.

Cornell University
Wason Collection
Olin Research Library
Ithaca, NY 14853-5301
607/255-4357
Holds 421,000 volumes and microforms covering China, Japan, Korea, Tibet, and Central Asia.

Harvard University
Harvard-Yenching Library
2 Divinity Avenue
Cambridge, MA 02138
617/495-3327
FAX: 617/495-0403
Covers humanities and social sciences of Japan, China, and Korea. Special collections include rare Chinese books and manuscripts, Chinese rubbings, Tibetan and Mongolian manuscripts, and more. Houses over 713,000 volumes.

Library of Congress
Asian Division
John Adams Building, Room 1024
101 Independence Avenue SE
Washington, DC 20540
202/287-5420
Contains 1.5 million volumes in Chinese, Japanese, Korean, and Southern Asian languages from Pakistani to Filipino, with much supporting material. Emphasis on history and current publications.

New York Public Library
Oriental Division
Fifth Avenue and Forty-second Street, Room 219
New York, NY 10018
212/930-0716
Covers history, languages, social sciences, and humanities of Far East, Middle East, ancient Middle East, and South and Central Asia. Special collections house Arabic manuscripts, Egyptology, rare Chinese books and manuscripts, printing in

India, and Tibetan language collection. Holdings include 250,000 volumes.

Princeton University
Gest Oriental Library and East Asian Collections
317 Palmer Hall
Princeton, NJ 08544
609/452-3182
Houses 430,700 books, 3,000 manuscripts, and 19,000 microforms about China, Japan, and Korea. Special collections include Buddhist sutras; Sung, Yang, and Ming editions; Hishi copies, and Japanese copies of Ming works; Chinese medicine; "Go"; and Mongolian, Tibetan, and Manchurian rare books.

University of California, Berkeley
Asian-American Studies Library
3407 Dwinelle Hall
Berkeley, CA 94720
415/642-2218
This collection of material on Asians in the United States has historical slant. Chinese American Research Collection contains archival materials in both English and Chinese. Includes slides, videotapes, and films as well as books.

University of California, Berkeley
Center for Chinese Studies Library
2223 Fulton Street
Berkeley, CA 94720
415/642-6510
Houses works in the humanities of People's Republic of China. Has videotapes of PRC television programs, reprints, and other materials.

University of California, Berkeley
South/Southeast Asia Library
438 Library
Berkeley, CA 94720
415/642-3095
Covers social sciences and humanities of the entire area including Indian subcontinent, Indonesia, and neighboring countries. Special collections include government publications on India and Indonesia; modern Hindi, Indonesian, and Malay literature; and Nepal Collection, Thai Collection, and others. Holds over 315,000 volumes, dissertations, maps, and other multimedia sources.

University of Chicago
East Asian Collection
Joseph Regenstein Library

1100 East Fifty-seventh Street
Chicago, IL 60637
312/702-8436
Covers humanities and social sciences of East Asia, China, Japan, and Korea. Special collections house Chinese classics and rare books. Holdings include 286,000 volumes in Chinese; 139,000 volumes in Japanese; 6,600 volumes in Korean; 6,400 volumes in Tibetan, Mongol, and Manchu; and 7,700 references in Western languages.

University of Chicago
Southern Asia Collection
Joseph Regenstein Library
1100 East Fifty-Seventh Street
Chicago, IL 60637
312/702-8430
Covers humanities and social sciences of Southern Asia, principally the Indian subcontinent. Holdings are in 30 South Asian and Western languages. Special collections hold Bhubaneshwar Archive on Modern Orissa and papers of well-known scholars. 203,000 volumes.

University of Hawaii
Asia Collection
Hamilton Library
2550 The Mall
Honolulu, HI 96822
808/948-8116
Covers Eastern, Southeastern, and Southern Asia. Special collections include the Sakamaki Collection on Ryukyus and Kajiyama Collection on Japanese language. Holds 550,000 volumes and supporting materials.

University of Michigan
Asia Library
Hatcher Graduate Library, 4th Fl.
Ann Arbor, MI 48109-1205
313/764-0406
Specializes in East Asia, mainly China and Japan. Has references on humanities and social sciences. Special collections include materials on the Red Guards and classified material on the Cultural Revolution, Ming literary collections, National Peking Library Rare Book Collection, British Public Record Office Archives on China, Japanese local history, materials on Allied occupation of Japan 1945–52, Japanese Diet Proceedings, and other collections. Holds 246,000 volumes in Chinese, 200,000 volumes in Japanese, 3,500 works in Korean, and supporting materials.

University of Texas, Austin
Asian Collection
General Libraries, MAI 316
Austin, TX 78713-7330
512/471-3135
FAX: 512/471-9241
Covers Chinese and Japanese linguistics, social sciences, and economics, and Indian, Bangladeshi, and Sri Lankan language, literature, and social sciences. Has special collections in English. Holds bound government documents in addition to 110,789 books.

University of Washington
East Asia Library
322 Gowen Hall, DO-27
Seattle, WA 98195
206/543-4490
Covers social sciences, humanities, literature and language, history, religion and philosophy. Holds 328,096 volumes, microfilm, microfiche, and pamphlets. Includes special collections in Chinese, Japanese, Korean, Tibetan, Thai, Vietnamese, Mongolian, Manchu, and Indonesian.

Yale University
East Asian Collection
Sterling Memorial Library
New Haven, CT 06520
203/432-1791
Covers all aspects of East Asian history and culture. Holds 460,982 volumes in Chinese, Japanese, and Korean and 5,124 reels of microfilm.

Yale University
Southeast Asia Collection
Sterling Memorial Library
New Haven, CT 06520
203/432-1859
Houses 200,000 volumes on the social sciences and humanities of Southeast Asia: Myanmar Burma, Thailand, Laos, Vietnam, Cambodia, Philippines, Malaysia, Brunei, Singapore, and Indonesia.

FEDERAL GOVERNMENT

Congressional Budget Office Library
House Office Building, Annex 2
Second and D Streets SW
Washington, DC 20515
202/226-2635
FAX: 202/226-2601
Has holdings on the federal budget and related studies, including files on budget proceedings of the 86th Congress to the present.

National Archives and Records Administration Library
Seventh Street and Pennsylvania Avenue NW
Washington, DC 20408
202/501-5400
Main repository for government records and publications down through the years.

FILM. *See* MOVIES.

FINANCE

American Bankers Association Library and Information Services
1120 Connecticut Avenue NW
Washington, DC 20036
202/663-5221
Holds 60,000 volumes, plus legislative documents stored on microfilm, about law, banking and finance, and economics.

Massachusetts Institute of Technology
Dewey Library
Hermann Building, E53-100
Cambridge, MA 02139
617/253-5677
Covers economics, management and finance, sociology, psychology, law, and political science. Has more than 375,000 volumes, 123,000 pamphlets, 26,000 technical reports, and 6,000 M.I.T. theses, plus more material on microfilm and microfiche. Includes special collections on industrial relations, United Nations documents, and corporate financial reports.

Securities and Exchange Commission Library
450 Fifth Street NW
Washington, D.C. 20549
202/272-2618
Holds 60,000 volumes and 5,000 bound periodical volumes relating to corporations, finance, government, securities, statistics, and stock exchanges.

Securities and Exchange Commission
Public Reference Library
Kluzynski Federal Building
230 South Dearborn, No. 3190
Chicago, IL 60604
312/353-7433
Emphasis is on securities laws and SEC releases. Holds 20,000 files of reports.

University of Chicago
Business and Economics Collection
Joseph Regenstein Library
1100 East Fifty-seventh Street
Chicago, IL 60637
312/702/8716
Covers economics, management, finance, and accounting. Holds 375,000 books.

FINE ARTS. *See also* GRAPHIC ARTS.

Archives of American Art/Smithsonian Institution
National Museum of American Art, 331 Balcony
Eighth and G Streets NW
Washington, DC 20560
202/357-2781
The Archives contain the largest collection of documentary materials reflecting the history of the visual arts in the United States. They gather, preserve, and microfilm the papers of artists, craftsmen, collectors, dealers, critics, museums, and art societies and house more than 8 million holdings. The Archives' chief processing and reference center is in Washington. Regional branch offices in Boston, Detroit, Los Angeles, New York, and San Francisco each house complete microfilm duplicates of the central collection.

Boston Athenaeum Library
10½ Beacon Street
Boston, MA 02108
617/227-0270
Covers history, fine and decorative arts, belles lettres, and biography. Holds 700,000 volumes, plus archives, maps, and manuscripts. Includes special collections of Confederate States imprints; books owned by George Washington, General Henry Knox, and the Adams family; the King's Chapel Library (1698); and early U.S. documents and tracts.

Columbia University
Avery Architectural and Fine Arts Library
Broadway and 116th Street
New York, NY 10027
212/854-3501
Holds 235,000 volumes plus 100,000 manuscripts and papers on architecture, planning, fine arts, and archaeology. Special collections holdings include 130,000 original architectural drawings of major firms.

Freer Gallery of Art. *See* ARTHUR M. SACKLER GALLERY.

Harvard University
Fine Arts Library
Fogg Art Museum
Cambridge, MA 02138
617/495-3373
Collection devoted to art history. Special collections include exhibition and auction catalogs, Islamic architecture, and Wendell Portrait Collection. Holds 227,000 volumes, archival material, 1.4 million photographs, and other materials.

Metropolitan Museum of Art
Thomas J. Watson Library
Fifth Avenue and Eighty-second Street
New York, NY 10028
212/879-5500
Founded in 1880. Houses more than 300,000 volumes on art, art history, and archaeology from ancient times through the 20th century. Has special collections of art auction and exhibit catalogs.

Museum of Fine Arts, Houston
Hirsch Library
Box 6826
Houston, TX 77265
713/526-1361
Holds 25,000 books, 2,000 bound periodical volumes, 137 vertical file drawers of exhibition and auction catalogs, 700 reels of microfilm, and 50,000 slides, all concerning art history and photography.

Museum of Modern Art Library
11 West Fifty-third Street
New York, NY 10019-5498
212/708-9433
FAX: 212/708-9889
Houses 100,000 books and catalogs, 6,000 bound periodical volumes, and 200,000 artist files, all concerning modern art from 1880 to present, including design, architecture, photography, and film. Includes special collections of Latin American art and artists' books.

National Gallery of Art Library
Sixth Street and Constitution Avenue NW
Washington, DC 20565
202/842-6511
Covers European and American architecture, painting, sculpture, drawings, and prints. Holds 129,000 books, 23,000 bound periodical volumes, and special collections of sale, exhibition, museum, and private catalogs.

New York Public Library
Miriam and Ira D. Wallach Division of Art, Prints and Photographs
Art and Architecture Collection
Fifth Avenue and Forty-second Street, Room 313
New York, NY 10018
212/930-0834
Houses 230,000 volumes and pamphlets, plus 100,000 clippings devoted to architecture, painting, drawing, sculpture, and allied arts. Includes Oriental art.

Philadelphia Museum of Art Library
Box 7646
Philadelphia, PA 19101
215/763-8100
FAX: 215/236-4465
Houses 130,000 books, periodicals, and pamphlets on fine arts. Includes special collection on arms and armor.

Princeton University
Department of Art and Archaeology
Index of Christian Art
McCormick Hall
Princeton, NJ 08544
609/452-3773
Specializes in Christian art before 1400. Has iconographic index of 700,000 cards, plus 200,000 photographs.

Arthur M. Sackler Gallery Library
1050 Independence Avenue SW
Washington, DC 20560
202/357-2091
The Gallery's permanent collection is founded on a large collection of art objects from China, South and Southeast Asia, and the Ancient Near East. The library holds 45,000 books and bound periodical volumes and a large collection of visual materials. Also functions as the library for the Freer Gallery of Art, which is closed for renovation until 1992.

Smithsonian Institution
Hirshhorn Museum and Sculpture Garden Library
Eighth Street and Independence Avenue SW
Washington, DC 20560
202/357-3223
The museum houses major collections of American and European painting and sculpture of the past 100 years. Also houses a collection research facility, a specialized 10,000-volume art library, a large collection of exhibition catalogs, and a photographic archive.

Smithsonian Institution
National Museum of Art/National Portrait Gallery Library
Eighth and F Streets NW
Washington, DC 20560
202/357-1886
This is the central library for the two art museums. Has 60,000 books and bound periodical volumes on American painting, sculpture, graphic arts, and related subjects.

Society for the Preservation of New England Antiquities Archives
141 Cambridge Street
Boston, MA 02114
617/227-3956
Covers New England art, architecture, and decorative arts. Holds 400,000 photographic prints, daguerreotypes, portraits, negatives, drawings, and the like.

Stanford University
Art and Architecture Library
Nathan Cummings Art Building
Stanford, CA 94305-2018
415/723-3408
Covers modern, ancient, medieval, Renaissance and Baroque art. Special collections include J.D. Chen collection of Chinese art and architecture. Houses 125,000 volumes.

University of California, Los Angeles
Art Library
2250 Dickson Art Center
Los Angeles, CA 90024
213/825-3817
Covers art and architecture, history, and design. Special collections house Judith A. Hoffberg Collection of Bookworks and Artists' Publications; 2,500 volumes. Materials include museum catalogs, exhibition catalogs, manuscripts, paintings, and photographs in addition to 95,000 volumes.

University of Chicago
Department of Art
Max Epstein Archive
Joseph Regenstein Library, Room 420
1100 East Fifty-seventh Street
Chicago, IL 60637
312/702-7080

Has holdings on art; special collections house Armenian Architectural Collection and photos of medals in the Courtauld Institute and the British Museum.

University of Pennsylvania
Fine Arts Library
Van Pelt Library
3420 Walnut Street
Philadelphia, PA 19104-6206
215/898-8325
Holds 96,000 volumes, 59,000 photographs, and rare books relating to art/architecture, historic preservation, and art history.

University of Texas, Austin
Fine Arts Library
General Libraries, FAB 3.200
Austin, TX 78713-7330
512/471-4777
FAX: 512/471-9241
Covers all areas of the fine arts. Houses 144,912 volumes, slides, CDs, bound scores, and bound periodical volumes.

University of Virginia
Fiske Kimball Fine Arts Library
Bayly Drive
Charlottesville, VA 22903
804/924-7024
Holds 108,000 volumes and 140,000 architecture slides. Covers art, architecture, theater, and allied arts.

University of Wisconsin, Madison
Kohler Art Library
General Library System
800 University Avenue
Madison, WI 53706
608/263-2256
Holds 103,000 volumes and 16,000 microforms on art, architecture, dance, and photography.

Yale University
Art and Architecture Library
Art and Architecture Building
Yale Station, Box 1605
New Haven, CT 06520
203/432-2641
Covers history of art, architecture, city planning, painting, sculpture, and graphic arts. Houses more than 92,000 volumes, 14,000 exhibition catalogs, 70 vertical file drawers, 290,000 slides, and 172,000 photographs. Includes special collection of books and photographs in color.

Yale University
Yale Center for British Art
Reference Library
1080 Chapel Street
Yale Station, Box 2120
New Haven, CT 06520
203/432-2846
Covers British art—paintings, drawings, prints, sculpture, and architecture, 1500–1945. Holds 9,000 books, 1,000 bound periodical volumes, 870 reels of microfilm, and 7,300 microfiche. Special collections include Sotheby and Christies sales catalogs 1734–1980 and Victoria and Albert Museum oils, watercolors, and miniatures, plus RIBA architectural drawings, satirical prints, and Huntington Library drawings.

FIREARMS

J.M. Davis Gun Museum Research Library
333 North Lynn Riggs Boulevard
Box 966
Claremore, OK 74017
918/341-5707
Covers firearms, edged weapons, Native American artifacts, steins, and musical instruments. Holds 830 volumes, old gun catalogs, World War I posters, pins, buttons, and badges.

FIRE PREVENTION

National Fire Protection Association
Charles S. Morgan Technical Library
Batterymarch Park
Quincy, MA 02269
617/770-3000
FAX: 617/471-5231
Has materials on fire prevention, arson, building codes, and related subjects. Special collections house the Association's archives, including historical file of old national fire codes.

FISH AND FISHERIES. *See also* AQUACULTURE; ICHTHYOLOGY; MARINE BIOLOGY; OCEANOGRAPHY.

U.S. Fish and Wildlife Service
National Fisheries Research Center
Technical Information Services
Box 700
Kearneysville, WV 25430
304/725-8451

Holdings of 20,000 volumes and 26,000 reprints cover aquaculture and all aspects of fish—nutrition, pathology, physiology, diseases, and other subjects. Depository for the government's Fish Disease Leaflets.

University of Washington
Fisheries–Oceanography Library
151 Oceanography Teaching Building, WB-30
Seattle, WA 98195
206/543-4279
Covers fisheries science, marine biology, food science and technology, marine policy, and oceanography. Includes special collection of Canadian publications in addition to 57,000 books and other research materials.

FOLKLORE

Cleveland Public Library
Fine Arts and Special Collections Department
Special Collections Section
John G. White Collection and Rare Books
325 Superior Avenue
Cleveland, OH 44114-1271
216/623-2818
Among the 160,000 volumes in this department of the Cleveland Library is a large collection of some 43,000 books and other materials devoted to folklore, with an emphasis on American tales, folk songs, and works on superstition, magic, and witchcraft.

Library of Congress
American Folklife Center
Thomas Jefferson Building, G108
Washington, DC 20540
202/707-6590
Specializes in folklore, ethnomusicology and folk music, and oral history. Owns 100,000 pages of manuscripts and includes Frances Densmore American Indian Collection recordings. Has 35,000 hours of unpublished field recordings and other research materials.

University of California, Los Angeles
Wayland D. Hand Library of Folklore and Mythology
Los Angeles, CA 90024
213/825-4242
Covers folklore, literature, and other ethnological materials and data. Special collections include Ralph Steele Boggs Collection of Latin American

Folklore. Has over 11,000 tapes and recordings in addition to books.

University of Pennsylvania
Archive of Folklore and Folklife
417 Logan Hall
Philadelphia, PA 19104
215/898-7352
Covers folklore and music of Newfoundland, West Indies, Virginia, and Pennsylvania. Includes special collections of folklore from Newfoundland, Nova Scotia, Jamaica, Great Britain, Ireland, and Western Pennsylvania; also collections of American humor. Library holds 4,000 recordings and other materials.

FOOD AND NUTRITION

General Foods Corporation
Tarrytown Technical Information Center
250 North Street
White Plains, NY 10625
914/335-6217
FAX: 914/335-6573
Covers food technology, science, microbiology, and enzymology, among other subjects. Holds 8,000 books, plus other supporting materials.

General Mills, Inc.
James Ford Bell Technical Center/Technical Information Services
9000 Plymouth Avenue, North
Minneapolis, MN 55427
612/540-3464
FAX: 612/540-7487
Holds more than 7,000 books and other research materials relating to food and food science.

Stanford University
Food Research Institute Library
Stanford, CA 94305
415/723-3943
Covers economic aspects of agriculture and food supply. Holds 76,500 volumes, plus other supporting materials.

U.S. Food and Drug Administration
Center for Food Safety and Applied Nutrition Library
200 C Street SW, Room 3321, HFF-37
Washington, DC 20204
202/245-1235
FAX: 202/426-1658
Holds reports, books, and documents on food

and cosmetics—latest information on toxicology, nutrition, and other concerns. Includes references on chemistry, analytic chemistry, biology, and other pertinent sciences.

FOOTBALL

Pro Football Hall of Fame Library/Research Center
2121 George Halas Drive, NW
Canton, OH 44708
216/456-8207
Houses more than 6,000 volumes, 6,000 game programs, 20,000 photographs and slides, 1,000 16mm films, and 1,000 team media guides. Includes special collections of Spaulding football guides 1892–1940, football scrapbooks, and pre-NFL player contracts.

FORD, GERALD R. *See* PRESIDENTIAL LIBRARIES.

FOREIGN LANGUAGES

New York Public Library
Donnell Library Center
Foreign Language Library
20 West Fifty-third Street
New York, NY 10019
212/621-0641
Houses representative works of both classical and contemporary writing in over 80 world languages. Holds 116,000 volumes.

FOREIGN POLICY. *See* INTERNATIONAL RELATIONS.

FORESTRY AND FOREST PRODUCTS

American Forestry Association
McArdle Memorial Library
1516 P Street NW
Washington, DC 20005
202/667-3300
Holds 6,000 books on forestry and related subjects: soil, water, wildlife, and recreation.

University of California, Berkeley
Forestry Library
260 Mulford Hall
Berkeley, CA 94720
415/642-2936
Covers forestry, agroforestry, ecology and conservation, wildlife management, and allied studies. Special collections house photographs of western forestry 1910–60, manuscripts, maps, and pamphlets as well as books.

University of Minnesota, St. Paul
Forestry Library
203 Green Hall
1530 North Cleveland Avenue
St. Paul, MN 55108
612/624-3222
Covers forestry, conservation, hydrology, pulp, and paper. Holds more than 24,000 volumes, 65,000 documents, 3,000 maps, and 2,000 microforms.

University of Washington
Forest Resources Library
60 Bloedel Hall, AQ-15
Seattle, WA 98195
206/543-7446
Covers wood science and technology, paper and pulp technology, fire control, conservation, and ecology. Holds 48,000 books.

Yale University
Yale Forestry Library
205 Prospect Street
New Haven, CT 06511
203/432-5130
FAX: 203/432-5942
Houses 130,000 volumes, government documents and reports, 175 newsletter titles, 900 dissertations, 500 maps, and 2,500 microforms, concerning environmental studies, ecology, natural resource management, conservation, and wildlife.

G

GAMBLING

University of Nevada, Las Vegas
Gaming Research Center
4505 Maryland Parkway
Las Vegas, NV 89154
702/739-3252
Covers studies of gambling and betting. Holds 5,000 volumes.

GARDENING. *See* HORTICULTURE.

GEMOLOGY

Gemological Institute of America Research Library
1660 Stewart Street
Santa Monica, CA 90404
213/829-2991
FAX: 213/458-6005

Covers gemology, mineralogy, and jewelry. Holds 4,000 volumes.

GENEALOGY. *See also* STATES AND TERRITORIES.

American Genealogical Lending Library
Box 244
Bountiful, UT 84010
801/298-5358
Has census records, mortality schedules, ship passenger lists, military records, vital records, deeds, wills, tax lists, and county and family histories, all recorded on 100,000 reels of microfilm.

Church of Jesus Christ of Latter-Day Saints
Family History Library
35 N.W. Temple
Salt Lake City, UT 845150
801/240-2331
Houses the largest genealogical collection in the world. Contains 180,000 volumes and 1.5 million reels of microfilm relating to family history, local history, and church and civil records.

Library of Congress
General Reading Rooms Division
Local History and Genealogy Reading Room
Section
Thomas Jefferson Building, Room LJ244
101 Independence Avenue SE
Washington, DC 20540
202/707-5537
Holds 400,000 volumes of U.S. genealogy, local history, and European heraldry. Includes military records, church records, and vital statistics.

National Society of the Sons of the American
Revolution
Genealogy Library
1000 South Fourth Street
Louisville, KY 40203
502/589-1776
Covers American Revolutionary War history and genealogy, as well as material on Colonial America. Special collections house genealogy of the signers of the Declaration of Independence, census records, and SAR archives.

New England Historic Genealogical Society Library
89-101 Newbury Street
Boston, MA 02116
617/536-5740
Covers genealogy, family history, and local history, with an emphasis on New England. Houses

200,000 volumes and other materials, including vital records and church histories.

New York Public Library
United States History, Local History and
Genealogy Division
Fifth Avenue and Forty-second Street, Room 315N
New York, NY 10018
212/930-0828
Covers European and American genealogy and heraldry, as well as local histories of towns and counties in the United States. Includes 100,000 photographs of New York City and election campaign materials. Holds 106,000 volumes.

National Genealogical Society Library
4527 Seventeenth Street, North
Arlington, VA 22207-2363
703/525-0050
Genealogy collection includes local history and biography. Holds the manuscript collections of the Society's former members. Publishes a newsletter and a quarterly journal as well as 54 special publications.

GEOGRAPHY. *See also* MAPS.

National Geographic Society Library
1146 Sixteenth Street NW
Washington, DC 20036
202/857-7787
FAX: 202/775-6141
Has holdings on past explorations including space, natural history, geography, and American history. Special collections include General A.W. Greely's Polar Library.

University of Washington
Geography Library
415 Smith Hall, DP-10
Seattle, WA 98195
206/543-5244
Covers geography, cartography, and regional science. Holds more than 15,000 volumes.

University of Wisconsin, Milwaukee
American Geographical Society Collection
Golda Meir Library
Box 399
Milwaukee, WI 53201
800/ 558-8993
In Wisconsin: 414/229-6282 or 414/229-3984
Covers exploration, cartography, earth sciences, social sciences, and history. Has more than 203,000

volumes, 421,000 maps, 6,000 atlases, 114,000 photographs, 70 globes, and 99,000 Landsat images.

GEOLOGY. *See also* EARTH SCIENCES.

Columbia University
Geology Library
601 Schermerhorn Hall
New York, NY 10027
212/280-4522
Holds 86,000 volumes on geology and related sciences such as geophysics, mineralogy, and remote sensing.

Harvard University
Bernhard Kummel Library of the Geological Sciences
24 Oxford Street
Cambridge, MA 02138
617/495-2029
Holds 28,000 volumes on geology and related topics such as mineralogy and petrology.

Princeton University
Geology Library
Guyot Hall
Princeton, NJ 08544
609/452-3267
Holds 60,000 volumes, 900 theses, 276,000 maps, and 450 technical reports about geology and related fields, such as crystallography, geochemistry, geomorphology, geophysics, mineralogy, oceanography, and paleontology.

U.S. Geological Survey
Library System
12201 Sunrise Valley Drive
National Center, Mail Stop 950
Reston, VA 22092
703/648-4302
Large collection of 765,000 volumes, 311,000 maps, 329,000 microforms, and other materials on geology and related subjects: mineralogy, mineral resources, water resources, petrology, and paleontology.

University of California, Los Angeles
Geology–Geophysics Library
Geology Building, Room 4697
Los Angeles, CA 90024-1567
213/825-1055
Covers geology, geophysics, and related sciences such as planetary sciences, paleontology, and geochemistry. Special emphasis on local California geology. Also holds theses and dissertations.

University of Missouri, Columbia
Geology Library
201 Geology Building
Columbia, MO 65211
314/882-4860
Covers geology and related sciences such as paleontology, geochemistry, and hydrology. Holds 39,000 volumes, 100,000 maps, and other materials.

University of Oklahoma
Geology Library
830 Van Vleet Oval, Room 103
Norman, OK 73019
405/325-6541
Covers geology and related sciences, oceanography, and hydrology. Holds more than 86,000 volumes, 120,000 maps, and other research materials.

University of Texas, Austin
Geology Library
General Libraries, GEO 302
Austin, TX 78713-7330
512/471-1257
FAX: 512/471-9241
Houses more than 79,000 books and other materials devoted to geology and and related sciences.

University of Wyoming
Geology Library
S.H. Knight Building
University Station, Box 3006
Laramie, WY 82071
307/766-3374
Covers geology and related sciences and remote sensing. Holds more than 50,000 books, 16,000 government documents, bound periodical documents, and 26,000 maps.

GEOPHYSICS. *See* EARTH SCIENCES.

GERONTOLOGY. *See* OLD AGE.

GOVERNMENT. *See also* FEDERAL GOVERNMENT; POLITICAL SCIENCE; STATES AND TERRITORIES.

Harvard University
John F. Kennedy School of Government Library
79 John F. Kennedy Street
Cambridge, MA 02138
617/495-1303
FAX: 617/495-1972
Covers public policy and government. Holds Center for Science and International Affairs library. Has 37,500 volumes.

New York Public Library
Economic and Public Affairs Division
Fifth Avenue and Forty-second Street, Room 228
New York, NY 10018
212/930-0750
Covers business-related subjects such as marketing, labor, banking and insurance; also government publications and demography. Houses publications of local, state, national, and international governmental bodies and census and other statistical information. Holds 1.5 million books and 1 million microforms.

University of Arizona
Government Documents Department
University Library
Tucson, AZ 85721
602/621-4871
FAX: 602/621-4619
Houses over 900,000 government documents, and supporting material, on business, environmental studies, American history and government, foreign relations, health care, and law enforcement. Special collections have copies of material from National Archives, U.S. Congressional hearings from 1869–1981, and Arizona state government documents.

University of California, Berkeley
Institute of Governmental Studies Library
Moses Hall, Room 109
Berkeley, CA 94720
415/642-1472
FAX: 415/642-3020
Concentrates on local government and metropolitan problems; also covers administration, planning, taxation, welfare, and other governmental studies.

University of California, Santa Barbara
Government Publications Department
University Library
Santa Barbara, CA 93106
805/961-2863
Holds publications from state and federal levels of government and international documents. 614,000 publications.

University of Texas, Austin
Wasserman Public Affairs Library
General Libraries
Sid Richardson Hall 3.243
Austin, TX 78713-7330

512/4471-4486
Subjects include public administration, politics and government, social problems, civil rights, and allied subjects. Houses collections of state documents and economic records; selective U.S. documents depository.

Yale University
Seeley G. Mudd Library
Government Documents Center
38 Mansfield Street
Yale Station, Box 2491
New Haven, CT 06520
203/432-3209 or 203/432-3212
Holds more than 605,000 items and 78 drawers of microfiche. Document depository for the following organizations: U.S. Federal Government 1869 to present, Canadian federal government, the United Nations, European Communities, and the Food and Agriculture Organization. Also has U.S. Congressional Committee Prints through 1969, U.S. Senate Unpublished Hearings 1824–1964, Index to Publications of the U.S. Congress, and the Declassified Documents Reference System.

GOVERNMENT—STATES. *See* STATES AND TERRITORIES.

GRAPHIC ARTS. *See also* FINE ARTS.

Cooper-Hewitt Museum of Design
Two East Ninety-first Street
New York, NY 10128
212/860-6887
Covers historical and contemporary decorative arts, design, textiles, and architecture. Holds 35,000 bound volumes; noted for its picture collection of over 350,000 items arranged by subject for use by designers.

New York Public Library
Mid-Manhattan Library
Literature and Language Department
Picture Collection
455 Fifth Avenue
New York, NY 10016
212/340-0877
Has more than 4.7 million pictures in classified collections covering costume, flora and fauna, history, geographic views, design, and other subjects.

New York Public Library
Miriam and Ira D. Wallach Division of Art, Prints and Photographs

Prints and Photographs Room
Fifth Avenue and Forty-second Street, Room 308
New York, NY 10018
212/930-0817
Houses original prints from the 15th century to
the present and photographs from 1839 to the
present. Holds 175,000 prints and 200,000 original
photographs, including 80,000 stereographs.

University of Houston
Architecture and Art Library
Houston, TX 77204-4431
713/749-7551
FAX: 713/749-3867
Holds more than 45,000 works on architecture
and urban design, art, and photography.

University of Illinois
Ricker Library of Architecture and Art
208 Architecture Building
Urbana, IL 61801
217/333-0224
Holds 59,000 volumes on architecture and the
fine arts—education, history, history of photography, and industrial and graphic design.

University of Kansas
Murphy Library of Art and Architecture
Helen Foresman Spencer Museum of Art
Lawrence, KS 66045-2800
913/864-3020
Covers architecture, design, photography, art, and
art history. Holds 84,000 volumes.

University of Maryland, College Park
Art Library
College Park, MD 20742
301/454-2065
Covers art history, art education, and decorative
and applied arts.
Holdings include 70,000 volumes, 27,000 art reproduction plates, picture collection, and related
materials.

University of Michigan
Art and Architecture Library
2106 Art and Architecture Bldg.
Ann Arbor, MI 48109
313/764-1303
Covers architecture, urban planning, design, landscape architecture, art, photography, and graphic
design. Special collections include Jens Jenson landscape drawings. Holds 55,000 volumes, software
programs, maps, and other supporting materials.

GREAT PLAINS

Museum of the Great Plains
Great Plains Research Library and Archives
601 Ferris
Box 68
Lawton, OK 73502
405/353-5675
Covers history, natural history, archaeology, anthropology, and agriculture of the Great Plains.
Holds more than 25,000 volumes, 30,000 photographs, manuscripts 1880–1940, Comanche County
newspapers 1901 to present, hardware, and agricultural catalogs. Includes special collections on
the settlement of southwestern Oklahoma and
the Southern Plains, and wagons and carriages
1869–1926.

University of North Dakota
Elwyn B. Robinson Department of Special
Collections
Chester Fritz Library
Grand Forks, ND 58202
701/777-4625
Covers North and South Dakota, as well as North-
ern Great Plains: history, archives, oral histories,
and government documents. Holds 11,000 books,
6,700 linear feet of archives.

H

HANDICRAFTS. *See* CRAFTS.

HEART DISEASE

National Heart, Lung, and Blood Institute
Education Programs' Information Center
University Research Corporation
4733 Bethesda Avenue, Suite 530
Bethesda, MD 20814
301/951-3260
FAX: 301/654-5976
Has materials on reducing risks of coronary disease and high blood pressure; emphasis on health
education. Operated by the U.S. National Institutes of Health.

HISPANIC AMERICANS

City University of New York
Hunter College
Centro de Estudios Puertorriqueños
695 Park Avenue

New York, NY 10021
212/772-5685
Houses books, periodicals, and a large microfilm collection of papers relating to Puerto Rican history, culture, literature, and Puerto Ricans in the United States, especially New York City.

Library of Congress
Hispanic Division
Thomas Jefferson Building, Room 204
101 Independence Avenue SE
Washington, DC 20540
202/287-5400
Devoted to Spanish-American and Caribbean studies. Holds 21 million volumes, some in Spanish and Portuguese. Includes special collections of Archives of Hispanic Literature and 8,000 Spanish plays.

University of California, Los Angeles
Chicano Studies Research Library
1112 Campbell Hall
405 Hilgard Avenue
Los Angeles, CA 90024-1544
213/206-6052
Covers all aspects of the Hispanic experience, with an emphasis on Americans of Mexican descent. Holds more than 10,000 books and other materials.

University of Texas, Austin
Benson Latin American Collection
General Libraries, SRH 1.108
Austin, TX 78713-7330
512/471-3818
FAX: 512/471-9241
Covers Latin American and Mexican humanities and social sciences and history of Hispanics in the United States. Holds more than 539,000 books, special collections, and archives.

HISTORY. *See also* ORAL HISTORY.

American:

American Antiquarian Society Library
185 Salisbury Street
Worcester, MA 01609
508/755-5221
Covers American history, literature, and culture through 1876. Includes special collections of newspapers, imprints, almanacs, directories, children's books, broadsides, prints, maps, manuscripts, genealogies, music, state and local histories, and periodicals. Holds 641,000 books, 150,000 bound periodicals, and newspapers.

John Carter Brown Library
Box 1894
Providence, RI 02912
401/863-2725
Covers discovery and exploration of North and South America to 1820; also maritime, science, and printing history. Includes special collections on marine history, cartography, and the American Revolution.

Brown University
Special Collections
John Hay Library, Box A
20 Prospect Street
Providence, RI 02912
401/863-2146
Holds 280,000 volumes; 40,000 broadsides; 60,000 prints, slides, drawings, and photographs; and 300,000 pieces of American sheet music. Includes special collections devoted to American poetry and plays, pamphlets, military history, Lincoln and John Hay, incunabula, Rhode Island history, Thoreau, whaling, and the history of science.

Columbia University
Oral History Collection
Butler Library
Box 20
New York, NY 10027
212/280-2273
Holds thousands of pages of edited transcripts of oral interviews on such subjects as national affairs, international relations, arts, welfare, business and labor, law, medicine, education, and religion. Special collections include the New Deal and origin of Social Security, aviation history, Vietnam veterans, and women's history.

Library of Congress
Manuscript Division
James Madison Memorial Building, Room 101-102
101 Independence Avenue SE
Washington, DC 20540
202/707-5383
Holds more than 40 million documents on persons and institutions including most Presidents from Washington through Coolidge and many national organizations. Also has reproductions from foreign archives that relate to U.S. history.

National Archives and Records Administration Library
Seventh Street and Pennsylvania Avenue NW
Washington, DC 20408
202/501-5400
Main repository for primary documents and manuscripts related to U.S. history, government, government records, and publications.

National Cowboy Hall of Fame and Western Heritage Center
Research Library of Western Americana
1700 North East Sixty-third Street
Oklahoma City, OK 73111
405/478-2250
Holds materials on cowboys, gauchos, and Western history. Includes special Collection of American Western art.

National Society, Daughters of the American Revolution Library
1776 D Street NW
Washington DC 20006-5392
202/879-3229
Primarily devoted to Revolutionary War history and documents—genealogies, regimental rosters, published archives of the states, Native American history, and transcripts of county records.

New York Public Library
U.S. History, Local History and Genealogy Division
Fifth Avenue and Forty-second Street, Room 315N
New York, NY 10018
212/930-0828
Broad collection specializing in histories of towns and counties in the United States. Includes 100,000 photographs of New York City, and election campaign materials. Holds 106,000 volumes.

Smithsonian Institution
National Museum of American History Library
Twelfth Street and Constitution Avenue NW
Washington, DC 20560
202/357-2414
Covers American history, with an emphasis on science, technology, and community life. Holdings include 165,000 volumes and a special collection of 275,000 trade catalogs.

University of California, Berkeley
Bancroft Library
Berkeley, CA 94720
415/642-3781

Houses the Bancroft Collection, covering the history of Western North America with an emphasis on California and Mexico; also has Regional Oral History Office records, history of science and technology related to California. Special collections include the Mark Twain Papers.

University of California, Davis
Michael and Margaret B. Harrison Western Research Center
Department of Special Collections
Shields Library
Davis, CA 95616
916/752-1621
Includes material on history and development of American West, from 19th century to present, Native Americans, ethnic studies, folklore, literature, art and architecture, and history of printing.

University of California, Los Angeles
Department of Special Collections
University Research Library, Floor A
Los Angeles, CA 90024-1575
213/825-4988
Covers California local history, entertainment media and popular culture, history of photography, Japanese in America, and American folklore and many other subjects. Manuscript collections include the papers of Franz Werfel, Henry Stevens, John Houseman, Ralph Bunche, Aldous Huxley, Edward Gordon Craig, Gertrude Stein, Raymond Chandler, and others. Includes collections of oral history interviews and Near Eastern manuscripts. Holds total of more than 19.7 million manuscripts, 660,000 photographs and pictures, 2,000 maps, and other media.

University of Texas, Austin
Barker Texas History Center
General Libraries, SRH 2.109
Austin, TX 78713-7330
512/471-5961
FAX: 512/471-9241
Covers Texas history, literature, and folklore and Southern and Western history. Holds 142,000 books, sound archives, Texas documents, historic newspapers, and photographs.

Ancient:

Harvard University
Center for Hellenic Studies Library
3100 Whitehaven Street NW
Washington, DC 20008

202/234-3738
Studies in ancient Greek history and civilization. Holds 42,000 books.

Yale University
Babylonian Collection
Sterling Memorial Library
120 High Street
New Haven, CT 06520
203/432-1837
Covers cuneiform; Sumerian, Akkadian, Hittite, and Mesopotamian literature, archaeology, and history; semitics; and Assyriology. Houses 7,000 books, 1,200 bound periodical volumes, 35,577 cuneiform tablets and inscriptions, and 3,000 cylinder seals and stamp seals, plus 1,000 other ancient Near Eastern artifacts.

British:

University of California, Los Angeles
William Andrews Clark Memorial Library
2520 Cimarron Street
Los Angeles, CA 90018-2098
213/731-8529
Covers English civilization from 1640-1750, with collections of Eric Gill, John Dryden, and Oscar Wilde.

Byzantine:

Harvard University
Dumbarton Oaks Research Library and Collection
Byzantine Library
1703 Thirty-second Street NW
Washington, DC 20007
202/342-3241
Has holdings on Byzantine history, archaeology, and civilization total 105,000 volumes.

Medieval:

University of Notre Dame
Medieval Institute Library
715 Memorial Library
Notre Dame, IN 46556
219/239-7420
FAX: 219/239-6772
Medieval studies, special collections of manuscripts, and seals. Holds 50,000 volumes.

University of Pennsylvania
Henry Charles Lea Library
Van Pelt Library
3420 Walnut Street

Philadelphia, PA 19104-6206
215/898-7088
Covers medieval and Renaissance history, church history, canon law, the Inquisition, magic, and witchcraft. Includes special collection of manuscripts. 18,000 volumes.

Pre-Columbian:

Harvard University
Dumbarton Oaks Center for Pre-Columbian
Studies Library
1703 Thirty-second Street NW
Washington, DC 20007
202/342-3265
Covers pre-Columbian archaeology and art; also ethnologies of Latin America and Central American linguistics. Includes special collection of the Mayan language.

HOOVER, HERBERT. *See* PRESIDENTIAL LIBRARIES.

HORSES AND HORSERACING

California Jockey Club at Bay Meadows
William P. Kyne Memorial Library
Box 5050
San Mateo, CA 94402
415/574-7223
Complete collection devoted to thoroughbred horseracing—breeding, training, history, personalities, and veterinary information. Includes special collection of Complete Racing Records, 1960 to present, photographs, and the Racing Calendar 1727–1958.

California State Polytechnic University
W.K. Kellogg Arabian Horse Library
3801 West Temple Avenue
Pomona, CA 91768-4080
714/869-3081
Has holdings on Arabian horses including rare books, the papers of the W.K. Kellogg Ranch, show programs, auction catalogs and specific related studies, on such areas as common veterinary problems of the breed.

California Thoroughbred Breeders Association
Carleton F. Burke Memorial Library
201 Colorado Place
Box 750
Arcadia, CA 91006-9986
818/445-7800
FAX: 818/574-0852
Holds reference materials concerning thoroughbreds,

common veterinary problems, breeding, and racing. Includes collection of foreign racing forms.

National Museum of Racing Library
Union Avenue
Saratoga Springs, NY 12866
518/584-0400
Mainly a historical collection, concentrating on origin and development of racing thoroughbreds.

HORTICULTURE. *See also* BOTANY.

Brooklyn Botanic Garden Library
1000 Washington Avenue
Brooklyn, NY 11225
718/622-4433
Large collection on horticultural and botanical subjects.

Harvard University
Arnold Arboretum and Gray Herbarium Library
22 Divinity Avenue
Cambridge, MA 02138
617/495-2366
Holds 152,500 volumes on botany and horticulture.

Massachusetts Horticultural Society Library
300 Massachusetts Avenue
Boston, MA 02115
617/536-9280
Holds 42,000 volumes, 4,000 documents, and 24 vertical file drawers of pamphlets and clippings about ornamental horticulture, garden history, landscape design, early agriculture, and flora of the world. Includes special collections of prints from the last six centuries, nursery catalogs 1771 to present, rare books, 19th-century books, and trade catalogs.

New York Botanical Garden Library
Bronx, NY 10458
212/220-8751
In addition to its magnificent gardens, this institution has a library of half a million books, periodicals, nursery catalogs and seed lists, microforms, photographs, and other materials relating to botany, horticulture, environmental sciences, and other subjects.

U.S. National Arboretum Library
3501 New York Avenue NE
Washington, DC 20002
202/475-4828
Has references on botany, horticulture, genetics, and taxonomy. Owns nursery and seed catalogs, a collection of floral prints, historical photographs from U.S. Department of Agriculture of early 20th-century agriculture, and U.S. Plant Patent File.

HOSPITALS

American Hospital Association Resource Center
840 North Lake Shore Drive
Chicago, IL 60611
312 280-6263
FAX: 312/280-5979
Holds 47,000 volumes, 20,000 microfiche, and hospital annual reports and audio cassettes about the administration, planning, and financing of health-care facilities and the administrative aspects of medical, nursing, paramedical, and prepayment fields. Includes special collections on the history of health-care administration and on management.

HOTELS

Cornell University
School of Hotel Administration Library
Statler Hall
Ithaca, NY 14835-6901
607/255-3673
Holds 25,000 volumes and other materials relating to hotel, motel, and restaurant administration; special collections include Menu Collection and rare cookbooks.

HOUSING

National Association of Home Builders
National Housing Center Library
Fifteenth and M Streets NW
Washington, DC 20005
202/822-0203
Houses references on all aspects of homebuilding. Publishes magazine and bimonthly bulletin.

U.S. Department of Housing and Urban Development Library
451 Seventh Street NW, Room 8141
Washington, DC 20410
202/755-6376
Holds research materials on departmental concerns such as urban planning, sociology, law, construction finance, architecture, and land use. Holdings are mainly journals, HUD publications, and HUD-commissioned reports.

HUMANITIES

Boston Public Library
Humanities Reference

Copley Square
Box 286
Boston, MA 02117
617/536-5400
Holds innumerable volumes on philosophy, psychology, religion, language, literature, bibliography, and library science.

New York Public Library
General Research Division
Fifth Avenue and Forty-second Street, Room 315
New York, NY 10018
212/930-0831
Has over 2.7 million volumes available to the public for reference use on all aspects of human activity, from American history, anthropology, and archaeology to psychology, religion, and sports.

University of Texas, Austin
Harry Ransom Humanities Research Center
Box 7219
Austin, TX 78713
512/471-9111
Covers American, English, and French literature, theater arts, book arts, and photography. Includes special collections, 10 million pages of manuscript, and 1 million books.

HYDROLOGY. *See* EARTH SCIENCES.

I

ICHTHYOLOGY. *See also* FISH AND FISHERIES.

American Museum of Natural History
Department of Ichthyology
Dean Memorial Library
Central Park West at 79th Street
New York, NY 10024
212/769-5798
Houses 2,800 volumes and 5,000 pamphlets on the anatomy, physiology, classification, ecology, and distribution of fish.

INDIANS. *See* NATIVE AMERICANS.

INTERNATIONAL RELATIONS

Columbia University
Herbert H. Lehman Library
International Affairs Building
420 West 118th Street
New York, 10027

212/854-4170
Covers political science, international affairs, and related subjects such as geography, sociology, and anthropology. Holds 249,000 volumes, 85,000 maps, and other materials.

Harvard University
Center for Science and International Affairs Library
John F. Kennedy School of Government
79 Kennedy Street, Rooms 369 and 371
Cambridge, MA 02138
617/495-1408
FAX: 617/495-4079
Holds 5,000 volumes on international relations and specific issues such as arms control and security.

Johns Hopkins University
School of Advanced International Studies
Sydney R. and Elsa W. Mason Library
1740 Massachusetts Avenue NW
Washington, DC 20036
202/785-6806
Covers international studies in such areas as international economics, law, history, and sociology. Emphasis on 1945 to present.

Princeton University
Woodrow Wilson School of Public and International Affairs
Princeton, NJ 08544
609/452-5455
FAX: 609/987-2809
Holds more than 19,000 volumes, on political science, economics, and international affairs.

U.S. Information Agency Library
301 4th Street SW
Washington, DC 20547
202/485-8947
FAX: 202/485-1879
Has holdings on international affairs, area studies, communications, and Americana. Depository for Agency archives.

U.S. Agency for International Development
A.I.D. Library
320 Twenty-first Street NW, Room 105, SA-18
Washington, DC 20523-0001
202/647-1850
Deals with methods, programs, suggestions for assisting foreign countries—especially Third World countries—with economic development and aid,

agriculture, education, health and population, energy, and transportation, among other subjects. Houses 50,000 books, A.I.D. documents and research reports, and technical publications. Publishes quarterly research abstract.

University of California, Berkeley
Institute of International Studies Library
340 Stephens Hall
Berkeley, CA 94720
415/642-3633
FAX: 415/643-5045
Works on international politics and organizations, economic development, area studies, and related fields. Special collections have newsletters from governments of several continents and journals from French-speaking Africa.

University of Southern California
Von Kleinsmid Library
University Park
Los Angeles, CA 90089-0182
213/743-7347
Covers international relations and allied fields, such as economics, urban and regional planning, and political science. Holds 184,700 books, as well as microfilm/microfiche.

INVESTMENTS

Securities and Exchange Commission
Public Reference Library
Kluzynski Federal Building
230 South Dearborn, No. 3190
Chicago, IL 60604
312/353-7433
Covers securities law, SEC releases, and special studies. Holds 20,000 files of reports and other financial/analytical documents.

IRISH AMERICANS

American Irish Historical Society Library
991 Fifth Avenue
New York, NY 10028
212/288-2263
Houses 25,000 books, plus archives and manuscripts, about Irish in the American colonies and United States.

ISLAM. *See also* MIDDLE EAST.

American Institute of Islamic Studies
Muslim Bibliographic Center
Box 10398

Denver, CO 80210
303 936-0108
Holds 7,500 volumes and 150 reels of microfilm on Islamic and Muslim culture and North African, Southeast Asian, and Near Eastern bibliography.

J

JEWS

American Jewish Committee
Blaustein Library
165 East 56th Street
New York, NY 10022
212/751-4000
Houses 30,000 volumes, 1,450 microforms, and 60 vertical file drawers on Jewish community organizations, contemporary Jewish issues, civil rights and liberties, ethnic groups, and interreligious relations.

American Jewish Historical Society Library
2 Thornton Road
Waltham, MA 02154
617/891-8110
Covers American Jewish history. Holds 80,000 books, 500,000 unbound periodicals, 8 million manuscript pieces, and 75,000 synagogue and other Jewish institutional items. Includes special collection of Judaica, including Yiddish sheet music and theater posters.

Jewish Theological Seminary of America Library
3080 Broadway
New York, NY 10027
212/678-8080
276,000 volumes devoted to theology, Jewish history, liturgy, Hebrew literature, and early Yiddish writings.

National Yiddish Book Center Library
Old East Street School
Box 969
Amherst, MA 01004
413/256-1241
In addition to Yiddish publications, special collections own the Aliza Greenblatt Collection on women Yiddish writers, Flexer Collection of Russian socialist literature, out-of-print books, and photographs. Publishes a newsletter.

New York Public Library
Jewish Division
Fifth Avenue and Forty-second Street, Room 84
New York, NY 10018
212/930-0601
Holds 227,000 volumes, newspapers, and periodicals in many languages covering Jewish history, literature, and traditions, plus general works in Hebrew and Yiddish.

Yivo Institute for Jewish Research Library and Archives
1048 Fifth Avenue
New York, NY 10028
212/535-6700
315,000 volumes and other holdings emphasize literature, drama, and folklore in Yiddish, as well as other related subjects.

JOBS. *See* EMPLOYMENT; LABOR.

JOHNSON, LYNDON B. *See* PRESIDENTIAL LIBRARIES.

JOURNALISM

Columbia University
Sulzberger Journalism Library
304 Journalism Building
Broadway and 116th Street
New York, NY 10027
212/854-3860
The library for the Columbia School of Journalism. Holdings of 15,000 volumes and other materials are focused on journalism and current events.

University of California, Berkeley
Graduate School of Journalism Library
140 North Gate Hall
Berkeley, CA 94720
415/642-0415
Has holdings on all types of journalism, including broadcasting and photojournalism.

University of Minnesota
Eric Sevareid Journalism Library
121 Murphy Hall
206 Church Street, SE
Minneapolis, MN 55455
612/625-7892
Subjects include mass communications, newspaper and broadcast journalism, advertising, public relations, graphic arts, and related subjects. Special collection holds the Eric Sevareid Papers.

University of Missouri, Columbia
Journalism Library
117 Walter Williams Hall
Columbia, MO 65202
314/882-7502
Covers newspaper and broadcast journalism, newspaper publishing, photography, public relations, advertising, and related subjects. Holdings include 22,600 volumes.

JUDAISM. *See also* JEWS.

American Jewish Historical Society Library
2 Thornton Road
Waltham, MA 02154
617/891-8110
Covers American Jewish history. Holds 80,000 books, 500,000 unbound periodicals, 8 million manuscript pieces, and 75,000 synagogue and other Jewish institutional items. Includes special collection of Judaica, including Yiddish sheet music and theater posters.

Jewish Theological Seminary of America Library
3080 Broadway
New York, NY 10027
212/678-8080
276,000 volumes devoted to theology, Jewish history, liturgy, Hebrew literature, and early Yiddish writings.

K

KENNEDY, JOHN F. *See* PRESIDENTIAL LIBRARIES.

L

LABOR

American Federation of Labor and Congress of Industrial Organizations Library
815 Sixteenth Street NW
Washington, DC 20006
202/637-5297
Holds 20,000 volumes and 75 vertical file drawers of pamphlets and clippings on labor, labor economics, trade unions, and industrial relations. Includes special collection on international union proceedings.

Cornell University
New York State School of Industrial and Labor Relations

Martin P. Catherwood Library
Ives Hall
Ithaca, NY 14851-0952
607/255-2277
Holdings of 165,000 volumes, 231,000 pamphlets
and documents, and other materials cover all aspects of labor–management relations, labor organizations, and related subjects.

National Labor Relations Board
Law Library
1717 Pennsylvania Avenue NW, Room 900
Washington, DC 20570
202/254-9055
Holdings deal with labor law, relations, history,
and allied subjects. Includes almost all primary
documents and publications of the NLRB. Publishes bimonthly newsletter.

New York University
Tamiment Library
70 Washington Square South
New York, NY 10012
212/998-2630
Holdings of 57,000 volumes and 500,000 items in
special collections cover the history of labor and
trade unionism. Special collections include the Eu-
gene V. Debs Collection, the American Socialist
Society Collection, the Robert F. Wagner Labor
Archives, and the Oral History of the American
Left.

U.S. Department of Labor Library
200 Constitution Avenue NW
Washington, DC 20210
202/523-6992
The holdings of 535,000 volumes and other materials date back to 1913 and focus on labor and
economics.

University of California, Berkeley
Institute of Industrial Relations Library
2521 Channing Way, Room 110
Berkeley, CA 94720
415/642-1705
Covers labor relations and allied social sciences.
Special collection houses papers of WWII Tenth
Regional War Labor Board.

University of Illinois
Institute of Labor and Industrial Relations Library
504 East Armory
Champaign, IL 61820
217/333-2380

Holds 11,500 volumes on labor law and related
studies.

LANDSCAPE ARCHITECTURE. *See also* ARCHI-
TECTURE.

California Polytechnic State University
Environmental Design Resource Center
3801 West Temple Avenue, Building 7
Pomona, CA 91768
714/869-2665
Library for study of landscaping, architecture, and
urban planning. Includes 60,000 slides.

Harvard University
Graduate School of Design
Frances Loeb Library
Gund Hall
Cambridge, MA 02138
617/495-2574
Subjects include architecture, landscape architec-
ture, and city and regional planning. Holds 244,000
volumes, 20,000 maps, 5,000 architectural draw-
ings, and supporting materials.

University of California, Berkeley
Environmental Design Library
210 Wurster Hall
Berkeley, CA 94720
415/642-4818
Library holdings include architecture, city planning, and landscape architecture. Houses the
Beatrix Jones Farrand Collection of historical
materials.

University of Kentucky
Hunter M. Adams Architecture Library
College of Architecture
200 Pence Hall
Lexington, KY 40506-0041
606/257-1533
FAX: 606/257-1563
Covers architecture and landscape architecture,
historic preservation, urban planning, design, and
alternative energy sources. Special collections house
rare books and works on Kentucky architecture.
Holds 20,000 volumes and supporting materials
including 600 sets of architectural plans.

University of Michigan
Art and Architecture Library
2106 Art and Architecture Building
Ann Arbor, MI 48109
313/764-1303

Covers architecture, urban planning, design, landscape architecture, art, photography, and graphic design. Special collection owns Jens Jenson landscape drawings. Holds 55,000 volumes, software programs, maps, and other supporting materials.

LAND TENURE

University of Wisconsin, Madison
Land Tenure Center Library
434 Steenbock Memorial Library
550 Babcock Drive
Madison, WI 53706
608/262-1240
FAX: 608/262-8852
Covers land tenure and reform in rural and Third World areas. Holds 25,000 books, bound periodical volumes, unbound reports, and other research materials.

LATIN AMERICA

Library of Congress
Hispanic Division
Thomas Jefferson Building, Room 204
101 Independence Avenue SE
Washington, DC 20540
202/287-5400
Devoted to Spanish-American and Caribbean studies. Houses 21 million volumes, some in Spanish and Portuguese. Includes special collections of Archives of Hispanic Literature and 8,000 Spanish plays.

University of Florida
Latin American Collection
Fourth Floor, Library East
Gainesville, FL 32611
904/392-0360
The Latin American Collection houses more than 177,000 books, plus periodicals and about 37,000 microform records relating to Latin America. There is an additional Caribbean Collection of 46,000 books and other materials.

University of Texas, Austin
Benson Latin American Collection
General Libraries, SRH 1.108
Austin, TX 78713-7330
512/471-3818
FAX: 512/471-9241
Covers Latin American and Mexican humanities and social sciences and history of Hispanics in the United States. Holds more than 539,000 books, special collections, and archives.

LAW. *See also* LAW ENFORCEMENT.

American Bar Association
Washington Office
Information Services
1800 M Street NW, 2nd Floor South
Washington, DC 20036
202/331-2207
Covers law, ethics, and legal education. Houses 3,900 volumes, plus ABA publications. Includes special collections of state and local bar journals and ABA Reports to the House of Delegates 1881 to present.

American Law Institute Library
4025 Chestnut Street
Philadelphia, PA 19104
215/243-1654
Holds 14,000 books, 1,000 pamphlets, 32 volumes of clippings, and 8 drawers of microfiche on law and legal education. Includes special collections of ALA publications and continuing legal education publications of various bar associations.

Columbia University
Law Library
Law School
435 West 116th Street
New York, NY 10027
212/280-3737
Houses more than 687,000 volumes on all kinds of law—Anglo-American, foreign, international, Roman, and medieval. Special collections hold League of Nations and United Nations documents, bar association reports, and other manuscript materials.

Federal Maritime Commission Library
1100 L Street NW
Washington, DC 20573
202/523-5762
Subjects include maritime law, economics, and marine transportation. Holds 11,120 books, in addition to documents, congressional hearing reports, and seven vertical file drawers of legislative histories.

Harvard University
Law School Library
Langdell Hall
Cambridge, MA 02138
617/495-3174
Holds 1.45 million volumes on Anglo-American law. Special collections house rare books and

manuscripts and works on foreign and international law.

International Monetary Fund
Law Library
700 Nineteenth Street NW
Washington, DC 20431
202/623-7707
Subjects include international, constitutional, and commercial law. Holds 55,000 volumes, collections of Central bank, and banking and monetary laws of member countries.

Massachusetts Institute of Technology
Dewey Library
Hermann Building, E53-100
Cambridge, MA 02139
617/253-5677
Covers economics, management and finance, sociology, psychology, law, and political science. Holds more than 375,000 volumes, 123,000 pamphlets, 26,000 technical reports, and 6,000 M.I.T. theses, plus more material on microfilm and microfiche. Includes special collections on industrial relations, United Nations documents, and corporate financial reports.

Ocean and Coastal Law Center Library
School of Law
University of Oregon
Eugene, OR 97403-1221
503/686-3845
FAX: 503/686-3985
Subjects include international law of the sea and coastline management and policy. Holds plans, maps, books, and other research materials.

Stanford University
Law Library
Stanford, CA 94305
415/497-2721
Emphasis is on Anglo-American legislative and administrative materials. Holds 325,000 volumes.

University of California, Berkeley
Law Library
230 Boalt Hall
Berkeley, CA 94720
415/642-4044
FAX: 415/643-6597
Houses 507,000 volumes on law—foreign, U.S., and international. Holds court briefs, theses, manuscripts, and other materials. Special collections

have materials on canon and ecclesiastical law, mining law, and medieval law.

University of California, Los Angeles
Law Library
School of Law Building
405 Hilgard Avenue
Los Angeles, CA 90024-1458
213/825-7826
Holds 322,000 volumes on Anglo-American law. Includes the David Bernard Memorial Aviation Law Library. Houses government documents, manuscripts, and maps, among other items.

University of Chicago
Law School Library
1121 East Sixtieth Street
Chicago, IL 60637
312/702-9631
FAX: 312/702-0730
Covers Anglo-American, foreign, and international law. Special collection has copies of U.S. Supreme Court Briefs and Records. Houses 500,000 volumes.

University of Houston
Law Library
Houston, TX 77204-6390
713/749-3191
FAX: 713/749-3867
Holds 194,000 volumes on law. Also owns 5,000 Texas Supreme Court briefs and other materials.

University of Illinois
Law Library
104 Law Building
504 East Pennsylvania Avenue
Champaign, IL 61820
217/333-2914
Holds 453,000 volumes on law and related subjects. Depository for U.S., Illinois, and European Economic Community documents. Also contains Archives of the American Association of Law Libraries.

University of Miami
School of Law Library
Box 248087
Coral Gables, FL 33124
305/284-2250
Covers Anglo-American, international, and foreign law, especially Latin American, Caribbean, and European law. Holdings include 266,000 volumes and supporting materials.

University of Michigan
Law Library
Legal Research Building
Ann Arbor, MI 48109-1210
313/764-9322
FAX: 313/936-3884
Covers Anglo-American, foreign, international, and old Roman law. Holds 653,000 volumes, journals, and other supporting materials.

University of Pennsylvania
Biddle Law Library
3400 Chestnut Street
Philadelphia, PA 19104-6279
215/898-7478
Covers American and foreign legislation, canon law, and Roman and international law. Holds more than 389,000 books and other research materials.

University of Texas, Austin
School of Law
Tarlton Law Library
727 East Twenty-sixth Street
Austin, TX 78705
512/471-7726
FAX: 512/471-6988
Holds 602,000 volumes, special collections of rare books, U.S government depository, and European communities depository.

University of Washington
Marian Gould Gallagher Law Library
School of Law
1100 North East Campus Parkway, JB-20
Seattle, WA 98105
206/543-4089
FAX: 206/543-5671
Holds more than 421,000 books and other references. Includes special collection of Japanese legal materials.

U.S. Department of the Interior
Information and Library Services Division
Law Branch
Eighteenth and C Streets NW, Room 7100W
Washington, DC 20240
202/343-4571
FAX: 202/289-4714
Covers U.S. law regarding public land, Native American claims, resources, and related environmental concerns. Special collections house archival material of DOI, Native American legal materials, legislative histories, publications of the Council of State Governments, and the like.

Yale University
Law Library
127 Wall Street
New Haven, CT 06520
203/432-1600
Large collection of 771,000 volumes covers Anglo-American, comparative, and international law. Also houses the Blackstone Collection.

LAW ENFORCEMENT

John Jay College of Criminal Justice of the City University of New York Library
899 Tenth Street
New York, NY 10019
212/237-8265
Covers criminal justice, police science, and related sujects. Holdings include 200,000 books and 20,000 bound periodical volumes.

University of Wisconsin, Madison
Law School Library
Criminal Justice Reference and Information Center
L140 Law Library
Madison, WI 53706
608/262-1499
Houses 29,000 volumes on criminal justice system, police science, correction, drug abuse, and alcoholism.

LEPROSY

American Leprosy Missions, Inc. Library
One Broadway
Elmwood Park, NJ 07407
800/543-3131
In New Jersey: 201/794-8650
Holds books, films, videotapes, slides, and ALM records on leprosy treatment, missionary efforts, reconstructive surgery, rehabilitation, and village health care. Includes special collection of photographs on the history of leprosy care facilities since 1930.

LIBRARY AND INFORMATION SCIENCE

American Library Association
Headquarters Library
50 East Huron Street
Chicago, IL 60611
312/944-6780
Holds 23,000 volumes, pamphlets, microfilm, and

microfiche on library science, library associations, and library architecture. Includes special collections of ALA publications, materials selection policy statements, library building programs, personnel and procedure manuals, and library surveys.

Simmons College
Graduate School of Library and Information Science Library
300 The Fenway
Boston, MA 02115
617/738-2226
Founded in 1902, the Library houses a collection of more than 23,000 volumes and other materials relating to library and information science, publishing, and media sources.

University of Arizona
Library Science Collection
Graduate Library School
1515 East First
Tucson, AZ 85721
602/621-3383
FAX: 602/621-4619
Has holdings on library and information sciences. More specialized subjects include bookbinding and printing and children's literature, including Historical Children's Collection.

University of California, Berkeley
Library School Library
2 South Hall
Berkeley, CA 94720
415/642-2253
Covers library science, printing and publishing, book trade, archives management, and related studies.

University of Illinois
Library and Information Science Library
306 Main Library
1408 West Gregory Drive
Urbana, IL 61801
217/333-3804
Holds 20,000 volumes on library and information science.

University of Maryland, College Park
College of Library and Information Services Library
Hornbake Library Building, Room 4105
College Park, MD 20742
301/454-6003

Holds 47,000 volumes on library science. Also has software programs, pamphlets, and other materials.

University of Michigan
Information and Library Studies Library
300 Hather Graduate Library
Ann Arbor, MI 48109-1205
313/764-9375
Covers library science, publishing, children's literature, and related topics. Holdings include 55,000 volumes and supporting materials.

University of North Carolina, Chapel Hill
School of Information and Library Science Library
114 Manning Hall, CB 3360
Chapel Hill, NC 27599
919/962-8361
FAX: 919/962-8071
Covers library science. Includes special collection of American children's literature.

University of Texas, Austin
Library and Information Science Collection
General Libraries, PCL 6.102
Austin, TX 78713-7330
512/471-7598
FAX: 512/471-9241
Holds 34,166 books on library science.

University of Wisconsin, Madison
School of Library and Information Studies
600 North Park Drive
Madison, WI 53706
608/263-2960
Covers library science and children's literature. Holds 60,000 volumes.

LIFE INSURANCE

American Council of Life Insurance
Information Resource Center
1001 Pennsylvania Avenue NW
Washington, DC 20004-2502
202/624-2475
Holds 54,200 volumes and 110 vertical file drawers of clippings and archives about life insurance, financial services, vital statistics, retirements, and pensions.

LIFE SCIENCES. *See also* NATURAL HISTORY; SCIENCE; *and related subjects, such as* BIOLOGY, ENTOMOLOGY, *and* ZOOLOGY.

California Academy of Sciences
J.W. Maillard, Jr. Library

Golden Gate Park
San Francisco, CA 94118-9961
415/221-4214
FAX: 415/750-7106
Owns materials on all biological sciences, especially marine biology; location of the Steinhart Aquarium. Also has an ecology/conservation section. Holds the Academy's archives.

Library of Congress
Science and Technology Division
John Adams Building, Room 5104
101 Independence Avenue SE
Washington, DC 20540
202/707-5639
Oversees all science and technology collections, which total 3.5 million volumes and 3.7 million technical reports, including those of NASA, the Department of Defense and its contractors, the International Science Organization, and others.

University of Alaska, Fairbanks
Bio-Medical Library
Fairbanks, AK 99775-0300
907/474-7442
Covers health sciences, veterinary medicine, fish biology, microbiology, and ocean sciences, among other areas. Includes Institute of Marine Science Library holdings.

University of California, Berkeley
Biosciences Library
40 Giannini Hall
Berkeley, CA 94720
415/642-2531
Has holdings in agriculture, anatomy, botany, biological sciences, and environmental sciences. Special collection has rare 17th- and 19th-century natural history books.

University of Massachusetts, Amherst
Morrill Biological and Geological Sciences Library
214 Morrill Science Center
Amherst, MA 01003
413/545-2674
Covers biology and biochemistry, botany, entomology, environmental sciences, forestry, geography and geology, earth sciences, public health, veterinary sciences, and zoology. Holds 100,000 volumes and 125,000 maps and other materials. Includes special collection on ornithology.

University of Texas, Austin
Life Science Library

General Libraries, MAI 220
Austin, TX 78713-7330
512/471-1475
Covers general biological sciences; includes Grey Herbarium Index. Holds more than 66,000 books, plus other research materials.

University of Wisconsin, Madison
Steenbock Memorial Library
550 Babcock Madison, WI 53706
608/262-9990
FAX: 608/263-3221
Covers life sciences, agriculture and allied fields, and family studies. Holds bound periodical volumes, documents, microforms, and monographs.

U.S. National Arboretum Library
3501 New York Avenue NE
Washington, DC 20002
202/475-4828
Houses references on botany, horticulture, genetics, and taxonomy. Owns nursery and seed catalogs, a collection of floral prints, historical photographs from U.S. Department of Agriculture of early 20th-century agriculture, and U.S. Plant Patent File.

LITERATURE. *See also* POETRY; RARE BOOKS; SHAKESPEARE.

Chicago Public Library Cultural Center
Literature and Language Department
78 East Washington Street
Chicago, IL 60602
312/269-2880
FAX: 312/419-1705
Covers American, English, and foreign literature, as well as foreign languages and language study. Holds more than 586,000 volumes and 5,000 language-instruction audio and videotapes.

New York Public Library
Berg Collection
Fifth Avenue and Forty-second Street
Room 318, 320
New York, NY 10018
212/930-0802
Houses 25,000 books, and 60,000 letters and manuscripts, on English and American literature of the 15th through the 20th centuries.

University of California, Los Angeles
English Reading Room
1120 Rolfe Hall
Los Angeles, CA 90024-1528

213/825-4511
Covers literature and criticism, also the Josephine Miles Poetry Collection.

University of Southern California
Department of Special Collections
American Literature Collection
University Park
Los Angeles, CA 90089-0182
213/743-0914
Covers American literature, especially 1850 to present. Includes special collections and archives on American authors. Holds 38,000 books, 19,000 manuscripts, and 10,000 clippings.

Children's:

Library of Congress
Children's Literature Center
Thomas Jefferson Building—Room 140H
101 Independence Avenue SE
Washington, DC 20540
202/707-5535
Holds 200,000 children's books, many in foreign languages. Also houses 20,000 rare books.

New York Public Library
Donnell Library Center
Central Children's Room
20 West Fifty-third Street
New York, NY 10019
212/621-0636
Contains fiction and nonfiction for children, histories of children's literature, and foreign-language literature. Owns 107,000 volumes and multimedia supporting materials.

New York Public Library
Donnell Library Center
Nathan Straus Young Adult Library
20 West Fifty-third Street
New York, NY 10019
212/621-0633
Holds books for young adults, including reference copies of books appearing on the New York Public Library's "Books for the Teen Age."

University of Florida
Baldwin Library
308 Library East
Gainesville, FL 32611
904/392-0369
Houses 84,000 books, periodicals, and manuscripts focusing on historical children's literature.

University of Minnesota
Children's Literature Research Collections
109 Walter Library
117 Pleasant Street, SE
Minneapolis, MN 55455
612/624-4576
Has children's literature of all kinds, including comic books, periodicals, manuscripts, and other subjects. Special collections include Children's Periodicals Collection of 19th-century magazines, Paul Bunyan Collection, studies of ethnicity in children's literature, and other collections.

University of Wisconsin, Madison
Cooperative Children's Book Center
Helen C. White Hall, Room 4290
600 North Park Street
Madison, WI 53706
608/263-3720
Has current and 19th-century coverage of children's and young adult literature and surrounding issues. Holds 25,000 volumes, including many special collections.

Classical:

Columbia University
Burgess-Carpenter Library
406 Butler Library
New York, NY 10027
212/854-4710
Library devoted to ancient Greek and Latin classics; also social sciences, history, and languages of the area. Owns 135,000 volumes.

University of Cincinnati
John Miller Burnam Classical Library
Carl Blegen Library, Room 320
Cincinnati, OH 45221-0191
513/556-1315
Covers classical Greek and Latin literature, archaeology, Byzantine and modern Greece, modern Greek language and literature, and ancient history. Holds 100,000 volumes, supplemented by maps, sound recordings, and other materials.

M

MANAGEMENT. *See also* BUSINESS.

American Management Associations Library
135 West 50th Street
New York, NY 10020

212/903-8182

Covers management, personnel, marketing, finance, production, and international operations. Holds 10,000 books and 175 file drawers of clippings, pamphlets, and company documents. Open to members only.

Columbia University
Thomas J. Watson Library of Business and Economics
130 Uris Hall
New York, NY 10027
212/280-4000

Library covers all business-related subjects including finance and management, marketing, labor relations, agriculture, banking, and transportation. Holds nearly 360,000 volumes and 566,000 microforms.

Harvard University
Harvard Business School
Baker Library
Soldiers Field Road
Boston, MA 02163
617/495-6044

Holds 540,000 volumes on all aspects of business management and economics. Special collections include corporate reports, manuscripts, and archives.

Massachusetts Institute of Technology
Dewey Library
Hermann Building, E53-100
Cambridge, MA 02139
617/253-5677

Covers economics, management and finance, sociology, psychology, law, and political science. Houses more than 375,000 volumes, 123,000 pamphlets, 26,000 technical reports, and 6,000 M.I.T. theses, plus more material on microfilm and microfiche. Includes special collections on industrial relations, United Nations documents, and corporate financial reports.

Stanford University
J. Hugh Jackson Library
Graduate School of Business
Stanford, CA 94305-5016
415/723-2161

Special collections emphasize Pacific Northwestern economics and business. Houses more than 364,000 volumes.

University of Chicago
Business and Economics Collection

Joseph Regenstein Library
1100 East Fifty-seventh Street
Chicago, IL 60637
312/702/8716

Covers economics, management, finance, and accounting. Holds 375,000 books.

University of Pennsylvania
Lippincott Library of the Wharton School
3420 Walnut Street
Philadelphia, PA 19104-6207
215/898-5924

Founded in 1927, the Wharton School's Lippincott Library covers business, management, finance, economics, multinational enterprises, and many other related subjects. The Library holds more than 202,000 volumes and 215,000 microform records.

University of Rochester
Management Library
Rush Rhees Library
River Campus
Rochester, NY 14627
716/275-4482

Covers management, accounting, finance, and allied fields and computer science and behavioral science in industry. Holds 10,000 business annual reports.

MAPS. *See also* GEOGRAPHY.

Harvard University
Pusey Library, Map Collection
Cambridge, MA 02138
617/495-2417

Holds 500,000 maps and atlases; worldwide coverage. Depository for U.S. Defense Mapping Agency, U.S. Geological Survey, and other government organizations.

Library of Congress
Geography and Map Division
James Madison Memorial Building, LMB01
101 Independence Avenue SE
Washington, DC 20540
202/287-6277

Holds over 4 million maps, as well as atlases on all subjects; worldwide coverage.

New York Public Library
Map Division
Fifth Avenue and Forty-second Street, Room 117
New York, NY 10018
212/930-0587

Holds 381,000 maps, atlases, and gazetteers illustrating history of cartography. Collections include American maps and atlases 1700 to present, European maps 1600 to present, 17th-century Dutch atlases, and other materials.

University of Arizona
Map Collection
University Library
Tucson, AZ 85721
602/621-2596
FAX: 602/621-4619
Holds books, maps, aerial photographs, and relief models dealing with geology, mines and mineral resources, history, topography, climate, water resources, and arid lands. Special collections include maps of the historical Southwest and the Frank A. Schilling Military Collection.

University of California, Berkeley
Map Room
137 Library
Berkeley, CA 94720
415/642-4940
Holds maps and atlases; worldwide coverage. Has over 287,000 maps, almost 40,000 aerial photographs, and 3,500 volumes.

University of California, Los Angeles
Henry J. Bruman Map Library
Bunche Hall, Room A-253
Los Angeles, CA 90024-1468
213/825-3526
Specializes in maps and atlases; worldwide coverage. Has nautical and aeronautical maps, with special coverage of Pacific Ocean and Latin America. Houses 508,000 maps, technical reports, photographs, and other materials.

University of California, Santa Barbara
Map and Imagery Laboratory Library
Santa Barbara, CA 93106
805/961-2779
FAX: 805/596-4676
Holds 357,000 maps, atlases, and 3.5 million remote sensing images; worldwide coverage. Special collections include Teledyne-Geotronics aerial photography 1927–84, U.S. Geological Survey, and U.S. Corps of Engineers back files of topographic mapping.

University of Chicago
Map Collection
Joseph Regenstein Library

1100 East Fifty-seventh Street
Chicago, IL 60637
312/702-8761
Holds 335,000 maps, plus atlases, charts, and aerial photographs; worldwide coverage. Special collections include 19th-century county atlases and topographic maps of Europe and America. Depository for U.S. Geological Survey, U.S. Defense Mapping Agency, CIA, and U.S. National Oceanic and Atmospheric Administration.

University of Florida
Map Library
Marston Science Library
Gainesville, FL 32611
904/335-8537
Holds 357,800 maps, 150,000 aerial photographs, and remote sensing images, specializing in Latin America, Africa, and Southeastern United States. Special collections include Erwin Raisz Collection of Maps and Cartographic Papers and Sanborn Historical Maps of Florida Cities, with 6,000 maps. Holdings include relief models and other supporting materials.

University of Wisconsin, Milwaukee
American Geographical Society Collection
Golda Meir Library
Box 399
Milwaukee, WI 53201
800/558-8993
In Wisconsin: 414/229-6282, or 414/229-3984
Covers exploration, cartography, earth sciences, social sciences, and history. Has more than 203,000 volumes, 421,000 maps, 6,000 atlases, 114,000 photographs, 70 globes, and 99,000 Landsat images.

MARINE BIOLOGY. *See also* AQUACULTURE; FISH AND FISHERIES; OCEANOGRAPHY.

Stanford University
Hopkins Marine Station Library
Cabrillo Point
Pacific Grove, CA 93950
408/373-0460
Holds 25,000 books, maps, reports, and other supporting materials relating to marine biology, neurobiology, ecology and population biology, and allied subjects.

University of Hawaii
Waikiki Aquarium Library
2777 Kalakaua Avenue

Honolulu, HI 96815
808/923-9741
Specializes in Hawaii and South Pacific region. Subjects include marine biology, oceanography, zoology, and environmental science. Holds Aquarium archives.

University of Miami
Dorothy and Lewis Rosenstiel School of Marine and Atmospheric Sciences Library
4600 Rickenbacker Causeway
Miami, FL 33149
305/361-4007
FAX: 305/361-9306
Covers marine sciences, concentrating on tropical waters, biology, oceanography, marine geology, and geophysics. Holdings include 48,000 volumes, 500 atlases, 2,500 nautical charts, and supporting materials.

University of Rhode Island, Narragansett Bay
Pell Marine Science Library
Narragansett, RI 02882
401/792-6161
Covers oceanography, marine biology and geology, and fisheries. Includes special collection of polar expeditionary reports.

University of Washington
Fisheries—Oceanography Library
151 Oceanography Teaching Building, WB-30
Seattle, WA 98195
206/543-4279
Covers marine biology, fisheries science, food science and technology, marine policy, and oceanography. Includes special collection of Canadian publications in addition to 57,000 books and other research materials.

University of Wisconsin, Milwaukee
American Geographical Society Collection
Golda Meir Library
Box 399
Milwaukee, WI 53201
800/558-8993
In Wisconsin: 414/229-6282 or 414/229-3984
Covers exploration, cartography, earth sciences, social sciences, and history. Has more than 203,000 volumes, 421,000 maps, 6,000 atlases, 114,000 photographs, 70 globes, and 99,000 Landsat images.

Woods Hole Oceanographic Institution Research Library

Woods Hole, MA 02543
508/548-1400
Covers oceanography, marine biology, and related subjects. Library has 12,000 books, 20,000 bound periodical volumes, plus charts, atlases, technical reports, and 160,000 underwater photographs.

MARITIME SCIENCES

California Maritime Academy Library
Box 1392
Vallejo, CA 94590-0644
707/648-4265
FAX: 707/648-4204
Collection includes technical reports on navigation, marine engineering, and related subjects.

National Maritime Museum
J. Porter Shaw Library
Building E, 3rd Floor
Fort Mason
San Francisco, CA 94123
415/556-9870
Contains maritime history in general but specializes in local and Pacific Ocean maritime history. Also has references on navigation and other nautical subjects. Has oral histories and taped interviews, Port of San Francisco records 1903–60, and a photographic collection.

U.S. Merchant Marine Academy
Schuyler Otis Bland Memorial Library
Steamboat Road
Kings Point, NY 11024
516/773-5501
Library covers subjects of use in Academy, such as maritime history, nautical science, and marine engineering. Contains the Bollman Collection on maritime history, material on oil spills, and tanker regulation lists. Operated by the Department of Transportation.

MATHEMATICS

American Mathematical Society Library
416 Fourth Street
Box 8604
Ann Arbor, MI 48107
313/996-5267
FAX: 313/996-2916
Holds 1,200 reference volumes, 50,000 unbound periodicals, and 1,000 reels of microfilm on mathematics. Includes special collection of Russian mathematical publications.

Massachusetts Institute of Technology
Lincoln Laboratory Library
244 Wood Street
Box 73
Lexington, MA 02173-0073
617/981-7171 or 617/981-2300
FAX: 617/981-0427
Covers electronics, electrical engineering, computer science, physics, mathematics, and space science. Holds 108,000 volumes, 400,000 technical reports, 3,000 maps, and 1 million other cataloged items.

Stanford University
Mathematical and Computer Sciences Library
Building 380, Sloan Mathematics Center
Stanford, CA 94305
415/723-4672
Holds more than 56,000 books and 60,000 reports on mathematics, statistics, operations research, and computer science.

University of Illinois
Mathematics Library
216 Altgeld Hall
1409 West Green Street
Urbana, IL 61801
217/333-0258
Covers pure and appled mathematics, statistics, and computer sciences. Owns 69,000 volumes.

University of North Carolina, Chapel Hill
Alfred T. Brauer Library
CB 3250 Phillips Hall
Chapel Hill, NC 27599
919/966-2323
Covers mathematics, statistics, computer science, operations research, and astronomy. Holds more than 78,000 volumes, reports, microfiche, and audiotapes.

MEDICINE AND HEALTH. *See also related subjects, such as* CANCER; HEART DISEASE; HOSPITALS; *and* PUBLIC HEALTH.

American Medical Association
Division of Library and Information Management
535 North Dearborn Street
Chicago, IL 60610-4377
312/645-4184
Covers clinical medicine, medical socioeconomics, U.S. medical history, and international health. Holds more than 157,000 volumes, 165,000 documents and artifacts, 500 linear feet of biographical data, and general medical files. Includes special collection of sociology and economics of medicine, worldwide, since 1962.

Harvard University
Schools of Medicine, Dental Medicine and Public Health
Boston Medical Library
Francis A. Countway Library
10 Shattuck Street
Boston, MA 02115
617/732-2136
Holds more than 529,000 volumes on medicine and related sciences such as physiology, public health, and microbiology. Special collections house items on the history of medicine, 14th-century Hebraic medical manuscripts, collection of medical medals and portraits, and national archive of medical illustrations, among other collections.

Johns Hopkins University
William H. Welch Medical Library
1900 East Monument Street
Baltimore, MD 21205
301/955-3411
Founded in 1929, this major medical library has more than 340,000 volumes and other materials. It also has 50,000 volumes in its Institute of the History of Medicine special collection.

National Library of Medicine
8600 Rockville Pike
Bethesda, MD 20894
301/496-6308
FAX: 301/496-2809
The largest medical library in the world, the National Library of Medicine has holdings of over 600,000 books and 1.74 million manuscripts on all aspects of medicine, health, and the life sciences. Special collections include manuscripts, rare prints and photographs, and a history of medicine collection.

New York Academy of Medicine Library
2 East 103rd Street
New York, NY 10029
212/876-8200
This library dates back to 1847. Its collection of more than half a million volumes cover medicine and related health sciences and includes more than 100 incunabula.

Stanford University
Lane Medical Library
Stanford University Medical Center

Stanford, CA 94305-5323
415/723-6831
Holds over 300,000 books plus other research materials, including the Barkan Ophthamological collection and the History of Medicine Collection.

University of California, Los Angeles
Louise Darling Biomedical Library
Center for Health Sciences
10833 Le Conte Boulevard
Los Angeles, CA 90024-1798
213/825-5781
FAX: 213/206-8675
Covers medical sciences, nursing, public health, and related subjects such as biology, microbiology, and zoology. Special collections include the Florence Nightingale Collection, the history of medicine, and some works in ornithology and mammology from the Donald R. Dickey Library of Vertebrate Zoology. Holds multimedia materials.

University of Cincinnati
Medical Center Information and Communications
Historical, Archival and Museum Services
121 Wherry Hall
Eden and Bethesda Avenues
Cincinnati, OH 45267-0574
513/872-5120
Houses materials on history of medicine and pharmacy. Special collections include Albert B. Sabin Archives of polio research, Robert A. Kehoe Archives in environmental health, Leon Goldman Archives on the history of lasers in medicine, Mussey Collection on 19th-century medicine, and hospital records from 1837–1900. Holds 30,000 volumes, videotapes, and historical medical instruments and pharmacy jars.

University of Florida
Health Science Library
Box J-206
Gainesville, FL 32611
904/392-4016
Covers medicine, nursing, dentistry, pharmacy, veterinary medicine, and allied health sciences. Holds 222,000 volumes and other materials.

University of Illinois at Chicago
Health Sciences Center
Library of the Health Sciences
1750 West Polk Street
Chicago, IL 60612
312/996-8974

FAX: 312/733-6440
Covers medicine, dentistry, nursing, pharmacy, and allied health sciences. Special collections include 500 volumes of herbals and pharmacopeias, Bailey Collection in neurology and psychiatry, and Kiefer Collection in urology. Library holds 563,000 volumes, 35,000 documents, the medical center archives, and other materials.

University of Michigan
Alfred Taubman Medical Library
1135 East Catherine
Ann Arbor, MI 48109-0726
313/764-1210
FAX: 313/763-1423
Houses 283,000 volumes on basic medical sciences, nursing, pharmacy, and allied health sciences. Special collections includes the Crummer collection on the history of medicine.

University of Minnesota
Biomedical Library
Owen H. Wangensteen Historical Library of
Biology and Medicine
505 Essex Street, SE
Minneapolis, MN 55455
612/626-6881
Holds 44,500 volumes on the history of medicine, surgery, nursing, pharmacy, and other health sciences. Special collections include Burch Ophthalmology Collection, College of American Pathology Manuscripts and Archives, and historical medical and pharmaceutical instruments.

University of Texas
Southwestern Medical Center, Dallas, Library
5323 Harry Hines Boulevard
Dallas, TX 75235
214/688-3368
Subjects include medicine, biochemistry, biological science, and medical specialties. Includes special collections on medical history. Holds more than 230,000 books, plus audiovisual programs, microforms, and other research materials.

U.S. National Institutes of Health Library
9000 Rockville Pike
Building 10, Room 1L-25
Bethesda, MD 20892
301/496-2447
Part of U.S. Public Health Service, the institutes provide references on general and specialized med-

icine. Main library has works on health sciences, medicine, and related fields.

METEOROLOGY. *See also* EARTH SCIENCES.

University of Arizona
Department of Atmospheric Sciences
Institute of Atmospheric Physics Library
PAS Building, Room 542
Tucson, AZ 85721
602/626-8631
Has holdings on meteorology. Special collections have manuscripts, publications, and library of Dr. James E. McDonald.

U.S. National Oceanic and Atmospheric Administration
Library and Information Services Division
Main Library
6009 Executive Boulevard
Rockville, MD 20852
301/443-8288
FAX: 301/443-0237
Subjects include oceanography, meteorology, and related topics, such as surveying, hydrographic surveying, geodesy, nautical and aeronautical cartography, geodetic astronomy, hydrology, and mathematics. Includes special rare book collection of scientific treatises from the 16th and 17th centuries. Holds nearly 654,000 books, as well as reports, maps, charts, and documents.

MEXICO

University of Texas, Arlington
Division of Special Collections
Box 19497
Arlington, TX 76019
817/273-3393
Covers Mexican history as it relates to Mexican-American war in Texas, with photographs, maps, sheet music and newspapers, as well as 20,000 books and other support materials.

University of Texas, Austin
Benson Latin American Collection
General Libraries, SRH 1.108
Austin, TX 78713-7330
512/471-3818
FAX: 512/471-9241
Covers Latin American and Mexican humanities and social sciences and history of Hispanics in the United States. Holds more than 539,000 books, special collections, and archives.

MICROFORMS

New York Public Library
Microforms Division
Fifth Avenue and Forty-second Street
New York, NY 10018
212/930-0838
Extensive collection has more than half a million microcards, microfiche, and reels of microfilm covering literature, science, and social science. Special collections include papers of the American Civil Liberties Union and FBI files on the assassination of President Kennedy.

MIDDLE EAST. *See also* FAR EAST.

Harvard University
Center for Middle Eastern Studies Library
Coolidge Hall
1737 Cambridge Street
Cambridge, MA 02138
617/495-2173
Covers ancient and modern history of Islam and the Middle East. Holds 5,000 volumes.

Library of Congress
African and Middle Eastern Division
John Adams Building, Room 1015
101 Independence Avenue SE
Washington, DC 20540
202/707-7937
Holds 600,000 volumes in general collections supplemented by area newspapers, manuscripts, and related material. Divided into African, Hebraic, and Near East sections, each of which has materials in the corresponding area languages as well as Western languages.

New York Public Library
Oriental Division
Fifth Avenue and Forty-second Street, Room 219
New York, NY 10018
212/930-0716
Covers history, languages, social sciences, and humanities of Far East, Middle East, ancient Middle East, and South and Central Asia. Special collections house Arabic manuscripts, Egyptology, rare Chinese books and manuscripts, printing in India, and Tibetan language collection. Holdings include 250,000 volumes.

Princeton University
Near East Collections
Firestone Library

Princeton, NJ 08544
609/452-3279
Holds more than 130,000 volumes and 12,000 manuscripts on Arabic, Persian, Turkish, and Hebrew languages and literature.

University of Chicago
Middle Eastern Collection
Joseph Regenstein Library, Room 560
100 East Fifty-seventh Street
Chicago, IL 60637
312/702-8425
Specializes in Middle Eastern and Islamic studies. Special collections have government documents, medieval archives, and manuscripts. Holdings include 250,000 volumes.

University of Chicago
Oriental Institute Archives
1155 East Fifty-eighth Street
Chicago, IL 60637-1569
312/702-9520
Covers ancient Middle East, archaeology, Egyptology, and Persian art among other subjects. Special collections hold files of Institute's director 1919 to present, prominent archaeologists' field records and papers, and field records and publication materials of archaeological expeditions in the Mideast. Holds 100,000 photographs.

University of Chicago
Oriental Institute Research Archives
1155 East Fifty-eighth Street
Chicago, IL 60637
312/702-9357
Contains volumes on Egyptology, archaeology, Semitic languages, and cuneiform studies. Includes maps and other items.

University of Texas, Austin
Middle East Collection
General Libraries, MAI 316
Austin, TX 78713-7330
512/471-4675
FAX: 512/71-9241
Covers Arabic, Persian, and Turkish language and literature. General Middle East studies in the vernacular. Houses 60,000 books, plus other research materials.

MILITARY

U.S. Army
Military History Institute

Carlisle Barracks, PA 17013-5008
717/245-3611
Houses large collection of 236,000 books, 9,200 bound periodical volumes, 700,000 photographs, and more than one million military publications, reports, interviews, and studies covering U.S. and foreign military history.

University of Pennsylvania
John Penman Wood Library of National Defense
516 Hollenback Center
3000 South Street
Philadelphia, PA 19104-6325
215/898-7757
Covers officer education and production, tactics, strategy, and related subjects. Holds more than 15,000 books and periodical volumes.

University of Texas, El Paso
S.L.A Marshall Military History Collection
Room 602
El Paso, TX 79968-0582
915/747-5697
FAX: 915/747-5327
Covers military history from antiquity to the present, with emphasis on the major world conflicts of the last 75 years. Includes special collections of military papers.

U.S. Air Force
Air University Library
FL 3368
Maxwell Air Force Base, AL 36112
205/293-2606
Holds over 280,000 books, 510,000 military documents, and 850,000 maps and charts. Topics are mainly aeronautics and military science, with political science as well. Stores the Air Force Regulations.

U.S. Air Force
Headquarters USAF Historical Research Center
HQ USAFHRC/HD
Building 1405
Maxwell Air Force Base, AL 36112-6678
205/293-5723
Contains history of the Army Air Force, which became a separate branch of the military in 1942, and U.S. Air Force. Holdings consist of 3 million documents, oral transcripts, and tapes. Special collections house the Karlsruhe Collection on the German Air Force, papers of selected personnel,

Air Corps Training materials from 1920s–30s, and other documents.

U.S. Army Military Academy Archives
West Point, NY 10966-1799
914/938-3833
Covers military science and history, U.S. Army history, engineering, and technology, plus social sciences and some humanities, particularly American literature. Special collections own archives and memorabilia of West Point Academy, manuscripts of early astronomy, and early atlases. Has a special catalog of official Civil War records.

U.S. Marine Corps
Historical Center Library
Washington Navy Yard, Building 58
Washington, DC 20374-0580
202/433-4253
Covers USMC history, history of amphibious warfare, and general military history. Special collections include USMC publications, some members' personal papers, and other documents.

U.S. Navy
Department Library
Building 44
Washington Navy Yard
Washington, DC 20374-0571
202/433-2386
Covers naval history, biography, maritime law, and polar studies. Special collections repository for Congressional documents, Secretary of the Navy reports, manuscripts, rare books, and historical maps and charts from the American Revolution.

U.S. Navy
Naval Historical Center Operational Archives
Building 57, Washington Navy Yard
Washington, DC 20374
202/433-3170
Holds material on U.S. Naval history, operations, and biography. Special collections have the naval archives, collected naval operations records, oral history transcripts, aviation history, and a collection of materials on China, plus miscellaneous records and publications.

MINING

University of Alabama
School of Mines and Energy Development
Coalbed Methane Resource Center
323 Farrah
Box 870164
Tuscaloosa, AL 35487
205/348-2839
FAX: 205/348-8882
Owns books, technical reports and logs, maps, and ephemera on gas and coal energy resources, alternative energy sources, and coalbed methane. Also contains work on gas and petroleum industries.

University of Missouri, Rolla
Curtis Laws Wilson Library
Rolla, MO 65401
314/341-4227
FAX: 314/341-4233
Subjects include mining and metallurgy, engineering, geology, and the earth sciences. Special collections include U.S. Geological Survey and U.S. Bureau of Mines publications. Holdings include 411,000 volumes.

University of Nevada, Reno
Mines Library
Getchell Library, Room 2
Reno, NV 89557-0044
702/784-6596
Subjects include mines and mining, earth science, chemical engineering, and physical geography. Special collections hold theses on Nevada geology. Holds more than 14,000 books, 115,800 maps and other materials.

MONEY

American Numismatic Association
818 North Cascade Avenue
Colorado Springs, CA 80903-3279
719/632-2646
Holds 10,000 books and 5,000 bound periodical volumes covering coins, medals, currency, and checks.

American Numismatic Society Library
Broadway at 155th Street
New York, NY 10032
212/234-3130
FAX: 212/234-3381
Holds 80,000 volumes, 10,000 other cataloged items, and 350 reels of microfilm. Special collections include David M. Bullowa Collection, George C. Miles Collection, and auction catalogs.

MOUNTAINEERING

American Alpine Club Library
113 East Ninetieth Street
New York, NY 10128
212/722-1628
Holds 12,000 books, maps, photographs, and slides.

MOVIES. *See also* PERFORMING ARTS.

Academy of Motion Picture Arts and Sciences
Margaret Herrick Library
333 South La Cienaga Boulevard
Beverly Hills, CA 90211
213/247-3020
FAX: 213/657-5193
Founded in 1927 and devoted to motion-picture history, biography, and production. Special collections cover many of the industry's most important pioneers. Has 17,000 books and millions of photographs.

American Film Institute
Louis B. Mayer Library
2021 North Western Avenue
Box 27999
Los Angeles, CA 90027
213/856-7660
Covers moving pictures, television, video, cable, and satellite. Houses more than 9,000 volumes, 5,000 movie and television scripts, 40 oral history transcripts, 1,100 seminar transcripts or audio tapes, and 31,000 files of clippings. Includes special collections of scripts, Buster Keaton scrapbooks, and RKO Radio Flash 1932–55.

University of California, Los Angeles
Theater Arts Library
22478 University Research Library
Los Angeles, CA 90024-1575
213/825-4880
Covers theater, but mainly film, television, and radio. Special collections include RKO Pictures Archive 1929–56; scripts; story submissions; music; Terence O'Flaherty Collection on television; Walter Lantz Collection of Animation Cels; Twentieth-Century Fox Motion Picture Stills Collection 1950–60 (3 million stills and proof sheets); Metro-Goldwyn-Mayer screenplay collection 1924–60; Film Poster Collection 1915–present; American, Polish, and Czechoslovakian productions; and much more.

University of California, Los Angeles
UCLA Film and Television Archives
Melnitz Hall, Room 1438
Los Angeles, CA 90024
213/206-8013
Covers U.S. films and broadcast television, as well as historically important films. Holdings include films from all major distributors, Hearst Newsreel Library, Jack Benny Radio and Television Collection, and Exploitation Film Study Collection.

University of Southern California
Cinema/Television Library and Archives of Performing Arts
Doheny Memorial Library
Los Angeles, CA 90089-0182
213/743-6058
Covers movies, radio, and television. Includes special collections of Hollywood memorabilia. Holds 18,000 books, as well as other media support materials.

MULTIPLE SCLEROSIS

National Multiple Sclerosis Society
Information Resource Center and Library
205 East Forty-second Street, 3rd Floor
New York, NY 10017
In New York: 212/986-3240
FAX: 212/986-7981
Houses references on medical research and the social and economic consequences of the disease. Has pamphlets as well as books on services for professionals and laypersons.

MUSIC

Berklee College of Music
150 Massachusetts Avenue
Boston, MA 02115
617/266-1400
Covers music, with an emphasis on jazz. Holds special collection of jazz music. Has more than 17,000 books, scores, and recordings.

Boston Public Library
Copley Square
Box 286
Boston, MA 02117
617/536-5400
Has 177,000 books and special collections of scores and recordings.

Columbia University
Music Library
701 Dodge Hall
New York, NY 10027
212/280-4711
Houses 59,000 scores, 16,000 recordings, 2,500 manuscripts, and supporting material. Includes work on ethnomusicology and musical instruments.

Eastman School of Music of the University of Rochester
Sibley Music Library
27 Gibbs Street
Rochester, NY 14604
716/274-1000
Holds 375,000 books and 85,000 recordings. Includes special collections of folk and chamber music.

Free Library of Philadelphia
Music Department
Logan Square
Philadelphia, PA 19103
100,000 volumes, 4,000 bound periodical volumes, and 45,000 recordings provide a broad coverage of music and dance.

Harvard University
Eda Kuhn Loeb Music Library
Cambridge, MA 02138
617/495-2794
Holds 104,000 books and scores, 40,000 recordings, and supporting material. Special collection houses Isham Memorial Library of rare books and manuscripts.

Indiana University
Archives of Traditional Music
Morrison Hall
Bloomington, IN 47405
812/855-8632
Emphasis is on folk music and ethnomusicological research. Collection has 35,000 tapes, 6,300 cylinder recordings, and more than 36,000 disk recordings. Has special collection of Hoagy Carmichael manuscripts and memorabilia.

Johns Hopkins University
Peabody Conservatory of Music Library
21 East Mt. Vernon Place
Baltimore, MD 21202
301/659-8154
FAX: 301/685-0657
Primarily a collection of music scores, including

ensemble parts. Also contains volumes on music and 21,000 sound recordings. Special collections contain the Caruso Collection and manuscripts and papers of other well-known musicians.

Library of Congress
Music Division
James Madison Memorial Building, Room 113
101 Independence Avenue SE
Washington, DC 20540
202/707-5507
Covers Western, especially American, music. Holdings include works in several world languages. Special collections hold copyrighted material on deposit, holograph manuscripts from 17th century to present, and instrument collection. All told, has over 6 million cataloged items. Library also commissions new works.

New York Public Library for the Performing Arts
Music Division
111 Amsterdam Avenue
New York, NY 10023
212/870-1650
Holdings include 400,000 books and scores, 700,000 pieces of sheet music, and 50,000 manuscripts. Special collections include rare books and manuscripts, Americana Collection, Beethoven Collection, and Toscanini Memorial Archives.

Oberlin College
Conservatory of Music Library
Oberlin, OH 44074
216/775-8280
Holdings include more than 91,000 books, in addition to archives and archival recordings.

University of California, Berkeley
Music Library
240 Morrison Hall
Berkeley, CA 94720
415/642-2623
FAX: 415/643-7891
Houses general works on music, especially fields of Western music history. Connick and Romberg Opera Collections on the history of opera have 10,000 scores; Cortot Opera Collection has 400 scores. Collections also include 18th-century instrumental music, contemporary art music, and ethnomusicology—especially African-American, Indic, Indonesian, and Japanese music. In addition to special collections already listed, library holds over 60 archival collections, 6,000 early mu-

sic manuscripts, 25,000 sound recordings, and 140,000 volumes.

University of California, Los Angeles
Music Library
1102 Schoenberg Hall
405 Hilgard Avenue
Los Angeles, CA 90024-1490
213/825-4881
Houses 52,000 volumes, 60,000 scores, and 37,000 recordings covering music, musicology, and music education.

University of Chicago
Music Collection
Joseph Regenstein Library
1100 East Fifty-seventh Street
Chicago, IL 60637
312/702-8451
Houses 100,000 books, 10,000 recordings, and scores. Special collection owns more than 1,700 hours of Chicago jazz recordings.

University of Michigan
Music Library
3250 Earl V. Moore Building, North Campus
Ann Arbor, MI 48109-2085
313/764-2512
Holds 84,000 volumes and scores and 22,000 recordings of music. Special collections include a women's music collection of 2,000 scores.

University of Washington
Ethnomusicology Archives
School of Music, DN-10
Seattle, WA 98195
206/543-0974
Covers world music, classical and indigenous. Has field recordings of Burmese, Korean, Romanian, Filipino, Pacific Northwest Indian, and Irish songs and stories.

Westminster Choir College
Talbott Library
Hamilton Avenue at Walnut Lane
Princeton, NJ 08540
609/921-7100
Houses scores, recordings, and books on performance, music education, and especially church music with an emphasis on sacred choral music. Includes special choral music collection; center for research in organology houses the archives of the Organ Historical Society and the Routley Collec-

tion of hymnology and church music. Stores the college archives.

Yale University
John Herrick Jackson Music Library
98 Wall Street
New Haven, CT 06520
203/432-0495
Houses more than 124,000 volumes, 80,000 pieces of sheet music, and 17,000 phonograph records. Includes special collections of church music, musical iconography, and the manuscripts and papers of Henry Gilbert, Benny Goodman, Charles Ives, Leo Ornstein, Virgil Thomson, and Kurt Weill.

N

NATIONAL PARKS

National Recreation and Park Association
Joseph Lee Memorial Library and Information Center
3101 Park Center Drive, 12th Floor
Alexandria, VA 22302
703/820-4940
Houses references on park services, conservation, public recreation, and the like. Holds the archives of NRPA.

U.S. Department of the Interior
Natural Resources Library
Eighteenth and C Streets NW
Washington, DC 20240
202/343-5815
Holds 600,000 books and other material on national parks, conservation and ecology, energy, land use, Native Americans, wildlife management, and law. Includes Department of the Interior published archives.

NATIVE AMERICANS

Museum of the American Indian Library
9 Westchester Square
Bronx, NY 10461
212/829-7770
This library, which maintains separate offices from the Museum of the American Indian, Heye Foundation (located in upper Manhattan), holds 17,000 volumes and other documents on the Native Americans of North America. The parent institution, housing the world's largest collection of Native American artifacts, became a part of the

Smithsonian Institution in 1989. A new facility to house this collection is now being planned by the Smithsonian. It will be located on the Mall in Washington, with a satellite facility in New York.

Smithsonian Institution
National Museum of Natural History
Anthropology Division Library
Natural History Building, Rooms 330/331
Tenth Street and Constitution Avenue NW
Washington, DC 20560
202/357-1819
Covers physical anthropology, ethnology, and archaeology, focusing on the Native Americans of North and South America. Holdings of 68,000 volumes and other materials include the Bureau of American Ethnology Library Collection.

Southwest Museum
Braun Research Library
Box 128
Los Angeles, CA 90042
213/221-2164
Collection of anthropological works, Native American studies, and history of the Southwest. Includes manuscripts; sound archives; the personal papers of John Fremont, George Grinnell, and others; and rare Western prints.

University of Alaska, Fairbanks
Alaska Native Language Center Research Library
Box 900111
Fairbanks, AK 99775-0120
907/474-7874
Houses studies of Aleut, Amerindian, and other native languages and linguistics. Holdings include unpublished papers, field notes, and archival materials. Contains nearly all written materials in or on Alaskan native languages, including those languages shared with groups in Soviet Union and Canada.

University of California, Los Angeles
American Indian Studies Center Library
3220 Campbell Hall
Los Angeles, CA 90024-1548
213/825-4591
Materials on Native Americans—government, history, literature, art, and language. Some emphasis on Native Americans of California. Holdings include Native American newspapers and journals.

University of North Dakota
Elwyn B. Robinson Department of Special Collections
Chester Fritz Library
Grand Forks, ND 58202
701/777-4625
Covers history of North and South Dakota, Northern Great Plains Indians, women, genealogy, and oral history. Houses 11,000 books and 6,700 feet of manuscript material.

NATURAL HISTORY. *See also* LIFE SCIENCES; SCIENCE; *and individual subjects, such as* BIOLOGY, ENTOMOLOGY, *and* ZOOLOGY.

American Museum of Natural History
Department of Library Services
Central Park West at Seventy-ninth Street
New York, NY 10024
212/769-5000
Houses more than 800,000 volumes, maps, and other materials relating to natural history and allied fields: anthropology, paleontology, entomology, malacology, zoology, geology, and travels and voyages. Includes special collections of rare books and films, manuscripts, and memorabilia, plus an extensive photograph collection.

Natural History Museum of Los Angeles County
Research Library
900 Exposition Boulevard
Los Angeles, CA 90007
213/744-3387
Contains materials on the life sciences: botany, zoology, and the earth sciences (paleontology and mineralogy), and collections pertaining to history of the American Southwest. Has collection of pre-1900 Southern California newspapers, natural history illustration and art, environmental reports, and Lepidopterists' Society Library.

Smithsonian Institution
National Museum of Natural History
Branch Library
Natural History Building, Room 51
Tenth Street and Constitution Avenue NW
Washington, DC 20560
202/357-1496
Holdings of 359,000 books and bound periodical volumes cover a wide range of natural history and related subjects.

University of Michigan
Museums Library
2500 Ruthven Museums Building
Ann Arbor, MI 48109
313/764-0467
Specializes in natural history, emphasizing taxonomy. Holds 106,000 volumes and other materials.

University of Minnesota
Bell Museum of Natural History Library
10 Church Street, SE
Minneapolis, MN 55455
612/624-1639
Holds 12,000 volumes on ornithology, ethology, taxonomy, mammalogy, and related subjects.

University of Washington
Natural Sciences Library
Suzzallo Library, FM-25
Seattle, WA 98195
206/543-1243
Subjects include zoology, geology, geophysics, atmospheric sciences, general sciences, history of science, and biology. Has more than 200,000 books.

NATUROPATHY

National College of Naturopathic Medicine Library
11231 SE Market
Portland, OR 97216
503/226-3745
Specializes in naturopathic medicine nondrug therapy, using foods and physical therapy. Related subjects include botanical medicine, acupuncture, nutrition, and allied fields.

NEUROLOGY

University of California, Los Angeles
Brain Information Service
Center for Health Sciences No. 43-367
Los Angeles, CA 90024
213/825-3417
Has holdings on neuroscience. Publishes quarterly journal *Alcohol, Drugs and Driving* and annual *Sleep Research.*

University of Virginia Medical Center
Department of Neurology
Elizabeth J. Ohrstrom Library
Box 394
Charlottesville, VA 22908
804/924-8378
Covers general and pediatric neurology, cardio-

vascular systems, and neuroscience. Holds 3,000 books, as well as rare and original texts.

NEWSPAPERS. *See* PERIODICALS.

NUCLEAR ENERGY. *See also* ENERGY AND POWER GENERATION.

Argonne National Laboratory
Technical Information Services Division
9700 South Cass Avenue, Building 203-D140
Argonne, IL 60439
312/972-4215
FAX: 312/972-3609
Eight centralized branches have extensive holdings on nuclear science, nuclear engineering, environmental sciences, energy, materials science, and related subjects. Attached to the U.S. Department of Energy and operated by the University of Chicago.

Brookhaven National Laboratory
Technical Information Division
Research Library
Upton, NY 11973
516/282-3485
FAX: 516/282-2090
The main library at Brookhaven, it holds research in mathematics, biology, and environmental sciences, as well as in the nuclear sciences. Special collections include reports from U.S. Department of Energy and Atomic Energy Commission and nuclear research reports from other countries. Contractually attached to U.S. Department of Energy.

University of California
Los Alamos National Laboratory Library
MS-P362
Los Alamos, NM 87545
505/667-4448
FAX: 505/667-4448
Covers nuclear engineering—military and civil—materials, science, earth sciences, engineering, mathematics, and computer sciences. In addition to books, library has over 1 million technical reports.

Westinghouse Electric Corporation
Power Systems Information Resource Center
Energy Center East 209
Box 355
Pittsburgh, PA 15230
412/374-4200
FAX: 412/374-5738

Holds volumes, technical reports, and documents on commercial nuclear power—science and technology, engineering, and related subjects. Special collections house material on the Three Mile Island and Chernobyl disasters.

NUMISMATICS. *See* MONEY.

NURSING. *See also* MEDICINE AND HEALTH.

National League for Nursing Library/Records Center
350 Hudson Street
New York, NY 10014
212/989-9393
Contains reports, statistics, books, and other materials on nursing education and administration. Special collection has archives of National League for Nursing Education 1894–1952.

University of Alabama
College of Community Health Sciences
Health Sciences Library
Box 870378
Tuscaloosa, AL 35487-0378
205/348-1360
Holds works on professional nursing, pharmacy, and allied health-care fields. Audiovisual programs on clinical medicine available.

University of Cincinnati
Medical Center Information and Communications
Nursing Educational Resources
College of Nursing and Health
Vine Street and St. Clair Avenue
Cincinnati, OH 42221-0038
513/558-8378
Holds 12,000 volumes on nursing, clinical medicine, gerontology, and history of nursing.

NUTRITION. *See* FOOD AND NUTRITION.

O

OCCUPATIONAL HEALTH

University of California, Berkeley
Institute of Industrial Relations
Labor Occupational Health Program Library
2521 Channing Way
Berkeley, CA 94720
415/642-5507
Specializes in particular occupational health hazards, on-the-job hygiene, health standards, and

workers' compensation and education. Special collections cover video terminals, AIDS in the workplace, hazardous waste, and indoor air quality. Publishes a bimonthly newsletter on worker safety.

OCEANOGRAPHY. *See also* AQUACULTURE; FISH AND FISHERIES; MARINE BIOLOGY.

U.S. National Oceanic and Atmospheric Administration
Library and Information Services Division
Main Library
6009 Executive Boulevard
Rockville, MD 20852
301/443-8288
FAX: 301/443-0237
Subjects include oceanography, meteorology, and related topics, such as surveying, hydrographic surveying, geodesy, nautical and aeronautical cartography, geodetic astronomy, hydrology, and mathematics. Includes special rare book collection of scientific treatises from the 16th and 17th centuries. Holds nearly 654,000 books, as well as reports, maps, charts, and documents.

University of California, San Diego
Scripps Institution of Oceanography Library
C-075C
La Jolla, CA 92093-0175
619/534-3274
Covers oceanography, marine biology, and geological sciences. Special collections include accounts of expeditions, rare books, and the Institution's archives. Holds 207,000 volumes and 60,000 maps.

University of Georgia
Skidaway Institute of Oceanography Library
Box 13687
Savannah, GA 31406-0687
912/356-2474
Holds 3,700 volumes on oceanography, marine biology, and geochemistry. Special collections include Gulf Stream data 1966 to present, climatological data for Georgia and neighboring states, and marine science reports.

University of Miami
Dorothy and Lewis Rosenstiel School of Marine and Atmospheric Sciences Library
4600 Rickenbacker Causeway
Miami, FL 33149
305/361-4007
FAX: 305/361-9306

Covers marine sciences, concentrating on tropical waters, biology, oceanography, marine geology, and geophysics. Holdings include 48,000 volumes, 500 atlases, 2,500 nautical charts, and supporting materials.

Woods Hole Oceanographic Institution Research Library
Woods Hole, MA 02543
508/548-1400
Covers oceanography, marine biology, and related subjects. Library has 12,000 books and 20,000 bound periodical volumes, plus charts, atlases, technical reports, and 160,000 underwater photographs.

OLD AGE

American Association of Retired Persons
National Gerontology Research Center
601 E Street NW
Washington, DC 20049
202/434-2277
Holds 18,000 books, pamphlets, and Congressional reports on social gerontology, retirement, preretirement planning, volunteerism, and allied subjects.

The National Council on the Aging, Inc.
Ollie A. Randall Library
600 Maryland Avenue SW, West Wing 100
Washington, DC 20024
202/479-1200
Houses works on subjects concerning the elderly, such as economics, employment, legal services, nursing homes, and health care.

National Council of Senior Citizens Library
925 Fifteenth Street NW
Washington, DC 20005
202/347-8800
Holds books and periodicals on gerontology.

National Institute on Aging
Gerontology Research Center Library
Baltimore City Hospitals
4940 Eastern Avenue
Baltimore, MD 21224
301/550-1730
Concentrates on gerontology research and geriatrics, psychology, biochemistry, and genetics.

University of Southern California
Gerontology Library
120 Gerontology, MC0191

Los Angeles, CA 90089-0191
213/743-5990
Covers gerontology with 10,000 books, bound periodical volumes, and other materials. Has large collection of dissertations on the subject.

OPHTHALMOLOGY AND OPTOMETRY

Harvard University
School of Medicine
Libraries of the Massachusetts Eye and Ear Infirmary
243 Charles Street
Boston, MA 02114
617/573-3196
Library devoted to ophthalmology and otolarnygology. Special collections contains exhibit of medical instruments and 1,500 rare books. Holds 16,000 volumes and supporting materials.

Johns Hopkins Hospital
Wilmer Ophthalmological Institute
Jonas S. Friedenwald Library
3/B 50 Woods Building
601 North Broadway
Baltimore, MD 21205
301/955-3127
Entire holdings devoted to ophthalmology.

University of California, Berkeley
Optometry Library
490 Minor Hall
Berkeley, CA 94720
415/642-1020
Covers all medical subjects related to optometry and ophthalmology. Multimedia holdings.

University of Houston
College of Optometry Library
Houston, TX 77204-6052
713/749-2411
FAX: 713/749-3867
Covers optometry, optics, public health services, and history of optometry. Owns 6,100 volumes and supporting materials.

University of Miami
School of Medicine
Bascom Palmer Eye Institute
Mary and Edward Norton Library of Ophthalmology
Anne Bates Leach Eye Hospital
900 N.W. Seventeenth Street
Box 016880

Miami, FL 33101
305/326-6078
Covers ophthalmology, optics, and physiology. Special collections include historical rare books. Houses 15,000 volumes.

OPTICS

University of Arizona
Optical Sciences Center Reading Room
Tuscon, AZ 85721
602/621-4022
Specialty library dealing with optics and optical engineering.

University of Rochester
Physics-Optics-Astronomy Library
374 Bausch and Lomb Building
Rochester, NY 14627
716/275-4469
Covers astronomy, astrophysics, and optics. Includes special collection preprints in High-Energy Physics. Holds more than 12,000 books, plus other research materials. Has quarterly list of new publications.

ORAL HISTORY

Columbia University
Oral History Collection
Butler Library
Box 20
New York, NY 10027
212/280-2273
Thousands of pages of edited transcripts of oral interviews on such subjects as national affairs, international relations, arts, welfare, business and labor, law, medicine, education, and religion. Special collections include material on the New Deal and origin of Social Security, aviation history, Vietnam veterans, and women's history.

ORCHIDS

Harvard University
Oakes Ames Orchid Library
University Herbarium
22 Divinity Avenue
Cambridge, MA 02138
617/495-2360
Small library devoted entirely to orchids.

ORNITHOLOGY. *See* BIRDS.

OSTEOPATHY

Chicago College of Osteopathic Medicine
Alumni Memorial Library
5200 South Ellis Avenue
Chicago, IL 60615
312/947-4380
Holds more than 20,000 books, including a collection on the history of osteopathic medicine.

Philadelphia College of Osteopathic Medicine
O.J. Snyder Memorial Medical Library
4150 City Avenue
Philadelphia, PA 19131
215/871-2821
Holds more than 60,000 volumes, 6,000 audio and videotapes, and 6,000 slides, plus microfilm, view-master reels, and filmstrips. Includes special collection of first-edition and autographed works on osteopathy.

University of Health Sciences
Mazzacano Hall Library
2105 Independence Boulevard
Kansas City, MO 64124
816/283-2451
51,000-volume medical library specializing in osteopathy. Contains radiographs, slides, and other supporting materials.

University of Osteopathic Medicine and Health Sciences Library
3200 Grand Avenue
Des Moines, IA 50312
515/271-1430
Covers osteopathic medicine, podiatry, and allied health sciences. Holds more than 28,000 volumes and archival collection.

P

PALEONTOLOGY. *See* EARTH SCIENCES.

PAPER AND PACKAGING

University of California, Berkeley
Forest Products Library
1301 South Forty-sixth Street
Richmond, CA 94804
415/231-9549
Specializes in wood chemistry, pulp and paper technology, and related technical fields.

University of Washington
Forest Resources Library
60 Bloedel Hall, AQ-15
Seattle, WA 98195
206/543-7446
Covers wood science and technology, paper and pulp technology, fire control, and conservation and ecology. Holds 48,000 books.

PATENTS AND TRADEMARKS

New York Public Library
Patents Collection
Fifth Avenue and Forty-second Street
New York, NY 10018
212/714-8259
Has copies of all U.S. and British patents issued; also contains patents from France, Germany, Belgium, Denmark, and Sweden. Holds 100,000 volumes, plus microforms.

U.S. Patent and Trademark Office
Scientific Library
Crystal Plaza Building 3
2021 Jefferson Davis Highway
Arlington, VA 22202
703/557-2955
Holds patents in technology and applied science. In addition to books and periodicals, library is depository for selected U.S. Government documents. Includes special collection of foreign patents.

PERFORMING ARTS. *See also* BROADCASTING; DANCE; MOVIES; RECORDINGS; THEATER.

Harvard University
Harvard Theatre Collection
Harvard College Library
101 Independence Avenue SE
Cambridge, MA 02138
617/495-2445
Encompasses theater and dance, circus and minstrel performance, and popular entertainments. Special collection features Melvin R. Seiden Collection of Hirschfeld drawings and works on ballet and modern dance. Includes 3 million playbills, 650,000 photos, and other supporting materials.

Library of Congress
Motion Picture, Broadcasting, and Recorded Sound Division
James Madison Memorial Building, Room 338
101 Independence Avenue SE
Washington, DC 20540
202/707-5840
Houses international collection of over 100,000 films, including earliest films, and 1.6 million sound recordings, including radio programs from 1920s to present and television 1948 to present.

New York Public Library
Donnell Library Center
Media Center
20 West Fifty-third Street
New York, NY 10019
212/621-0609
General collection of films, recordings, and other media; subjects range from documentaries for various age groups to recordings of music, drama, and speeches. Also includes language instruction.

New York Public Library for the Performing Arts
Billy Rose Theatre Collection
111 Amsterdam Avenue
New York, NY 10023
212/870-1639
Collections cover all aspects of performing arts, including stage, film, circuses, radio, television, and other areas. Special collections include the archives of many studios, the Society of American Magicians, Universal Pictures Still Books, scrapbooks and memorabilia of theater groups and persons such as the Actor's Workshop, Edward Albee, Brooks Atkinson, David Belasco, Katharine Cornell, Harold Clurman, the Group Theater, Burl Ives, Bert Lahr, the Living Theater, the Neighborhood Playhouse, Clifford Odets, Hal Prince, Richard Rodgers, and many others. The theater department also maintains files on all active theater groups in New York area, including amateur and university groups. Collection also has original designs by world-famous designers and original drawings by Al Hirschfeld and others. There are more than 1 million books, documents, prompt books, scripts, scrapbooks, scenery and costume designs, posters, prints, photographs, letters, and business papers, and 20 million clippings.

University of Texas, Austin
Humanities Research Center
Theater Arts Collections
Box 7219
Austin, TX 78713
512/471-9122
Houses 15,000 books, in addition to special collections of plays, manuscripts, programs, photo-

graphs, letters, and other memorabilia from the theater.

PERIODICALS

Library of Congress
General Reading Rooms Division
Microform Reading Room Section
Thomas Jefferson Building—LJ 140
101 Independence Avenue SE
Washington, DC 20540
202/287-5471
Holds 3.5 million reels of microforms covering everything from early English and American periodicals to underground newspapers, press summaries, broadcast transcriptions, corporation annual reports, and many other subjects.

Library of Congress
Serial and Government Publications Division
James Madison Memorial Building, Room LM-133
101 Independence Avenue SE
Washington, DC 20540
202/287-5690
Contains official and nonofficial serial publications, in bound volumes and on microforms. Includes microfilm of newspapers in Western and Slavic languages dating from 17th century.

New York Public Library
Newspapers and Other Research Materials Collection
Fifth Avenue and Forty-second Street
New York, NY 10018
212/714-8520
Especially strong on New York City newspapers, both English and foreign language. Also has copies of selected U.S. newspapers and some foreign publications and holds directories, public documents, and other materials. Has more than 2 million items.

PETS

American Kennel Club Library
51 Madison Avenue
New York, NY 10010
212/696-8245
Holds 15,000 volumes, 36 vertical file drawers of clippings, photos and pamphlets, 160 videotapes, and a fine-arts collection, devoted entirely to dog breeding, training, health, literature, art, and sports. Includes special collections of domestic and foreign stud books.

PHARMACOLOGY. *See* DRUGS AND MEDICINES.

PHILATELY. *See* STAMPS AND STAMP COLLECTING.

PHILOSOPHY

Harvard University
Robbins Library
Emerson Hall
Cambridge, MA 02138
617/495-2193
Houses works in philosophy and mathematical logic. Includes special collection on Kierkegaard, among others.

Stanford University
Tanner Memorial Philosophy Library
Department of Philosophy
Stanford, CA 94305
415/723-1539
Holds 5,500 books and dissertations on logic and philosophy.

University of Southern California
Philosophy Library
University Park
Los Angeles, CA 90089-0182
213/743-2634
Holds 60,000 books, with 11,000 volumes in special collections.

PHOTOGRAPHY

International Center of Photography Archives and Collections
1130 Fifth Avenue
New York, NY 10028
212/860-1750
Houses collections of Photography in the Fine Arts, original photographic prints, and manuscripts, as well as 8,000 original prints.

International Museum of Photography at George Eastman House
900 East Avenue
Rochester, NY 14607
716/271-3361
Holds 18,000 books and 600,000 photographic prints. Includes special collection of 19th-century books illustrated with photographs.

New York Public Library
Miriam and Ira D. Wallach Division of Art, Prints and Photographs
Prints and Photographs Room

Fifth Avenue and Forty-second Street, Room 308
New York, NY 10018
212/930-0817
Houses original prints from the 15th century to the present and photographs from 1839 to the present. Holds 175,000 prints and 200,000 original photographs, including 80,000 stereographs.

University of Arizona
Center for Creative Photography
Olive Street at Speedway Boulevard
Tucson, AZ 85721
602/621-7968
Specializes in photography. Holds 10,000 books, periodicals, biographical data on photographers, oral history transcripts, and photographic archives, especially archives of Ansel Adams.

University of California, Santa Barbara
Arts Library
Santa Barbara, CA 93106
805/961-3613
Covers art and photography history and music. Special collections include Archive of Art Auction Catalogs and Archive of Recorded Vocal Music, with 25,000 78 rpm recordings. Holds 145,000 volumes.

University of Chicago
Art and Architecture Collection
Joseph Regenstein Library, Room 420
1100 East Fifty-seventh Street
Chicago, IL 60637
312/702-8439
Specializes in art, architecture, and history of photography. Houses 60,000 volumes.

University of Louisville
Photographic Archives
Belknap Campus
Louisville, KY 40292
502/588-6752
Houses photographs of historic Louisville, 20th-century social history, and American industry among other subjects. Special collections include antique cameras and equipment, erotic photography, Forensic Photography Collection, film stills, and World Wars I and II. Holds 1 million photographs, 1,000 volumes, and 10,000 pages in manuscript.

PHYSICS. *See also* SCIENCE.

American Institute of Physics
Center for History of Physics

Niels Bohr Library
335 East Forty-fifth Street
New York, NY 10017-3483
212/661-9404
FAX: 212/949-0473
Covers history and philosophy of physics and of science in general. Holds 21,500 volumes; also notebooks, photographs, manuscripts, autobiographies, dissertations, and oral histories.

Massachusetts Institute of Technology
Lincoln Laboratory Library
244 Wood Street
Box 73
Lexington, MA 02173-0073
617/981-7171 or 617/981-2300
FAX: 617/981-0427
Covers electronics, electrical engineering, computer science, physics, mathematics, and space science. Houses 108,000 volumes, 400,000 technical reports, 3,000 maps, plus 1 million other cataloged items.

Stanford University
Physics Library
Stanford, CA 94305
415/723-4054
Holds 47,000 books on physics, astronomy, and astrophysics.

University of Notre Dame
Chemistry/Physics Library
231 Nieuwland Science Hall
Notre Dame, IN 46556
219/239-7203
FAX: 219/239-6772
Covers chemistry and physics, pure and applied. Houses more than 41,000 volumes.

University of Wisconsin, Madison
Physics Library
1150 University Avenue
Madison, WI 53706
608/262-9500
Holds 16,000 volumes on theoretical and experimental physics.

PODIATRY

California College of Podiatric Medicine
Schmidt Medical Library
Rincon Annex, Box 7855
San Francisco, CA 94120
415/563-3444
General medical library with special collections in

podiatry, orthopedics, and sports medicine. Publishes biennial research guide and holdings lists.

POETRY. *See also* LITERATURE.

Amherst College
Robert Frost Library
Special Collections and Archives Department
Amherst, MA 01002
413/542-2068
Houses nearly half of the collected papers of Emily Dickinson; also has large Robert Frost collection. Special collections contain thousands of acting editions of English and American plays.

Brown University
John Hay Library, Box A
20 Prospect Street
Providence, RI 02912
401/863-2146
Among the Hay Library's special collections is the Harris Collection of American Poetry and Plays, which contains 500,000 items covering the 17th century to the present. All movements or schools of American poetry are represented.

Harvard University
Woodberry Poetry Room
Harvard College Library
Cambridge, MA 02138
617/495-2454
Devoted exclusively to 20th-century English-language poetry and poetics. Holdings include 11,000 books and audiotape materials.

State University of New York (SUNY) at Buffalo
Poetry/Rare Books Collection
University Libraries
420 Capen Hall
Buffalo, NY 14260
716/636-2918
Specializes in 20th-century poetry in English and in translation; holds 94,000 books and ephemera, 110,000 letters, and other materials.

University of Arizona
Poetry Center
1086 North Highland Avenue
Tucson, AZ 85719
602/621-7941
Houses poetry collections, periodicals, and recordings. Publishes newsletter and, in 1985, an Anniversary Anthology.

University of Cincinnati
George Elliston Poetry Collection
646 Langsam Library
Cincinnati, OH 45221-0033
513/556-1570
Specializes in 20th-century poetry. Includes special collection of rare books.

University of Toledo
Ward M. Canaday Center
William S. Carlson Library
Toledo, OH 43606
419/537-4480
FAX: 419/537-2726
Holds 20,000 books on 20th-century American poetry and Southern and black authors, among other subjects. Special collections include the Ezra Pound and William Faulkner collections.

University of Wisconsin, La Crosse
Center for Contemporary Poetry
Murphy Library
1631 Pine Street
La Crosse, WI 54601
608/785-8511
Specializes in contemporary poetry, with an emphasis on Midwestern poetry. Special collections cover August Derleth, private presses, and fantasy and science fiction. Holds 4,700 volumes.

POLITICAL SCIENCE. *See also* GOVERNMENT.

Columbia University
Herbert H. Lehman Library
International Affairs Building
420 West 118th Street
New York, 10027
212/280-4170
Covers political science, international affairs, and related subjects such as geography, sociology, and anthropology. Holds 249,000 volumes, 85,000 maps, and other materials.

Massachusetts Institute of Technology
Dewey Library
Hermann Building, E53-100
Cambridge, MA 02139
617/253-5677
Covers economics, management and finance, sociology, psychology, law, and political science. Holds more than 375,000 volumes, 123,000 pamphlets, 26,000 technical reports, and 6,000 M.I.T. theses, plus more material on microfilm and mi-

crofiche. Includes special collections on industrial relations, United Nations documents, and corporate financial reports.

POPULATION AND VITAL STATISTICS. *See* DEMOGRAPHICS.

POSTAL SERVICES

U.S. Postal Service Library
475 L'Enfant Plaza SW
Washington, DC 20260
202/268-2904
FAX: 202/554-1388
General business library has books on marketing, management, economics, and law. Depository for government documents and USPS archives.

PRESIDENTIAL LIBRARIES

Jimmy Carter Library
One Copenhill Avenue
Atlanta, GA 30307
404/331-3942
Records of Carter presidency. Holds 27 million manuscript pages from his personal papers.

Dwight D. Eisenhower Library
South East Fourth Street
Abilene, KS 67410
913/263-4751
Holds more than 19 million manuscript pages, 12,000 government documents, 250,000 photos, and 675,000 feet of film from National Archives and Records Administration, on life and career of Dwight D. Eisenhower and associates. Repository for Eisenhower's personal papers.

Gerald R. Ford Library
1000 Beal Avenue
Ann Arbor, MI 48109
313/668-2218
Holds records and other documents from Gerald Ford presidency. Includes Ford biography, U.S. party politics, archives and manuscripts, Ford papers 1948 to present, and 780,000 feet of film.

Herbert Hoover Library
West Branch, IA 52358
319/643-5301
Records of Hoover presidency and 20th-century history 1920–60. Houses Hoover and associates' personal papers, 150,000 feet of film, oral history transcripts, and other media.

Lyndon B. Johnson Library and Museum
2313 Red River Street
Austin, TX 78705
512/482-5137
Holds records of the Johnson presidency and American political history, 1937 to present. Houses Johnson's family and personal papers, transcripts of oral interviews, 38 million manuscript pages, 825,000 feet of film, transcripts of Congressional hearings, and supporting materials.

John F. Kennedy Library
Columbia Point on Dorchester Bay
Boston, MA 02125
617/929-4500
Records of Kennedy presidency and history of American politics at midcentury. Also houses papers of Robert Kennedy and Ernest Hemingway, as well as Seymour Harris Economics Collection. Holds 28 million manuscript pages, 2.2 million pages of Democratic National Committee records, oral interview transcripts, museum objects, 6.5 million feet of film, and other media.

Franklin D. Roosevelt Library
259 Albany Post Road
Hyde Park, NY 12538
914/229-8114
Houses material on New Deal, World War II, American naval history 1775-1945, and Roosevelt himself. Special collections include repository for papers of Franklin and Eleanor Roosevelt and associates, collection of 18th- and 19th-century children's books, FDR's naval history library and ship models, local history of Hudson Valley and other Americana, archives of the Livingston family 1680–1880, and papers of Henry Morgenthau, Jr. Holds more than 16 million manuscript pages, 21,000 museum objects, and 300,000 feet of film, plus other media.

Harry S Truman Library
Independence, MO 64050
816/833-1400
Houses records of Truman presidency and Truman's career. Holds 13.5 million manuscript pages, documents, oral history, and taped interviews.

PRIMATES

University of Washington
Regional Primate Research Center
Primate Information Center

SJ-50
Seattle, WA 98195
206/543-4376
An indexing service providing literature-based information to scientists worldwide. Publishes *Current Primate References* monthly.

University of Wisconsin, Madison
Wisconsin Regional Primate Research Center
Primate Center Library
1223 Capitol Court
Madison, WI 53715-1299
608/63-3512
Subjects include primatology, neurosciences, reproductive physiology, behavioral endocrinology, and animal behavior. Includes special collections of primate vocalizations, videotapes, slides, and other nonprint media. Holds 5,000 books, periodical volumes, reprints, and other supporting materials.

PSYCHIATRY

American Psychiatric Association Library and Archives
1400 K Street NW
Washington, DC 20005
202/682-6080
FAX: 202/682-6114
Holds rare book collection, APA archives, and 17,000 books relating to psychiatry—community and social, child and adolescent, and forensic, among other types—and history of psychiatry.

University of Rochester
School of Medicine and Dentistry
Edward G. Miner Library
601 Elmwood Avenue
Rochester, NY 14642
716/275-3364
FAX: 716/275-4799
Holds 200,000 volumes on a variety of medical disciplines: medicine, dentistry, nursing, psychiatry, and dental research. Includes special collections, journals, and bound periodical volumes.

University of Texas Mental Sciences Institute
UT Psychiatry Library
1300 Moursund Avenue
Houston, TX 77030
713/792-7711
Holds more than 10,000 books on psychiatry, clinical psychology, psychopharmacology, gerontology, and drug abuse.

PSYCHIC RESEARCH

American Society for Psychical Research, Inc.
ASPR Library
5 West Seventy-third Street
New York, NY 10023
212/799-5050
Holds 7,500 books as well as other supporting materials relating to psychical research, parapsychology, spiritualism, philosophy, psychology, and religion.

Association for Research and Enlightenment
Edgar Cayce Foundation Library
Box 595
Virginia Beach, VA 23451
804/428-3588
Has more than 55,000 items on parapsychology and psychic research, including a collection of the works of Edgar Cayce.

PSYCHOANALYSIS

Chicago Institute for Psychoanalysis
McLean Library
180 North Michigan Avenue
Chicago, IL 60601
312/726-6300
Holds 13,000 books, plus other supporting materials relating to psychoanalysis, psychosomatic medicine, and allied social and behavioral sciences.

PSYCHOLOGY. *See also* SOCIAL SCIENCES.

American Psychological Association
Arthur W. Melton Library
1200 Seventeenth Street NW
Washington, DC 20036
703/247-7747
Home to the APA central office, division, and state association publications. Houses 4,400 books and journals relating to psychology and allied disciplines.

California School of Professional Psychology
Los Angeles Library
2235 Beverly Boulevard
Los Angeles, CA 90057
213/483-7034
FAX: 213/413-5323
Library of clinical psychology including more specialized studies on such areas as public policy, women's issues, and homosexuality.

Massachusetts Institute of Technology
Dewey Library
Hermann Building, E53-100
Cambridge, MA 02139
617/253-5677
Covers economics, management and finance, sociology, psychology, law, and political science. Holds more than 375,000 volumes, 123,000 pamphlets, 26,000 technical reports, and 6,000 M.I.T. theses, plus more material on microfilm and microfiche. Includes special collections on industrial relations, United Nations documents, and corporate financial reports.

National Institute of Mental Health
Division of Intramural Research Programs Library
NIMH Neurosciences Center at St. Elizabeth's
Washington, DC 20032
202/373-6071
Holds research materials on psychology and related fields such as neuroscience and biochemistry. Also houses papers by the Institute's research staff, past and present.

Princeton University
Psychology Library
Green Hall
Princeton, NJ 08544
609/452-3239
Holds more than 29,000 volumes and 4,000 microfiche about perception, personality, neuropsychology, psychotherapy, artificial intelligence, and psychology: cognitive, developmental, social, experimental, health, and physiological.

University of Akron
Archives of the History of American Psychology
Simmons Hall
Akron, OH 44325
216/375-7285
Houses the papers of some eminent American psychologists, historical laboratory equipment, films, documents, written histories, and other materials.

PUBLIC HEALTH

California State Department of Health Services
Vector Surveillance and Control Library
2151 Berkeley Way
Berkeley, CA 94704
415/540-2356
Houses books and mainly reports from the department covering public health, waste management, health education, and related subjects. Smaller libraries are attached to local field offices as well.

Johns Hopkins University
School of Hygiene and Public Health
Abraham M. Lilienfeld Memorial Library
615 North Wolfe Street
Baltimore, MD 21205-2179
301/955-3028
Library for the study of public health, epidemiology, and related subjects such as population, psychology, and sociology.

University of California, Berkeley
Public Health Library
42 Earl Warren Hall
Berkeley, CA 94720
415/642-2511
Covers all subjects related to public health, especially epidemiology, hospital administration, biomedical science laboratory, occupational health, and toxicology.

University of Cincinnati
Department of Environmental Health Library
Kettering Laboratory Library
3223 Eden Avenue
Cincinnati, OH 45267-0056
513/558-1721
Covers environmental health and toxicology and related subjects such as industrial safety, and analytical chemistry. Holds technical reports and translations in addition to books.

University of Hawaii
School of Public Health Library
1960 East-West Road, Room D 207
Honolulu, HI 96822
808/948-8666
Subjects include public health and health services, population studies, health education, nutrition, family planning, and gerontology. Special collections include the Kaiser-Hawaii Health Care Microfiche Collection. Holds 14,000 volumes and supporting materials.

University of Michigan
School of Public Health
Public Health Library
M2030 School of Public Health
Ann Arbor, MI 48109
313/764-5473

Covers epidemiology, demography, and family planning. Holds 500 books, reports, and related materials.

PUBLISHING

American Booksellers Association Library
137 West Twenty-fifth Street
New York, NY 10001
212/463-8450, 212/867-9060
Holds 3,000 books, 700 bound periodical volumes, and 5,000 publisher's catalogs about book publishing. Includes special collection of the library of the Association of American Publishers.

Q, R

RAILROADS. *See* TRANSPORTATION.

RARE BOOKS

American Antiquarian Society
185 Salisbury Street
Worcester, MA 01609
508/755-5221
Founded in 1812, the Society's 641,000 bound volumes and 150,000 bound periodical volumes cover American history through 1876. Has special collections of early American newspapers, almanacs, directories, broadsides, prints, maps, music, and genealogical material.

Brown University
Special Collections
John Hay Library, Box A
20 Prospect Street
Providence, RI 02912
401/863-2146
Main focus is on American literature and history. Collection includes 280,000 books; 300,000 historical and literary manuscripts, including the writings of John Hay; and large holdings of broadsides, prints, drawings, photographs, and sheet music.

Folger Shakespeare Library
201 East Capitol Street
Washington, DC 20003
202544-4600
Houses largest collection of Shakespeariana in the world, along with many other volumes and manuscripts relating to English and Western civilization in the 16th and 17th centuries. Holds 230,000 volumes and 50,000 manuscripts.

Harvard University
Houghton Library
Cambridge, MA 02138
617/495-2440
Houses major collection of 360,000 rare books and manuscripts with an emphasis on literature, history, theater history, and typography.

Indiana University
Lilly Library
Bloomington, IN 47405
812/855-2452
Holds 345,000 volumes and 6.2 million manuscripts on British and American literature, especially Poe, Riley, Sinclair, and Plath. Special collections include the papers of Wendell Wilkie and Orson Welles.

Johns Hopkins University
John Work Garrett Library
Evergreen House
4545 North Charles Street
Baltimore, MD 21210
301/338-7641
Houses original manuscripts of 15th–17th-century Bibles, English literature, and architecture books. Special collections house documents by the signers of the Constitution.

Library Company of Philadelphia
1314 Locust Street
Philadelphia, PA
212/546-3181
Founded in 1732, emphasizes pre-1860 Americana, especially Pennsylvania and Philadelphia; pre-1820 medical material; and black history prior to 1906. Holds 450,000 books, 160,000 manuscripts, and 50,000 prints and photographs.

Library of Congress
Manuscript Division
James Madison Memorial Building, Room 101-102
101 Independence Avenue SE
Washington, DC 20540
202/707-5383
Holds more than 40 million documents of persons and institutions, including most Presidents from Washington through Coolidge and many national organizations. Also has reproductions from foreign archives that relate to U.S. history.

Library of Congress
Rare Book and Special Collections Division

Thomas Jefferson Building, Room 204
Washington, DC 20540
202/707-5434
Special collections range from American almanacs through World War II propaganda and include writings and materials collected by many prominent Americans. Holds 600,000 items, including the largest collection of incunabula in the Western Hemisphere.

New York Public Library
Carl H. Pforzheimer Shelley and His Circle
Collection
Fifth Avenue and Forty-second Street, Room 319
New York, NY 10018
212/930-0717
Covers Caxton and other early English authors, manuscripts of Shelley and his circle, and women writers 1790–1840.

New York Public Library
Rare Books and Manuscripts Division
Manuscripts and Archives Collection
476 Fifth Avenue, Room 324
New York, NY 10018
212/930-0801
From handwritten materials to present-day forms, this collection emphasizes American Revolutionary sources and 18th-, 19th-, and 20th-century correspondence, papers, diaries, and account books.

New York Public Library
Rare Books and Manuscripts Division
Rare Book Collection
Fifth Avenue and Forty-second Street
New York, NY 10018
212/930-0801
Houses early Bibles, including the Gutenberg; records of early travels and voyages; newspapers; and Americana before 1801. Has 110,000 books and more than 3,000 bound periodical volumes.

New York Public Library
Spencer Collection
Fifth Avenue and Forty-second Street, Room 308
New York, NY 10018
212/930-0818
Holds illustrated books and illuminated manuscripts showing the history of book illustration and the book arts in the West from the Middle Ages to the present; also includes work from China, Japan, India, Arabia, and Persia.

Pierpont Morgan Library
Thirty-sixth Street and Madison Avenue
New York, NY 10016
212/685-0008
Houses 100,000 volumes of Medieval and Renaissance illuminated manuscripts and early printed books; papers of European and American cultural figures; drawings from the 14th century; and Rembrandt etchings.

Princeton University
Rare Books and Special Collections
Firestone Library
Princeton, NJ 08544
609 452-3184
Holds 250,000 books, 1,000 manuscript collections, 210,000 maps and charts, and 25,000 prints and drawings on topics as diverse as papyrii and Babylonian clay tablets; medieval, Renaissance, Ethiopian, and Batak manuscripts; English and American history and literature; New Jersey; bookmaking and printing; Mormons; and motion-picture history. Innumerable special collections include collections on chess, Grover Cleveland, Jonathan Edwards, fables, incunabula, the history of women, Horace and Virgil, Woodrow Wilson, and the papers of F. Scott Fitzgerald, Hemingway, Pirandello, John Foster Dulles, and the ACLU.

University of Chicago
Special Collections
Joseph Regenstein Library
1100 East 57th Street
Chicago, IL 60637
312/702-8705
Among many collections are Ludwig Rosenberger Collection of Judaica, Donnelley Collection on the history of printing, Grant Collection of English Bibles, William E. Barton Collection of Lincolniana, Croue Collection of Balzac's Works, early theology and Bible criticism, Littlefield Collection of early American schoolbooks, Samuel Harper Collection of Russian political pamphlets 1902–46, Eckels Collection of Cromwelliana, *Chaucer Life Records*, and photostats of *Canterbury Tales* manuscripts. Holds more than 6 million manuscripts.

Yale University
Beinecke Rare Book and Manuscript Library
Wall and High Streets
New Haven, CT 06520
203/432-2959

Holdings include special collections devoted to the work of approximately 200 major literary and cultural figues, such as Matthew Arnold, Joseph Conrad, Robert Penn Warren, and Richard Wright, as well as many other subjects. Has 495,000 volumes and 2.25 million manuscripts.

REAL ESTATE

Federal Home Loan Bank Board Research Library
1700 G Street NW
Washington, DC 20552
202/377-6296
Subjects include real estate, finance, banking, and loans. Holds 25,000 volumes.

National Association of Realtors Library
430 North Michigan Avenue
Chicago, IL 60611-4087
313/329-8292
Has substantial holdings on real estate, architecture, and related subjects.

RECORDINGS

Library of Congress
Motion Picture, Broadcasting, and Recorded Sound Division
James Madison Memorial Building, Room 338
101 Independence Avenue SE
Washington, DC 20540
202/707-5840
Houses international collection of over 100,000 films, including earliest films, and 1.6 million sound recordings, including radio programs from 1920s to present and television 1948 to present.

New York Public Library
Donnell Library Center
Media Center
20 West Fifty-third Street
New York, NY 10019
212/621-0609
General collection of films, recordings, and other media; subjects range from documentaries for various age groups to recordings of music, drama, and speeches. Also includes language instruction.

New York Public Library for the Performing Arts
Rodgers and Hammerstein Archives of Recorded Sound
111 Amsterdam Avenue
New York, NY 10023
212/870-1663

Houses audio and video recordings and related materials. Special collections include Benedict Stambler Memorial Collection of Recorded Jewish Music, Jan Holcman collection of Recorded Piano Music, Metropolitan Opera Archives, WNYC local radio-station archives, Mapleson cylinders of Metropolitan Opera performances, Marian McPartland's Piano Jazz Radio Series on tape, and more. Has 450,000 records, disks, tapes, and other types of recordings.

Yale University
Yale Collection of Historical Sound Recordings
Sterling Memorial Library
Box 1603A, Yale Station
New Haven, CT 06520
203/432-1795
Houses phonograph recordings of historical interest, with emphasis on history of performance practice in the arts, and concert music, jazz, drama, politics, and literature. Has 125,800 sound recordings, plus catalogs, books, photographs, autograph letters, manuscripts, and other relevant documents.

REGIONAL AND URBAN PLANNING

California Polytechnic State University
Environmental Design Resource Center
3801 West Temple Avenue, Building 7
Pomona, CA 91768
714/869-2665
Library for study of landscaping, architecture, and urban planning. Includes 60,000 slides.

Harvard University
Graduate School of Design
Frances Loeb Library
Gund Hall
Cambridge, MA 02138
617/495-2574
Subjects include architecture and landscape architecture and city and regional planning. Holds 244,000 volumes, 20,000 maps, 5,000 architectural drawings, and supporting materials.

Massachusetts Institute of Technology
Rotch Library of Architecture and Planning
Room 7-238
Cambridge, MA 02139
617/258-5599
Covers architectural history and design, urban and environmental studies, and regional planning. Holds more than 100,000 books, bound periodical

volumes, technical reports, pamphlets, maps and plans, and M.I.T. theses.

University of California, Berkeley
Environmental Design Library
210 Wurster Hall
Berkeley, CA 94720
415/642-4818
Holdings include architecture, city planning, and landscape architecture. Houses the Beatrix Jones Farrand Collection of historical materials.

University of California, Los Angeles
Architecture and Urban Planning Library
1302 Perloff Hall
Los Angeles, CA 90024-1467
213/825-2747
Holds 25,000 volumes on architecture and urban planning.

University of North Carolina, Chapel Hill
F. Stuart Chapin, Jr. Planning Library
CB 3140 New East
Chapel Hill, NC 27599
919/962-3985
Covers urban planning, landscaping, community development, transportation, environmental planning, and regional economics. Holds more than 16,000 books and a planning document collection.

RELIGION. *See* BUDDHISM; CHRISTIANITY; ISLAM; JUDAISM.

ROOSEVELT, FRANKLIN DELANO. *See* PRESIDENTIAL LIBRARIES.

RUBBER

American Chemical Society, Rubber Division
John H. Gifford Memorial Library and Information Center
1155 Sixteenth Street NW
Washington, DC 20036
202/872-4600
Covers rubber, polymers, and rubber history. Holds books, periodicals, reports, and symposia.

S

SAFETY

National Safety Council Library
444 North Michigan Avenue

Chicago, IL 60611
312/527-4800
FAX: 312/527-9381
Holds safety education books, research reports, and other items. Includes material on industrial health and accident prevention. Stores the NSC archives.

U.S. National Highway Traffic Safety Administration Technical Reference Division
400 Seventh Street SW, Room 5108
Washington, DC 20590
202/366-2768
Part of Department of Transportation, library is dedicated to motor-vehicle safety—emergency medical services, highway safety, and reports on drinking and driving. Houses Administration Research Reports, Federal safety standards, and defects investigations reports, among other items.

University of North Carolina, Chapel Hill
Highway Safety Research Center Library
CB 3430 Craige Trailer Park
Chapel Hill, NC 27599
919/962-8701
Covers highway safety, statistics, highway safety program evaluations, and related subjects. Holds 17,000 books and 38,000 reports. Special collections include North Carolina traffic data.

University of Southern California
Institute of Safety and Systems Management
SSM Library
University Park—MC 0021
Los Angeles, CA 90089-0021
213/743-6253
Covers safety, systems and decision science, systems management, human factors, and biomechanics. Holds 10,000 books, plus reports, abstracts, and other research materials.

SCIENCE. *See also* EARTH SCIENCES; LIFE SCIENCES; NATURAL HISTORY; *and individual subjects, such as* BIOLOGY, CHEMISTRY, *and* PHYSICS.

American Philosophical Society Library
105 South Fifth Street
Philadelphia, PA 19106
215/627-0706
Covers the history of American science, including European background. Holds the collected papers of Benjamin Franklin, Charles Darwin, Lewis and Clark, Thomas Paine, Franz Boaz, and others.

Brown University
Sciences Library
Brown University Library, Box 1
Providence, RI 02192
401/863-2405
Holds 453,665 volumes on the general, life, and health sciences.

California Institute of Technology
Millikan Library
1201 East California Boulevard
Pasadena, CA 91125
818/356-6405
General science library including the social sciences and some humanities volumes. The archives house impressive history-of-science collections.

Harvard University
Godfrey Lowell Cabot Science Library
Science Center
1 Oxford Street
Cambridge, MA 02138
617/495-5351
Covers all general sciences, mathematics, and theoretical statistics. Holds 146,000 volumes.

Library of Congress
Science and Technology Division
John Adams Building, Room 5104
101 Independence Avenue SE
Washington, DC 20540
202/707-5639
Oversees all science and technology collections, which total 3.5 million volumes and 3.7 million technical reports, including those of NASA, the Department of Defense and its contractors, the International Science Organization, and others.

Massachusetts Institute of Technology
Science Library
Room 14S-100
Cambridge, MA 02139
617/253-5685
Provides broad coverage of mathematics, astronomy, biology, nutrition and food science, physics, engineering, and related subjects. Includes special collections of early works in mathematics and physics, Eastham collection of books on microscopy, and Kayser collection of pamphlets on spectroscopy. Holds 25,000 books, 109,000 volumes of bound periodicals, and many thousands of microforms.

National Science Foundation Library
1800 G Street NW
Washington, DC 20550
202/357-7811
Collection features general and applied science and technology. Includes related studies on such areas as environmental policy, computer sciences and mathematics, social sciences, and economics.

New York Public Library
Science and Technology Research Center
Fifth Avenue and Forty-second Street, Room 121
New York, NY 10018
212/930-0574
FAX: 212/869-7824
Covers all science and applied science subjects including automobiles, communications, mathematics and computers, earth sciences, engineering, meteorology, mining, navigation, materials science, radio, railroads, history of science, and technology. Holds 1.2 million volumes; also technical reports.

University of California, Santa Barbara
Sciences-Engineering Library
Santa Barbara, CA 93106
805/961-2765
All general sciences represented including biology, engineering, earth and environmental sciences, computer science and mathematics, materials science, and physics. Holds 425,000 volumes and 750,000 technical reports.

University of Chicago
John Crerar Library
5730 South Ellis
Chicago, IL 60637
312/702-7715
FAX: 312/702-3022
Covers all major branches of science, including astronomy and astrophysics, biological sciences, chemistry, clinical medicine, mathematics and computer sciences, earth and environmental sciences, history of science and medicine, and physics. Special collections feature John Crerar Collection of Rare Books. Holdings include 375,000 volumes.

University of Georgia
Science Library
Athens, GA 30602
404/542-4535
Holds 700,000 volumes on science and technol-

ogy, agriculture, medicine, veterinary medicine, and economics.

University of Massachusetts, Amherst
Morrill Biological and Geological Sciences Library
214 Morrill Science Center
Amherst, MA 01003
413/545-2674

Covers biology and biochemistry, botany, entomology, environmental sciences, forestry, geography and geology, earth sciences, public health, veterinary sciences, and zoology. Holds 100,000 volumes and 125,000 maps and other materials. Includes special collection on ornithology.

University of Minnesota
Science and Engineering Library
206 Walter Library
117 Pleasant Street, SE
Minneapolis, MN 55455
612/624-0224

Covers engineering, general sciences, and history of science. Special collections include Archive for the History of Quantum Physics. Holds 331,000 volumes, 91,500 maps, 200,000 government documents, and other materials.

SCIENCE FICTION

American Science Fiction Association
ASFA Library
421 East Carson, Suite 95
Las Vegas, NV 89101

Holds more than 26,000 volumes and 10,000 manuscripts of science-fiction and fantasy works. Also owns the SF Gold Medal Books collection. Telephone number not listed.

Massachusetts Institute of Technology
Science Fiction Society Library
Room W20-473
Cambridge, MA 02139
617/258-5126

Holds 40,000 books as well as bound periodical volumes on science fiction, fantasy, and horror, plus fan magazines.

University of California, Riverside
Special Collections
Box 5900
Riverside, CA 92517
714/787-3233

Among the special collections is the Eaton Collection of science fiction and fantasy containing 50,000 volumes and 6,500 periodicals.

SEISMOLOGY. *See also* EARTH SCIENCES.

California Institute of Technology
Earthquake Engineering Research Library
201 Thomas Laboratory
Pasadena, CA 91125
818/356-4227

Has holdings in seismology and allied fields such as structural mechanics and disaster recovery. Has exchange program with foreign institutions.

University of California, Berkeley
Earthquake Engineering Research Center Library
1301 South 46th Street
Richmond, CA 94804
415/231-9401
FAX: 415/231-9471

Covers seismology, earthquake engineering, geology, and allied subjects. Publishes the *Abstract Journal in Earthquake Engineering*, semiannually. Library holdings are in multiple languages, including principal Asian languages.

SHAKESPEARE

Folger Shakespeare Library
201 East Capitol Street
Washington, DC 20003
202544-4600

Largest collection of Shakespeariana in the world, along with many other volumes and manuscripts relating to English and Western civilization in the 16th and 17th centuries. Holds 230,000 volumes and 50,000 manuscripts.

University of Pennsylvania
Horace Howard Furness Memorial Library
Van Pelt Library
3420 Walnut Street
Philadelphia, PA 19104-6206
215/898-7552

Covers Shakespeare, medieval to 17th-century British drama, theater, and history. Includes special collections of playbills, promptbooks, and pictures. Houses 20,000 books.

SKIING. *See also* SPORTS.

National Ski Hall of Fame and Museum
Roland Palmedo National Ski Library
Box 191
Ishpeming, MI 49849
906/486-9281

Holds material pertaining to skiing—books, pamphlets, and magazines.

SLAVIC LANGUAGES AND LITERATURE

New York Public Library
Slavic and Baltic Division
Fifth Avenue and Forty-second Street, Room 217
New York, NY 10018
212/930-0714
Holds 268,000 volumes and other materials devoted to Slavic and Baltic literature and linguistics, with special collections devoted to Slavic rare books and Russian imprints before 1860.

Yale University
Slavic and East European Collections
Sterling Memorial Library
New Haven, CT 06520
203/432-1861
Specializes in East Europe—social sciences, humanities, linguistics, and history. Holds more than 252,000 books in Slavic and East European languages, 72,000 bound periodical volumes, clippings, 40 archival collections, and 2.25 aisles of Free Europe material. Includes special collections of Joel Sumner Smith, Harrison Thomson, Mikhail Tostovtseff, George Vernadsky, Vasilii Tutcheff, and the Pilsudski archives.

SMOKING. *See* SUBSTANCE ABUSE; TOBACCO.

SOCIAL SCIENCES. *See also* ANTHROPOLOGY; ECONOMICS; POLITICAL SCIENCE; PSYCHOLOGY; SOCIOLOGY.

Chicago Public Library Central Library
Social Sciences and History Division
400 North Franklin Street
Chicago, IL 60610
312/269-2830 or 312/269-2929
Holds more than 337,000 volumes. Covers all social sciences, plus history, law, philosophy, religion, sports, and travel.

Columbia University
Burgess-Carpenter Library
406 Butler Library
New York, NY 10027
212/854-4710
Houses works in the social sciences, history, linguistics, and some literature, particularly classic Greek and Latin works. Holds 135,00 volumes, plus dissertations and other essays.

University of California, Los Angeles
Public Affairs Service
405 Hilgard Avenue

Los Angeles, CA 90024-1575
213/825-3135
Holds nearly 306,000 volumes on social and economic problems, government, labor relations, ethnic studies, welfare, and politics.

University of Illinois
Education and Social Sciences Library
100 Main Library
1408 West Gregory Drive
Urbana, IL 61801
217/333-2305
Houses references on education and general social sciences such as anthropology, psychology, and sociology. Has 131,000 volumes and other materials.

Yale University
Social Science Library
140 Prospect Street
Yale Station, Box 1958
New Haven, CT 06520
203/432-3304
Holds 70,000 volumes covering administrative sciences, economics and economic development, finance, health services administration, management, political science, and sociology. Includes special collections on economic growth, social science data, and Roper public opinion polls.

SOCIAL WORK

Columbia University
Whitney M. Young, Jr. Memorial Library of Social Work
309 International Affairs Building
New York, NY 10027
212/280-5159
Has holdings on social work; community organization and development; mental health and retardation; social services such as day care, aging, alcoholism, and drug addiction; urban education; intergroup relations; and social and physical rehabilitation, among other subjects. Special collections include Dorothy Hutchinson Collection on the Child and Brookdale Collection on Gerontology. Houses 130,000 volumes.

University of Chicago
Social Services Administration Library
969 East Sixtieth Street
Chicago, IL 60637
312/702-1199
Has studies dealing with public policy, social ser-

vices, foreign social work, urban studies, welfare and child welfare, mental health, and psychotherapy.

University of Michigan
Social Work Library
1548 Frieze Building
Ann Arbor, MI 48109
313/764-5169
Holds 37,000 volumes on social work. Special collections include studies of minority representation in educational curriculum, National Assessment of Juvenile Corrections, and other supporting materials.

University of Minnesota
Social Welfare History Archives
101 Walter Library
117 Pleasant Street, SE
Minneapolis, MN 55455
612/624-6394
Holds 10,000 volumes and other materials on social welfare, social work, history of voluntary associations, and related subjects.

University of Southern California
Social Work Library
University Park
Los Angeles, CA 90089-0411
213/743-7932
Covers social work, welfare, and allied subjects. Special collections include the California Social Welfare History Archives and Hispanic Mental Health Collection. Houses 35,000 books.

University of Washington
Social Work Library
Social Work/Speech-Hearing Building, JH-30
Seattle, WA 98195
206/545-2180
Holds more than 26,000 volumes and pamphlets relating to social work and welfare, agency administration, social research, community organizations, and public policy and services.

SOCIOLOGY. *See also* SOCIAL SCIENCES.

Massachusetts Institute of Technology
Dewey Library
Hermann Building, E53-100
Cambridge, MA 02139
617/253-5677
Covers economics, management and finance, sociology, psychology, law, and political science.

Holds more than 375,000 volumes, 123,000 pamphlets, 26,000 technical reports, and 6,000 M.I.T. theses, plus more material on microfilm and microfiche. Includes special collections on industrial relations, United Nations documents, and corporate financial reports.

THE SOUTH. *See* AMERICAN SOUTH.

SOVIET UNION

Harvard University
Russian Research Center Library
Coolidge Hall Library
1737 Cambridge Street
Cambridge, MA 02138
617/495-4030
Has holdings on the Soviet Union and post-World War II Eastern Europe. Focuses on history, political science, economics, and military. Holds Harvard Project on the Soviet social system.

SPACE TECHNOLOGY. *See also* AERONAUTICS.

California Institute of Technology
Jet Propulsion Laboratory Library
4800 Oak Grove Drive
Pasadena, CA 91109
818/354-4200
Primarily emphasizes astronautics and astronomy and related fields such as satellite communications. Special collection devoted to oceanic remote sensing.

Massachusetts Institute of Technology
Lincoln Laboratory Library
244 Wood Street
Box 73
Lexington, MA 02173-0073
617/981-7171 or
617/981-2300
FAX: 617/981-0427
Covers electronics, electrical engineering, computer science, physics, mathematics, and space science. Holdings include 108,000 volumes, 400,000 technical reports, 3,000 maps, plus 1 million other cataloged items.

National Space Society
Von Braun-Oberth Memorial Library
922 Pennsylvania Avenue SE
Washington, DC 20003
202/543-1900
FAX: 202/546-4189

Topics include development of the space program and transportation.

Smithsonian Institution
National Air and Space Museum Library
National Air and Space Museum, Room 3100
Seventh Street and Independence Avenue SW
Washington, DC 20560
202/357-3133
In addition to its superb display of authentic, historic air and spacecraft, the library holds 40,000 books, 7,000 bound periodical volumes, and a large collection of photographs covering all aspects of aeronautics and astronautics, with special emphasis on aeronautic and space history.

SPELEOLOGY

National Speleological Society Library
1 Cave Avenue
Huntsville, AL 35810
205/852-1300
Has works on cave exploration, geology, and archaeology. Special collections house foreign publications on speleology, newsletters, and other items.

SPORTS. *See also* SPORTS MEDICINE *and individual sports, such as* BASEBALL, FOOTBALL, *and* SKIING.

National Library of Sports
San Jose Public Library
180 West San Carlos Street
San Jose, CA 95113-2096
408/287-0093
Collection covers over 95 different sports. Includes baseball guides from 1871 to present, college and pro sports brochures, football programs, and sports histories.

National Sporting Library, Inc.
Box 1335
Middleburg, VA 22117
703/687-6542
Has collection on outdoor and field sports such as fox hunting, thoroughbred racing, polo, fishing, shooting, falconry, and cockfighting. Specializes in horse sports; owns a large polo collection, a collection of 16th–19th-century books on horses, and a collection of sporting paintings.

Seattle Public Library
Education, Psychology, Sociology, and Sports Department
1000 Fourth Street
Seattle, WA 98104
206/625-2663
Holds more than 70,300 volumes, including works on sports.

United States Sports Academy Library
One Academy Drive
Daphne, AL 36526
205/626-3303
FAX: 205/626-3874
Covers aspects of sports, coaching, fitness, medicine, and management. Materials in various media such as films, audio tapes, and newspaper clippings available.

SPORTS MEDICINE

U.S. Olympic Committee
Sports Medicine and Science Information Center
Sports Medicine Division
Department of Education Services
1750 East Boulder Street
Colorado Springs, CO 80909
719/632-5551
Library of all sports-related medical sciences—physiology, sports psychology, injury treatment and prevention—and other sport subjects, such as training and conditioning. Also has sports rule books, USOC files, and photographs. Publishes quarterly newsletter.

STAMPS AND STAMP COLLECTING

American Philatelic Research Library
Box 8338
State College, PA 16803
814/237-3803
Holds over 12,000 books and 4,000 periodical volumes on stamp collecting and U.S. postal history. Includes special collection American First Day Cover Society Archives.

National Association of Precancel Collectors, Inc.
Chester Davis Memorial Library
5121 Park Boulevard
Wildwood, NJ 08260
609/522-2569
Books, periodicals, and color prints on precanceled stamps from the United States, Canada, Great Britain, and Europe.

STANDARDS

National Standards Association, Inc.
Techinfo

1200 Quince Orchard Boulevard
Gaithersburg, MD 20878
301/590-2352 or 800/638-8094
FAX: 301/990-8378
Holds U.S. Federal and military safety standards and specifications. Also has lists of legal industry standards. Special collections house DOD Index of Specifications and Standards and NASA standards. Publishes several bulletins throughout year.

STATES AND TERRITORIES

Alabama:

University of Alabama
William Stanley Hoole Special Collections Library
Box 870266
Tuscaloosa, AL 35487-9784
205/348-5512
Covers Alabama local history, university archives, oral history, maps, state documents, and recordings of folk music, among other materials.

Birmingham Public and Jefferson County Free Library
Linn-Henley Library for Southern Historical Research
Tutwiler Collection of Southern History and Literature
2100 Park Place
Birmingham, AL 35203
205/226-3665
Specializes in local history and Southern genealogy. Holds state, county, and municipal documents, 60,000 books, and other support materials.

Alaska:

Alaska State Division of State Libraries
Historical Library
Box G
Juneau, AK
907/465-2925
Covers Alaskan, Arctic, and Russian culture. Holds 33,000 books, documents, records, and special collections (noncirculating).

University of Alaska, Anchorage, Library
Archives and Manuscripts Department
3211 Providence Drive
Anchorage, AK 99508
907/786-1849
Holds special collection of historical manuscripts. Repository for University archives. Covers Alaskan social, political, and cultural organizations and business records, as well as papers of individuals and families.

University of Alaska, Anchorage, Library
Special Collections
3211 Providence Drive
Anchorage, AK 99508
907/786-1873
Holds special collection of Alaskan cultural rarities —sheet music, rare books, and maps.

University of Alaska, Fairbanks
Alaska and Polar Regions Department
Elmer E. Rasmuson Library
Fairbanks, AK 99701
907/479-7261
Covers Alaskan history, business, and sciences and material on Arctic and Antarctic. Special collections house historical photographs, rare books and maps, oral history transcripts, books on Alaska, and the papers of several of Alaska's senators and congressmen. Includes film, manuscripts, and government documents.

Arizona:

Arizona State Department of Library
Archives and Public Records
State Capital
1700 West Washington
Phoenix, AZ 85007
602/542-4035
Covers Arizona and Southwestern history, law, and genealogy. Holds state archives. Houses 1.1 million volumes and federal document depository.

Arizona Historical Society Library
949 East Second Street
Tucson, AZ 85719
602/628-5774
Covers Southwestern Americana, Mexicana, military history, ranching, and Southwestern Indians. Holds 48,000 books, special collections of papers, documents, and photographs.

University of Arizona
Special Collections Department
University Library
Tucson, AZ 85721
602/621-6423
Holds 150,000 volumes and 800 manuscript collections. Subjects include Arizona, Arizona archives, Southwest, science fiction, and history of science.

University of Arizona
Arizona State Museum Library
Tucson, AZ 85721
602/621-4695
Subjects include Southwestern and Mesoamerican anthropology, museum studies, and Latin American art and architecture.

University of Arizona
Special Collections Department
University Library
Tucson, AZ 85721
602/621-6423
FAX: 602/621-4619
Holds University archives, materials on Southwestern history, history of science collection, and collections of science fiction and poetry. Includes archives of Black Sparrow Press.

  Arkansas:

Arkansas State Library
One Capital Mall
Little Rock, AR 722901
501/682-1527
Holds 144,278 volumes on Arkansas.

University of Arkansas, Fayetteville
Special Collections Division
Fayetteville, AR 72701
501/575-4101
Holds University archives, material on Arkansas history, literature, folklore, Ozark folklore, a Dime Novel Collection, a Robert Owen collection, and rare maps and photographs.

University of Arkansas
Monticello Library
Special Collections
Box 3599
Monticello, AR 71655
501/367-6811
Mainly houses the Arkansas Collection miscellaneous items. Also has government documents.

  California:

California Historical Society
History Center
4201 Wilshire Boulevard, No. 202
Los Angeles, CA 90010
213/937-1848
Holds local and state history. Publishes quarterly *California History*. Owns 75,000 historical photographs.

California Historical Society
Schubert Hall Library
2099 Pacific Avenue
San Francisco, CA 94109-2235
415/567-1848
Houses rare books, maps, and numerous historical photos from the San Franciso Photographic Archives. Includes special collections of California printing and publishing.

California State Archives
Archives Building, Room 130
1020 O Street
Sacramento, CA 95814
916/445-4293
Holds 58,000 volumes on California government and politics. Includes collection of Spanish land grants and Robert F. Kennedy Investigation papers, among others.

California State Library
Library and Courts Building
914 Capitol Mall
Box 942837
Sacramento, CA 94237-0001
916/445-2585
Holds materials concerning state government, such as population and other statistics, education, law, state administration, and related studies. Special collections own a Braille library and other materials for the blind and physically handicapped.

California State Library
Sutro Library
480 Winston Drive
San Francisco, CA 94132
415/557-0421
Has holdings on a variety of humanities and science subjects with emphasis on American genealogy and local history. Also covers history of science, Mexican history, and Hebrew studies, among others. Holdings include 20,000 manuscripts and papers of Sir Joseph Banks, 1760–1820. Publishes quarterly journal on local history and genealogy.

California State University, Fullerton
Henry Madden Library
Department of Special Collections
Fresno, CA 93740
209/294-2595
Covers local history, concentrating on viticulture and oenology. Includes merchant's catalogs, pam-

phlets from international fairs, and related studies and documents, such as federal water irrigation regulations.

California State University, Fullerton
University Archives and Special Collections

Box 4150
Fullerton, CA 92634
714/773-3444

Houses the University archives as well as local history. Contains the Kerridge Angling Collection and popular culture archives, and is a depository for Science Fiction Writers of America (SFWA).

California State University, Northridge
Urban Archives Center

South Library, Room 205
Northridge, CA 91330
818/885-2487

Covers local Los Angeles and San Fernando Valley history; also urban social sciences and labor history. Archives include labor newspapers, documents, union papers, and photographs.

Los Angeles Public Library
History and Genealogy Department

630 West Fifth Street
Los Angeles, CA 90071
213/612-3314

Houses 38,000 volumes in genealogy collection; also Californiana, history, local history, heraldry, and newspapers. Holds 290,000 books and other supporting materials.

University of California, Berkeley
Bancroft Library

Berkeley, CA 94720
415/642-3781

Covers history of western North America, concentrating on California and Mexico. Also holds the Mark Twain papers, American incunabula, rare imprints, medieval manuscripts, and oral history archives.

University of California, Los Angeles
Department of Special Collections

University Research Library, Floor A
Los Angeles, CA 90024-1575
213/825-4988

Covers history of California and history of various performing arts, as well as photography, folklore, and popular culture. Holds 174,155 volumes, pictures, photographs, recordings, and other supporting materials.

University of California, Santa Cruz
Regional History Project

Dean East McHenry Library
Santa Cruz, CA 95064
408/429-2847

Covers local social, economic, and agricultural history, focusing on central California coast. Has oral interview transcripts and photographs of interviewees. Transcripts also available in Bancroft Library, UC Berkeley.

Colorado:

Colorado Historical Society
Stephen H. Hart Library

Colorado State History Museum
1300 Broadway
Denver, CO 80203
303/866-2305

Covers Colorado and business history, railroads, mining, cattle industry, and social and cultural movements. Holds 47,000 volumes, photographs, maps, and atlases.

University of Colorado, Boulder
Western Historical Collection and University Archives

Norlin Library
Campus Box 184
Boulder, CO 80309
303/492-7242
FAX: 303/492-8775

Focus on Colorado in the historical American West—politics, organizations, business, and industry. Special collections include Women's International League for Peace and Freedom Papers, National Farmers' Union Archives, Western Federation of Miners Archives, and personal papers of Gary Hart and others. Also holds University archives. Includes over 150,000 photographs.

Connecticut:

Connecticut Historical Society Library

1 Elizabeth Street
Hartford, CT 06105
203/236-5621

Covers New England and Connecticut history and genealogy and colonial sources. Holds 100,000 books, children's books, sermons, broadsides, and trade catalogs, and 2,500 volumes of 18th- and early 19th-century newspapers.

Connecticut State Library
231 Capitol Avenue
Hartford, CT 06106
203/566-4777
Covers local history and genealogy and state and
federal law. Includes collections of Connecticut
newspapers, town documents, probate records,
and archives. Holds 700,000 books, plus other
research materials.

Delaware:

**Delaware State Division of Historical and Cultural
Affairs**
Delaware State Archives
Hall of Records
Dover, DE 19901
302/736-5318
Holds Delaware history and government, county,
and city records. Has 60,000 photographs and
slides and 2,000 books.

Historical Society of Delaware Library
505 Market Street Mall
Wilmington, DE 19801
302/655-7161
Holds 50,000 volumes on Delaware history, business, industry, politics and diplomacy, law, religion, and genealogy, along with 150,000 photographs.

District of Columbia:

District of Columbia Public Library
Washingtoniana Division
Martin Luther King Memorial Library
901 G Street NW
Washington, DC 20001
202/727-1213
Covers history, current affairs, government, and
biography, including history of the District of Columbia from its founding to the present.

Florida:

**Florida State Division of Libraries and Information
Services**
Bureau of Archives and Records Management
Florida State Archives
R.A. Gray Building
500 South Bronough Street
904/487-2073
Holds both the Florida Photographic Collection
and the Florida Genealogy Collection. Contains
25,000 square feet of state archival materials.

State Library of Florida
R.A. Gray Building
Tallahassee, FL 32399-0250
904/487-2651
Houses 253,682 books on Floridian history and
social sciences. Holds state and federal documents.

University of Florida
P.K. Yonge Library of Florida History
404 Library West
Gainesville, FL 32611
904/392-0319
Covers Florida history and prehistory. Holds 25,000
volumes and collection of papers from Spanish
colonization.

University of South Florida Library
Special Collections Department
Tampa, FL 33620
813/974-2731
Covers Floridiana and 19th- and early 20th-century
children's literature. Includes collections of juvenile fiction, children's toys, photographs, and cigar-
box art.

Georgia:

Georgia Historical Society Library
501 Whitaker Street
Savannah, GA 31499
912/651-2128
Has collections of genealogical records and the
Central of Georgia Railroad collection. Holds 20,000
books, manuscripts, private papers, and naturalization and court records.

**Georgia State Department of Archives and His-
tory Reference Services**
330 Capitol Avenue SE
Atlanta, GA 30334
404/656-2358
Holds 17,000 books, along with other research
materials on Georgian and Southeastern U.S. history and genealogy.

University of Georgia
Hargrett Rare Book and Manuscript Library
University of Georgia Libraries
Athens, GA 30602
404/542-7123
Covers Georgiana, Civil War, small press and fine
printing, Southern culture, and American and En-

glish literature. Holds 100,000 rare books and 4 million papers.

Guam:

University of Guam
Micronesian Area Research Center
Pacific Collection
U.O.G. Station
Mangilao, GU 96923
671/734-2921
FAX: 671/734-3118
Holds works on Micronesia's history, languages, and role in World War II; also area anthropology and marine biology. Special collections include Spanish manuscripts, South Pacific Commission depository, Guam Constitutional Convention Papers, and A.B. Won Pat Papers. Includes 25,000 volumes, 15,000 photographs, and other supporting materials.

Hawaii:

Hawaii State Public Library System
Hawaii State Library
Hawaii and Pacific Section I
478 South King Street
Honolulu, HI 96813
808/548-2346
Holds the Hawaii and the Pacific Collection, State Documents Collection, Admiral Thomas Papers, and other research materials relating to Hawaii and the Pacific.

University of Hawaii
Special Collections—Hawaiian Collection
Hamilton Library
2550 The Mall
Honolulu, HI 96822
808/948-8264
Houses references on Hawaiian Islands history, Captain Cook, Hawaiian language, children's literature, and state and local government documents. Special collections include 19th-century Hawaiian manuscripts, rare books, and Hawaiiana. Holds 93,000 volumes and supporting materials.

Idaho:

Idaho State Historical Society Library and Archives
610 North Julia Davis Drive
Boise, ID 83702
208/334-3356
Covers state government, labor, law, genealogy,

and Pacific Northwest. Includes collections of manuscripts and archival material. Holds 5,000 books.

Idaho State Library
325 West State Street
Boise, ID 83702
208/334-2150
Holds 117,000 books on the Pacific Northwest and Idaho, library science, and public administration.

Illinois:

Chicago Historical Society Research Collections
Clark Street at North Avenue
Chicago, IL 60614
312/642-4600
Specializes in the history of Chicago, Illinois, the Civil War, and Abraham Lincoln. Holds 133,300 volumes, 501,000 architectural drawings, 1 million photographs, and 12,000 reels of news film, plus maps, atlases, posters, clippings, miscellanea, and manuscripts. Includes special collections of lake and river disasters, historic American city prints, the personal papers of Chicago residents and organizations, and photos from the morgues of Chicago newspapers 1900–65.

Illinois State Historical Library
Old State Capitol
Springfield, IL 62701
217/782-4836
Holds the Abraham Lincoln Collection and material on history of Illinois, Mormons, Lincoln, Native Americans, and genealogy. Holds 160,000 books and other research materials.

Illinois State Library
Centennial Building
Springfield, IL 62756
217/782-2994
Covers U.S. and Illinois history and government and business. Includes special collections of state and federal documents. Holds 4.5 million items.

Indiana:

Indiana Historical Society
William Henry Smith Memorial Library

315 West Ohio Street
Indianapolis, IN 46202-3299
317/232-1879
Holds collections on architectural history, railroads, Civil War, Old Northwest history, charitable organizations, and Jewish Welfare Federation manuscripts. Houses 28,000 books.

Indiana State Library
140 North Senate Avenue
Indianapolis, IN 46204
317/232-3675
Covers genealogy, history, and federal and state documents. Includes special collection of Braille and talking books. Holds 1.3 million items.

Indiana State Library
Indiana Division
140 North Senate Avenue
Indianapolis, IN 46204
317/232-3668
Covers state and local history, with books by Indiana authors and about Indiana. Holds 55,000 volumes, clippings, vertical file drawers, and 3.25 million manuscripts.

Iowa:

State Historical Society of Iowa Library/Archives
600 East Locust
Des Moines, IA 52240
515/281-5111
Devoted to the history of the region, its indigenous peoples, and its immigrants. Holds 130,000 books, vertical file drawers, pamphlets, and other supporting materials. Special collections include historical photographs and Iowa Industry house organs.

State Historical Society of Iowa Library
402 Iowa Avenue
Iowa City, IA 52240
319/335-3916
Holds 130,000 books on Iowa history, history of the frontier, agriculture, Native Americans of the area, and genealogy.

State Library of Iowa
East 12th and Grand
Des Moines, IA 50319
515/281-4118
Subjects include state government, law, medicine,

and library science. Holds 262,480 books, vertical file drawers, pamphlets, state and federal documents, and other research materials.

Kansas:

Kansas State Historical Society Library
Historical Research Center
120 West Tenth Street
Topeka, KS 66612
913/296-3251
Covers Kansas history, local history of other states, genealogy, Native Americans, and the West. Holds more than 129,000 volumes, plus other supporting materials.

Kansas State Library
Statehouse, 3rd Floor
Topeka, KS 66612
913/296-3296
Covers public administration, census, and Kansas government and legislation. Includes collections of federal and state documents.

University of Kansas
Kansas Collection
220 Spencer Research Library
Lawrence, KS 66045-2800
913/864-4274
Covers Kansas and Great Plains history and sociology and regional Afro-American history. Includes collections of diaries and photographs.

Kentucky:

Kentucky Historical Society
KHS Library
Old Capital Annex
300 West Broadway
Box H
Frankfort, KY 40602-2108
502/564-3016
Holds 60,000 books on Kentucky history and genealogy.

Kentucky State Department for Libraries and Archives
Public Records Division, Archives
300 Coffee Tree Road
Box 537
Frankfort, KY 40602
502/875-7000
Holds more than 1 million documents and micro-

forms relating to Kentucky history and genealogy, politics, and health services.

University of Kentucky
Margaret I. King Library
Special Collections and Archives
11 King Library North
Lexington, KY 40506-0039
606/257-8611
Covers Kentuckiana, Victorian and American literature, and Appalachia. Holds 120,972 volumes, documents, and other research materials.

Louisiana:

Louisiana State Library
Box 131
Baton Rouge, LA 70821
504/342-4923
Covers Louisiana genealogy and U.S. government documents and photographs.

Louisiana State Museum
Louisiana Historical Center
751 Chartres Street
New Orleans, LA 70116
504/568-8214
Covers New Orleans and Louisiana history. Includes judicial papers of both French and Spanish regimes.

Louisiana State Office of the Secretary of State
Division of Archives, Records Management and
History
Box 94125
Baton Rouge, LA 70804
504/922-1206
Holds Confederate government records, legal archives, and oral-history tape library. Houses 7,800 books.

Louisiana State University
Special Collections
Hill Memorial Library
Baton Rouge, LA 70803-3300
504/388-6551
Covers Southern history and politics, botany, slavery, Civil War, travel, and exploration. Holds 100,000 books and 5 million manuscript pieces.

Maine:

Maine Historical Society Library
485 Congress Street
Portland, ME 04101

207/774-1822
Covers Maine and New England history and genealogy. Holds 60,000 books.

Maine State Library
Cultural Building
State House Station 64
Augusta, ME 04333
207/289-5600
Covers Maine history, genealogy, and state, county, and local histories. Holds 400,000 books and supporting materials.

University of Maine, Orono
Raymond H. Fogler Library, Special Collections
Orono, ME 04469
207/581-1680
Holds 1.5 million documents relating to government, Canada, New Brunswick, agriculture and forestry, and maps and atlases.

Maryland:

Maryland Historical Society Library
201 West Monument Street
Baltimore, MD 21201
301/685-3750
Holds 80,000 books and 3 million manuscripts relating to Maryland and U.S. history.

Maryland State Law Library
361 Rowe Boulevard
Annapolis, MD 21401
301/974-3395
Covers Marylandia, genealogy, early English reports and statutes, and U.S. Supreme Court records and briefs.

University of Baltimore
Langsdale Library Special Collections Department
1420 Maryland Avenue
Baltimore, MD 21201
301/625-3135
Covers history and development of Baltimore, urban renewal, welfare, oral histories, documents of Baltimore organizations and associations, and business records. Special collections house corporate annual reports, WMAR-TV Newsfilm Collection, Steamship Historical Society of America Library, and state document depository.

Massachusetts:

Essex Institute
James Duncan Phillips Library

132-134 Essex Street
Salem, MA 01970
508/744-3390
Holds 400,000 books, bound periodical volumes, and other items relating to Massachusetts and New England regional history.

Massachusetts Historical Society Library
1154 Boylston Street
Boston, MA 02215
617/536-1608
Holds 250,000 books, diaries, maps, and prints relating to Massachusetts, New England, and U.S. history.

Massachusetts State Library
341 State House
Boston, MA 02133
617/727-2590
Covers public law, public affairs, government, politics, Massachusetts, and U.S. history. Includes collections of Massachusetts historical documents and prints, State House architectural plans, and city directories.

Michigan:

Michigan Bureau of History Archives
717 West Allegan
Lansing, MI 48918
517/373-1408
Official Michigan Archives. Holds 19,500 feet of state, local, and private records.

Michigan State University
University Archives and Historical Collections
East Lansing, MI 48824-1048
517/355-2330
Holds university archives; covers Michigan history and industry. Includes special collections of biblical and liturgical texts, 1470–1927, and industrial records.

University of Michigan
Michigan Historical Collections
Bentley Historical Library
1150 Beal
Ann Arbor, MI 48109-2113
313/764-3482
Covers history, religion, urban affairs, education, business, politics and government, and ethnic groups. Includes collections on temperance and prohibition in United States, Sino-American relations, and the Philippines.

Minnesota:

Minnesota Historical Society
Library Reference Services
690 Cedar Street
St. Paul, MN 55101
612/296-2143
Covers Minnesota, Upper Midwest, Scandinaviana, and ethnic groups in United States and Canada. Holds 500,000 monographs, government documents, vertical file drawers, 200,000 photographs, and other supporting materials.

Mississippi:

Mississippi State Department of Archives and History
Archives and Library Division
100 South State Street
Box 571
Jackson, MS 39205
601/359-1424
Covers Mississippiana, genealogy, and Confederate history. Holds 40,000 volumes, 200 manuscript collections, and other research materials.

Mississippi State University
Mitchell Memorial Library, Special Collections
Drawer 5408
Mississippi State, MS 39762
601/325-3060
Covers state, Southern, and local history and politics. Includes collections of private and public papers. Holds 21,614 books.

University of Southern Mississippi
McCain Library and Archives
Southern Station, Box 5148
Hattiesburg, MS 39406-5148
601/266-4345
Holds 65,000 books, as well as collections of children's literature, Confederate and Civil War history, Mississippiana, and genealogy.

Missouri:

Missouri Historical Society Research Library
Jefferson Memorial Building
Forest Park
St. Louis, MO 63112
312/361-1424
Holds 122,000 volumes and 2,500 maps concerning St. Louis, the Missouri, Western, and Mississippi rivers, the fur trade, and biography/genealogy.

Includes special collections on the Mississippi River, rare Western Americana, and music and theater.

Missouri State Library

Box 387
Jefferson City, MO 65102
314/751-3615
FAX 314/751-3612
Holds 94,194 volumes, 75,000 microforms, plus federal and state documents about state government, social services, taxation, and statistics.

State Historical Society of Missouri

1020 Lowry Street
Columbia, MO 65201
314/882-7083
Holds books by and about Missouri history and Missourians. Special collections include the J. Christian Bay Rare Book collection and the Alice Irene Fitzgerald Collection of Missouri's Literary Heritage for Children and Youth.

Montana:

Montana Historical Society Library/Archives

225 North Roberts
Helena, MT 59620
406/444-2681
Holds 35,000 volumes, 50,000 state publications, and 20,000 government documents, with photographs, plus private papers and microfilm of Montana newspapers. Subjects include the Lewis and Clark Expedition, George Armstrong Custer, Charles M. Russell, mining, cattle and range, homesteading, the Montana Indians, and Montana biography/genealogy. Includes special collections of photographs on Western cattle and range, the Northern Pacific Railroad, and Yellowstone National Park; the papers of T.C. Powers, Senator Lee Metcalf, and the Anaconda Copper Mining Company; and state government archives.

State Law Library of Montana

Justice Building
215 North Saunders
Helena, MT 59620-3004
406/444-3660
Holds 65,000 books on law.

University of Montana
Maureen and Mike Mansfield Library
K. Ross Toole Archives

Missoula, MT 59812
406/243-2053

Holds 1,000 oral histories, 30,000 photographs, and 8,000 feet of manuscripts about business history, forest industries, and Montana politics and government. Includes special collections on Senator Mike Mansfield, James W. Gerard, Chet Huntley, Dorothy M. Johnson, James E. Murray, and Joseph M. Dixon.

Nebraska:

Nebraska State Historical Society Library

1500 R Street
Box 82554
Lincoln, NE 68501
402/471-4751
Subjects include the history of Nebraska, the Great Plains, and the Great Plains Indians, and archaeology and genealogy. Holds 95,000 volumes, 150,000 photographs, maps, and atlases of Nebraska from 1854 to present, and Nebraska state government publications since 1905.

University of Nebraska, Lincoln
Center for Great Plains Studies

205 Love Library
Lincoln, NE 68588-0475
402/472-6220
Covers Midwestern history. Special collections include William Henry Jackson photographs and Patricia J. and Stanley H. Broder Collection of Indian Painting.

University of Nebraska, Lincoln
University Archives and Special Collections

308 Love Library
Lincoln, NE 68588-0410
402/472-2531
Subjects include Nebraska, World Wars I and II, and American folklore; houses the university archives. Special collections include Mari Sandoz Collection, Christlieb Collection of Western Americana, Latvian Collection, Mazour Collection of Russian History and Culture, and Czech Heritage Collection. Holds 44,000 volumes.

Nevada:

Nevada Historical Society

1650 North Virginia Street
Reno, NV 89503-1799
702/789-0190
Holdings include 15,000 volumes, 100,000 photographs, 20,000 maps, plus manscripts and microfilm,

about Nevada history, mining, Native Americans, and agriculture.

Nevada State Library and Archives
Capitol Complex
Carson City, NV 89710
702/885-5160
Covers Nevada history, public administration, and library science. Holds 60,650 volumes, 250,000 government publications, vertical file drawers of Nevada and local history materials, and microfilm of Nevada newspapers. Includes special collection of state, county, and municipal documents.

University of Nevada, Reno
Special Collections Department/University Archives
University Library
Reno, NV 89557-0044
702/784-6538
Special collections include Nevada Collection, Great Basin Anthropological Collection, Nevada fiction, Women in the West, University of Nevada, Reno Archives, Nevada Architectural Archives, and Virginia and Truckee Railroad Collection. Includes 43,000 volumes, 100,000 photographs, 1,500 maps, 15,000 architectural drawings, and other materials.

New Hampshire:

New Hampshire Historical Society Library
30 Park Street
Concord, NH 03301
603/225-3381
Holds 50,000 volumes, 20,000 photographs, plus early New Hampshire newspapers concerning New Hampshire history, New England history, genealogy, architecture, and decorative arts. Includes special collections of New Hampshire maps, 18th- and 19th-century account books and diaries, and papers of Daniel Webster, Franklin Pierce, General John Sullivan, William E. Chandler, and Josiah Bartlett.

New Hampshire State Library
20 Park Street
Concord, NH 03301-6303
603/271-2393
FAX 603/271-2205
Focuses on history, law, political science, and government documents. Holds 469,400 volumes, 16,011 manuscripts, and 195,500 microforms, plus scores, sound recordings, and motion pictures.

Includes special collections on New Hampshire history and genealogy.

University of New Hampshire
Special Collections
Diamond Library
Durham, NH 03824
603/862-2714
FAX 603/862-2714
Holds 45,000 volumes, plus manuscripts, about New Hampshire. Includes special collections of University dissertations, Robert Frost, angling, Early New Hampshire Imprints, and historical juvenile books.

New Jersey:

New Jersey Historical Society Library
230 Broadway
Newark, NJ 07104
201/483-3939
Holds 68,000 volumes, plus manuscripts, about New Jersey history and genealogy and neighboring states.

New Jersey State Library
185 West State Street
Trenton, NJ 08625-1520
609/292-6220
Houses 750,000 volumes on law, New Jersey history and newspapers, political science, public administration, and genealogy. Includes special collections of New Jerseyana, manuscripts, and U.S. Government documents. Is a library for the blind and handicapped and a Foundation Center depository.

New Mexico:

New Mexico State Records Center and Archives
404 Montezuma Street
Santa Fe, NM 87503
505/827-8860
Holds 4,300 volumes on the history of New Mexico and the Southwest. Includes special collections of Spanish, Mexican, Territorial, and Statehood Archives pertaining to New Mexico.

New Mexico State University Library
Rio Grande Historical Collection
Box 30006
Las Cruces, NM 88003-0006
505/646-4727
Covers history of New Mexico from 1800 and

New Mexico State University. Collections made up of organizational records, papers of individuals and families, audiovisual programs, and programs on education, farming and ranching, business, water resources management, mining, politics, culture, and pioneer life.

University of New Mexico
Special Collections Department
General Library
Albuquerque, NM 87131
505/277-6451
Holds 36,700 volumes, 17,000 photographs, plus manuscripts, audio tapes, and videotapes on Native Americans and architecture of the Southwest and the history of New Mexico, Mexico, Latin America, and the American West. Includes special collection of oral history tapes.

New York:

New-York Historical Society Library
170 Central Park West
New York, NY 10024
212/873-3400
Covers history of New York State, New York City, and the Civil War, and naval history to 1898, as well as genealogy, art and museum reference, and American painting and decorative arts. Holds 635,000 volumes, 2 million manuscripts, 175,000 pamphlets and broadsides, 1 million prints and photographs, and 30,000 maps. Includes special collections of 18th-century newspapers and printed ephemera.

New York State Historical Association Library
Lake Road
Box 800
Cooperstown, NY 13326
607/547-2509
Holds 70,000 volumes, plus manuscripts, on central New York genealogy and New York State history, American social history and art, and agricultural history. Includes special collection of James Fenimore Cooper first editions and folklife archives.

New York State Library
Manuscripts and Special Collections
Cultural Education Center
Empire State Plaza
Albany, NY 12230
518/474-4461
Covers American, state, and local history, cartog-

raphy, and historic iconography. Holds 5,400 volumes; 35,000 prints, pictures, and glass negatives; 176,300 maps and atlases; and 25,000 pieces of sheet music, plus posters and broadsides. Includes special collections of historic manuscripts (11 million) and rare books.

North Carolina:

North Carolina State Department of Cultural Resources
Division of the State Library
109 East Jones Street
Raleigh, NC 27611
919/733-2570
FAX 919/733-5679
Covers public policy, Southern history, library science, and general nonfiction. Holds 200,000 volumes, 600,000 state and federal documents, 166,000 talking books, and 38,950 microforms, plus 16mm films and videotapes. Includes special collections of books for the blind, North Carolina state documents, and genealogy.

University of North Carolina, Chapel Hill
North Carolina Collection
CB 3930 Wilson Library
Chapel Hill, NC 27599-3930
919/962-1172
Specializes in North Caroliniana and books by and about North Carolinians. Holds 179,242 volumes, 12,667 manuscripts, 200,000 pictures, and 175,000 mounted clippings, plus maps, broadsides, and microfilm. Includes special collections on Sir Walter Raleigh, Thomas Wolfe, and fine and rare North Caroliniana.

North Dakota:

North Dakota State Library
Liberty Memorial Building
Capitol Grounds
Bismarck, ND 58505
701/224-2492
Holds 110,000 volumes, 20,000 audio tapes, and state documents since 1904. Topics include North Dakota, state government, music, education, and library science.

State Historical Society of North Dakota
State Archives and Historical Research Library
Heritage Center
Bismarck, ND 58505
701/224-2668

Covers the history and social sciences of the region, including ethnohistory, and historic preservation. Holds 92,000 volumes, plus other documents, manuscripts, and supporting materials.

University of North Dakota
Elwyn B. Robinson Department of Special Collections
Chester Fritz Library
Grand Forks, ND 58202
701/777-4625
Holds 11,000 volumes and 6,700 linear feet of manuscripts about oral history, genealogy, agrarian radicalism, the Nonpartisan League (North Dakota), and history of North and South Dakota, the Northern Great Plains, the Plains Indians, women, and the environment.

Ohio:

State Library of Ohio
65 South Front Street
Columbus, OH 43266-0334
614/644-7061
Covers management, social sciences, education, public administration, Ohio history, and genealogy. Holds 569,706 books and 1.2 million state and federal documents.

Oklahoma:

Oklahoma Historical Society
Archives and Manuscript Division
Historical Building
Oklahoma City, OK 73105
405/521-2491
Holds 29,900 reels of microfilm, 27,000 photographs, and 4,500 oral history tapes about Oklahoma and Indian territories, pioneer life, missionaries, territorial court records, explorers, and Native American tribes of Oklahoma.

Oklahoma Historical Society
Division of Library Resources
Wiley Post Historical Building
Oklahoma City, OK 73105
405/521-2491
Holds 55,000 volumes on Oklahoma and Native American history, genealogy, and the American West. Also has both the U.S. Census (1790–1910) and Oklahoma newspapers since 1893 on microfilm.

Oklahoma State Department of Libraries
200 NE Eighteenth Street

Oklahoma City, OK 73105
405/521-2502
FAX 405/525-7804
Houses 299,184 volumes; 704,484 microforms; 37,733 cubic feet of state records, archives, and manuscripts; plus films, U.S. Government documents, pamphlets, and clippings about law, Oklahoma government, and history.

University of Oklahoma
Western History Collections
630 Parrington Oval, Room 452
Norman, OK 73019
405/325-3641
Holds 50,000 volumes, 250,000 photographs and prints, 20,000 microforms, and 8,000 linear feet of manuscripts, plus maps, oral history tapes, pamphlets, documents, posters, and newspapers, about the American Southwest, Native Americans, and Oklahoma.

Oregon:

Oregon Historical Society Library
1230 SW Park Avenue
Portland, OR 97205
503/222-1741
Subjects include history of Oregon; history, social, political, and economic growth of the Pacific Northwest; explorations and voyages of the Northwest; and cartography. Holds 100,000 volumes, 17 million manuscripts, 1.5 million photographs, and 16,000 reels of microfilm, plus 15,000 maps and 10,000 reels of TV film. Includes special collections on the Oregon Provisional Government, Oregon imprints by Belknap, and Russian-American studies.

Oregon State Library
State Library Building
Summer and Court Streets
Salem, OR 97310
503/378-4274
FAX 503/378-4498
Houses 1.1 million books and government documents, 18,636 maps, plus videotapes, clippings, and pamphlets, concerning the history, government, and business of Oregon, as well as the social sciences, humanities, sciences, and librarianship. Includes special collection of Oregoniana; also has materials for the blind and handicapped, and is a Patent Depository Library.

University of Oregon
Special Collections Department
University Library
Eugene, OR 97403
503/686-3068
FAX: 503/686-3094

Covers political, social, and economic history of Oregon and the Pacific Northwest in the 19th and 20th centuries. Includes special collections of Pacific Northwest authors, politicians, architects, and business figures; photographs of Pacific Northwest, Alaska, and Far East; and rare books. Holds 70,000 volumes and 20 million manuscripts.

Pennsylvania:

Historical Society of Pennsylvania Library
1400 Locust Street
Philadelphia, PA 19107
215/732-6201
FAX 215/732-2680

Holds 564,000 volumes, 14 million manuscripts, and 29,000 microforms, plus maps, prints, drawings and paintings, newspapers, and ephemera on U.S. and Pennsylvania history from 1783–1865; also genealogy and Afro-Americana.

Pennsylvania State Department of Education
State Library of Pennsylvania
Box 1601
Harrisburg, PA 17105
717/787-2646
FAX 717/783-2070

Houses 972,221 volumes on government, law, education, public welfare and administration, genealogy, and Pennsylvania history and biography. Includes special collections on Americana, Pennsylvania Imprints, and the Colonial Assembly.

Pennsylvania State Historical and Museum Commission Library
Box 1026
Harrisburg, PA 17108
717/783-9898

Holds 17,500 volumes on Pennsylvania history and museum technology.

Rhode Island:

Rhode Island Historical Society Library
121 Hope Street
Providence, RI 02906
401/331-8575

Holds 150,000 volumes, plus manuscripts, about Rhode Island and local history and New England genealogy. Includes special collections of film, newspapers, and imprints relating to Rhode Island, and business history.

South Carolina:

South Carolina Historical Society Library
Fireproof Building
10 D Meeting Street
Charleston, SC 29401
803/723-3225

Holds 30,000 volumes, 9,000 pamphlets, 2,000 architectural drawings and 2,000 photographs, plus manuscripts and ephemera about architecture, slavery, literature, politics, genealogy, and South Carolina history.

South Carolina State Department of Archives and History
Archives Search Room
Capitol Station, Box 11669
Columbia, SC 29211
803/734-8577

Holds 2,250 volumes on all aspects of South Carolina's history. Includes special collections of non-current public records of the state, Revolutionary War accounts, Confederate service records, and executive, legislative, judicial, and probate records of the colony.

University of South Carolina
South Caroliniana Library
Columbia, SC 29208
803/777-3131

All about South Caroliniana. Holds 84,230 books, 2.1 million manuscripts, and 14,000 pictures on the subject, plus maps, sheet music, and an extensive collection of South Carolina newspapers.

South Dakota:

South Dakota State Historical Society
Office of History
South Dakota State Archives
900 Governors Drive
Pierre, SD 57501
605/773-3458

Holds 26,000 volumes and 4,000 maps, plus records and photographs about South Dakota history, culture, and government and the Great Plains.

South Dakota State Library
800 Governors Drive

Pierre, SD 57501-2294
605/773-3131
Houses 149,949 volumes, 396,343 microforms, and 30,000 talking book titles, plus pictures, maps, films, filmstrips, and videotapes. Includes special collections of large-print books and South Dakota documents, and on South Dakota in general.

Tennessee:

Tennessee State Department of State
Tennessee State Library and Archives
403 Seventh Avenue North, Main Floor
Nashville, TN 37219
615/741-7996
Holds 400,800 volumes, 3 million manuscripts, 40,000 photographs, and 27,500 audio tapes on Tennesseana, U.S. and local history, state and local government, law, and genealogy. Includes special collections of the papers of Andrew Jackson and Richard Ewell, land records (1777–1903), state agencies and legislative records and governors' papers since 1796, state Supreme Court records (1815-1955), prints and cartoons of Tennessee subjects, and Tennessee newspapers.

Texas:

Daughters of the Republic of Texas Library
Box 1401
San Antonio, TX 78295-1401
512/225-1071 or 512/225-8155
Holds 13,000 volumes, 10,000 manuscripts, 10,000 photographs, and archival materials, plus maps and clippings on Texas history, the Alamo, San Antonio, and the Republic of Texas. Includes special collections on Theodore Gentilz, Spanish Kings and Viceroys, and the Grandjean Photograph Collection.

Texas State Library
Information Services Division
Box 12927
Austin, TX 78711
512/463-5455
Houses U.S. and Texas documents, genealogy, Texas history, biography, and folklore. Holds 106,500 volumes and 1.1 million federal and state government documents. A clearinghouse for state publications and documents and a regional depository for U.S. government publications.

Texas State Library
State Archives Division

1201 Brazos
Box 12927
Austin, TX 78711
512/463-5480
Holds 38,000 volumes, 6,000 maps, 70,000 photographs, and 2,350 historical manuscript collections on Texas history. Also holds the archives of both the Republic and the State of Texas.

Texas Tech University
Southwest Collection
Box 4090
Lubbock, TX 79409
806/742-3749
Holds 40,000 volumes, 17 million leaves of business and personal documents, 300,000 photographs, and 1,200 reels of movie film. Subjects include social, economic, and religious affairs of West Texas, literature, and the "man-land confrontation in the arid and semi-arid Southwest, including the struggle of the pioneer settlers, especially women; cattle industry; land colonization; mining; mechanized agriculture and the water problem."

University of Houston Libraries
Special Collections
Houston, TX 77204-2091
713/749-2726
Holds 52,000 volumes on Texas history; Houston, British, and American writers; and Latin drama. Includes special collections of Texana, manuscripts of Larry McMurtry and Aldous Huxley, and historical railroad and Western hemisphere maps.

University of Texas, Austin
Barker Texas History Center
General Libraries, SRH 2.109
Austin, TX 78713-7330
512/471-5961
Covers Texas history, literature, and folklore and Texas state documents. Holds 142,025 volumes, 29,579 maps, 518,000 photographs, and 25,500 linear feet of records, plus historic Texas and Southwest newspapers, slides, clippings, and oral history tapes. Includes special collections of sound recordings, dime novels, the frontier, and the papers of prominent Texans.

Utah:

University of Utah
Special Collections Department

Marriott Library
Salt Lake City, UT 84112
801/581-8863
Subjects include Utah, the Mountain West, Mormons, and Native Americans. Holds 83,000 books, pamphlets, federal documents, archival records, and other support materials.

Utah State Historical Society Library
300 Rio Grande
Salt Lake City, UT 84101
801/533-5808
Holds 73,000 volumes, 300,000 photographs, and 30,000 maps, plus pamphlets, oral history tapes, manuscripts, and clippings about Utah, Mormon, Western, and Native American history. Includes special collections of Utah water records and Works Progress Administration (WPA) records.

Utah State Library
2150 South 300 West, Suite 16
Salt Lake City, UT 84115
801/466-5888
Devoted to state and federal government. Holds 36,284 volumes and 73,468 federal and state documents.

Vermont:

University of Vermont
Department of Special Collections
Bailey/Howe Library
Burlington, VT 05405
802/656-2595
Subjects include Vermontiana; history of books, printing, and photography; and illustrated editions of Ovid. Holds 85,900 volumes, 225,000 photographs, and 7,500 maps, plus manuscripts and census reports (1810–80, 1900). Includes special collections of papers and manuscripts of several Vermont public figures and companies.

Vermont Historical Society Library
Pavilion Office Building
109 State Street
Montpelier, VT 05602
802/828-2291
Holds 40,000 volumes, 30,000 photographs, and 1,000 maps, plus pamphlets, broadsides, and manuscripts about Vermont and New England state and local history, Vermontiana, and genealogy. Includes special collection of Vermont imprints.

Vermont State Department of Libraries
Pavillion Office Building
109 State Street
Montpelier, VT 05602
802/828-3261
FAX 802/828-2199
Holds 595,033 volumes, plus films, records, tapes, and state and federal documents, about law, Vermontiana, and general subjects.

Virginia:

Virginia Historical Society Library
428 North Boulevard
Richmond, VA 23221
804/358-4901
Houses Virginiana and 16th–19th-century Americana. Holds 265,000 volumes and 7 million manuscripts, plus prints, engravings, maps, newspapers, paintings, and sheet music. Includes special collections of Confederate imprints and 17th- and 18th-century English architecture.

Virginia State Library and Archives
11th Street at Capitol Square
Richmond, VA 23219
804/786-8929
Holds 628,600 volumes, 86,115 maps, 30.3 million manuscripts, and 222,900 reels of microfilm about Virginiana, Southern and Confederate history, U.S. colonial history, genealogy, and the social sciences. Includes special collections of Virginia newspapers, public records and maps, and Confederate imprints.

Virgin Islands:

Virgin Islands Department of Planning and Natural Resources
Division of Libraries, Archives and Museums
23 Dronningens Gade
Charlotte Amalie
St. Thomas, VI 00802
809/774-3407
General and reference library. Holds 119,000 books; manuscripts; clippings; archives; U.N., U.S., and Virgin Islands government documents; and ephemera. Includes special collections on the Caribbean, West Indies, and Virgin Islands and newspapers, 1770 to present.

Washington:

State Capital Historical Association Library and Photo Archives

211 West Twenty-first Avenue
Olympia, WA 98501
206/753-2580
Holds 3,000 historic photographs on such sub-
jects as pioneering, state government, Native
American art, Victoriana, and state history.

Washington State Historical Society Library
315 North Stadium Way
Tacoma, WA 98403
206/593-2830
Holds 15,000 volumes, 200,000 photographs, 4,000
manuscripts, and 3,000 pamphlets about Washington State and Pacific Northwest history. Includes special collection of photographic negatives.

Washington State Library
State Library Building, AJ-11
Olympia, WA 98504-0111
206/753-5592
FAX 206/753-3546
Subjects include public administration, applied and
behavioral sciences, public health, transportation,
ecology, and energy. Holds 451,511 volumes, 1.3
million U.S. and state documents, and 436,111
microforms, plus clippings and audiovisual programs. Includes special collections on Pacific Northwest history and Washington authors.

West Virginia:

**West Virginia State Department of Culture and
History**
Archives and History Library
Cultural Center, Capitol Complex
Charleston, WV 25305
304/348-0230
Covers West Virginia, U.S., Civil War, colonial,
and military history and genealogy. Holds 80,200
volumes, 30,000 photographs, and 25,000 microforms, plus newsfilm and videotape from West
Virginia TV stations (1955–82). Includes special
collections of governors' papers, manuscripts,
agency records, state documents, county court
records, newspapers, and military and land records.

West Virginia University
West Virginia and Regional History Collections
University Library
Colson Hall
Morgantown, WV 26506
304/293-3536
Covers Appalachian, regional, state, and local his-

tory, literature, and genealogy. Holds 27,000 volumes, 100,000 photographs, and 1,200 newspapers,
plus manuscripts, archives, oral histories, and folk
music.

Wisconsin:

State Historical Society of Wisconsin
Archives Division
816 State Street
Madison, WI 53706
608/262-3338
Subjects include Wisconsin history, labor and industrial relations, socialism, civil rights, and contemporary social action movements. Holds 82,813
cubic feet of both public and nongovernmental
records, 17,000 maps and atlases, 6,600 sound
recordings, and 1.5 million iconographic items.
Includes special collections of Nazi papers and
World War II memorabilia, the frontier, agriculture and agricultural manufacturing, mass communications history, film and theater research,
and Jewish archives.

State Historical Society of Wisconsin Library
816 State Street
Madison, WI 53706-1482
608/262-3421
Subjects include history of the region; Canadian,
local, labor, and women's history; ethnohistory;
and genealogy. Holds 2.2 million items.

Wisconsin State Legislative Reference Bureau
Reference and Library Section
State Capitol, Room 201 North
Madison, WI 53702
608/266-0341
Holds 100,000 volumes, plus many unbound or
microfilmed clippings, on all aspects of state and
local government, regulation, law, and jurisprudence. Includes special collections of state laws,
statutes, legislative journals, and Supreme Court
reports (1848—), Opinions of the Attorney General (1904—), Blue Books (1858—), departmental
reports archives, and legislative bill drafting records (1927—).

Wyoming:

**Wyoming State Archives, Museums and Histori-
cal Department**
Barrett Building
Cheyenne, WY 82002-0130
307/777-7519 or 307/777-7014

Covers Wyoming and Western history, ethnology, and archaeology. Holds 6,500 volumes, plus Wyoming newspapers from 1867 to the present, National Archives materials, manuscripts, maps, documents, letters, ledgers, diaries, census records, oral histories, folklore, and territorial and state government records.

Wyoming State Library
Supreme Court and State Library Building
Cheyenne, WY 82002
307/777-7281
FAX 307/777-6289
Subjects include Wyoming, Western Americana, Native Americans, cookbooks, and art and architecture. Holds 152,264 volumes, plus U.S. Government and Wyoming publications. Includes special collection of large-print books.

STATISTICS

Harvard University
Statistics Library
Science Center, 6th floor
1 Oxford Street
Cambridge, MA 02138
617/495-5496
Devoted entirely to statistics and applied statistics.

SUBSTANCE ABUSE

American Health Foundation
Naylor Dana Institute for Disease Prevention Library
Dana Road
Valhalla, NY 10595
914/592-2600
FAX: 914/592-6317
Special collection of research on smoking and health.

National Clearinghouse for Alcohol and Drug Information Library
Box 2345
Rockville, MD 20852
301/468-2600
Emphasis is on prevention of abuse. Houses books, abstracts, and other media. Branch of U.S. Public Health Service.

National Institute on Drug Abuse
Addiction Research Center Library
Box 5180

Baltimore, MD 21224
301/955-7502
Collection emphasizes science and includes works on pharmacology, psychology, and biochemistry. Branch of U.S. Public Health Service.

National Woman's Christian Temperance Union
Frances E. Willard Memorial Library
1730 Chicago Avenue
Evanston, IL 60201
312/864-1396
Houses works on history of temperance movement and prohibition, biographies of temperance workers, and material on drug education and the women's movement. Also houses collection on Frances Willard.

U.S. Centers for Disease Control
Office on Smoking and Health Technical Information Center
Park Building, Room 1-16
5600 Fishers Lane
Rockville, MD 20857
301/443-1690
Holds books, journals, and technical reports on smoking and health, behavior and addiction, clinical tests on tobacco and nicotine, and methods of breaking smoking habit. Publishes several bulletins.

SURGERY

American College of Surgeons Library
35 East Erie Street
Chicago, IL 60611
312/664-4050
Holds 25,000 books and other supporting materials on surgery, and material on the history of medicine and related subjects.

SWIMMING

International Swimming Hall of Fame Museum and Library
One Hall of Fame Drive
Fort Lauderdale, FL 33316
305/462-6536
Holds special collection of swimming memorabilia and 5,200 books relating to swimming history, instruction, sports medicine and psychology, diving, and water polo.

T

TECHNOLOGY. *See also* COMPUTERS; ELECTRONICS.

Chicago Public Library Central Library
Business/Science/Technology Division
400 North Franklin Street
Chicago, IL 60611
312/269-2814 or 312/269-2865
Covers all business topics, including marketing, small business, investments, and personnel, as well as related scientific topics: technology, patents, medicine, physics and biology, and computer science. Has more than 60,000 volumes and SEC reports and 50 drawers of corporate annual reports. Includes special collections of complete U.S. and British patents, gazettes, domestic and foreign auto manuals, career information, electrical and computer schematics, and industrial, corporate, and product directories.

Harvard University
Division of Applied Sciences
Gordon McKay Library
Pierce Hall
29 Oxford Street
Cambridge, MA 02138
617/495-2836
Holds nearly 100,000 volumes on applied mathematics and computer science, electronics, and mechanics, plus almost 200,000 technical reports on microforms.

Library of Congress
Science and Technology Division
John Adams Building, Room 5104
101 Independence Avenue SE
Washington, DC 20540
202/707-5639
Oversees all science and technology collections, which total 3.5 million volumes and 3.7 million technical reports, including those of NASA, the Department of Defense and its contractors, the International Science Organization, and others.

Massachusetts Institute of Technology
Lincoln Laboratory Library
244 Wood Street
Box 73
Lexington, MA 02173-0073
617/981-7171 or 617/981-2300
FAX: 617 981-0427
Covers electronics, electrical engineering, computer science, physics, mathematics, and space science. Holds 108,000 volumes, 400,000 technical reports, 3,000 maps, and 1 million other cataloged items.

New York Public Library
Science and Technology Research Center
Fifth Avenue and Forty-second Street, Room 121
New York, NY 10018
212/930-0574
FAX: 212/869-7824
Covers all science and applied science subjects, including automobiles, communications, mathematics and computers, earth sciences, engineering, meteorology, mining, navigation, materials science, radio, railroads, and history of science and technology. Holds 1.2 million volumes; also has technical reports.

U.S. Office of Technology Assessment Information Center
Congress of the United States
Washington, DC 20510
202/228-6150
FAX/: 202/228-6098
Holds references dealing with future of science and technology, and assessment of present technologies. Publishes biweekly newsletter. Operated under auspices of the U.S. Senate.

TELECOMMUNICATIONS

AT&T Bell Laboratories
Libraries and Information Systems Center
600 Mountain Avenue
Murray Hill, NJ 07974
201/582-2854
FAX: 201/582-3146
Covers computerized systems, cataloging, and related subjects.

Federal Communications Commission Library
1919 M Street NW
Washington, DC 20554
202/632-7100
Holds the legislative histories of Communications Act of 1934 and allied statutes and covers congressional hearings in telecommunications. Houses 45,000 books.

TEXTILES. *See* CLOTHING AND TEXTILES.

THEATER. *See also* PERFORMING ARTS.

American Academy of Dramatic Arts Library
120 Madison Avenue
New York, NY 10016
212/686-9244
Holds 7,000 books, audiotapes, and cassettes.

Chicago Public Library Cultural Center
Visual and Performing Arts/Art Information Center
78 East Washington Street
Chicago, IL 60602
312/269-2858
FAX: 312/368-0918
Houses picture collection, folk dance collection, 85,000 books, and other supporting materials.

International Theatre Institute of the United States, Inc.
International Theatre Collection
220 West Forty-second Street, Suite 1710
New York, NY 10036-7202
212/944-1490
Holds 11,000 plays, yearbooks, playbills, and other memorabilia. Includes 5,700 books relating to contempory international theater.

Princeton University
William Seymour Theatre Collection
Firestone Library
Princeton, NJ 08544
609/452-3223
Covers performing arts: theater, musical theater, popular music, dance, circus, and film. Houses 14,000 books plus thousands of programs, pictures, pamphlets, and other materials. Includes special collections of the papers of Sarah Enright and Woody Allen.

Shubert Archive
Lyceum Theatre
149 West Forty-fifth Street
New York, NY 10036
212/944-3895, 212/944-4156
Business and artistic records in the Archive cover every aspect of the Shubert theatrical organization's productions and operations from the 1890s through the 1930s. Includes correspondence, business papers, photographs, paintings, and memorabilia.

University of Texas, Austin
Humanities Research Center
Theater Arts Collections
Box 7219
Austin, TX 78713
512/471-9122
Holds 15,000 books, in addition to special collections of manuscripts, playbills, photographs, recordings, letters, and other memorabilia.

University of Washington
Drama Library
145 Hutchinson Hall DX-20
Seattle, WA 98195
206/543-5148
Holds more than 20,000 volumes on all aspects of dramatic theory, history, and practice.

Yale University
Collection of the Literature of the American Musical Theatre
Sterling Memorial Library
Box 1603A Yale Station
New Haven, CT 06520
203/432-1795
Holds books, theater programs, clippings, phonograph records, sheet music, and scores relating to musical shows produced on Broadway for profit. Includes special collection of manuscripts of Cole Porter and E.Y. Harburg.

Yale University
School of Drama Library
222 York Street
Yale Station Box 1903A
New Haven, CT 06520
203/432-1554
Houses plays by American, British, and international playwrights; criticism; theater history; and materials on costume, set design, lighting, acting, directing, and related subjects. Holdings include more than 25,000 volumes and other materials.

TOBACCO

American Tobacco Company
Department of Research and Development Library
Box 899
Hopewell, VA 23860
804/51-7517
Holds over 10,000 books, pamphlets, and patents relating the tobacco industry, mathematics, plant physiology, ecology, and quality control.

New York Public Library
Arents Tobacco Collection
Fifth Avenue and Forty-second Street, Room 324
New York, NY 10018
212/930-0801
Has holdings on tobacco, herbals, history, law, and medicine. Special collections contain English and American drama, poetry, and prose that mention tobacco, as well as tobacco ephemera, manuscripts, and first editions.

Philip Morris, U.S.A.
Research Center Library
Box 26583
Richmond, VA 23261
804/274-2877
Holds 40,000 volumes, 11,500 microforms, 250 audio-visual programs, and 21 vertical file drawers of clippings on tobacco, biochemistry, and plant physiology.

TRANSPORTATION

Association of American Railroads Library
50 F Street NW, Room 5800
Washington, DC 20001
202/639-2334
FAX: 202/639-5546
Holds 19,000 volumes, collections of railroad statistics, and memorabilia.

California State Department of Transportation
Transportation Library
1120 N Street, Room 1315
Box 1438
Sacramento, CA 95807
916/445-5830
FAX: 916/324-6016
Holds materials on public transportation, highway and bridge design, and related studies. Contains departmental archives.

California State Railroad Museum Library
111 I Street
Sacramento, CA 95814
916/323-8073
Concentrates on history of the Western railroads. Special collections include corporate records of many of the Western railroads. Also holds large photograph collection.

Federal Maritime Commission Library
1100 L Street NW
Washington, DC 20573
202/523-5762
Subjects include maritime law, economics, and marine transportation. Has holdings of more than 11,000 books, in addition to documents, congressional hearing reports, and legislative histories.

Interstate Commerce Commission Library
Twelfth and Constitution Avenue NW, Room 3392
Washington, DC 20423
202/275-7328
Subjects include U.S. transportation law and regulations, economics, administrative law, account-

ing, and statistics. Houses 94,000 books, plus other research documents.

National Railway Historical Society
Library of American Transportation
Box 58153
Philadelphia, PA 19102
215/557-6606
Houses collection of materials on railroads, trolleys, and other transportation. Has negatives of American Locomotive Works. Holds 20,000 photographs.

National Research Council
Highway Research Information Service
Transportation Research Board
2101 Constitution Avenue NW
Washington, DC 20418
202/334-3250
Main holdings are abstracts of technical literature and outlines of current research topics in highway transport, design, construction, and maintenance.

Transportation Museum Association
Transportation Reference Library
3015 Barrett Station Road
St. Louis, MO 63122
314/965-6885
Houses assemblage of a wide variety of books, pamphlets, blueprints, and phonograph records having to do with transportation and communication.

University of California, Berkeley
Institute of Transportation Studies Library
412 McLaughlin Hall
Berkeley, CA 94720
415/642-3604
Holds 126,000 volumes, maps, visual aids, and microfiche on transportation.

University of Michigan
Transportation Research Institute Library
2901 Baxter Road
Ann Arbor, MI 48109-2150
313/764-2171
FAX: 313/936-1081
Houses documents and periodicals on highway safety, accident investigation, and related subjects, as well as shipbuilding and the auto industry.

U.S. Department of Transportation
Library and Distribution Services Division

400 Seventh Street SW
Washington, DC 20590
202/366-0746
Holdings represent all kinds of transportation, especially aviation. Also covers urban mass transit, law, and related subjects. Special collections own thousands of aviation reports and technical publications. Also contains Coast Guard law collection.

TRUMAN, HARRY S. *See* PRESIDENTIAL LIBRARIES.

TYPOGRAPHY

Yale University
Arts of the Book Collection
Sterling Memorial Library
New Haven, CT 06520
203/432-1712
Covers typography, book illustration and design, calligraphy, bookbinding, bookplates, private presses, and fine printing. Holds 14,000 books, 10,000 prints, 1 million bookplates, type specimens, and masters' theses from Yale School of Graphic Design. Includes special collections of caricature, Western Americana prints, engravings of Vienna, historic printing material, and engraved woodblocks, and special archives of Fritz Kredel, Fritz Eichenberg, and Carl P. Rollins.

U

URBAN PLANNING. *See* REGIONAL AND URBAN PLANNING.

U.S.S.R. *See* SOVIET UNION.

V

VETERANS AFFAIRS

American Legion
National Headquarters Library
700 North Pennsylvania Street
Box 1055
Indianapolis, IN 46206
317/635-8411
Covers veterans' affairs, children and youth, national defense, patriotism, and American Legion. Holds 8,500 volumes, 300 periodicals, and 1,140 vertical file drawers of pamphlets, reports, manuscripts, and correspondence. Includes special collection of American Legion national, state, and local archives.

U.S. Department of Veterans Affairs
Central Office Library (143B4)
810 Vermont Avenue NW
Washington, DC 20420
202/535-7337
FAX: 202/535-7539
Holds information of significance to veterans—particularly health care and medicine. System is composed of many smaller libraries, computer linked, throughout the United States. In addition to 700,000 books, system has audiovisual materials, government documents, and Veterans Administration archives. Contact office above for information on the nearest local VA library.

VETERINARY MEDICINE

American Veterinary Medical Association
930 North Meacham Road
Schaumburg, IL 60196
312/605-8070
Holds 5,000 books on veterinary medicine.

Cornell University
Flower Veterinary Library
Schurman Hall
Ithaca, NY 14853-6401
607/253-3510
Holds 78,000 volumes devoted to veterinary medicine and related biomedical subjects.

University of Alaska, Fairbanks
Bio-Medical Library
Fairbanks, AK 99775-0300
907/474-7442
Covers health sciences, veterinary medicine, fish biology, microbiology, and ocean sciences, among other works. Includes Institute of Marine Science Library holdings.

University of Georgia
Science Library
Athens, GA 30602
404/542-4535
Holds 700,000 volumes on science and technology, agriculture, medicine, veterinary medicine, and economics.

University of Massachusetts, Amherst
Morrill Biological and Geological Sciences Library
214 Morrill Science Center
Amherst, MA 01003
413/545-2674
Covers biology and biochemistry, botany, ento-

mology, environmental sciences, forestry, geography and geology, earth sciences, public health, veterinary sciences, and zoology. Holds 100,000 volumes and 125,000 maps and other materials. Includes special collection on ornithology.

University of Pennsylvania
School of Veterinary Medicine
C.J. Marshall Memorial Library
3800 Spruce Street
Philadelphia, PA 19104-6008
215/898-8874
Covers veterinary and comparative medicine and animal husbandry. Holds 28,627 books, along with other support materials. Figures include holdings at the New Bolton Center Library.

W

WEATHER. *See* METEOROLOGY.

WELFARE

American Public Welfare Association Resource Center
1125 Fifteenth Street NW, Suite 300
Washington, DC 20005
202/293-7550
Subjects include public and child welfare, public health, immigration, and homelessness. Holds the U.S. Department of Health and Human Services grant appeal decisions, the Association archives, and the history of welfare reform.

THE WEST. *See* AMERICAN WEST.

WOMEN

American Association of University Women
Education Foundation Library and Archives
2401 Virginia Avenue NW
Washington, DC 20037
202/785-7763
FAX: 202/785-7797
Subjects include education and higher education, status of women, and women's accomplishments. Holds 4,500 books and association publications and archival records.

Radcliffe College
Arthur and Elizabeth Schlesinger Library on the History of Women in America
10 Garden Street
Cambridge, MA 02138

617/495-8647
Founded in 1943; covers the history of American women in all phases of public and private life. Has 30,000 volumes, 3,000 bound periodical volumes, and a picture collection of 55,000 items. Special collections devoted to Harriet Beecher Stowe, Emma Goldman, Jeannette Rankin, the National Organization for Women, and many others.

Smith College
Sophia Smith Collection
Women's History Archive
Northampton, MA 01063
413/585-2970
Covers American women's history, 1820 to present, with attention to birth control, social welfare, professions, rights, families, and international affairs. Special collections include papers of Margaret Sanger, Planned Parenthood, and others.

WOOL. *See* CLOTHING AND TEXTILES.

WRESTLING. *See also* SPORTS.

National Wrestling Hall of Fame Library
405 West Hall of Fame Avenue
Stillwater, OK 74075
405/377-5243
Specialty library concentrates on amateur and Olympic, as opposed to professional, wrestling. Includes biographies of wrestlers and their trainers.

WRITING

National Writers Club Library
1450 South Havana, Suite 620
Aurora, CO 80012
303/751-7844
Houses books on writing, markets for writing, and biographies of writers.

X, Y, Z

ZOOLOGY. *See also* LIFE SCIENCES.

Harvard University
Museum of Comparative Zoology Library
Oxford Street
Cambridge, MA 02138
617/495-2475
Holds collection on zoology, paleontology, evolution, and oceanography. Special collections in-

clude rare books, original drawings, manuscripts, and archives. Holds 236,000 volumes.

University of North Carolina, Chapel Hill
John N. Couch Biology Library—Zoology Section
213 Wilson Hall, CB 3280
Chapel Hill, NC 27599-3280
919/962-2264
Holds more than 38,000 books relating to vertebrate and invertebrate biology and related subjects.

6.

Electronic Databases

Fueled by the widespread use and availability of personal computers, the explosion in the amount of information available through electronic databases has been almost nuclear in size. From 1988 to 1989 alone, according to Martha E. Williams in her Foreword to the 1990 edition of *Computer Readable Databases*, more than 3.5 *billion* records were added to databases in that one year. That is an average of about *9.6 million new records added every day* in 1988. Computer databases never sleep, it seems.

Fortunately, the very computers that made this information explosion possible have also made it manageable. The computer can search huge masses of electronic data quickly and accurately and display an answer to most queries in a matter of seconds and then, if desired, send it off to a computer printer for a permanent copy.

A person does not have to be a computer expert to search computer databases. As electronic databases have evolved, they have also become easier and more logical to use. And you don't need a computer of your own to tap into this vast electronic inventory of information. Many public library systems, special collections, schools, corporate offices, and other institutions subscribe to online services such as BRS, DIALOG, or ORBIT. Libraries without their own subscriptions to an online service can usually forward your request to an affiliate for fulfillment.

Electronic Text Processing

Another major factor in the explosive growth of electronic databases has been the use of computers for text processing, typesetting, and composition throughout the publishing business. All publications—newspapers, magazines, books, and virtually everything else that finds its way into print these days—are processed electronically. Reporters and writers do their original work on word processors, editors edit in front of computer screens, and typesetting and composing programs prepare this electronic output for the printing presses.

When the electronic data goes to the printer, it is a simple matter to send a duplicate set to a database, where it can be quickly reformatted and placed online or on a CD-ROM. This permits updating of the full text of newspapers every day and comparable freshness for other periodicals. (See NEWS AND CURRENT EVENTS below for some of the daily newspapers offered this way.)

The easy transfer of data from publishers to online services has another important consequence. Very large directory or bibliographic publications, such as *Books in Print*, can be stored efficiently in electronic form and easily revised and updated by keying in the changes to the online version. There is no need to go through the full, laborious process of producing printed, bound volumes. Thus large directory and bibliographic publications can be kept more accurate and up-to-date than ever before. Publishers can now have the best of two worlds. Printed versions are still essential for permanent reference and use in situations where an electronic database is impractical or too costly; electronic versions are attracting a wider audience because they are easier to keep current and can organize great masses of information in a form that can be easily searched.

CD-ROM

One of the most rapidly growing types of electronic database is the CD-ROM (Compact Disk-Read Only Memory). The disk itself is almost identical to that used in stereo music systems; the player, however, is a computer, rather than a sound system. Each CD-ROM disk can store a tremendous amount of data. For example, the thirteen volumes of the 1933 edition of the *Oxford English Dictionary* are stored on just one CD-ROM disk.

Many CD-ROM databases are available as subscriptions that deliver updated disks on a periodic basis, perhaps monthly or quarterly. Others, like the *Oxford English Dictionary*, are one-time purchases. Most CD-ROM databases are also available through online services. The one drawback to CD-ROMs at this writing is that the disk players themselves are not standardized. One provider's hardware may not necessarily access the disks of another provider.

As a sample of the variety of databases now available on CD-ROMs, the General Research Division of the New York Public Library currently provides the following on CD-ROM players accessible to the general public in its main reading rooms:

Art Index
Biography Index
Cumulative Book Index
Dissertation Abstracts
Electronic Encyclopedia
General Periodicals Index
Humanities Index
MLA International Index
National Newspaper Index
Oxford English Dictionary
Periodical Abstracts
PsycLIT
Reader's Guide to Periodical Literature
Social Sciences Index
Sociofile

Online Services

Thousands of individual databases, such as *Books in Print*, are now offered to the public through online services. Online services are analogous to libraries; the individual databases they offer are comparable to the volumes in a library. DIALOG, a large, general online service, houses over 300 databases. Many online services also offer shopping, games, bulletin boards, travel reservations, and other nonreference features.

This chapter is a subject-by-subject guide to the hundreds of individual databases available through four major, widely used general online "libraries": BRS, CompuServe, DIALOG, and ORBIT. Databases are listed alphabetically by subject, along with the online service, or services, offering the database and a brief description. Here is an example from the NEWS AND CURRENT EVENTS—GENERAL category:

UPI News   CompuServe, DIALOG
The full text of items carried on the United Press International wire is available 48 hours after release to the news media. Also included are UPI columns, standing features, and commentaries. Covers 1983 to present. Updated daily. Provider: United Press International, Inc.

For further information on the four major online services providing the databases in this chapter, contact them as shown below. One call to the listed 800 number can usually establish a new account and provide the basic information needed to get started. This information will include local access telephone numbers, identification or account numbers, passwords, and other items needed to start using the service.

Here are the four services listed in this chapter:

BRS Information Technologies
8000 Westpark Drive
McLean, VA 22102
800/468-0908
In Virginia: 703/442-0900
FAX: 703/893-4632

CompuServe Information Services, Inc.
5000 Arlington Centre Boulevard
Department L, Box 477
P.O. Box 18161
Columbus, OH 43272-4630
800/848-8199
In Ohio: 614/457-0802

Dialog Information Services, Inc.
3460 Hillview Avenue
Palo Alto, CA 94304
800/3-DIALOG (800/334-2564)
In California: 415/858-3785
FAX: 415/858-7069

ORBIT Search Service
8000 Westpark Drive
McLean, VA 22102
800/45-ORBIT (800/456-7248)
In Virginia: 703/442-0900
FAX: 703/893-4632

Other Services

There are approximately 1,000 online services and 5,000 databases currently available, plus almost 500 databases available on CD-ROM. An excellent source of information on all online services and databases is this annual directory:

Computer Readable Databases: A Directory and Data Sourcebook, Kathleen Young Marcaccio, editor.
Gale Research Inc.
835 Penobscot Building
Detroit, MI 48226-4094
800/347-GALE (800/347-4253)
In Michigan: 313/961-2242
FAX: 313/961-6241

Costs

Costs depend on the type of service provided. A common arrangement consists of a basic fee plus charges for the actual time spent working with the specific database. These "connect time" charges can vary widely. The databases offered by DIALOG, for example, range from $15 to $300 per hour, billed in minutes at the hourly rates. Discounts may be available for heavy users.

In addition to their basic packages, many online services offer lower-priced introductory packages. These starter packages usually provide manuals and instructions for using the service along with a limited amount of free connect time to reduce the cost of the inevitable trial-and-error period while learning a new system. The introductory package may also have options such as tutorials, practice databases, videotapes, and new-user seminars. Rates and fees are always subject to change, and there are often discounts and special services available in addition to the introductory and basic packages.

Tips on Database Searches

1. Know your databases. You can conduct a search much more quickly—and save money—if you know which database contains the information you want. Keep an informal log to note which databases were useful and which weren't. Log your information alongside the appropriate entry in this chapter for quick reference.

If other people are doing the search for you, it will help them if they also know which databases you consider most productive.

2. Be as specific as you can. Database searches are based on "keywords." The main computer of the online service will search for your keywords throughout your chosen database. If your keywords are too broad, don't be surprised if your screen turns up page after page of not terribly useful information.

3. Become familiar with the basics of Boolean searches. They can save time and focus the computer's powerful search capabilities more closely on exactly what you want. This may sound esoteric, and Boolean algebra is certainly not for beginners, but the basic concept of a Boolean search is a simple one. The

search is based on three basic extra instructions to the computer to link keywords by using the logical operators AND, OR, or NOT.

Suppose you are interested in locating books about women military pilots. If you queried the computerized card catalog of the New York Public Library (called CATNYP for short) you would discover 15,625 books in the New York Public Library System relating to women—far too many, obviously, for a reasonable research effort.

However, querying CATNYP for titles about women AND pilots would turn up eighteen titles dealing with women pilots. Further refining the query to women AND pilots AND military would produce only two titles. If you had no interest in women pilots in the military services, a Boolean query framed as "women AND pilots and NOT military" would produce a total of 16 titles.

Boolean searches can be conducted on both online databases and CD-ROMs.

4. As might be expected from a high-technology reference source, online databases are especially good when researching rapidly changing high-tech subjects such as biotechnology, space technology, and telecommunications. Familiarity with the electronic databases in high-tech areas of special interest to you can save you countless hours of searching other reference media only to find that they are out of date.

Electronic Databases
Subject Index

A

ACCOUNTING

Accountants Index   CompuServe, ORBIT
Database indexes worldwide English-language journals in accounting, taxation, data processing, and financial reporting. Covers 1974 to present. Updated quarterly. Provider: American Institute of Certified Public Accountants.

ADVERTISING. *See also* MARKETING; PUBLIC RELATIONS.

Electronic Shopping News CompuServe
Newsletter examines the selling of merchandise and financial products by cable and broadcast television home shopping services along with video and online retailing. Full text; updated monthly. Provider: NewsNet, Inc.

Media Week CompuServe
Magazine reports news on media buying and selling. Includes pricing and schedules, advertising, editorial policies, and circulation/viewing trends. Full text; covers July 1986 to present. Updated weekly. Provider: Profile Information.

Mintel Daily Digest CompuServe
The *Digest* gives news of advertising, public relations, and market research business in the United Kingdom and Europe with some coverage of other countries as well. Covers September 1986 to present. Updated daily. Provider: Profile Information.

PTS Marketing & Advertising Reference Service (MARS) CompuServe, DIALOG
PTS MARS has data on many types of goods and services as well as the companies that provide them, their advertising agencies, chosen advertising media, and marketing strategies. It consists of abstracts from over 70 sources including key advertising journals and newsletters, consumer-oriented trade magazines, business-method journals, and the advertising columns of major newspapers. Covers 1984 to present. Updated daily. Provider: Predicasts.

AERONAUTICS. *See also* MILITARY; MILITARY—PROCUREMENT; SPACE TECHNOLOGY.

Helicopter News CompuServe
This trade newsletter looks at business and technology developments in the helicopter industry. Full text; updated every two weeks. Provider: NewsNet, Inc.

Japanese Aviation News: Wing CompuServe
Newsletter covers the Japanese aerospace and aviation industry. Topics include transport, defense, space, industry, marketing, and Japanese involvement in Southeast Asia. Full text; updated weekly. Provider: NewsNet, Inc.

AGRICULTURE. *See also* FOOD AND NUTRITION; FORESTRY AND FOREST PRODUCTS; PESTICIDES.

Abstracts of Tropical Agriculture CompuServe, ORBIT
Provides an index of worldwide technical literature on tropical and subtropical agriculture. Included as well are economic and sociological aspects, animal husbandry, fisheries, forestry, and public health. Covers 1975 to present. Updated monthly. Provider: Koninklijk Instituut voor de Tropen (Royal Tropical Institute), The Netherlands.

Agribusiness U.S.A. CompuServe, DIALOG
Database covers all aspects of the agricultural business with abstracts from some 300 trade journals. Topics include crop and livestock industries, agricultural chemicals, biotechnology, agricultural finance, farm equipment manufacturing, and agricultural marketing, among others. Covers 1985 to present. Updated biweekly. Provider: Pioneer Hi-Bred International, Inc.

Agricola BRS, CompuServe, DIALOG
This is the database of the U.S. National Agricultural Library covering worldwide agricultural journal and monograph literature (abstracts may or may not be included). Related topics include animal husbandry, botany, chemistry, entomology, fertilizers, forestry, hydroponics, soils, and more. Covers 1970 to present. Updated monthly. Provider: U.S. National Agricultural Library.

Agris International CompuServe, DIALOG
Agris International provides an exhaustive compilation of worldwide agricultural literature with a view toward identifying problems in world food supply. It corresponds, in part, to *AgrIndex* published monthly by the Food and Agricultural Organization of the U.N. Some of the subjects covered are general agriculture, geography and history, education, extension and advisory work, administration and legislation, economics, development and rural sociology, plant production, protection of plants and stored products, forestry, animal production, aquatic sciences and fisheries, machinery and buildings, natural resources, food science, home economics, pollution, and more. Covers 1975 to present. Updated monthly. Provider: U.S. National Agricultural Library.

The Agrochemicals Handbook DIALOG
Agrochemicals Databank - CompuServe
Both databases provide information on the chemical makeup of agrochemical products used worldwide, including chemical names (including synonyms and tradenames), CAS Registry Number, molecular formula and weight, manufacturer's names, chemical and physical properties, toxicity,

mode of action, activity, health and safety, and more. Covers current products. Updated twice a year. Provider: The Royal Society of Chemistry, Nottingham, UK (DIALOG); Data-Star (Compu-Serve).

Biological and Agricultural Index CompuServe
Index focuses on agriculture with broad coverage of biochemistry, microbiology, and nutrition. Covers July 1983 to present. Updated semiweekly. Provider: H.W. Wilson Company.

CAB Abstracts BRS, CompuServe, DIALOG
This index of agricultural biological literature contains abstracts of major papers and citations of less important works. Over 8,500 journals in 37 languages along with books, reports, theses, conference proceedings, patents, and annual reports are contained in 26 main abstract reports published by the Commonwealth Agricultural Bureaux (United Kingdom). Among the subjects included are agricultural engineering, animal breeding and disease, arid lands, dairy science, forestry, horticulture, nutrition, veterinary science, entomology, plant breeding and pathology, rural recreation and tourism, soils and fertilizers, weeds, world agricultural economics, and more. Covers 1972 to present. Updated monthly. Provider: CAB International, Farnham Royal Slough, UK.

Coffeeline CompuServe, DIALOG
Coffeeline covers all aspects of coffee production from growing to marketing. References are chosen from 5,000 worldwide journals. In addition, references are provided for books, patents, reports, and theses. Online file corresponds to *International Coffee Organization Library Monthly Entries*. Covers 1973 to present. Updated bimonthly. Provider: International Coffee Organisation, London, UK.

CRIS/USDA DIALOG
The Current Research Information System reports on current research in agriculture and related sciences sponsored or conducted by the USDA, state agricultural experiment stations, state forestry schools, and other cooperating state institutions. Research reported includes agricultural-related biological, physical, social, and behavioral sciences; marketing and economics; food and nutrition, consumer health and safety; family life, housing, and rural development; environmental protection; forestry; outdoor recreation; community, area, and regional development; and more. Covers currently active or recently completed projects. Updated monthly. Provider: U.S. Department of Agriculture.

European Directory of Agrochemical Products DIALOG
Extensive data on over 20,000 agrochemical products manufactured and/or used in Europe is provided by EDAP. Data are broken out by country, product, and active ingredient proportions. Details provided are active ingredient proportions, preharvest intervals, application timing, product name, company name, toxicity, formulation type, uses, and limitations. Covers current products. Updated semiannually. Provider: The Royal Society of Chemistry, Nottingham, UK.

Tropical Agriculture ORBIT
Database covers tropical and subtropical agriculture. Topics include crop production, crop protection, fertilizers, soils, and more. Provider: Koninklijk Instituut voor de Tropen (Royal Tropical Institute), The Netherlands.

Viticulture and Enology Abstracts ORBIT
This index, with abstracts, covers grape and grapevine science and technology. Areas include plant pathology and breeding, biochemistry, soils, economy of wine making, and more. Provider: International Food Information Service.

AIDS

AIDS Abstracts from the Bureau of Hygiene and Tropical Diseases BRS
Database has abstracts of papers on viruses in the HIV/HTLV family, AIDS-related retroviruses, and associated infections. Coverage includes treatment, etiology, pathology, epidemiology, immunology, and more. Provider: Bureau of Hygiene and Tropical Diseases.

AIDS Database CompuServe
Service provides selected articles on all aspects of Acquired Immune Deficiency Syndrome (AIDS) and AIDS-related research. Covers 1982 to present. Updated monthly. Provider: Data-Star.

AIDS Knowledge Base from San Francisco General Hospital and the University of California, San Francisco BRS
This is an online textbook on acquired immunodeficiency syndrome and includes epidemiology, diagnosis, prevention, treatment, social concerns, and more. Provider: Massachusetts Medical Society.

Aidsline DIALOG
Database is an index, with abstracts to about 40 percent of the references, to worldwide literature on AIDS. References are to 3,363 journals from over 70 countries. About 6,000 new entries are added yearly, with over 84 percent of the articles indexed written in English. Covers 1980 to present. Updated monthly. Provider: U.S. National Library of Medicine.

Medline Reference on AIDS BRS
This portion of Medline indexes the clinical and research material on AIDS. Updated monthly. Provider: U.S. National Library of Medicine.

ALCOHOLISM. *See* SUBSTANCE ABUSE.

ANTARCTICA. *See* EARTH SCIENCES.

APPLIED SCIENCE. *See* TECHNOLOGY.

AQUACULTURE

Aquaculture CompuServe, DIALOG
This bibliographical database is an index of monographs, periodicals, and conference proceedings. All aspects of the growing of marine and freshwater organisms are covered, including disease, economics, engineering, food and nutrition, growth requirements, and legal aspects of water organisms. Covers 1970 to January 1984. Provider: National Oceanic and Atmospheric Administration.

Aquatic Sciences and Fisheries Abstracts
DIALOG
ASFA provides broad coverage of the science, technology, and management of salt- and freshwater environments. Database includes citations to 5,000 primary journals, monographs, conference proceedings and technical reports. Covers 1978 to present. Updated monthly. Provider: NOAA/Cambridge Scientific Abstracts.

Aqualine ORBIT
Database indexes literature from around the world on water resources and supplies. Topics include water quality, low-cost technology, water treatment, wastes, pollution, and much more. Provider: Water Research Centre.

ARCHAEOLOGY. *See* HUMANITIES.

ARCHITECTURE

Architecture Database DIALOG
This service is the online version of *The Architec-*

tural Periodicals Index and *The Architectural Books Catalog* along with other catalog records. Over 400 worldwide periodicals are indexed along with about 2,000 cataloged items from around the world such as monographs, proceedings, exhibition catalogs, pamphlets, and technical literature. Covers *Architectural Periodicals Index* from 1978 to present and *Architectural Books Catalog* from 1984 to present. Updated monthly. Provider: British Architectural Library at the Royal Institute of British Architects, London, UK.

ICONDA ORBIT
Database has international literature on construction, civil engineering, architecture, and town planning. Topics include structural design, material testing, bridges, tunnels, steel, concrete and masonry, energy conservation, design, and much more. Provider: ICONDA Agency c/o Information Centre for Regional Planning and Building Construction of the Fraunhofer Society.

ART. *See* FINE ARTS; HUMANITIES.

ASSOCIATIONS. *See* ORGANIZATIONS.

AUTOMOTIVE ENGINEERING. *See also* ENGINEERING.

SAE Global Mobility ORBIT
Society of Automotive Engineers Meetings - CompuServe
Database has abstracts of papers given at meetings and conferences of the Society of Automotive Engineers and the International Federation of Automotive Engineering Societies. Covers 1965 to present. Updated quarterly. Provider: Society of Automotive Engineers, Inc.

B

BANKING. *See* FINANCE.

BENEFITS

Department of Health and Social Security
CompuServe
Database has information on health services and hospital administration and associated fields ranging from health-service buildings to social security pensions. Covers November 1983 to present. Updated weekly. Provider: Data-Star.

EBIS - Employee Benefits Infosource DIALOG
Database covers all aspects of employee benefit

plans by indexing and abstracting English-language material pertinent to the United States, Canada, and other countries. A very broad range of topics are offered running from compensation to stock option plans, to laws and regulations, to workers' compensation, and much, much more. Covers 1986 to present. Updated monthly. Provider: International Foundation of Employee Benefit Plans.

BEVERAGES. *See* SOFT DRINKS; WINES AND SPIRITS.

BIBLIOGRAPHIES—BOOKS. *See also* BIBLIOGRAPHIES—PERIODICALS.

Books Information   CompuServe
This index references hard-to-find publications including monographs, texts, small press books, juvenile books, and English-language books from foreign publishers. Updated monthly. Provider: BRS Information Technologies.

Books in Print   CompuServe, BRS, DIALOG
Major source of information on current books in the United States. Provides a record of forthcoming books, books in print, and books recently out of print. Covers scientific, technical, medical, scholarly, popular, and children's books. The file includes several print publications: *Books in Print, Subject Guide to Books in Print, Books in Print Supplement, Paperbound Books in Print, Forthcoming Books,* and *Subject Guide to Forthcoming Books.* Entries include basic bibliographic information (author, title, publisher, and date), as well as Library of Congress Card number, International Standard Book Number (ISDN), and price. Covers current in-print and forthcoming books. Updated monthly. Provider: R.R. Bowker.

British Books in Print   DIALOG
Database is a thorough index of books published in the United Kingdom plus other English-language books published elsewhere and available in the British Isles. Corresponds to the printed version of the same title. Covers Current Edition. Updated monthly. Provider: J. Whitaker & Sons, Ltd., London, UK.

LC MARC-Books   CompuServe, DIALOG
The Library of Congress's MARC catalog of holdings from 1968 to the present. Foreign-language books from 1970 to 1979 are included. Searches can be made by the usual methods such as author, title, subject, publication date, and more. (For books prior to 1968, see REMARC, below.)

Covers 1968 to present. Updated weekly. Provider: U.S. Library of Congress.

REMARC   CompuServe, DIALOG
REMARC covers the Library of Congress's cataloged collections from 1897 to 1968. Searches can be made by the usual methods such as author, title, subject, publication date, and more. (For books after 1968, see LC MARC, above.) Covers 1897 to 1968. Updated irregularly. Provider: UTLAS International, Toronto, Ontario, Canada.

BIBLIOGRAPHIES—PERIODICALS. *(Specific magazines, journals, newsletters, and other periodicals are listed with their appropriate subjects.)*

Academic Index   BRS, DIALOG
Bibliographic database of over 400 academic and general-interest publications representing the most commonly held titles in over 120 college and university libraries. AI expands the coverage of Magazine Index, below, providing information in the social sciences and humanities. Indexing for articles, news reports, editorials on major issues, product evaluations, biographies, short stories, poetry, and reviews is provided. AI also indexes the following general areas: art, anthropology, economics, education, ethnic studies, government, history, literature, political science, general science, psychology, religion, sociology, and leisure. Covers 1976 to present. Updated monthly. Provider: Information Access Company.

Associations' Publications in Print   CompuServe
Database is an index of U.S. and Canadian trade association publications including newsletters, journals, proceedings, and more. Corresponds to the printed version of the same name. Updated monthly. Provider: BRS Information Technologies.

Business Periodicals Index   CompuServe
This index of major English-language business magazines focuses on management, marketing, economics, industry, and finance. It corresponds to the printed version of the same title. Covers June 1982 to present. Updated twice a week. Provider: H.W. Wilson Company.

California Union List of Periodicals   CompuServe
Detailed information on the journal and periodical holdings of public and private California libraries is provided. Updated monthly. Provider: BRS Information Technologies.

Magazine ASAP   BRS, CompuServe, DIALOG
Magazine ASAP has full text and indexing for over
one-quarter of the magazines indexed in *Magazine
Index* (see below). Articles, editorials, columns,
reviews, product evaluations, and recipes are
included. Covers 1983 to present. Updated
monthly. Provider: Information Access Company.

Magazine Index   BRS, CompuServe, DIALOG
Created for general reference, the database indexes over 435 popular magazines covering current affairs, performing arts, business, sports,
recreation and travel, consumer product evaluations, science and technology, leisure-time activities, and more. Covers 1959 to March 1970 and
1973 to present. Updated monthly. Provider: Information Access Company.

Readers' Guide to Periodical Literature
CompuServe
The Readers' Guide indexes articles from general-
interest magazines published in the United States
and Canada. Online edition corresponds to the
printed Readers' Guide. Covers 1983 to present.
Updated biweekly. Provider: H.W. Wilson Company.

Ulrich's International Periodicals Directory
CompuServe, DIALOG
Database corresponds to the printed version of
the *Directory* along with *Irregular Serials and Annuals*, *Sources of Serials*, and *Ulrich's Quarterly*. Over
100,000 regularly and irregularly published periodicals from 65,000 publishers worldwide are referenced here. Publications range from consumer
magazines to conference proceedings. Covers current editions. Updated monthly. Provider: R.R.
Bowker.

UMI Article Clearinghouse   BRS
Index has citations for over 11,000 periodicals and
conference proceedings on business, computer science, education, engineering, humanities, life sciences, medicine, and social sciences. Provider:
UMI Article Clearinghouse.

BIOGRAPHY

American Men and Women of Science
CompuServe, DIALOG
Biographical information on over 127,000 U.S. and
Canadian scientists is presented. Each entry in-
cludes basic biographical details, positions held,
awards and honors, and research specialties. Cov-

ers 1979 to present. Updated on a three-year cycle. Provider: R.R. Bowker.

Biography Index   CompuServe
Provides an index to biographies coming from
books, journals, autobiographies, memoirs, dia-
ries, book reviews, bibliographies, and interviews.
Covers August 1984 to present. Updated biweekly.
Provider: H.W. Wilson Company.

Biography Master Index
CompuServe, DIALOG
This master index provides citations to biographical data found in over 700 publications. Information is arranged by surname and includes dates of
birth and death, and names and dates of the
source publications that have information on the
person. Coverage runs from scientists to sports
figures, including both historical and living persons. Covers current edition. Updated irregularly.
Provider: Gale Research Company.

Marquis Who's Who   CompuServe, DIALOG
Contains detailed biographies of over 101,000 people in business, sports, government, the arts, entertainment, science, and technology. Each entry
contains career history, education, creative works,
publications, family background, current address,
political activities and affiliation, religion, and special achievements. Database corresponds to the
Marquis Who's Who in America and *Who's Who in
Science and Technology*. Covers current edition. Updated quarterly. Provider: National Register Publishing Company.

Standard and Poor's Register - Biographical
CompuServe, DIALOG
Corresponding to the printed *Standard & Poor's
Register of Corporations, Directors, and Executives*,
Volume Two, the *Register* contains profiles of top
executives of U.S. and foreign corporations with
sales of $1 million or more. Each profile details
the executive's or director's personal, professional,
and educational accomplishments. Covers current
edition. Updated semiannually. Provider: Standard & Poor's Corporation.

Who's Who in Technology   ORBIT
Database has brief biographies of leading persons
in American technology. Entries include name,
title, employer, career history, education, publications and patents, and honors and awards. Provider: Research Publications, Inc.

BIOTECHNOLOGY

Biotechnology Abstracts DIALOG, ORBIT
Service provides indexing and abstracts of publications describing research in all areas of biotechnology from genetic engineering to waste disposal. One to two thousand new documents are added each month. About 27 percent of the entries are patent records. Covers 1982 to present. Updated monthly. Provider: Derwent Publications, Ltd., London, UK.

Current Biotechnology Abstracts CompuServe, DIALOG
This bibliographic reference also contains abstracts and covers all areas of biotechnology from genetic manipulation to single-cell proteins to fermentation technology. Patents, forthcoming events, and book announcements are included. Covers 1983 to present. Updated monthly. Provider: The Royal Society of Chemistry, Nottingham, UK.

BONDS. *See* INVESTMENTS.

BOOK REVIEWS

Book Review Digest CompuServe
Look here for references to current English-language fiction and nonfiction (adult and children's). Covers April 1983 to present. Updated twice weekly. Provider: H.W. Wilson Company.

Book Review Index CompuServe, DIALOG
This is an index to book reviews from over 380 journals, oriented toward the humanities, including literature, fine arts, history, social science, education, and more. Each listing shows author, book title, and source of review. Covers 1969 to present. Updated three times per year. Provider: Gale Research Company.

Kirkus Book Reviews CompuServe
Database provides the full text of brief reviews of new fiction and nonfiction books. Reviews are usually available two months prior to publication. Updated every two weeks. NewsNet, Inc.

BROADCASTING. *See* TELECOMMUNICATIONS.

BULLETIN BOARDS. *See* COMPUTER BULLETIN BOARDS.

BUSINESS EXECUTIVES

Standard and Poor's Register - Biographical
CompuServe, DIALOG
Corresponding to the printed *Standard & Poor's Register of Corporations, Directors, and Executives*,

Volume Two, the *Register* contains profiles of top executives of U.S. and foreign corporations with sales of $1 million or more. Each profile details the executive's or director's personal, professional, and educational accomplishments. Covers current edition. Updated semiannually. Provider: Standard & Poor's Corporation.

BUSINESS—GENERAL. *See also* BUSINESS EXECUTIVES; BUSINESS—INTERNATIONAL; COMPANIES—INTERNATIONAL; COMPANIES—U.S.; FINANCE; INDUSTRIES; MERGERS AND ACQUISITIONS.

Arthur D. Little/Online DIALOG
Industry forecasts, technology assessments, product and market overviews, public opinion surveys, and management commentaries are to be found here. The industries and technologies covered are chemical (including specialty chemicals), health care, pharmaceuticals, medical equipment, diagnostic products, health-care delivery services, biotechnology, advanced materials, food processing, environmental issues, and information processing and telecommunications (includes office automation, computers, equipment manufacturers, and services). Covers 1977 to present. Updated every two months. Provider: Arthur D. Little Decision Resources.

Business America CompuServe
Covers 1983 to present. Updated monthly. Provider: DIALOG Information Services (drawn from the Trade & Industry ASAP database).

Business Dateline BRS, CompuServe, DIALOG
Here is the full text of 110 regional U.S. and Canadian business publications as well as Crain News Service publications, nine daily newspapers, and BUSINESSWIRE. Topics include regional business activities and trends, small companies, new start-ups, products and services, executives, and more. Covers 1985 to present. Updated weekly. Provider: UMI/Data Courier.

Business Periodicals Index CompuServe
This index of major English-language business magazines focuses on management, marketing, economics, industry, and finance. It corresponds to the printed version of the same title. Covers June 1982 to present. Updated twice a week. Provider: H.W. Wilson Company.

BUSINESSWIRE CompuServe, DIALOG
The full text of over 10,000 news sources includ-

ing companies, public relations firms, government agencies, and much more are available here. About 90 percent of news releases are business or financial, covering all types of businesses. Covers 1986 to present. Updated continuously. Provider: BUSINESSWIRE.

Economist CompuServe
Database has the full text of the premier British economics and business magazine, which covers worldwide developments. Covers December 1981 to present. Updated weekly. Provider: Profile Information.

Financial Times & The Economist CompuServe
Database has the full text of both the *London Financial Times* and the *Economist*, which report on business, economic, and financial events. Provider: Profile Information.

Financial Times Fulltext CompuServe, DIALOG
Database has the full text of all *Financial Times* articles, which give detailed data on industries, companies, and markets worldwide. Government regulation, labor and management issues, technology, and more are included. Covers 1986 to present. Updated daily. Provider: Financial Times Business Information, Ltd., London, UK.

Financial World CompuServe
Full-text magazine has industry reviews, trends and forecasts, company profiles, and issues ratings. Covers 1983 to present. Updated monthly. Provider: DIALOG Information Services (drawn from the Trade & Industry ASAP database).

Forbes CompuServe
Full-text magazine covers business news, case histories, and personal profiles. Covers 1983 to present. Updated monthly. Provider: DIALOG Information Services (drawn from the Trade & Industry ASAP database).

Fortune CompuServe
The full text of this business and industry magazine is available. Coverage includes economic forecasts, personal investing, company information, and corporate performance. Covers 1983 to present. Updated monthly. Provider: DIALOG Information Services (drawn from the Trade & Industry ASAP database).

Industry Week CompuServe
This business newsweekly is aimed at business executives and reports on all aspects of business.

Covers 1983 to present. Updated monthly. Provider: DIALOG Information Services (drawn from the Trade & Industry ASAP database).

Information Report CompuServe
Newsletter looks at free and low-cost business data sources such as magazines, directories, and databases provided by federal and state governments, unions, and other groups. Updated monthly. Provider: NewsNet, Inc.

Inc. CompuServe
Here is the full text of this magazine of small business. Topics include trends, management policies, and solutions to small-business problems along with articles on successful entrepreneurs and small businesses. Covers 1983 to present. Updated monthly. Provider: DIALOG Information Services (drawn from the Trade & Industry ASAP database).

Innovator's Digest CompuServe
Newsletter reviews worldwide reports on innovations in many fields including technical management, marketing, and regulatory aspects of a wide range of topics. The newsletter also looks at the "business" of innovating. Full text; updated every two weeks. Provider: NewsNet, Inc.

McGraw-Hill News DIALOG
The full text of current news stories of important business events are presented here. Stories come in from McGraw-Hill news bureaus around the world and are made available as soon as they are written. Covers June 18, 1987 to present. Updated every fifteen minutes from 8 A.M. to 6 P.M. Eastern time, Monday to Friday. Provider: McGraw-Hill Information Network.

Moody's Corporate News - U.S. CompuServe, DIALOG
This database has current, detailed coverage of business news and financial data on about 13,000 public U.S. companies. Both tabular and text records are provided on business news announcements and financial data. Covers 1983 to present. Updated weekly. Provider: Moody's Investor Services, Inc.

Nation's Business CompuServe
The full text of this journal covers business news, the economy, company and manager profiles, management trends, and government trends. Covers 1983 to present. Updated monthly. Provider: DI-

ALOG Information Services (drawn from the Trade & Industry ASAP database).

Newswire ASAP DIALOG
This service has the full text and indexing of news releases and wire stories from PR Newswire, Kyodo, and Reuters. These cover current and previous data on companies, industries, products, economics, and finance in the United States and worldwide. Covers PR Newswire, January 1985 to present; Kyodo, July 1987 to present; Reuters, June 1987 to present. Provider: Information Access Company.

PR Newswire CompuServe, DIALOG
This service has the full text of news releases from companies, public relations firms, trade associations, domestic and foreign governments, and other sources. About 80 percent of the items contained here are business/financial. Covers May 1, 1987 to present. Updated continually. Provider: PR Newswire Association, Inc.

PTS F&S (Funk & Scott) Indexes
BRS, CompuServe, DIALOG
The Index has data on domestic and international companies, products, and industries. Acquisitions and mergers, new products and technologies, and sociopolitical factors are covered. In addition, analyses and forecasts by securities firms are included. Covers 1972 to present. Updated weekly. Provider: Predicasts.

PTS Newsletter Database DIALOG
The full text of over 100 major specialized industry newsletters from the United States and abroad are available here. Covers 1988 to present. Updated daily. Provider: Predicasts.

PTS PROMT BRS, CompuServe, DIALOG
Predicasts Overview of Markets and Technology contains abstracts of all important information from thousands of newspapers, business magazines, trade journals, bank letters, and special and government reports worldwide. Further, regional business news and abstracts of corporate and industry research reports by securities/investment firms are also covered. Covers 1972 to present. Updated daily. Provider: Predicasts.

Sales Prospector/USA CompuServe
This full-text newsletter covers industrial, commercial, and institutional expansions and reloca-

tions. Arranged by regions in the United States. Updated monthly. Provider: NewsNet, Inc.

Standard & Poor's News CompuServe, DIALOG
Database covers general news and financial information on over 10,000 publicly owned U.S. companies in such areas as earnings, management changes, litigation, and much more. Covers June 1979 to present. Updated daily. Provider: Standard & Poor's Corporation.

Thomas Regional Industrial Suppliers
CompuServe, DIALOG
Similar to the *Thomas Register* below, the regional directory lists local manufacturers, distributors, and manufacturers' representatives in the eastern and central United States broken down into 14 regions. Database corresponds to the printed *Regional Industrial Purchasing Guide*. Covers current edition. Updated quarterly. Provider: Thomas Publishing Company.

Thomas Register Online CompuServe, DIALOG
Contains the full text of the printed *Thomas Register of American Manufacturers*, making it possible to find virtually any product made in the United States. Over 133,000 manufacturers of over 55,000 classes of products with over 106,000 brand names are covered. Overall, there are listings for over 1,000,000 product and service providers. Covers current edition. Updated annually. Provider: Thomas Publishing Company.

Trade & Industry ASAP BRS, CompuServe, DIALOG
The full text and indexing for over 85 journals selected from the *Trade & Industry Index* along with news releases from *PR Newswire* are contained here. Covers 1983 to present. Updated monthly. Provider: Information Access Company.

Trade & Industry Index DIALOG
This database provides an index to and selected abstracts of over 300 trade and industry journals plus thorough but selective coverage of business and trade information from an additional 1,200 publications. Also included are full-text records from over 85 of the covered journals and the *PR Newswire* from 1983 to the present. The database also contains the *Area Business Database*, which contains indexing and abstracts from over 100 local and regional business publications from 1985 to the present. Subjects include banking, insur-

ance, agriculture, public utilities, taxation, construction, wholesale and retail trade, and much more. Covers 1981 to present. Updated monthly. Provider: Information Access Company.

BUSINESS—INTERNATIONAL

Asian Intelligence CompuServe
Full-text newsletter looks at economic trends, market and credit climate, and exchange rates in Asia. Covers March 1986 to present. Updated every two weeks. Provider: NewsNet, Inc.

Asia-Pacific DIALOG
Database covers business, economics, and new industries of the Pacific Rim nations (East and Southeast Asia, Indian Subcontinent, Middle East, Australia, and Pacific Islands). Two data types are available: abstracts and citations for journal articles and other print material, and company thesaurus records. Covers 1985 to present. Updated every two weeks. Provider: Aristarchus Knowledge Industries.

Business Database CompuServe
This database contains listings of worldwide trade leads for manufacturing, marketing, and sales. Covers October 1983 to present. Updated monthly. Provider: Data-Star.

Canadian Business and Current Affairs
CompuServe, DIALOG
This is an index to over 100,000 articles per year that appear in over 500 Canadian business magazines and 10 newspapers. In addition to broad business coverage, all aspects of Canadian current affairs ranging from local to national affairs are presented. Covers July 1980 to present. Updated monthly. Provider: Micromedia Ltd., Toronto, Ontario, Canada.

China Express CompuServe
Service lists new Chinese opportunities for business and investments for Western businesses. Listings are, from time to time, added to *China Express Contracts* (see below). Updated every two weeks. Provider: NewsNet, Inc.

China Express Contracts CompuServe
A companion to *China Express*, this service provides a list of Chinese projects needing Western export or partners. Updated weekly. Provider: NewsNet, Inc.

East Asian Business Intelligence CompuServe
Newsletter reports on government tenders and current and future business opportunities in East Asia. Updated every two weeks. Provider: NewsNet, Inc.

Economist CompuServe
Database has the full text of the premier British economics and business magazine, which covers worldwide developments. Covers December 1981 to present. Updated weekly. Provider: Profile Information.

Exporter CompuServe
This is the full text of the *Exporter Newsletter*, which reports on developments affecting exporters. Covered are credit and financial news, tariff matters, and government activities, plus listings of publications, conferences, and training providers. Updated monthly. Provider: NewsNet, Inc.

Financial Times & The Economist CompuServe
Database has the full text of both the *London Financial Times* and the *Economist*, which report on business, economic, and financial events. Provider: Profile Information.

Financial Times Fulltext CompuServe, DIALOG
Database has the full text of all *Financial Times* articles that give detailed data on industries, companies, and markets worldwide. Government regulation, labor and management issues, technology, and more are included. Covers 1986 to present. Updated daily. Provider: Financial Times Business Information, Ltd., London, UK.

Frost & Sullivan's Political Risk Letter
CompuServe
Political events affecting foreign business conditions are the subject of this full-text newsletter. Ratings are given for exporting, manufacturing, and financial risks over the following 18 months along with a five-year stability report. Updated monthly. Provider: NewsNet, Inc.

GAS International Surveys CompuServe
Database has reports on political and economic developments in 95 countries. Updated two to three times a year. Provider: Profile Information.

German American Commerce CompuServe
This is the newsletter of the German-American Chamber of Commerce with coverage of the German commercial climate along with U.S.-German business connections. Full text; updated every two weeks. Provider: NewsNet, Inc.

German Business Scope CompuServe
Newsletter lists German firms seeking U.S. partners and has dates of industrial fairs, conferences, and other meetings. Full text; updated monthly. Provider: NewsNet, Inc.

Infomat International Business DIALOG
BIS Infomat World Business - CompuServe
Infomat contains abstracts of articles from over 400 business publications translated into English from 10 languages. Covers April 1984 to present. Updated weekly. Provider: Predicasts.

International Businessman News Report
CompuServe
Newsletter gives information on international business opportunities along with contact lists of financiers and banks. Additional coverage includes business personalities, projects, travel, and more. Full text, updated every two weeks. Provider: NewsNet, Inc.

Japan High Tech Review CompuServe
Japanese high-technology markets are the subject of this full-text newsletter. Areas include products, technologies, and analysis of marketing and competition. Updated monthly. Provider: NewsNet, Inc.

McCarthy Press Cutting Service CompuServe
Daily service covers company, industry, and market information taken from more than 60 newspapers and business magazines worldwide. Updated daily. Provider: Profile Information.

Mid-East Business Digest CompuServe
This is the full text of the newsletter that reports on business news from the Middle East. Material is taken from the region's news wires and newspapers. Updated weekly. Provider: NewsNet, Inc.

Middle East Business Intelligence CompuServe
Newsletter gives details of current Middle East business opportunities including contracting, financing, and sales leads along with contact persons. Laws and regulations that affect foreign investment and operation are covered. Full text, updated every two weeks. Provider: NewsNet, Inc.

Opportunities for Export CompuServe
Searchable by SIC codes, this full-text newsletter provides listings of specific U.S. products, services, and commodities sought by government agencies, companies, and persons worldwide who are seeking to purchase or represent. Contact data is included. Updated weekly. Provider: NewsNet, Inc.

Sales Prospector/Canada CompuServe
This full-text newsletter covers industrial, commercial, and institutional expansions and relocations in Canada. Updated monthly. Provider: NewsNet, Inc.

C

CANCER

Cancerlit BRS, CompuServe, DIALOG
Database indexes and abstracts all cancer-related articles from a large number of sources. Topics range from experimental and clinical therapy to biochemistry to mutagen testing. Covers 1963 to present. Updated monthly. Provider: U.S. National Library of Medicine.

Physician Data Query Cancer Information File
BRS, CompuServe
Database has current data on more than 85 cancers including symptoms, prognosis, cellular classification, standard and experimental treatments, and more. References to medical literature are provided. Updated monthly. Provider: National Cancer Institute.

Physician Data Query Patient Information File
BRS
Addressed to nonmedical persons dealing with cancer, this database has information on general prognosis, stage explanations, treatment overview, and options. Updated monthly. Provider: National Cancer Institute.

Physician Data Query Directory File
BRS, CompuServe
This is a directory of the names, addresses, and telephone numbers of over 10,000 physicians and organizations that care for cancer patients. Updated monthly. Provider: National Cancer Institute.

Physician Data Query Protocol File
BRS, CompuServe
Database has data on over 1,000 active cancer treatment protocols. Included are clinical trials supported by the National Cancer Institute and those

submitted by other investigators. Updated monthly. Provider: National Cancer Institute.

CENSUS STATISTICS. *See* DEMOGRAPHICS.

CERAMICS. *See also* ENGINEERING.

Ceramic Abstracts   DIALOG, ORBIT
This is the online version of the printed *Ceramics Abstracts*. It provides abstracts of worldwide technical literature on all aspects of ceramics. Most nonpatent entries are in English, regardless of the original language of publication. Covers 1980 to present. Updated every two months. Provider: The American Ceramic Society.

World Ceramic Abstracts   ORBIT
Covers worldwide literature on ceramics. Topics include high-tech ceramics, whitewares, vitreous enamels, clay-based building materials, glasses, and more. Provider: Rapra Technology, Ltd. and Ceram Research.

CHEMICAL ENGINEERING. *See also* CHEMISTRY; ENGINEERING.

Chemical Engineering Abstracts   CompuServe, DIALOG
Abstracts in this database are taken from worldwide journals and cover all aspects of industrial practice and theoretical chemical engineering. Covers 1971 to present. Updated monthly. Provider: Royal Society of Chemistry, Nottingham, UK.

Kirk-Othmer Online (Kirk-Othmer Encyclopedia of Chemical Technology)   BRS, CompuServe, DIALOG
Corresponding to the printed version, this is an exhaustive treatise of applied chemistry and industrial technology. Subject areas covered include agricultural chemicals, drugs, fibers, fossil fuels, glass and ceramics, metals, semiconductors, and much more. (Note: Both BRS and CompuServe also include the Wiley *Encyclopedia of Polymer Science and Engineering* as well.) Covers current edition. Updated irregularly. Provider: Wiley Electronic Publishing.

CHEMISTRY. *See also* CHEMICAL ENGINEERING.

Analytica   ORBIT
Database covers worldwide literature on analytical chemistry. Provider: Royal Society of Chemistry, Nottingham, UK.

Analytical Abstracts   CompuServe, DIALOG, ORBIT

Covering all aspects of analytical chemistry, the database provides references from some 1,300 journals of which 300 are core journals along with material from conference papers, books, standards, and technical reports. Each record includes chemical names with synonyms/tradenames, CAS Registry Numbers, analyte and matrices data, and more. Covers 1980 to present. Updated monthly. Provider: The Royal Society of Chemistry, Nottingham, UK.

Beilstein Online   DIALOG, ORBIT
Database combines the printed *Handbuch de Organischen Chemie* (Beilstein's Handbook) with a file of unevaluated chemical data not yet in the printed version. This vast compendium of organic compounds covers constitution and configuration, preparation data, physical properties, chemical reaction data, and much more. Covers 1830 to present. Updated periodically. Provider: Springer Verlag, Heidelberg, Germany.

CA Search (Chemical Abstracts)
BRS, CompuServe, DIALOG, ORBIT
This database contains citations to chemical literature. It contains the basic bibliographic information that appears in the printed *Chemical Abstracts*. Each index entry has CA General Subject headings and CAS Registry numbers. Covers 1967 to present. Updated every two weeks. Provider: Chemical Abstracts Service.

Chemical Abstracts Source Index   CompuServe, ORBIT
Database provides a bibliography and record of library holdings of scientific and technical primary literature related to chemistry. Covers 1907 to present. Updated quarterly. Provider: Chemical Abstracts Service.

Chemical Dictionary   ORBIT
A companion file to *Chemical Abstracts*, above, the dictionary has all compounds cited in the literature from 1972 to date. Covers 1972 to present. Provider: Chemical Abstracts Service, American Chemical Society.

Chemical Exposure   CompuServe, DIALOG
Covers chemicals identified in the tissues of humans and wild and domestic animals. References are made to selected journal articles, conferences, and reports. Information reported includes chemical properties, synonyms, CAS Registry Num-

bers, formulas, tissue measured and analytical method used, demographics, and more. Covers 1974 to present. Updated annually. Provider: Science Applications International Corporation.

Chemical Hazards in Industry CompuServe
Database contains data on all documented hazards and health and safety information needed by those working in the chemical industry worldwide. Covers 1984 to present. Updated monthly. Provider: Data-Star.

Chemical Reactions Documentation Service
ORBIT
Covers the latest developments in synthetic organic chemistry. Provider: Derwent Publications, Ltd., London, UK.

Chemname CompuServe, DIALOG
Chemname is a dictionary for substances cited two or more times in *CA Search*, above. Each item shows CAS Registry Number, molecular formula, CA Substance Index name and synonyms, complete ring data, and more. Covers 1967 to present. Updated monthly. Provider: Dialog Information Services, Inc. and Chemical Abstracts Service.

Chemquest ORBIT
This is a catalog of 60 international research chemical suppliers. Search can be made by chemical and trade name, molecular formula, CAS Registry Number, or supplier name. Provider: Molecular Design Ltd.

Chemsis CompuServe, DIALOG
This is a directory of chemical substances cited once during a Collective Index Period of *Chemical Abstracts*. Each substance listing shows CAS Registry Number, molecular formula, CAS Substance Index name and synonyms, complete ring data, and more. Covers 1967 to present. Updated monthly. Provider: Dialog Information Services, Inc. and Chemical Abstracts Service.

Chemzero CompuServe, DIALOG
Chemzero is a directory of chemical substances for which there is no listing in other Chemical Abstracts databases. Information on listed substances includes CAS Registry Number, molecular formula, CA Substance Index name and synonyms, and complete ring data. Covers 1965 to present. Updated monthly. Provider: Dialog Information Services, Inc. and Chemical Abstracts Service.

Heilbron DIALOG
This chemical properties database contains the full text of the *Dictionary of Organic Compounds*, *Dictionary of Organometallic Compounds*, *Carbohydrates, Amino Acids, and Peptides*, *The Dictionary of Antibiotics and Related Compounds*, and the *Dictionary of Organophosphorus Compounds*. Other publications will be added as time goes on. Covers current editions. Updated twice a year. Provider: Chapman & Hall Ltd., London, UK.

Janssen CompuServe
Janssen is a catalog of research and industrial chemicals. All data are in English. Updated quarterly. Provider: Telesystems/Questel, Inc.

Kirk-Othmer Online (Kirk-Othmer Encyclopedia of Chemical Technology) BRS, CompuServe, DIALOG
Corresponding to the printed version, this is an exhaustive treatise of applied chemistry and industrial technology. Subject areas include agricultural chemicals, drugs, fibers, fossil fuels, glass and ceramics, metals, semiconductors, and much more. (Note: Both BRS and CompuServe include the Wiley *Encyclopedia of Polymer Science and Engineering* as well.) Covers current edition. Updated irregularly. Provider: Wiley Electronic Publishing.

Laboratory Hazards Bulletin CompuServe
Database indexes worldwide technical literature on chemical laboratory safety with topics including hazardous chemicals, legislation, and safety practices. Covers 1981 to present. Updated monthly. Provider: Pergamon Financial Data Services.

The Merck Index Online CompuServe, DIALOG
This is an updated and expanded version of *The Merck Index*, an internationally acknowledged, single-volume encyclopedia of chemicals, drugs, and other substances of biological importance. Covers late 19th century to present. Updated twice a year. Provider: Merck & Co.

National Union Catalog Codes ORBIT
Database has names, addresses, and National Union Catalog codes for all libraries mentioned in the *Chemical Abstracts Source Index*, above. Provider: Maxwell Online.

TSCA Chemical Substances Inventory DIALOG
Toxic Substances Control Act - CompuServe, ORBIT
This directory lists chemical substances in com-

mercial use in the United States as of June 1, 1979. Data are taken from the *Initial Inventory* of the *Toxic Substances Control Act Chemical Substances Inventory*; toxicity, however, is not the only criterion for inclusion. Covers May 1983 edition. Updated irregularly. Providers for DIALOG: Dialog Information Services, Inc. and Environmental Protection Agency, Office of Toxic Substances; CompuServe, ORBIT: Office of Toxic Substances, U.S. Environmental Protection Agency.

CHILD ABUSE

Child Abuse and Neglect CompuServe, DIALOG
This is an index of material ranging from research project descriptions to legal references in the field of child abuse in the United States. Also found here are abstracts of court decisions. Covers current edition. Updated twice a year. Provider: National Center on Child Abuse and Neglect, Children's Bureau, U.S. Department of Health and Human Services.

CHRISTIANITY

Bible (King James Version)
CompuServe, DIALOG
The full text of the modern revision of the 1769 King James Version of the Bible is available here. Provider: Thomas Nelson Publishers.

Churchnews International CompuServe
Newsletter has news of churches and religious agencies, associated with the National and World Council of Churches. Topics include peace, ethnicity, corporate responsibility, human rights, women's concerns, and more. Covers November 1982 to present. Full text, updated daily. Provider: NewsNet, Inc.

Lutheran News Service CompuServe
Newsletter gives news of the different denominations of the Lutheran Church worldwide. Covers July 1986 to present. Full text, updated weekly. Provider: NewsNet, Inc.

Religion Index BRS, CompuServe, DIALOG
Indexing, with abstracts, of articles from over 200 journals, over 300 multiple-author works, and book reviews covering church history, biblical literature, psychology of religion, and more. Covers 1975 to present. Updated monthly. Provider: American Theological Library Association.

RNS Daily News Reports CompuServe
Newsletter by the Religious News Service has news and analysis of major religious denominations around the world. Associated economic, political, and social concerns are included. Full text; updated daily. Provider: NewsNet, Inc.

United Methodist Information CompuServe
Taken from the news releases of the United Methodist Church, this full-text service has news, information, and features about the Church. United Methodist News Service articles and conference news are included. Updated daily. Provider: NewsNet, Inc.

CIVIL ENGINEERING. *See also* ENGINEERING.

ICONDA ORBIT
Database has international literature on construction, civil engineering, architecture, and town planning. Topics include structural design, material testing, bridges, tunnels, steel, concrete and masonry, energy conservation, design, and much more. Provider: ICONDA Agency c/o Information Centre for Regional Planning and Building Construction of the Fraunhofer Society.

COLLEGES AND UNIVERSITIES

ACS Directory of Graduate Research
CompuServe
This is a directory of college and university programs in chemistry, biochemistry, chemical engineering, and other chemical disciplines. Listings include program description and information on the faculty. Updated every two years. Provider: BRS Information Technologies.

Gradline DIALOG
Over 2,600 accredited institutions in the United States and Canada offering graduate study are covered here. Each graduate program at each school is included and its position within the administrative hierarchy of the parent institution is indicated. Coverage is for current year. Updated annually. Provider: Peterson's Guides, Inc.

National College Databank BRS
Directory contains descriptions of undergraduate institutions and programs in the United States and Canada. Data include majors, college size, location, financial aid, and more. Provider: Peterson's Guides, Inc.

Peterson's College Database
CompuServe, DIALOG
With information taken from the printed Peterson's guides, this online version provides descriptions to two- and four-year degree programs in the United States, Puerto Rico, Guam, the Virgin Islands, and Canada. Listings give general information on the governance of each college, profile of students, admissions data, costs, financial assistance, and more. Covers current data. Updated annually. Provider: Peterson's Guides, Inc.

COMPACT DISKS (CDs)

CD Computing News CompuServe
This newsletter covers compact disks and peripheral products focusing on developments, applications, and business ventures. Updated monthly. Provider: NewsNet, Inc.

CD Data Report CompuServe
Newsletter looks at developments in the compact disk industry including technical advances in hardware and software, markets, and top industry people. Covers June 1986 to present. Updated monthly. Provider: NewsNet, Inc.

CD-ROM Databases CompuServe
This is a catalog of available CD-ROM databases. Listings have title, price, and subject category along with the names, addresses, and telephone numbers of vendors. Updated monthly. Provider: NewsNet, Inc.

COMPANIES—INTERNATIONAL

Cancorp Canadian Corporations DIALOG
Here is comprehensive current financial data for over 5,600 Canadian public and private companies, with up to five years of historical information. Directory information includes name, address, telephone number, rankings, holding company data, officers, and more. Financial data include annual financial ratios, key accounts from balance sheets and income statements, and more. Textual information covers a description of the business, mergers and acquisitions, President's letter to shareholders, and ownership information. Updated weekly. Provider: Micromedia, Ltd., Toronto, Ontario, Canada.

D&B - Canadian Dun's Market Identifiers
CompuServe, DIALOG
This directory contains the name, address, and financial and marketing data for some 350,000 public and private Canadian companies. Covers current data. Updated quarterly. Provider: Dun's Marketing Services.

D&B - International Dun's Market Identifiers
CompuServe, DIALOG
This international directory includes names, addresses, sales and marketing data, parent companies (where applicable), and much more, for over 500,000 leading companies from over 130 foreign countries. Covers current data. Updated quarterly. Provider: Dun's Marketing Services.

Financial Times Company Abstracts
CompuServe, DIALOG
Abstracts of articles about more than 30,000 companies published in the London and Frankfurt editions of *The Financial Times* newspaper are presented here. Covers 1981 to present. Updated weekly. Provider: Financial Times Business Information, Ltd., London, UK.

Foreign Traders Index CompuServe, DIALOG
The *Index* is a directory of manufacturers, service organizations, agent representatives, retailers, wholesalers, distributors, and cooperatives in 130 foreign countries. Listings for each firm show the kind of business activity, product or service, officers, relative size, number of employees, and date of founding. Covers current four years. Updated three times a year. Provider: U.S. Department of Commerce.

Hoppenstedt Directory of German Companies
DIALOG
This directory covers 35,000 major German companies with sales of over 2.5 million DM or a minimum of 40 employees. Listings show company name, address, type of business, sales, and more. Entries are in both German and English. Covers current data. Updated quarterly. Provider: Hoppenstedt Wirtschaftsdatenbank, Darmstadt, Germany.

ICC British Company Directory CompuServe, DIALOG
All corporations in Scotland, United Kingdom, and Wales are covered. Each listing has company name, address, financial data, and more. Also included are records for about 500,000 dissolved companies. Covers current data. Updated weekly. Provider: ICC Information Group Ltd., London, UK.

ICC British Company Financial Datasheets
CompuServe, DIALOG
Financial information for over 100,000 British companies plus abridged information for more than 5,000. Data include company name, address, business type, sales, and more. Covers the last four years. Updated weekly. Provider: ICC Information Group Ltd., London, UK.

ICC International Business Research   DIALOG
All kinds of reports on British and European businesses are available, including annual reports, stockbroker reports, company account records, and more. Covers current data. Updated weekly. Provider: ICC Information Group Ltd., London, UK.

Key British Enterprises   CompuServe
Database contains profiles of important British companies ranked by annual sales. Updated monthly. Provider: Pergamon Financial Data Services.

McCarthy Company Fact Sheets   CompuServe
Service has detailed data on top companies worldwide. Provider: Profile Information.

Moody's Corporate News - International
CompuServe, DIALOG
Look here for detailed coverage of over 3,900 major corporations from over 100 countries. Both tabular and text records are provided on business news announcements and financial data. Covers 1983 to present. Updated weekly. Provider: Moody's Investor Services, Inc.

NTT Topics   CompuServe
This is the full text of the Nippon Telegraph & Telephone Corporation's newsletter with coverage of NTT activities, research and development, new technology and hardware, and procurement plans. Updated weekly. Provider: NewsNet, Inc.

COMPANIES—U.S.

BOC Week   CompuServe
Newsletter covers the Bell Operating Companies, looking at new products, services, construction, marketing plans, current Requests for Proposals, contracts awarded, and rates. Updated weekly. Provider: NewsNet, Inc.

Corporate Affiliations   CompuServe, DIALOG
Equivalent to the printed *Corporate Affiliations*, the online version is a directory showing corporate family linkage. Parent company entries show the corporate tree while affiliate company entries show where in the corporate family it fits. In addition, financial, executive, and much more data are given for each company. Covers current data. Updated quarterly. Provider: National Register Publishing Company.

Corptech   ORBIT
Database contains profiles of over 30,000 U.S. companies that make or develop high-technology products. Provider: Corporate Technology Information Service.

D&B - Dun's Financial Records Plus   DIALOG
Database contains up to three years of detailed financial statements for more than 750,000 public and private companies. History and operations background only is given for an additional 700,000 companies. Covers current data. Updated quarterly. Provider: Dun & Bradstreet Credit Services.

D&B - Dun's Market Identifiers   CompuServe, DIALOG
This service provides detailed data on more than 2,250,000 U.S. companies having five or more employees or with $1 million or more in sales. Product, financial, and marketing information for both private and public companies is given. Covers current data. Updated quarterly. Provider: Dun's Marketing Services.

D&B - Dun's Electronic Yellow Pages
CompuServe (not all categories), DIALOG
This business directory has information on almost 8.5 million businesses and professionals in the United States. Each listing includes name, address, telephone numbers, and more. The directory is broken down into 14 broad categories ranging from agriculture to wholesale. Covers current data. Updated quarterly. Provider: Dun's Marketing Services.

D&B - Million Dollar Directory   CompuServe, DIALOG
Directory has comprehensive business data on more than 160,000 U.S. companies with a net worth of $500,000 or more. Also included is hard-to-find information on privately held companies. Covers current data. Updated annually. Provider: Dun's Marketing Services.

Disclosure Database   BRS, CompuServe, DIALOG
Disclosure consists of detailed financial information on over 12,000 companies. Data are taken from Securities and Exchange Commission filings.

In addition annual report extracts are available. Covers current data. Updated weekly. Provider: Disclosure, Incorporated.

Disclosure/Health BRS

This portion of the *Disclosure Database* provides annual and quarterly financial and management data on publicly traded health-care, pharmaceutical, and medical equipment companies. Provider: Disclosure, Incorporated.

Disclosure/History BRS

Database has historical financial and text data taken from Securities and Exchange Commission filings of more than 12,000 U.S. and foreign publicly traded companies. Provider: Disclosure, Incorporated.

Disclosure/Spectrum Ownership

BRS, CompuServe, DIALOG

Database has public corporation ownership as taken from Securities and Exchange Commission filings. Common stock holdings of institutions, insiders, and 5-percent beneficial owners of some 5,000 companies is available. Covers current data. Updated quarterly. Provider: Disclosure, Incorporated.

Edge On & About AT&T CompuServe

Newsletter has news and analysis of American Telephone and Telegraph Company product development, marketing, strategy, and organization changes along with the outside events affecting the company. Full text; updated every two weeks. Provider: NewsNet, Inc.

Moody's Corporate Profiles

CompuServe, DIALOG

Profiles gives descriptive and financial details on significant publicly held U.S. companies. These include all companies listed on the New York and American Stock Exchanges and some 1,300 of the most active new companies traded over-the-counter. In addition, analyses of over 900 companies of high investor interest are given. Covers current data. Updated weekly. Provider: Moody's Investor Services, Inc.

Outlook on AT&T CompuServe

Full-text newsletter provides information on all areas of the activities of the American Telephone and Telegraph Corporation. Updated monthly. Provider: NewsNet, Inc.

PTS Annual Reports Abstracts (ARA)

CompuServe, DIALOG

Abstracts of the text and statistical data from the annual reports of over 3,000 publicly held U.S. and selected foreign companies are available here. Covers current data. Updated monthly. Provider: Predicasts.

Publishers, Distributors, and Wholesalers

DIALOG

This directory contains complete address information for over 21,000 *Books In Print* publishers, 15,000 associations, 400 audiocassette publishers, 7,000 software publishers, 500 microcomputer hardware manufacturers, 1,000 microcomputer peripheral manufacturers, 2,500 distributors, and 1,500 wholesalers. Covers current data. Updated monthly. Provider: R.R. Bowker.

Report on AT&T CompuServe

Newsletter has news and analysis of the American Telephone and Telegraph Corporation, looking at telephone equipment, computers, long-distance service, marketing, joint ventures, and other matters. Full text, updated weekly. Provider: NewsNet, Inc.

Report on IBM CompuServe

Containing news and analysis of the International Business Machines Corporation, this full-text newsletter includes detailed descriptions of product and pricing announcements and comprehensive reports on key company issues. Updated weekly. Provider: NewsNet, Inc.

Sid Cato's Newsletter on Annual Reports

CompuServe

Newsletter reports on production and uses of company annual reports. Topics include discussion of Securities and Exchange Commission requirements and comments on the design, content, and influence of annual reports. Full text; updated monthly. Provider: NewsNet, Inc.

Standard & Poor's Corporate Descriptions

DIALOG

This is a source for detailed descriptions of more than 9,000 publicly owned U.S. companies. Data include a complete company background, financial statement figures, and stock and bond data. Covers current data. Updated every two weeks. Provider: Standard & Poor's Corporation.

Standard & Poor's Register - Corporate

CompuServe, DIALOG

Key facts on over 45,000 U.S. public and private companies and some foreign companies with sales usually in excess of $1 million are available here. Data are provided on companies and their subsidiaries, divisions, and affiliates. Entries include address, financial, marketing, and key personnel. Covers current data. Updated quarterly. Provider: Standard & Poor's Corporation.

Trinet Company Database
CompuServe, DIALOG
The database gives financial data on U.S. public and private businesses with 20 or more employees. Aggregate company information is given here while data on individual branches (if any) is given in *Trinet Establishment Database*, below. Current address and financial and marketing information is given for each business. Covers current data. Updated quarterly. Provider: TRINET, Inc.

Trinet Establishment Database CompuServe, DIALOG
A companion to the *Trinet Company Database*, this compilation provides information on company branch locations. Two types of reports are available: one gives a company's line of business; the other, market share. Covers current data. Updated quarterly. Provider: TRINET, Inc.

COMPUTER BULLETIN BOARDS

Bulletin Board Systems CompuServe
Newsletter reports on electronic bulletin board systems and includes news on legal issues and uses to which such systems are put. Newsletter also has profiles and telephone numbers of selected systems. Full text; updated monthly. Provider: NewsNet, Inc.

COMPUTER DATABASES

Cuadra Directory of Online Databases
CompuServe
Database is a directory of online databases worldwide with public access. Each entry shows database type, subject, language, hours of operation, and name and address. Updated quarterly. Provider: Data-Star.

Database of Databases CompuServe, DIALOG
This directory gives details on publicly accessible databases available through an online service, batch processor, direct lease, license, or purchase (tape, diskette, or other). Covers varying dates. Updated irregularly. Provider: Gale Research Company.

Data Informer CompuServe
This newsletter covers free and low-cost online databases. Emphasis is on free databases and advice is given on cost-effective methods of using online services. Updated monthly. Provider: NewsNet, Inc.

Electronic Information Report CompuServe
Covering the online database business, this newsletter reports on new developments and markets, highlights of recent meetings, and people in the field. In addition, lists and descriptions of new databases are included. Covers March 1982 to present. Updated monthly. Provider: NewsNet, Inc.

Knowledge Industry Publications Database BRS, CompuServe
Directory contains descriptions of all publicly accessible online databases in North America. Entries show producer, vendor, price information, subjects, and more. Updated quarterly. Provider: Knowledge Industry Publications, Inc.

Online Chronicle CompuServe, DIALOG
Look here for expanded full-text coverage of news from *Online* and *Database* magazines. News items include online industry events and people, new databases, search aids, and computer equipment. A *Jobline* section has job listings and ads from professionals seeking new positions. Covers October 1981 to September 1982 and September 1983 to present. Updated every two weeks. Provider: Online, Inc.

COMPUTERS. *See also* COMPUTER BULLETIN BOARDS; COMPUTER DATABASES; COMPUTER SOFTWARE.

Advanced Military Computing CompuServe
Newsletter covers military computer research, procurement, and uses. Updated twice a month. Provider: NewsNet, Inc.

Business Computer CompuServe
This full-text service has articles and reviews expanded from newspaper columns on computer products and the business applications of computers. Also has software and hardware comparisons, compatibility tests, and innovations. Updated twice a week. Provider: NewsNet, Inc.

Computer ASAP DIALOG
The full text and indexing for 70 percent of the articles indexed in *Computer Database*, below, are contained here. Included are product reports, comparisons, best buys, and articles on rapidly growing high-tech fields. Company names are indexed

for easy access to information. Covers 1988 to present. Updated weekly. Provider: Information Access Company.

Computer Book Review CompuServe
This full-text newsletter reviews books on all areas of computers including programming languages, computer education, employment opportunities, and more. Updated monthly. Provider: NewsNet, Inc.

Computer Cookbook CompuServe
This is the full text of the book about all areas of small and midsized computer systems and applications. Price comparisons and purchase advice is included. Covers current edition. Updated annually. Provider: NewsNet, Inc.

Computer Database BRS, CompuServe, DIALOG
This database has abstracts and indexing from journals covering most aspects of computers, telecommunications, and electronics. Included are product reports, comparisons, best buys, and profiles and financial data on computer, telecommunications, and electronics companies. Additionally, the full text of articles from over 50 magazines dating from 1983 are included. Covers 1983 to present. Updated weekly. Provider: Information Access Company.

Computer Decisions CompuServe
The full text of this trade magazine is presented. News and analysis of the computer industry includes systems and data processing. Covers 1983 to present. Updated monthly. Provider: DIALOG Information Services (drawn from the Trade & Industry ASAP database).

Computergram International CompuServe
This is the full text of the largest daily newspaper covering data processing, communications, microelectronics, and high-tech investing. Updated daily. Provider: NewsNet, Inc.

Computing Today! Journal CompuServe
Full-text newsletter has computer industry news announcements with particular coverage of microcomputer products, both hardware and software. Also included are in-depth reviews of microcomputer software. Covers February 1986 to present. Updated weekly. Provider: NewsNet, Inc.

Data Channels CompuServe
This newsletter of data communications news and applications includes new technologies, products,

regulation and business trends in data transmission, electronic mail, local area networks, and office automation. Covers 1982 to present. Updated weekly. Provider: NewsNet, Inc.

Datamation CompuServe
The full text of this key computer and dataprocessing journal is available. Covers 1983 to present. Updated monthly. Provider: DIALOG Information Services (drawn from the Trade & Industry ASAP database).

EDI News CompuServe
This full-text newsletter provides coverage only of electronic data interchange including emerging technologies, trends, and strategies. Updated monthly. Provider: NewsNet, Inc.

HR/PC Online CompuServe
Newsletter looks at human resource management's use of personal computers. Topics include news, product reviews, and case studies of effective applications. Full text; updated monthly. Provider: NewsNet, Inc.

IDB Online - The Computing Industry Daily
CompuServe
Full-text newsletter reports on the computer industry and related areas including telecommunications, artificial intelligence, and CAD/CAM. Coverage includes technology, products, and business news with emphasis placed on European events. Updated daily. Provider: NewsNet, Inc.

InfoWorld CompuServe
Look here for the full text of this newsmagazine of the microcomputer industry. Topics include news, product reviews, and analysis of industry trends. Updated weekly.

Interactivity Report CompuServe
Covers worldwide videotex industry giving reports and statistics on products, companies, and industry trends. Full-text newsletter; updated monthly. Provider: NewsNet, Inc.

Japan Computer Industry Scan CompuServe
Taken from *Feedback from Fujitsu*, this full-text service focuses on the Japanese computer industry looking at technical, product, company, and business developments. Updated every two months. Provider: NewsNet, Inc.

Lawyers' Micro Users Group Newsletter
CompuServe
Newsletter focuses on the use of microcomputers

in law offices and looks at hardware, software, databases, and applications. Updated monthly. Provider: NewsNet, Inc.

Microcomputer Index   CompuServe, DIALOG
The *Index* is a subject and abstract guide to articles from over 50 computer publications. Subjects include general articles on microcomputer matters, book, software, and hardware reviews, new products, and more. Each entry includes a brief abstract and complete citation. Covers 1981 to present. Updated monthly. Provider: Learned Information, Inc.

Microcomputer Resources   CompuServe
This full-text service contains reviews of products in the data processing, telecommunications, and fiber optics areas. Updated monthly. Provider: NewsNet, Inc.

Microcomputer Software & Hardware Guide
CompuServe, DIALOG
These guides have information of almost all microcomputer software and hardware made in the United States. Bibliographic entries are available for all types of software from business to education. Each entry has ordering information, technical specifications, a brief description, and more. Covers current data. Updated monthly. Provider: R.R. Bowker.

Microsearch   CompuServe, ORBIT
Database has abstracts of articles on microcomputer hardware, software, and peripherals including reviews and interviews with industry personalities. Covers 1981 to present. Updated every two weeks. Provider: Information, Inc.

Online Products News   CompuServe
Newsletter covers videotex/teletext products and services. Topics include hardware, online databases, bulletin boards, electronic mail, and broadcast and cable television, with emphasis on personal computer products. Full text, updated monthly. Provider: NewsNet, Inc.

Optical Information Systems Update
CompuServe
Full-text newsletter provides news of optical-based information systems such as videodisk, optical disk, and CD-ROM. New product releases, software, conference news, and contract announcements are provided. Updated every two weeks. Provider: NewsNet, Inc.

PC Magazine   CompuServe
This is the full text of the magazine, which focuses on IBM and compatible personal computers. Topics include product news, reviews, product comparisons, advice, utilities, and more. Covers 1983 to present. Updated monthly. Provider: DIALOG Information Services (drawn from the Trade & Industry ASAP database).

PC Week   CompuServe
This full-text newsweekly focuses on IBM and compatible personal computers. Topics include product news, reviews, and more. Covers 1983 to present. Updated monthly. Provider: DIALOG Information Services (drawn from the Trade & Industry ASAP database).

Seybold Outlook: Professional Computing
CompuServe
The impact of computers in business and offices along with industry news and trade show reports is the focus of this full-text newsletter. Updated monthly. Provider: NewsNet, Inc.

Supertech   CompuServe, DIALOG
Supertech corresponds to the printed abstract journals *Telegen Reporter*, *Artificial Intelligence Abstracts*, *CAD/CAM Abstracts*, *Robomatix Reporter*, and *Telecommunications Abstracts*. It covers the fields of biotechnology, artificial intelligence, computer-aided design and manufacturing, robotics, and telecommunications. Covers 1972 to present (robotics/biotechnology), 1984 to present (artificial intelligence/CAD/CAM/telecommunications). Updated monthly. Provider: R.R. Bowker.

TDS Computer Calendar   CompuServe
This is a listing of events (seminars, conferences, trade shows, association meetings, and others) of interest to computer professionals. Updated twice a week. Provider: NewsNet, Inc.

TDS Computer Report Search   CompuServe
Weekly digest has brief summaries of reports on new technical applications, developments, and marketing strategies relating to computer markets. Updated weekly. Provider: NewsNet, Inc.

Telecom A.M.   CompuServe
Daily weekday service gives news of telecommunications such as meetings, hearings, and other government activities. Full text; updated daily. Provider: NewsNet, Inc.

Telecommuting Report   CompuServe
Newsletter has articles and case studies on work in nontraditional places using computers and telecommunications. Full text; updated monthly. Provider: NewsNet, Inc.

COMPUTER SOFTWARE

Business Software Database   BRS, CompuServe, DIALOG
This database has descriptions of business application software for micro- and minicomputers. Information includes description of software; manufacturer's name, address, and telephone; and price and number of units sold. In addition, details on availability, machine compatibility, description of documentation, customer assistance, and more are provided. Covers current data. Updated quarterly. Provider: Information Sources, Inc.

Buyer's Guide to Micro Software   BRS
Service has descriptions of software packages along with costs, applications, hardware requirements, and more. Provider: Online, Inc.

.Menu - The International Software Database
CompuServe, DIALOG
.Menu is an inclusive directory of commercially available software for micro- and minicomputers. Each entry contains a brief description, publisher's name, distributor, availability, computer compatibility, price, and more. Covers current offerings. Updated monthly. Provider: Black Box Corporation.

Micro Software Directory   DIALOG
This directory of business and professional software available in the U.S. has product, technical, and bibliographic data on leading software packages. The database is highly selective, listing only software that gets at least a "good" rating by the technical press, all software from major publishers even if badly reviewed, and software unique to specific businesses (including library and medical software). Each entry has an abstract and full citation when available. Covers current data. Updated monthly. Provider: Online, Inc.

NASA Software Directory   CompuServe
Full-text directory describes software sponsored and developed by the U.S. National Aeronautics and Space Administration. Listings include program specifications and potential applications. Covers current annual edition. Updated monthly. Provider: NewsNet, Inc.

Online Microcomputer Software Guide and Directory
CompuServe
Full-text directory has descriptions and evaluations of microcomputer programs. Updated monthly. Provider: BRS Information Technologies.

CONFERENCES. *See* FAIRS, CONFERENCES, AND MEETINGS.

CONGRESS. *See* FEDERAL GOVERNMENT.

CONSUMER PRODUCTS INFORMATION. *See also* INDUSTRIAL PRODUCTS INFORMATION.

Consumer Drug Information Fulltext
BRS, CompuServe, DIALOG
Database contains the full text of the *Consumer Drug Digest* and has detailed descriptions of over 260 compounds making up more than 80 percent of all prescription drugs and some important nonprescription drugs. Such information as side effects, interactions, mode of action, dosage and use, and more is included. Covers current edition. Updated quarterly with annual reloads. Provider: American Society of Hospital Pharmacists.

Consumer Reports   CompuServe, DIALOG
The full text of this major consumer products testing organization's 11 monthly issues is available. Testing covers all areas of consumer products from automobiles to cleaning supplies, financial services, consumer law, and more. Consumers Union does not allow use of its material, name, or work (including this database) in advertising or as an endorsement of any product or service or for any commercial purpose. Covers 1982 to present. Updated monthly. Provider: Consumers Union.

CONSUMER RESEARCH. *See* MARKETING.

D

DATABASES. *See* COMPUTER DATABASES.

DEFENSE. *See* MILITARY.

DEMOGRAPHICS

American Marketplace   CompuServe
Newsletter provides information on Census Bureau demographic data. Full text, updated every two weeks. Provider: NewsNet, Inc.

Cendata   CompuServe, DIALOG
Cendata makes available selected statistical data,

the 20 most recent press releases, and product information from the Census Bureau. Data areas include agriculture, business, construction and housing, foreign trade, government, international, manufacturing, population, and more. Demographic data is excerpted from *Current Population Reports,* the 1980 census, and includes limited data on more than 200 countries. Covers current information. Updated daily. Provider: U.S. Bureau of the Census.

D&B - Donnelley Demographics   CompuServe, DIALOG
Database provides access to data from the 1980 U.S. census plus estimates and projections prepared by Donnelley Marketing Information Services. Covers current data. Updated annually. Provider: Donnelley Marketing Services.

Population Bibliography   CompuServe, DIALOG
Population is the focus of this database that indexes monographs, journals, technical reports, dissertations, unpublished reports, and more. Topics include abortion, family planning and fertility, demography, policy and law, research methodology, and much more. Covers 1966 to 1984. No updates. Provider: Carolina Population Center, University of North Carolina.

DIAGNOSTIC TESTS

Health Instrument File   BRS
Database has descriptions of evaluative tests used in the health and psychosocial fields. Provider: Behavioral Measurement Database Services.

DISABILITIES. *See also* SPECIAL EDUCATION.

Abledata   BRS, CompuServe
Database contains data on products for rehabilitation and technical aids for the disabled, which can include devices and educational and vocational materials. Updated monthly. Provider: Adaptive Equipment Center; Newington Children's Hospital.

DISSERTATIONS

Dissertation Abstracts Online   BRS, CompuServe, DIALOG
This is a subject, title, and author guide to almost every U.S. doctoral dissertation since 1861 in all subject areas. Additional listings are for thousands of Canadian dissertations and an increasing number of international papers. British dissertations since 1988 are available. From 1980 on, the vast majority of listings include abstracts. Covers 1861 to present. Updated monthly. Provider: University Microfilms International.

DOCTORS

ExpertNet   DIALOG
ExpertNet contains profiles of over 1,000 medical experts who have agreed to do medico-legal consulting. Most are physicians in active practice or teaching. All geographic areas and almost all medical specialties are represented. Note that though most have medico-legal experience, "professional witnesses" are discouraged from participating in ExpertNet. Each entry shows the expert's medical specialties, education and clinical training, board certification, past experience, and current positions. Any travel limitations, willingness to testify, usual hourly fees, and other comments are included. Covers current listings. Updated five to six times per year. Provider: ExpertNet, Ltd.

DRUG ABUSE. *See* SUBSTANCE ABUSE.

DRUGS AND MEDICINES. *See also* SUBSTANCE ABUSE.

Consumer Drug Information Fulltext
BRS, CompuServe, DIALOG
Database contains the full text of the *Consumer Drug Digest* and has detailed descriptions of over 260 compounds making up more than 80 percent of all prescription drugs and some important nonprescription drugs. Such information as side effects, interactions, mode of action, dosage and use, and more is included. Covers current edition. Updated quarterly with annual reloads. Provider: American Society of Hospital Pharmacists.

De Haen Drug Data   CompuServe, DIALOG
This comprehensive database contains information taken from more than 1,200 worldwide biomedical journals, over 20 secondary references, and many abstracts/summaries of conference papers. Topics range from adverse drug reactions to investigational drugs to pharmaceutical chemistry and much more. The database is divided into four sections, *De Haen's Drugs in Prospect, De Haen's Drugs in Use, De Haen's Drugs in Research,* and *De Haen's ADRIS* (Adverse Drug Reactions & Interactions System). Covers 1980 to present. Updated every two months. Provider: Paul de Haen International, Inc.

Deltabank CompuServe
Information on drug and other interactions with medical tests is the subject of this database. Covers 1970 to present. Updated quarterly. Provider: Data-Star.

Diogenes BRS, CompuServe, DIALOG
Database covers Food and Drug Administration regulatory data. Included are news stories and unpublished documents regarding U.S. regulation of pharmaceuticals and medical devices. Full text is provided for key material. Covers 1976 to present. Updated weekly. Provider: DIOGENES.

DRUGINFO and Alcohol Use and Abuse BRS, CompuServe
Database covers the educational, sociological, and psychological aspects of drug and alcohol use and abuse and includes material concerning treatment, evaluation, chemical dependence, and alcoholism in different populations. Covers 1968 to present. Updated quarterly. Provider: Drug Information Services, University of Minnesota.

Drug Information Fulltext BRS, CompuServe, DIALOG
Database corresponds to two printed works, *The American Hospital Formulary Service* and *The Handbook on Injectable Drugs,* which together have data on 1,217 commercially available and 57 investigational drugs in use in the United States. Material covers drug stability, action, usage, interactions, and more. Covers current data. Updated quarterly. Provider: American Society of Hospital Pharmacists.

Drug Topics CompuServe
This retail drug trade magazine reports on trends in health care, medical and pharmaceutical developments, and legislation affecting the industry. Covers 1983 to present. Updated monthly. Provider: DIALOG Information Services (drawn from the Trade & Industry ASAP database).

International Pharmaceutical Abstracts BRS, CompuServe, DIALOG
Over 650 pharmaceutical, medical, and related journals yield 17,000 citations a year for this database that covers all aspects of the development and use of drugs and of professional pharmaceutical practice. Starting in 1985, information is also available on state regulations, salaries, manpower studies, laws, and more. All abstracts are in English. Covers 1970 to present. Updated monthly. Provider: American Society of Hospital Pharmacists.

Iowa Drug Information Service BRS
Index covers over 160 biomedical journals and provides citations to articles on human drug therapy. Each entry shows drugs, diseases, and clinical concepts covered by the article. Covers 1965 to present. Provider: Iowa Drug Information Service.

Martindale Online DIALOG
This is a full-text database on drugs and medicines that is related to the printed *Martindale, The Extra Pharmacopoeia* but has more data and is updated more frequently. Detailed information on each substance includes nomenclature, CAS Registry Numbers, properties, precautions, actions, uses, and much more. Covers current edition. Updated approximately once a year. Provider: The Pharmaceutical Society of Great Britain, London, UK.

The Merck Index Online CompuServe, DIALOG
This is an updated and expanded version of *The Merck Index,* an internationally acknowledged, single-volume encyclopedia of chemicals, drugs, and other substances of biological importance. Covers late 19th century to present. Updated twice a year. Provider: Merck & Co.

Pharmaprojects BRS, CompuServe
This database is a register of pharmaceutical, biotechnological, new formulation, and combination development projects around the world. Over 3,500 drugs believed to be in active development are included. Selected literature references are provided as well. Corresponds to the printed *Pharmaprojects.* Updated monthly. Provider: PJB Publications, Ltd.

Pharmline CompuServe
Service covers data on the adverse effects, bioactivity, and clinical pharmacokinetics of drugs. Covers 1978 to present. Updated weekly. Provider: Data-Star.

Ringdoc DIALOG, ORBIT
This database contains data of concern to the pharmaceutical industry. Information includes chemistry, biochemistry, pharmacology, action, toxicology, preparation and testing, and much more. Available to subscribers only by contacting Derwent offices in the United States or the United King-

dom. Covers 1964 to present. Updated monthly. Provider: Derwent Publications, Ltd., London, UK.

Sedbase   DIALOG

This full-text service provides critical analysis of the literature of side effects of drugs in current use. All material is prepared by recognized authorities who assess and distill some 9,000 journal articles each year. In addition, the full text of the last 12 years of *Meyler's Side Effects of Drugs*, *Side Effects of Drugs Annual*, and *Marler's Pharmacological & Chemical Synonyms* are available. Covers current data. Updated quarterly. Provider: Elsevier Science Publishers B.V., Amsterdam, The Netherlands.

Standard Drug File   ORBIT

Directory contains some 7,500 known drugs and other compounds and includes full name, standard registry name, pharmacological classification of standard activities, and more. Provider: Derwent Publications, Ltd., London, UK.

Toxline   BRS

Database has citations to more than 850,000 sources of information on pharmacological, biomedical, physiological, and toxicological effects of drugs and other chemicals. Covers 1965 to present. Provider: National Library of Medicine.

E

EARTH SCIENCES. *See also* SCIENCE.

Antarctic Bibliography   CompuServe

Database has references only to materials on the Antarctic region including exploration, navigation, transportation, and more. Covers 1962 to present. Updated quarterly. Provider: ORBIT Search Service.

COLD   ORBIT

Database covers the Antarctic and subantarctic islands. Areas include snow, ice, frozen ground, navigation on ice, civil engineering in cold regions, and more. Provider: Cold Regions Research and Engineering Laboratory of the U.S. Army Corps of Engineers.

Geoarchive   CompuServe, DIALOG

This index provides comprehensive references to material in the geosciences. Over 100,000 items are added each year from more than 5,000 serials, books from over 1,000 publishers, conferences, dissertations, and technical reports. In addition,

some 100,000 geological maps from the Institute of Geological Sciences libraries are indexed. Areas include geophysics, geochemistry, geology, paleontology, and mathematical geology. Covers 1974 to present. Updated monthly. Provider: Geosystems, Oxon, UK.

Geobase   DIALOG

This international database indexes material on geography, geology, ecology, and related areas. Database has all references published in *Geological Abstracts, Parts A through G*; *International Development Abstracts*; *Geological Abstracts Series*; *Mineralogical Abstracts*; and *Ecological Abstracts*. More than 2,000 journals are completely indexed with partial coverage of 3,000 more along with over 2,000 books, monographs, and so on. Covers 1980 to present. Updated monthly. Provider: Geo Abstracts Ltd., Norwich, UK.

Geomechanics Abstracts   CompuServe, ORBIT

Abstracts of articles from selected scientific and technical sources on rock and soil mechanics and engineering geology are contained in this database, which corresponds to the printed book of the same title. Covers 1977 to date. Updated every two weeks. Provider: Rock Mechanics Information Service.

Georef   CompuServe, DIALOG, ORBIT

Extensive coverage of all areas of geology, geochemistry, geophysics, mineralogy, paleontology, petrology, and seismology is included in this index. References are given for over 4,500 worldwide journals, and books, conference papers, dissertations, maps, and government publications. About 40 percent of the material indexed is U.S.-published. For-profit organizations that spend over $500 per year for *Georef* use must become *Georef* subscribers or pay a surcharge. Covers 1785 to present (North American material) and 1933 to present (worldwide material). Updated monthly. Provider: American Geological Institute.

Meteorological and Geoastrophysical Abstracts   DIALOG

This index provides English citations, most with abstracts, for worldwide meteorological and geoastrophysical research. Over 200 sources that include journals, monographs, proceedings, and so on are scanned for inclusion. Topics covered include meteorology, astrophysics, physical oceanography, environmental sciences, and more. Covers

1972 to present (abstracts for 1972–73 and 1976 to present). Updated irregularly. Provider: American Meteorological Society.

ECOLOGY

Enviroline   CompuServe, DIALOG, ORBIT
This database has abstracts from over 5,000 international primary and secondary source publications covering all environmental areas. Fields included range from management to political science to chemistry as they apply to environmental issues. Covers 1971 to present. Updated monthly. Provider: R.R. Bowker.

Environmental Bibliography
CompuServe, DIALOG
Database provides an index to over 300 publications in the fields of general human ecology, atmospheric studies, energy, land and water resources, and nutrition and health. Covers 1973 to present. Updated every two months. Provider: Environmental Studies Institute.

Environmental Compliance Update   CompuServe
Publication watches legislative, economic, and technical developments that affect businesses complying with environmental regulations. Updated monthly. Provider: NewsNet, Inc.

Ground Water Monitor   CompuServe
Newsletter monitors regulation, legislation, and technology in connection with groundwater resources. Topics include contamination and protection. Full text, updated weekly. Provider: NewsNet, Inc.

National Environmental Data Referral Service
BRS
This is a catalog and index of publicly accessible environmental information including climatology, meteorology, ecology, pollution, geography, geophysics, geology, hydrology, limnology, oceanography, and satellite data. Provider: National Environmental Data Referral Service, U.S. Department of Commerce.

ECONOMICS. *See also* SOCIAL SCIENCES.

Abstracts of Working Papers in Economics
CompuServe
Database contains abstracts of major economics research studies and papers from around the world. Covers 1982 to present. Updated monthly. Provider: BRS Information Technologies.

Boot Cove Economic Forecast   CompuServe
Full text of newsletter that analyzes and forecasts the economy and covers the Gross National Product (GNP), stock market, finance, currency, and more. Also provides key economic data and economic analysis of important political events. Updated monthly. Provider: NewsNet, Inc.

Econbase   CompuServe, DIALOG
Econbase provides a broad range of economic and business statistics including economics, business conditions, finance, manufacturing, household income distribution, and demographics. U.S. regional and international data can also be found, along with forecast data on several of the areas. Covers as early as 1948 for some time series. Updated monthly. Provider: WEFA Group.

Economic Literature Index
CompuServe, DIALOG
This is an index of articles and book reviews from 260 economics journals and from approximately 200 monographs per year. Abstracts for about 25 percent of the entries are available starting June 1984. These are in English, written by the author/editor of the article, and are about 100 words long. The *Index* corresponds to the printed quarterly index of the *Journal of Economic Literature* and the annual index of *Index of Economic Articles*. Covers 1969 to present. Updated quarterly. Provider: American Economic Association.

Economic Trends in Germany   CompuServe
Newsletter covers the economy of the Federal Republic of Germany with information and analysis on the different industrial sectors and financial markets. Full text; updated monthly. Provider: NewsNet, Inc.

Economist   CompuServe
Database has the full text of the premier British economics and business magazines that covers worldwide developments. Covers December 1981 to present. Updated weekly. Provider: Profile Information.

Foreign Trade and Economic Abstracts
CompuServe, DIALOG
Provides abstracts of some 1,800 journals plus books, reports, and directories in all areas of economics and international economics. Broad coverage includes markets, specific industries, import regulations and management, and much more.

Covers 1974 to present. Updated semimonthly. Provider: Netherlands Foreign Trade Agency, The Hague, The Netherlands.

GAS Statistics and Ratings CompuServe
Service has statistical data on money supply, exchange rates, and gross domestic product for all countries. Updated every six weeks. Provider: Profile Information.

Latin American Debt Chronicle CompuServe
Newsletter provides reports and analyses of the Latin American and Caribbean debt crisis. Topics include negotiations, balance of payments, internal developments, and foreign debt updates by country. Updated twice a week. Provider: NewsNet, Inc.

Metra National Development Plans CompuServe
Service has analyses and progress reports on developing and communist countries' economic developments and budgets. Provider: Profile Information.

PTS International Forecasts
CompuServe, DIALOG
Look here for abstracts of published forecasts of economics, industries, and products of all countries (except the United States). Historical data are also provided. Data are taken from over 1,000 international sources ranging from annual reports to United Nations publications. Covers 1971 to present. Updated monthly. Provider: Predicasts.

PTS U.S. Forecasts CompuServe. DIALOG
Abstracted are published forecasts of economics, industries, and products for the United States. Historical data are also provided. Sources range from trade journals to government reports. 25,000 records from the *Census of Manufacturers* for 1967, 1972, and 1977 are also included. Covers July 1971 to present. Updated monthly. Provider: Predicasts.

PTS U.S. Historical Time Series CompuServe, DIALOG
The *Time Series* is in two parts. The first (*Predicasts Composites*) contains 500 time series of historical data (since 1957) and projections from published forecasts through 1990. Population, GNP, production, and other economic data are included. The other section (*Predicasts Basebook*) has annual data (since 1957) for about 47,000 series providing figures for many types of industries, products, and services. Years included in *Time Series* vary,

with earliest start 1957. Updated quarterly. Provider: Predicasts.

Standard & Poor's Economic Report CompuServe
Full-text service gives statistics along with analysis of the economy and interest rates. Also includes predictions for major economic indicators and interest rates. Updated twice a month. Provider: NewsNet, Inc.

EDUCATION. *See also* COLLEGES AND UNIVERSITIES; DISSERTATIONS; EDUCATIONAL MATERIALS; SPECIAL EDUCATION; TESTING; VOCATIONAL AND TECHNICAL EDUCATION.

Base d'Information Robert Debre CompuServe
Database provides information in English, French, and Spanish on children's education, development, and health worldwide with a concentration on developing countries. Covers 1980 to present. Updated monthly. Provider: G. Cam Serveur, Paris, France.

British Education Index DIALOG
Database combines the *British Education Index* (BEI) and the *British Education Theses Index* (BETI), providing broad coverage of literature on education and teaching of specific subjects. All aspects of education from preschool to higher and adult education such as cognitive development, computer-assisted learning, educational policy, science education, and much more is indexed. Covers 1976 to present for BEI and 1950 to present for BETI. Updated quarterly (BEI) and annually (BETI). Provider: British Education Index, Leeds, UK.

D&B - Dun's Electronic Directory of Education
CompuServe, DIALOG
Database provides directory listings for over 100,000 U.S. schools, 15,000 school districts, 3,000 colleges and universities, and 15,000 public libraries. School listings include public, private, and Catholic schools. Library listings cover both main and branch libraries. Additional information includes names of staff and demographic data (enrollment, expenditures, and special facilities). Covers current data. Updated twice a year. Provider: Dun's Marketing Services.

Education Index CompuServe
This index of major English-language periodicals provides references for all areas of education. Covers September 1983 to present. Updated twice a week. Provider: H.W. Wilson Company.

ERIC (Educational Resources Information Center)
CompuServe, DIALOG, ORBIT
Corresponding to two printed indexes, *Resources in Education* and *Current Index to Journals in Education*, *ERIC* indexes material in all educational fields and related disciplines. Listings are derived from research reports and over 700 periodicals. Covers 1966 to present. Updated monthly. Provider: U.S. Department of Education, OERI, and the ERIC Processing and Reference Facility.

Ontario Educational Resources Information BRS, CompuServe
All references in this bibliographic database are in English and French. It is a comprehensive listing of educational research, curriculum guidelines, reports, and learning materials, which include educational software for primary and secondary schools. Covers 1970 to date. Updated three times a year. Provider: Ontario Ministry of Education, Toronto, Ontario, Canada.

School Practices Information File CompuServe
Database contains descriptions of current educational practices, programs, tests, and materials. Updated irregularly. Provider: BRS Information Technologies.

EDUCATIONAL MATERIALS

A-V Online CompuServe, DIALOG
This database of nonprint educational material lists material ranging from preschool to professional and graduate school. References cover film and filmstrips (16 and 35mm), transparencies, audio and video tapes, disk recordings, motion-picture cartridges, and slides. Covers 1964 to present, with selective earlier records. Updated quarterly. Provider: Access Information, Inc.

Microcomputers in Education CompuServe
Full-text newsletter reports on educational microcomputer applications. Topics include technical developments, industry news, public domain software, book reviews, software news, and reviews. Updated monthly. Provider: NewsNet, Inc.

ELECTRONIC PUBLISHING. *See* PUBLISHING.

ELECTRONICS. *See also* INDUSTRIES: ELECTRONICS.

Electronic Design CompuServe
The full text of this magazine on the design of electronic circuit boards, chips, and associated parts is presented. Coverage includes new technologies,

techniques, and products. Covers 1983 to present. Updated monthly. Provider: DIALOG Information Services (drawn from the Trade & Industry ASAP database).

Electronic Materials Information System BRS
Database provides data on properties of substances used in microelectronics and includes numeric data on 250 electronic materials. Full text. Provider: INSPEC.

Electronics CompuServe
Magazine looks at new trends, processes, and products in all areas of electronics. Covers 1983 to present. Full text, updated monthly. Provider: DIALOG Information Services (drawn from the Trade & Industry ASAP database).

High Fidelity CompuServe
Magazine covers high-fidelity (stereo) equipment, music, and musicians and has reports on audio and video equipment and recordings. Covers 1983 to present. Updated monthly. Provider: DIALOG Information Services (drawn from the Trade & Industry ASAP database).

Integrated Circuit Parameter Retrieval Database (ICPR) CompuServe
Database has abstracts of the functional, technological, and numeric parameters for integrated circuits along with vendor information. Covers 1986 to present. Updated monthly. Provider: BRS Information Technologies.

Semiconductor Parameter Retrieval Database
CompuServe
Database identifies semiconductor devices by functional, technological, and numeric parameters. Full-text printed records are available from the producer. Updated every four months. Provider: BRS Information Technologies.

Stereo Review CompuServe
Magazine covers high-fidelity (stereo) equipment and has reports on audio equipment and recordings. Covers 1983 to present. Updated monthly. Provider: DIALOG Information Services (drawn from the Trade & Industry ASAP database).

EMPLOYEE BENEFITS. *See* BENEFITS.

EMPLOYMENT

Career Placement Registry
CompuServe, DIALOG
The *Registry* contains résumés for over 25,000

persons looking for employment. Experienced applicants as well as students seeking first jobs are included. Résumés, which remain active for six months, include the person's name, colleges attended, degrees, occupational preferences, experience, past job history, geographic preference, and unique qualifications. Covers current listings. Updated weekly. Provider: Career Placement Registry.

U.S. Employment Opportunities–Advertising/PR; Banking/Finance; Federal Government; The Computer Field   CompuServe

These four files contain full newsletter text of job listings in these fields nationwide. Also reported are employment and recruitment trends. Coverage is current. Updated monthly. NewsNet, Inc.

ENCYCLOPEDIAS

Academic American Encyclopedia   CompuServe, BRS, DIALOG

The online edition of Grolier's *Academic American Encyclopedia* contains the full text of this major 21-volume reference work. The 34,000 articles are written by 2,300 contributors in such fields as the arts, business, history, law, politics, the social sciences, science, and technology. Covers latest edition (1980). Updated quarterly. Provider: Grolier Electronic Publishing.

Everyman's Encyclopaedia   DIALOG

Complete text of the 6th Edition of the 12-volume British encyclopedia. This comprehensive work covers all areas of knowledge, including science, technology, medicine, mathematics, history, geography, languages, literature, religion, the arts, biographies, social sciences, current affairs, and more. Each article is by an expert in the field. Covers current (6th) edition. Updated irregularly. Provider: J.M. Dent and Sons, Ltd.; Learned Information, Abingdon, Oxford, UK.

ENERGY AND POWER GENERATION. *See also* NUCLEAR ENERGY.

DOE Energy   DIALOG

The U.S. Department of Energy's database provides references to literature in energy and related fields. Material is drawn from journals, dissertations, books, patents, conference papers, and more. Energy topics covered are nuclear, wind, fossil, geothermal, tidal, and solar. Allied topics include environment, energy policy, and conser-

vation. Covers 1974 to present. Updated every two weeks. Provider: U.S. Department of Energy.

Electric Power Database   CompuServe, DIALOG

Corresponding to the printed *Digest of Research in the Electric Utility Industry*, this online version provides references to research and development projects in the United States and Canada. Entries have abstracts of project summaries for past and ongoing research projects. Covers 1972 to present. Updated monthly. Provider: Electric Power Research Institute.

Electric Power Industry Abstracts   CompuServe, ORBIT

Service indexes and abstracts literature on electric power plants and similar installations. Also provides sources on the effects of power plants on the environment. Covers 1975 to present. Updated six times a year. Provider: Edison Electric Institute.

Energy Bibliography & Index   CompuServe, ORBIT

Database has citations of international literature on energy contained in the Texas A&M University library, which includes German documents from World War II on synthetic fuel technology. Covers 1919 to present. Updated irregularly. Provider: Texas A&M University Library.

Energyline   CompuServe, DIALOG, ORBIT

The online version of *Energy Information Abstracts* also includes 8,000 energy and environment records from *The Energy Index*. The database covers energy issues both from technical and political/economic viewpoints. References and abstracts are provided to books, journals, Congressional committee prints, and more. Covers 1971 to present. Updated monthly. Provider: R.R. Bowker.

Energy User News   CompuServe

Covers 1983 to present. Updated monthly. Provider: DIALOG Information Services (drawn from the Trade & Industry ASAP database).

Hydrowire   CompuServe

Newsletter covers the North American hydroelectric industry. Full text; updated every two weeks. Provider: NewsNet, Inc.

P/E News (Petroleum/Energy News)
CompuServe, DIALOG

This index covers current political, social, and economic information as it applies to the energy industry in general and the petroleum industry in particular. Among the 16 main publications indexed are *International Petroleum Finance* and *National Petroleum News*. In addition, about 300 business-related items each month covered by API Abstracts/Literature are included. Covers 1975 to present. Updated weekly. Provider: Central Abstracting and Indexing Service, American Petroleum Institute.

Power   CompuServe, ORBIT
Power is the catalog of the Energy Library at the U.S. Department of Energy. The collection covers all areas of energy worldwide and includes books, monograph proceedings, and more. Covers current holdings. Updated every two months. Provider: Energy Library, U.S. Department of Energy.

Purpa Lines   CompuServe
Full-text newsletter keeps current on small power production including regulation, finance, licensing, and the environment. Updated every two weeks. Provider: NewsNet, Inc.

Utility Reporter - Fuels, Energy & Power
CompuServe
Newsletter covers worldwide energy and power production, looking at resources, research and development, equipment and distribution, management, legislation, and regulation. Full text, updated monthly. Provider: NewsNet, Inc.

ENGINEERING. *See also* AUTOMOTIVE ENGINEERING; CERAMICS; CHEMICAL ENGINEERING; CIVIL ENGINEERING; HYDRAULICS; MATERIALS; MECHANICAL ENGINEERING; TEXTILE ENGINEERING.

Cambridge Scientific Abstracts Engineering   BRS
Database consists of five Cambridge abstracts services: *Computer & Information Systems Abstracts*, *Electronics & Communications Abstracts*, *ISMEC: Mechanical Engineering Abstracts*, *Health & Safety Science Abstracts*, and *Solid State/Superconductivity Abstracts*. Provider: Cambridge Information Group.

Compendex Plus   CompuServe, DIALOG, ORBIT
Corresponding to the printed *Engineering Index*, this database indexes and abstracts important engineering and technological literature from some 4,500 journals and selected government reports and books. Topics include civil, energy, geological, biological, electrical and electronics, automotive, and nuclear engineering, and much more. In addition, over 480,000 items from conferences are

included. Covers 1970 to present. Updated monthly. Provider: Engineering Information, Inc.

Conference Papers Index   CompuServe, DIALOG
This is an index to over 100,000 scientific and technical papers given at more than 1,000 important regional, national, and international meetings each year. The main subjects covered include life sciences, chemistry, physical sciences, geosciences, and engineering. Covers 1973 to present. Updated six times per year. Provider: Cambridge Scientific Abstracts.

Current Contents Search   BRS, DIALOG
This service reproduces the tables of contents from issues of important journals in a number of disciplines and is the online version of the *Current Contents* series: *Clinical Medicine; Life Sciences; Engineering; Technology and Applied Sciences; Agriculture; Biology and Environmental Sciences; Physical, Chemical, and Earth Sciences; Social and Behavioral Sciences;* and *Arts and Humanities*. Covers 1988 to present. Updated weekly. Provider: Institute for Scientific Information.

Directory of Federal Laboratories   CompuServe
Service gives descriptions of U.S. national laboratory and technology facilities and capabilities that can be used by the private sector. Updated twice a year. Provider: NewsNet, Inc.

Engineering Microsoftware Review   CompuServe
Newsletter is concerned with microcomputer software for engineering applications and has articles and in-depth software reviews written by engineers. Full text; covers August 1984 to present. Updated monthly. Provider: NewsNet, Inc.

Federal Applied Technology Database   BRS
Database is a directory of U.S. government laboratory engineering, technical, and research and development projects with possible commercial applications. Provider: National Technical Information Service, U.S. Department of Commerce.

Federal Research in Progress   CompuServe
(abridged version), DIALOG
All federally funded ongoing research projects in the physical sciences, engineering, and life sciences are listed here. Each item shows title, principal investigator, performing organization, sponsoring organization, and often a description of the research. Covers current data. Updated monthly. Provider: National Technical Information Service, U.S. Department of Commerce.

ISTP Search ORBIT
Multidisciplinary database covers major worldwide
scientific and technical proceedings and literature
in the fields of chemistry, clinical medicine, computer science, earth sciences, engineering, life sciences, mathematics, and technology. Provider:
Institute for Scientific Information.

**SSIE Current Research (Smithsonian Science In-
formation Exchange)** CompuServe, DIALOG
Database has reports of government and privately
funded research projects in progress or started in
1978 to 1982. Basic and applied research in the
life, physical, social, and engineering sciences are
covered. Ninety percent of the data comes from
federal government agencies. For current data on
federally funded research projects see *Federal Research in Progress*, above. Covers 1978 to February
1982. No updates. Provider: National Technical
Information Service, U.S. Department of Commerce.

**Scientific and Technical Books & Serials in
Print** ORBIT
Database lists over 120,000 book titles and more
than 18,000 serial titles in the scientific and technical fields. Provider: Bowker Electronic Publishing.

Wiley Catalog/Online CompuServe
The complete publications catalog of John Wiley
& Sons, specialists in scientific and technical sub-
jects. Includes out-of-print, current, and forth-
coming books, journals, software, and databases.
Covers 1940 to present. Updated every two months.
Provider: DIALOG Information Services, Inc.

ENVIRONMENT. *See* ECOLOGY.

EXECUTIVES. *See* BUSINESS EXECUTIVES.

F

FAIRS, CONFERENCES, AND MEETINGS

EI Engineering Meetings CompuServe
Index lists published proceedings and papers from
worldwide engineering and technical conferences
and meetings. There is a print version entitled
Engineering Conference Index. Covers 1982 to present. Updated monthly. Provider: ORBIT Search
Service.

FAIRBASE BRS
Worldwide directory lists upcoming trade fairs,
exhibitions, and conferences. Provider: FAIRBASE
Database Ltd.

Meeting CompuServe
This directory provides a list of upcoming meetings, conferences, exhibitions, and fairs in the
United States and abroad in all scientific and technical fields plus the humanities and social sciences. Covers current data. Updated twice a
month. Provider: Telesystems/Questel, Inc.

TDS Computer Calendar CompuServe
Listing of events (seminars, conferences, trade
shows, association meetings, and others) of interest to computer professionals. Updated twice a
week. Provider: NewsNet, Inc.

TDS Telecom Calendar CompuServe
Listing of events (seminars, conferences, trade
shows, and government and regulatory hearings)
for the next six months that are of interest to the
telecommunications industry. Updated three times
a week. Provider: NewsNet, Inc.

Telecom A.M. CompuServe
Daily weekday service gives news of telecommunications events such as meetings, hearings, and
other government activities. Full text; updated
daily. Provider: NewsNet, Inc.

FAMILIES

Family Resources BRS, CompuServe, DIALOG
References to more than 1,200 books, journals,
audiovisual material, newsletters, dissertations, and
much more provide coverage of psychosocial literature on the family. This includes information
from the fields of medicine, psychology, education, and sociology. Topics include marriage and
divorce, family trends, sexual attitudes, services,
therapy, and more. Covers 1970 to present (non-
journal) and 1973 to present (journals). Updated
monthly. Provider: National Council on Family
Relations.

FEDERAL COMMUNICATIONS COMMISSION

FCC Daily Digest CompuServe
This is the online version of the official Federal
Communications Commission digest containing
all notices, texts, press releases, and schedules.
Updated daily. Provider: NewsNet, Inc.

FCC Daily Tariff Log   CompuServe
Service shows tariff transmittals received by the Federal Communications Commission. Covers August 1986 to present. Updated daily. Provider: NewsNet, Inc.

FCC Week   CompuServe
Newsletter reports on federal regulation of the telecommunications industry. Full text; updated weekly. Provider: NewsNet, Inc.

FEDERAL GOVERNMENT. *See also* FREEDOM OF INFORMATION; GOVERNMENT PROCUREMENT; GOVERNMENT PUBLICATIONS; GOVERNMENT REGULATIONS; GOVERNMENT SURPLUS; POLITICAL SCIENCE; TAXES.

CIS   DIALOG
Congressional Information Service - CompuServe
This is the online version of the *Index to Publications of the United States Congress*. Included are citations of material that records the investigatory, oversight, and legislative analysis activities of the Congress. Covers 1970 to present. Updated monthly. Provider: Congressional Information Service.

Congressional Activities   CompuServe
The full text of this newsletter gives a schedule of upcoming congressional activities, placing emphasis on those concerned with energy and the environment. Included are lists of pending and enacted bills and an index of the *Congressional Record*. Updated weekly. Provider: NewsNet, Inc.

Congressional Record Abstracts   CompuServe, DIALOG
This database has indexing and abstracts of each issue of the *Congressional Record*, the official record of the activities of the U.S. Congress. Covers 1981 to present. Updated weekly. Provider: National Standards Association.

CRecord   CompuServe
Database contains an index to the *Congressional Record*. Topics include legislation, resolutions, committee and floor activities, speeches, and inserts. Covers 1981 to present. Updated weekly. Provider: ORBIT Search Service.

Federal Index   CompuServe, DIALOG
Federal actions (proposed rules, regulations, bill introductions, speeches, hearings, roll calls, reports, vetoes, court decisions, executive orders, and contract awards) from Fall 1976 to Fall 1980 are presented. Covers October 1976 to November 1980. No updates. Provider: Capitol Services International.

PACS and Lobbies   CompuServe
Newsletter covers federal actions that affect campaign financing and lobbying and provides lists of recent Political Action Committee, lobby, and foreign agent registrations. Full text; updated every two weeks. Provider: NewsNet, Inc.

Washington Presstext   CompuServe, DIALOG
Contained here are the complete texts of White House and U.S. State Department news releases, policy statements, and background information. Broad coverage of domestic and world news is provided as well as in-depth profiles of over 170 countries. Covers 1981 to present. Updated daily. Provider: Presstext News Service.

FEDERAL TRADE COMMISSION

FTC FOIA Log   CompuServe
Newsletter summarizes pending Freedom of Information Act requests filed with the Federal Trade Commission. Full text; updated weekly. Provider: NewsNet, Inc.

FTC: Watch   CompuServe
This full-text newsletter covers Federal Trade Commission activities with the stress on political analysis and forecasting enforcement trends. Updated every two weeks. Provider: NewsNet, Inc.

FIBER OPTICS. *See* OPTICS.

FINANCE. *See also* INSURANCE; INVESTMENTS; TAXES.

American Banker Full Text
CompuServe, DIALOG
Equivalent to the printed version of the *American Banker*, this service covers local, regional, and international financial services, technology, applications, law, international trade, regulations, and much more. Special features not available in the print version are quarterly reports on bank earnings, results of *American Banker* surveys, and complete text of speeches and articles by industry personalities. Covers November 1981 to present. Updated daily. Provider: American Banker-Bond Buyer.

American Banker News   DIALOG
This menu-driven version of *American Banker Full Text*, above, covers the last five days' news sto-

ries. Updated daily. Provider: American Banker-Bond Buyer, New York, NY.

Banking Regulator CompuServe
This full-text newsletter covers federal regulation of U.S. banks, providing drafts of proposed rules (and final rules) before their printing in the Federal Register. Updated daily. Provider: NewsNet, Inc.

Business Credit Database CompuServe
Up-to-date financial data on public and private companies in all industries presented in report format that includes credit and payment information. Updated daily. Provider: NewsNet, Inc.

Credit Market Analysis CompuServe
Newsletter covers the credit markets by looking at Federal Reserve Board and Treasury Department actions, interest-rate fluctuations, and relative value of credit market instruments. Full text; updated daily. Provider: NewsNet, Inc.

Consumer Credit Letter CompuServe
This full-text newsletter covers consumer credit regulation, reporting on Congress, courts, the FTC, and other agencies. Updated weekly. Provider: NewsNet, Inc.

Credit Union Regulator CompuServe
Full-text service covers federal actions affecting credit unions, providing proposed and final rules before publication in the Federal Register. Updated daily. Provider: NewsNet, Inc.

Financial Industry Information Service (FINIS)
BRS, CompuServe, DIALOG
FINIS contains abstracts from over 200 journals, books, press releases, brochures, and reports on the financial services industry. Topics include bank activity, brokers, credit unions, insurance companies, and more. Covers 1982 to present. Updated every two weeks. Provider: Bank Marketing Association.

Financial Services Week CompuServe
Comprehensive coverage of the financial services industry is provided by this full-text database. Topics include banking, real estate, insurance, and stockbrokerage, along with company profiles. Updated weekly. Provider: NewsNet, Inc.

Financial Times & The Economist CompuServe
Database has the full text of both the *London Financial Times* and the *Economist*, which report on

business, economic, and financial events. Provider: Profile Information.

Financial Times Fulltext CompuServe, DIALOG
Database has the full text of all *Financial Times* articles, which give detailed data on industries, companies, and markets worldwide. Government regulation, labor and management issues, technology, and more are included. Covers 1986 to present. Updated daily. Provider: Financial Times Business Information, Ltd., London, UK.

Financial World CompuServe
Full-text magazine has industry reviews, trends and forecasts, company profiles, and issues ratings. Covers 1983 to present. Updated monthly. Provider: DIALOG Information Services (drawn from the Trade & Industry ASAP database).

Japan Weekly Monitor CompuServe
Full-text newsletter covers economic and financial activity in Japan, reporting on the Japanese Stock Exchange, yen/dollar movements, and economic statistics. U.S.–Japanese relations and important Japanese news stories are presented. Updated weekly. Provider: NewsNet, Inc.

Knight-Ridder Financial News CompuServe, DIALOG
Service provides full-text financial and commodity market news worldwide. Financial news focuses on credit markets, foreign exchange, mortgage-backed securities, financial futures, and more, while commodities news includes both cash and futures markets. Covers January 5, 1987 to present. Updated continuously (DIALOG) and daily (CompuServe). Provider: Knight-Ridder Financial Information.

Latin American Debt Chronicle CompuServe
Newsletter provides reports and analyses of the Latin American and Caribbean debt crisis. Topics include negotiations, balance of payments, internal developments, and foreign debt updates by country. Updated twice a week. Provider: NewsNet, Inc.

Money Paper CompuServe
Full-text financial advisory newsletter has articles on business, investment, taxation, consumer issues, and banking. Updated monthly. Provider: NewsNet, Inc.

FINE ARTS. *See also* HUMANITIES.

Art Index   CompuServe
Database indexes worldwide literature on the arts. Topics include archaeology, art history, museum studies, photography, and city planning. Covers November 1984 to present. Updated twice a week. Provider: H.W. Wilson Company.

Art Literature International (RILA)   CompuServe, DIALOG
Database indexes and abstracts publications on the history of art and corresponds to the printed *RILA* (International Repertory of the Literature of Art). All areas of Western art since the fourth century are included. Covers 1973 to present. Updated twice a year. Provider: RILA, J. Paul Getty Trust.

Artbibliographies Modern
CompuServe, DIALOG
Database is a bibliography of material including articles, books, dissertations, and exhibition catalogs. While complete coverage of 19th- and 20th-century art and design is provided, major artists and movements of the 18th century are included as well. Topics run from architecture to folk art to textiles and much more. Covers 1974 to present. Updated twice a year. Provider: ABC-CLIO.

FOOD AND NUTRITION

Food Science and Technology Abstracts
CompuServe, DIALOG
Indexing over 1,200 journals from over 50 countries, patents from 20 countries, and books in many languages, FSTA covers research and development in fields related to food science and technology. Such areas as agriculture, chemistry, biochemistry, and physics are also included. Where relevant, such fields as engineering and home economics are indexed. Included as well is VITIS, a subfile on viticulture and oenology (covering grapes, grapevine science, and technology). Covers 1969 to present. Updated monthly. Provider: International Food Information Service, Reading, Berkshire, UK.

Foods Adlibra   CompuServe, DIALOG
Brief abstracts from over 250 trade periodicals on the latest developments in food technology, packaging, marketing, management, and world food economics can be found in Foods Adlibra. Additionally, material from over 500 highly technical journals is included as appropriate. All aspects of the food industry are included, such as retailers, processors, brokers, equipment suppliers, gourmet food importers, and general company and food association news. Covers 1974 to present. Updated monthly. Provider: General Mills, Foods Adlibra Publications.

FOREIGN EXCHANGE

Forex Commentary   CompuServe
Full text of the newsletter, which reports on foreign exchange markets. Coverage includes worldwide prices, comments on futures trading, and assessment of factors affecting foreign exchange. Full text; updated daily. Provider: NewsNet, Inc.

GAS Statistics and Ratings   CompuServe
Service has statistical data on money supply, exchange rates, publication, and gross domestic product for all countries. Updated every six weeks. Provider: Profile Information.

FORESTRY AND FOREST PRODUCTS

Forest Products   CompuServe, ORBIT
This index of worldwide technical literature covers the wood products industry from harvesting to marketing the final product. Covers 1947 to present. Updated bimonthly. Provider: Forest Products Research Society.

FREEDOM OF INFORMATION

Access Reports/Freedom of Information
CompuServe
Newsletter watches legislation and regulatory matters affecting access to government records. Full text; updated every two weeks. Provider: NewsNet, Inc.

FUTURES. *See* INVESTMENTS.

G

GEOLOGY. *See* EARTH SCIENCES.

GEOPHYSICS. *See* EARTH SCIENCES.

GIFTED CHILDREN. *See* SPECIAL EDUCATION.

GOVERNMENT PROCUREMENT

Commerce Business Daily
CompuServe, DIALOG
This is the full text equivalent of the printed CBD, which provides information on products and ser-

vices needed or offered by the U.S. Government. All proposed procurements and contract awards of $25,000 or more are given. In addition, non-U.S. standards that may affect U.S. exports are mentioned. Covers October 1982 to present. Updated daily. Provider: Commerce Business Daily, U.S. Department of Commerce.

DMS Contract Awards   CompuServe, DIALOG
Awards provides information on all government contracts awarded for more than $25,000 for research, systems, and services in defense, aerospace, energy, and transportation. Also included is analysis of contracting trends by fiscal year or quarter. Covers 1981 to present. Updated quarterly. Provider: Jane's Information Group, Alexandria, VA.

Privatization   CompuServe
Newsletter reports on the contracting out of U.S. government services to private companies. Areas included are prisons, traffic, education, fire and police, airports, and more. Full text, updated every two weeks. Provider: NewsNet, Inc.

TDS RFP/Tender Search   CompuServe
The full text of this publication lists current federal, state, and local requests for proposals for telecommunications equipment open for bidding. Updated weekly. Provider: NewsNet, Inc.

GOVERNMENT PUBLICATIONS

ASI (American Statistics Index)   CompuServe, DIALOG
This is an extensive index, with abstracts, of all federal statistical publications. Data indexed covers an extremely wide range including population and economic censuses, international trade, vital statistics, education, and much more. Covers 1973 to present. Updated monthly. Provider: Congressional Information Service, Inc.

CIS   DIALOG
Congressional Information Service - CompuServe
This is the online version of the *Index to Publications of the United States Congress*. Included are citations of material that records the investigatory, oversight, and legislative analysis activities of the Congress. Covers 1970 to present. Updated monthly. Provider: Congressional Information Service, Inc.

GPO Monthly Catalog
BRS, CompuServe, DIALOG

Equivalent to the printed *Monthly Catalog of United States Government Publications*, this online version is an index of Federal Government publications. Listings include studies, fact sheets, maps, records of all Senate and House hearings, and other materials. Subjects covered include agriculture, economics, energy, health, law, and much more. Covers July 1976 to present. Updated monthly. Provider: U.S. Government Printing Office.

GPO Publications Reference File   CompuServe, DIALOG
The *Publications Reference File* indexes public documents available for sale by the U.S. Government Printing Office. Current, forthcoming, and recently out-of-print items are listed along with availability, prices, and stock numbers. Covers 1971 to present. Updated biweekly. Provider: U.S. Government Printing Office.

Index to U.S. Government Periodicals   BRS
Over 185 publications from more than 100 U.S. government agencies are indexed by subject and author. Provider: Infordata International, Inc.

NTIS   CompuServe, DIALOG, ORBIT
Through NTIS, unclassified, unlimited distribution reports from such agencies as NASA, DDC, DOE, HUD, DOT, and some state and local government agencies are made available for sale. References are to government-sponsored research, development, engineering, and analyses furnished by federal agencies, contractors, and grantees. A vast range of subjects are covered such as administration and management, agriculture and food, sociology, business and economics, the sciences, military science, transportation, and much more. Covers 1964 to present. Updated every two weeks. Provider: National Technical Information Service, U.S. Department of Commerce.

NTIS Bibliographical Database   BRS
Database provides references to U.S. and foreign government-sponsored research reports in physical sciences, technology, engineering, biological sciences, medicine, agriculture, and social sciences. Provider: National Technical Information Service, U.S. Department of Commerce.

GOVERNMENT REGULATIONS

Banking Regulator   CompuServe
This full-text newsletter covers federal regulation

of U.S. banks providing drafts of proposed rules (and final rules) before their printing in the Federal Register. Updated daily. Provider: NewsNet, Inc.

Chemical Regulations & Guidelines System
CompuServe, DIALOG
This database provides an index to U.S. federal regulations on the control of chemicals. Federal statutes, regulations, guidelines, standards, and support documents are included. Covers regulations in effect as of October 1982. No updates. Provider: U.S. Interagency Regulatory Liaison Group, CRC Systems, Inc.

Credit Union Regulator   CompuServe
Full-text service covers federal actions affecting credit unions, providing proposed and final rules before publication in the Federal Register. Updated daily. Provider: NewsNet, Inc.

Federal Register Abstracts   BRS, CompuServe, DIALOG, ORBIT
This service indexes and abstracts all federal regulations as reported in the *Federal Register*. Federal regulations, rules, legal notices, public laws, executive orders, and more are included. Covers March 1977 to present. Updated weekly. Provider: National Standards Association, Bethesda, MD.

GOVERNMENT SURPLUS

Surplus & Business Alert   CompuServe
Full-text newsletter lists government surplus sales that include equipment, land, buildings, vehicles, and more. Updated weekly. Provider: NewsNet, Inc.

GRANTS. *See* PHILANTHROPY.

H

HAZARDS. *See also* POLLUTION AND WASTE MANAGEMENT.

Chemical Exposure   CompuServe, DIALOG
Coverage is of chemicals identified in the tissues of humans and wild and domestic animals. References are made to selected journal articles, conferences, and reports. Information reported includes chemical properties, synonyms, CAS Registry Numbers, formulas, tissue measured and analytical method used, demographics, and more. Covers 1974 to present. Updated annually. Provider: Science Applications International Corporation.

Chemical Hazards in Industry   CompuServe
Database contains data on all documented hazards and health and safety information needed by those working in the chemical industry worldwide. Covers 1984 to present. Updated monthly. Provider: Data-Star.

Hazardous Waste News   CompuServe
This full-text newsletter focuses on hazardous waste regulation enforcement and compliance. Updated weekly. Provider: NewsNet, Inc.

Industrial Health & Hazards Update
CompuServe
This is a newsletter of worldwide workplace health and safety reporting on regulation, litigation, standards and testing, and medical and environmental matters. Full text; updated monthly. Provider: NewsNet, Inc.

Laboratory Hazards Bulletin   CompuServe
Database indexes worldwide technical literature on chemical laboratory safety with topics including hazardous chemicals, legislation, and safety practices. Covers 1981 to present. Updated monthly. Provider: Pergamon Financial Data Services.

Nuclear Waste News   CompuServe
The full text of this newsletter reports on such issues regarding nuclear waste as management, regulation, transportation, disposal, and more. Updated weekly. Provider: NewsNet, Inc.

Toxic Materials News   CompuServe
Full text of this newsletter covers matters affecting toxic materials control in the United States. Topics include legislation, regulation and enforcement, litigation, technology, state and local programs, and business news. Updated weekly. Provider: NewsNet, Inc.

Toxic Materials Transport   CompuServe
Newsletter watches regulations and other legal matters dealing with the transport of toxic materials. Topics include route restrictions, accident preparedness, compliance, and more. Full text, updated every two weeks. Provider: NewsNet, Inc.

TSCA Chemical Substances Inventory   DIALOG
Toxic Substances Control Act - CompuServe, ORBIT
This directory lists chemical substances in commercial use in the United States as of June 1, 1979, with their toxicity and other properties. Data are taken from the *Initial Inventory* of the *Toxic*

Substances Control Act Chemical Substances Inventory. Covers May 1983 edition. Updated irregularly. Providers for DIALOG: Dialog Information Services, Inc. and Environmental Protection Agency, Office of Toxic Substances; CompuServe, ORBIT: Office of Toxic Substances, U.S. Environmental Protection Agency.

HEALTH-CARE ADMINISTRATION

Health Planning and Administration
BRS, CompuServe
This is an index, with abstracts, of worldwide publications on health-care planning, organization, financing, and other nonclinical topics. Covers 1975 to present. Updated weekly. Provider: National Library of Medicine.

HISTORY. *See also* HUMANITIES.

Historical Abstracts   CompuServe, DIALOG
This service provides an index, with abstracts, of over 2,000 worldwide periodicals in history and related social sciences and humanities. Corresponding to the printed *Historical Abstracts*, parts A and B, the database covers world history from 1450 to present with the exception of the United States and Canada, which can be found in *America: History and Life*, below. Covers 1973 to present. Updated quarterly. Provider: ABC-CLIO.

American:

America: History and Life
CompuServe, DIALOG
This is an index, with abstracts, of more than 2,000 sciences and humanities journals along with monographs and dissertations covering U.S. and Canadian history and current affairs. Corresponding to the printed version, parts A to C, the database covers American and ethnic studies, history, urban affairs, and much more. Covers 1964 to present. Updated two times a year. Provider: ABC-CLIO.

HOSPITALS AND HEALTH SERVICES

Department of Health and Social Security
CompuServe
Database has information on health services and hospital administration and associated fields ranging from health service buildings to social security pensions. Covers November 1983 to present. Updated weekly. Provider: Data-Star.

Hospitals   CompuServe
This hospital administrator magazine reports on discharge planning, emergency care, consumer satisfaction, and the business aspects of hospital operation. Covers 1983 to present. Updated monthly. Provider: DIALOG Information Services (drawn from the Trade & Industry ASAP database).

HOUSING AND URBAN DEVELOPMENT, DEPARTMENT OF

HUD User Online   BRS
Service has U.S. Department of Housing and Urban Development report abstracts on housing and urban development. Provider: U.S. Department of Housing and Urban Development.

HUMANITIES

Arts & Humanities Search   BRS, CompuServe, DIALOG
Corresponding to the *Arts & Humanities Index*, this database fully indexes 1,300 of the leading arts and humanities and 5,000 social and natural science journals worldwide. Topics range from archaeology to classics to music to filmographies and much more. Covers 1980 to present. Updated every two weeks. Provider: Institute for Scientific Information.

Humanities Index   CompuServe
This index is drawn from U.S., Canadian, British, and Dutch periodicals and covers archaeology, classical studies, area studies, folklore, language, literature, philosophy, and history. Covers February 1984 to present. Updated twice a week. Provider: H.W. Wilson Company.

HYDRAULICS. *See also* ENGINEERING.

Fluidex   CompuServe, DIALOG
Database is an index with abstracts of all areas of fluid engineering, both theoretical and practical. Almost 1,000 technical journals are indexed along with books, conference proceedings, standards, research reports from around the world, and some British patents. Included are aerodynamics, fluid dynamics, river and flood control, jet cutting, materials properties, and much more. Covers 1974 to present. Updated monthly. Provider: BHRA, The Fluid Engineering Center, Bedford, UK.

HYDROELECTRIC POWER. *See* ENERGY.

I

INDUSTRIAL PRODUCTS INFORMATION. *See also* CONSUMER PRODUCTS INFORMATION.

IHS Vendor Information Database CompuServe
Database is a catalog of industrial products from many vendors and concentrates on components, machinery, and engineering equipment. Full text; updated monthly. Provider: BRS Information Technologies.

Kompass Europe DIALOG
Produced by a group of five European publishers, this directory gives information on some 2,000 classes of products from about 210,000 European companies from Denmark, France, Italy, Norway, Sweden, Germany, and the United Kingdom, along with company name, address, telephone and telex numbers, executive names, description of business, and more. Covers current data. Updated on an annual rotating basis for each country. Provider: Reed Information Services, Ltd., Sussex, UK.

Kompass UK DIALOG
This database covers companies producing some 45,000 classes of products in the United Kingdom. Emphasis is on manufacturing, industrial, and service sectors and provides company name, address, phone number, product information, and top executives. Covers current data. Updated quarterly. Provider: Information Services Ltd., West Sussex, UK.

PTS New Product Announcements/Plus
CompuServe, DIALOG
Announcements contains the full text of company press releases concerning new products. Along with product descriptions, announcements often contain details about new products and technologies, technical specifications, availability, and so on. Contacts and phone numbers are included. *Plus* has additional coverage of new facilities, merger and acquisition activity, contracts, litigations, and more. Covers 1985 to present. Updated weekly. Provider: Predicasts.

Thomas New Industrial Products CompuServe, DIALOG
Prepared from new product press releases, this database provides information on product attributes, specifications, and use, trade name, and model number, along with company name, address, and telephone number. Covers 1985 to present. Updated weekly. Provider: Thomas Publishing Company, Inc.

Thomas Regional Industrial Suppliers
CompuServe, DIALOG
Similar to the *Thomas Register*, below, the regional directory lists local manufacturers, distributors, and manufacturer's representatives in the eastern and central United States broken down into 14 regions. Database corresponds to the printed *Regional Industrial Purchasing Guide*. Covers current edition. Updated quarterly. Provider: Thomas Publishing Company.

Thomas Register Online CompuServe, DIALOG
Containing the full text of the printed *Thomas Register of American Manufacturers*, makes it possible to find virtually any product made in the United States. Over 133,000 manufacturers of over 55,000 classes of products with over 106,000 brand names are covered. Overall, there are listings for over 1,000,000 product and service providers. Covers current edition. Updated annually. Provider: Thomas Publishing Company.

Transin CompuServe
Database is a listing of requests and offers for new products and processes and acts as a technology exchange clearinghouse. Listings are from international private and public sources. Covers last three years' data. Updated twice a month. Provider: Telesystems/Questel, Inc.

INDUSTRIES

Biotechnology:

BioBusiness BRS, CompuServe, DIALOG
This database has current abstracts combined with multiple citations of source journals of information about the business applications of the biological sciences. Covers 1985 to present. Updated weekly. Provider: BIOSIS.

Biocommerce Abstracts CompuServe, DIALOG
Database contains indexing to and abstracts of material concerned with business aspects of biotechnology. Sources include over 100 papers, trade journals, popular scientific magazines, and technical publications. Covers 1981 to present. Updated twice a month. Provider: BioCommerce Data Ltd., Slough, UK.

Chemicals:

Chemical Business Newsbase
CompuServe, DIALOG
The *Newsbase* contains summaries and citations of worldwide chemical business news with emphasis on European news. Items summarized are from such sources as journals, press releases, company reports, advertisements, and more. Covers October 1984 to present. Updated weekly. Provider: Royal Society of Chemistry, Nottingham, UK.

Chemical Economics Handbook ORBIT
Database has supply/demand and price data for the chemical industry worldwide. Full text. Provider: SRI International.

Chemical Industry Notes CompuServe, DIALOG, ORBIT
This index of over 80 journals, newspapers, and other material covers business-related chemical industry news. Covers 1974 to present. Updated weekly. Provider: Chemical Abstracts Service and the American Chemical Society.

Chemical Regulations & Guidelines System
CompuServe, DIALOG
This database provides an index to U.S. federal regulations on the control of chemicals. Federal statutes, regulations, guidelines, standards, and support documents are included. Covers regulations in effect as of October 1982. No updates. Provider: U.S. Interagency Regulatory Liaison Group, CRC Systems, Inc.

Chem-Intell DIALOG
Chem-Intell provides information on chemical manufacturing plants and trade and production figures for over 100 chemicals. Plant reports show company name, location, capacity, and trade and production statistics for the last 10 years. Covers within 10 years. Updated monthly. Provider: Chemical Intelligence Services, London, UK.

Clothing and Textiles:

Womens Wear Daily CompuServe
This is the full text of this key fashion-industry newspaper covering trends in fashion, pricing, buying, and personal profiles. Covers 1983 to present. Updated monthly. Provider: DIALOG Information Services (drawn from the Trade & Industry ASAP database).

Electronics:

Consumer Electronics CompuServe
Newsletter looks at the consumer electronics industry (telephones, computers, entertainment equipment, and more). Full text; updated weekly. Provider: NewsNet, Inc.

Corporate EFT Report CompuServe
This full-text newsletter looks at techniques for electronic funds transfer, including intercorporate programs and developments in funds transfer software and methods. Updated every two weeks. Provider: NewsNet, Inc.

EFT Report CompuServe
This full-text newsletter covers areas of electronic funds transfer including automated teller machines, home banking, government activities, and privacy issues. Updated every two weeks. Provider: NewsNet, Inc.

Electronic News CompuServe
Magazine reports on company news, new products, and government activities affecting the electronics industry. Covers 1983 to present. Updated monthly. Provider: DIALOG Information Services (drawn from the Trade & Industry ASAP database).

Japan Semiconductor Industry Scan CompuServe
Published by the Electronics Industries Association of Japan, this newsletter looks at the semiconductor industries of Japan and the United States and the competition and cooperation between them. Updated weekly. Provider: NewsNet, Inc.

Semiconductor Industry & Business Survey
CompuServe
Newsletter covers the worldwide semiconductor industry looking at products, markets, plants, licensing, and more. Updated every two weeks. Provider: NewsNet, Inc.

Footwear:

Footwear News CompuServe
This is the full text of the footwear trade news publication. Covers 1983 to present. Updated monthly. Provider: DIALOG Information Services (drawn from the Trade & Industry ASAP database).

Materials:

American Metal Market CompuServe
The full text of this trade journal has detailed coverage of metals industry news. Covers 1983 to

present. Updated monthly. Provider: DIALOG Information Services (drawn from the Trade & Industry ASAP database).

Materials Business File   CompuServe, DIALOG, ORBIT

References are provided to over 1,300 sources covering commercial developments in iron and steel, nonferrous metals, composites, plastics, and more. Sources include magazines, company reports, dissertations, conference proceedings, and others. Among the nine categories listed are plant developments, engineering, applications, and economics. Covers 1985 to present. Updated monthly. Provider: ASM International.

Petroleum:

APILIT (American Petroleum Institute)
CompuServe, ORBIT

Database is an index to journals, meetings, papers, and government reports on petroleum refining, air and water conservation, petrochemicals, synthetic fuels, transportation and storage, and more. Oilfield chemicals covered since 1981. Covers 1964 to present. Updated monthly. Provider: The American Petroleum Institute, Central Abstracting & Indexing Service.

IPABASE   ORBIT

Provides references to worldwide literature on oil field exploration and development, and oil refining, products, and economics, along with pollution and safety. Provider: The Institute of Petroleum.

Oil Daily   CompuServe

Newspaper covers the oil and gas industry around the world giving news and summaries of U.S. supply and demand. Covers 1983 to present. Updated monthly. Provider: DIALOG Information Services (drawn from the Trade & Industry ASAP database).

P/E News (Petroleum/Energy News)
CompuServe, DIALOG

This index covers current political, social, and economic information as it applies to the energy industry in general and the petroleum industry in particular. Among the 16 main publications indexed are *International Petroleum Finance* and *National Petroleum News*. In addition, about 300 business-related items each month covered by API Abstracts/Literature are included. Covers 1975 to present. Updated weekly. Provider: Central Abstracting and Indexing Service, American Petroleum Institute.

TULSA   ORBIT

Database covers international literature on oil and natural gas exploration, development, and production, and includes patents. Provider: The University of Tulsa, Information Services Division.

Pharmaceuticals:

Diogenes   BRS, CompuServe, DIALOG

Database covers Food and Drug Administration regulatory data. Included are news stories and unpublished documents regarding U.S. regulation of pharmaceuticals and medical devices. Full text is provided for key material. Covers 1976 to present. Updated weekly. Provider: DIOGENES.

Drug Topics   CompuServe

This retail drug trade magazine reports on trends in health care, medical and pharmaceutical developments, and legislation affecting the industry. Covers 1983 to present. Updated monthly. Provider: DIALOG Information Services (drawn from the Trade & Industry ASAP database).

Pharmaceutical and Healthcare Industry News Database   BRS

Four international pharmaceutical, device and diagnostic, veterinary, and agrochemical industry newsletters are presented here. Full text. Provider: PJB Publications, Ltd.

Pharmaceutical News Index (PNI)
BRS, CompuServe, DIALOG

PNI indexes some 20 major publications covering pharmaceuticals, cosmetics, medical devices, and related health fields. Product news, regulations, corporate news, legal actions, and much more is referenced. Covers 1974 to present. Updated weekly. Provider: UMI/Data Courier.

Pharmacontacts   BRS

Directory lists the names and addresses of more than 7,000 European and American pharmaceutical companies plus an additional 2,400 veterinary health products companies around the world. Provider: PJB Publication, Ltd.

SCRIP   CompuServe

This full-text newsletter reports on products, markets, companies, and regulatory matters as they affect the worldwide pharmaceutical industry. Covers 1986 to present. Updated daily. Provider: Data-Star.

Restaurants:

Nation's Restaurant News CompuServe
This is the full text of this restaurant business
magazine, which reports on food trends, advertising, new products, and government activities
affecting the food service business. Covers 1983
to present. Updated monthly. Provider: DIALOG
Information Services (drawn from the Trade &
Industry ASAP database).

Restaurant Business Magazine CompuServe
Look here for the full text of this commercial food
service news magazine. Coverage includes legal
tips, menu planning, bar management, and more.
Covers 1983 to present. Updated monthly. Provider: DIALOG Information Services (drawn from
the Trade & Industry ASAP database).

Retailing:

Chain Store Age CompuServe
This is the full text of the publication, which reports on the chain-store industry. Topics include
merchandising trends and company profiles. Covers 1983 to present. Updated monthly. Provider:
DIALOG Information Services (drawn from the
Trade & Industry ASAP database).

Discount Store News CompuServe
Publication provides news and reports on trends,
marketing, companies, consumer preferences,
products, brands, and merchandising. Covers 1983
to present. Updated monthly. Provider: DIALOG
Information Services (drawn from the Trade &
Industry ASAP database).

HFD (Home Furnishings Daily) CompuServe
Newspaper gives news of the many areas of the
home furnishings business. Covers 1983 to pres-
ent. Full text; updated monthly. Provider: DIA-
LOG Information Services (drawn from the Trade
& Industry ASAP database).

Supermarketing CompuServe
The full text of the trade newspaper *Super Marketing*
is addressed to senior managers in the food retailing industry of the United Kingdom. Nonfood
markets such as toys and do-it-yourself are also
mentioned. Updated weekly. Provider: Profile
Information.

Supermarket News CompuServe
Full-text publication reports on supermarket business and product news. Covers 1983 to present.

Updated monthly. Provider: DIALOG Information Services (drawn from the Trade & Industry
ASAP database).

Service Businesses:

Service Dealer's Newsletter CompuServe
Newsletter covers managing repair businesses by
looking at such topics as innovations, labor relations, computer applications, and marketing. Updated monthly. Provider: NewsNet, Inc.

INFECTIOUS DISEASES. *See also* AIDS.

Diack's Indicator CompuServe
Database contains summaries of research reports,
conferences, articles, and other sources on new
progress in infection control with emphasis on
the sterilization of medical devices. Updated every two months. Provider: NewsNet, Inc.

MMWR Plus AIDS CompuServe
This is the full text of the Center for Disease
Control's *Morbidity and Mortality Weekly Report*,
which covers diseases, toxic exposure, adverse
drug/vaccine reactions, substance abuse, and trends
in the spread of infectious diseases. Updated
weekly. Provider: NewsNet, Inc.

INSURANCE

Federal & State Insurance Week CompuServe
Full-text newsletter covers legislative and political
affairs as they affect the insurance industry and consumers. Updated weekly. Provider: NewsNet, Inc.

IMS Weekly Marketer CompuServe
Newsletter provides news, analyses, and editorials on developments in insurance and financial
services. Full text, updated weekly. Provider:
NewsNet, Inc.

Insurance Abstracts CompuServe, DIALOG
This is an index, with abstracts, of literature covering life, property, and liability insurance taken
from more than 100 journals. Covers 1979 to 1984.
No updates. Provider: University Microfilms International.

Insurance Periodicals Index DIALOG
Database indexes and abstracts 35 of the most-
read insurance periodicals. Articles cover a wide
number of topics from accounting to advertising,
to Lloyd's, to worker's compensation, and much
more. Covers 1984 to present. Updated every two
weeks. Provider: NILS Publishing Company.

Liability Week CompuServe
Legal and political matters, and proposed Congressional reforms affecting liability insurance, are the subjects of this full-text newsletter. Updated weekly. Provider: NewsNet, Inc.

INTERNATIONAL RELATIONS

Logos CompuServe
Logos provides reports on French Cabinet meetings and other political developments in France, including the speeches by officials and news clippings from the French press. Covers 1970 to present. Provider: Telesystems/Questel, Inc.

PAIS International BRS, CompuServe, DIALOG
This is a bibliographic index to worldwide public policy material regarding business, economics and finance, law, international relations, government, political science, and other social sciences. All references are in English and all manner of material from pamphlets to books are covered. Covers 1972 to present. Updated monthly. Provider: Public Affairs Information Service, Inc.

INVESTMENTS

Biotechnology Investment Opportunities
CompuServe
Newsletter looks at the investment possibilities in genetic engineering. Coverage includes new companies, markets, regulations, applications, and the commercial implications of new biotechnologies. Full text, updated monthly. Provider: NewsNet, Inc.

Bond Buyer Full Text CompuServe, DIALOG
Equivalent to the printed *Bond Buyer* and *Credit Markets*, the online version covers the fixed-income investment market with daily coverage of government and Treasury securities, financial futures, corporate bonds, and mortgage securities along with reports on government actions, international monetary and fiscal policies, and regulatory actions. Also included are planned bond issues, bond calls and redemptions, and bond sale results. Covers November 1981 to present. Updated daily. Provider: American Banker-Bond Buyer.

Corporate and Industry Research Reports Online Index CompuServe
This is an index of company and industry research reports prepared by U.S. and Canadian securities and institutional investment businesses.

Covers 1982 to present. Updated quarterly. Provider: JA Micropublishing, Inc.

Daily Industrial Index Analyzer CompuServe
This technical investment advisory service watches fluctuations in industrial averages as they indicate possible market shifts. Full text; updated daily. Provider: NewsNet, Inc.

Daily Metals Report CompuServe
Newsletter analyzes each day's trading in gold and silver coins, bullion, and other metals. Market forces are also analyzed and stop-loss positions suggested. Covers October 1983 to present. Updated daily. Provider: NewsNet, Inc.

Daily Petro Futures CompuServe
Service shows previous day's results in petroleum market actions and futures on the New York Mercantile Exchange. Prices and chart analysis are provided. Covers four weeks of full-text newsletters. Updated twice a day. Provider: NewsNet, Inc.

Defotel CompuServe
Database contains data of French companies traded on the French Stock Exchange and has company profiles, product lines, officers, subsidiaries, capitalization, six years of stock/bond figures, and two years of balance sheet/revenue figures. Updated irregularly. Provider: Telesystems/Questel, Inc.

Dialog Quotes and Trading DIALOG
Current (delayed at least 20 minutes) stock and option quotations from the New York and American Stock Exchanges, NASDAQ, and the four major options exchanges are provided. Any stock or option listed in the *Wall Street Journal* can be purchased or sold as well. Up to 75 portfolios can be set up to track gains/losses and pertinent tax information. Covers current data. Updated continuously (20 minute delay). Provider: Trade*Plus, Palo Alto, CA.

Fastock II CompuServe
Service has historical investment data on markets including daily prices, trading volumes, dividends, interest payments for principal stocks, put-and-call options, money market and mutual funds, and bonds (corporate, municipal, and federal) traded on U.S. markets. Data covers U.S. and Canadian exchanges. Updated daily. Provider: ADP Network Services.

Ford Investment Review   CompuServe
This is the full text of this investment advisory service that follows a selected group of high-performance stocks and also has special reports with analysis of stock selection and performance. Updated monthly. Provider: NewsNet, Inc.

Futures Focus   CompuServe
This investment-advisory newsletter focuses on futures trading and includes market news, overviews, trading advice, and recommendations. Updated weekly. Provider: NewsNet, Inc.

Health Industry Research Reports   BRS
This is an index of reports on companies in the health industry prepared by large U.S. and Canadian securities and institutional investment firms. Provider: JA Micropublishing, Inc.

Insider Trading Monitor   DIALOG
Taken from SEC records, this database has transaction details of all insider trading filings along with the holdings of over 100,000 officers, directors, and major shareholders (10 percent or more) in over 8,500 U.S. public companies. Details include insider name and position, company name and address, SIC code, filing date, price per share, and CUSIP number. Covers 1984 to present. Updated daily. Provider: Invest/Net, Inc.

Insider Weekly Summary   CompuServe
This full-text newsletter has information on insider trading. Provider: NewsNet, Inc.

Investext   CompuServe, DIALOG
This full-text service has reports from more than 50 leading research firms in the United States, Europe, Canada, and Japan with sales and earnings forecasts, market-share projections, research and development expenses, and similar information for about 7,500 of the biggest publicly traded U.S. corporations plus 500 emerging firms. Foreign sources provide data on about 1,500 large companies listed on European and Canadian stock exchanges. Covers July 1982 to present. Updated weekly. Provider: Technical Data International.

Investor's Daily   BRS, CompuServe
Contains abstracts of the financial newspaper *Investor's Daily*, which covers financial and stock-market information and highlights companies, industries, and the New York and American stock exchanges. Covers 1986 to present. Updated monthly. Provider: JA Micropublishing, Inc.

Limited Partnership Investment Review
CompuServe
Newsletter covers syndications and their marketing, reporting on the latest news of limited partnership offerings and trends as well as regulations and Internal Revenue Service and Securities and Exchange Commission actions. Full text; updated monthly. Provider: NewsNet, Inc.

Media General Plus   CompuServe, DIALOG
Database contains detailed financial and stock price data for some 5,100 public corporations from the New York and American Stock Exchanges as well as all NASDAQ National Market System companies and designated over-the-counter issues. Covers last five years. Updated weekly. Provider: Media General Financial Services, Inc.

Ober Income Letter   CompuServe
Newsletter looks at partnership performance, important new offerings, legislation, news, and trends for real estate and oil and gas investment partnerships. Updated every two months. Provider: NewsNet, Inc.

OTC Insight   CompuServe
Investment advisory newsletter covers selected over-the-counter stocks and has comments on significant stocks, market outlook, and investment strategies. Updated monthly. Provider: NewsNet, Inc.

OTC Newswire Daily   CompuServe
Service gives the full text of press releases put out by companies traded over-the-counter. Updated daily. Provider: NewsNet, Inc.

Perspectives on Hard Assets   CompuServe
This investment advisory newsletter looks at physical assets such as coins, gems, and real estate. Full text; updated weekly. Provider: NewsNet, Inc.

Profit Report   CompuServe
Newsletter reports on the political and economic forces that affect international financial markets. In addition, economic trends are monitored and buy/sell recommendations made. Full text; updated every two weeks. Provider: NewsNet, Inc.

RateGram Online   CompuServe
Newsletter reports on the highest available federally insured interest rates from bank, savings-and-loan, and money-market fund investments. Full

text; updated every two weeks. Provider: NewsNet, Inc.

Silicon Mountain Report   CompuServe
The full text of this newsletter covers high-technology companies in the Colorado Rockies area that include biotechnology, electronics, software, and communications. Product, contract, financial, and personnel news is given along with company profiles. Updated monthly. Provider: NewsNet, Inc.

Simon's Mutual Fund Monthly   CompuServe
Publication is a directory of mutual funds registered with the Securities and Exchange Commission and includes such data as fees, redemption and deposit requirements, officers, and investment objectives. Full text; updated monthly. Provider: NewsNet, Inc.

Stanger Report   CompuServe
Newsletter provides news and advice on tax shelters. Among those reported on are real estate, oil and gas, and limited partnerships. Tax and regulatory developments are also included. Full text; updated monthly. Provider: NewsNet, Inc.

Street Talk   CompuServe
This full-text newsletter scans the top investment newsletters and summarizes the investment ideas and advice they give. Stocks, bonds, precious metals, and tax-saving information are included. Updated every three weeks. Provider: NewsNet, Inc.

Trendvest Ratings   CompuServe
This investment letter rates market indicators for stocks, bonds, and gold. Individual common stocks are rated also. Full text; updated twice a week. Provider: NewsNet, Inc.

Wall Street Monitor: Weekly Market Digest
CompuServe
Newsletter is a digest of investment newsletters and brokerage house reports. Market analysis and outlook and stock recommendations are provided. Full text; updated weekly. Provider: NewsNet, Inc.

Wall Street S.O.S.   CompuServe
Full-text newsletter gives recommendations for buying and selling common stocks listed on the New York and American stock exchanges and has analysis of trading, updates on performance of recommended stocks, and forecasts. Updated daily. Provider: NewsNet, Inc.

Wall Street S.O.S. Options Alert   CompuServe
Newsletter gives daily recommendations for index options. Updated daily. Provider: NewsNet, Inc.

J

JOBS. *See* EMPLOYMENT.

JUSTICE, DEPARTMENT OF

Antitrust FOIA Log   CompuServe
Newsletter tracks freedom of information requests filed with the Department of Justice's Antitrust Division and shows the name and address of requester, documents requested, and date of request. Full text; covers July 1986 to present. Updated weekly. Provider: NewsNet, Inc.

K, L

LABOR. *See also* EMPLOYMENT.

LaborDoc   CompuServe, ORBIT
Database catalogs international journal literature about labor relations. Topics include industrial relations, economic and social development, demography, education, law, and rural development. Covers 1965 to present. Updated monthly. Provider: International Labor Organization.

LaborLaw I & II   CompuServe, DIALOG
LaborLaw I provides references and summaries of U.S. court decisions regarding labor relations, fair employment, wages and hours, and occupational safety and health from 1938 to the mid-1980s. LaborLaw II indexes and abstracts U.S. federal, state, court, and administrative agency decisions in labor relations. Its seven areas are labor management relations, labor arbitration awards and settlements, fair employment practices, wages and hours, occupational safety and health, mine safety and health, and individual employment rights. Covers LaborLaw I, 1938 to mid-1980s (depending on file), and LaborLaw II (varies depending on file). Updates: LaborLaw I, none; LaborLaw II, monthly. Provider: The Bureau of National Affairs.

LANGUAGE. *See also* HUMANITIES.

Linguistics and Language Behavior Abstracts
BRS, CompuServe, DIALOG
Worldwide material on language and linguistics is indexed and abstracted for this database. Entries

are derived from approximately 1,000 journals. Covers 1973 to present. Updated quarterly. Provider: Sociological Abstracts, Inc.

MLA Bibliography   CompuServe, DIALOG
All publications of the Modern Language Association are indexed in this database. Major categories are modern languages, literature, and linguistics. Literatures and folklore of the Americas, Europe, Asia, and Africa are covered along with theoretical, descriptive, comparative, and historical linguistics and information on specific languages and communication behavior. Covers 1964 to present. Updated annually. Provider: Modern Language Association.

LAW

Bowne Digest - Corp/Sec Article Abstracts
CompuServe
Newsletter summarizes important new articles on corporate and securities law. Updated monthly. Provider: NewsNet, Inc.

Child Abuse and Neglect   CompuServe, DIALOG
This is an index of material ranging from research project descriptions to legal references in the field of child abuse in the United States. Also found here are abstracts of court decisions. Covers current edition. Updated twice a year. Provider: National Center on Child Abuse and Neglect, Children's Bureau, U.S. Department of Health and Human Services.

Criminal Justice Periodical Index   CompuServe, DIALOG
Database has complete indexing for over 100 journals, newsletters, and law reporters. All areas of criminal justice are included, ranging from arrest to legal aid to victimless crimes. Covers 1975 to present. Updated monthly. Provider: University Microfilms International.

Index to Legal Periodicals   CompuServe
Corresponding to the printed publication of the same name, the online version is an index to all areas of jurisprudence. Emphasis is placed on patent law, tax law, international law, malpractice statutes, case notes, and book reviews. Updated twice a week. Provider: H.W. Wilson Company.

Legal Resource Index
BRS, CompuServe, DIALOG
This is a complete index of more than 750 major law journals, six law newspapers, and legal mono-

graphs. Pertinent law articles from Magazine Index, National Newspaper Index, and Trade and Industry Index are indexed here as well. Covers 1980 to present. Updated monthly. Provider: Information Access Company.

NCJRS (National Criminal Justice Reference Service)   CompuServe, DIALOG
All aspects of law enforcement and criminal justice are indexed in this database. Material cited includes both U.S. and foreign research reports, published papers, books and articles, and audiovisual productions. Covers 1972 to present. Updated monthly. Provider: National Institute of Justice/National Criminal Justice Reference Service.

Reports of Interest to Lawyers   CompuServe
Sources outside the normal legal press are scanned for reports on matters affecting legal practice. Full text; updated every two months. Provider: NewsNet, Inc.

LIBRARY AND INFORMATION SCIENCE

American Library Directory   DIALOG
This directory of U.S. and Canadian libraries contains information on public, academic, armed forces, special, and religious libraries plus information on library consortia and networks and institutions granting degrees in library science. Covers current data. Updated annually. Provider: R.R. Bowker.

Friday Memo   CompuServe
Public policy positions of the U.S. information industry, a calendar of major events of the Information Industry Association, and other information-oriented groups, along with reports on new products, services, and industry trends are the subjects of this newsletter. Full text; updated monthly. Provider: NewsNet, Inc.

Information Science Abstracts   CompuServe, DIALOG
Database indexes and abstracts journal articles, patents, proceedings, government reports and documents, and more on information science and associated fields. Among the topics are information science documentation; libraries; information services and generation, reproduction, and distribution; storage and retrieval, techniques, and more. Covers 1966 to present. Updated every two months. Provider: IFI/Plenum Data Company.

Library Literature   CompuServe
Database covers library and information science

worldwide. Data is drawn from periodicals, books, pamphlets, and theses. Covers November 1984 to present. Updated twice a week. Provider: H.W. Wilson Company.

LISA (Library and Information Science Abstracts) BRS, CompuServe, DIALOG, ORBIT
LISA indexes worldwide literature in library and information science, and over 550 journals from 60 countries are scanned for indexing. From 1980, abstracts are provided for reports, conference proceedings, theses, and monographs. Among the topics are librarianship and library services, online information retrieval, word processing, storage and retrieval, and more. Related topics include publishing and bookselling, nonbook materials, education, and more. Covers 1969 to present. Updated monthly. Provider: Library Association Publishing, London, UK.

OCLC EASI Reference BRS, CompuServe
This service allows searching the OCLC library catalog of 20 million books, serials, sound recordings, music scores, software, and audiovisual materials. Covers last four years. Updated quarterly. Provider: OCLC Online Computer Library Center, Inc.

LIFE SCIENCES. *See also* MARINE BIOLOGY; ZOOLOGY.

BIOSIS Previews BRS, CompuServe, DIALOG
This online service has citations from both *Biological Abstracts* and *Biological Abstracts/RRM*. Together these works are the main English-language index of worldwide research in the biosciences and medicine. Abstracts are available from July 1976 on. Covers 1969 to present. Updated twice a month. Provider: BIOSIS, Philadelphia, PA.

Current Awareness in Biological Sciences BRS, ORBIT
Database has references to worldwide literature in the biological sciences including biochemistry, cell biology, genetics, pharmacology, plant science, cancer research, and much more. Provider: Current Awareness in Biological Sciences.

Life Sciences Collection CompuServe, DIALOG
This is a collection of abstracts of literature in the life sciences ranging from animal behavior to virology. Coverage is worldwide and is taken from journals, books, conference proceedings, and reports. Covers 1978 to present. Updated monthly. Provider: Cambridge Scientific Abstracts.

LITERATURE. *See also* HUMANITIES.

MLA Bibliography CompuServe, DIALOG
All publications of the Modern Language Association are indexed in this database. Major categories are modern languages, literature, and linguistics. Literature and folklore of the Americas, Europe, Asia, and Africa are covered along with theoretical, descriptive, comparative, and historical linguistics and information on specific languages and communication behavior. Covers 1964 to present. Updated annually. Provider: Modern Language Association.

M

MAGAZINE ARTICLES. *See also listings under specific subject headings.*

McGraw-Hill Publications Online CompuServe, DIALOG
The full text of many McGraw-Hill business and industry publications are available here. These include *Aviation Week & Space Technology, Biotechnology Newswatch, Business Week, Byte, Chemical Engineering, Clean Coal/Synfuels Letter, Coal Week, Coal Week International, Cogeneration Report, Data Communications, Electric Utility Week, Electrical Marketing, ENR, Green Markets, Inside Energy/With Federal Lands, Inside FERC, Inside FERC's Gas Market Report, Inside NRC, Metals Week, Nuclear Fuel, Nucleonics Week, Platt's International Oilgram Petrochemical Report, Platt's Oilgram News, Platt's Oilgram Price Report, Securities Week,* and *Waste-to-Energy Report.* Covers 1985 to present. Updated weekly. Provider: McGraw-Hill, Inc., New York, NY.

Popular Magazine Review Online BRS
Database contains descriptions of articles from more than 200 general interest magazines such as *Time, Newsweek, FDA Consumer, Natural History* and many more. Provider: Ebsco Industries, Inc.

MAGAZINES. *See* BIBLIOGRAPHIES—PERIODICALS; MAGAZINE ARTICLES.

MANAGEMENT. *See also* BENEFITS; LABOR.

ABI/Inform BRS, CompuServe, DIALOG, ORBIT
Designed for managers, this service provides references to articles in over 800 publications in business and allied fields including management, law, taxation, finance, advertising, employee benefits, and much more. Covers August 1971 to present. Updated weekly. Provider: UMI/Data Courier.

Harvard Business Review BRS, CompuServe, DIALOG

This is the complete text of the *Review* from 1976 to date along with abstracts of articles from 1971 to 1975 and 700 earlier articles. Articles cover a broad range of business topics such as automation, business ethics, strategic planning, and more. Covers 1971 to present. Updated every two months. Provider: Wiley Electronic Publishing.

Management and Marketing Abstracts
CompuServe

Database has abstracts from worldwide journal articles on the theoretical and practical aspects of management and marketing. Covers 1976 to present. Updated twice a month. Provider: Pergamon Financial Data Services.

Management Contents
BRS, CompuServe, DIALOG

Information on many business and management topics is indexed and abstracted. Sources include over 120 journals, plus proceedings, transactions, course materials, newsletters, and research reports. Topics include accounting, decision sciences, industrial relations, marketing, public administration, and more. Covers September 1974 to present. Updated monthly. Provider: Information Access Company.

MARINE BIOLOGY

Oceanic Abstracts CompuServe, DIALOG

Marine-related topics are abstracted and indexed in this database. Over 9,000 citations from some 3,500 sources worldwide are added each year. Chief areas covered are oceanography, marine biology and pollution, legal aspects of marine resources, and much more. Covers 1964 to present. Updated every two months. Provider: Cambridge Scientific Abstracts.

MARKETING. *See also* ADVERTISING; DEMOGRAPHICS.

Cambridge Reports Trends and Forecasts
CompuServe

Full-text newsletter analyzes and interprets U.S. consumer opinion. Areas reported on include marketing, government relations, management, and public affairs. Updated monthly. Provider: NewsNet, Inc.

Electronic Shopping News CompuServe

Newsletter examines the selling of merchandise and financial products by cable and broadcast television home-shopping services along with video and online retailing. Full text; updated monthly. Provider: NewsNet, Inc.

FINDEX CompuServe, DIALOG

Corresponding to the printed *FINDEX: The Directory of Market Research Reports, Studies and Surveys*, this online version indexes and describes all such reports available for purchase from U.S. and international publishers. Also included are reports written by investment research companies on individual firms and industries. The purchase price of each report is given and each can be ordered from the National Standards Association through Dialorder. Covers 1972 to present. Updated twice a year. Provider: Information Group Directories.

Index to Frost & Sullivan Market Research Reports
CompuServe

Database is an index to market research reports covering products, industries, market size and distribution, and forecasts. Full text is available from the provider. Covers 1978 to present. Updated monthly. Provider: BRS Information Technologies.

Industry Data Sources CompuServe, DIALOG

Drawn from U.S. and foreign sources, this database gives primary and secondary sources of market research reports, investment banking studies, special issues of trade journals, economic forecasts, and numeric databases. Each item includes a brief abstract and all information needed to order the report from the publisher. Covers 1979 to present. Updated monthly. Provider: Information Access Company.

Management and Marketing Abstracts
CompuServe

Database has abstracts from worldwide journal articles on the theoretical and practical aspects of management and marketing. Covers 1976 to present. Updated twice a month. Provider: Pergamon Financial Data Services.

Marketing CompuServe

This is the full text of the printed magazine, which looks at new marketing strategies, product development, case histories, and analyses of statistical data. Covers September 1985 to present. Updated weekly. Provider: Profile Information.

Marketing Research Review CompuServe

Newsletter abstracts and reviews publicly available technology assessment and marketing research studies plus reviews of executive-oriented books. Updated monthly. Provider: NewsNet, Inc.

Marketing Surveys Index CompuServe
This is an extensive directory of published research on British, European, and world markets. Covers 1983 to present. Updated monthly. Provider: Profile Information.

Mintel Daily Digest CompuServe
The *Digest* gives news of advertising, public relations, and market research businesses in the United Kingdom and Europe with some coverage of other countries as well. Covers September 1986 to present. Updated daily. Provider: Profile Information.

PR Week CompuServe
Look here for information on all areas of public relations activity in the United Kingdom. It includes reports of new campaigns, account moves, and executive changes. Covers August 1985 to present. Updated weekly. Provider: NewsNet, Inc.

PTS Marketing & Advertising Reference Service (MARS) CompuServe, DIALOG
PTS MARS has data on many types of goods and services as well as the companies that provide them, their advertising agencies, chosen advertising media, and marketing strategies. It consists of abstracts from over 70 sources including key advertising journals and newsletters, consumer-oriented trade magazines, business method journals, and the advertising columns of major newspapers. Covers 1984 to present. Updated daily. Provider: Predicasts.

MATERIALS. *See also* ENGINEERING.

Corrosion ORBIT
Database has information on the effects of over 600 substances on commonly used metals, plastics, and other nonmetallics and rubbers from 40 to 560 degrees Fahrenheit. Provider: Maxwell Online.

Engineered Materials Abstracts DIALOG, ORBIT
This is an index, with abstracts for most items, of worldwide literature on polymer, ceramic, and composite material science along with the practices of materials science and engineering as related to those materials. Covers 1986 to present. Updated monthly. Provider: ASM International, Metals Park, OH and Institute of Metals, London, UK.

Iron Age CompuServe
Iron Age gives news of iron industry economic conditions, management trends, and new technology. Covers 1983 to present. Updated monthly.

Provider: DIALOG Information Services (drawn from the Trade & Industry ASAP database).

Metadex CompuServe, DIALOG, ORBIT
Metadex indexes and abstracts worldwide literature on metallurgy and is the most comprehensive such index available. Six basic areas of metallurgy are included: materials, processes, properties, products, forms, and influencing factors. Some 3,500 new references and abstracts are added each month. Covers 1966 to present. Updated monthly. Provider: ASM International and The Metals Society, London, UK.

Metals Data File ORBIT
Metals Information Designations and Specifications - CompuServe
Online directory has designation and specifications numbers for ferrous and nonferrous metals and alloys along with composition, properties, applications, and more. Updated monthly. Provider: Materials Information, ASM International.

Nonferrous Metals Abstracts
CompuServe, DIALOG
Corresponding to the printed *BNF Abstracts*, the online version indexes and abstracts worldwide literature on all aspects of nonferrous metallurgy and technology. While the majority of items indexed are in English, a large number of French and German publications are listed as well. Covers 1961 to 1983. No updates. Provider: British Non-Ferrous Metals Technology Centre, Wantage, Oxfordshire, UK.

Weldasearch CompuServe, DIALOG
This is an index of worldwide material on all facets of joining of metals and plastics along with related areas such as metal spraying and thermal cutting. Topics include welded design, metallurgy, fatigue and fracture mechanics, welding equipment, and more. About 5,000 new listings are added each year from several thousand journals and other sources. Covers 1967 to present. Updated monthly. Provider: The Welding Institute, Cambridge, UK.

World Aluminum Abstracts
CompuServe, DIALOG
This service covers technical literature on aluminum (except mining) from ore processing through fabrication. Citations and abstracts are taken from some 1,900 patents, government reports, conference proceedings, dissertations, books, and jour-

nals. Major topics include the industry in general, ores, casting, metallurgy, and much more. Covers 1968 to present. Updated monthly. Provider: ASM International.

World Surface Coatings Abstracts ORBIT

This index provides references to worldwide literature on paint and surface coatings including synthetic resins, adhesives, polymers, hazards, solvents, marketing, legislation, and more. Provider: Paint Research Association.

Zinc, Lead and Cadmium Abstracts CompuServe

This is an index of worldwide publications dealing with zinc, lead, cadmium, and their compounds and alloys. Areas include production, properties, uses, economics, and health and environmental matters. Covers 1975 to present. Updated monthly. Provider: Pergamon Financial Data Services.

MATHEMATICS

Mathsci BRS, CompuServe, DIALOG

Pure and applied mathematical literature is indexed and, since 1980, contains abstracts and reviews as well. Some 1,600 journals are scanned for inclusion and 400 of these are core mathematics journals that are completely indexed. About one-third of the items are in languages other than English with heavy emphasis on Russian journals. Covers 1959 to present. Updated monthly. Provider: American Mathematical Society.

MECHNICAL ENGINEERING *See also* ENGINEERING.

ISMEC (Information Service in Mechanical Engineering) DIALOG

This index of nearly 750 international journals covers all aspects of mechanical and production engineering and engineering management. Books, reports, and conference proceedings are indexed as well. Major areas listed are mechanical, electrical and electronic, civil, optical, energy and power, plus much more. Covers 1973 to present. Updated every two months. Provider: Cambridge Scientific Abstracts.

MEDICAL DEVICES

Health Devices Alerts DIALOG

This is a database of reported medical device problems, hazards, recalls, evaluations, and updates. Devices covered range from sutures to magnetic resonance equipment. Covers 1977 to present. Updated weekly. Provider: ECRI.

Health Devices Sourcebook DIALOG

The *Sourcebook* has names, addresses, and marketing information on North American manufacturers and distributors of over 4,000 classes of medical equipment, reagents, furniture, and so on. Covers current data. Updated annually. Provider: ECRI.

MEDICINE AND HEALTH, *See also related subjects, such as* AIDS; ALCOHOLISM; CANCER; *and* DIAGNOSTIC TESTS.

BIOSIS Previews BRS, CompuServe, DIALOG

This online service has citations from both *Biological Abstracts* and *Biological Abstracts/RRM*. Together these works are the main English-language index of worldwide research in the biosciences and medicine. Abstracts are available from July 1976 on. Covers 1969 to present. Updated twice a month. Provider: BIOSIS, Philadelphia, PA.

Clinical Abstracts CompuServe, DIALOG

Covering all aspects of clinical medicine, this database draws on more than 300 major English-language medical journals. Key topics include pediatrics, family practice, internal medicine, and general and cardiovascular surgery. Covers 1981 to present. Updated monthly. Provider: Medical Information Systems, Reference & Index Services, Inc.

Combined Health Information Database BRS, CompuServe

Database contains references only to materials on AIDS, Alzheimer's disease, arthritis, diabetes, and other health topics, plus information and education programs. Covers 1973 to present. Updated quarterly. Provider: Combined Health Information Database.

Comprehensive Core Medical Library
BRS, CompuServe

Full text database contains current editions of medical reference and textbooks plus over 70 key medical and scientific journals. Covers 1982 to present. Updated every two weeks. Provider: BRS Information Technologies.

Computer Retrieval of Information on Scientific Projects BRS

Database contains information on research projects supported by the U.S. Public Health Service.

Provider: National Institutes of Health, Division of Research Grants.

Current Contents Search   BRS, DIALOG
This service reproduces the tables of contents from issues of important journals in a number of disciplines and is the online version of the *Current Contents* series: *Clinical Medicine; Life Sciences; Engineering; Technology and Applied Sciences; Agriculture; Biology and Environmental Sciences; Physical, Chemical, and Earth Sciences; Social and Behavioral Sciences;* and *Arts and Humanities.* Covers 1988 to present. Updated weekly. Provider: Institute for Scientific Information.

Embase   BRS (since 1980 only), CompuServe (since 1980 only), DIALOG
The *Excerpta Medica* database has citations and abstracts of articles from more than 4,000 worldwide biomedical journals covering the entire field of human medicine and allied subjects. While the online database corresponds to the printed *Excerpta Medica*, it also contains 100,000 entries annually that are not in the printed version. Covers June 1974 to present. Updated weekly. Provider for BRS and CompuServe: Elsevier Science Publishing Co. Provider for DIALOG: Excerpta Medica, Amsterdam, The Netherlands.

Health Planning and Administration
BRS, CompuServe
This is an index, with abstracts, of worldwide publications on health-care planning, organization, financing, and other nonclinical topics. Covers 1975 to present. Updated weekly. Provider: National Library of Medicine.

ISTP Search   ORBIT
Multidisciplinary database covers major worldwide scientific and technical proceedings literature in the fields of chemistry, clinical medicine, computer science, earth sciences, engineering, life sciences, mathematics, and technology. Provider: Institute for Scientific Information.

Journal Watch   BRS
Service provides summaries of key new articles from 20 leading medical journals including *JAMA, The New England Journal of Medicine, The Lancet,* and *Annals of Internal Medicine.* Provider: Massachusetts Medical Society.

Life Sciences Collection   CompuServe, DIALOG
This is a collection of abstracts of literature in the life sciences ranging from animal behavior to virology. Coverage is worldwide and is taken from journals, books, conference proceedings, and reports. Covers 1978 to present. Updated monthly. Provider: Cambridge Scientific Abstracts.

Medical and Psychological Previews
BRS, CompuServe
This on-line index provides references from some 240 key medical and psychological journals within 10 days of their receipt in libraries. After three months, the entries are abstracted and transferred to *Medline.* Covers current three months. Updated weekly. Provider: BRS Information Technologies.

Medical Science Research Database   BRS
IRCS Medical Science Database - CompuServe
The complete text of articles from the *Medical Science Research* (formerly *IRCS Medical Science*) series is available. The series covers biomedical research experiments, findings, and methods. Covers 1981 to present. Updated twice a month. Provider: Medical Science Research.

Medline   BRS, CompuServe, DIALOG
This an index of more than 3,000 biomedical journals published in the U.S. and 70 other countries. It corresponds to the printed *Index Medicus, Index to Dental Literature,* and the *International Nursing Index.* Covers 1966 to present. Updated monthly. Provider: U.S. National Library of Medicine.

Scientific American Medicine   BRS
This is the full text of this internal medicine textbook, which includes up-to-date information on patient management, diagnostic techniques, basic medical science, and much more. Provider: Scientific American, Inc.

MEETINGS. *See* FAIRS, CONFERENCES, AND MEETINGS.

MENTAL HEALTH

Mental Health Abstracts   DIALOG
Database has references to 1,200 international journals, books, monographs, Far Eastern literature, nonprint materials, and more in the area of mental health. Covers 1969 to present. Updated monthly. Providers: National Clearinghouse for Mental Health Information, National Institute of Mental Health (through 1982), and IFI/Plenum Data Company (from 1983 to present).

National Institute for Mental Health
CompuServe
Database has abstracts of articles, books, reports,

and audiovisual materials on all areas of mental health. Material after 1981 is contained in the database *Mental Health Abstracts*. Covers 1969 to 1981. Not updated. Provider: BRS Information Technologies.

MERGERS AND ACQUISITIONS

IDD M&A Transactions DIALOG

Data on all partial or completed mergers, acquisitions, or divestitures of $1 million or more of undisclosed value are detailed here. Each item includes, among other information, detailed data on both target and acquirer companies, transaction terms and amount, advisor and fee information, financial data, deal status, and defensive techniques. Covers January 1984 to present. Updated semiweekly. Provider: IDD Information Services, Inc.

M&A Filings DIALOG

Abstracts of all original and amended merger and acquisition documents made available by the Securities and Exchange Commission since April 1985 are contained here. Copies of the full text of each filing or exhibit are available from the provider. Covers April 1985 to present. Updated daily. Provider: Charles E. Simpson & Company.

Mergers DIALOG

This is a menu-driven version of *M&A Filings*, above. Many users will find *Mergers* easier to use. Covers April 1985 to present. Updated daily. Provider: Charles E. Simpson & Company.

METALS. *See* MATERIALS.

METEOROLOGY. *See* EARTH SCIENCES.

MILITARY. *See also* MILITARY PROCUREMENT.

Defense Daily CompuServe

This newsletter looks at defense and aerospace industry developments, reporting on such things as progress of defense-related legislation in the Congress, foreign military sales, and contract awards. Covers August 1986 to present. Full text, updated daily. Provider: NewsNet, Inc.

Defense Industry Report CompuServe

This full-text newsletter reports on Defense Department contracting, following contract and budget processes for all weapons systems. Updated every two weeks. Provider: NewsNet, Inc.

Defense R&D Update CompuServe

Newsletter focuses on Defense Department research and development programs in aeronautics, space, and electronics and includes budgets, contracts, and Congressional oversight. Full text; updated monthly. Provider: NewsNet, Inc.

IHS International Standards and Specifications DIALOG

Database provides references to industry, military, and federal standards in engineering and related fields. Referenced are 90 percent of the world's most used standards from over 70 domestic, foreign, and international standardizing groups. Also available are active and historical U.S. military and federal specifications and standards. Covers current data. Updated weekly for military specifications, every two months for others. Provider: Information Handling Services.

Jane's Defense & Aerospace News/Analysis DIALOG

The full text from *Jane's Defense Weekly*, *Interavia International Defense Review*, *Interavia Aerospace Review*, *Interavia Space Markets*, *Aerospace Intelligence*, *Defense Budget Intelligence*, *International Defense Intelligence*, *Turbine Intelligence*, *O&M Intelligence*, and *Contracting Intelligence* are available. These publications collectively summarize and interpret defense and aerospace industry worldwide. Covers 1982 to present. Updated weekly. Provider: Jane's Information Group.

MILITARY PROCUREMENT

C31 Report CompuServe

This full-text newsletter gives information on the design and procurement of military command, control, and communications programs. Areas covered include technical, budgetary, and political developments. In addition, contract awards and contact information is provided. Updated every two weeks. Provider: NewsNet, Inc.

DMS Contractors DIALOG

This online directory has data on defense/aerospace companies. Listings show title of program, name and address of the company involved (plus subcontractors), description of work performed, and the market intelligence report having additional information (see *DMS Market Intelligence Reports* below). Covers 1960 to present. Updated weekly. Provider: Jane's Information Group.

DMS Market Intelligence Reports DIALOG

Service has detailed and up-to-date full-text reports on the defense/aerospace industry. Almost all major defense companies, programs, and products are covered with data including forecasts, major activity, funding, location, military posture, and much more. Covers current data. Updated weekly. Provider: Jane's Information Group.

PTS Aerospace/Defense Markets & Technology
CompuServe, DIALOG

More than 100 key defense journals are thoroughly abstracted along with selective abstracts of articles from over 1,500 other pertinent sources. All major U.S. Defense Department contracts are included as well as annual reports and press releases from the defense industry. Database corresponds to the printed PTS ADM&T. Covers 1982 to present. Updated daily. Provider: Predicasts.

MINERALOGY. *See* EARTH SCIENCES.

MINING

Ecomine CompuServe

Ecomine indexes international technical literature on mining economics, production, policies, and legislation. Covers 1984 to present. Updated monthly. Provider: Telesystems/Questel, Inc.

MONEY. *See* FOREIGN EXCHANGE.

MOVIES

Magill's Survey of Cinema
CompuServe, DIALOG

This database has full-text articles on more than 1,800 outstanding films. It also includes short listings on hundreds of other films with an abstract and credit listing for each. Covers 1902 to present. Updated every two weeks. Provider: Salem Press, Inc.

Hollywood Hotline CompuServe

This is the newsletter's full text of news of movies, television, music, and personalities, plus movie reviews. Updated daily. Provider: NewsNet, Inc.

MUSIC

RILM Abstracts (Repertoire International de Litterature Musicale) CompuServe, DIALOG

This international database abstracts all important literature on music taken from over 300 journals. The broad range of topics includes historical musicology, performance practice, theory, esthetics, acoustics, and much more. Covers 1971 to December 1979. Updated irregularly. Provider: Inter-

national RILM Center, City University of New York, New York, NY.

MUTUAL FUNDS. *See* INVESTMENTS.

N

NEWS AND CURRENT EVENTS—GENERAL

AP News DIALOG

The full text of national, international, and business news from the AP Data Stream Service is available 48 hours after release to the news media. Covers 1984 to present. Updated daily. Provider: Associated Press.

BUSINESSWIRE CompuServe, DIALOG

The full text of over 10,000 news sources including companies, public relations firms, government agencies, and much more is available here. About 90 percent of news releases are business or financial covering all types of businesses. Covers 1986 to present. Updated continuously. Provider: BUSINESSWIRE.

Courier Plus DIALOG

Comprehensive indexing (with 25-word abstracts) of articles from more than 25 national and regional newspapers and over 300 general-interest, professional, and scholarly periodicals. Photocopies of most articles can be ordered through DIALOG's Dialorder. Covers 1988 to present (periodicals) and 1989 to present (newspapers). Updated weekly. Provider: UMI/Data Courier.

Facts on File CompuServe, DIALOG

Drawn from worldwide news sources, this weekly record of current history is divided into four sections: international affairs, U.S. affairs, world news, and miscellaneous. The news summaries are comprehensive and precise. Covers 1982 to present. Updated weekly. Provider: Facts on File, Inc.

Keesing's Record of World Events CompuServe

Database has reference data on world politics, economics, events, and defense along with budget and fiscal data. Covers December 1986 to present. Updated monthly. Provider: Profile Information.

McGraw-Hill News DIALOG

The full text of current news stories of important business events is presented here. Stories come in from McGraw-Hill news bureaus around the world and are made available as soon as they are written. Covers June 18, 1987 to present. Updated every 15 minutes from 8 A.M. to 6 P.M. Eastern time, Monday to Friday. Provider: McGraw-Hill Information Network.

Mediawire   CompuServe
Service has full text of press releases and similar announcements from organizations in the Mid-Atlantic states of Pennsylvania, Delaware, Maryland, and West Virginia and provides a source for regional corporate and political news. Reports of arrests are included. Covers August 1983 to present. Updated twice a week. Provider: VU/TEXT Information Services, Inc.

National Newspaper Index   BRS, CompuServe, DIALOG
This index provides complete indexing for the *Christian Science Monitor*, the *New York Times*, and the *Wall Street Journal*. The only items not indexed are weather charts, stock market tables, crossword puzzles, and horoscopes. Additionally, international news stories written by staff reporters of the *Washington Post* and the *Los Angeles Times* are covered with other types of articles indexed selectively. Covers 1979 to present. Updated monthly. Provider: Information Access Company.

Newsearch   BRS, CompuServe, DIALOG
This daily index covers over 2,000 news items, information articles, and book reviews from more than 1,700 key newspapers, magazines, and periodicals. This database also has two other features: the Area Business Databank, which has indexing and abstracts from over 100 local and regional business publications, and the full text of *PR Newswire*. Covers current month only. Updated daily. Provider: Information Access Company.

Newspaper Abstracts   DIALOG
This indexing and abstract service has complete indexing for 19 regional, national, and international newspapers and short article abstracts. Indexed are *American Banker*, *Atlanta Constitution*, *Atlanta Journal* (selected articles), *Boston Globe*, *Chicago Tribune*, *Christian Science Monitor*, *Denver Post*, *Detroit News*, *Guardian* and *Guardian Weekly* (London), *Houston Post*, *Los Angeles Times*, *New Orleans Times-Picayune*, *New York Times* (no sports), *Pravda* (English-language edition), *St. Louis Post-Dispatch*, *San Francisco Chronicle*, *USA Today*, *Wall Street Journal*, and the Black newspaper collection. Covers 1984 to present (most papers). Updated weekly. Provider: University Microfilms International.

Newswire ASAP   DIALOG
This service has the full text and indexing of news releases and wire stories from PR Newswire, Kyodo, and Reuters. These cover current and previous data on companies, industries, products, economics, and finance in the United States and worldwide. Covers PR Newswire, January 1985 to present; Kyodo, July 1987 to present; and Reuters, June 1987 to present. Provider: Information Access Company.

PR Newswire   CompuServe, DIALOG
This service has the full text of news releases from companies, public relations firms, trade associations, domestic and foreign governments, and other sources. About 80 percent of the items contained here are business/financial. Covers May 1, 1987 to present. Updated continuously. Provider: PR Newswire Association, Inc.

Reuters   DIALOG
The complete text of the Reuter Library Service newswire is available online. International news is continually updated and news "flashes" containing headlines and/or stories presented before the complete story is written are made available. Covers 1987 to present. Updated continuously. Provider: Reuters U.S., Inc.

UPI News   CompuServe, DIALOG
The full text of items carried on the United Press International wire is available 48 hours after release to the news media. Also included are UPI columns, standing features, and commentaries. Covers 1983 to present. Updated daily. Provider: United Press International, Inc.

USA Today Decisionline   DIALOG
This command-driven service contains capsules of significant events in 18 news categories from advertising to international news. The companion service of this same database, *USA Today* is menu-driven. Covers the last two weeks. Updated daily. Provider: Gannett News Media.

U.S. News and World Report   CompuServe
This is the full text of the magazine that reports U.S. and international news. Covers 1983 to present. Updated monthly. Provider: DIALOG Information Services (drawn from the Trade & Industry ASAP database).

World Affairs Report   CompuServe, DIALOG
This database provides a digest of world news

from the perspective of the Soviet Union. A country-by-country, subject-by-subject analysis of the Soviet view of world developments based on Soviet and non-Soviet sources is presented. Covers 1970 to present. Updated monthly. Provider: California Institute of International Affairs.

NEWS AND CURRENT EVENTS— INTERNATIONAL

BBC Summary of World Broadcasts CompuServe
Database is jointly compiled and translated by the British Broadcasting Corporation and the U.S. government's Broadcast Information Service. It provides a record of international events, speeches, and policy statements not ordinarily covered by the media. Covers 1982 to present. Updated daily. Provider: Profile Information.

Africa:

Africa News CompuServe
Newsletter reports news and provides background analysis of African political, economic, and cultural events along with U.S.–African relations. Updated weekly. Provider: NewsNet, Inc.

Central America:

Central America Update CompuServe
Focusing on Nicaragua and El Salvador, this newsletter covers Central American political, military, economic, and social developments along with U.S. policy toward the region. Covers February 1986 to present. Updated twice a week. Provider: NewsNet, Inc.

France:

AFPE CompuServe
Database contains the full text of the *Agence France Presse* newswire, which gives coverage of French and international news. Covers December 1985 to present. Updated daily. Provider: G.Cam Serveur.

Japan:

Asahi News Service CompuServe
This Japanese newswire service contains news of Japan and the Far East. Emphasis is placed on Japanese policy and international relations, trade, communications, computers, electronics, pharmaceuticals, medicine, and agriculture. Covers August 1982 to present. Updated daily. Provider: Profile Information.

Japan Economic Newswire Plus DIALOG
This database has all English-language newswires reported by Kyodo News Service, Tokyo, Japan, including both the Japan Economic Daily and Kyodo English Language News. Coverage includes both business and general news from Japan along with international news in regard to Japan. Covers 1984 to present. Updated daily. Provider: Kyodo News International, Inc., New York, NY.

Middle East:

APS Diplomat CompuServe
Newsletter watches Middle East politics and contains reports on political and defense matters, balance-of-power analyses, and country surveys. Material is compiled by the Arab Press Service. Covers February 1984 to present. Full text, updated weekly. Provider: NewsNet, Inc.

APS Review CompuServe
Compiled by the Arab Press Service, the *Review* covers and forecasts Middle East technical, economic, and business developments in the oil and natural gas markets. Prices, sales contracts, and market events are reported. Full text, updated weekly. Provider: NewsNet, Inc.

Soviet Union:

Current Digest of the Soviet Press DIALOG
Equivalent to the English-language journal of the same name, this online version provides up-to-date translations and abstracts from Soviet newspapers and a large number of magazines without elaboration or comment. Covers 1982 to present. Updated weekly. Provider: The Current Digest of the Soviet Press.

United Kingdom:

BBC External Services News CompuServe
Database contains compilations of key British and worldwide news stories from the British Broadcasting Corporation's External Services. Covers 1982 to present. Updated daily. Provider: Profile Information.

NEWS AND CURRENT EVENTS—SPECIFIC NEWSPAPERS

Akron Beacon Journal CompuServe
This is the full text of this Akron, Ohio newspaper. Akron is a center for the rubber and auto industries. Covers 1985 to present. Updated daily. Provider: VU/TEXT Information Services, Inc.

Albany Times Union/Knickerbocker News
CompuServe
The full text of these midstate New York newspapers is available. The *Times Union* is published every morning and the *News* every evening. Stories include news on state government, the General Electric Company, the Saratoga Performing Arts Center, and mid-state New York. Covers *Times Union* from March 1986 to present; *Knickerbocker News* from January 1986 to present. Updated daily. Provider: VU/TEXT Information Services, Inc.

Allentown Morning Call   CompuServe
The full text of all stories, features, and editorials regarding the Allentown area of Pennsylvania is provided. Covers 1984 to present. Updated three times a week. Provider: VU/TEXT Information Services, Inc.

Anchorage Daily News   CompuServe
The full text of this Alaskan newspaper provides particular coverage of Alaskan political, energy, resource, and development news along with northern defense systems and arctic regional studies. Covers October 1985 to present. Provider: VU/TEXT Information Services, Inc.

Annapolis Capital   CompuServe
Look here for the full text of stories, features, syndicated columns, and editorials about Maryland and Annapolis. Important coverage includes the U.S. Naval Academy, state government, maritime industries, and the Chesapeake bay environment. Covers June 1986 to present. Updated daily. Provider: VU/TEXT Information Services, Inc.

Arizona Republic/Phoenix Gazette   CompuServe
The full text of both of these Phoenix, Arizona newspapers is presented. Particular attention is paid to area news, real estate development, tourism, desert environment, and high technology. Covers *Republic* from June 1986 to present and *Gazette* from January 1986 to present. Updated daily. Provider: VU/TEXT Information Services, Inc.

Arkansas Gazette   CompuServe
Full text of the newspaper covering Arkansas business, political, and general news. Covers October 1984 to present. Updated daily. Provider: DataTimes.

Baton Rouge Advocate & Times   CompuServe
The full text of these Louisiana newspapers has particular coverage of regional energy industry

affairs. Covers 1985 to present. Updated daily. Provider: DataTimes.

Bergen Record   CompuServe
This daily newspaper has state and regional news for northern New Jersey and the New York metropolitan area. Covers June 1985 to present. Updated daily. Provider: DataTimes.

Boston Globe   CompuServe
Newspaper covers local, national, and international news with attention paid to local Boston/Massachusetts political issues, the Kennedy family, and regional technology. Covers 1980 to present. Full text; updated daily. Provider: VU/TEXT Information Services, Inc.

Charlotte Observer   CompuServe
The full text of this newspaper covers this North Carolina financial and transportation center along with national and international news. Covers July 1985 to present. Updated daily. Provider: VU/TEXT Information Services, Inc.

Chicago Sun Times   CompuServe
Look here for the full text of this newspaper covering local, national, and international news. Covers July 1985 to present. Updated daily. Provider: DataTimes.

Chicago Tribune   CompuServe, DIALOG
The full text of the newspaper is available. National, international, local, and business coverage is provided. Covers 1988 to present. Updated daily. Provider: Chicago Tribune Co.

Columbus Dispatch   CompuServe
The full text of this newspaper from this Ohio center for business and research is available. Covers July 1985 to present. Updated daily. Provider: VU/TEXT Information Services, Inc.

Daily Oklahoman   CompuServe
This is the full text of this Oklahoma newspaper that covers business, political, and general news. Covers November 1981 to present. Updated daily. Provider: DataTimes.

Daily Texan   CompuServe
The newspaper of the University of Texas covers state political and general news along with university and educational matters. Covers September 1984 to present. Full text; updated daily. Provider: DataTimes.

Dallas Morning News CompuServe
The full text of this major Texas newspaper covers local, national, and international news. Covers August 1984 to present. Updated daily. Provider: DataTimes.

Detroit Free Press CompuServe
This auto-center newspaper reports local, national, and international news with a special focus on the automobile industry and labor issues. Covers March 1982 to present. Updated daily. Provider: VU/TEXT Information Services, Inc.

Fort Lauderdale News & Sun-Sentinel
CompuServe
The full text of this south Florida newspaper is presented here. Regional coverage focuses on agriculture, business, tourism, sports, and recreation on Florida's southeast coast. Covers 1985 to present. Updated daily. Provider: VU/TEXT Information Services, Inc.

Fresno Bee CompuServe
All stories, features, columns, editorials, letters to the editor, obituaries, and articles by special correspondents are available. The paper has local coverage of California's San Joaquin Valley along with national and international news. Covers March 1986 to present. Updated daily. Provider: VU/TEXT Information Services, Inc.

Harrisburg Patriot and Evening News
CompuServe
The full text of this newspaper has south-central Pennsylvania and state news along with major newswire items. Covers August 1986 to present. Updated daily. Provider: DataTimes.

Houston Chronicle CompuServe
Online service has the full text of this Texas newspaper covering Houston and southeastern Texas. Covers February 1985 to present. Updated daily. Provider: DataTimes.

Houston Post CompuServe
This is the full text of all news stories, columns, feature stories, editorials, and letters to the editor. Local, state, national, and international news is provided with focus on energy, space, and international business and trade. Covers 1985 to present. Updated five times a week. Provider: VU/TEXT Information Services, Inc.

Journal Record CompuServe
The full text gives news of Oklahoma and Oklahoma City business along with detailed coverage of the Oklahoma legislature. Covers April 1985 to present. Updated daily. Provider: DataTimes.

Lexington Herald-Leader CompuServe
The full text of this Kentucky newspaper has particular coverage of thoroughbred horse racing and breeding, collegiate sports, state and local news, and other regional matters. Covers 1983 to present. Updated daily. Provider: VU/TEXT Information Services, Inc.

Los Angeles Daily News CompuServe
Service has the full text of all staff-written stories, features, columns, editorials, letters to the editor, and wire-service stories relating to California. Paper provides regional coverage plus a focus on high technology, the entertainment and citrus industries, and business. Covers October 1985 to present. Updated daily. Provider: VU/TEXT Information Services, Inc.

Los Angeles Times CompuServe
This is the full text of this key California newspaper with local, state, national, and international news. Particular attention is paid to business and finance, banking, high technology, entertainment, aerospace, and Far Eastern trade. Covers 1985 to present. Updated daily. Provider: VU/TEXT Information Services, Inc.

Miami Herald CompuServe
El Miami Herald (Spanish-language) - CompuServe
The online version of this major Florida newspaper contains the full text of all stories, features, columns, and editorials. The paper has local, state, national, and international news reports with special focus on Latin America, the Middle East, and sun-belt agriculture. Covers 1983 to present. Updated daily. Provider: VU/TEXT Information Services, Inc.

Minneapolis Star and Tribune CompuServe
The full text of this Minnesota newspaper includes broad coverage of local and state economic conditions and key businesses in the state. Updated daily. Provider: DataTimes.

Montreal Gazette CompuServe
The full text of this daily newspaper is provided here. Canadian and international news along with politics, business, sports, and fashion news of Montreal and Quebec province is available. Cov-

ers 1985 to present. Updated daily. Provider:
DataTimes.

Orange County Register CompuServe
Look here for stories and newswire items from
California's third largest newspaper. Extended cov-
erage of the defense and computer industries is
included. Covers 1986 to present. Updated daily.
Provider: DataTimes.

Orlando Sentinel CompuServe
The full text of this newspaper concentrates particularly on Orlando and central Florida with emphasis on tourism, high technology, agriculture,
citrus growers and processors, and business. Covers April 1985 to present. Updated daily. Provider: VU/TEXT Information Services, Inc.

Ottawa Citizen CompuServe
Canadian newspaper covers local, national, and
international news. Excellent coverage of events
on Parliament Hill and the Canadian federal government is provided. Covers September 1985 to
present. Updated daily. Provider: DataTimes.

Philadelphia Daily News CompuServe
The full text of this Pennsylvania newspaper features local news, features, and sports. Covers 1980
to present. Updated daily. Provider: VU/TEXT Information Services, Inc.

Philadelphia Inquirer CompuServe
The full text of this Pennsylvania newspaper has
national and international news plus detailed reporting on local and regional business and economics, education, and the arts. Covers 1981 to
present. Updated daily. Provider: VU/TEXT Information Services, Inc.

Reading Times and Eagle CompuServe
The full text of locally written stories and selected
wire-service stories from these two southeastern
Pennsylvania newspapers are provided. Covers
1987 to present. Updated daily. Provider: Data-
Times.

Richmond News Leader/Times Dispatch
CompuServe
The full text of both of these Virginia newspapers
covers city, regional, and state news with special
attention being given to the tobacco industry, agriculture, and business. Covers August 1985 to
present. Updated daily. Provider: VU/TEXT Information Services, Inc.

Sacramento Bee CompuServe
Service has the full text of news stories, features,
and editorials from this northeastern California
paper. Strong coverage is provided for state government, business, investments, and securities.
Covers March 1984 to present. Updated three times
a week. Provider: VU/TEXT Information Services,
Inc.

San Francisco Chronicle CompuServe
The full text of this California newspaper has
local, state, national, and international news with
a special interest in Silicon Valley. Covers 1985 to
present. Updated daily. Provider: DataTimes.

San Jose Mercury News CompuServe
Newspaper has regional and state news with emphasis on coverage of Silicon Valley developments,
real estate, science, and medicine. Covers June
1985 to present. Updated daily. Provider: VU/
TEXT Information Services, Inc.

Seattle Post-Intelligencer CompuServe
Newspaper has strong coverage of the Puget Sound
region including the maritime, timber, aviation,
nuclear energy, and waste industries. Covers June
1986 to present. Updated daily (weekdays). Provider: VU/TEXT Information Services, Inc.

Seattle Times CompuServe
Providing one-third national and international
news, the *Times* also has excellent coverage of
Seattle and the Pacific Northwest including extensive business news. Covers 1985 to present. Updated daily. Provider: DataTimes.

St. Petersburg Times CompuServe
The full text of this west Florida newspaper contains local, national, and international news. Covers November 1986 to present. Updated daily.
Provider: DataTimes.

Toronto Star CompuServe
The full text of Canada's largest newspaper is
presented, which covers local, regional, and na-
tional events along with financial news. Covers
April 1986 to present. Updated daily. Provider:
DataTimes.

USA Today CompuServe, DIALOG
This menu-driven service contains capsules of significant events in 18 news categories from advertising to international news. The companion service
of this same database, *USA Today Decisionline,* is

command-driven. Covers the past two weeks. Updated daily. Provider: Gannett News Media, Washington, DC.

USA Today Decisionline   DIALOG
This command-driven service contains capsules of significant events in 18 news categories from advertising to international news. The companion service of this same database, *USA Today*, is menu-driven. Covers the past two weeks. Updated daily. Provider: Gannett News Media, Washington, DC.

Washington Post Online   CompuServe, DIALOG
This is the electronic version of the daily and Sunday *Washington Post*, published in Washington, DC. Covers April 1983 to present. Updated daily. Provider: The Washington Post Company.

Wichita Eagle-Beacon   CompuServe
This is the full text of this Kansas newspaper from a regional agriculture, energy, transportation, and aviation center. Covers October 1984 to present. Updated daily. Provider: VU/TEXT Information Services, Inc.

Windsor Star   CompuServe
Look here for daily coverage of politics, business, and local news in the Windsor, Canada area. Covers October 1986 to present. Full text; updated daily. Provider: DataTimes.

NEWSPAPERS. *See* NEWS AND CURRENT EVENTS—SPECIFIC NEWSPAPERS.

NUCLEAR ENERGY. *See also* ENERGY AND POWER GENERATION.

DOE Energy   DIALOG
The U.S. Department of Energy's database provides references to literature in energy and related fields. Material is drawn from journals, dissertations, books, patents, conference papers, and more. Energy topics covered are nuclear, wind, fossil, geothermal, tidal, and solar. Allied topics include environment, energy policy, and conservation. Covers 1974 to present. Updated every two weeks. Provider: U.S. Department of Energy.

Nuclear Science Abstracts   DIALOG
Database is an index with abstracts of worldwide material on nuclear science and technology for the years 1948 to 1976 and is the companion to *DOE Energy* (above), which covers the field since 1976. Covers 1948 to 1976. Provider: U.S. Department of Energy.

Nuclear Waste News   CompuServe
The full text of this newsletter reports on such issues regarding nuclear waste as management, regulation, transportation, disposal, and more. Updated weekly. Provider: NewsNet, Inc.

NURSING

Nursing and Allied Health   BRS, CompuServe, DIALOG
Database is an index of over 300 English-language nursing journals and the publications of the American Nurses' Association and the National League for Nursing. Also indexed are primary journals in over 12 related health fields, nearly a dozen library science journals, pertinent citations from the *Index Medicus* and various psychological and management journals, and popular literature. Covers 1983 to present. Updated every two months. Provider: Cumulative Index to Nursing and Allied Health Literature Corporation.

O

OCEANOGRAPHY. *See also* EARTH SCIENCES.

Oceanic Abstracts   CompuServe, DIALOG
Marine-related topics are abstracted and indexed in this database. Over 9,000 citations from some 3,500 sources worldwide are added each year. Chief areas covered are oceanography, marine biology and pollution, legal aspects of marine resources, and much more. Covers 1964 to present. Updated every two months. Provider: Cambridge Scientific Abstracts.

OIL. *See* ENERGY AND POWER GENERATION; INDUSTRIES: PETROLEUM.

OLD AGE

AgeLine   BRS, CompuServe
This is an index, with abstracts, on materials on aging. Topics include psychological, medical, economic, and political considerations. Covers 1978 to present. Updated every two months. Provider: American Association of Retired Persons; National Gerontology Resource Center.

OPTICS

Fiber/Optics News   CompuServe
Newsletter covers the fiber optics and laser industries, reporting on government and private industry. Topics include communications, television,

computers, and more. Updated weekly. Provider: NewsNet, Inc.

Military Fiber Optics News   CompuServe
Newsletter covers U.S. Government fiber optics developments, contract awards, industry standards, legislation, and proposed and continuing activities. Full text; updated every two weeks. Provider: NewsNet, Inc.

ORGANIZATIONS

Encyclopedia of Associations
CompuServe, DIALOG
The full text of the printed *Encyclopedia* is presented here. All kinds of associations including several thousand trade, professional, fraternal, and patriotic associations, labor unions, and other voluntary associations are represented. Listings include name, address, phone number, size of membership, scope and purpose, and publications. Covers current edition. Updated annually. Provider: Gale Research Company.

National Foundations   CompuServe, DIALOG
National Foundations gives descriptions of foundations without regard to assets or amount of giving. Many of these smaller foundations restrict giving to local or regional recipients. Covers current year's data. Updated annually. Provider: The Foundation Center.

P

PACKAGING. *See* PAPER AND PACKAGING.

PALEONTOLOGY. *See* EARTH SCIENCES.

PAPER AND PACKAGING

Packaging Science and Technology Abstracts
CompuServe, DIALOG
This service indexes research and development literature of all areas of packaging science. Over 400 journals, along with books, reports, patents, legislation, and more sources, are indexed. Covers 1982 to present. Updated monthly. Provider: International Food Information Service, Frankfurt am Main, Germany.

Paperchem   CompuServe, DIALOG
Paperchem indexes and abstracts scientific and technical literature of the pulp and paper industry including raw materials, processes, and technol-

ogy. Also covered are related subjects such as graphic arts, forestry, carbohydrate chemistry, and more. Some 50 percent of the entries are on patent information. Covers July 1967 to present. Updated monthly. Provider: Institute of Paper Chemistry.

Paper, Printing, Packaging, & Nonwovens Abstracts   ORBIT
PIRA Abstracts - CompuServe
Database has abstracts of articles in all areas of paper, nonwoven materials, printing, and packaging including technology, processes, waste treatment, management, marketing, and more. Covers 1975 to present. Updated twice a month. Provider: Paper & Board, Printing & Packaging Industries Research Association.

PATENTS AND TRADEMARKS

APIPAT   CompuServe, ORBIT
APIPAT provides references to petroleum-related patents from the United States and eight other countries. Areas include processes, fuels, petrochemicals, tankers, pollution control, synthetic fuels, and more. Covers 1964 to present. Updated monthly. Provider: The American Petroleum Institute, Central Abstracting & Indexing Service.

British Trade Marks   ORBIT
Database contains data on registered and applied-for trademarks in the United Kingdom. Also included are marks that have expired since January 1, 1976. Provider: The Patent Office State House.

Chinese Patent Abstracts in English   DIALOG
A complete listing of patents issued by the People's Republic of China along with English-language abstracts are available in this database. Covers 1985 to present. Updated every two weeks. Provider: INPADOC, Vienna, Austria.

Claims/Citation   CompuServe, DIALOG
This database contains the answers as to which patents are cited by a later one. More than 5 million patents cited in U.S. patents since 1947 are referenced. Covers 1947 to present. Updated quarterly. Providers: Search Check, Inc. and IFI/Plenum Data Corp.

Claims/Classification   ORBIT
Claims/Reference - DIALOG
This is a dictionary index to the U.S. Patent Office's classification codes. Provider: IFI/Plenum Data Corp.

Claims/Compound Registry CompuServe, DIALOG, ORBIT
This dictionary of chemical compounds gives the IFI compound term number, main compound name, synonyms, molecular formula, and fragment codes and terms. Database is primarily for assistance in finding patents in *Claims/Uniterm*, below. Covers current data. Updated annually. Provider: IFI/Plenum Data Corp.

Claims/Reassignment & Reexamination CompuServe, DIALOG, ORBIT
This service tracks patents whose ownership has been reassigned from the original assignee and those patents that have reexamined by the Patent Office at the request of another party who challenges the patentability of one or more claims. Covers reassigned patents from 1980 to present; reexamined patents from 1981 to present; expired patents from 1985 to present. Updated every two months. Provider: IFI/Plenum Data Corp.

Claims/US Patent Abstracts CompuServe, DIALOG
Patents in the general, chemical, electrical, and mechanical sections of the *Official Gazette* of the U.S. Patent Office are available. Chemical patents have claims from 1950 to 1970 and from 1971 to present along with abstracts from 1971 to the present. Citations only can be had for electrical and mechanical patents from 1963 to present and claims for 1965 to 1970 plus 1978 to the present. Design patents have citations and abstracts only from 1980 to present. Covers 1950 to present (see above). Updated monthly. Provider: IFI/Plenum Data Corp.

Claims/U.S. Patent Abstracts Weekly CompuServe, DIALOG
The newest U.S. patents can be found here before they are added to the database above each month. Covers current month only. Updated weekly. Provider: IFI/Plenum Data Corp.

Claims/Uniterm DIALOG
This index covers chemical and chemically related patents only. See also *Claims/Compound Registry*, above. Covers 1950 to present. Updated quarterly. Provider: IFI/Plenum Data Corporation, Alexandria, VA.

Computerpat CompuServe, ORBIT
Database contains abstracts of all U.S. patents issued for data processing and computers. Cover-

age includes processors, input/output devices, storage elements, storage management devices, error detection and diagnostic methods, communications systems, and applications. Covers 1942 to present. Updated monthly. Provider: Maxwell Online.

EDOC CompuServe
Database is an index of relationships between European and worldwide patents. Covers 1969 to present. Updated every three weeks. Provider: Telesystems/Questel, Inc.

EPAT CompuServe
This is an index of all published European patent applications. Covers 1978 to present. Updated weekly. Provider: Telesystems/Questel, Inc.

FPAT CompuServe
All French patents applied for and published since 1969 are indexed in French. Covers 1969 to present. Updated weekly. Provider: Telesystems/Questel, Inc.

Inpadoc/Family and Legal Status Dialog
Inpadoc/Inapnew - CompuServe, ORBIT
Service lists new patents issued in 55 countries. Listings contain title, inventor, and assignment along with data on priority application numbers, countries, and dates. *Family and Legal Status* shows equivalent patents for patents issued by the 55 countries and legal status data for 10 of the issuing countries. All areas of technology are covered. Covers 1968 to present. Updated weekly. Provider: INPADOC, Vienna, Austria.

JAPIO CompuServe, ORBIT
Database has references, with abstracts, to Japanese unexamined patent applications. Covers 1976 to present. Updated monthly. Provider: Japan Patent Information Organization.

Legal Status ORBIT
Look here for information on the actions that can affect a patent's legal status after it has been granted. Provider: International Patent Documentation Centre.

LitAlert ORBIT
This directory lists patent and trademark infringements suits filed in U.S. District Courts. Included are suit status, names of litigants, patent/trademark numbers, and more. Provider: Rapid Patent Service, Research Publications Inc.

Patdata BRS
Database has abstracts of all utility patents issued by the U.S. Patent and Trademark Office. Covers: 1971 to present; reissue patents from July 1, 1975 to present. Provider: U.S. Patent and Trademark Office.

Patent Abstracts of China CompuServe
Database is an index of patents from the People's Republic of China. Covers 1985 to present. Updated weekly. Provider: Pergamon Financial Data Services.

Patsearch CompuServe
Database provides short abstracts of U.S. patents. Covers 1970 to present. Updated weekly. Provider: Pergamon Financial Data Services.

Patent Status File ORBIT
Service gives notice of more than 20 types of actions affecting over 150,000 issued U.S. patents. Covers 1969 to present. Provider: Rapid Patent Service, Research Publications Inc.

RAPRA Trade Names ORBIT
Directory has trademarks and tradenames used in the rubber and plastics industries and includes company names and addresses. Provider: Rapra Technology Ltd.

Trademarkscan CompuServe, DIALOG
Trademarkscan consists of two files, one for federal and one for state trademarks. The federal database has records of over 800,000 active trademark applications and registrations on file with the U.S. Patent and Trademark Office. Each listing shows serial or registration number, trademark, U.S. classification of goods and services, owner, image, and more. The state database has records of trademarks registered in the 50 states and Puerto Rico. Each listing shows the trademark, state of registration and number, U.S. and international class numbers, description of goods and services, current status, and owner. Covers federal, 1884 to present; state (active registrations), 1986 to present. Updated: federal, weekly; state, every two weeks (each state on its own cycle). Provider: Thomson & Thomson.

U.S. Classification CompuServe, ORBIT
Database has classifications, cross-reference classifications, and unofficial classifications for all U.S. patents. Covers 1798 to present. Updated every two weeks. Provider: Derwent Publications, Ltd., London UK.

U.S. Patent Office CompuServe
U.S. Patents - ORBIT
This online service has complete U.S. patent data including complete front-page information and all claims. Covers 1970 to present. Updated weekly. Provider: Derwent Publications, Ltd., London, UK.

U.S. Trademark Watch ORBIT
Service gives details of registered and pending trademarks from the U.S. Patent and Trademark Office. Covers latest twelve weeks. Provider: U.S. Patent and Trademark Office.

World Patents Index CompuServe, DIALOG, ORBIT
This index aids in finding almost 3 million inventions covered in over 6 million worldwide patents. In addition to citations, most entries have a full abstract (1981 to present) and other information. Covers 1963 to present (pharmaceuticals from 1963; agricultural chemicals from 1965; polymers and plastics from 1966; other chemicals from 1970). Updated weekly and monthly. Provider: Derwent Publications, Ltd., London, UK.

PESTICIDES

Pestdoc ORBIT
Database indexes international literature on pesticides, herbicides, and plant protection and is aimed at manufacturers of agricultural chemicals. Provider: Derwent Publications, Ltd., London, UK.

Pesticide Databank DIALOG, ORBIT
Databank provides information on agricultural, veterinary, and public health products, including fungicides, herbicides, insecticides, acaridices, molluscicides, rodenticides, repellents, synergists, herbicide safeners, and plant growth regulators (both microbial agents and chemicals). Common name, properties, uses, toxicology, and analysis are provided. Covers 8th edition (1987). Updated quarterly. Provider: The British Crop Protection Council and CAB International.

Standard Pesticide Databank ORBIT
This is a list of some 3,900 known pesticides plus other common compounds. Each entry includes full name, standard registry name, pesticidal classification of standard activities, and more. Provider: Derwent Publications, Ltd., London, UK.

PHARMACOLOGY. *See* DRUGS AND MEDICINES.

PHILANTHROPY

Federal Research Report   CompuServe
This full-text newsletter reports on research grants (with deadlines, contacts, and addresses) from federal agencies and private foundations. Updated weekly. Provider: NewsNet, Inc.

Foundation Grants Index   CompuServe, DIALOG
The *Index* gives information on grants to organizations of $5,000 or more that are awarded by over 400 major American philanthropic foundations. Approximately 200,000 new grants are added each year and are given mainly for education, health, welfare, sciences, international activities, and religion. Covers 1973 to present. Updated every two months. Provider: The Foundation Center.

Grants   CompuServe, DIALOG
This is a database of grants offered by federal, state, and local governments, commercial organizations, and foundations in over 90 academic areas. Areas include arts, education, humanities, sciences, building grants, writing, and more. Grants detailed have application deadlines of up to six months ahead. Entries include a full description, qualifications, funds available, and renewability along with the name, address, and phone number of each grantor (when available). Covers current data. Updated monthly. Provider: The Oryx Press.

National Foundations   CompuServe, DIALOG
National Foundations gives descriptions of foundations without regard to assets or amount of giving. Many of these smaller foundations restrict giving to local or regional recipients. Covers current year's data. Updated annually. Provider: The Foundation Center.

PHILOSOPHY. *See also* HUMANITIES.

Philosopher's Index   CompuServe, DIALOG
Over 270 journals of philosophy and associated fields are indexed and abstracted in this database. Topics include aesthetics, epistemology, ethics, logic, metaphysics, and the philosophy of other fields such as education, history, religion, law, and science. Covers 1940 to present. Updated quarterly. Provider: Philosophy Documentation Center, Bowling Green State University.

PHOTOGRAPHY

Imaging Abstracts   ORBIT
Service provides references, with abstracts, to worldwide literature on the science and technology of photography and imaging. Topics include theory, processing, cameras, lighting, systems, radiology, filters, and holography. Provider: Royal Photographic Society.

Photobulletin   CompuServe
Full text service is a comprehensive listing of the photo needs of major buyers such as advertising and public relations firms, companies, and major publishers. Updated weekly. Provider: NewsNet, Inc.

Photoletter   CompuServe
This is a full-text listing of the photo needs of smaller buyers. Each entry includes a specific description of the photo desired, deadlines, and price range. Updated every two weeks. Provider: NewsNet, Inc.

Photomarket   CompuServe
Full-text listing of the photo needs of midsized buyers such as advertising and public relations firms, companies, government agencies, and publishers. Updated every two weeks. Provider: NewsNet, Inc.

PHYSICS

SPIN (Searchable Physics Information Notices)   CompuServe, DIALOG
This database has indexing and abstracts of a selected group of the most important physics journals. This set includes all journals from the American Institute of Physics with the Russian translations and some other American physics journals. Some 2,500 new entries are added each month. Covers 1975 to present. Updated monthly. Provider: American Institute of Physics.

PLASTICS AND RUBBER

RAPRA Abstracts   CompuServe, ORBIT
Database has abstracts of articles on all aspects of rubber, plastics, and polymer composites including chemical modification, machinery, and compounding properties. Covers 1972 to present. Updated twice a month. Provider: Rapra Technology Ltd.

POLITICAL SCIENCE

PAIS International   BRS, CompuServe, DIALOG

This is a bibliographic index to worldwide public policy material regarding business, economics and finance, law, international relations, government, political science, and other social sciences. All references are in English and all manner of material from pamphlets to books are covered. Covers 1972 to present. Updated monthly. Provider: Public Affairs Information Service, Inc.

U.S. Political Science Documents CompuServe, DIALOG
Database has comprehensive indexing and detailed abstracts of material from some 150 key American scholarly journals in the area of political science. Topics include foreign policy, behavioral sciences, law and contemporary problems, and much more. Covers 1975 to present. Updated quarterly. Provider: NASA Industrial Applications Center, University of Pittsburgh.

POLITICS. *See* FEDERAL GOVERNMENT; POLITICAL SCIENCE.

POLLUTION AND WASTE MANAGEMENT. *See also* HAZARDS.

Air/Water Pollution Report CompuServe
Full-text newsletter watches air and water pollution with particular respect to the Clean Air and Water Acts and similar environmental laws and court actions. Updated weekly. Provider: NewsNet, Inc.

Aptic (Air Pollution Technical Information Center) CompuServe, DIALOG
Thorough coverage of all aspects of air pollution, its effects, and control for the years 1966 to 1976 (with some data to 1978) can be found here. Areas include social, legal, and political aspects; atmospheric interaction, effects on materials, plants, and livestock, social aspects, and more. Covers 1966 to 1976 (with some additions through 1978). No updates. Provider: Manpower and Technical Information Branch, U.S. Environmental Protection Agency.

Ground Water Monitor CompuServe
Newsletter monitors regulation, legislation, and technology in connection with groundwater resources. Topics include contamination and protection. Full text; updated weekly. Provider: NewsNet, Inc.

Pollution Abstracts CompuServe, DIALOG
Database has abstracts and citations of information on air, noise, and water pollution, environ-

mental quality, pesticides, radiation, and solid wastes. Covers 1970 to present. Updated every two months. Provider: Cambridge Scientific Abstracts.

Solid Waste Report CompuServe
Newsletter looks at nonhazardous waste collection, recycling, and processing. Federal and state regulations and new technology is also reported. Full text, updated every two weeks. Provider: NewsNet, Inc.

WasteInfo ORBIT
Database has references only to literature on nonradioactive waste management including waste disposal and treatment, recycling, environmental hazards, environmental impact, regulations, and much more. Provider: Waste Management Information Bureau, Harwell Laboratory.

POPULATION AND VITAL STATISTICS. *See* DEMOGRAPHICS.

PSYCHOLOGY

Health Instrument File BRS
Database has descriptions of evaluative tests used in the health and psychosocial fields. Provider: Behavioral Measurement Database Services.

Medical and Psychological Previews
BRS, CompuServe
This online index provides references from some 240 key medical and psychological journals within 10 days of their receipt in libraries. After three months, the entries are abstracted and transferred to *Medline*. Covers current three months. Updated weekly. Provider: BRS Information Technologies.

Mental Measurements Yearbook CompuServe
Containing the full text of the printed *Yearbook*, the online version provides a source for information on psychological, personality, and aptitude tests. Included are critical reviews, reliability-validity data, and test descriptions. Covers 1974 to present. Updated monthly. Provider: Buros Institute of Mental Measurements, University of Nebraska-Lincoln.

PsychALERT CompuServe, DIALOG
A companion to *PsychINFO*, below, this database holds references only to the most recent material in psychology and related behavioral sciences. When indexed and abstracted, each item is transferred to *PsychINFO*. Covers most recent data.

Updated weekly. Provider: American Psychological Association.

PsychINFO BRS, CompuServe, DIALOG
Database provides coverage of worldwide literature on psychology and related behavioral sciences. Taken from over 1,300 journals, reports, monographs, and dissertations, coverage includes original research, reviews, theory, description of apparatus, and more. See also *PsychAlert*, above. Covers 1967 to present. Updated monthly. Provider: American Psychological Association.

PUBLIC RELATIONS. *See also* ADVERTISING.

Mediawire CompuServe
Service has full text of press releases and similar announcements from organizations in the Mid-Atlantic states of Pennsylvania, Delaware, Maryland, and West Virginia and provides a source for regional corporate and political news. Reports of arrests are included. Covers August 1983 to present. Updated twice a week. Provider: VU/TEXT Information Services, Inc.

PR Newswire CompuServe, DIALOG
This service has the full text of news releases from companies, public relations firms, trade associations, domestic and foreign governments, and other sources. About 80 percent of the items contained here are business/financial. Covers May 1, 1987 to present. Updated continuously. Provider: PR Newswire Association, Inc.

PR Week CompuServe
Look here for information on all areas of public relations activity in the United Kingdom. It includes reports of new campaigns, account moves, and executive changes. Covers August 1985 to present. Updated weekly. Provider: NewsNet, Inc.

PUBLISHING

Electronic Publishing Abstracts CompuServe
Database has abstracts from worldwide sources of information on electronic publishing, information technology, and information storage and retrieval. Covers 1975 to present. Updated every two weeks. Provider: Pergamon Financial Data Services.

Morgan Report on Directory Publishing
CompuServe
The *Report* looks at the directory buying guide and yellow pages markets with articles on new

products, business acquisitions, and company profiles. Updated monthly. Provider: NewsNet, Inc.

NA Hotline CompuServe
Publishing industry newsletter covers Congressional activity, federal regulations and publications, direct-mail law, and electronic publishing. Updated every two weeks. Provider: NewsNet, Inc.

Seybold Report on Publishing Systems
CompuServe
Newsletter reports on computer-based equipment used in publishing ranging from text editors to full publishing systems. Included are detailed product descriptions, and industry and trade-show news. Full text; updated every two weeks. Provider: NewsNet, Inc.

Q, R

REAGENTS

Linscott's Directory of Immunological and Biological Reagents ORBIT
Directory covers immunological and biological reagents including 3,300 commercially available monoclonal antibodies, 9,000 conventional antisera and conjugates, and over 14,000 other reagents used in biomedical research. Provider: Linscott's Directory.

REAL ESTATE

Real Estate Buyers Directory CompuServe
Directory lists real estate buyers. Listings include buyer's profiles, types and locations of purchases, and investment limits. Updated monthly. Provider: NewsNet, Inc.

Real Estate Sellers Directory CompuServe
Full text service lists commercial, industrial, institutional, residential, and recreational properties and land with asking prices of $500,000 or more. Updated monthly. Provider: NewsNet, Inc.

Real Estate & Venture Funding Directory
CompuServe
This full-text listing of real estate lenders includes information on real estate types, area preferences, and loan amounts. In addition, sources of business loans and venture capital are listed. Updated monthly. Provider: NewsNet, Inc.

RECORDINGS

High Fidelity CompuServe
Magazine covers high-fidelity (stereo) equipment, music, and musicians and has reports on audio and video equipment and recordings. Covers 1983 to present. Updated monthly. Provider: DIALOG Information Services (drawn from the Trade & Industry ASAP database).

Stereo Review CompuServe
Magazine covers high-fidelity (stereo) equipment and has reports on audio equipment and recordings. Covers 1983 to present. Updated monthly. Provider: DIALOG Information Services (drawn from the Trade & Industry ASAP database).

Videodisk Monitor CompuServe
Newsletter looks at interactive video, compact disc, and similar technologies with an eye toward their effect on business. Full text; updated monthly. Provider: NewsNet, Inc.

Video Week CompuServe
This home-video industry newsletter reports on business news, technology, marketing, and programming with regard to videocassettes, videodiscs, pay television, and similar media. Full text; updated weekly. Provider: NewsNet, Inc.

REGIONAL AND URBAN PLANNING

ICONDA ORBIT
Database has international literature on construction, civil engineering, architecture, and town planning. Topics include structural design, material testing, bridges, tunnels, steel, concrete and masonry, energy conservation, design, and much more. Provider: ICONDA Agency c/o Information Centre for Regional Planning and Building Construction of the Fraunhofer Society.

Urbamet CompuServe
Database has English- and French-language abstracts from periodicals and other materials on all areas of urban and regional planning and development. Covers 1976 to present. Updated monthly. Producer: Telesystems/Questel, Inc.

ROBOTS

Robot News CompuServe
Newsletter covers Japanese robotics technology and applications and includes artificial intelligence, vision systems, and vehicles. Updated monthly. Provider: NewsNet, Inc.

Robotics Age Newsletter CompuServe
Publication reports on design, manufacturing, applications, and management issues pertaining to the robotics industry. Full text, updated every two weeks. Provider: NewsNet, Inc.

Supertech CompuServe, DIALOG
Supertech corresponds to the printed abstract journals *Telegen Reporter, Artificial Intelligence Abstracts, CAD/CAM Abstracts, Robomatix Reporter,* and *Telecommunications Abstracts*. It covers the fields of biotechnology, artificial intelligence, computer-aided design and manufacturing, robotics, and telecommunications. Covers robotics and biotechnology 1972 to present; artificial intelligence and CAD/CAM telecommunications 1984 to present. Updated monthly. Provider: R.R. Bowker.

RUBBER. *See* PLASTICS AND RUBBER.

S

SAFETY AND HEALTH. *See also* HAZARDS.

Chemical Safety Newsbase DIALOG, ORBIT
This database gives information on hazardous and possibly hazardous effects of chemicals and processes found in the workplace along with workplace microbiological and radiation hazards. The range of data includes microorganisms, chemical reactions, emergency planning, fires, laboratory design, legislation, waste management, and more. Covers 1981 to present. Updated monthly. Provider: The Royal Society of Chemistry, Cambridge, UK.

Hazardline BRS, CompuServe
Database has full-text data on 3,000 hazardous substances as taken from government agencies, court decisions, books, and journals. Entries include name, formula, properties, toxicity, and overexposure and accident measures. Updated monthly. Provider: Occupational Health Services, Inc.

Health and Safety Executive ORBIT
Database covers international literature on health and safety in manufacturing, agriculture, occupational hygiene, explosives, engineering, mining, nuclear technology, and industrial air pollution. Provider: Health and Safety Executive.

HSELINE: Health and Safety CompuServe
Online index, with abstracts, covers worldwide

literature on occupational health and safety. Fields include agriculture, mining, manufacturing, nuclear engineering, and more. Covers 1977 to present. Updated monthly. Provider: Data-Star.

Occupational Safety and Health (NIOSH)
CompuServe, DIALOG
Contains citations to over 400 journal titles plus more than 70,000 monographs and technical reports. All parts of occupational safety and health are covered, 1973 to present. Updated quarterly. Provider: U.S. National Institute for Occupational Safety and Health Technical Information Center.

Safety Science Abstracts   ORBIT
Database abstracts material in the safety field focusing on transportation, aviation and aerospace, environmental and ecological, and medical safety. Provider: Cambridge Scientific Abstracts.

SCIENCE. *See also* EARTH SCIENCES; LIFE SCIENCES; *and specific subjects, such as* CHEMISTRY *and* PHYSICS.

American Men and Women of Science
CompuServe, DIALOG
Biographical information on over 127,000 U.S. and Canadian scientists is presented. Each entry includes basic biographical details, positions held, awards and honors, and research specialties. Covers 1979 to present. Updated on a three-year cycle. Provider: R.R. Bowker.

Cambridge Scientific Abstracts Life Science   BRS
Database consists of four Cambridge abstracts services: *The Life Sciences Collection, Aquatic Sciences and Fisheries Abstracts, Oceanic Abstracts,* and *Pollution Abstracts.* Provider: Cambridge Information Group.

Conference Papers Index   CompuServe, DIALOG
This is an index to over 100,000 scientific and technical papers given at more than 1,000 important regional, national, and international meetings each year. The main subjects covered include life sciences, chemistry, physical sciences, geosciences, and engineering. Covers 1973 to present. Updated six times per year. Provider: Cambridge Scientific Abstracts.

Current Contents Search   BRS, DIALOG
This service reproduces the tables of contents from issues of important journals in a number of disciplines and is the online version of the *Current Contents* series: *Clinical Medicine; Life Sciences; Engineering; Technology and Applied Sciences; Agriculture; Biology and Environmental Sciences; Physical, Chemical, and Earth Sciences; Social and Behavioral Sciences;* and *Arts and Humanities.* Covers 1988 to present. Updated weekly. Provider: Institute for Scientific Information.

Directory of Federal Laboratories   CompuServe
Service gives descriptions of U.S. national laboratory and technology facilities and capabilities that can be used by the private sector. Updated twice a year. Provider: NewsNet, Inc.

Federal Research in Progress   CompuServe (abridged version), DIALOG
All federally funded, ongoing research projects in the physical sciences, engineering, and life sciences are listed here. Each item shows title, principal investigator, performing organization, sponsoring organization, and often a description of the research. Covers current data. Updated monthly. Provider: National Technical Information Service, U.S. Department of Commerce.

General Science Index   CompuServe
This is an index to articles, symposia, conferences, and reviews in the physical, life, and health sciences. Covers 1977 to present. Updated monthly. Provider: H.W. Wilson Company.

ISTP Search   ORBIT
Multidisciplinary database covers major worldwide scientific and technical proceedings literature in the fields of chemistry, clinical medicine, computer science, earth sciences, engineering, life sciences, mathematics, and technology. Provider: Institute for Scientific Information.

Scientific and Technical Books & Serials in Print   ORBIT
Database lists over 120,000 book titles and more than 18,000 serial titles in the scientific and technical fields. Provider: Bowker Electronic Publishing.

SSIE Current Research (Smithsonian Science Information Exchange)   CompuServe, DIALOG
Database has reports of government and privately funded research projects in progress or started in 1978 to 1982. Basic and applied research in the life, physical, social, and engineering sciences are covered. Ninety percent of the data comes from federal government agencies. For current data on federally funded research projects see *Federal Research in Progress,* above. Covers 1978 to February 1982. No updates. Provider: National Technical

Information Service, U.S. Department of Commerce.

Wiley Catalog/Online   CompuServe
The complete publications catalog of John Wiley & Sons, specialists in scientific and technical subjects. Includes out-of-print, current, and forthcoming books, journals, software, and databases. Covers 1940 to present. Updated every two months. Provider: DIALOG Information Services, Inc.

SEISMOLOGY. *See* EARTH SCIENCES.

SOCIAL SCIENCES. *See also* ECONOMICS; HUMANITIES; POLITICAL SCIENCE; PSYCHOLOGY; SOCIOLOGY.

Social Planning/Policy & Development Abstracts
BRS
A companion to *Sociological Abstracts*, below, this database covers the applied and social problems-oriented aspects of social science literature worldwide. Provider: Sociological Abstracts, Inc.

Social Sciences Index   CompuServe
Index provides references to English-language periodicals in the social sciences including current events in politics, business, and foreign affairs. Covers February 1984 to present. Updated monthly. Provider: H.W. Wilson Company.

Social Scisearch   BRS, CompuServe, DIALOG
All important items from 1,500 key social sciences journals, monographs, and social sciences articles from 3,000 other journals in the hard sciences are indexed. All areas of the social and behavioral sciences are found here. Covers 1972 to present. Updated monthly. Provider: Institute for Scientific Information.

SSIE Current Research (Smithsonian Science Information Exchange)   CompuServe, DIALOG
Database has reports of government and privately funded research projects in progress or started in 1978 to 1982. Basic and applied research in the life, physical, social, and engineering sciences are covered. Ninety percent of the data comes from federal government agencies. For current data on federally funded research projects see *Federal Research in Progress*, above. Covers 1978 to February 1982. No updates. Provider: National Technical Information Service, U.S. Department of Commerce.

SOCIAL SECURITY. *See* BENEFITS.

SOCIAL WORK

Social Work Abstracts   BRS
Database has abstracts of articles from over 350 social-work journals and those from related fields. Topics include aging, alcoholism and drug abuse, crime and delinquency, employment, public assistance, housing, health, and more. Provider: National Association of Social Workers, Inc.

SOCIOLOGY

International Review of Publications in Sociology
BRS
This index lists book reviews appearing in journals abstracted by *Sociological Abstracts*, below, and includes detailed abstracts of books in sociology and its sister fields. Provider: Sociological Abstracts, Inc.

Sociological Abstracts
BRS, CompuServe, DIALOG
This index, with abstracts, covers worldwide literature in sociology and associated disciplines in the social and behavioral sciences, scanning over 1,200 journals and other publications. Covers 1963 to present. Updated three times a year. Provider: Sociological Abstracts, Inc.

SOFT DRINKS

Washington Beverage Insight   CompuServe
Here is the full text of this trade newsletter on federal actions concerning the soft drink and alcoholic beverage industries. Coverage includes Congressional, administrative, and court matters. Updated weekly. Provider: NewsNet, Inc.

SOFTWARE. *See* COMPUTER SOFTWARE.

SPACE TECHNOLOGY. *See also* MILITARY.

Aerospace Database   DIALOG
References to and abstracts of important scientific and technical documents, books, reports, and conferences dealing with aerospace research and development are provided from over 40 countries, including Japan, Eastern Europe, and the Soviet Union. The database combines two publications, *Scientific and Technical Aerospace Reports*, published by NASA, and *International Aerospace Abstracts*, published by the American Institute of Aeronautics and Astronautics. Covers 1962 to present. Updated twice a month. Provider: American Institute of Aeronautics and Astronautics/Technical Information Service.

Military Space CompuServe
This full-text newsletter reports on government policy on space-based military programs. Updated every two weeks. Provider: NewsNet, Inc.

Satellite Week CompuServe
Satellite communications and space applications are the focus of this newsletter. Topics include business, technical, and regulatory developments worldwide. Full text; updated weekly. Provider: NewsNet, Inc.

SDI Intelligence Report CompuServe
Newsletter reports on the Strategic Defense Initiative procurement process including contracts, appropriations, expenditures, and political issues. Full text; updated every two weeks. Provider: NewsNet, Inc.

SDI Monitor CompuServe
Full-text newsletter provides information on Strategic Defense Initiative requests for proposals, contract awards, and technical developments. Updated twice a month. Provider: NewsNet, Inc.

Soviet Aerospace CompuServe
Monitors space launches, technology, weapons systems, and programs of the Union of Soviet Socialist Republics. Full text; updated weekly. Provider: NewsNet, Inc.

Space Business News CompuServe
Newsletter looks at developments in the commercial uses of outer space. Full text; updated every two weeks. Provider: NewsNet, Inc.

Space Commerce Bulletin CompuServe
Biweekly newsletter on the commercial uses of outer space. Full text; updated every two weeks. Provider: NewsNet, Inc.

Space Daily CompuServe
Aerospace industry news worldwide is the purview of this full-text newsletter. Coverage includes U.S. and foreign political developments, company activities, and industry conferences. Updated daily. Provider: NewsNet, Inc.

Space Station News CompuServe
Newsletter reports on developments in the program to build the first U.S. space station, the latest news about the Soviet space station, and other advanced technology projects. Full text. Covers 1988 to present. Provider: NewsNet, Inc.

Strategic Defense CompuServe
Defense industry newsletter covers the Strategic Defense Initiative. Full text; updated weekly. Provider: NewsNet, Inc.

SPECIAL EDUCATION

Exceptional Child Education Resources BRS, CompuServe, DIALOG
Both published and unpublished material dealing with all aspects of the education of handicapped and gifted children is indexed here. Sources include books, journal articles, teaching materials, and reports. Covers 1966 to present. Updated monthly. Provider: The Council for Exceptional Children.

Rehabdata BRS, CompuServe
Database is an index to a wide variety of materials dealing with the rehabilitation of the physically and mentally handicapped including articles, books, reports, and audiovisual productions. Covers 1950 to present. Updated monthly. Provider: NARIC.

SPORTS

Gold Sheet CompuServe
This is the full text of this football and basketball handicapping newsletter. Updated weekly from September to April. Provider: NewsNet, Inc.

Sport BRS, CompuServe, DIALOG
This international bibliography provides references to over 2,000 sports journals, monographs, book analyses, and theses in English and other languages. All areas of sport, fitness, and recreation are included. Covers 1949 to present. Updated monthly. Provider: Sport Information Resource Centre, Ottawa, Ontario, Canada.

Sport & Fitness Thesaurus BRS
Corresponding to the printed *Sport Thesaurus*, the online version has all terminology used in the index of the *Sport Database* including descriptor terms and hierarchal relationships. Provider: Sport Information Resource Centre, Ottawa, Ontario, Canada.

Sport Database BRS
Database has references, with abstracts, to serials and monographs on sports, recreation, exercise physiology, sports medicine, sport training psychology, and more. Provider: Sport Information Resource Centre, Ottawa, Ontario, Canada.

STANDARDS

Industry and International Standards
CompuServe
Database provides references to engineering standards from U.S. organizations plus some from foreign and international organizations. Updated every two months. Provider: BRS Information Technologies.

Military and Federal Specifications and Standards
CompuServe
Database provides references to all unclassified standards of the U.S. Defense Department and other federal standards. Active and historical standards are indexed. Updated weekly. Provider: BRS Information Technologies.

National Bureau of Standards Bulletin
CompuServe
Newsletter reports on the activities of the National Bureau of Standards including projects, cooperative programs, and documentation. Updated monthly. Provider: NewsNet, Inc.

Standards & Specifications
CompuServe, DIALOG
Database provides an index to government and industry standards, specifications, and associated documents specifying terminology, testing, safety, materials, products, and other requirements and characteristics. Most items have been issued since 1950 but some go back to 1920. Covers 1950 to present. Updated monthly. Provider: National Standards Association, Inc.

Standards Search   ORBIT
This database contains standards, specifications, and test procedures developed by the Society of Automotive Engineers and the American Society for Testing and Materials. Provider: Society of Automotive Engineers, Inc. and American Society for Testing and Materials.

STATES

CCH Tax Day: State   CompuServe
Newsletter watches tax matters in all 50 states including legislation, regulations, court decisions and actions, and administrative decisions. Updated daily. Provider: NewsNet, Inc.

State Capitals: Alcoholic Beverages; Banking Policies; Insurance Regulation; Pollution Control; Property Taxes; Public Health; Public Utilities; Taxation & Revenue; Water Supply CompuServe
State Capitals is a series of newsletters that cover state legislation and regulations in each of the areas listed above. Full text; updated weekly. Provider: NewsNet, Inc.

State Regulation Report: Toxics   CompuServe
Newsletter covers states' management of toxic substances and hazardous wastes and looks at legislative actions, worker safety regulations, transportation, disposal, and more. Full text; updated every two weeks. Provider: NewsNet, Inc.

STOCK MARKET. *See* INVESTMENTS.

STOCKS. *See* INVESTMENTS.

SUBSTANCE ABUSE

Alcohol and Alcohol Problems Science Database
BRS
Database covers alcoholism research. Topics include psychology, biochemistry, animal studies, treatment, education, legislation and public policy, and much more. Providers: National Institute on Alcohol Abuse & Alcoholism; Alcohol, Drug Abuse, and Mental Health Administration; Public Health Service.

Alcohol Information for Clinicians and Educators
BRS
Database is an index to the Project Cork Resource Center's collection on alcohol and alcoholism. Provider: Project Cork Institute, Dartmouth Medical School.

DRUGINFO and Alcohol Use and Abuse   BRS, CompuServe
Database covers the educational, sociological, and psychological aspects of drug and alcohol use and abuse and includes material concerning treatment, evaluation, chemical dependence, and alcoholism in different populations. Covers 1968 to present. Updated quarterly. Provider: Drug Information Services, University of Minnesota.

Smoking and Health   CompuServe, DIALOG
Corresponding to the printed *Smoking and Health Bulletin*, the online version provides citations to and abstracts of material on the effects of smoking on health. Topics covered run from chemistry and pharmacology to disease to tobacco processing and economics. Covers 1960 to present. Updated every two months. Provider: U.S. National Institute of Health, Office of Smoking and Health.

T

TAXES. *See also* STATES.

CCH Tax Day: Federal CompuServe
This is the full text of the newsletter that covers federal taxation including legislation, court decisions and actions, and Internal Revenue Service and Treasury Department announcements. Updated daily. Provider: NewsNet, Inc.

IRS Taxinfo CompuServe, DIALOG
The full text of 71 Internal Revenue Service individual tax return publications is available. In addition, sections of IRS Publication 17, *Your Federal Income Tax*, on how to prepare a tax return are included. Illustrative examples are provided. Covers current tax year. Updated annually. Provider: U.S. Internal Revenue Service.

Small Business Tax Review CompuServe
In addition to containing tax saving ideas, this newsletter provides news and articles on taxes that apply to small businesses. Coverage includes legislation, rulings, and court decisions. Full text; updated monthly. Provider: NewsNet, Inc.

Tax Directory CompuServe
This online directory has names, addresses, and telephone numbers of Internal Revenue Service, Treasury Department, and U.S. Congress officials and includes the status of proposed Internal Revenue Service regulations. Updated weekly. Provider: NewsNet, Inc.

Taxnotes International CompuServe
Newsletter has international news as taken from the newsletter *Tax Notes* and looks at federal tax matters affecting multinational corporations and U.S. citizens working abroad. Full text; updated weekly. Provider: NewsNet, Inc.

Tax Notes Today CompuServe, DIALOG
Database has the most up-to-date documents in all areas of taxation. Also provided are analytical summaries and the full text of key legislative, regulatory, judicial, and policy documents on federal taxation. State tax news is also reported. Covers 1987 to present. Updated daily. Provider: Tax Analysts.

TNT DIALOG
This is the menu-driven version of *Tax Notes Today*, above.

TECHNOLOGY. *See also* BIOTECHNOLOGY; ELECTRONICS; ENERGY AND POWER GENERATION; NUCLEAR ENERGY.

Applied Science & Technology Index
CompuServe
Index provides references to literature in aeronautics, chemistry, computer science, construction, food science, marine technology, metallurgy, physics, robotics, telecommunications, and energy-related technologies. Covers November 1983 to present. Updated twice a week. Provider: H.W. Wilson Company.

Cambridge Scientific Abstracts Engineering BRS
Database consists of five Cambridge abstracts services: *Computer & Information Systems Abstracts, Electronics & Communications Abstracts, ISMEC: Mechanical Engineering Abstracts, Health & Safety Science Abstracts*, and *Solid State/Superconductivity Abstracts*. Provider: Cambridge Information Group.

Conference Papers Index CompuServe, DIALOG
This is an index to over 100,000 scientific and technical papers given at more than 1,000 important regional, national, and international meetings each year. The main subjects covered include life sciences, chemistry, physical sciences, geosciences, and engineering. Covers 1973 to present. Updated six times per year. Provider: Cambridge Scientific Abstracts.

Current Contents Search BRS, DIALOG
This service reproduces the tables of contents from issues of important journals in a number of disciplines and is the online version of the *Current Contents* series: *Clinical Medicine; Life Sciences; Engineering; Technology and Applied Sciences; Agriculture; Biology and Environmental Sciences; Physical, Chemical, and Earth Sciences; Social and Behavioral Sciences*; and *Arts and Humanities*. Covers 1988 to present. Updated weekly. Provider: Institute for Scientific Information.

Current Technology Index
CompuServe, DIALOG
Database is an index of British journals from all fields of modern technology ranging from acoustic engineering to space science. Covers 1981 to present. Updated monthly. Provider: Library Association Publishing Ltd., The Library Association, London, UK.

Directory of American Research and Technology
ORBIT
This online directory gives the research and development (R&D) abilities of corporations and non-profit and privately financed companies in the United States that perform R&D for industry. Entries include name, address, key personnel, staffing, and areas of research. Provider: Bowker Electronic Publishing.

Directory of Federal Laboratories CompuServe
Service gives descriptions of U.S. national laboratory and technology facilities and capabilities that can be used by the private sector. Updated twice a year. Provider: NewsNet, Inc.

Federal Applied Technology Database BRS
Database is a directory of U.S. government laboratory engineering, technical, and research and development projects with possible commercial applications. Provider: National Technical Information Service, U.S. Department of Commerce.

Federal Research in Progress CompuServe
(abridged version), DIALOG
All federally funded, ongoing research projects in the physical sciences, engineering, and life sciences are listed here. Each item shows title, principal investigator, performing organization, sponsoring organization, and often a description of the research. Covers current data. Updated monthly. Provider: National Technical Information Service, U.S. Department of Commerce.

High Tech International CompuServe
Full-text newsletter reports on U.S. and German technology trends. Topics include developments in electronics, energy, ecology, commentary on social and policy implications, and more. Updated monthly. Provider: NewsNet, Inc.

IBSEDEX: Mechanical and Electrical
CompuServe
Database indexes and abstracts technical literature about buildings' mechanical and electrical service. Covers 1979 to present. Updated monthly. Provider: Pergamon Financial Data Service.

Inspec BRS, CompuServe, DIALOG, ORBIT
Inspec covers physics, electronics, electrical engineering, computer and control, and information technology. Abstracted and indexed are journals, conference proceedings, technical reports, books, and theses. Covers 1969 to present. Updated

monthly. Provider: The Institute of Electrical Engineers, London, UK.

ISTP Search ORBIT
Multidisciplinary database covers major worldwide scientific and technical proceedings literature in the fields of chemistry, clinical medicine, computer science, earth sciences, engineering, life sciences, mathematics, and technology. Institute for Scientific Information.

Japan Technology CompuServe
Corresponding to the printed *Japanese Technical Abstracts*, this online version has English-language abstracts of articles from key Japanese technical journals in applied sciences, engineering, technology, and business management. Covers 1986 to present. Provider: DIALOG Information Services, Inc.

New Scientist CompuServe
This is the full text of this British magazine of science that focuses on scientific and technological developments and their economic, social, and commercial consequences. Covers May 1985 to present. Updated weekly. Provider: Profile Information.

Scisearch CompuServe, DIALOG, ORBIT
This index covers every area of the pure and applied sciences. Ninety percent of important world scientific and technical literature is indexed. The database contains all items from the printed *Science Citation Index* plus items from *Current Contents*. Covers 1974 to present. Updated every two weeks. Provider: Institute for Scientific Information.

Soviet Science and Technology CompuServe, DIALOG
This database is an index of journal articles, patents, technical reports, and conference papers from the Soviet Union and Eastern Europe. A wide range of science and technology is indexed ranging from aerospace to pollution abatement. Covers 1975 to present. Updated monthly. Provider: IFI/Plenum Data Corporation.

SSIE Current Research (Smithsonian Science Information Exchange) CompuServe, DIALOG
Database has reports of government and privately funded research projects in progress or started in 1978 to 1982. Basic and applied research in the life, physical, social, and engineering sciences are covered. Ninety percent of the data comes from

federal government agencies. For current data on federally funded research projects see *Federal Research in Progress*, above. Covers 1978 to February 1982. No updates. Provider: National Technical Information Service, U.S. Department of Commerce.

Supertech CompuServe, DIALOG
Supertech corresponds to the printed abstract journals *Telegen Reporter, Artificial Intelligence Abstracts, CAD/CAM Abstracts, Robomatix Reporter,* and *Telecommunications Abstracts*. It covers the fields of biotechnology, artificial intelligence, computer-aided design and manufacturing, robotics, and telecommunications. Covers robotics and biotechnology 1972 to present; artificial intelligence and CAD/CAM telecommunications 1984 to present. Updated monthly. Provider: R.R. Bowker.

Who's Who in Technology ORBIT
Database has brief biographies of leading persons in American technology. Entries include name, title, employer, career history, education, publications and patents, and honors and awards. Provider: Research Publications, Inc.

World Translations Index DIALOG
This is an index to translations of material in all scientific and technical fields. Starting in 1983, translations from all languages to Western languages are included. Prior to 1983, only translations from East European and Asiatic languages into Western languages were indexed. Covers 1977 to present. Updated 10 times a year. Provider: International Translation Centre, Delft, The Netherlands.

TELECOMMUNICATIONS

Broadcasting CompuServe
Service covers radio, television, cable, satellite, home video, and similar areas with emphasis on industry news, technology, legislation, and FCC regulation. Covers 1983 to present. Updated monthly. Provider: DIALOG Information Services (drawn from the Trade & Industry ASAP database).

Cable and Satellite TV News CompuServe
Full text newsletter reports on the cable and satellite industries, products, and software in Western Europe. Political and regulatory matters are included. Covers February 1985 to present. Updated weekly. Provider: NewsNet, Inc.

Cellular Sales and Marketing CompuServe
Newsletter looks at the advertising and marketing of cellular telephones, peripherals, and services. Full text; updated monthly. Provider: NewsNet, Inc.

Common Carrier Week CompuServe
Newsletter looks at the U.S. telephone industry with coverage of new products and services, legislative and judicial actions, and regulation (federal, state, and local). Covers April 1984 to present. Full text; updated weekly. Provider: NewsNet, Inc.

Communications Daily CompuServe
The full text of this newsletter covers all areas of the communications industry. Included are television, cable, telephone, data transmission, and electronic publishing. Topics reported on are new technology, legislation and regulation, and company news. Covers 1982 to present. Updated daily. Provider: NewsNet, Inc.

FCC Daily Digest CompuServe
This is the online version of the official Federal Communications Commission digest containing all notices, texts, press releases, and schedules. Updated daily. Provider: NewsNet, Inc.

FCC Daily Tariff Log CompuServe
Service shows tariff transmittals received by the Federal Communications Commission. Covers August 1986 to present. Updated daily. Provider: NewsNet, Inc.

FCC Week CompuServe
Newsletter reports on federal regulation of the telecommunications industry. Full text; updated weekly. Provider: NewsNet, Inc.

Long Distance Letter CompuServe
Newsletter covers the long-distance telephone market with reports and analyses of current developments. Topics include new technology, corporate finances, and government regulation. Full text; updated monthly. Provider: NewsNet, Inc.

Mobile Phone News CompuServe
The full text of this newsletter looks at cellular radio and associated technologies. Topics include regulations, emerging applications, industry news, and business opportunities. Updated every two weeks. Provider: NewsNet, Inc.

New Era: Japan CompuServe
Newsletter provides coverage of the Japanese tele-

communications industry. Topics include research and development, equipment, regulations, policies, and systems applications. Updated every two weeks. Provider: NewsNet, Inc.

Netweaver CompuServe
Netweaver reports on electronic communications focusing on human—computer interaction. Full text, updated monthly. Provider: NewsNet, Inc.

Online Products News CompuServe
Newsletter covers videotex/teletext products and services. Topics include hardware, online databases, bulletin boards, electronic mail, and broadcast and cable television with emphasis on personal computer products. Full text; updated monthly. Provider: NewsNet, Inc.

PR Hi-Tech Alert CompuServe
Newsletter covers application of electronic media for marketing and business communications executives. Broadcasting, satellites, cellular radio, cable television, electronic mail, videotex, and more are included. Full text, updated every two weeks. Provider: NewsNet, Inc.

Public Broadcasting Report CompuServe
Newsletter reports on matters of concern to public television and radio broadcasting such as legislation, regulations, programming, and personnel. Full text; updated every two weeks. Provider: NewsNet, Inc.

Satellite News CompuServe
Reporting on the satellite communications industry, this newsletter covers new technology, networks, and markets; regulation; worldwide developments; and satellites' impact on telecommunications. Full text; updated weekly. Provider: NewsNet, Inc.

State Telephone Regulation Report CompuServe
Newsletter is concerned with telephone regulation at the state level. Topics include rate cases, tariffs, state legislative matters, and court rulings. Updated weekly. Provider: NewsNet, Inc.

Supertech CompuServe, DIALOG
Supertech corresponds to the printed abstract journals *Telegen Reporter*, *Artificial Intelligence Abstracts*, *CAD/CAM Abstracts*, *Robomatix Reporter*, and *Telecommunications Abstracts*. It covers the fields of biotechnology, artificial intelligence, computer-aided design and manufacturing, robotics, and telecommunications. Covers 1972 to present (robo-

tics/biotechnology); 1984 to present (artificial intelligence/CAD/CAM/telecommunications). Updated monthly. Provider: R.R. Bowker.

TDS Equipment Registration CompuServe
Service lists new registrations with the Federal Communications Commission of customer premises (telephone) equipment. Updated weekly. Provider: NewsNet, Inc.

TDS Market Report Search CompuServe
Newsletter reports on new technology, regulations and proposed regulations, and marketing strategies as they affect telecommunications markets. Updated weekly. Provider: NewsNet, Inc.

TDS Tariff Search CompuServe
Full text newsletter lists tariffs filed with the Federal Communications Commission by telecommunications carriers. Updated three times a week. Provider: NewsNet, Inc.

TDS RFP/Tender Search CompuServe
The full text of this publication lists current federal, state, and local requests for proposals for telecommunications equipment open for bidding. Updated weekly. Provider: NewsNet, Inc.

TDS Telecom Calendar CompuServe
This is a listing of events (seminars, conferences, trade shows, government and regulatory hearings) for the next six months that are of interest to the telecommunications industry. Updated three times a week. Provider: NewsNet, Inc.

Telecommunications Reports CompuServe
Newsletter gives telecommunications news with emphasis on telephone and regulatory matters. In addition, in-depth reports on trends are provided. Updated weekly. Provider: NewsNet, Inc.

Telecommunications Week CompuServe
The full text of this newsletter has brief reports on measures affecting the telecommunications industry that are taken by the Federal Communications Commission, courts, Congress, and the Department of Justice plus additional coverage of business news. Updated weekly. Provider: NewsNet, Inc.

Telecommuting Report CompuServe
Newsletter has articles and case studies on work in nontraditional places using computers and telecommunications. Full text; updated monthly. Provider: NewsNet, Inc.

Telephone Engineer and Management
CompuServe
Publication covers all areas of telephone engineering. Covers 1983 to present. Full text; updated monthly. Provider: DIALOG Information Services (drawn from the Trade & Industry ASAP database).

Telephone News CompuServe
Covering all areas of the telephone industry, this newsletter provides information on new products, technology, regulation, and more. Full text; updated weekly. Provider: NewsNet, Inc.

Television Digest CompuServe
This television industry newsletter reports on technology, regulation, company news, marketing, and programming. Full text; updated weekly. Provider: NewsNet, Inc.

Video Week CompuServe
This home-video industry newsletter reports on business news, technology, marketing, and programming with regard to videocassettes, videodiscs, pay television, and similar media. Full text; updated weekly. Provider: NewsNet, Inc.

Viewdata/Videotex Report CompuServe
Look here for reports and analyses of the videotex industry. Topics include company strategies, technological developments, marketing, industry trends, and more. Full text; updated monthly. Provider: NewsNet, Inc.

Viewtext CompuServe
Covers interactive telecommunications around the world. Coverage includes videotex, teletext, online databases, microcomputers, and interactive cable television, industry news, technology, regulation, markets, and trends. Full text; updated monthly. Provider: NewsNet, Inc.

Worldwide Videotex Update CompuServe
Newsletter provides news of videotex/teletext projects and products worldwide with a focus on marketing (including customer groups and emerging markets). Updated monthly. Provider: NewsNet, Inc.

TESTING

Educational Testing Service Test Collection BRS, CompuServe
Database contains data on a large number of educational tests along with those used by psychological services, business, and health science plus assessment/screening devices used in assessing skills, aptitude, interests, attitudes, and achievement. Updated quarterly. Provider: Educational Testing Service.

TEXTILE ENGINEERING. *See also* ENGINEERING.

Textile Technology Digest
CompuServe, DIALOG
References with abstracts are given for all areas of textile technology. Sources include over 650 journals along with books, theses, patents, standards, conferences, and directories. Topics range from dyeing to fibers to apparel design. Covers 1978 to present. Updated monthly. Provider: Institute of Textile Technology.

World Textiles CompuServe, DIALOG
Corresponding to the printed *World Textiles Abstracts*, the online version indexes worldwide textile and textile-related literature from some 500 journals, U.S. and British patents, U.S. and British and international standards, books, conference proceedings, and more. Material indexed ranges from textile technology and science to economics to production and management to applications. Covers 1970 to present. Updated twice a month on CompuServe, monthly on DIALOG. Provider for CompuServe: Pergamon Financial Data Services; provider for DIALOG: Shirley Institute, Manchester, UK.

TEXTILES. *See also* INDUSTRIES: CLOTHING AND TEXTILES; TEXTILE ENGINEERING.

World Textiles CompuServe, DIALOG
Corresponding to the printed *World Textiles Abstracts*, the online version indexes worldwide textile and textile-related literature from some 500 journals, U.S. and British patents, U.S. and British and international standards, books, conference proceedings, and more. Material indexed ranges from textile technology and science to economics to production and management to applications. Covers 1970 to present. Updated twice a month on CompuServe, monthly on DIALOG. Provider for CompuServe: Pergamon Financial Data Services; for DIALOG: Shirley Institute, Manchester, UK.

TOXIC WASTES. *See* HAZARDS.

TRADEMARKS. *See* PATENTS AND TRADEMARKS.

TRANSPORTATION. *See also* TRAVEL.

Electric Vehicle Progress   CompuServe
Full-text newsletter covers the electric-vehicle industry dealing with such things as manufacturers, demonstration projects, research and development, and battery technology. In addition, analyses, forecasts, and interviews on technical and
management matters are provided. Updated every two weeks. Provider: NewsNet, Inc.

TRIS (Transportation Research Information Service)
CompuServe, DIALOG
TRIS has transportation research data in the form
of either abstracts of documents and data holdings or résumés of research projects. Covering
air, rail, highway, maritime, mass, and other transportation modes, topics include regulations, energy and environmental technology, traffic control,
and more. Covers 1968 to present. Updated
monthly. Provider: U.S. Department of Transportation and Transportation Research Board.

TRAVEL

Business Traveler's Letter   CompuServe
Newsletter has up-to-date data on airlines, hotels,
and other such services. Full text, updated monthly.
Provider: NewsNet, Inc.

International Travel Warning Service
CompuServe
Newsletter gives danger and medical warnings
issued by the Department of State, World Health
Organization, and the Center for Disease Control.
Additionally, it contains a directory of passport,
visa, and vaccination requirements for all coun-
tries. Full text, updated monthly. Provider: News-
Net, Inc.

OAG Electronic Edition   DIALOG
OAG (Official Airline Guide) gives detailed flight
information for over 1,500,000 direct and connect-
ing airline schedules around the world plus over
600,000 North American fares on all licensed carriers. Data include departure and arrival times,
aircraft type, meals, and number of stops. Reservations and ticket purchase can be made while
online with payment by major credit card. Information is also available on North American, European, and Pacific area hotels. Covers current data.
Updated weekly for schedules, daily for fares.
Provider: Official Airline Guides, Inc.

U

URBAN PLANNING. *See* REGIONAL AND URBAN
PLANNING.

V

VETERINARY MEDICINE

VETDOC   ORBIT
Service indexes worldwide literature on veterinary uses of drugs, hormones, vaccines, and more
as given to domestic animals and livestock. Provider: Derwent Publications, Ltd., London, UK.

VIDEO CASSETTES, VIDEODISKS. *See* RECORD-
INGS.

VOCATIONAL AND TECHNICAL EDUCATION

AIM/ARM   DIALOG
Database indexes material on vocational and technical education plus allied areas of manpower
economics and development, employment, job
training, and vocational guidance. Materials after
1977 are indexed in *ERIC*, under EDUCATION
above. Covers 1967 to 1976. No updates. Provider: The Center for Vocational Education, Ohio
State University, Columbus, OH.

Resources in Vocational Education
BRS, CompuServe
Database has brief summaries of research, curriculum, and professional development projects in
vocational education that are state or federally
funded. Covers 1978 to present. Updated quarterly. Provider: Graduate School of Education, University of California, Berkeley.

Vocational Education Curriculum Materials   BRS,
CompuServe
Look here for references to print and nonprint
materials on vocational and technical education.
Covers 1979 to present. Updated quarterly. Provider: Graduate School of Education, University
of California, Berkeley.

W

WASTE MANAGEMENT. *See* POLLUTION AND
WASTE MANAGEMENT.

WATER. *See also* POLLUTION.

Waternet   CompuServe, DIALOG
Waternet is an index to the publications of the American Waterworks Association and the AWWA Research Foundation. Everything from books to water-quality standard test methods are included. Emphasis is placed on technical reports and studies from water utilities, regulatory agencies, and research groups in the United States, Canada, Mexico, and Latin America. European and Asian data are also given. Covers 1971 to present. Updated every two months. Provider: American Water Works Association.

Water Resources Abstracts
CompuServe, DIALOG
Abstracts and citations to material from over 50 U.S. water research centers and institutes are collected here. Topics include water resource economics, hydrology, regional planning, water-related nuclear radiation and safety and more. Water planning, cycle, and quality are emphasized. Covers 1968 to present. Updated monthly. Provider: U.S. Department of the Interior.

WINES AND SPIRITS

Fearless Taster   CompuServe
Database has the full text of this magazine of wine tasting which covers wine news, reviews, and recipes. Updated monthly. Provider: NewsNet, Inc.

Washington Beverage Insight   CompuServe
Here is the full text of this trade newsletter on federal actions concerning the soft-drink and alcoholic beverage industries. Coverage includes Congressional, administrative, and court matters. Updated weekly. Provider: NewsNet, Inc.

WOMEN

Catalyst Resources for the Workplace and Women
CompuServe
Database contains references, with abstracts, to published data on women's issues with regard to working conditions. Topics include careers, affirmative action, day care, benefits, and more. Covers 1963 to present. Updated quarterly. Provider: BRS Information Technologies.

WRITING

Editors Only   CompuServe
Providing advice for effective editing, writing, and management, this newsletter includes case studies, surveys, conference reports, and an event calendar. Covers October 1983 to present. Full text; updated monthly. Provider: NewsNet, Inc.

X, Y, Z

ZOOLOGY

Zoological Record   BRS, CompuServe, DIALOG
For this index of worldwide zoological literature, some 6,000 journals are scanned for inclusion. Emphasis is on systematic/taxonomic data, and 27 sections provide coverage of different animal groups ranging from protozoa to mammalia. Covers 1978 to present. Updated monthly. Provider: BIOSIS, Philadelphia, PA.

Index